India and Pakistan
Two Dominions

About the Author

Dr. Shree Govind Mishra (Born 1923), an Indian educationalist, Historian and Author, *Education:* M.A. (History), M.A. (Political Science), Ph.D. (History) Patna University. Positions Held: Head of the Department of History, D.A.V. College, Siwan (Saran), Principal, K.M.D. College, Parvatta, Munger, Lecturer/Reader, University Department of History, T.M. Bhagalpur University, Bhagalpur, U.N. Colombo Plan Reader in Modern History, Tribhuvan University Kathmandu (Kritipur) Nepal. Dr. Mishra was appointed Colombo Plan Reader in Modern History by the External Affairs, Government of India on the recommendations of the U.P.S.C., New Delhi. He retired from the Bhagalpur University service in December 1983. His name has figured in *Who is Who in India* (1985 and 1986), *International Biography* (1991-1992), Vols. III and IV, and *Twentieth Century Admirable Achievers*, (1999). He has written more than 130 papers which have been published in the proceedings of the Indian History Congress and Friend's Group of Archives, New Delhi; His book *Constitutional Development and National Movement 1919-1947* has been selected by the Ministry of Information and Broadcasting, Government of India under the heading of *Constitutional and Administration* and is on the Government record from 1981. He was the member of the Indian History Congress, Friend's Group of Archives and Author's Guild of India, New Delhi. Dr. Mishra was a Research Award winner in 1977 sponsored by Hamdard University, New Delhi.

India and Pakistan
Two Dominions

By

Dr. Shree Govind Mishra
Retired Professor of History
Tilka Manjhi University,
Bhagalpur

CONCEPT PUBLISHING COMPANY PVT. LTD.,
NEW DELHI-110059

ISBN-13-978-81-8069-871-2

First Published 2012

Published and Printed by

Concept Since 1974

Concept Publishing Company Pvt. Ltd.
A/15-16, Commercial Block, Mohan Garden
New Delhi-110059 (India)
T: 25351460, 25351794, *F*: 091-11-25357109
E: publishing@conceptpub.com W: www.conceptpub.com
Editorial Office: H-13, Bali Nagar, New Delhi-110 015, India.

Cataloging in Publication Data--Courtesy: D.K. Agencies (P) Ltd. <docinfo@dkagencies.com>

Mishra, Shree Govind.
India and Pakistan : two dominions / by Shree Govind Mishra.
p. cm.
Includes bibliographical references and index.
ISBN 9788180698712

1. India—History—Partition, 1947. 2. India—Politics and government—1919 1947. 3. Pakistan movement. 4. Hindus—India. 5. Muslims—India. I. Title.

DDC 954.0359 23

Dedicated

to

My Elder Brothers

Pandit Satya Narayan Mishra
Acharya, A Sanskrit Scholar

and

Mr. Abadh Kishore Mishra
M.A., Retd. Head Master,

Who are no more.

Acknowledgements

This acknowledgement is written on behalf of my father, Shri Govind Mishra, who left us bereft. This book is an untiring effort of my father. I being his daughter Dr. (Mrs) Asha Mishra an Associate Professor of History in Mahila College Chaibasa Jharkhand have taken keen interest in the writings of my father's manuscript. I lived his dream and tried to bring his unpublished record in the shape of his book. It was a Herculean task to get a publisher which difficult situation was eased by Shri A.K. Mittal, Director, Concept Publications. I must thank the typist B.K. Pandit, Bhagalpur and C.R. Dey, Chaibasa who put their effort in typing the hand-written notes of my father at the odd hours of the day. I am also indebted to the colleagues of my father Dr. P. Mishra, Dr. P. Pathak, Sri T.N. Ray, Advocate and mine colleagues Dr. (Mrs) P. Sen, Dr. Ashok Sen, Dr. C.K. Paty who encouraged and helped me from time to time. This book could not have been successful without the contribution of my daughter Ms. Shruti Sharma and my husband Sri Pradeep Kumar, Advocate who helped me through thick and thin to get the unpublished record transferring to personal computer and then preparing hard disc etc. This book preparation was also dream of my real brother D.K. Mishra and sisters Veena Dixit, Sunita Choubey, Anita Jha and Nita Mishra. I once again thank Mr. A.K. Mittal and his team, Concept Publications for lending me immeasurable support for bringing out the publication of this book.

Asha Mishra
D/o Late Dr. Shree Govind Mishra

Contents

Acknowledgements vii
Introduction xiii

1. Nation and Nationalism 1
2. Nation and Nationality 12
3. Lord Minto and the Muslims : The Simla Deputation 1906 24
4. Formation of the Muslim League and the Lucknow Pact (1906-1916) 34
5. The Indian Independence Movement 70
6. Rahmat Ali Iqbal and the Lahore Session of 1940 78
7. Road to Pakistan 111
8. 1946 : Year of Decision 160
9. Nehru's Press Conference in Bombay on July 10 and the London Conference 180
10. Lord Mountbatten presided over the Partition of India : An Introduction 205
11. Plan Balkan—The Balkanization of India 238
12. Orderly Partition of India and Transfer of Power 260
13. Partition through the Pages of History 325
14. Jawaharlal Nehru and Edwina's Relationship 367
15. Jinnah as a Man, as a Politician and his Achievement 403
16. BBC Documentary on Jinnah 423

Appendices

I.	Carnage of Partition	445
II.	Liaquat Ali Khan wanted to Avert India's Partition	448
III.	Jinnah's Blunder	450
IV.	If Churchill had won in 1945—Would he agree to part with Pakistan?	451
V.	The Transfer of Power and Partition	453
VI.	History was on Nehru's Side (Inside of the Simla Conference, 1945)	456
VII.	Diaries of a Troubled Time (1829-1945) : *The Empire at Bay*	459
VIII.	Nizam considered Pakistan Shadow without Reality	462
IX.	Last of the Imperial Lords : *An Interview of Govind Talwalkar with Lord Listowel*	464
X.	August 15, 1947—Freedom : *One Era Ends and a New Begins*	467
XI.	New Insight into History of Congress	469
XII.	Gandhi and Ambedkar—*Commercial Awards and the Poona Pact*	472
XIII.	Legacy of the Raj	474
XIV.	Acharya Narendra Dev	475
XV.	Sardar Patel	476
XVI.	Jai Prakash Narayan	477
XVII.	Communist Role in Freedom Struggle	478
XVIII.	Dandi Revisited: A Monument and a Memorial	481
XIX.	Mahatma Gandhi was not chosen for the Nobel Peace Prize	483
XX.	Gopal Krishan Gokhale's Ideas have Continuing Relevance	488

XXI. The Film that could have averted India's Partition 490
XXII. Jinnah's Negativism and Partition 492
XXIII. Jawaharlal Nehru's Call for Socialism in India 493
XXIV. CPI and Partition 495
XXV. The Man Behind Socialist Movement 496
XXVI. Patel's Letter to Golwalkar 498
XXVII. The Hindu Mahasabha and the RSS 500
XXVIII. Rise of Urdu and Partition 501

Index 506

Introduction

The relation between the two communities 'Hindus and Muslims' were not always free from suspicion or distrust. Sometimes there was rejection by one group of the habits and social practices of the other. Occasionally the conflicts were painful and sometimes there were events of murder and arson. The first instance of a communal riot was in 1809 in Banaras though Hindus and Muslims allegedly slaughtered each other in large numbers, the riot is known to the researchers only through what British administrators chose to record about it. Gyan Pandey has studied colonial documents from 1809-1810 and has put the numbers more than 30 and the site of the disturbances Lal Bhurray, outside the city. Over the years as the need to find evidence for the ancient antagonism between Hindus and Muslims increased the riot description became more fanciful. By 1909, the District Gazetteers was confidently asserting that 'several hundred have been killed'. The riot location was also conveniently shifted to the Gyan Vapi mosque, site of the old Vishwanath temple and more volatile and durable zone of contestation than the Lal Bhurray.[1]

But moments of communal frenzy and malevolence, were rare and transient. Alok Bhalla writes: "the experience of a life lived together was sufficiently secure and routed to enable the communities to have evolved mechanisms for contending tensions and even outrage so that even if these were disruptions, the rich heterogeneity of the life of the two communities were never seriously threatened the Hindus never ceased from paying homage at *dargahs*, the Muslims continued to participate in Hindu festivals, traders of both the communities carried on with their usual exchange of goods and services in bazaars, learned men sought each other out to gather information and knowledge about the best of both traditions, and princes never stopped to consider the religion of the mercenaries they recruited into their armies.[2]

Had there been a history of irreconcilable hatred between the two communities in the medieval period, it would have been clearly reflected in the cultural and social practices of the two groups. The pain of living together would have been extensively recorded in the popular stories and amusement of songs and chronicles, while popular tales talked about Muslims conquests and destruction or about Hindu intolerance and retaliation, there are hardly any account of conflagrations between the two communities in their ordinary lives, which were so serious as to have threatened the very structure of a life of independence in the various regions of the subcontinent.[3]

But soon this phase came to an end. The Hindus and Muslims had thrown a great challenge to the British rule in 1857. There were several regional leaders of both communities, who fought against the company's rule but they were defeated. Now the British government took over the administration of India from 1858. India was slowly being modernized. English education had started in the country from 1835. Hindus received English education in large numbers but Muslims in large numbers refused to take the English education. The English educated people soon established a political association known as the Indian National Congress in 1885 with a view to introduce representative type of government in the country. The Indian National Congress was the greatest political association in the country. The Muslims in large number did not take the membership of the Indian National Congress. Sir Syed Ahmad Khan had emerged a leader of the Muslims in upper India. He had established an Anglo-Oriental College at Aligarh in 1876 for imparting English education to the Muslims of the country. He threw his powerful influence in favour of the isolation of his community from the National Movement, when the Indian National Congress started its political career. Sir Syed raised the great question mark which was to overshadow Indian politics for the next sixty years. Did Sir Syed sow seeds of partition of the country? Did he sow seeds of the Muslim separatism?

Partition: Pakistan's Historical Approach

I.H. Qureshi, who happens to be the leading spokesman of Pakistan nationalist historiography, talks of at the glorious past of the Muslims and cites the historical, cultural and civilization deeply rooted in medieval history. He projects the Muslims as the near-opponents of India's throne. What a fantastic idea? British rule is highlighted by him as the source of trouble, while the Indian National Congress portrayed as the main obstacle in the Muslim search for identity. It is an absurd idea, rather the national movement of India helped Muslims to find out their identity. The same line of thought is conveyed by Hafiz Malik describing the Muslims as a nation in themselves. Sir Syed Ahmad's ideal had influenced H. Malik. K.K. Aziz also talks about the growing cultural gulf between the two communities. So does Aziz Ahmad by explaining it as a case of two civilizations. Mumtaz Hasan presents the political and geographical disunity of India as also the cultural rivalry in the country as the reason for the difficult co-existence. S.M. Ikran talks of the Indian soil as being not congenial for the two communities. It is an unhistorical idea.

S. Mujahid gives the same analysis and tried to convince that it was Jinnah's dexterity that translated the surging condition into a reality. M. Munir and Jalaluddin Ahmad also use the same expression in their works but the Indian scholars did not agree to this simplistic conceptualization of the historical, cultural and civilizations divide.

The concept of nationalism or religion as the basis of self-determination through which Pakistan came into existence is highlighted by K.K. Aziz in his study on nationalism. He points to the personal feeding on religion as the basis of nationalism. Choudhary Mohammad Ali also tries to see disunity at the social level, later reflected in political outlook as an important concomitant of nationalism. S.M.M. Qureshi suggests that in this phase Muslim nationalism was a reaction to the Congress evil design. I.H. Qureshi holds that Muslims were a nation in themselves. So does A. Aziz who mentions that Muslims were so accepted as a nation in themselves. So does A. Aziz who mentions that Muslims were so accepted till as late as 1857.

S.M.M. Qureshi writing after the experience of the formation of Bangladesh that Muslim nationalism was a forged concept invented on the basis of religion. He adds it was the Congress absence from the political scene from 1942-1945 that helped Muslim nationalism to strike ground as a reaction to a united India. It was Muslim League, an elitist nationalism, which could not adjust itself with mainstream nationalism called Indian nationalism. It was neither for the concern religion nor its followers Anwar Hussein Syed suggests that Muslims nationalism in its pure form was totally ideological. It was in the cultural rather than the religious form that Muslim nationalism worked that too under pressure.

As far as the interpretations of political events are concerned, I.M. Qureshi, S.M.M. Qureshi, Chaudhary Mohammed Ali, M.A.H. Isphan, K.K. Aziz, S. Pirzada, M.A. Chaudhary and M. Hassen are all unanimous about the Congress quest to monopolize power in an independent India. They interpret the entire event from 1937 to 1947 as their onward march towards attainment of self-determination to which at every step was to be destructed by the Congress. They say that the Lahore Resolution of 1940 was the first step of their assertion to become a separate nation. The Cripps Mission of 1942 considered their claim of being a nation. The Gandhi-Jinnah talks of 1944 strengthened the idea of separateness. The Cabinet Mission of 1946 recognized and explored the possibility of their secession. All of them try to impress the point that till 1946 there had been the utmost desire to become a united India but in their own way, which the Congress was not ready to accept and, therefore, there was no alternative to Pakistan.

Prof. K.K. Aziz, a well-known historian of Pakistan writing as late as 1968, begins his version of the events leading up to the Partition by reasserting that the "Indian Nationalism" espoused by the Congress was, from its very inception, a 'Hindu nationalism": in essence, "which the Muslims could not possibly have supported a fantastic and unhistorical idea. He quotes with approval a statement by Ameer Ali published in 1906, when the Congress was not yet in complete control of the national movement, urging the Muslims not to join the Congress, for otherwise, "tied to the wheels of the Juggernaut of majority they would in the end be crushed out of the semblance of nationality. Since this declaration has little historical substance and can only be provoked by repetition. Prof. Aziz goes on to do so by evoking the authority of an article by Maulana Shaukat Ali published in the Empire Review in 1931. In this article Maulana Shaukat Ali called upon the Muslims to place their faith in the British because the Hindus were trying to coerce them into accepting a subordinate position in the nation. After this conventional call to the faithful to be vigilant against Hindu subversion, Maulana Shaukat Ali's argument which Aziz accepts without a murmur of dissent becomes a little baroque, unlike the Hindus who are used to being subjects, Maulana Shaukat Ali says that the Muslims are remarkably free from servility and know how to maintain their poise and dignity in adversity. The Muslims being a constitutionally minded people should trust the British because they have made fair laws and treated them justly. Moreover, Hindu agitation politics as advocated by the victims of Satyagraha is not only unconstitutional, it is also against the Islamic injunctions about obeying the rulers. Indeed, it is reasonable for the Muslims to try to establish closer ties with the British, with whom they have greater social intellectual and spiritual affinity than with the 'idol worshipping Hindus'. The most bizarre part of this argument is that since the British had established the greatest "Muslim Empire in the world, and had intimate relations with all the independent Muslim states", it was to be expected that the Indian Muslims would wish to remain within the security of the Empire for their own well-being. Given this kind of thinking, it is not surprising to find that people like Aziz regards the Partition as "*azadi*" from the *fasadat* (riots) caused by Hindus—for them the creation of Pakistan becomes a vindication of their presuppositions, history becomes a tautology instead of an explanation.[4]

If the historians of Pakistan movement manufacture facts to justify the existence of a separate Muslim consciousness, which naturally constitute a nation, the historians of the Hindu Rashtra conjure up a past in order to assure the Muslims of discretion and betrayal, as well as, to assert the presence of a Hindu brotherhood which has a primal right to the inheritance of India. But their construction of a fundamental entity called a "Hindu" who could become the basis of a new collectivity of true leaders turns out to be as confusing and mythical as that of Islamic brotherhood.

Thus Bharatendu Harish Chandra who was not perhaps a communal thinker but was passionately concerned with the shape of the Hindu civilization, in a lecture in 1884, defines the "Hindus" as people who lived in Hindustan and includes the Janis, Buddhists, Sikhs, Brahmos and Muslims in his sweep. In order to give substance to such a Meta-religious category, Bharatendu translated parts of the Koran into Hindi (1884), wrote brief biographies of the Prophet, Hassan and Hussain (1875), and a long poem praising Kabir, Tansen and Pirzadi Bibi (it is worth noting here that Sir Syed Ahmad Khan also described the "Hindus" in a lecture in 1884 precisely in the same terms as Bharatendu and included the Muslims in his definitions). By 1924, however, Lala Lajpat Rai and Swami Shraddhanand began to speak forcefully about the old antagonism between the Hindus and the Muslims and even urged the formation of two distinct religious nations for the sake of peace. As the years went by, the terms "Hindu" became sharper and Mahatma Gandhi, the architect of the Indian freedom and who was one of the finest witnesses to the possibility of a Hindu spiritual and democratic life in modern India and in modern History, was assassinated on January 30, 1948 at Birla Bhawan Campus by Hindus. The "Hindu" came to be defined, by the more communally committed historians, as one who was first an unrelenting enemy of Islam and only after that as someone who had a particular set of ideals and practices.[5]

Regarding the Lahore Resolution, I.H. Qureshi says that it was an expression of being an unwilling partner of second class citizen in a united India. Isphani calls it a manifestation of the suffocating Muslims nationhood, when the doors of an alternative were closed. S.S. Pirzada characterises it as the beginning of the end of India's unity. S.M.M. Qureshi points that it was the insistence of the Congress to monopolize the negotiation, which forced the League to draft the Lahore Resolution. K.K. Aziz calls it a desperate oppression of Congress domination.

Communalism and National Fragmentation

Approach to religion and religious system is not communalism. Exploitation of religion is communalism. Attachment to a religious community or religiosity is not communalism. Affiliation to any social, cultural and service organ of a religious community may also not be communalism. But restricting one's sympathy, help, social obligations and range of services as citizens of a secular republic just only to community of one's birth can be communalism. 'Affiliation' to ritualism, superstition, obscurantism, magic charm and ociult and practices like astrology is not communalism. These are mainly unnatural, unscientific and primordial orientations, due to conformism to traditions, or to fear of the unknown and unbounded ambition. Even commitment to conservative values and practices in social life and conservative orientation in politics is not communalism. It can be called social backwardness and political reaction. However, it should be recognized that all these aspects can be imparted into the development of communal consciousness and indeed the communalists in various permutations and combinations have utilized most of these aspects, in order to build their communal, and political base. But

"Communalism" as a specific phenomenon in Indian polity is something different and more specific.[6]

It is wrong to assume that communalists are religious people in the real sense of the world. Even these few, who are both 'religious' and 'communal' act as communalists in politics largely by emphasizing the dubious and contentious belief that their religion is a complete code of life and hereafter for all time, hence they agreed that politics and civic affairs cannot be segregated from religion. A communalist may not even respect and adhere to a religion expect as a public posture, for a communalist is basically interested in 'using' religion and that too not for any religious spiritual or moral ends but on the contrary for, secular ends (in the sense of statecraft and politics), communalism is the enemy of progress, revolution, democracy and of federal nation state building on rational scientific lines.

In spite of this detailed discussion, the question is how do we define communalism? Communalism is a modern phenomenon, and not a phenomenon of the medieval past. It is a sectarian, restrictive and negative response to the process of modernization and modern national leading communalism envisages a religious community alone as a base of its political assertion and action. Communalism is a political orientation that recognizes religious community and not the nation and the nation-state as a terminal community—the final point of political allegiance. Therefore, communalism is a political strategy opposed to nationalism as aggregation of multi-ethnic, multi-religious and multi-lingual communities. Communalism is opposed to secularism as a pattern of socio-cultural co-existence and political integration. Communalism perceives majorities and minorities as segments and detection within a policy and a nation-based essentially on religious communities and not on any other abscriptive basis (like that of family, clan, tribe, *jati*, language, region or domicile) and certainly not on the basis of political, ideological, party, class, interests or strata considerations, which is the hallmark of a modern political system.

Colonialism and Communalism

It is very interesting to recall that communalism as a term used in the connotations of religious and social antagonism especially in India from the mid-nineteenth century, when the British Crown became the Imperial Sovereign in 1858. It has to be explained that communities in the same religious sense existed before 1850 and that antagonism between them ninety per cent absent. The point is that in the anticipation of this very antagonistic and its transformation from the latent and inward looking religious cleavage into the most articulate socio-political division conflict. The presence of policy of British imperialism played a decisive role.

Separatism in politics and the politicization of religious communities have been the two most detrimental contribution of British colonial administration in the emerging body politics of the divided India. It should be understood that it was the structure, style and process of politics which eventually resulted in the vivisection of the nation and the partition of the country.

The 'Two-Nation Theory' implied that Hindus and Muslims were two separate monolith religious communities. It was historically and sociologically a fallacious assumption. The false slogan that Hindus and Muslims constituted separated nations and, therefore, were entitled to separate 'territorial sovereignty' is irrelevant. It was the most monumental blunder of contemporary Indian leaders. This approach destroyed not only the civilization unity built over the centuries and the dominant pattern of composite culture even by the long drawn historic process of interactions, assimilation and synthesis of diverse ethnic groups and trends, but also violated the time-tested and universally accepted basic assumptions of modern federal nation-building. It gave a disastrous stake of some of the cherished traditions of Indian polity and social life. This thought projected an irrational, invidious and untenable proposition that 'religion' alone is the criteria of identifying a nation and, therefore, of state-building.

The recognition of principle of religion alone as the basis of modern state-formation and statecraft, had far reaching repercussions on the polity and policies of the sub-continent of South Asia, or what is historically referred to as the Hindustan subcontinent. The consequence of this development was the Birth of a Muslim communal state of Pakistan. Creation of Pakistan, has been on irrational lines, which distorted the process of democratic federal nation-building in India.[7]

Repercussion of Communalism on the Indian Polity

Communalization of politics is the effect of the two-nation theory.

India today appears a society prior to continuing violence and political destabilization. What are the current manifestations of communalism in India? To use the issues of the bygone past for setting scores in the present against another community is communalism. Communalism is also an attempt to generate inter-communal psychotics is ranking up events and episodes of the medieval past. The communalists seek to use the past as a continuum of the present, for promoting inter-communal discord. They overlook themselves and confuse the other people about the basic characteristic of the ancient and medieval ages marked as they were by feudal aristocracy, religious bigotry, dynastic ambitions, migratory movements, for empire building invasions, annexative, conquest and tyranny. To punish innocent members of the community due to acts of commissions of few rulers or leaders of the same community in the past or in the present time is communalism. To attack and murder of a human being is frenzy or not, only because he belongs to another community is the worst form of communalism. To incite communal animosity and riots by word of mouth or persecution, particularly by using one's privileged position in profession and society especially the media is wrecked and manifest communalism.

Today communalism in the varied shapes has acquired a most dangerous form and an alarming position. It is a multi-pronged challenge that seeks to disrupt India's multi-religious fraternity. It is an affront to India's nationalist identity and tragic setback to our evolving secular culture. It is subversive of our political stability and economic development, and, therefore, manifests itself as enemy number one of our democratic society.

To be clearer, it should be recapitulated that in the medieval period, there was no struggle based on religion. The Mogul Empire had fought with the Bijapur Muslims. The siege of city started on 11th April, 1685 and Aurangzeb himself went there in July 1686. Bijapur surrendered on September 1686. Bijapur lost its independence. Aurangzeb was influenced in this conquest by imperial interests more than religious considerations. The Nizam had joined hands with the Peshwa and the English in the battle with Tipu Sultan in 1799. Tipu was defeated on the 5th March, 1799 and again on the 27th of March. The Mysore Sultan died, while defending his capital Seringapatam on the 4th May, 1799. Madhojee Sindhia had advised the young Peshwa Madhava Deo II not to wage war against the English. The British government had accepted Madho Jee Sindhia as an independent prince. Unfortunately Madho Jee Sindhia died on the 12th February, 1794 at Poona.

Genesis of the Two-Nation Theory

The Hindu view of the Indian Nation found one of its most coherent expression in the writings of V.D. Savarkar solicitor propounded the two-nation theory first in 1923 in his book *Hindutva* and reiterated it in his presidential address to the Hindu Mahasabha on December 30th, 1937. Savarkar stated that India belongs to those who subscribed to the Hindu religion and were naturally as it was equipped to the bearers of its *sanskriti* of the Hindu converts to Christianity and Islam, who shared with the Hindus a common culture and the common homeland were excluded from the Hindu fold. M.A. Jinnah, whose grandfather was a Hindu, wrote forcibly about a Muslim view of the Indian Nation, believed that the Indian subcontinent contained the territorial frontier of two distinct political formations, each having its own religion, philosophy, customs and literature. To yoke together two such nations under a state, one of a numerical minority and the other as a majority must lead to growing discontent and find destruction of any fabric that may be built up for the government of such a state,[8] Jinnah propounded it in an article in *Time and Tide*, London, March 9, 1940. Exactly a fortnight later came to Leagues Pakistan's resolution.

Democratic methods based upon the majoritarian principle could only lead to a 'Hindu Raj'. Jinnah further declared that the case of the Indian Peninsula was not unique. The Balkan area, Europe, which was much smaller, was recognized as containing seven to eight different states and in the Iberian Peninsula the Portuguese and the Spanish had become two independent nations.[9]

Pandit Jawaharlal Nehru believed that both the Hindu and Muslim views of the Indian Nation were followed because they identified culture and religion, when culture was only one area of the manifestation. Cultural types are national not religious". In the opinion of Jawaharlal Nehru Hindustan was a faith which was a vague, amorphous, many-sided all things to all men. In the present form and even in the past, it embraces many beliefs and practices, often opposed to and contradictory to each other. Nehru rejected Jinnah's claim that the Muslims in India could be regarded as a culturally advanced monolith. There was difference among the rich and the poor and social differences similar to those associated with caste. There was no art or music which could be regarded as typically Muslim. At the mundane level culture was evident in the choice of clothes, hair styles and personal effects. In the urban areas at the mass level a distinction could be indeed drawn between the Hindu and Muslim, for instance in the preference for a *dhoti* rather than a *payjama*. However, the limited base of this phenomenon needed to noted: the Muslim peasantry and industrial workers were hardly distinguished from the Hindu counterparts. In addition, technological advance assumed to be pulling the way for the emergence of an industrial stereotype. The belief that a majoritarian rule would be Hindu rule was a fallacy. A federal democratic constitution which safeguards for minorities held equally the prospect of well-being to all communities.

Jinnah referred to the Balkans for the purpose of indicating a design for the political development of the Muslim community. He ignored the example of other Muslim majority nations, such as Turkey, which had deliberately opted for secularism so that they could benefit their ordinary citizens. Partition in the Indian context was a wholly impractical proposition for the seventy million Muslims were scattered. If each area was asked to decide the independent status on the basis of religion, there would be "vast numbers of small states are incredible and fantastic development". Also ironically the end would be relatively more disadvantageous to the Muslim majority and then the Hindu majority once because important mineral resources and face of industrial activity in the later. The Muslim areas would be economically backward and often different areas which cannot exist without a great deal of existence.

Vinayak Damodar Savarkar became the first president of Hindu Mahasabha and continued till Mahatma Gandhi was assassinated on January 30, 1948 at the Birla Bhawan complex. It was Savarkar's belief that Hindutva was the obvious basis for nationalism in India. But it may be called Hindu nationalism and not Indian nationalist. In his book *Hindutva* (1923), he said: A Hindu is one who looks upon the land that extends from Sindhu to Sindhu, i.e. from the Indus to the sea as the land of his forefathers. Savarkar was of the view that the prospects of Hindutva blossoming as a dominant sentiment—M.S. Golwakar, the supreme leader of the RSS from 1940 to 1973 was prominent among those who elaborated upon it.

From Nehru's point of view, Hindutva was a contrived concept legitimating and upholding India's nationalist stories though from the eighth century A.D. for about a thousand years the word Hindu was used to refer to those, who live in a particular area in the other side of the Indus. For a number of centuries in a more recent historical period, it had begun to mean those who followed the Hindu religion. In this view, the contemporary English political theorist C.E.M. Joad, defined India's unique national skill aptly when he wrote 'whatever the reason' in fact the India's special gift to mankind has been the ability and willingness of Indians to effect sympathies of many different elements both of thought and peoples, to create in fact unity out of diversity.

According to Nehru, the supporters of Hindutva were not wrong in equating Hindu culture with Indian culture and enlisting it. After the Aryan conquest for hundreds of years Hindu social forms, beliefs and ideas largely determined the authoritative content of Indian culture. With the coming of Greeks, Persians, Scythians, Kushans, Huns and Muslims, who proceeded to settle here, changed the whole context. This culture, at first imperceptibly, became more varied in the typical Indian assimilative geneses found expression in religion, literature and other spheres. In retrospect, it summed to him that ancient Aryan civilization represented one of the most interesting creative pellets of Indian History.

Nehru believed that the anti-Party of the supporters of Hindutva towards the Congress Party should be a significant factor in evaluating ideology. The Congress Party, according to him, represented an All India multi-religious, multi-class movement, for national regeneration at all levels, for political emancipation from British rule, for economic transformation and social equality. Those who believe in 'Hindutva' are men of narrow outlook.

Such a context of 'Hindu Nation' was compared to the Muslim concept of 'Muslim Nation' associated with M.A. Jinnah. However, in the context if India's future evolution as a nation, it was more dangerous. In an article which was published in the *Tribune* on November 27, 1933, he wrote: In the thirties and forties the major cultural political organization, which sought to promote Hindutva, was the Hindu Mahasabha. Referring to their leaders, Nehru said: It was for the rest of Indian Hindu and non-Hindus to face them equally and oppose them and tried them as enemies of freedom and all that we are striving for.

Religion and its Effects

The role of religion in the political and social life of India has been far more divisive than either of war, insurgencies and language. Large numbers of people have identified themselves as adherents to a particul r religion, i.e. Hindus, next to Hindus are Muslims. The Muslims are identified with the religion of foreign conquerors.

The communal riots between Hindus and Muslims were frequent till 1947. The Direct Action Day of 1946 was very devastating. In Calcutta, Noakhali, Bihar and U.P. thousands of persons lost their lives. But what were the reasons for the riots during the period of the national movement in the nineteenth and twentieth centuries? There was multitude of causes. The general one was surely the social situation identified on the Deport of Linguistic states; the promise of democracy opened up new possibilities of action for individuals to express their economic and social discontents. As early as 1926, a politician pressed the position at apathy comment. Until I call the other community names and damn them before my electorate, I have absolutely no chance of being elected.

The result was religion and politics were morgue. As India was ruled by the British rulers, so the detrimental result of religion on politics was not felt. The Muslim League, the Hindu Mahasabha and the RSS started to exploit religion for their political ends. The two theories developed in such a way that the vivisection of India took place and a Pakistan was created a new state in 1947. Prime Minister Pandit Nehru had argued that in the cardinal doctrine of modern democratic practice is the separation of the state from religion. The founding father of the Constitution of India, 1950, guaranteed freedom of religion and denied to any religion a privileged place of any kind in relation to the state. The place of religion in defining the national culture had a long history during the period of the Indian National Movement, 1885-1947.

NOTES

1. The *Times of India*, New Delhi, February 27, 2000.
2. Alok Bhalla, *Stories about the Partition of India*, Vol. I, p. viii.
3. *Ibid.*, p. viii.
4. A. Bhalla, *The Partition of India,* Vol. I, pp. xi-xviii.
5. *Ibid.*, pp. xiii-xiv.

6. *Mainstream*, May 1993, p. 1.
7. *Mainstream,* May 1993, p. 21.
8. M.A. Jinnah, *Times and Tide,* ed. London, March, 1940, p. 9.
9. *Mainstream,* January 1992, p. 11.

1

Nation and Nationalism

Was India a Nation in the ancient period? There is a misconception that India was a nation in the ancient period. Some members of the BSP, the RSS and other reactionary bore their liberal attack on the father of the Nation on January 3rd, 2000. Pramod Mahajan said at a press conference. I do not feel that Gandhi was the father of Nation, to calll him the father of Nation is not valid and India was not born in 1947 but has a history of 2000 years. Such concepts of "Hindu Nation" are to be found in the works of Golwakar and Savarkar. To think that India was a nation in the ancient period is a historical and parochial and cannot furnish the basis for a viable, modern India.

Was India a nation in the pre-colonial period ? In reality, pre-colonial periods have been marked by different relationship, between and within the state, society, religion, ritual and culture. It is simply false to think of Hinduism as arising from the Vedic culture or Sanatan Dharma. Hinduism, as D.D. Kosambi, a scholar of History but not a professional historian, says, was always divided into sects and institutions. There is an ongoing controversy as to whether Harsh Vardhan of Kanouj was a Buddhist or a Shaiva? Harsh Vardhan the Shaiva sects of Kashmir had destroyed Buddhist monasteries and killed Buddhist monks. The Chalukyas of Gujarat built a mosque for Arabs, which was destroyed by the Paramaras of Malwa. Mughal endowments to Brahmans, Jogis and temples are recorded even those of Aurangzeb.[1]

Is it true that Hinduism was a 'natural religion' of India? Indeed the term 'Hindu' itself originating in Arabia and Persia, was used for a long time connotate territorial identity. Islam entered in India and became a strong power in 871 A.D. Kerala's Syrian Christians were in India six centuries before Brahmanism consolidated itself. India's uniqueness has for centuries been not in Hinduism, but in cultural-religious pluralism, whose defense was the duty of the king. "Has protection of *dharma* was not religion in the modern sense for it enveloped in the entire range of social delegation of which religion ritual was a part", says a Retired Professor of History, Dr. Romila Thaper.

Because political power was relatively open throughout Indian history. It could pass on to local or alien groups, which offset ranked socially low, but which (as Kusumbi shows) raised their ritual status with origin myths and a little help from priests, power could equally easily pass on to "others". This complicates the whole idea of the "Foreigner". Within is assimilative society "invaders" mixed freely with the "Locals", practicing similar rituals. What mattered was not so much religion, as systems of patronage, loyalty and rewards, a code of honour, and accommodation of others interests.

There is an example that Shivaji's general was a Muslim and the language of record of this "Hindu" founder of a "Hindu-Nation State" was Persian Ashrafs and Sayyades, who claimed high status by virtue of being "outsiders" often held elevated position in "Hindu" courts. Often, *jati* or caste fragmentation prevailed over religious identities. Romila Thaper says, "The religious reality for the majority of Indians has been the recognition of a multiplicity of religions drawing marginally perhaps from the established once, but far more rooted in local cults, beliefs and rituals and identified less by religion and more by *jati*.... This gave them a certain freedom to worship a stone, an icon or a deity with which they alone had a dialogue."

"These were groups entwined by socio-regulations but of a local kind. This maintained a distance from the Brahmanas and the Ulemas governed—as they were by their own customary observations. This distance was not idyllic but—resulted from the segmentation of *jati.*"

"To claim of exceptional religious tolerance in India is also open to question", says Dr. Thaper. In fact it was the juxtaposition of various kinds of religious practices and belief—which was the basis of both a relative religious tolerance and a heightened intolerance based on social outcasting. Religious practices and belief could overlap among adjoining castes, but social distinctions were firmly demarcated. Religious intolerance was possible because of the enforcement of social boundaries, but when these were transgressed or seen as competitive, as per example, between the Shaivas and the

Jain in Karnataka, the tolerance disappeared and the conflict took a religious form.

Was there secularism in the ancient period of Indian History? The co-existence of many religions, sects and practices does not amount to secularism. But it does open up the possibility of a transition to secular order, and secularization of society, in ways different from what happened in Europe, where a single religion was dominant before the advent of the modern age and entered into a confrontation with the state as a focus of power. In India's transition to modernity, the state did not have to confront one or all religions. It is easier for us to regard religion as a personal matter than as a concern, or guiding philosophy of the state.

This is the premise on which the leadership of the freedom movement (1885-1947) defined the notions of a 'composite culture and unity in adversity'. The freedom struggle and the making of the Indian Republic were founded on secularism. The Indian union became a secular-democratic country. This was challenged by parochial groups that largely evolved their conception of monolithic communities from colonialist history and embraced a narrow communalized Europe model of the nation-state.

Important among them were the Rashtriya Swayamsevak Sangh, Hindu Mahasabha and others which rejected the modernist secular premises of the freedom struggle. They only had a tenuous relationship with that struggle, and did not participate significantly in it. This current was long reluctant to accept the secular, tricolour and Jana, Gana, Mana as national symbols. "They insisted on the Bhagwa Flag and devotion to a sanctified and yet paranoid image of Bharat Mata".

This narrow approach found its counterpart in the Muslim League, which was formed in 1906, with its agenda of separatism. Indeed, Hindu and Muslim-communal models of the state are in some respect mirror images of each other. This same current now finds an expression in the statements of the Thackeray, and other conservative leaders. This trend would be registered for the preservation of a composite culture and secularism.

At stake is the legacy of the freedom struggle. The composite culture and secularism are the legacy of the freedom struggle. India's religious pluralism is for wealth, but at the same time is what makes it difficult for the country to function. I think India has taken on an extraordinary courageous challenge in accepting a secular constitution, though circumstances were adverse against secularism. The worst migration in history was taking place but the founding father opted for secularism. In certain cases fundamental rights are opposed to the directive principles of the Constitution. The situation becomes clearer with the Supreme Court judgment concerning the 'Ramshila' at Ayodhya. The Supreme Court explained that it could not rule against fundamental rights enshrined in the Constitution—total freedom to practice his religion. It is left to every state government to maintain law and order. As a student of History I say that nationalism is a modern contemporary concept and phenomenon. It will be wrong and historically untenable to extrapolate nationalism into the Vedic period. It is as contemporary as the 'Middle Class'. Dr. B.B. Mishra, an eminent Historian, has written a well-documented book on the 'Middle Class'. Nationalism and secularism are ingredients of Modern History and Modern Age. Modern Age started after the breakdown of the feudal age.

Nationalism is the product of historical development. A nation is neither something present from the beginning of time nor is its advent sudden. The accumulation of experience leading to the shaping of the distinctive and shared identity results in the emergence of a nation. That specific moment is almost universally associated with a movement secluding in winning a state to which willing even joyful allegiance is extended by those whose loyalty has made the movement what it is.

The movement, however, has to be of a specific kind and it has to build upon historical inscriptive. The movement has to embrace all religions, languages, communities and classes which have in varying measure, shaped by it. Conflict cannot be avoided but the point is to internationalize it and even to use it to advance the existing unity.

It is somewhat facile though fashionable to define the nation as an "imagined community". Such a definition begs the question, what is the community which does the beginning? Why should and when does the imagination result in the birth of national feeling? Moreover the devotion and even separation of segments of a community can still not always prevent the birth of a nation.

India's emergence and continuation as a nation and the persistence of its national state is a copybook example of the historical generation mentioned earlier. Its inferior was treasure unified diversities. Colonial rule came in the way of this inheritance becoming the foundation of modern state. The national movement was much more in reassertion and enriching of this inheritance than even a movement of resistance to and eliminating of foreign rule.[2]

Before the birth of nationalism, India consisted of several nationalities and provinces. In its memorandum to the cabinet mission, the nationalities were defined as follows:

Tamil Nadu, Andhra Desha, Kerala, Karnataka, Maharashtra, Gujarat, Rajasthan, Sindh, Baluchistan, Pathanland, Kashmir, Western Punjab, Central Punjab, Hindustan (U.P. and Haryana), Bihar, Assam, Bengal and Orissa.[3]

Sapru was the leader of the Indian National Federation and was at the top of the legal profession in Allahabad. He was lavish in hospitality. His house was the rule of politics, for he did not relish small talk. According to him, nationalism in the case of India must be very different for the treaty of Vienna (1815) and which has been accentuated in Europe by trace rivalries. Nationalism in India maintain, for a long time to come, at reducing the internal parts of conflict too minimum, multiplying the parts of contact and flattering a sense of community of interest. This will require very conscious and continued effort.

> *"Personally speaking, I have very little evidence of such nationalism in India. Each Party is using democratic phrases and slogans really for the establishment of its own supremacy."*[4]

Nationalism provides a separate, distinct identity to a racial type which in turn establishes a nation of sovereign states and with distinct political, social and cultural identity. Nationalism as a decisive factor developed only in the nineteenth century and its founder was Rousseau, who rejecting the endorsement of the nation in the personal sovereign of the ruling class, identified 'nation' and 'people'. And this became the fundamental principle both of the American and French revolutions. Internal relations, as E.H. Carr observes, were henceforth to be governed not by the personal interests, ambition and emotitions of the monarch, but by the collective interests, ambitions and emotitions of the nation. Again, nationalism got an economic orientation in the early twentieth century when national policies in countries like Great Britain came to be founded on the support of the masses, and the counterpart was the loyalties the masses to a nation which has become instrumental of their collective interest and ambition. Perhaps this concept gave birth to 'Jingoism' in Great Britain indicating nationalism of the masses.

Thus, the nationalism which has been so decisive in the formation of nation-state in modern times is the nationalism which is both democratic and socialistic but not the altered ego of the person of the sovereign of the earlier days.

Nationalism by its very meaning presupposes the existence of separate, independent nation-state or countries. Even some scholars have pointed that whole patriotism is a positive concept, nationalism is a negative one based on collective grievances against the foreigners. So nationalism is always indicative of the existence of separate nations.

According to S. Bahera, the nation-state were continue to exist and it has not lost its relevance. According to Bahera, India is a multi-nation-state and we have succeeded in forging a common nationalism which can be safely timed as Indian nationalism or non-Indian nationalism.

Historian Tom Navim has persuasively argued that "The arrival of nationalism in a distinctively modern sense was tried to the political baptism of the lower classes". This thesis holds true as much for India as the West. The strengthening of nationalism in India was rapid after taking over the leadership of the Indian National Congress by Mahatma Gandhi in 1920 because of his indomitable capacity to mobilize lower class peasants and farmers for the achievement of 'Swaraj'. In India, there is no better way of preserving diversity and enabling local communities to extend their democratic space than through the secular-liberal-modernist route.

What I have discussed is clear that India was not a nation in the Vedic period. Groups of people had started to inhabit after defeating the non-Aryans. Even the sense of nationality had not struck deep root. They were tribal and fought for political supremacy among themselves. Soon they came under foreign domination from 1206. There was no nation in India till the Indian National Congress brought them to the common platform and they become political conscious for the liberation of the country. So a modern nation was born in India in 1947. India was a heterogeneous till 1885. Gradually the society became heterogeneous. All sections of the people including the downtrodden and the tribal started to think in terms of India.

Until there is modernity, there cannot be a nation. Nations are both out of travail and sufferings.

To be modern a community needs to grow into a self-conscious nation. To be an established nation, it needs to cross the threshold of modernity. Independence, territorial integrity and popular cohesion are the principle ingredients of nationhood. To be a nation, they must think they are a nation, language, religion, territory, political skill and economic necessity can all help a nation first come into being and thereafter endurance, to have common glories in the past, a common will in the present, to have accomplished great things together, to wish to do so again, that is essential condition for long a nation.[5]

The more modern a society, the more capacity, it will have to cement all groups and the larger ones and thereby create complicated and flexible forms of organization. The modern nation is essentially an achievement in the making of a nation, Ernest Rennin said: "The nation, like the individual, is the product of a long period of work sacrifice and dereliction." Britain first became valid nation or nation-state and thereafter went inquest of modernity. Germany first opted for modernity and then became nation-state. Japan became a nation-state and introduced modernity in the country. Argentina is still struggling for full modernity but has attained imperfect nationhood. In this world the modern nations undergo great strains to preserve their achievements. A modern nation will never arise on the foundation of a traditional society or liberated colony of adventurous settlement if the circumstances are not promoting. There are examples of "the achieving society" in the world and such societies have combined modernity and nationhood in their policies. There are differences between nation on the move and the nation left to rot lies in the realm of character and of attitude. For the last decades India is rolling between the political leaders have lost their visions. The concept of modernity and the nationhood has been much weakened. In the nation on the move, restlessness, hope and effort combine to produce a genuinely 'modern spirit'. In the words of Glows Dickerson, a dissatisfaction with the world in which we live and a determination to relies of one that shall be better and the spirit may be more powerful influence in the progress of the nation than the accidental possession of fertile soil or bubbling oil.[6] Nations are born, develop, modernize and endure only under the leadership of skilled and dedicated leaders. Unfortunately we have no dedicated leader in our midst, which is politically strong. Hence castes and communalism are raising their heads again. Nation is in doldrums.

The elite of India should be unified and clear minded. Unless the elite provide alert and functional leadership, the nation will not make progress in the field of political, social, economic or cultural development. Politics is the key that men must sooner or later turn energetically it a modern nation is to come into being and then to be preserved. India is an example of emerged nation that has searched for nationhood and modernity with the method grounded on democratic ideas.

My findings are that India was not a nation during the period of *Rig Veda* and the *Rig Veda* has been assigned the time bracket, *c.* 1700-900 B.C. The Vedic people remained to the west of Jamuna-Ganga doab until *c.* 850 B.C. The large scale settlement of the Gangetic plain took place only when the use of iron became widespread and perhaps when population increased. During their migration, the Indo-Aryans canoe with them not only their poetry and religious beliefs and no political system. The Indo-Aryan consisted of several tribal groups often clashed and the Bharata battle place only in *c.* 900 B.C. It is evident that large scale settlement of Ganga plain took only in the Iron Age, after *c.* 900 B.C. Since the bulk of the *Rig Veda* is by all account older than 900 B.C., the *Rig* Vedic Aryans must have been confined to the religion west of Ganga, no matter where they came from.

The composition of *Rig Veda* was taken upon South Afghanistan a few centuries after the demise of the mature Harappan phase. The later parts of the *Rig Veda* as well as the later Vedic texts were, however, composed in India so there was no nation in India either in the period of *Rig Veda* or the later *Veda*. The freedom struggle brought the concept of nation in our country.

It might be instructive to remember that modern system of political governess-democracy and constitution came in the wake of the Industrial Revolution which began in the middle of the eighteenth century in England. As feudalism begin to melt with the advent of Industrial Revolution, the old way of governance gave way to the new. In other words, new technology which spurred the industrial revolution also brought about a new system of governance.

I conclude that our Nation is fifty-three and to think that India was a nation in the ancient period of our history is against the spirit of History, and it is untenable. India began in Mohanjodaro and become a nation on August 14/15, 1947 at the midnight. So India emerged and continues as a nation. The idea of nation is relatively new, although countries have existed for a long time. The United States is the first modern nation. The notion of modernity also begins with the United States. For the first time people consciously decided to become a nation. The French, during the French Revolution in 1789, followed the American example. However, they had to deal with a past. So did every other country which decided to become a nation in the past 2000 years. The American did not have the past but they were unique. They did only for the future.[7]

We, in India, got the American idea of founding a nation from England, but our inspiration was American. Unlike Americans, our project of nationhood has to deal with the difficult terrain of "our golden past". It is particularly exhausting because we do not have homogeneous history. It is a devise past of many religion, many languages and many people. The Americans solved their problem of diversity by throwing their many immigrant communities into the 'melting past'. Their ethnic immigrant monotonous did not form separatist movements. They eagerly followed the English language and American way of life in order to get ahead in the land of opportunity. In India, we historically dealt with the problem of diversity through the caste system. The minority became sub-caste. This solution worked except when it came to the Islamic minority who were the product of a separate religion which has spread from Spain to China and they were unwilling to be assimilated as a sub-caste.[8]

If Americans are melting pot, we are a mosaic. A good mosaic has a unity of style, however, and India's unity is provided by its civilization and "the Indian way of life". Most scholars admit the India's diversity makes a profound unity.

When Hinduism found that it was unable to accommodate Islam into the caste fabric, it withdrew within itself unable to deal with or the challenge of Islam, it slowly lost its vitality. After the thirteenth century, when our last great temples were built it lost its way in superstitions and rituals and it did not recover from its stupor until the nineteenth century, when it was challenged by another universal civilization, the Christian civilization of the West newly invigorated by science, technology and the modernist idea of the enlightenment.

Modern India, which started from 1757 A.D., is thus a product of clash of Hindu tradition with the universal religion of Islam and with Western civilization. The search for a modern Indian nation has been the overwhelming obsession of the educated Indian for the past 100 years and it continues to this day. The British education first spread in Bengal, Bombay and Madras did not lag behind but the early settlers were primarily Bengalese, the first lateral products of the Macaulay's education policy. They adopted a critical attitude towards the past. They helped to reform the Indian society (both Hindu and Muslim). They gave birth to the political movement for independent and they ushered in modern India.

Mahatma Gandhi took modernity to the masses. Yet he suffered deeply from the same trammel of modernity, which afflicts other educated Indians. He vigorously used the railways and the telegraph but they hated them. He could not reconcile to the idea that Western technology was a national approach in solving universal problems and its products were a universal purpose of all human beings.

In the past 53 years our Constitution and democracy have provided a great school for teaching modernist attitude to the average Indian. Especially in the past decade our experience with many coalition governments, with a general change in Prime Ministers has removed some of the traditional areas of authority. So also has the recent working of checks and balances in the government. The prospect of a cabinet minister or a chief minister being disciplined by a Judge of the Election Commission and has taken some of the share out of the authority in the eye of the common man so used to despotic authority. The self-restraint displayed by our military has similarly been instructive for, it has provided the base for civil order, unlike the Latin America, where the Army is the principle catalyst of civil disorder. Having seen the mighty fall has introduced a little sense of justice in the terribly unjust world of the average Indian.

The modern India of today should feel self-confident. He must not—after swadeshi, which betrays an inferiority complex. He must repose trust in his own reason, and be able to discriminate between the 'modern' and the 'western'. Above all, he must have confidence, that the diverse civilization of India will survive the phony Global culture.[9]

Historian Tom Nairn has advanced this argument that "the arrival of nationalism in a distinctively modern sense was true to the political baptism of the lower class". This thesis holds true as much for India as the West. The spread of nationalism in India was rapid after the arrival of Mahatma Gandhi on the scene because of his indomitable capacity to mobilize the peasants, workers and *dalits* for the sake of Swaraj. Nationalism's convenient marriage with the institutions of the state gradually reversed that process. The nation-state after the initial euphoria became very much alienated from the subaltern classes.

NOTES

1. Prophet Bidow, 'India: Nation or Republic', *Frontline*, February 2001, p. 21.
2. The *Times of India*, New Delhi, December1997, p. 11.
3. *Mainstream,* January 1995, p. 28.
4. Durga Das, *Current National Affair*, p. 197.
5. Clinton Rossetar, *The American Quest,* 1790-1860, p. 41.
6. *Ibid.*, p. 79.
7. The *Times of India*, New Delhi, 10/12, 1997.
8. *Ibid.*
9. *Ibid.*

2

Nation and Nationality

Two-nation Theory and its Origin

Before defining two-nation theory, it is essential that the word nation and nationality should be defined. The word 'nation' is derived from the Latin word *natio* means birth or descent. In the etymological sense the word 'nation', therefore, refers to a group of people descended from the same stock. But for the political scientists, the two term nation and nationality have acquired a new meaning. A nationality is a group of people found together by the identities of race, language, religion or by communities of interest, history and tradition, while a nation is a group of men united under the same sovereignty. A nation is a nationality when it organized itself into a political body either independent or desiring to be independent. When a nationality forms an independent political organization it acquires statehood; it emerges into a nation. Thus the difference between nation and nationality rests on the attainment of independent statehood. A nationality invested with political consciousness is a nation and a nation divested of political consciousness is a nationality. So in order to be a nation, a state must have the feeling of oneness among the people. Language, religion, territory, political skill and economic necessity can all help a nation first come into being and thereafter endure. To have common glories in the past, a common will in the present to have accomplished great things together, to wish to do so again that is the essential condition for being a nation. A modern nation will never arise on the foundation of a traditional society, if the circumstances are not promising. Nations are born, develop, modernize and endure only under the leadership of a dedicated leader. The modern nation is essentially an achievement.

The nation like the individual is the product of long period of work, sacrifice and devotion. A nation is the product of a concrete historical process. In Western Europe nation was largely, though not wholly the result of common language and culture. Nation is a word used often but defined seldom, language, territory, religion or race may contribute to the making of a nation but do not quite make it. A useful clue may be a joint family which has members speaking more than one language, praying to different gods but living under one roof. They can live together only because they have an average commitment to one another as member of a family. A joint family is the charpoy or perhaps the miniature of a nation.

The widespread distinction between state and nation may be opted from the following situations:

1. One nation, one state. In the contemporary world there is hardly any case of such a pure type, however, Japan and Portuguese could be cited as example.
2. Parts of different nations come together to constitute a state for geo-political reasons, i.e. Switzerland.
3. One nation is divided into two or three states for ideological reasons, i.e. Korea, Arabia.
4. Part of a nation is constituted into one state and the remaining part is attached or affiliated to another state, i.e. Bangladesh and West Bengal.
5. A nation may be divided between two or more states and constitute parts of them along with other nations, i.e. Kurtz.
6. A number of nations came to constitute a state, i.e. India, United Kingdom.
7. A set of migrants drawn from a multiplicity of nations constitute a state, i.e. the United States of America.

The cases of the U.S. indicate the specificity of ethnicity in comparison to nationality. While nationality is a product of coterminality between culture and territory, ethnicity emerges out of the dissociation between the two; ethnicity is a product of immigration, colonization or conquest. But if an ethnic group succeeds in establishing a moral claim over the territory into which it moves, it becomes a nation. However, it is not necessary that the nation should make an exclusive legal claim over the territory. If it does not succeed it becomes a state but the claim even to nationhood may be contested (as in the case of Fiji Indians) or conceded (as in the case of Malthusian Indians) depending upon a varieties of factors. What is pertinent to my argument is that ethnic group is treated as outsiders by the nationals. In a nation all are insiders; the nationality of the constituting elements is not question. Yet often the only difference of consequence between nation on the move and a nation left to not lies in the realm of character and attitude. Britain and France stand on a different pattern. Britain and France were not ethnically or linguistically homogeneous till the nineteenth century and are not fully so even today.

In India, nation is not the result of ethnicity or common language of a dominant position acquired by anyone ethnic group or region but nation and nationalism is basically the product of the freedom struggle by the entire common people to achieve freedom of the country.

The time has come to define the word 'nation' in the Indian context. The Indian nation means coming into being of the Indian people as a historical entity. The nation was formed in India not only because their society or culture became homogeneous but also because of their economic and political interests and the interest of their social and cultural development became one even when they continued to be differentiated by language and ethnicity.

Nation formation is a big interesting process in India. The British period helped the process of the formation of the nation in India. The foreign rulers ruled in their own interests so the Indian people were unified and fought against the mighty British Empire. So before the British rule and the freedom struggle, India was not a nation. In the ancient period and the medieval period, India could not be regarded as a nation. The people of India had not been unified before a British rule. This aspect had been studied by Prof. John Seley, he said that India was not a nation and he described India as a "geological expression" but he wrote that the British government might bring the Indian nation into being by providing a common target to its people. Simultaneously the liberation struggle brought the people in one bond and the Indian nation was born. Perhaps without the Indian freedom movement (1885-1947), Indians might have been considered as the inhabitants of a geographical region on the map of the world. In short India was a nationality before 1885.

But political scientists have the different approach, they assume that first a nation is formed then the freedom struggle starts. The conversationalists are more extreme in their arguments. They say that nationality was present in the country even before the British period. They quote Raphael Samuel, who says "Nationality is something unproblematic and progressive, a unity which defines time and space and links past and present in a mystic union." If at all it is to be believed, nationality did not develop into a nation. Raphael Samuel's argument is not tenable. A nation is a process of becoming, in the case of India, it is different. Here the formation of nation and the struggle for the freedom struggle started together. National consciousness motivated struggle and struggle stimulated consciousness.

It is evident from my discussion that the British rule constituted to the growth of the concept of nation. India became a nation in 1947 but the question is 'were Muslims a nation in India?' Mahatma Gandhi and Jinnah differed widely on this issue. Gandhi's letter to Jinnah dated September 15, 1944 read, "I find no parallel in history for a body of converts and their descendents claiming to be a nation apart from the parent stock. If India was one nation before the advent of Islam, it remains one in spite of the change of faith of a very large body of her children." Jinnah's rejoinder to Gandhi came on September 19, 1944: can you not appreciate our point of view that we claim the right of self-determination as a nation and not as territorial unit, and that we are entitled to exercise our inherent right as a Muslim nation, which is our birth right? Whereas you are labouring under a wrong idea that 'self-determination' means only that of territorial unit which by the way is neither demanded nor defined.

At this stage it is proper to understand Sir Syed Ahmed Khan's political ideas, did he believe in two-nation theory? Two-nation theory means that Hindus and Muslims were both a nation before 1947.

Sir Syed Ahmad Khan (1807-1893)

Syed Ahmad is regarded as the greatest Indian Muslim leader after Bahadur Shah Zafar and before M.A. Jinnah. He wanted to help the Muslims against the British hostility in the post-1857 period. He felt shocked to discover that the Muslims were discussed as vile treacherous and contemptible. He developed his thesis in 1860 describing his community as the loyal Mohammedans of India. In the seventies, W.W. Hunter's work *The Indian Musalmans* was published. Hunter made an academic study of the conditions of the Muslims. Syed Ahmad studied why Muslims were mentally isolated?

Syed Ahmad was the first leader of the country, who thought that the Muslims of the country first should receive the English education and then they should take the membership of the Indian National Congress. Impelled by this motive, he established the Mohammedan Anglo-Oriental College at Aligarh on May 24, 1875.[1] On January 8, 1877, Lord Lytton, the Viceroy of the country, laid the foundation stone of the Mohammedan Anglo-Oriental College at Aligarh. The founders of college regarded the British rule in India as 'the most wonderful phenomena the world ever has seen'. Aligarh became not merely a place for Anglo-Oriental learning but also a centre of a new political ideology to further Mohammedan interests. The leaders of the Aligarh school of thought projected their policies for safeguarding the interest of the Muslim community. In other words, their line of approach encouraged directly and indirectly political separatism, within the broader framework of national politics, which had taken share from 1885.

Syed Ahmad had his reactionary view "the system of representation by election he declared in 1883" means the representation of the views and interest of the majority of the population and in the countries where the population is composed of one race and one creed. It is no doubt that the best system that can be adopted but, my lord, in a country like India, where caste distinction still flourish, where there is no fusion of the various races, where religious distinctions are still violent, where education in its modern sense has not made an equal and proportionate progress among all sections of the population. I am convinced that the introduction of the principle of election, pure and simple, for representation of various interests on the Local Boards and District Councils, would be attended with evils of greater significance than purely economic considerations.[2]

Sir Syed Ahmad followed the lofty ideas of modernizing the Muslim through education but he did not work a common cause with his fellow Hindus and question foreign domination. Just as we blame several of nineteenth century, Hindu nationalist for their failure to distinguishing between Hindu nationalism and Indian nationalism. So we should have no hesitation in condemning Muslim moderates like Sir Syed for their failure towards building the secular Indian nationalism. As this type of nationalism could not develop, two-nation theory developed.

Before the birth of the Congress, the National Mohammedan was the mouth of the advance section of Mohammedans and in 1882 the body was negotiating with the Government regarding the improvement of the conditions of the Muslim people. It was to the body that the Congress appeared a phenomenon to reckon with. Amer Ali, the Honorary Secretary of the Central National Mohammedan Association wrote a letter to the secretaries to the National Congress explaining why the Association should abstain from participation in the proposed Congress. It was the beginning of a parochial tendency from the side of the largest religious minority of India towards a national organization, which wanted to be all comprehensive but which by circumstances was bound to represent to a larger degree the feelings and assignations of the preponderant majority, namely the Hindus.

The Muslim apathy towards National Congress, both from progressive and conservative sections, did cause concern to the Founding Father of the Congress, though they did not consider it either as final or likely to endanger the national cause. After all these were the inceptive days of a great Party. It needed time for all sections common to its fold. Badruddin Tyabjee was the president of the third session of the Congress in 1887. Tyabjee tried to bring Muslims in the Congress and he wanted to strengthen the foundation of the National Congress but Tyabjee could not succeed in his policy.

Sir Syed Ahmad wrote in 1893 just before his death, "India is like a balance whose two puns are of equal weight, and to equalize them in compensating weight is required to make the lighter equal to the heavy. This compensating weight will always be a foreign nation and it is an occasion of congratulation that God has entrusted the British nation with this duty, who was generous and free people. He developed the 'two-nation theory' which went in favour of the British government and it was an obstacle before the Indian nation.

In the first part of his political life he was progressive. The following quotations are from the book of Urdu, *Sayyed Ahmad Khan Ka Safarnama* written by Ali Sayyed Iqbal and printed by the Aligarh Institute Gazette Press Aligarh, 1884.

> *"A community*[3] *is constituted by those who inhabit one and the same country. The term Hindu and Muslim have*

denominational reference only. In fact all communities domiciled in India are one people. Their political interest ought to be distinguished. There is no time to allow religion to draw a dividing line between the citizens of a state."

Addressing a deputation of Aryasamagists at Lahore, Sir Syed Ahmad is reported to have said, "You distinguish yourself from the others by the appellation of 'Hindus'. I cannot agree to this, Hinduism is not orthodoxy; everybody living in this country can style himself a Hindu. I am sorry to penetrate that you do not take me for a Hindu although I am as much a son of soil."

Replying to an address of welcome by the Indian association of Lahore, he observed: I regard Hindus and Muslims as my two eyes. The people would generally make a difference by calling one the right and other left eye but I regard the Hindus and Muslims as one eye. I wish I had only one eye, in which case I would compare them with advantage to that single eye.

Syed Ahmad was following a different path. Syed Ahmad was explaining to the people how the political demands of the Congress would endanger the Muslims. Referring to elective principles in India he said, "We can prove by mathematics that there will be four votes for the Hindu to every one vote for the Mohammedan. And how can the Mohammedan guard his interests? It would be like a game of dice, on which one man had four dice and the other only one— Now, I ask you oh, Mohammedan I weep at your condition. Have you such wealth that you can compete with the Hindus?—Now I ask you to pardon me for saying something which I say with a sore heart. In the whole nation, there is no person who is equal to the Hindus in fitness for the work." Now there were three parties to the Indian problem, the Congress, the British and the Muslims.

Jawaharlal Nehru has stated that the 'Mao College' failed to inspire its students with the kind of intellectual struggle that forces people to break out of the mould of past categories of thought develop new sensibility and social loyalties. "For a nationalist and socialist, the ideology that Aligarh stood for, served only to frustrate a multitude of glorious aspirations, for many religious Muslims as well as Indian nationalists, Muslims identity as construed at Aligarh seemed shallow."

Till 1885, Syed Ahmad was a liberal leader. He believed in one nation but the foundation of the Indian National Congress brought to an end to his liberalism and the change had appeared in his liberal attitude much before 1885. Syed Ahmed told a gathering of students in Ludhiana in 1882, in this way: 'Dear Children' if someone becomes a star of heaven but ceases to be a Muslim, what is he to us? He is no longer a member of our nation. Sir Syed Ahmad's speech advising Muslims to keep aloof from the Congress came in 1887. "When our Hindu breathes or Bengali friends wish to make a move which involves a loss to us and humiliation to our nation, we cannot remain friendly and undoubtedly it is our duty to protect our nation from the attack of Hindus and Bengalis, which we are sure, are going to harm our nation." Another statement came in 1893 just before his death: "The proposals of the Congress are exceeding inexpedient for a country which is inhabited by two different nations. Now suppose that all the English were to leave India then who would be ruler of India?" It is possible that under these circumstances two nations the Hindus and the Mohammedans could sit on the same throne and remain equal in power. Most certainly not, it is necessary that one of them should conquer the other and thrust it down. To hope that both could remain is to desire the impossible and the irreconcilable.

Sir Syed Ahmad established the Indian Patriotic Association in 1888. He had established this association to assure the British government of the loyalty of the association. He gave the membership of it to Muslims and such categories of Hindus who were opposed to the Congress. Sir Syed Ahmad was helped by a prominent Taluqdar discord between of Banaras Raja Shiv Prasad but soon there was a discord between Syed Ahmad and Shiv Prasad regarding the attitude towards the Congress. Syed Ahmad was recognized the patriotic association under the name called the United Indian Patriotic Association. Syed Ahmad was not clear about the meaning of community and the nation. The word 'Nation' has been defined by the Western scholars but Syed Ahmad did not apply the meaning of nation as it was understood in Europe. Moreover, as I have explained the meaning of nation, Syed Ahmad used the word community for the nation. It was misnomer, sometimes the Maulvis managed to get an authenticated Fatwa from the Imam of Mecca, on this ground that he was propagating the English education in India. Govind Ballabh Pant said that Syed Ahmad was not a communalist or separatist but historical facts are opposed to this. While giving credit for the liberalism and nationalism of Syed Ahmad I emphasize the essential communal was of his outlook.

Mr. B.R. Nanda, an eminent non-professional historian in his article entitled "Sir Syed sowed seed of partition" published in the *Times of India* in November 1988 has called Syed Ahmad as separatist. Prof. V.N. Dutta, retired University Professor and Head of the Department of History, Kurukshetra University, Haryana, in his two well-written articles, which were published in the *Times of India* dated December 21/22, 1988, has agreed with the view points of B.R. Nanda. He has written nothing on the two-nation theory. Dr. Rafiq Zakaria, the Chancellor of Urdu University Aligarh, in his article "two-nation theory and its origin" published in the *Times of India*, New Delhi, Zakaria had called that Sir Syed Ahmad was not separatist. Lala Lajpat Rai was a Congress leader and he joined the Hindu Mahasabha in 1925. In those days a member of Hindu Mahasabha used to attend the meeting of Congress Party and *vice versa*. The constitution of Congress Party permitted this addressing the Hindu Mahasabha in 1925. Lajpat Rai denounced the talk of Hindu Raj or Muslim Raj. He has written about thirteen articles on 'Hindu Muslim Problems' which was published in the *Tribune* in November-December 1924. In the 11th of the 13-series article he wrote: "If communal representation with separate electorates is to be the rule, then Maulana Hasrat Mahani's[4] scheme, as to smaller provinces, seems to be the only workable proposition. Under his scheme, Muslims would have achieved four Muslim States: (1) The Pathan Province of North-West Frontier, (2) Western Punjab, (3) Sindh, and (4) Eastern Bengal. It was said that if there were compact Muslim area in any part of India, sufficiently large too from a province, they should be similarly constituted but it should be distinctly understood that this is not a united India. It means a clear partition of India into a Muslim India and non-Muslim India.

Lala Lajpat Rai's arguments is in a historical prospective but it was not his original statement. He simply explained Maulana Hasrat Mohani's scheme. Accordingly it was that there should be smaller province. Small province was to be constituted only to strengthen communal representation and separate electorates. If this formula was implemented, the entire province of Bengal and Punjab might have gone to the Muslim League. Lajpat Rai was a member of the Indian National Congress and Hindu Mahasabha. He understood the implication of the scheme of Mohani and he said that small province means Western Punjab and Eastern Bengal. Dr. Zakaria had said that Lala Lajpat Rai was the first leader who talked for the division of Punjab and Bengal on communal lines. So he talked of the two-nation theory and he was a separatist but there is fallacy in his arguments. Lajpat Rai was not a communalist in 1925, he simply explained the scheme of Mohani, Dr. Zakaria should call Mohani a communalist.

Sir Syed Ahmad Khan was not a progressive man. He said that the Muslims were a nation. He believed in two-nation theory from 1885. In the early part of his political career he was liberal. But from 1885, he slowly moved towards communalism and he developed his faith on two-nation theory. Gradually, he became a separatist and strong propagator of two-nation theory. Subsequently the two-nation theory was developed by Dr. Iqbal, Rahamat Ali, and M.A. Jinnah.[5] Exactly a fortnight later came the League's Pakistan resolution. Much before Jinnah, V. Savarkar had propounded two-nation theory, first time in 1923 in his book *Hindutva* and reiterated it in his presidential address to the Mahasabha on December 30, 1937. In the old days the Congressmen could work in both the organizations, namely the Hindu Mahasabha and the Congress. But the Congress abolished this practice in 1938 and from 1938 no Congress could be the member of the Hindu Mahasabha and *vice versa*. The two-nation theory of Syed Ahmad, M.A. Jinnah and connived at by the British colonial rulers had proved grossly fallacious within less than half a century.

Sir Syed and the Congress

While Lord Daffrin was criticizing the activity of the Congress, Sir Syed Ahmad launched his campaign against the Indian National Congress. He utilized the forum of Muslim Education conference for this conference.

Sir Syed public speech on 28th December, 1887 was the beginning of his tirade against this national organization, which was holding its third Annual conference in 1887 at Bombay. He condemned all the previous resolutions of the Congress. The Congress had passed a resolution in the first session in Bombay in 1885 on the I.C.S. examination. The Congress was in favour that I.C.S. examination be held simultaneously in England and India. But Sir Syed Ahmad was opposed to the simultaneous examination of I.C.S. in India. He thought that the Muslim candidates could not compete with the Bengalis.[6]

Syed Ahmad opposed even the expansion of the legislative councils, as in his view only respectable persons, i.e. high born belonging to aristocratic families could become members of the Viceroy's Executive Council. He asserted that "The respectable communities of India would not like any person of low creed and caste whom they fully know, to rule over them."[7]

The Anglo-Indian press and the Aligarh Institute Gazette criticized the pamphlets of Hume. Reckless abuse was hurled on the author and the Bengali Babus. Pandit Ajudhianath was aware of the anti-Bengalis feeling prevalent among his contemporaries and in one office speech he said that the time was not ripe for joining the Congress.[8]

Syed Ahmad was opposed to any agitation by the Congress, which according to him, if unchecked, "will end in a mutiny followed by horrors and massacres in comparison in which the mutiny of 1857 was more child's play and may finally end in a disastrous catastrophe."[9]

In the beginning people thought that Syed Ahmad was the author of the criticism against Hume, but subsequently it was found that he was not and the criticism appeared in the Gazette as 'communicated'.[10]

The *Pioneer* Allahabad went a step further. It soiled its columns with much foul matter by unjustly abusing two very worthy Englishmen, Messers Hume and Cotton. Pandit Ajudhianath, although still not in the Congress, did not allow such culinary to go unnoticed. His journal *Indian Union* wrote: "these gentlemen have, in the eye of our contemporary the unpardonable aspirations and must, therefore, be given no quarter."[11]

I conclude that Sir Syed Ahmad gave birth to the idea of two-nation theory—a direct offshoot of religious fundamentalism. The divisive two-nation theory, considers religious differences to be the basis of nationalhood. To accept that is to justify acts like ethnic cleansing and the holocaust.

NOTES

1. K.R. Narendra Nath, *Sardar Panikar*, p. 30.
2. Proceeds of the Indian Legislative Council, *Syed Ahmad Khan on Local Self-government Bill*, March 1883.
3. Ali Syed Iqbal, *Sayyed Ahmad Khan Ka Safarnama,* printed by the Aligarh Institute Gazette Press, Aligarh, 1884.
4. President of the Muslim League at Ahmedabad in 1921.
5. M.A. Jinnah propounded the two-nation theory in an article in *Time and Tide*, ed., London, March 1940, p. 9.
6. The *Aligarh Institute Gazette*, 1st March, 1890.
7. *Ibid.*
8. The Bengalis, February 18, 1888.
9. The *Aligarh Institute Gazette*, March 1, 1880.
10. *The Tribune*, December 11, 1886.
11. *Ibid.*

3

Lord Minto and the Muslims : The Simla Deputation 1906

Lord Minto succeeded Curzon in 1905. Never since the dark days of Lord Lytton's viceroyalty (1876-80) had India been so distracted, disconnected and the victim of so many misfortunes as it was in 1905. Minto arrived in India as Viceroy on November 17, 1905. He succeeded a brilliant Viceroy, Lord Curzon, whose reign, ending in storm and stress left troubled waters for his successor to navigate. He maintained the partition of Bengal. The Swadeshi movement was supported all walks of the people. Even Rabindranath Tagore took part in many partition protest meetings for some time. Another important effect of the movement was the split between the Moderates and the Extremists divided along ideological lines. Anti-British sentiment was powerful and widespread. The feelings of the educated class of the country were imitated because Curzon had treated with open contempt and they were denied a share in the administration. The revolutionary movement had also started in Bengal in 1905. Lord Minto had to face this challenge.

However the most significant development which confronted the new Viceroy was Muslim awakening and further growth of Indian nationalism. The Muslims, specially the Western educated and younger generation among them, were showing signs of awakening, their thoughts ran into the "Congress mould". With the growth of English education among the Muslim youth religious differences between the Hindus and Muslims for political purposes loomed large before the eyes of Viceroy. As he said, "I think that caste and religious differences certainly in respect to the two groups of Mohammedans and Hindus are showing signs of weakening and that in the next generations there is a great prospect of the disappearance of the separation of caste and religions in deference to the calls of political aims.[1]

Warning of a possible Hindu-Muslim unity and cooperation for political purposes reached Minto from other sources as well. Sir Theodore Morrison, formerly principle of Aligarh Oriental Mohammedan College, Aligarh, who was regarded as 'particularly competent' to speak, on behalf of the Mohammedans, told Morley about the possibility of Mohammedan sympathies by and by gaining over to the Congress Party.[2] He belied that as a result of the spread of education, a young generation of Mohammedans was coming up in all the big towns of northern India whole, thoughts run easily in the "Congress mould" and he did not think that the Mussalmans will long stand out against the blandishment of the Congress.[3] A similar warning came from the Denzil Ibbotson, member of the Viceroy's executive council, "I have heard from other quarters also what Mohsin-ul-Mulk, says about the aspirations of the younger generation of Mohammedan. Their aspirations are perfectly natural but it could be a calamity if they were to drive them into the aims of the Congress Party, for at present the educated Mohammedan is the most conservative element in Indian society."[4]

So Minto wanted to weaken the forces of nationalism by preventing the Muslims from joining the Indian National Congress. It became the policy of the Viceroy Lord Minto to bring about Anglo Mohammedan rapprochement. The Viceroy wanted to recognize the Muslims as a separate and historically important community. He also liked that the Muslims should have the large share in the civil services of the country and should also enjoy separate representation in the legislative councils.

The genesis of the Simla deputation could be traced from the behaviour of the Principal of the Anglo Oriental College. The principal of the M.A.O. College was W.A.J. Archibald. He was taking a keen interest for the deputation itself was a collection of individuals, hard-packed for the purpose; in disregard this fact that the All India Muslim League was the reciprocated forum of politically minded Muslims in the country.

Welfare of the Muslims, Principal Archibald asked Mohsin-ul-Mulk, the Honorary Secretary of the College, to despatch a representation to the Government of India for the sake of the Muslims, Mr. Archibald stressed that loyalty of the Muslims should only be stressed in the address to be presented to the Viceroy. Nawab-ul-Mulk enlisted the support of the leading Muslims of India and a deputation was formed. This deputation considered of thirty-five members of the Muslims. In spite of pressure, a strong nationalist like M.A. Jinnah refused to join the deputation. They were all Muslim nobilities. The Aga Khan III was the leader of the deputation. An address was presented by Aga Khan to Viceroy Lord Minto on October 1st, 1906 at 11 A.M. and this memorandum was signed at Simla by nobles, ministers of various states, great landowners, lawyers, merchants and many others of His Majesty's Mohammedan subjects.

The chief feature of an address was that the Muslim rights should be protected. The deputationists requested the Viceroy for recognition of Muslim political status. So they demanded political concessions separately. The deputationists stressed separate electoral constituency for the Muslims. There were other minor demands also.

Viceroy Minto remarked "the pith of your address, as I understand it, is a claim that in any system of representation, whether it affects a municipality, a district board or a legislature in which it is proposed to introduce or to increase. The electoral organization, the Mohammedan community should be represented as a body. You justly claimed that your position should be estimated not merely in your numerical strength but in respect to the political importance of your community and the services that it has rendered to the Empire." The Viceroy assured the deputationists that adequate attention should be paid to the Muslim point of view. He concluded in this way: "please do not misunderstand me. I make no attempt to indicate by what means the communities can be obtained, but I am as firmly convinced as I believe to be, that any electoral representation to India would be doomed to mischievous failure, which aimed at granting a personal enfranchisement regardless to beliefs and traditions of the communities comprising the population of the continent." So the deputationists were much satisfied. Now the Muslims were assured separate electorates, which were introduced in 1909. The hereditary spiritual head, of the Lama II sect, of Muslims are claiming descent from Fatima.

The Aga Khan III urged the case for increased Muslim participation in the political life of the country and pressed that they should be regarded as a nation within a nation with rights and obligations safeguarded by statute, with adequate and separate representations both in local bodies and on legislative councils and with a communal franchise of electoral roll. Lord Minto's reply was reassuring. The Viceroy had a pro-Muslim attitude.

The Simla deputation appears to be a got up affair and fully engineered by interested officials—so the All India Mohammedan Deputation is neither an Indian, nor all Mohammedans, not even the deputation, properly so called. It is only an instrument in the hands of the officials to whitewash their doings. In other words, the authorities wanted a few simple-minded men of position to give them a certificate of good conduct. They knew the Hindus would not do it. So they began operating among the older classes of Mussalmans[5].

The Indian nationalist press also questioned the views of the British owned press like *The London Times*, *The Pioneer* and *The Englishman* that the Simla deputation was a thoroughly representative body of the Indian Muslims.

The *Tribune* wrote Sir Syed Ahmad's opposition to the Congress was not at all creditable to him. There are many Mohammedans of position, culture and influence who wholly disapproves of the unholy alliance he entered into with Sir Auckland Colvin and the Anglo-Indian press to verify the Hindus and their political agitation.[6]

To Minto the deputation was a welcome event, coming at the critical juncture of History, when the feeling between the people and the government ran high and the extreme section of the Indian National Congress had the upper hand, Minto searched for allies who could be loyal and faithful to the British and counteract the activities of the Congress. In the Mohammedans he found one such useful ally. After receiving the deputation the Viceroy informed Morley that "the recent expression of Mohammedans feeling will do an enormous[7] amount of good" and a month later he added that, the Mohammedans deputation and the display of Mohammedan feeling generally has undoubtedly done much to minimize the importance of Bengalee vapourings.[8] Minto was satisfied with his performance and the Simla success went a long way in weaning the Muslim away from the Congress. Minto was the first Governor General who introduced Communalism for the first time in the polity of the Indian states. The Simla deputation was a command performance by the Viceroy which was started by Maulana Mohammad Ali who presided over the Congress at Gowanda in 1923. The memorandum was published in full both in the *Pioneer* of Lucknow and the *Mail* of Madras on October 5, 1906. Both the papers were British papers then and it showed that behind the deputation the British hand was clear.

Lord Minto inaugurated another trend giving preference to Muslims in the recruitment to civil services. Sir Lancelot Hare, the Lieutenant Governor of Eastern Bengal and Assam noticed the vast disparity in public services between the two communities. He, therefore, submitted privately a circular for Viceroy's approval, which he proposed to make public in his province, drawing attention to the 'great disproportion' between the Mohammedans and Hindus employed in the public offices and instructing his subordinate officers to follow certain tales for increasing the number of the former. Minto's reaction speaks for itself.

"Hare's proposal seemed sound enough at first sight but luckily we found that the necessary instructions for a proportionate employment of Mohammedans had been in existence since 1885, and there was no necessity to give the public at the present moment reason to think that we are arranging matters in order to meet Mohammedans' claims. The Mohammedans are no doubt very much underrepresented but still feel sure it would be a mistake (it is one of which Fuller was accused) to show any appearance of playing off Mohammedans against Hindus. The machinery to put things right is in existence and it is only necessary quietly to draw attention to it, so I stopped the circular.[9]

What Fuller did openly and avowedly, Minto wanted to do 'quietly' and without arousing the fears of the Hindus. Similarly in connection with the appointment of Judges to the Calcutta High Court, Minto wrote significantly; 'there are bigger questions involved in the possible appointment of the Mohammedans to the Calcutta High Court than those of mere legal capacity'.[10]

The Muslim community was given separate representation in the separate legislative councils. This was an introduction of a principle in Indian politics about which conflicting opinions have been expressed and will continue to be expressed. Undoubtedly, the Muslims, an important section of Indian society, could not be ignored in the matter of representation in these enlarged councils. But the creation of separate electorates for them was not the only alternative. A just and satisfactory solution would have been found in the scheme of Electoral colleges proposed by the Secretary of State in his dispatch of November 27, 1908. By adopting this scheme, Morley was convinced that the Minorities of the country would be protected against exclusion by majorities and all large and important sections of the population would have the opportunity of returning members in proportion to their ratio to the total population.[11] It would have ensured sufficient representation of all classes and interests without introducing the invidious destruction between one community and another. But it was wonder that Minto himself rejected this scheme. He called this scheme as unworkable, impracticable 'full of mischief' and contrary to the pledges given to the Mohammedans. Minto was against the joint electorate in all possible ways. He wrote to Sir Arthur Lawley, the Governor of Madras; 'I don't for instant think the Secretary of State will push but please say all you can against them'.[12] To his friend Lansdowne, in London, Minto wrote: "the electoral colleges are absolutely impossible—mud and distinctly contrary to pledges I had given to the Mohammedans, and of which the Government of India approved. We simply cannot have them. I am so glad you saw the meaning of deputation to me—it was by far the most important event that has happened during my time".[13] The trouble that arose, later on, the question of Mohammedans representation, Minto attributed to those d-d' 'Electoral College' which put the fate in the fire, and if accepted by themselves, would have knocked Mohammedans altogether.[14] The Viceroy believed that in the scheme of Electoral College a Mohammedan representative of advanced Hindu political inclination, and not of *bona fide* Mohammedan interests, could be elected. The most important reason that weighed with Minto was that he was keen to secure the support of conservative and 'old fashioned' Mohammedans against the younger generation which was interestingly participating in the political agitation. He said, "......the old fashioned Mohammedans, who are such a local mainly to us, are not likely to push themselves forward and will be left in the lurch if opportunity is given for the election of manipulated Hindu votes to secure seats for a younger Mohammedan generation that is being drawn into the vortex of political agitation.[15] In his monograph 'Muselmann ka Rashan Musteffel', Tufail Ahmad Manglori suggested that the divisive political agenda of the All India Muslim League during the 1930s was preceded by the introduction of the separate electorate under the constitutional reforms of 1909.

It is pointed out by Tufail Ahmad that the seed of the communal divide of the 1930s were sown by the British authorities themselves with the help of the 'Loyalists' among the leaders of the Aligarh movement.

The introduction of the principle of separate electorates accentuated the difference between the two communities. The Hindus and Muslims stood in two different camps: hopes of unity between the two communities for political purposes receded in the background. Minto, thus, succeeded in dividing and weakening the forces of nationalism. Separate electorates for Muslims helped to entrench separatism and communalism. The rise of Muslim communities signified the irreverent failure of the composite Indian Nationalism. After the final budget debate in the new imperial legislative council, Minto gave expression to his unmixed delight. The debate had far more life and honour in it than usual. The most delightful incident has been the utter demolition of the partition cry! Bhupendra Nath Basu entirely kicked over the traces in respect to rules, and notwithstanding my repeatedly calling him to order managed to introduce some of the old arguments into the budget decision, the result being that the Mohammedan members flew at his throat one after another and tore partition to pieces.[16] The presence of Muslim members in the enlarged council was source of satisfaction to the government. In the opinion of Mian Muhammad Shafi their presence would not only safeguard the interests of the Muslims but also secure the stability of the British Government—and would prevent the Hindu dream of *Swaraj* from being realized.[17]

Thus Minto was able to secure the help of large number of Muslims in dealing with agitation. A *fatwa* was prepared by Hakim Razi-ul-Din and Maulbi Abdul Haque of Delhi regarding the duties and delegations of the Muslims not only to keep aloof but also to take practical steps against the "improper agitation which is being carried on for some time in this country".[18] It reiterates that "we, the ulema and those who follow us numbering about six crores of Mohammedans are sincerely loyal and faithful to British Government".[19] Mian Mohammed Safi of Punjab assured the British Government that his community constituted 'the real and truly loyal' section of the population. The Muslims he proudly declared regard the British Government as their very own and refuse to take part in anything calculated. In the slightest degree, to ensure British interests had weakened the stability and performance of the British rule in India.[20] Similarly the trustees of the Aligarh College assured Minto that aim of their college was to train young men imbedded by sentiments of deep loyalty to the government.[21] The Viceroy succeeded in winning over a large majority of the Muslims to the side of the government assessing them that their interests were safe within British. In a letter to the King, Minto proudly wrote, "His Majesty's Mohammedan subjects have been the most loyal supporters of the *Raj* throughout the recent seditious agitation."[22]

So the Simla deputation succeeded. The deputationists represented the interests of landlords on one hand and those of professional middle class on the other. Its members were all educated urban elites. Later on the separate electorates brought disaster for the country. Patrick French has remarked in his book *Liberty to Death* that 'perfidious Mussalmans and scheming Britishers join hands to assure the ultimate breakup of united mother India'.[23] Lady Minto wrote in her diary that Lord Minto's work prevented sixty-two million people from joining the ranks of the seditious opposition. The Congress did not like that Muslims should be granted separate electorates. The Congress did not pass a resolution either in the meeting of the working committee of the A.I.C.C. Now there was a rift between the Congress and the Muslim League. Subsequently the Muslim League was established. The Muslim League was a communal Party. So the Simla deputation brought communalism in Indian politics.

The Separate Electorate

Lord Minto was behaving as a pro-Muslim and he linked that the Muslims should enjoy the privilege of the separate electorate. The Secretary of State, John Morley understood the game of the Viceroy. The Viceroy wanted to divide Hindus and Muslims in the name of reforms. So Morley advanced his famous scheme of 'Mixed Electoral College'. His scheme was containing in his dispatch of November 27, 1908. In this college, if there are 12 vacancies, 9 shall be Hindus and 3 Muslims. In each area, an electoral college shall be constituted. If there are 100 members to be elected, 75 should be Hindus and 25 Mohammedans.

The Indian National Congress meeting at Madras on

December 28-30, 1908, congratulated the government of their reform proposals. Jinnah at that time a veteran nationalist and an opponent of Aligarh communalists thanked the government for the concession it wanted to faction and called upon the Muslims to approve of the mixed electoral system just after the end of the session of the Congress, Viceroy Lord Minto decided to disobey the concept of a joint or mixed electorate. He wrote to the Secretary of State on December 31, 1908 rejecting Morley's mixed electoral system.[24]

Minto took the Nawab of Dacca into confidence. So, too Immam Ali the League prepared the memorandum. Minto wrote a letter to Lord Lander mentioning that "electoral colleges are absolutely impossible". The result was that the mixed electoral system was dropped. In the opinion of Muslim League, Lord Minto was their champion in their struggle for self-presentation and self-defence against an aggressive majority. After some time the Indian Council Act came into operation. By the end of the year 1909, elections were held in India and Muslims captured large seats.

The Congress viewed the whole situation with great agony at the Lahore session in 1909. The Morley-Minto era thus ended with a new turn in Indian political scene. As the result of the special circumstances the Congress and the Muslim League came together in 1916.

Communalism is the political, economical and social assertiveness of an organized aggregation of individuals identifying themselves with a particular group preferably a religious group. This assertiveness is antagonistic in its form and contents towards other religious groups. Religion is used by communalist to protect and promote their own interests and damage that of their rivals.

NOTES

1. Letter, June 5, 1907, Minto to Morley, *Minto Papers.*
2. Letter, June 22, 1906, Morley to Minto, *Ibid.*
3. Proceedings, *Indian History Congress*, Lord Minto and the Muglone, 1973.
4. Letter, August 10, 1906, Ibbetson to Dunlop Singh, *Minto Papers.*
5. *Amrit Bazar Patrika*, October 4, 1906.
6. *The Tribune*, October 4, 1906.
7. Letter, October 9, 1906, Minto to Morley, *Minto Paper.*
8. Letter, 11th October, 1906, *Ibid.*

9. Letter, December 19, 1906, *Ibid.*
10. Letter, November 4, 1906, *Ibid.*
11. Dispatch No. 193, November 27, 1908, Secretary of State to Governor General, Para 13.
12. Letter, January 19, 1909, Minto to Morley, *Minto papers.*
13. Letter, 21st January, *Ibid.*
14. *Ibid.*
15. Letter, December 1908, Minto to Morley, *Minto Papers.*
16. Letter, March 31, 1910, *Ibid.*
17. Letter, April 30, 1909, Md. Shafi to Dunlop Smith, *Ibid.*
18. Enclosure to Letter, January 20th 1909, *Public Proceedings*, February 1909, No. 14
19. *Ibid.*
20. Letter No.455, June 18, 1909, Safi to Dunlop Smith.
21. Letter, September 21, 1908, *Minto Papers.*
22. Letter, August 20, 1908, *Minto Papers.*
23. Patrick French, in his book *Liberty to Death*, p. 43.
24. Minto to Morley, Vol. 12, December 31, 1908.

4

Formation of the Muslim League and the Lucknow Pact (1906–1916)

Just after two months of the Simla deputation, the Muslim League was formed on November 30, 1906, the Nawab, Salim-ullah of Dacca took an interest and he assured to all the prominent Muslim persons of the country to establish "the Muslim All India Confederacy". He played the most to the gathering; Nawab Mohsin-ul-Mulk played the role of the chief organizer. M.A. Jinnah, who later on founded Pakistan, was the member of the Indian National Congress from 1906. He was not associated with the conference. Jinnah was a secular leader by his merit. The person who had been invited to attend had not been elected or they were the office bearer of any association. It was the personal choice of the Nawab of Dacca. All members were loyal to the government. The president of the conference was Nawab Viqar-ul-Mulk.[1] The conference opened on December 30, 1906 and the Muslim League was formed at Dacca. The president had no English education and he spoke in Urdu. Viqar-ul-Mulk, the president, was a feudal landlord. He was very obstinate in his behaviour. He was a resident of Aligarh and he believed in traditional society. The Western education had not made any impact on his feudal mind.[2] He spoke for the rights of the *quam*. He did not explain what he understood by *quam*. Sir Syed Ahmad Khan had also talked about the *Quam*. Sir Syed understood the meaning of the word *quam* as community and not the nation.

The president's speech was in Urdu. The president said: "The Mussalmans[3] are not only a fifth in number as compared with the total population of the country and it is manifest that if at any remote period the British Government ceases to exist in India, the rule of India would pass into the hands of the community which is nearly four times as ourselves—then our life, our property, our honour and our faith will all be in great danger—woe betide the time when we become the subjects of our neighbours and answer to them for sins, real or imaginary, of Aurangzeb, who lived and died two centuries ago, and other Mussalman conquerors, and rulers who went before him. In his opinion, Muslims should help to stamp our sedition, side by side with the British Government. The role of Muslims communalism signified the incipient failure of the composite Indian nationalism. The result was that side by side with Indian nationalism and Hindu nationalism began to grow and spread, bringing about the denouncement loyal to the government.

The creation of separate electorates for the Muslims brought new problems for the country. The Private Secretary of Viceroy brought it to the kind notice of the Viceroy that the minorities of the country were now demanding separate educational institution and separate judicial courts. Many Hindus thought that the Muslims were getting favour by the Government. It was pointed out that Muslim tenants were being evicted, Muslim merchants were refused credit and in Agra Muslim prostitutes were boycotted. So the impacts of the separate electorates were devastating on the community.

Many nationalists[4] interpreted that the idea behind the separate electorates was to spread disharmony among the various communities in the country and to start the 'Divide and Rule' strategy to weaken the national movement of the country. By weaning the Muslim the Muslims from the Hindu fold, the Viceroy liked to strengthen British imperialism. As Patrick French remarks, "In the view of many Indians today, the creation of divided electorates was a deliberate strategy to provoke the demand for a Muslim homeland and thereby destroy the coherence and unity of India.[5]

Nationalists of the country believed that the policy of Divide and Rule started from 1906 and in 1909 it was evident. Under the Morley-Minto Reforms of 1909, the Muslims were granted separate electorates and this policy remained in operation till 1947. It was said that before the British period there was communal harmony in the country. Various statements of British officials prove that the policy of Divide and Rule had started from 1860. Colonel Coke stated in 1860 that 'divide et impera'[6] should be our principle aim. This policy continued till 1946. According to Intelligence Bureau Report in 1946, "communal disorder must not be disturbing us into action which would reintroduce anti-British agitation". The report pointed out that there are advantages of keeping disorder on 'the appropriate plan of communalism'.

British followed the policy of 'Divide and Rule' without any break. The conservative, the liberal and the labour Prime Ministers all followed this policy. The Secretary of State for India Lord Birkenhead encouraged this policy in 1920. It was followed by Lord Linlithgow, 1936-1943, and Prime Minister Winston Churchill supported it. But this policy was followed in such a way so that there should not be Hindu-Muslim hatred in the country. In the words of V.P. Menon,[7] 'the policy of British Government in India was evolved merely the exigencies of time and circumstances than as a result of deliberate planning.'

Jinnah was opposed to separate electorates. The President of session of the League at Nagpur in December 1910 noted that Jinnah had acknowledged that in his opposition to the extension of separate electorates to local bodies, "he did not represent the opinion of the community". In 1934 he agreed to a pact with Rajendra Prasad based on the principle that 'joint electorates shall replace separate electorates in all the provinces and in the country'.

Objects of the Muslim League

Its objective was to promote among the Musalmans of India feeling of loyalty to the British Government.[8] "The Muslims recoil from Congress Nationalism", according to Prof. Coupland, "was mainly Ahmad's (Sir Syed) doing".[9] The British apparently groomed and used it as a counter-weight to Indian National Congress which, since its formation in 1885, had been insisting on self-rule for India. The Muslim League was thus the King's own Party.[10] The Aga Khan was the President of the Muslim League from 1906 to 1912.

There were three main objectives of the Muslim League:

(a) To promote among Musalmans of India feeling of loyalty to the British Government and to remove any misconception that may arise as to the intention of the government with regard to any of its measures.
(b) To protect and advance the political rights and interest of the Musalmans of India and to respectfully represent their needs and aspiration in the government.

(c) To prevent the rise among the Musalman of India of any feelings of hostility towards other communities without prejudice to other aforementioned objects of the League.

In this way was established a political and a communal platform, which was anti-national. Its only one aim was to promote loyalty of the Muslims of the country towards the British Government. The Anglo Mohammedan rapprochement and the birth of the Muslim League came at a significant juncture of modern history. The conference of the All India Muslim League was held at Amritsar with Sir Syed Ali as the President. The League leaders attending the conference passed a resolution for more weightage to the Muslims in the legislative councils and in civil services. The Muslims also wanted equality of representation with the Hindus in the Governor-General's Executive Council. These two demands were also raised in the conference of 1909 and 1910.

But the entire Muslim intellectuals did not take the membership of the Muslim League due to its communal character. There were secular Muslims also in the country. They refused to join the Muslim League. Badruddin Tyabjee was the President of the Indian National Congress in 1887. Even M.A. Jinnah did not join the League. Jinnah took the membership of the Indian National Congress in 1906. Such Muslims were known as the nationalist Muslims. In Allahabad[11] session of the Indian National Congress in 1910, Jinnah moved a resolution in the open session of the Congress condemning the system of communal representation. His resolution was seconded by Maulana Mazhar-ul-Haq of Bihar. He pleaded for greater friendship and cooperation between the Hindus and the Muslims for the welfare of the country. All the Muslim leaders except few were happy at the Indian Council Act of 1909, under which the Muslims got the system of separate electorates. Nawab Syed Mohammed,[12] Maidana Shibli Naumani, Maulana Mohammed Ali and Maulana Abul Kalam Azad, these leaders had no link with the Muslim League and they condemned the communal organization like the Muslim League. Maulana Mohammed Ali started an English paper *Comrade* and an Urdu paper *Hamdard* to propagate his anti-League views. Maulana Azad established the 'Al-ttilal' press and the first number of journal *Al-ttilal* was published in 1912.[13] The *Al-ttilal* created a revolutionary stir among the masses. The demand for *Al-ttilal* was very great. The leadership of the Muslim politics at this time was in the hands of

Aligarh Party.[14] Their basic trend was that the Muslims must be loyal to the British Crown and remain aloof from the freedom movement. When *Al-ttilal* raised a different slogan and its popularity and circulation increased fast, they felt that their leadership was threatened. Therefore, they began to oppose *Al-ttilal.* The Government was also disturbed by this success of *Al-ttilal.* The Government confiscated the *Al-ttilal* press in 1915. Besides these leaders, there were other progressive Muslim leaders like Syed Wazir Hussain, Hasan Imam and Hakim Ajmal Khan.[15]

Changed Attitude of the Muslim League and the Lucknow Pact

Under the influence of the secular Muslim leaders, the Muslim League had to change its aims and objects. The Muslim League had to amend its constitution. There was one development; Maulana Mohammed-ul-Hussain established another organization called 'Jamait-ul-Ulema Hind'.[16] This organization proved in the long run a strong rival of the League. Soon it acquired the national status and it spread gradually throughout the country. A mighty challenge was drawn to the Muslim League. The Jamait-ul-ulema vigorously opposed the communal character of the Muslim League and tried to bring the Muslims into the Indian National Congress, the Nationalist Muslims were becoming very much popular and the influence of the Muslim League was waning. The Muslim League was faced to give up its communal approach. Hence, the League amended its constitution and promotion of goodwill between Hindus and the Muslims became its objective. It also declared its goal of attainment of '*Swaraj*'[17] under the British Crown.

At this stage M.A. Jinnah, who was a member of the Indian National Congress from 1906, took the membership of the Muslim League in 1913. Jinnah was a secular leader at this time. There were many factors which were compelling the Muslim League to move towards the Congress and also to withdraw loyalty from the British Government. As the First World War[18] was being fought on the principle of self-determination and also for strengthening democracy, so movement had started in the South-East European countries to throw off the political domination of Turkey for the achievement of freedom. Russia extended its support to those countries which were struggling against Turkey, England, France and Russia was the member of the Triple Entente, which had been formed in 1907. So England supported Russia mildly. Turkey was a Muslim power so the Muslim League felt that Britain was an anti-Muslim power and the Muslim loyalty was shaken. Another reason was that Turkey had joined Germany in the First World War against the Triple Entente. The Sultan of Turkey was a religious head of the entire Muslims of the world. The Indian Muslims felt that Britain was an enemy of the Muslims of the world. Now the League thought that co-operation with the Congress was essential. The Indian National Congress wanted self rule for the country. It was not possible unless the Muslim League backed the Congress. These factors brought Congress and Muslim League together for different reasons.

At the time of the outbreak of the First World War in 1914, the Indian National College had completed 30 years. The Congress leaders of the first generation, many of them the founding-fathers were dead or nearing death. W.C. Bannerjee, Anand Mohan Bose and Tyabji had died in 1906, P. Ananda Charlu in 1908, Lal Mohan Bose in 1909 and A.O. Hume in 1912. During the period of war, died Pheroz Shah Mehta, Gopal Krishna Gokhale and Henry Cotton in 1915, B.N. Dar in 1916, Dadabhai Naoroji in 1917 and William Wedderbeum in 1918. Bal Gangadhar Tilak, Annie Besant, Mohammed Ali Jinnah and Madan Mohan Malvia were called upon by the circumstances to guide the Congress politics in the war period. Mohan Das Karamchand Gandhi entered the Indian public life in 1915.

The Indian National Congress and the Muslim League were coming very close. The committee of the Indian National Congress and the All-India Muslim League met in Calcutta in November 1916 and finalized a scheme in the spirit of mutual trust and goodwill.

The Lucknow Pact

Much before the Government of India Act, 1919, the leaders of the Indian National Congress from which extremist leaders like Bal Gangadhar Tilak, Lala Lajpat Rai and Bipin Chandra Pal had kept away and was dominated by moderate leaders like Gopal Krishna Gokhale, Pheroz Shah Mehta and Surendra Nath Banerjee. These leaders decided to have closer links with Muslim League. According to Maulana Mohammed Ali, who along with Maulana Shaukat Ali had entered in Baitul Jail at the time of the First World War, had suggested to Maulana Mazhurul Haque the veteran Congressman, who had been elected president of the Muslim League in 1915, to come to terms with the Congress which was also having its session in Bombay at the same time under the presidentship of (Lord) S.P. Sinha.

The Indian National Congress and the Muslim League were to hold their annual session in 1916. M.A. Jinnah was trying to bring the Indian National Congress and the Muslim League in one platform. Jinnah had prepared his proposals known as the Lucknow Pact. The significance of the Lucknow Pact was the introduction of the Indian self-government within the British Empire with weightage in favour of the minorities. In December 1916, he told the Muslim League in his speech that this proposal and the scheme of guarantees offered to Indian Muslims would decide the fate of India's future, unity of India and a desire on the part of the Indian National Congress and the Muslim League for constitutional freedom. So Jinnah was initiating a new-born movement in the direction of national unity which was to bring Hindus and Muslims together involving brotherly service for the common use.[19] Jinnah had been shouted in 1915 by the Muslim League Mullahs for his Western dress, for smoking cigarettes and for the use of English rather than Urdu. The Governor of U.P. attended the Congress session and addressed to it. It was for the first time that a British governor addressed the Indian National Congress.

The Morley-Minto Reforms of 1909 gave to the Muslims the right of separate electorates. Among those opposed to the separate electorates was M.A. Jinnah, the Indian National Congress did not like the separate electorates too. The Indian National Congress and the Muslim League had come closer during the war period. The Indian National Congress and the Muslim League met at Lucknow in December 1916. A.C. Majumdar presided over the session of the Indian National Congress and Jinnah over the Muslim League. In the Congress there was a reunion of the moderates and the extremists, which had been separated from the Congress split of 1907. The Congress accepted the principle of the separate electorates extended to Muslims under the reforms of 1909. Mahatma Gandhi, who had returned from South Africa in 1915 had attended the Lucknow Congress but his presence was nominal. Tilak had attended the session, Motilal Nehru and Jawaharlal Nehru were mere delegates or visitors and did not wield any influence on the working of the

Congress as such a secular organization like the Congress recognized for the first time the division of people on religious basis, which helped Pakistan to be created in 1947.

At Lucknow, Tilak not only reasserted his tall stature but also re-established the appeal of his extremist philosophy. Tilak now stood for complete Home Rule. Gandhi was steadily emerging as a national leader. He was in close touch with various leaders like Tilak, Annie Besant, Lala Lajpat Rai, Madan Mohan Malviya and others. After the Champaran movement of 1917, Gandhi attracted many followers including Vinoba Bhave, Mahadev Desai, Rajendra Prasad, J.B. Kriplani, C.F. Andrews and others. Gandhi's rise to power and prominence was sudden and spectacular. Many Indians did not know about his South African adventure. The Rowlett Act of March 1919 gave Gandhi chance to press his mettle. Indian nationalism was strengthening itself. The growth of Indian nationalism signified the decline of the British Empire. The Congress was the most remarkable political organization of the country.

As Jinnah was a brilliant legal practitioner so the Lucknow Pact was 'a carefully framed legal document'.[20] Even Tilak, who was an extremist and who had just been released from 'Mendalay Jail' in Burma, where he was kept as a prisoner from 1908 to 1914, he accepted the 'Lucknow Pact' so the entire Congress accepted the Lucknow Pact. It was the climax of Jinnah's political career as a true nationalist leader. But the Congress of the Lucknow Pact faded away soon and by 1925 communalism again raised its ugly head. It has to be accepted that the acceptance of the principle of the separate electorates by the Congress leaders did not bring any positive gain to country. Neither the cause of nationalism nor the principle of secularism was made stronger. The seed of partition was latent in this pact.

Background and Emergence of Mahatma Gandhi

It has to be recapitulated that A.O. Hume was the father of the Indian National Congress. He was the General Secretary of the Congress from 1885 to 1906. The Congress was the secular organization from its inception. The first president of the Congress, W.C. Banerjee was a Christian. The second president Badruddin Tyabjee was a Muslim. Tyabjee was followed by few Englishmen like George Yule, Sir William Wedderburn, Alfred Web and Sir Henry

Cotton. Other persons who acted as president of the Congress were parties like Sir Feroz Shah Mehta, D.E. Wacha and Muslims like Rahimatullah Sayan, Nawab Syed Mohammed Bahadur and Hussain Imam. The resolution of the Congress at that time spoke about the people as a whole and not about a section of the people.

The Congress had become a strong organization by 1897. It was a great challenge to the British rulers. George N.M. Curzon of Hedlaston was 39, when he was appointed Viceroy and Governor-General of India. He was the youngest man to occupy the office held from 1899 to 1905. Lord Curzon remains one of the most controversial British Viceroy. Most Indians regarded him as the antitype of Western imperialism, self-assured, a migrant totally committed to the theory that it was the White men's vision to civilize the Asian. Even today he is remembered, above all, for the partition of Bengal in 1905, which was subsequently annulled by the King Emperor George V at the Coronation Durbar on December 1911 at Delhi. India had much to be grateful to him but for him our frontiers along Tibet may have remained undemarcated. But for him, our monuments might have disappeared, many without a trace, the beautiful carved friezes from Amrati were being used to lay down railway lines when he saw the horror of it and promulgated the Act for the protection of monuments. He passed the Ancient Monuments Preservation Act in 1904. Pandit Nehru thanked him later on for preserving all that was beautiful in India. But when he left India, he was not given farewell. He left behind him a disturbed and disgust India. At this Curzon's rival Lord Kitchiner jumped with joy. Lord Curzon had the brain of an I.C.S. man and an enormous sense of his own importance.

The original name of Mahatma Gandhi was Mohandas Karamchand Gandhi. He, like Jinnah, belonged to the upper middle class family. Mohandas Karamchand Gandhi was born on 2nd October, 1869 in Porbander, a coastal town which was then part of Bombay Presidency, British India. He was born in his ancestral home, now known as Kirti Mandir, Porbander. His father, Karamchand Gandhi, who belonged to the Hindu Modh community served as a Diwan (a high official) of Porbander state, a small Princely State in the Kathiawar Agency of British India.* which was then part of Bombay Presidency. At the age of thirteen, Mohandas was married

* Fisher, Louis (1954), Gandhi : His Life and message for the Word mentor.

to Kasturba. He passed the Matriculation examination at the age of 17. Then he went to Britain for the Bar-at-law examination. He returned to Gujarat at the age of 21. Then he came to Bombay but he could not do well at the legal practice. At this stage he did his chamber practice for two years then he came to Netal in South Africa in 1893 to work in a Law Firm but he did not prove as a successful lawyer there also. He took up the cases of Indians. Indians had no political rights. He launched a mass-based campaign against the Government of South Africa. General Smith was the Prime Minister of South Africa. Gandhi agitated against the Transvaal Government's Asiatic Registration Bill. His movement was peaceful. By 1914 Gandhi succeeded in his endeavour. General Smith agreed to such acts which were against the interest of Indians. He then left Netal at the age of 43 and reached Bombay on January 9, 1915, after a gap of 21 years, wearing a loin cloth and travelling from London in the lowest class size ship. This Gandhi has little or no relation to the M.K. Gandhi, the 23 years old Barrister in a suit, who had started from Bombay in April 1893 by First class in the hope of finding opportunities in the land.

Gandhi was awarded the prestigious Kaisar-i-Hind Gold Medal in the New Year Honour's list by the British Government. Gandhi surrendered his Gold Medal and titles to Viceroy, Lord Chelmsford on August 1, 1920, due to Non-cooperation Movement. After his coming to Bombay he decided to settle at Ahmedabad and the place he decided to settle was known as Satyagrah Ashram. It was his simple life style that attracted Sardar Patel, Ravi Shanker Maharaj and the host of others. Later on the Ashram was shifted to Sabarmati, two years later, following an outburst of an epidemic at Kochorole. However, the building remains at Ahmedabad tended by Gujarat Vidyapeeth. He offered the Sabarmati Ashram to the Harijan Sevak Sangh in September 1933 for the use of the "Harijan cause".

From Sabarmati he made a tour to many parts of India. In 1917, he came to Champaran in Bihar against the Tinkathia system and he succeeded. It was the first peasant movement in which he struggled against the government. As a result of the Jallianwala Bagh tragedy in 1919, Montagu-Chelmsford Act of 1919 and British policy towards Turkey, Gandhi decided to start a movement against the government. It was known as the Non-cooperation Movement of 1920. Gandhi went into the frame of eventful history in the period of the freedom struggle and Nehru appeared rising the white horse like flash of lightning on the horror of hope and frustration. Before the non-cooperation movement of 1920, the Indian National Congress was in the hands of the elitist middle class. The Indian middle class had been influenced by the West. The middle class in the West immediately connotes democracy, nationalism, dignity of the person and a public commitment to citizenship. At this time Tilak died on August 1, 1920.

Gandhi's emergence in the Indian political scene began within leadership of a nation-wide agitation against the Rowlett's Act in 1919. Under this draconian legislation a person could be detained anywhere, arrested without a warrant and house search. The Act was direct negation of Rule of Law, which the British Raj claimed to be the most striking feature of the system of administration.

Gandhi was present in the public following of the Imperial legislative council during the debate on the Rowlet Bills in the 1918-19 in the winter session in Delhi. He was hardly noticed as he was still an unknown political quantity. Indian coined a slogan which truly characterised the new law as "no *vakil* to detect his appeal" it was called the "Black Acts".

Gandhi's rise to unrivalled leadership reserved a political impetus. From the popular favour at the resignation of Sir Sankera Nair from the Viceroy's Executive Council and Rabindra Nath Tagore's renunciation of his knighthood as a protest against the Jallianwala Bagh massacre.[21]

Now Gandhi decided to start the Non-cooperation Movement. At the Nagpur session of the Congress held on December 24, 1920, the resolution of Non-cooperation was adopted by the Congress by 1855 votes to 873. Gandhi had the backing of Motilal Nehru, the delegates from the South and Muslim delegates. In fact, all the Muslim members of the subjects committee except Jinnah supported the main resolution. This matter had been discussed at the special session of the Congress held at Calcutta from 6th to 9th September, 1919 to consider the findings of the Hunter Commission. The Khilafat wing and the final attitude to the question of reforms in view of the impending election, C.R. Das and B.C. Pal wanted to defeat the non-violent, non-cooperation campaign. Motilal was with Gandhi and Gandhi was victorious at the Nagpur Congress.

The Muslim League had also met in Calcutta on September 7, 1919. Jinnah found it too difficult to sworn against the tide of popular opinion. Jinnah conceded that there was no course open except to support the non-cooperation. But Jinnah made it clear that he did not necessarily approve Gandhi's programme. The resolution adopted by the League supported non-cooperation.

The Nagpur session of Indian National Congress in December 1920 handed over the reins of the freedom struggle to Gandhi. Gandhi, dressed in loin cloth and carrying a handspun togci, presented an odd figure amidst the elite of formal costumes. He persuaded the Congress to adopt a new constitution which declared the attainment of *swaraj* (self-rule) "—" by peaceful and legitimate replacing the word "Constitutional" means as the aim of the Congress. The non-cooperation movement started in practice with the boycott of the Duke of Connaught's visit to India for the inauguration of the reformed legislatures. But the movement could not run its full course. In 1920, Gandhi, declining to travel in a higher class than third, said: "I can no more effectively deliver my message to millions by travelling first class than the Viceroy can rule over the hearts of India's millions from his unapproachable Simla heights.

Lord Reading assumed the Viceroyalty in April 1921. and immediately plunged into a study of the Indian scence. Reading, who was the former Chief Justice of England was at the pilgrimage centre of Madurai, in Madras, Gandhi had his head shaved and, discarding his ordinary wear, donned only a loin cloth, a dress which led to his being described later by Churchill as a 'half naked fakir'. Now everything was ready and Gandhi announced that civil disobedience would begin on November 17, 1920, when the Prince of Wales was due to land in Bombay. The next Congress session was held in December 1921 in Ahmedabad. Hakim Ajmal Khan was the President of the Congress. This conference set the seal of Gandhiji's mastery over the Congress.[22]

Jinnah's Resignation from the Indian National Congress

In order to understand the cause that led Jinnah to resign from the Congress, I have to discuss Gandhi's political life briefly. By 1920 Gandhi emerged as the unchallenged leader of the Congress. Jinnah did not like Gandhi's rise. Jinnah was in the Congress from 1906. After the death of Congress leader, Bal Gangadhar Tilak, Madan Mohan Malviya, Annie Besant and M.A. Jinnah were in the field. They all wanted to become the leader of the Congress. But Gandhi was a very shrewd politician and he became the leader of the

Congress. Now for various reasons as elaborated earlier Gandhi decided to start the non-cooperation movement. Gandhi liked that students should break the law for the success of the movement. Now Jinnah intervened.

I have written earlier that Jinnah was a constitutionalist. He did not like that Gandhi should teach the younger generation to break the law of the country. He asked this question to Gandhi, if the Congress government was established at the centre at the earliest, then how the administration of the country would be carried on, if people break the law? So the movement should not be unconstitutional. The second point was that the peasants and workers had joined the Congress organization in large numbers. Jinnah argued that the peasants and the workers were illiterates. They do not understand the politics of the country. They are ill-dressed and had no shoes in their feet. So they should not be given the membership of the Congress. Jinnah was best-dressed man in the British Empire. He was the successful barrister so he thought that he would not be able to sit and participate in the discussion with peasants and workers. He told Jawaharlal Nehru that he should suggest to Gandhi that only matriculates should be enrolled as a member of Congress. Jinnah told Gandhi at Nagpur Congress in 1920. "Mr. Gandhi, for God's sake, do not mix up religion with politics, you do not know what you are doing." The factor was that Jinnah was an ambitious man. But his ambition received a jerk when he could not become the leader of the Congress. The possible reason of his resignation was the political disappointment of being side tracked by the leadership in the Congress. Finding no alternative he resigned from the Indian National Congress[23] and began to take a keen interest in the activity of Muslim League. It was not in the interest of the country that a strong nationalist and secular leader like Jinnah ceased to be member of a secular organization like the Indian National Congress. Though Jinnah was not member of the Congress, still he had faith in the Congress ideology and he believed in Indian nationalism, secularism and all India citizenship. Communalism was growing from the time of the Khilafat movement and Swami Shradhanand was born at Talisan near Jalandhar. He practiced as a pleader at Jalandhar for some time. He plunged into the freedom struggle and lent support to the Khilafat movement. He was active during the non-cooperation movement. He was a prominent leader of the Hindu Mahasabha and Shradhanand was assassinated in December 26,

1926 in Delhi by a Muslim fanatic, who on the pretext of paying his respect to the ailing Swami, had shot him dead. His staying was the outcome of a fanatical outburst against the publication of a book maligning the Prophet. Its author had been cleared in judicial proceedings, but a Muslim had murdered Shradhanand in Lahore.[24]

All Parties Conference and Jinnah's Fourteen Point

The boycott of the Simon Commission was the major event in India during 1928. This year was followed by a second significant development: appointment of an All Parties Conference, which, was the result of Birkenhead's challenge. Birkenhead threw challenges in this way[25] : I have twice in three years, during which I have been Secretary of State invited our critics in India to put forward their own suggestions for a constitution to indicate to us the form, in which in their judgment any reform of constitution may take place. That offer is still open.

The Congress leader took up the challenge and it was discussed by the Madras Congress in 1927. The Madras Congress Committee had directed the Congress Working Committee to draft a '*Swaraj*' constitution in consultation with other parties. So an all Parties conference met in Delhi in February 1928, Dr. Ansari, the Congress President, was the President of the conference. This conference liked full responsible government, the conference met in Bombay. The All parties conferance appointed a sub-committee to decide the principles of an Indian Constitution. The sub-committee presided over by Motilal included Sir Ali Imam and in 1928 Shuib Qureshi (Muslims), M.S. Aney and M.R. Jayakar (Hindu Mahasabha), Mangal Singh (Sikh League), Tej Bahadur Sapru (Liberals), M.M. Joshi (Labour), G.P. Pradhan (Non-Brahmin) and Subhas Chandra Bose. Pt. Jawaharlal Nehru, who was the General Secretary of All India Congress Committee, also acted as the Secretary of the committee. It was known as the Nehru Committee. The committee had to draw up a constitution for India. On the whole twenty-nine parties participated in it, after discussing the preliminaries the conference held its sittings in Bombay on May 19, 1928.

The Nehru Committee[26] had to find a solution of the Muslims. Jinnah pleaded that Muslim would not remain satisfied simply on assurances. They wanted statutory protection and Muslims should have reservation in central legislature. Some Congress leaders liked to support Jinnah but the Hindu Mahasabha opposed.

Motilal, Jinnah and Sapru were making Herculean efforts to bring about a national identity of views on the pattern of self-government and adjustment of communal claims through an all Party convention. The outcome of their attempts was the Nehru Report. Fazli Hussain in conjunction with Chetu Ram, who represented the Hindu Rural interests in East Punjab and had been a Congressman from 1917 to 1920, formed the Punjab Nationalist Unionist Party. Fazal's political beliefs were the same as Jawaharlal Nehru. So Fazal Hussain was campaigning for the acceptance of his own political beliefs. Bhim Rao Ambedkar, who had emerged as a powerful spokesman of the depressed classes walked in the stage. The British Raj, on its side, was aiming at exposing the weakness of the Indian case for self-rule through the investigation of the Simon Commission. Finally, there was the rivalry between Srinivasa Iyangar and Motilal. Srinivasa Iyangar stood for complete independence at the Congress session held in Madras in December 1927. Subhas Bose and Jawaharlal Nehru joined the independence League and Iyangar formed its secretaries.

The British Raj looking for ways of driving a wedge into the National Movement devised a method of giving substance to the group of Muslim politicians raged behind Fazal and to Ambedkar's demand for special safeguard for the untouchables. The aim of bureaucracy was to neutralize the caste Hindus, who it felt, was the major political force antagonistic to the continuance of British rule. At this stage the conflict was brought to a head of state by two closely connected events; the publication of the Nehru Report on constitutional reforms in August 1928 and the arrival of Simon and his colleagues for public hearing in October 1928.

The following were the highlights of Nehru Report :

1. *Dominion Status and Full Responsible Government*

The majority opinion favoured dominion status and minority liked complete independence. Hence a compromise formula was evolved. Dominion status was accepted not as the ultimate but the immediate goal. All the parties which pressed for complete independence were told to pursue their goal. The report also demanded a full responsible government on the lines of self-governing dominions.

2. *Provincial Autonomy and Residuary Powers*

The committee envisaged a future federation in India. It emphasized the need of giving as much autonomy to the province as was safely possible. The subjects were to be divided into the central and provincial lists, the residuary powers to be exercised by the centre. There should be unicameral legislation in a province.

3. Rejection of Communal Electorate

The report admitted that there was communal problem in India and expressed its faith that free India would be able to solve the problem satisfactorily. It held the British element in India as partly responsible for creating communal tension. The report further said that India should be a secular state where there would be no state religion. It suggests cultural autonomy, safeguards and guarantees to be promised to minority communities but it rejected the system of communal electorate. In its place it offered the system of joint electorate with reservation of seats.

4. Creation of New Province

The sub-committee in its report conceded the demand of the Muslim to create a separate province of Sindh and to give N.W.F.P. a footing of equality with other provinces although the motive behind such a demand was to have four Muslim majority provinces in India, viz. Bengal, Punjab, Sindh and N.W.F.P.

5. Fundamental Rights

"Where did the sovereignty reside"? This problem had arisen in the seventeenth century in England and it became the chief causes of the civil war between the two, first Stuart Kings and their parliaments in the seventeenth century. The report said that sovereignty belongs to the people of India and it was to be exercised through their representatives in accordance with the constitution. To ensure freedom to the individual, the report mentioned nineteen fundamental rights to be included in the constitution. Some notable rights were equality of men and women in regard to rights and freedom of faith of every individual.

6. Parliament

According to the report, India's Parliament should be bi-cameral. It should consist of the Senate and the House of Representative. The

Crown was to be an integral part of parliament. The senate should have 200 members elected by the members of the provincial legislature. Each province was to be represented in the senate in proportion to its population. The house of representative should have 500 members directly elected on the basis of adult franchise. The life of lower house should be five years. In foreign affairs, the Indian parliament was to exercise the same right as exercised by the dominion parliament.

7. Indian State

In this connection, the report said that the Indian Parliament should have the same rights and discharge the same obligations towards the Indian states as the then existing government of India did. In case of the conflict between the state and parliament, the governor general should have the power to refer the issue to the Supreme Court for arbitration.

8. Central Executive

The Crown accepted the principle that the Crown was to remain the highest executive exercising the powers through his representative, i.e. the Governor General of India. But the report said that the Governor General should act perfectly in accordance with the constitution and parliamentary laws. His executive should consist of one Prime Minister and six Ministers collectively responsible to the Dominion Parliament of India.

9. Supreme Court

The report suggests that the setting up of a Supreme Court in India whose duty would be to interpret the constitution and deciding points of conflict between one province and the other. It is recommended that no appeal would lie to the Privy Council.

10. Defence

The report suggests that a Defence Committee should be constituted consisting of the Prime Minister, the Defence Minister, Commander-in-Chief, Chief of the Naval and Air Force, Chief of the General Staff and two military experts. The Defence budget should be put to the House for approval, and that in emergency the Central Executive should have the right to sanction any sum it liked.

11. All powers of the government and all authority, legislative, executive and judicial are derived from the people and the same shall be exercised in the Commonwealth of India through organizations established by or under and in accord with this constitution.

> *"There shall be no state religion, men and women shall have equal rights as citizen".*
>
> *"Separate electorate shall be abolished. Every person of the age of 21 shall have the vote".*
>
> *"A Supreme Court shall be set up".*

The report, having recommended adult franchise, attempted to appease Communal sentiment by proposing a balance between the Hindu majority and Muslim majority provinces. It recommended the advancement of the North-West Frontier to full provincial status and the separation of Sindh from Bombay presidency.[27]

Reaction to Nehru Report

According to Dr. Rafiq Zakaria, the Nehru Report was "a masterly and statesman like report". For the first time in India's history, all the political parties laid their heads together to discuss constitutional problems and their mutually agreeable solutions. No greater tribute can be paid to it than that it supplied the blue print of the present Indian constitution.

In August 1928, report was accepted unanimously by the all parties' conference at Lucknow. But soon difficulty cropped up when such political Party began to consider the report threadbare separately. The Muslim League was divided on the issue. Maulana Azad, Hakim Ajmal Khan, Dr. Ansari and other nationalist Muslims were in favour of accepting the report in the original form. Mohammed Shafi wanted to reject it. The third section was led by M.A. Jinnah, who wanted amendments in the Nehru report. The Muslim conference pressed for weightage representation of Muslims in all the legislatures and also in the Central and Provincial Cabinets. It also differed with the report on the question of residuary powers.[28]

The All-Parties Convention at Calcutta

The Congress was itself divided in its attitude to the Nehru report.

The radical group was led by Pt. Jawaharlal Nehru and Subhas Bose stood for complete independence. The other group led by Pt. Motilal wanted that the Nehru Report should be accepted *in toto*. This group wanted dominion independence. Jinnah did not like this report. So he prepared his fourteen points formula as an amendment. This formula had been presented before the Muslim League and the League had ratified it. The fourteen points were as follows:

1. The form of the constitution for free India should be federal and the residuary powers should be vested in the provincial government.
2. Every province should enjoy a uniform measure of autonomy.
3. The minorities should be adequately represented to all the Legislative Assemblies and local bodies. No attempt should be made to reduce their majority in any province to a minority or even equality.
4. One-third of the total seats in the Central Assembly should be reserved for the Muslims.
5. Representation of all the communities should be on the basis of separate electorate. It should, however, be open to any group to abandon the system of separate electorate in favour of joint electorate.
6. Any territorial redistribution should not in any way affect the Muslim majority in the Punjab, Bengal and N.W.F.P.
7. Full religious liberty should be guaranteed to every individual.
8. No legislature or an elected body should adopt a bill or resolution which was opposed to three-forth of the members of that community in that body on the ground that it was injurious to the interest of that community.
9. Sindh to be separated from Bombay presidency.
10. N.W.F.P. and Baluchistan should not be discriminated against in respect of reforms.
11. Adequate share for Musalmans should be provided in the constitution of all services, subject to requirements of efficiency.
12. Adequate safeguards and state help should be given for the protection and promotion of Muslim culture, religion, language, education, laws and religious institutions.

13. At least one-third of total number of ministers to the central and provincial cabinets should be drawn from Muslim community.
14. No change in the constitution should be made by central assembly except with the concurrence of the units constituting the Indian Federation.[29]

Jinnah was under impression that if the all-parties conference would agree to accept the 14-points, communal problem of the country would be solved. According to Dr. Rajendra Prasad, these 14 points had an importance of their own as they were adopted in their entirety by Mr. Macdonald's communal award. Jinnah had prepared a federal Indian constitution with various safeguards for Muslims' culture and religion.

The 14-points were discussed in the all-parties convention at Calcutta in December 1928. Some Congress leaders along with Hindu Mahasabha did not appreciate the 14-points. These members did not like the modifications of the Nehru report. His 14 points were rejected one by one. The members of the all-parties conference were of this opinion that Jinnah had no strong base in the Muslim League and several eminent Congress Muslims were willing to accept the Nehru report. The meeting rejected Jinnah's claim to special treatment. He was also treated with having no right to represent the Muslims. It broke his heart and hurt his pride and he gave up all hope of Hindu-Muslim Unity which was his life's mission. These proposals were not only rejected but his representative capacity as a spokesman of the Muslims was questioned. Jinnah was the nationalist politician from 1906. He had taken membership of the Indian National Congress. But these events brought to an end Jinnah's career as an Indian nationalist politician. He had tears in his eyes[30] as he said Jamshed (his Parsee friend) "this is the parting of the ways". The positions hardened on both sides and Jinnah now became a better enemy to the Congress. It was a tragedy for the nationalists that a staunch nationalist like Jinnah now turned into a separatist and took shelter under a communal organization like the Muslim League. Patrick French remarks: "from now he (Jinnah) came to believe, quietly at first, in separation, either in form of powerful, autonomous provinces within a federal system or ultimately in an independent state. Now in March 1929, Jinnah put forward his famous "fourteen points".

Had the Congress members followed a conciliatory policy, Jinnah would not have parted with the Congress. To be a successful politician one has to follow the policy of give and take. Had few points, out of 14, had been accepted by the all-parties conference, the situation would not have been so tragic. But the Congress representatives and the Hindu Mahasabha were very rigid. They even teased Jinnah. So slowly the country moved towards the partition of India.

The Simon Inquiry

The conservative British Government appointed the Simon Commission to investigate the working of the Government of India Act, 1919, to inquire into desirability of introducing responsible government and to the extent which constitutional reform might be introduced. It was an all white commission which was headed by Sir John Simon. Indian political opinion was outraged by the exclusion of Indians from the Commission.

The Commission reached India in February 1928 and was met a country *hartal*. The Commission worked under these hostile circumstances. Major Attlee was one of the members of the commission. Attlee frankly admitted that the more he studied the situation the more puzzled he became. India seemed to him too big a country to be brought under the British system of parliamentary democracy. The term of reference ruled out the projection of schemes like the presidential system, alike the U.S. as being more suited the Indian conditions. Further it was very difficult, he said, to see how hundreds of states big and small could remain islands of autocracy in a country with parliamentary institutions.[31]

The Simon report was published in June 1930. As was expected, it aroused better disappointment in every segment of Indian opinion. The Commission relegated to an uncertain future the establishment of an all India federation. It failed to make even a passing reference to dominion status. Indeed, the report expressed scepticism about the suitability of the parliamentary system for India and threw out a hint that the provinces might develop different constitutional practices later on.

The Crises and the Gandhi-Irwin Pact

The political situation was getting out of control. So to stir public opinion in India, the Labour Party leader, Ramsay MacDonald declared in a speech before becoming Prime Minister: 'I hope that within a period of months rather than years there will be a new Dominion' added to the commonwealth of our nations, a Dominion of another, a dominion which will find self-respect as an equal within the commonwealth. I refer to India, to improve the situation, grown promised Dominion status but Gandhi dismissed Irwin's promise of Dominion status as "undated and unidentified". Vithalbhai Patel, who had been helping to build a bridge between the Viceroy and Gandhi, called a leader's conference at his house and succeeded in persuading Gandhi to modify his stand. The conference resulted in a statement signed by Gandhi, Malviya, Motilal, Sapru, Ansari, Jawaharlal and Mrs. Besant conceding the sincerity underlying the declaration and the desire of the British Government to satisfy Indian opinion.

To resolve the difference the difference, Irwin invited Gandhi and other leaders to meet him on 23rd December, 1929. Somebody placed a bomb on the track of the train bringing Irwin to Delhi. But nothing happened to the Viceroy and the Viceroy was safe. Under this tense situation talk between Irwin and Gandhi took place but the talk failed. Irwin maintained that it could not be concluded that the conference would fail on liberty of parliament could be restricted. Gandhi insisted that the conference must prepare a constitution based on Dominion status and this constitution should come into operation immediately.

In this background the Lahore session of 1929 was held under the presidentship of Pt. Jawaharlal Nehru, who was young and dynamic. The most important achievement of the session was that the declaration of independence was adopted at mid-night of 31st December, 1929. The banner of independence was unfurled on the banks of the Ravi river. The declaration of independence was read out as a pledge all over the country on 26th January, 1930.[32]

In resolution adopted at the Lahore session split the Congress Party and the Congress Democratic Party was born. The members of the Congress Democratic Party did not respond to the call issued to Congress members of the legislatures to resign their seats. Jayakar was the leader of this Party and he assumed the role of the leader of the opposition in the Central Assembly.

The fact that the Congress had voted for independence had an interesting reaction in the U.S., where within a week of its adoption a resolution was tabled in the Senate urging the American Government to recognize this Indian aspiration. An important off shoot of resolution was that the 26th January was designed Independence Day, to be celebrated officially, with the Congressmen, renewing the independence pledge.[33]

Gandhi-Irwin Pact, 1931

The Dandi March was the one and only assertion of the right to revolution in modern India. The die was cast; Gandhi felt that the country was ripe for mass movement. He decided the inauguration of the movement with the breach of salt laws. As the sun rose on March 12, 1930, Gandhi with his 78 disciples set out for the Arabian Sea from the Sabarmati Ashram, at a distance of 241 miles. The number was as follows: Karnataka-1, Andhra Pradesh-1, Kutch-6, U. P.-0, Bihar-1, Maharashtra-13, Tamilnadu-11, Bengal-1, Bombay-2, Punjab-3, Kerala-4, Sind-1, Gujarat-32, Orissa-1, and Rajasthan-1.[34] Out of 78, there were two Muslims in this march. After Gandhi picked up a salty mud on the sea shore at Dandi, Gandhi staged in a specially built palm-leaf hut a few miles away from Dandi. He wondered what to do next. He knew that Irwin and his advisors were in a quandary 'the government's plight is that of the serpent who has swallowed a rat'. Gandhi said, 'it would find hard to resort to either course of action allowing me to remain out or putting me behind the bars! Patrick French says that Gandhi was arrested by the British Government after mid-night on May 4, 1930, under Bombay Regulation 25 of 1827, which provided for detention without trial.[35]

Gandhi was arrested very late because the very idea of unseating the King-Emperor by boiling sea water in a kettle was considered absurd and impractical. When the movement gathered momentum, the Viceroy struck hard, and issued a series of drastic ordinances to arm the executive with vast powers to suppress the movement.[36]

The government dealt with the movement very harshly. Webb Millo of New York Telegram reported: "I have never witnessed such harrowing scene as at Dharsena". The western mind can grasp violence returned by violence, can understand a fight, but it is, I find, perplexed and baffled by the site of men advancing coldly and deliberately and submitting to beatings without Defence. Sometimes the scenes were so painful; I had to turn away momentarily.

The Dharsena raid was not an isolated episode. William L. Shirer, a well-known journalist and author of "The Rise and Fall of Adolf Hitler", who covered the Salt Satyagraha for the *Chicago Tribune* in 1930, has become testimony to police beatings in Bombay, Calcutta, Delhi, Lahore, and other places. "It was a sickening sight", he writes in his memoirs, "I had marvelled, at the magnificent discipline of non-violence which the genius Gandhi had taught them. They had not struck back, they had not even defended themselves except to try to shield their faces and heads from lathi blows."

The civil disobedient movement was in full swing. The report of Simon Commission was published in June 1930. Its recommendation did not evoke enthusiasm to even conservative people in India. Mahatma Gandhi and other leaders were in jail, when the first Round Table Conference met in London on November 12, 1930 to discuss possible changes in the manner in which India was to be governed in the future. The Congress did not attend the conference. Nothing was achieved and the conference was adjourned.

The Congress had refused to participate in the First Round Table Conference. So Lord Irvin wanted to find a solution of the problem. Irvin decided to appeal to Gandhi himself. He delivered a speech on the floor of the Legislative Assembly in January 1931. He spoke to Gandhi in such terms that had never been used by any Viceroy, when speaking of an opponent in jail for sedation. "No one can fail to recognize the spiritual force which impels Mr. Gandhi to count no sacrifice too great in the cause as he believes of India he loves." Irvin followed up this speech by releasing Gandhi and the members of the Congress Working Committee from prison. Gandhi agreed to meet the Viceroy. Gandhi got an official invitation from the Viceroy to meet him. Gandhi reached the Viceroy's palace. A platoon of peon in smart uniform bowed low as Gandhi entered the Conference room and this ritual was repeated when he left. The Gandhi Irwin parlay began on the afternoon of February 17, 1931 at the Viceroy house. The Mahatma in his loin cloth had parleyed with the Viceroy. To cover up the discussion Durga Das was in the A.D.C's room at vice-regal Lodge. The Viceroy was parlaying with the 'rebel' leaders behind closed doors. The moments were enlivened by the broad sides fired by Churchill from London. He declared it "nauseating to see Gandhi striding half naked up the steps of the viceregal palace which he is still organizing and conducting a difficult campaign of civil disobedience of equal terms with the representative of the King Empire."

When the talks appeared to be moving towards a settlement, Churchill fumed: "the loss of India would be final and fetal to us. It could not fail to be part of a process that would reduce us to the scale of a money power". His outburst increased the zeal of the participants in the talks to make them fruitful.

Irwin listened to Gandhi's monologues with patience such as no other Viceroy can have possessed in such abundance. As a Viceroy who was both willing and able to adjust in the Gandhian negotiation style. He was uniquely qualified to come to an agreement with that 'little strange man'. He also understood the springs that gave the Mahatma have the astonishing power. Irwin's own religion made him see Gandhi as something much more than what he appeared to people like Churchill. It enabled the tall, brilliant, aristocratic Viceroy to talk to the half-naked *fakir*.

The first sitting of the parley which started on the afternoon of February 17, 1931 continued in the night. The parley came to an end because of dinner time. Durga Das was present in the courtyard, Gandhi then boarded in the car. Durga Das dashed to his side and asked "Mahatmajee, will you issue a statement about the agreement". Gandhi perhaps must have taken Durga Das in the dark for a number of the Viceroy's staff and answered, "Ask the private secretary". Now Durga Das addressed Irwin as he was about to walk back to his office room. 'What are you doing here at this hour?' Irwin asked Durga Das. He was surprised and said, 'at the post of duty, your Excellency, even as you are'. Durga Das said and added "is a communiqué on the agreement being issued tonight? With a smile, Irwin said: "you will know tomorrow".

Durga Das then went to the Central Telegraph Office and he flashed a message announcing the news that Gandhi and Irwin had reached an agreement and that the pact now only awaited ratification by the Congress Working Committee. This message took one minute to reach London and another five minutes to reach New York. There were eight sittings between Irwin and Gandhi and they signed an agreement at noon on 5th March, 1931. Durga Das asked Gandhi how the ceremony went off. Gandhi told him that we had joked about Churchill's broad sides and drunk to each other's health; Irwin in tea and Gandhi in nimbu pani (lemon juice) flavoured with a pinch of salt.

The Indian Freedom Movement became very popular in the U.S. at this period Dr. J. Haynes Holmes of the community, Churchill of New York, who had attended the Congress session at Kanpur in 1925 regarding Gandhi and Christ reborn and was the most powerful American Advocate of the cause of Indian freedom. Loms Fischer was for a time a favourite American commentator in Indian affairs and he did much to sell the freedom movement in the U.S. and the West generally by interpreting the phenomenon that was Gandhi as the new star on the Indian horizon and Jawaharlal Nehru. Among Indians Syed Husain did more than anyone else to sell India and Gandhi to Americans.[37]

As a result of the Gandhi-Irwin Pact, 1931, Gandhi attended the Second Round Table Conference[38] as the only representative of the Indian National Congress. In spite of persistent efforts, the question of communal representation was not solved. The separate electorates were demanded not only by Muslims but by depressed castes, Indian Christians, Anglo-Indians and Europeans. All these groups came together in a 'minorities' pact for joint action on November 13.

So the conference failed and was adjourned on December 1, 1931. Gandhi landed at Bombay on December 28, 1931. Irwin was replaced by Wallington as Viceroy. The British had miscalculated, however, the effect of Gandhi's failure to make an impression at the Round Table Conference. His activities received wide publicity in the U.S., and the British establishment was blamed for sending Gandhi back empty handed.

The King and Fakir

When the Round Table Conference was in session in London in 1931, it was decided to hold a reception for the delegates in Buckingham Palace. The question arose whether Gandhi, who was attending the conference as the side representative of the Indian National Congress, should be invited. Sir *Samuel Hoare*, the Secretary of State for India, the Minister in-Charge of Indian affairs in the British cabinet sought an audience with King George V. The King's reaction to the proposed was that Sir Samuel had feared. "What" he exclaimed, "have their rebel Fakir in the Palace after he has been behind all these attacks on my officers."

After the King had let off steam, Sir Samuel procceded to discuss the arrangements for the Party. By the time the interview was over, His Majesty was reconciled to Gandhi's presence. But he expressed himself strongly against the Indian leader coming to the Party with "no proper clothes on and bare knees". Ultimately, as Sir Samuel wrote, the King was mollified and an invitation was issued without any condition to clothes.

The invitation created a dilemma as acute for Gandhi as it had been for the King. The Mahatma had long since ceased to take part in such social functions but there were other reasons for his wanting to stay away. The proceedings of the Round Table Conference had been disappointing from the Congress point of view. They had been conducted so as to marshal together all the communal and reactionary elements among the Indian delegates to isolate Gandhi and create a stalemate. The news from India was also ominous. The Gandhi-Irwin Pact was on the verge of breaking down. In such circumstances the Mahatma did not have the heart to attend the Party.

At the meeting with the Quaker friends, he did some loud thinking. He was, he said, in an embarrassing position. It was a moral issue. He was the guest of the English people and could not be discourteous to the hosts. It was, Mahadev Desai noted at the time 'the morality of things' ultimately prevailed with Gandhi. He wrote a courteous letter to Lord Chamberlain thanking him for the royal invitation and informing him that he would attend the reception in his usual dress.

At last the day came when the 'half naked fakir' as Churchill had described Gandhi stepped into Buckingham Palace. All the other delegates to the Round Table, the British Ministers and other eminent people at the reception were of course in formal dress. It had been arranged that *Sir Samuel Hoare* would introduce Gandhi to the King. The conversation seemed to be growing well, when *Hoare* saw with trepidation that the King had began staring at the Mahatma's bare knees. And just as Gandhi was about to leave, the King burst out: "remember Mr. Gandhi, I would not have any attacks on my Empire".

Hoare wrote later that when he heard the King's remark, he held his breath in fear of an unpleasant scene. The Mahatma's 'savoir faire' saved the situation. I must not be drawn into a political argument he told the King in His Majesty's palace after receiving His Majesty's hospitality. Hoare heaved a sigh of relief and many years later in his memoirs concluded the account of this episode with the words: what exquisite manners the unworldly successes.

Irwin's Departure

At the time of Irwin's departure, Bhagat Singh's execution had dominated the Indian political scene. In the assembly case, Bhagat Singh and Rajguru were convicted and sentenced to transportation for life on June 12, 1929. In the first Lahore Conspiracy Case, the judgment was delivered on October 7, 1930. Bhagat Singh was convicted to death along with Sukhdeo and Rajguru under ordinance number of 1930. Bhagat Singh, Sukhdeo and Rajguru were placed in the Lahore Central Jail. There was a feeling in the country that Bhagat Singh's life should be protected. Gandhi met Irwin on March 19, 1931 and pleaded for the reprieve of Bhagat Singh and his two colleagues from the death sentence to which they had been condemned. He reinforced his oral request with the powerful appeal to the charity of a 'great Christian' in *Young India*. Irwin took the public into confidence on his reasons for rejecting Gandhi's appeal. Irwin's farewell speech on 26th March, 1931 at a local club in New Delhi was very forthright and a sort of political stocktaking.

In the course of the speech Irwin remarked, as I listened the other day to Mr. Gandhi putting the case for commutation formally before me. I reflected first on what significance it surely was that the apostle of non-violence should be earnestly pleading the cause of devotees of a creed fundamentally opposed to his own, but I should regard it was wholly to allow my judgment on these matters to be influenced or deflected by purely political consideration. I could imagine no case in which under the law the penalty had been directly deserved. Later on the Viceroy explained he had been caught before two stools. He said, "There are extremists who would condone violence. I have saved Gandhi from falling from his own moral standard."

Then Durga Das asked Irwin to name the outstanding events during his tenure of office besides the pact with Gandhi. He replied he was deeply moved when he opened council (now parliament) house and thereby inaugurated the new centre of government in New Delhi. This was on 18th January, 1927 and everybody was struck by the circular edifice as the emblem of permanence of eternity. What troubled Irwin most was the growing estrangement of the Hindus and the Muslims? He added: 'I wonder whether I have not missed an opportunity to bring Gandhi and Fazli together.'

Gandhi's failure to save the life caused much indignation in Congress circles. Gandhi tried to pacify Irwin's critics by stating that commutation of the sentences was no part of Gandhi-Irwin Pact: "we may not accuse them of breach of settlement", on 23rd March, 1931, three young men Bhagat Singh, Rajguru and Sukhdeo were hanged to death at 7.15 p.m. in the Lahore Central Jail on account of their devotion to the country and the people. Their bodies were cremated on the bank of the Sutlej. Two days later Sir Abdur Rahim, leader of the opposition and Sir Cowasit Jehangir, deputy leader of the independent walked out of the Central Assembly as a protest against the executions, showing that the non-Congress parties were equally indignant. Jawaharlal Nehru declared that "the corpse of Bhagat Singh shall stand between us and England".

Under this tragic event, the Congress session was held at Karachi in March 1931 presided over by Sardar Patel. It was held in March instead of December for this reason that this month suited for lawyer-members, as the courts recessed during this time. Secondly, the Karachi audience being large, the session was held in an open stadium, a practice which has been followed since then.

As Irwin's departure drew near, so Gandhi went to Bombay to bid farewell to Lord and Lady Irwin on 18th April. In this way Gandhi showed his faith in the Viceroy's sincerity in trying to further a peaceful and honourable settlement between Indian nationalism and Britain. At this time it was not clear that with the departure of Irwin, the chapter of bipolar politics (the contenders being the *Raj* and the Congress) would come to an end.[39]

Giants of the Central Legislature

Vithalbhai Patel was the first member of the central legislature, who became speaker of the house. He was an impressive figure with his flow gray beard with a Turkish cap. He was an upholder of the dignity and independence of his office. He asserted his right to occupy a seat beside the Viceroy, when the latter attended the House for the former opening of the legislative session. But his successor, Sir Abdur Rahim was not very assertive and he was contended to occupy a seat on the floor of the House facing. It was left to G.V. Mavalankar, the first speaker of the Lok Sabha to reassert the Speaker's prerogative in the matter as the 'best'.

Vithalbhai's mental equipment was formidable. There was not the smallest detail of British parliamentary rules which he had not mastered. He did not like that the British Secretary should control the legislative department. The speaker demanded an independent Secretariat for the Assembly. He took up the case with Irwin. The Viceroy was prevailed upon to ensure for the speaker, as a master of the house, a large degree of independence by creating the assembly secretariat his own portfolio. Vithalbhai's sympathies were with the nationalist opposition. He always conferred with Motilal Nehru on political questions.

Few examples are sufficient to indicate that he championed his rights as speaker once, when he was apprised of a whispering campaign in the lobby attacking his impartiality, he lodged a protest with the Viceroy. As this turn of events the Home member had to apologise in the House. Even more sensational was his snub to the Commander-in-Chief, Sir William Birdwood, who was found absent from the House, when he had to answer a question. The Army Chief was obliged to make amends on the floor of the House. The Speaker insisted that security control in the chamber be vested in the Speaker's watch and ward. During a crisis over his right to control admission to the assembly galleries, he ordered them to be closed until he won his point.

Irwin considered Vithalbhai as a link between him and the Congress High Command. So the Viceroy extended his full cooperation to Vithalbhai and he agreed to make the separated assembly department his portfolio by delinking it from the bureaucracy-ridden legislative department. But Irwin also administered few snubs to the Speaker. The day the Swarajists, led by Motilal Nehru, walked out of the house in response to the Congress mandate, the Speaker, Patel ordered an adjournment, declaring that it had become unrepresentative. Irwin conveyed his displeasure at this procedure and the speaker expressed regret for this action. In another occasion, Vithalbhai refused to allow the Public Safety Bill to be introduced on the ground that it was unconstitutional. The Viceroy had the rules amended to ensure that the Speaker could not throw out a Bill as being unconstitutional, an authority with which the judiciary was empowered with.

Motilal Nehru was another dominant leader of the House. On the death of C.R. Das in 1925 he became President of Swaraj Party. The Swaraj Party merged in 1926 with the Congress under his leadership in the House. Motilal Nehru, the leader of opposition was a striking personality. An astute tactician, an eloquent debater and orator and a stern disciplinarian with a dignified presence in his white homespun *dhoti* and *Kurta*, he was a formidable opposition leader.[40]

Tall and handsome, he looked as imposing in his homespun *dhoti* and *kurta* as he had in the elegant Western attire of his princely lawyer days at Allahabad. The shawl he affected was draped around his shoulders much like a Roman toga. Motilal was intolerant of opposition. He could not keep peace with his deputy leaders, Vithalbhai Patel and Srinivasa Iyengar, a formal Advocate General of Madras. They considered themselves possessed of sharp intellects than he had believed in aggressive opposition. He was also responsible for the resignation of Jayaker and his Lieutenants from his Party. "They are a diseased limb, and I have amputed it". He remarked to me when he got rid of Maharashtrian leaders.

Though he followed Gandhian principles, Motilal retained much of his aristocratic way of life. He would not completely abjure alcohol, nor would he deny himself the luxury of rich food, one day in the assembly lobby, Durga Das pointed out to Motilal that the European Members spoke of his habit of drinking with Sir Alexander Muddiman, the leader of the house; he protested that he took alcohol strictly on medical grounds. C.R. Das, Motilal added by way of explanation, hastened to death by giving up the kind of food and drink he has been accustomed to as a lawyer with a flourishing practice. Motilal had his European friends, Motilal took wine. His all friends knew it. Sir Harcourt Butler visited Motilal in jail. He promised to Motilal that he would send him whisky and champagne. According to Mahabir Tyagi, a fellow prisoner, the liquor never reached Motilal.

The third giant was Mohammed Ali Jinnah. He was the leader of the independent group who was tall and thin and liked European dress. He was an excellent debater. He spoke very good English and was an astute politician. There is one example, the Governor had succeeded in originating the Muslim conference. This event led him to revise his stand. So he prepared a programme to be placed before the Muslim League council. At this stage Durga Das went to meet Jinnah. Jinnah remarked: "Durga, I want your help urgently. Please use your journalistic talent to enumerate our stand by amalgamating our resolutions with the demands made by the all-party Muslim conference. We must appear before the Muslim as the best protectors of their interests."

Jinnah was always friendly and communicative so Durga Das scrutinized the resolution and reduced it to thirteen points. Jinnah had a glance at thirteen points and suggested that it should be fourteen, like Wilson's 14-point. He said: 'no Cabinet either provincial or central should be formed without their being a proportion of at least one-third Muslim Ministers'. This is a genesis of fourteen points which Jinnah placed at the all-Party conference in 1928. Jinnah was not thinking in terms of demands but of tactics. He was keeping himself afloat as a political leader. His last point was thus motivated by the desire to champion the cause of the Muslims on area where they were a minority. His main support at the time was in Bombay and the U.P. and this provision was meant to strengthen his hold on these provinces.[41]

Durga Das went to the meeting of the League Council with Jinnah at a cinema hall in old Delhi. The opposition had mobilized rowdies to break up the meeting and they did succeed in their design. But Jinnah adjointly outman oeuvre them by announcing amidst den and confusion that his 14-points had been adopted. At this time cheers were flying and Jinnah rushed out and drove back to Western Court, the residential block for legislatures. From that time Jinnah's 14-points became famous in History. There were a minor difference between Jinnah's 14-points and the demand of the all parties' Muslim conference. Jinnah was condolatory only to the extent that he kept issue of separate electorate only to the extent that he kept the issue of separate electorate open to negotiation. It was left to the community to abandon separate electorate in favour of joint electorate.

After the Poona Pact of 1932 and the failure of the third Round Table Conference in 1933, Gandhi announced his retirement from the Congress on September 17, 1934. The Government of India Act, 1935, came into force on July 3, 1936, and the act in its totality on April 1, 1937. Although the part relating to Federal was not to become operative until a given number of princely states had concerted to it, the province gained a separate legal entity and their financial resources and the central government's power of direction and control were limited to specific spheres. The British policy was undergoing a change. Irwin had recognized the Congress as a vital force and signed an agreement with Gandhi. The British Government after 1931 began to whittle down their pledges. They thought if they could promote communal clashes, they could retain control of the country. They had begun for the first time to think of the Muslim question in terms of their own safety.

Fazli Husain, a member of the Viceroy's executive council brought another communal thinking. He was not satisfied with securing separate electorates and a fix number of seats in the legislatures. Fazli talked of creating Muslim majority zone as a counterpoise to Hindu-majority areas. He said that the British were now building up a new power triangle designed to retain their hold in India. They were planning to divide the country into Hindu, Muslim and princes would outvote the nationalist Hindus in a federal set-up.

But this was not how several Britain's viewed the prospect. Sir Malcolm Hailey, the Governor of U.P. was retiring from the I.C.S., speaking in a farewell dinner in Lucknow in 1934. He said it is impossible to suppress a nationalist movement. We have tried to suppress it with all the force at our disposal but even you cannot be sure that the Congress will not come up again. There is no safeguard for the civil service in a democracy, except that trained officials will be necessary to execute mainstream policy and not merely deal with law and order. The future Government of India would be largely socialistic.

Churchill's speech, during the second reading of the bill, on February 11, 1935 spoke in a contrasting way. He said, "We have as good a right to be in India as anyone there except, perhaps, the depressed classes, who are the original stock. Our Government is not irresponsible government. It is a government responsible to the Crown and to the Parliament. It is incomparably the best government that India has ever seen or ever will see. It is not true to say that the Indians whatever their creed, would not rather have their affairs deal with in many cases by British courts and British officers than by their own people, especially their own people of the opposite religion." Seeing the widely divergent interpretations put on it by labour and young spokesmen, politicians in India naturally found it difficult to assess the true worth of the Reforms Act.[42]

The Seeds of Pakistan : Fazli's Views

The Congress Party stood for a united India. It was a secular Party. The Muslim League was a communal Party and this Party was loyal to the British Government. Now a general election was to take place in the country under the Government of India Act, 1935. Slowly the rift between the Congress and the League had started. Fazli Husain was both a communalist and nationalist. If any issue flavoured the interest of the Muslims Fazli forgot nation and behaved like a strong communalist otherwise he was a nationalist. In 1935, he told to Durga Das that most Muslims of today were Hindus, not so long ago he told that the ancestors of Mohammed Iqbal and M.A. Jinnah were Hindus. In his self-interest the Muslims were inclined to flatter the British by protestations of loyalty.

Fazli threw considerable light on the plan for Pakistan. Those who gave birth to this idea in the early thirties had been financed by British intelligence in London according to Fazli. But the Indian leaders either the Congress or Muslim League were not influenced at all. Sir Mohammed Zafrullah Khan placed Fazli's views before the consultative committee set up in London to consider the White Paper on proposed reforms had for instance dismissed it as chimerical. The Aga Khan had made a vague allusion to Pakistan in a letter to Fazli as a means of safeguarding Muslim interests under a democratic regime in India. The Aga Khan was providing funds to unionist Party in the Punjab, All-India Muslim Conference and the Praja Krashak Party of Khwaja Nazimuddin and Fazlul Haque in Bengal. Fazli had published the letter only after expunging this reference. He believed that until adult franchise was introduced in the country the separate electorate should continue. Fazli, like the All India Congress stood for a united states of India in which both Hindu and Muslim states would contribute to a composite culture. He held his opinion that communal differences were not based on religion but on sharing political power and the meagre economic resources of the country. He had the poor opinion of Jinnah, whom he considered an anti-chair politician. He thought Jinnah stood for joint electorates with reservation of seats merely to earn kudos from Congress and moderate leaders. He thought that Jinnah's main contribution to the national movement was his consistent advocacy of industrialization of the commissioned rank in the Army.

Fazli expressed total opposition to Jinnah's plan to fight the elections through the Muslim League, a communal Party. Fazli liked that Muslim should join secular parties. He was greatly surpassed that the people took Jinnah seriously. He recalled that Jinnah had written to the *Times of India* on October 3, 1925 during the charge that the Congress was a Hindu body. Speaking in a legislative Assembly, he had declared: "I am a nationalist first, a nationalist second and a nationalist last." He wanted the assembly to become a 'real nationalist parliament'. Jinnah joined the boycott of the Simon Commission in 1928 and split the League. He did not cooperate with the Muslim delegates at the Round Table Conference in London. His League is on paper and has no organization.

Fazli reached Lahore on April 1, 1935. He requested Aga Khan to attend a meeting of the Executive Board of the All India Muslim Conference in Delhi in February 1936 and the Executive Board adopted a resolution: "that the Muslims put India first, being as much their motherland as of other races that inhabit India". The Aga Khan gave funds to help counter the propaganda of Jinnah's League, which received financial support from the Hindu mill owners of Bombay because of its tacit alliance with the Congress in the coming elections.

In order to capture all India leadership of the Muslims, Jinnah prepared a purely communal programme and invited Fazli to preside over the next session of the League. Fazli rejected this offer. Jinnah in anger reported: "I shall smash Fazli". On April 1, 1936, Fazli reorganized the Unionist Party under his own chairmanship. He prepared a manifesto to fight the elections of 1937. But destiny did not help him. Fazli, a communalist turn nationalist was determined to extend his cooperation to the Congress on the economic plan, but Jinnah, a nationalist turned communalist sought a coalition with the Congress on the communal basis. But as ill luck would have it, Fazli fell ill on 1st July and died on 9th July. Had he survived for two years more India's fate would have been different. Now Jinnah had to obstacle and he gave a tough challenge to the Congress in the ensuing elections. The idea of partitioning the country took a concrete shape after Fazli's sudden death.[43]

NOTES

1. Patrick French, *Liberty or Death,* p. 43.
2. *Ibid.*
3. Pirzada Syed Saifuddin, *Foundation of Pakistan*, Karachi, 1969-1990, quoted by P. French, p. 43.
4. Members of the Indian National Congress and certain categories of Muslims.

5. Patrick French, p. 44.
6. Mansargh and Moon, *Transfer of Power*, Vol. 9, pp. 542-543.
7. Menon, V.P., *Transfer of Power,* p. 1
8. Mishra, S.G., *Freedom Movement,* p. 51.
9. *Ibid.*
10. *Ibid.*
11. Agarwala R.C., *C.H.* and *National Movement*, p. 151.
12. *Ibid.*
13. Azad, M.K., *India Wins Freedom,* p. 8.
14. *Ibid.*
15. *Ibid.*
16. Agarwala, R.C., *C.H. and National Movement*, p. 152.
17. *Ibid.*
18. *First World War*, 1914-1918.
19. Quoted *Wolpart Stanley*, p. 47
20. Patrick French, *Liberty or Death,* p. 46.
21. Durga Das, *India from Curzon to Nehru and After*, pp. 63-64.
22. *Ibid.*, pp. 72 to 96.
23. "The Lonely Road to Pakistan" written by Stanley Wolpart, *Times of India*, November 13, 1984
24. Durga Das, p. 124.
25. Nanda, B.R., *The Nehrus*, p. 287.
26. Norman Jorothy, *Nehru II*, p. 169.
27. Durga Das, *India from Curzon to Nehru and After*, pp. 127-128.
28. Mishra, S.G., *Freedom Movement,* p. 8.
29. Aggarwala, R.N., *Natonal Movement.*
30. Sarkar, Sumit, *Modern India,* p. 263.
31. Durga Das, p. 31.
32. Durga Das, *India from Curzon to Nehru and After*, p. 135.
33. When India became a republic, the new Constitution was brought into force on this day, now observed as Republic day.
34. *Tribune*, Lahore March 10, 1930.
35. Patrick French, *Liberty or Death*, p. 79.
36. *The Times of India*, New Delhi, June 9, 1985.
37. Durga Das, *India from Curzon to Nehru and After*, p. 141.
38. September-December 1931.
39. Durga Das, pp. 146-148.
40. D. Weavers (ed.), *The Dictionary of National Biography*, London, 1912, 1921, 1968, pp. 648-649.
41. Durga Das, *India from Curzon to Nehru and After*, pp. 144-145.
42. *Ibid.*, p. 168.
43. *Ibid.*, pp. 169-173.

5

The Indian Independence Movement

According to Mrinal Dutta Chaudhary, Economist and Head of Delhi School of Economics, India's Independence movement grew out of the modernization of the Indian society, which began in the early nineteenth century. The process was set in motion by the creation of presidential and with the consolidation of the British rule in India. The presidency of Calcutta, Madras and Bombay developed first. Subsequently other urban centres were established to support the emerging system of administration and commerce. The administrative apparatus as well as the commercial organizations needed the service of local functionaries, who in turn required not only some knowledge of the English language but also a degree of familiarity with the administrative and legal system of the new rulers. This inevitably led to the emergence of English educated elite groups in the three presidencies. The growth of English education started in the country from 1835.

A remarkable achievement of these elite groups was that they promptly engaged in a creative interaction with the Western invaders in diverse call and spheres, such as literature and religious, social and political values. They took into initiatives in spreading Western education and started various movements for social reform in the light of the valuable emanating from the European enlightenment.[1]

Gradually their aspiration grew; firstly, they wanted more jobs in the higher echelon of the administration, then, local self-government and finally, independence from foreign rule. However, the social values, which led earlier, sustained the various movements for social reform, continued to be important motivating factors in the new movement for independence. The ideals of liberty and representative government became integral parts of the national movement for self-rule.

The pre-1885 period was not a peaceful period. After the uprising of 1857, many of the participants were exiled to the Andaman and these islands were governed by a chief commissioner. In 1874, Lord Mayo, the Viceroy of India, was assassinated by a brave prisioner called Sher Ali while he was inspecting the Cellular Jail which popularly known as silver Jail.[2] Gradually political associations were being established in the different parts of the country in 1839. In 1867, the Poona Sarvajanik Sabha was organized for communication to the government the wishes and opinion of the people. But the P.S. Sabha was weakened in 1868 and it was rejuvenated in 1870. The Sabha represented the wealth and influence of the local community Mahadev Govind Ranade, a subordinate judge became the life-blood of the Sabha from 1871. The Poona Sarvajanik Sabha did much to stimulate political activity in western India.

The civil service recruitment was a burning topic before the English educated students. They were invested to sit in the I.C.S. examination in London. The Indian demand for holding simultaneous examination for the civil services in India grew from 1856 but it was argued for example that the holding of civil services examination in India would benefit only the English educated classes, particularly the Bengalese and the Brahmins, who lacked ruling power, that it would be unfair to the martial races, such as the Sikhs and the Pathans.

The I.C.S. was regarded as the "Heaven-born services". The first Indian Satyendra Nath Tagore competed in the Indian Civil Services in 1863 but according to Dr. B.B. Mishra it was 1864 and not 1863. In 1869 four Indians succeeded in passing the civil services examination of the 40 Indians who competed for the civil services between 1862 and 1875, not more than 10 were successful and those successful only 6 were Bengalis.

In 1866, Lord Salisbery as Secretary of State for India reduced the maximum age of which the civil services examination might be set from 21 to 19 for the educated Indians. The age reduction from 22 to 21 in 1866 was being prejudiced to their interests. The reduction of 1876 was disliked.

The civil service question became the all India question. It became the national question, irrespective of provinces, language and region; the educated community mingled together and raised their voices against the age reduction.[3]

With the active interest of Allan Octavian Hume, the first session of the Indian national Congress was held in Bombay on December 28, 1885. So 1885 saw the generation of Dadabhai Naoroji, Pherozshah Mehta, Mahadev Govind Ranade, Ananda Charry, Badruddin Tyabji, Dineshaw Wacha, Subramania Iyer and Woomesh Chandra Banerjee, passing away.[4]

Allan Octavian Hume, William Wedderbaurn, and Charles Bradlaugh and the British leaders also belonged to the rank of passing generation. Contemporaries Bal Gangadhar Tilak was 29, Gopal Krishan Gokhale 19 and Mohandas Karamchand Gandhi, who took over the leadership of the national movement in 1920, was doing his matriculation in a school and he was a boy of 16 only.

Allan Octavian Hume was the son of a distinguished member of British Parliament, Joseph Hume. He belonged to Scotland. Hume was a radical. Joseph Hume (1777-1855) was also a radical man. A.O. Hume was born in 1829 and came to India at the age of twenty and began his career as a District Officer. He was appointed in Bengal civil service in 1849. He worked in different capacities and he was promoted to the rank of secretary in the central department. He was a radical man. He had his differences with the government. He was demoted in 1879 and sent as a member of the Board of Revenue of the North-West Provinces. Subsequently he resigned and settled down at Simla in 1882. He lived in his own house at Simla called Rothney Castle above the ridge. The house became the rendezvous of the Founding Father of the Congress. The Rothney Castle had become the historical place. Hume watched the agitation over the Ilbert Bill anxiously. The Ilbert Bill crises enabled Hume to establish himself at the head of a network of contents extending throughout India. This was the most significant event of his life. This event helped him to establish the Indian National Union, which took the name of the Indian National Congress in 1885. Lord Duffrin was the Viceroy of the country. W.C. Banerjee was the President of the National Congress. According to Banerjee, A.O. Hume first conceived the idea that it would be of great advantage to India if the leading politicians of the country could be brought together once a year to discuss social matters and that politics should form no part of their discussion.

The President elected W.C. Banerjee described the gathering as the 'First National Assembly' ever yet convened in India. The aims and objectives of the Congress were: the promotion of personal intimacy and friendship amongst all the more earnest workers in the country's cause in the various parts of the Empire and the fuller development and consolidation of the sentiments of national unity.

The President spoke in this way: I think that our desire to be governed according to the ideas of governments prevalent in Europe is in no way incompatible with our thorough loyalty to the British Government. All that we desire is that the basis of the government should be widened and that the people should have their proper and legitimate share in it.

The Congress passed a series of resolutions. It demanded reform and expansion of the central and local legislative councils by the admission of a considerable proportion of elected members. Hume pointed out that "this conference will form the germ of a national parliament, and, if properly conducted will in a few years constitute an answerable reply to the assertion that India is unfit for any form of representative institutions". Annie Besant said, "India was realizing herself as a Nation". When the Congress was born, Lord Randalph Churchil was the Secretary of State. It is evident that the Congress had not asked the British to withdraw.

Dufferin was keeping an alert eye on the political situation and in November 1988, he informed the new Secretary of State, Lendcross that he had decided to establish an intelligence department all over India.

The second session of the Congress met in Calcutta, the capital of the British Indian Empire. The first session was attended by 72 delegates only; 18 from Bombay, 8 from Madras, 8 from Poona, 6 from Surat, 3 from Calcutta and the rest from the rest of India. The second session claimed to represent the whole of India in a more definite manner. According to Dr. M.N. Das, nearly 500 delegates had attended the session; Dadabhai Naoroji was the President of the second session. Dadabhai wanted to be a link between the Indian Congress and British Parliament. Lord Dufferin was confused on that point, what should be the policy of the government towards the Congress? Should he welcome them? By way of compromise, the Viceroy received some of the leading Congressmen just as 'distinguished visitors' and entertained several others at the Garden Party, without recognizing them as the representative of any Party.

Dadabhai Naoroji reminded the Congress delegates from all parts of India that an assemblage of that kind could not have been imagined even in the most glorious days of the ancient Hindu rule or even in the days of the great Akbar when people of the different provinces composed of all classes and communities could have met, all speaking one language and all having common and high aspirations of their own. He tried to assure the authorities that the Congress was not nursery for sedition and rebellion against the British Government; on the other hand it was yet another piece of mile stone in the foundation of the stability of that government.[5]

The third session was held at Madras in 1887 and Badruddin Tyabji presided over the session. Badruddin Tyabji was the first Indian Barrister. He told the delegates that wholesome general questions affected India as a whole, India was in no sense one nation. He tried to persuade Congress to modify its claims so as to attract Muslim members. But Muslim fears spread quickly. Most middle class Muslims lacked Tayabji's self-confidence. Within a year of first Congress, rival Muslim organizations sprung up to oppose the dangerous idea of a single voice for Indian interests.[6]

By early 1888, Lord Dufferin was seriously thinking of laying down the viceroyalty of India after the expiry of his fourth year of office at the end of the year. He was thinking to resign on domestic difficulties. In November 1888, Lord Dufferin drafted a Minute on the Congress for official purpose. In an elaborate thesis he did not try to show that the Congress had neither any root in the country nor was it capable of contributing much for the welfare of the people. Among vast millions of men there were 'only a few thousands' who possessed qualifications for taking any intelligent view of even local public affairs. And, the number of those men who could at all comprehend the larger problems would have to be counted rather by tens than by hundreds. The chief concern of the Government of India writes Dufferin is to protect and foster the interests of the people of India, and the people of India are not the seven or eight thousand students who have graduated at the universities, or the pleaders recruited from their numbers who are practicing in our courts of justice, or the newspaper writers, of the Europeanized zamindars or the wealthy traders, but the voiceless millions neither education nor civilization for the influence of Europe ideas or modern thoughts, have in the slightest degree transfigured or transformed from what their forefathers were of thousand years ago. In the concluding portions of Minute, Dufferin noted that "the Congress was the product of that infantilisms section of the Indian community".[7]

Dufferin made a famous speech in his St. Andrews farewell

dinner in Calcutta on November 30, 1888. It was considered invective paragana. He described the educated people of his empire as a 'microscopic minority'. At the day break on December 3, 1888, Dufferin's successor Lansdown reached Bombay and spent three days there, on December 10, 1888, Dufferin left Calcutta. His successor entered the capital and was given an impressive reception. By the end of month the fourth session of the Congress was meeting at Allahabad and George Yule was the elected president. Auckland Colvin, the Lieutenant Governor of the province did not like that the session of the Congress should be held at Allahabad.

The Great Maharaja

When India's national prestige was at stake, the Maharaja of Darbhanga vindicated the honour of the nation by taking Luther Castle on lease in 1888. This Castle was just in front of the then Government House in Allahabad. The Maharaja made the building available to the reception committee for holding the session of the Indian National Congress. But for the timely patriotic move on the part of Maharaja Lakshmeshwar Singh Bahadur, the session perhaps would not have been held.

The Congress sent requests to the Viceroy to receive a small deputation which was to come from Allahabad to Calcutta to lay before him the resolution adopted at that session, but the Viceroy declined. The fifth session of the Congress was held in Bombay in December 1899 with William Wedderlean as its President. Wadderlean was a good friend of India and he was second only to Allan Octavian Hume. Charles Brad Laugh had come from England to attend the Congress.

From its inception the Congress was a secular body. The first, second, third, fourth and fifth presidents of the Congress were Christian, Parsi, Muslim and Englishmen. The Congress was born to make demands. In the first session of the Congress in 1885, the Congress raised the demand for admission of a considerable proportion of elected members in the existing legislative councils. The Allahabad Congress of 1888 laid emphasis on elective principles. When the Congress met in Calcutta in 1890, the chairman of the reception committee, Man Mohan Ghose, expressed his feeling thus: "to divide and rule is a wicked policy and unworthy of the great

English people as it is practicably impossible". The Indian Council Act of June 20, 1892 contained the provisions regarding the enlargement of the Indian councils.

From 1885 to 1900 the Congress was on the whole a moderate and loyal organization, through less moderate voices were also making their influence felt. It was, by and large, wedded to peaceful and constitutional struggle.

With the opening of the twentieth century, times and minds changed rapidly, and the Indian National Congress underwent a great transformation. It was Curzon's viceroyalty—"hectic, eventful and highly provocative—that was responsible, in a large measure for this change."

Minto's regime had seen the seeds of Muslim separatism being sown. Chelmsford viceroyalty marked the mobilization of the princely states as a counterpoise to the nationalist upsurge Chelmsford answers at the second conference of princes and chiefs held in Delhi on November 5, 1917, that he contemplated the early establishment of a council of princes. This was later to become the chamber of princes, which embraced most members of the timely order eligible for membership.

The policy of divide and rule has given new dimension because whole Muslim separatism could take care of the situation in the Indo-Gangetic Plane; the regions below the Vindhyas had to tackle differently. A beginning was made with the sponsoring of the non-Brahmin movement. This was followed by a subtle attempt to drive a wedge between the Dravidian and the Aryan.

The final bid to split in Hindu community was even more ingenious, the untouchables were encouraged to claim they were a sub-nation entitled to separate electorates.[8]

NOTES

1. India, *The First 50 Years*, p. 23.
2. Bhalla, Alok, *'Stories About the Partition of India'*, Vol. I, p. 242.
3. Mehratra, S. R, *The Emergence of Congress*, pp. 272-273.
4. Das, M. N., *Indian National Congress* versus *the British*, Vol. I. pp. 31-32.
5. Das, M. N., p. 53.
6. Brian Lapping, "End of Empire", *Review of India*, Sunday, June 16, 1985, p. 5.

7. Das, M. N., Lord Dufferin's *Minute on the Congress*, November 1888, p. 69.
8. Durga Das, *From Curzon to Nehru and After*, p. 59.

6

Rahmat Ali Iqbal and the Lahore Session of 1940

Chaudhary Rahmat Ali was a Punjabi and he came from a poor background. He was born in 1897. He had received his education at Islamia College, Lahore. He then became tutor to the Nawab of Bhawalpur. He was admitted in the Cambridge University in 1931. At Cambridge he began to take interest in politics and he wanted a separate homeland for the Muslims. At Cambridge[1] he saw the word 'Paktan' or 'Pakastan' written on the upper deck of a London Bus. He thought about these two words and coined a new word' 'Pakistan' which Liaquat Ali later on defined 'Land of the pure'. In 1933, Rahmat Ali published a pamphlet under the title 'now and never'. The contents of the pamphlet were based on Iqbal's speech. It was for the first time that some one talked about separation and partition. The new nation, Rahmat wrote, symbolized 'the proclamation of our freedom from British[2] Bania domination, the release of our nation from the bonds of minorities. Rahmat Ali pursued his campaign from Cambridge vigorously. He tried to meet Jinnah. Jinnah had settled at London after 1933 and was practicing at the Privy Council. In 1934, he attempted to see him for discussion on his pamphlet but Jinnah was very busy in his legal practice and he did not give him time. Soon they differed and Rahmat Ali criticized Jinnah. Soon Rahmat Ali's ideas were becoming eccentric. He was proposing a term Muslim 'stand across Paksia, ranging from 'Maplistan' in Southern India through 'Siddiquestan' and 'Haideristan' to a union of Bengal and Assam with the wondrous name of 'Bang-i-Islam'. This word form part of a series of hamdards for the world's Muslim community, or Millat.

Rahmat Ali wanted Muslim Hamdard as early as 1933. His 'Pakistan National Movement' has found a reference in a German book on Islam, published in 1933 in Berlin. He wanted to return Karachi in 1940 but he was refused a Pakistan passport. He was suspicious that some one would poison him. He was dejected and disappointed. He was nearly living in exile from 1948 and he died in Cambridge in 1951. He was buried there leaving substantial debts.

The British Parliament committee had dismissed the nation of Pakistan in 1933 as only a student's scheme—Chimerical and impracticable but after ten years it was being taken seriously by Jinnah and other leaders of the Muslim League. For some time the demand for a separate homeland was a bargaining point for the Muslim League. It was a direct challenge for the Indian National Congress, a national organization founded in 1885.

Dr. Mohammed Iqbal (1877-1938)

Dr. Mohammed Iqbal, a great Urdu poet and one of the spiritual founders of Pakistan made the birth of Pakistan possible and like Jinnah, ancestors of Iqbal were Hindu. So Jinnah and Iqbal were converted Muslims. Iqbal's father was a Kashmiri Brahmin and he was called Sapru. On April 21, 1988, the Government of India had issued a ticket in his memory. Still there are people of India who think that Iqbal was one of Pakistan's founders. So it is necessary to understand Iqbal's political thought. Iqbal was like Jinnah, a barrister from Lincon's Inn and he was respected Islamic scholar and philosopher.

Dr. Iqbal presided over the session of the Muslim League at Allahabad in 1930. He delivered his presidential address on December 29, 1930. He said that he wanted a free state consisting of N.W.F.P., Sind, Baluchistan and Punjab. He made it clear that this Free State would be under the Indian Federation. It would continue as a unit of the federation.

Later on the chairman of the minority committee Mr. S.M.H. Barne explained that Dr. Iqbal wanted an independent Muslim state within the Indian federation. After some time, Edward Thompson in 1935 called the scheme of Iqbal under the name of Pakistan. Dr. Iqbal contradicted the view point of Thompson and wrote a letter, 'you call me a supporter of Pakistan but my scheme is not Pakistan'. Before this, Dr. Iqbal had written a letter to Raghib Atsan on March 6, 1934 in this way: "I am sending you two copies of review which has been done by Edward Thompson. You will see by yourself that Thompson had called my scheme as Pakistan".

Mr. S.M.H. Barne has said further that Pandit Jawaharlal Nehru did not think Iqbal as a supporter of Pakistan. Barne has proved his point with few lines from the *Discovery of India* where Jawaharlal says, 'Iqbal had supported Pakistan in the early part of his political career but towards the end he thought Pakistan irrelevant'. When Jawaharlal began to leave Iqbal's house, then he said, "What are the similarities between you and Jinnah. Jinnah is a politician and you are a patriot."

About Iqbal's Free State, an eminent historian Dr. Tarachand has written in his book *History of Freedom Movement* that this scheme had nothing to do with the partition of India. His scheme would not create two sovereign states. Iqbal simply demanded redistribution of states—only those states where Muslims are in a majority. Iqbal had not discussed two-nation theory. It has not been said that there are contradictions in the Hindu culture and the Muslim culture.

Mr. K.K. Aziz a Pakistani Historian has said in his book *The Making of Pakistan* that Iqbal did not plead for a separate Muslim state—he simply demanded a Muslim state under an Indian federation. "It will be a false conclusion if Iqbal is considered as an originator of the idea of Pakistan or he should be thought a poet—a poet that had dreamed about the partition of India."

Barne had discussed those things which Mr. K.K. Aziz had analysed in his book *Iqbal: Poet-Patriot of India*. According to Barne, Iqbal was not supporter of Pakistan but Berney's materials which have been collected, is incomplete. A new book had been published titled *Quaid-i-Azam* Jinnah's correspondence. This had been edited by Jinnah's honorary secretary Mr. Syed Sarifuddin Pirazada. There are some letters had been written by Iqbal to Jinnah. Iqbal wrote the first letter on June 21, 1937: "In my opinion there is the provision of an All India Federation under the new constitution, this is disappointing." I have talked to you about a new federation consisting of Muslim province, this is the only alternative. This will bring a peace loving India and Muslims could save out of the Hindu dominion. Muslim inhabiting North-West Frontier Province and Bengal should be treated as a nation and like other nations Indian Muslims should be given the right of self-determination.

Dr. Iqbal had argued before this letter in this way: "the Congress

President has rejected the political existence of Muslims in a clear language. There is another Hindu political congregation known as the Hindu Mahasabha, to which body I regard the true real representative of the Hindus. That Hindu Mahasabha had declared more than once that there is no possibility of a composite Hindu-Muslim unity. So it is evident that there should be redistribution of India on the basis of caste, religion and language." He had written another letter to Jinnah on May 28, 1937, "it is a matter of rejoicing that the solution of this problem is in Islamic laws and situation can develop in the background of modern thoughts. But without a free Muslim state, Islamic Shariat cannot develop. This is my true opinion for so many years and still I hold this opinion that I think that this is the only alternative."

Mr. S.M.H. Barne quoted Jawaharlal out of context, there is chapter titled "Asian Nationalism" in *Discovery of India* if one reads it, it becomes clear that Pandit Jawaharlal Nehru had no doubt on this point that Iqbal had provided philosophical background to the separatist movement going on in the country and also for the struggle of the partition of India. In the last part of his life, Iqbal possibly felt the contradiction of Pakistan but still the poet did not cut off his connections from the separatist's movement. On the contrary he maintained his relations with the Muslim League and continued to give his statement in favour of a separate country for the Muslims of the North-West Frontier Province.

Like M.A. Jinnah, Dr. Mohammed Iqbal was also a nationalist in the first part of his political life. Iqbal had composed, "*Sare Zahan Se Acha Hindustan Hamara*". In "*Naya Shivala* (The New Temple")" Iqbal said with full claim; '*Khake Batan Ka Mujhko Har Zarra Deveta Hai*'. His patriotic poems are found in "*Himlaya, Tajbir and Dard*". In this way he was nationalist. But his ideas changed from 1930. He was convinced that the entire world would be benefited by Islam. From this time Iqbal began to preach Islam in his writings. He wrote, "Your country is Islam. You are Musulfa also". Again he wrote in *Tarane-e-Mill* we are Muslims, it is our country; whole world belongs to us (*Muslim Hay Hum, Batan Hay, Sara Jahan Hamara*). His conception of Nation was like this: "*Kom Mahajab Se Hay*"/"*Rastra Dharam Par Nirver Raheta Hay.*" Iqbal wrote at another place "*Aah Arab Desh Hay, Muslim Ka Tu, Maba Hay To*" (*Oh Arab, Aap Musalmano Ke Desh Hay Aur Musalmano Ke Ashray Hay*).

In the later part of his life he was convinced that Islam alone could deliver the goods to the world. Since then, he preached Islam and Islam alone through his work. He called upon the Muffins of the world to unite in the case of Islam.

These thoughts of Iqbal compelled the Muslims of the country not to regard India as their motherland. Now the Muslims were encouraged to demand a separate homeland for themselves. The foreign government helped this movement to blossom. So there is no doubt to hold this opinion that Dr. Iqbal was not a secular leader. He was the spiritual and ideological father of Pakistan. He was also protagonist of a reactionary ideology. Dr. Iqbal and modern India, which is based on the concept of socialism and secularism, nothing is common.

These developments were affecting the communal problems of the country. Pandit Jawaharlal Nehru was very anxious at these developments. M.J. Akbar has written in his book *Life of Nehru* that Nehru wrote few letters to Jinnah in this connection. Jinnah sent a reply to these letters but failed to bring any advantage instantly. After some months Nehru's letters changed the situation. Mr. S. Wazir Hasan was influenced by Nehru's letters. Wazir Hasan was the President of Muslim League at Bombay in 1936. Wazir Hasan was not satisfied with communalism being spread by Jinnah. Wazir Hasan wrote a letter to Nehru on February 11, 1938 in this way: "False, untruth, religious and communal rivalry has spread in the country, propaganda is going on. This propaganda has affected not only Hindus and Muslims but between Muslims and Muslims. The glimpses of other developments could be traced from the session of the Muslim League held at Lucknow in October 1937. This propaganda spread at the great speed after the Lucknow session. Facts are twisted and then spoken from 1937, false things are said in the name of minority, and religious jealousy was spread. Wazir Hasan suggested that Nehru and Maulana Azad should start a counter offensive. But Nehru was tired. The developments of Haripura Congress (1938) had destroyed his mental peace. Spanish Civil War had started in Spain and democracy was being trampled by General Frenco and Hitlar. Nehru wanted to go to Spain to help the Republican government of the country. In 1938, Nehru went to Spain and addressed a public meeting in Barcelona. As Jawaharlal Nehru was outsider, communalism was making a rapid progress.

Conclusion

Iqbal was a unique personality, whose poetic and philosophical creations have profoundly influenced three successive questions, raising fundamentally controversial issues in both literary and political domains. He proceeded to Europe for higher studies after completing his university[3] education in public literature, law and philosophy. After three years of intimate acquaintance with Western socio-political institutions and academic personalities, he arrived at credentials identical to the other drawn by Swami Vivekananda; 'the spiritually starved West is strongly sitting on the top of volcano and eruption is imminent."

Islamic Brotherhood

Iqbal rejected the Western mode of nationalism and gradually veered around to the concept of Islamic brotherhood transcending all geographical and political boundaries. He opined that Islamic Pantheism could forge an effective weapon for the liberation of the East and the Muslim world simultaneously. The liberating sword could only be sharpened on the whetstone of soft-hood that is self-consciousness. Hence this aspiration to see the publication of his thought provoking Persian poem 'Asrari-khadi' (seeds of selfhood) in Europe. The first was translated by Prof. Nicholson of Cambridge University and took the literary world by storm.

The carnage of World War I and the treaty of Versailles only confirmed his worst suspicion about Western civilisation. But the catastrophic also produced two unforeseen and far-reaching chaims of events, the socialist revolution and the sudden upsurge of national liberation movement in the East. Iqbal thus found himself engulfed by two powerful currents. However, it was too early for him to infer that active nationalism of the colonial and exploited people during its development imbibes elements of the anti-imperialist struggle and in the long run aligns itself with the broad based international movements for the emancipation of humanity.[4]

At this stage Iqbal was universally regarded as the spokesman of Pan-Islamism and he became the target of severe criticism in patriotic circles of India, while presiding at All India Muslim League session in 1930 at Allahabad, he categorically advocated autonomous status for the North-West Provinces. He was dubbed a separatist fundamentalist for saying so, both in India and abroad. This image was reinforced on the eve of partition. Significantly Iqbal as declared "Poet Laureate" of Pakistan, Sir Mohammed Iqbal, the great Urdu poet and one of the spiritual founders of Pakistan claimed that it was impossible to fuse the various Indian communities.

The Depressed Class

The first session of the All India Depressed Classes Congress opened at Nagpur on August 8, 1930 before a large gathering of delegates from all over the country. Dr. B.R. Ambedkar, Bar-at-Law, ex-M.L.C., Bombay presided.

In the course of his presidential address Dr. Ambedkar said that it was quite possible for the peoples of India to become one united self-governing community. If Latvia, Luthawa, Czechoslovakia, Hungry and Rumania with all their differences of race, creed, language and culture could function as united self-governing communities, he said, there was no reason why India could not, at the same time he held that the diversity of conditions and peoples prevalent in India must be taken into account in framing the constitution for a self-governing India.[5]

The Communal Award and the Poona Pact

In August 1932, the British Government introduced constitutional changes in India entitled "the communal award". This Award was first published on August 17, 1932.[6] This scheme provided communal electorate not only for the Muslims but for the depressed classes, Hindus, Sikhs, Indian Christians and Europeans. The depressed classes were to enjoy the double vote for their own separate constituencies as well as for the general, Hindu, constituencies. Mahatma Gandhi protested against this award. The communal award treated the untouchables as politically separate from the Hindus. They were also to enjoy the double vote. McDonald's Communal Award created separated electorate for untouchables. Mahatma Gandhi announced on September 13, 1932 that he would 'fast unto death' because of the Communal Award of British Prime Minister Ramsay McDonald. It should be recalled in mind that Gandhi had been lodged in the Yervada prison in Poona.

This news that Gandhi would 'fast unto death' was like a bombshell and it shook India. The fast began on September 13,

1932 but according to B.R. Nanda it was on September 20, 1932. Gandhi wanted that the depressed classes should remain part of the general constituencies. To save Gandhi's precious life, a conference of leaders of caste Hindus and deprived classes were held to replace the Communal Award. The Hindu leader's conference met at Bombay, Madan Mohan Malviya, Tej Bahadur Sapru, M.R. Tayokar, C. Rajgopalachari, N.C. Kelkar, Rajendra Prasad and Moorji wanted quick solution, but the solution required Dr. Ambedkar's cooperation. The fast led ultimately to negotiations with Ambedkar culminating in the Poona Pact of September 24, 1932,[7] which conceded for more parliamentary representations to the untouchables than they had been allotted under the British Award. It was the price which the Indian National Congress had to pay to keep the untouchables within the Hindu fold. The British Government set its seed of approval on the Poona Pact on September 26, 1932. Now Gandhi broke the fast, the Hindu joint electorate continued with reserved seats for untouchables.

The Poona Pact doubled the representation for the depressed classes in the provincial legislatures. The electoral system was also revised. Communal Award had granted seventy two seats to the depressed class in the provincial legislatures but Poona Pact conceded 148, and was to be revised after ten years. The reservation of seats was to continue until it was ended by mutual agreement as desired by the Pattabhi Sitaramayya, leaders of the untouchables had every reason to be grateful, since the Pact secured them double the number of seats granted in Prime Minister McDonald's previous Award was substituted by the Poona Pact and a measure of representation somewhat in excess of the proportion of their population was confined on the depressed classes. If the Muslims had separate electorates from 1909, depressed classes also enjoyed the same facility from 1932. Thus communalism was strengthened in the Indian politics. No doubt the Hindu community stood intact, later on the term of ten years was retained in the Constitution of India but it is extended every ten years without a chance of it being taken out of the statute born at my time.

Before setting out on the 'Dandi March' in 1930, Gandhi had vowed that he would not return to Sabarmati Ashram until the attainment of *Swaraj*, Jamnalal Bajaj pleaded with Gandhi to make wards at the centre of his activities. Gandhi came to Wardha in 1933. Initially he stayed at Mahila Ashram and the Jamanlal's garden.

Finally, Segaon a village about five miles from Wardha was also selected; first Miraben went to Segaon and constructed a small kutcha mud-hut. She began to live there, on the morning of April 30, 1936 Gandhi came to Segaon to establish his Ashram. Segaon was a typical Indian village. Sardar Patel jointly named it 'Oxford'. Segaon was named as Sevagram in 1939-40. All the leaders of Congress including Pandit Nehru used to come to this place. The working committee of the Congress met here. Distinguished foreign guests also arrived.

The General Election of 1937 and Islam in Danger

The Lucknow Congress of 1936 and the Faizpur Congress of 1937 accepted the Government of India Act, 1935 after a long discussion. Jawaharlal Nehru and the left wing strongly urged rejection. Jawaharlal termed the Act of 1935 as a "charter of slavery" but the majority of Congressmen hungered for power after many years of sacrifices. A compromise fomula was finally evolved by Gandhi and Congress decided to contest the elections of 1937 a socialist nation was defeated by 467 votes to 255. Pandit Jawaharlal Nehru was the President of the Congress. But Jawaharlal Nehru was under a great mental strain. His wife Kamla Nehru had died of tuberclosis at the age of 37 on February 28, 1936. In 1926, it was known that Kamla was suffering from tuberculosis. He was re-elected and led the Congress to a sweeping victory at the polls. His election compaign can only be described as a fury of activity. He covered some 50,000 miles in less than five months, using every conceivable means of transport. Out of 1,585 seats, the Congress won 711,[8] a particularly striking success since it had run candidates in only 1,161 seats. But the Congress had run candidates in only 58 of the 482 separate Muslim constituencies. The Congress sweep is all the more impressive when it is borne in mind that of the 1,585 seats less then half, 657,[9] were 'General' or 'open' not allotted to a separate, closed electoral group. The balance was fragmented among Muslims, Sikhs, Christians, Europeans, Landholders and others. Of the eleven provinces in British India, the Congress won an absolute majority in five and was the largest Party in three others. By contrast, the Muslim League, which attained separate state of Pakistan in 1947, secured only 48 per cent[10] of the total Muslim votes. Nor did it win a majority of seats in any of the four Muslim provinces. At this time Lord Linlithgow replaced Willingdon as the Viceroy of the country.

The Muslim League fought the election on the issue of Hindu domination; united India and the consequent need it a separate Muslim homeland, i.e. Pakistan. The results were astonishing; the League won all 30 Muslim seats in the Central Assembly with 81 per cent of the Muslim vote and 427 out of 527 Muslim seats in the provincial legislature with 74 per cent of the Muslim votes. Its only setback was in the north-west province where the Khan Brothers captured a clear majority. The Congress won 56 seats in the Central Assembly with 91 per cent of the 'General votes' and 930 in the provinces.

There were two fundamental reasons for the Congress victory, a broadly based organizational network throughout the country and the mass appeal of its election manifesto, especially its pledge of agrarian reform. As *The Times of London* remarked on March 9, 1937,[11] the Party had won its victories on issues, which interested millions of Indian rural voters and scores of millions who had no votes. To Nehru goes most of the credit for the Congress stressed on land reform and it was he who carried the message so effectively in the countryside.

The following numbers of seats were won by the Congress in the legislative assembly of six provinces. Madras 159 out of 315, U.P. 134 out of 228, Bihar 98 out of 151, Bombay 86 out of 175, Central Provinces 70 out of 112, and Orissa 36 out of 60 seats. Out of 664 candidates for the 218 seats in the U.P., 152 were from the National Agricultural Party as against 168 Congressmen and Muslim League. The National Agricultural Party won 21 seats and the Muslim League 21 seats.[12]

After elections the Congress emerged as the strongest Party to form the Ministry in U.P. but out of 64 provincial seats reserved for Muslims, 26 were won by the Muslim League, 28 by Independent, 9 by the National Agriculture Party and only one by the Congress.[13] The Muslim League led by Jinnah, however, met with an electoral disaster. It was 39 out of 107 Muslim seats in Punjab, 3 out of 33 in Sind and 10 in Madras. It did not win a single Muslim seat in the legislature of Bihar, U.P., Orissa and N.W.F.P. In U.P. and Bombay it did comparably better. In Bombay it won 27 out of 60 Muslim seats and 20 out of 29 in U.P.[14] with this poor showing the League hardly qualified for a coalition in any province.

The case of U.P. should be understood thoroughly because Maulana Azad has accused Nehru on the formation of the U.P.

Ministry. In this election in U.P. the Indian National Congress and the Muslim League were facing challenges from the N.W.F.P. The National Agricultural Party of Awadh and Agra was formed in 1934.[15] On the eve of the 'General Election' Sir Malcolm Hailey, the Governor of U.P. had inspired the big landlords supported by business interests to form the National Agriculturists Party in U.P. to fight the Congress.

During the period of general elections there was not much conflict between the Congress and the Muslim League. It was desire of both parties to avoid a conflict as much as possible and to accommodate each other. In the early stages of the election campaign a number of Muslims who were more or less Congressmen were doubtful if they would stand on behalf of Congress or the League. So they dressed gradually to the League side. The League election board in U.P. was a curious affair. There were some fairly good and old Congressmen in it. This election was a tussle with the Agricultural Party which was wholly a Government Party. The League also was opposing them and so the Congress opposition to the League weakened.

There was "no kind of arrangement"[16] between the U.P. Congress and League, but a kind of convention had developed. In one or two instances the Congress opposed League candidates and defeated them during the election the outstanding and most powerful worker on behalf of the League.

After the election there was a tussle between the League and the reactionary elements seemed to gain the upper hand. Relation between the U.P. Congress and the U.P. League became more strained. During the convention at Delhi this matter was discussed by the Congress with the Jamait leaders who had so far supported the League fully but who were now worked at the reactionary turn it was taking.

After the convention the U.P. League board became even more reactionary and its President Raja Shaben Ali Khan of Salimpur[17] had joined the interim Ministry. This created crises in the League which resulted in the resignation of many members from the parliamentary board. Among those who had resigned was Maulana Husain Ahmad, most of those who resigned were not MLA's but one MLA Hafiz Ibrahim who resigned and finally joined the Congress Party.[18]

Walli, a Congressman of Lucknow, in his letter of March 28,

1937 informed the Congress president, Jawaharlal Nehru that Khaliq-uz-Zaman had been drifting away from the Congress and should not be brought back through any alliance or coalition with the Muslim League in the assembly. Walli further wrote a letter to Jawaharlal Nehru on March 30, 1937 informing him that "a scheme is being hatched with the help of Pantji or coalition between us and the Muslim League will be highly injurious".[19]

In this respect, Jawaharlal wrote a letter on the same day to Govind Ballabh Pant, the leader of the U.P. Congress legislature Party in this way: "I have been informed that a scheme is being hatched with your help and Mohanlal. I am personally convinced that any kind of pact of coalition between the Congress and the Muslim League will be highly injurious." Nehru issued a statement on April 25, 1937 at Allahabad: "those who talk of Congress entering into the alliance with Muslim and others fail to understand of the new forces that are moving over people."[20]

Towards the end of June 1937, the U.P. Muslim League leader Khaliq-uz-Zaman and Nawab Mohammad Ismail Khan made an approach towards Congress. This had obviously some connection within possibility of ministers. They pointed out that their parliamentary board had offered cooperation to the U.P. Congress Party on the basis of 'Warsaw Programme' as laid down by the working committee and were prepared to work under the discipline of the Congress Party.

At this stage Maulana Abul Kalam Azad went to Lucknow from Wardha. Azad was a member of three-man Congress parliamentary sub-committee.[21] Khaliq-uz-Zaman was negotiating on the coalition ministry with Azad. Azad had been authorized by the Congress working committee to deal with the Congress affairs in U.P. and nothing seems to have been done against the wishes, Pant was also with Azad.[22] Azad saw Khaliq who told him that he was practically prepared to give him a blank cheque provided two or three members were included in the ministry—one himself and other Nawab Ismail Khan, the President of U.P. Parliamentary Board. Azad looked at all with some suspicion but he felt attracted by the possibility of the whole Muslim League ceasing to exist as a separate group and being practically absorbed by the Congress.

Thereafter Maulana Azad and Govind Ballabh Pant came to Allahabad. They discussed the question of the formation of the coalition ministry with Jawaharlal Nehru. He disliked this bargaining for seats in the ministry. Azad and Pant shared the feeling of Nehru.

All of them disliked taking two persons, who from the Congress point of view were weak. They feared reaction among them, Congressmen in general and the Congress Muslims in particular, who would have been initiated at their being excluded in preference for those who had been fighting the Congress, what of those who had stood by the Congress during all that years. What of the Jamait which was supporting the Congress and opposing the League.[23]

Nehru, Azad and Pant thought over this matter seriously and they decided to workable proposition. This was the winding of the Muslim League group in the U.P. and its absorption in the Congress. This would have been a great effect not only in U.P. but all over India. This would mean a freehold for the Congress programme without communal troubles.

After much discussion in which two other members of the U.P., Acharya J.B. Kripalani and Narendra Dev joined. They all came to the conclusion that Congress should offer stringent conditions to the U.P. Muslim League group and if they accept them *in toto*, then we should offer two ministers of their group. Besides them, one minister would be Rafi Ahmad Kidwai.

So the conditions were drawn up. The March resolution of the working committee and the Congress policy in the legislature were to be accepted. The Muslim League would be wounded up including the U.P. Parliamentary Board. All Muslim League MLAs were to become full members of the Congress Party. All of them were to be abided by the discipline of the Party. But they did not ask them to sever all connections with the parent Muslim League.

The Azad and Pant went to Lucknow. They sent for Nawab Ismail Khan but he was ill in Meerut and could not come. There were talks with Khaliq-uz-Zaman, who agreed to all the conditions except two, the winding up of the parliamentary board and not to set up separate candidates at bye-election. These were vital conditions. Khaliq-uz-Zaman said that he personally could agree but he had no authority to do so. They said that he could not give a final answer and returned to Allahabad.

While rumours had spread that Azad and Pant were talking with the Muslim League. There was consternation among all Congress people especially the Muslim Congressmen, the Jamait people and young Muslims. At this stage Nehru felt that trouble would follow and the settlement would be temporary only. Azad was also distracted, ultimately a word was sent that "we regretted, we could not alter our previous conditions at all, if they were accepted *in toto*, we would agree, not otherwise we had no authority to go beyond this without consulting the working committee." So the matter dropped and Azad went off to Bombay. Khaliq-uz-Zaman said that he was unable to agree. In the words of A.G. Noorani, the Congress wanted merger not coalition.

Nehru's Role

To blame Nehru for the failure of the negotiations with the Muslim League of the U.P. is unjustifiable. Azad was in charge of the negotiations in U.P. He had carried on negotiation with Khaliq-uz-Zaman. His memory played trick with him, as facts are otherwise. He twisted them to blame Nehru. His role in these negotiations was relatively small. He was keeping indifferent health. He was being consulted by Azad, who was in touch with G.B. Pant, R.A. Kidwai, K.M. Ashraf, P.D. Tandon and other important members of the U.P. legislature. The most important consideration with provincial Congress leaders as with Nehru was that if the Muslim League with its landlord support came into cabinet, the Congress programme for agrarian reforms partially the abolition of zamindari would be jeopardized.[24]

There is no doubt on this point that if a coalition ministry had been formed with the Muslim League in 1937 and other provinces on Jinnah's terms, the paralysis which struck the interim government in the centre in 1946-47 would have overtaken the provincial government ten years earlier. But it is difficult to agree with V.N. Dutta, who had suggested in his article No. 1985 that "a successful working of Congress League coalition would have prevented the possibility of the Pakistan Resolution of 1940". Under the circumstances there can be any alliance of a secular Party with a communal Party. If there would have been any alliance between them, the alliance would never have been permanent. The question is how Nehru can be blamed, if the coalition ministry could not be formed in the U.P.

The Congress wanted the League to accept the principle of joint responsibility which the League refused. The League also wants itself to be accepted as the sole arbitrator of the matters pertaining to Muslims. Fortunately, P.D. Tandon, a journalist and Congressman of Allahabad is still alive. He was involved in the negotiation with the U.P. Muslim League. P.D. Tandon covered Congress politics in the 40s and 50s also as a journalist. Commenting on the Prof. Humayun Kabir, Tandon said, "Kabir had some hidden hostility towards Nehru". Commenting about the proposed release of the concealed pages 30 years[25] after Azad's death, he said, "how will it help history to release a doubtful document. Those who could do no harm to Nehru in his life time now won to have some sadistic pleasure defaming after his death".[26]

Gowher Devi in his book, published in 1988, *Linlithgow and India* had contested Abul Kalam Azad's claim that failure to form a Congress-Muslim League coalition in U.P. turned Jinnah into an implacable foe of the Congress, revitalized the League and ultimately led to partition.[27] Rizvi said that a close examination of the evidence, it was possible to conclude that there was no breach of faith, when Congress failed to include League nominees in the U.P. cabinet. He says in the end that it is surely difficult to attribute protection to so trifling a case. An error of the series of errors in tactical judgment cannot explain such a momentous event. These were more fundamental forces at work.

So there is no doubt in this point that the discussion of the 1937 election in "India wins freedom" is flowed by numerous errors of fact as well as of judgment. There are no evidences to hold this opinion that the negotiation with the Muslim League failed because of Nehru's interference and obstinacy. Prof. C.H. Philips had observed in his introduction to the book *the partition of India*, 1970, and had contended Azad's conclusion in this way: "In the light of this success at the polls, there was justification in the refusal of its leader to accept any play of forming coalition ministries with other parties, and certainly not with the Muslim League which, in failing almost entirely to bring out with the Muslim votes, had been humiliated in the general election. On the contrary, by offering places to many Congress Muslims in the new Ministries was able to point the morale and in this context Nehru's declaration that Congress must actively pursue a policy of mass Muslim contact made excellent sense."

The book titled *Gandhi, His Life and Thought*, 1970, Acharya J.B. Kriplani, who was the General Secretary of the Congress, described the account of the events in the Maulana's book *India Wins Freedom* as a curious mixture of facts and fancies and says "it is not a question of correcting a passage here and there. It would require a volume as big as had written to correct all his misstatements and misconception."

Jawaharlal Nehru may be opposed in 1937 to any opportunistic alliance by the Congress with the Muslim League in the then United Provinces but no personal responsibility could be fixed on him for the failure of negotiations for League cooperation with the Congress government in return for two seats in the State cabinet says Dr. S. Gopal, former Prof. of Contemporary History, JNU, New Delhi. Dr. Gopal contests the stand taken by the Maulana that Nehru's action gave the League in the U.P. a new lease of life and enabled Jinnah to start "an offensive which ultimately led to Pakistan".

At a press conference before his death Nehru said: "The Maulana's thinking that I was deciding and ordering things was not quite correct. These things are seldom done by an old individual. I was not in the ministry or going to be in the ministry. There were others too, may be my views counted by senior people to some extent, and I will tell you quite frequently that I was worried about at that time. I was anxious that since Congress ministers came in, they should take up the question of land reforms, viz. zamindari abolition and I did not want that question stymied by any agreement with the Muslim League which was largely representative of big zamindars of U.P., therefore, it was not so much a question of principles but policies to be adopted by the Congress ministry.

In 1938, Tufail Ahmad appeared to be arguing that the communal divide could still be overcome by inducing common Muslim to join the Congress in large numbers. It was in this sense that he then regarded their future as bright. So it was clear that there was a communal divide before Lahore resolution of 1940.

Provincial Autonomy at Work (1937-1939)

In the general election of 1937, the Congress got clear majority in Bombay, Madras, C.P., U.P., and Bihar. The Working Committee of the Indian National Congress met and on July 7, 1937, it was decided to permit acceptance of cabinet responsibilities. Within a few days of this resolution of the Working Committee, the leaders of Congress parties in the six provinces were invited to form cabinet and they accepted the invitation. Subsequently ministries were formed in Bombay, Madras, C.P., U.P., Bihar, Orissa, N.W.F.P., and Assam by July 1937.

Rajendra Prasad's Surprise Choice (1937)

Rajendra Prasad's task to choose one of the two contenders of the Congress Legislature Party leader become all the more difficult because he was a Kayastha, the community which had its bearings towards the Rajputs for over a decade or so of the two candidates for the post, while one was a Bhumihar and the other was Rajput. If Rajendra Prasad chose Anugraha Narain Sinha, he would at once be condemned by the Bhumihars and also other sections of the Party. And if he chose Sri Krishan Sinha, his own caste man, then Rajputs would condemn him for his lack of courage.

In such a delicate situation, Rajendra Prasad was placed in a most uncomfortable position. Not only was he the topmost Congress leader of Bihar but was also an all India leader by virtue of being a member of the Congress Working Committee. For this ability and integrity he was respected not only by all the CWC members but also by Mahatma Gandhi himself. So the problem now was to extricate him from such an embarrassing situation. He took time to give his verdict, and thought over the question for two or three days. Then ultimately he announced his decision. To the surprise of everyone, he nominated Sri Krishna Sinha. There was anger and shock among both the Rajput and the Kayasthas over his decision but there was no defiance of any demonstration because that was not the culture of Congressmen in those days. They accepted the decision with grace. Anugraha Narain Sinha was the first to go and embrace Sri Krishna Sinha and garlanded him to the great joy of all Congressmen. Political rivalries did not stand in the way of social relationships.

Jawaharlal was the President of the Indian National Congress in 1937. He was not happy at the formation of the Congress ministry. He said, "Acceptance of the office does not mean by an iota acceptance of the slave constitution. It means a fight against the coming of the federation by all means in our power—we have taken a new step involving new responsibilities and some risks, but if we are true to our objectives and are ever vigilant, we shall overcome those risks and gain, strength and power......".

The immediate and most far-reaching effect of the Congress victory at the polls was a widening of the breach with Muslim League. Flashed with success the Congress Party adopted an imperious attitude to all other political parties. It was a big mistake on the part of the Congress. The Muslim League was dissatisfied with this approach.

Nehru himself set the tone with his remark in March 1937; "there are only two forces in India today, British imperialism and Indian Nationalism as represented by the Congress". Jinnah was quick to resort: "No, there is a third Party—Mussalmaan".[28] This remark turned correct and Pakistan was born as a sovereign and independent state on August 14, 1947 just after ten years.

After being formerly elected, on the appointment day, Sri Krishna went to meet the Governor. It was expected that the Governor would readily administer the oath of office and appoint him the premier and would request him to take over the administration of the province. It may be stated that Sri Krishna Sinha was not an excellent lawyer but was also an ardent reader of the reports of the Joint Parliamentary Committee's proceedings in London. During his discussion with the Governor, he put the condition for acceptance of office that there would be no gubernatorial interference. The Governor under instructions either from the Viceroy or the Secretary of State refused to give such an assurance. Thus the fond hope of millions of people of Bihar and of seeing the installation of a popular ministry was dashed to pieces. Similar incident occurred in all the eight provinces where the Congress had secured an absolute majority. The Governor of Bihar thus was forced to form an Interim Ministry. The Governor knew very well that when Congress had 98 MLAs in a house of 150, no Ministry would last if the legislative assembly was summoned. Yet, he formed an Interim Ministry with Mohammed Yunus, the leader of the Bihar Muslim Independent Party.

U.P. Election—1937

Pandit Jawaharlal Nehru was the President of the Indian National Congress. The number of persons enfranchised was about five and a half million as compared with a million and a half voters under the Montague-Chelmsford Reforms. Although the franchise was very much broad based but only 13 per cent of the population of the province enjoyed the privilege of vote.

Number of Candidates

The number of candidates in the field was unrepresented. For 228 seats in the U.P. Legislative Assembly, Lower House, the Congress had nominated 138 candidates, the Nationalist Agricultural Party, both Agra and Oudh, 38, the Muslim League 36 and the Hindu Mahasabha 22. Large number of Independents mainly landlords had also contested.

For 52 seats in the U.P. Legislative Council, Upper House, the Nationalist Agriculturist Party nominees numbered 18, Congress 19 and the Hindu Mahasabha 3. The Muslim League did not contest any seat.

Six out of 15 candidates for the assembly who had been returned unopposed belonged to the Nationalist Agriculturist Party and 4 to the Congress, while four are independents, two Europeans and the last a member of Muslim League.

Five candidates have been returned unopposed to the council. One of them was a member of the National Agricultural Party.[29]

When the coalition ministry was not established in U.P. in 1937, Jinnah took a very strong attitude at this development. In July 1937, just after the formation of the Congress ministry in the Indian provinces, Jinnah, who was the President of Muslim League from 1934, called upon the Muslims to consolidate their strength for the next political election? The annual session of the Muslim League called in October 1937, where it was decided to frame a comprehensive social, economical and educational programme to win the support of the Muslim masses. Jinnah was disturbed at the 1937 election result. He now wanted to appeal the ignorant Muslim peasants. He took the shelter of religion. He was a complete communal. "Islam is in danger" he cried and got the response from the Muslims.[30] The atmosphere began to turn gloomy and the relationship between Hindus and Muslims began to deteriorate. In 1937 the Muslim League was still a small upper and middle class organization which had little contact with or interest in the Muslim landlords and princes and to ensure greater opportunities in government service for the growing Muslim middle class. At this stage Jinnah had few Muslim supporters. The Congress had great support from the Muslim intellectuals including the nationalist Muslims. Nehru had tremendous support from the Muslim community in the 1937 elections. Even the Muslims regarded Nehru not communal.[31] Nehru's attitude was a consistent extension of his general political ideology. He often spoke against the communalist approach to politics. He did not like the Muslim League or the Hindu Mahasabha or the R.S.S. In free India Mr. M.C. Chagla, was the head of the Nationalist Muslims. Nehru was a prophet of secularism. Just after freedom, Nehru declared that whatever Pakistan might have done, he would not let India shape into Hindu state. He said, 'India is not a communal state, but a democratic state'. He opposed separate electorates for Muslim because he felt that this weakened the groups that were already weak or prevented the growth of National unity. He always looked upon such measures as a negation of democracy which created vested interests of the most reactionary kind, thus diverting the people's attention from the real economic problems which were common to all. He hated communalism because he thought that his main struggle was against British rule. He thought that the League was mainly a stumbling block to the marshalling of complete national support against the British imperialism. He wrote, "All third parties' have to real importance in this historic sense".

Nehru was a liberal and tolerant. He was not rigid in his views. He was not an enemy to the Muslim League. It is a fact that Nehru did not accept the Muslim League as the authoritative representative of all Indian Muslims; still he was willing to meet Jinnah to reduce the growing friction with the League after 1937 elections. There were exchange of letters between him and Jinnah in the early month of 1938.

The correspondence began from Nehru. Nehru requested Jinnah to elaborate the points of dispute and end this period of uncertainties. Jinnah retorted 'surely you know what the point are?' Jinnah indicated a willingness to meet him. Nehru agreed and said what we shall talk so issue must be defined through correspondence. Jinnah then reiterated the "Fourteen Points" which he had raised at the All-Party Conference in 1928 and subsequently it was published in 1929. Nehru termed the "Fourteen Points" outdated and said that he was willing to talk on certain issues of the "Fourteen Points". Nehru said that the Congress still opposes the communal Award. He agreed that the minorities must have a just share in the services of the country. He pointed out that as for Muslim cultural and religious rights; the Congress resolution of 1931 at Karachi was emphatic. Redistribution of provincial boundaries was certainly in order if the interested parties consented. Jinnah had also demanded that Urdu be made the National language. It was an unreasonable demand, how Urdu could be the National language in India? Nehru did not like Jinnah's demand. Nehru rejected the Muslim League's claim to represent nine crore Muslims. The Muslim League also criticized the use of the Congress flag on public buildings. Nehru was also following the policy of conciliation. He invited Jinnah to come to Allahabad for a talk. Jinnah replied that he was pained to read your letter. Your letter had misrepresented the League's views and it seemed that the Congress had assumed total power of administration in the country. Jinnah suggested that the League must be considered as an equal with the Indian National Congress. Both are political parties and so there should be equality of status. If it was not conceded, then a trial of strength was the logical conclusion. Besides a political leader, Nehru was a gentleman *par excellence*. He at once conveyed his regret to Jinnah for having caused pain to him and he wrote that he was very sincere in his attempt of reducing tension between the Congress and the League. He expressed his desire to reach an agreement with him. Jinnah invited Nehru to come to talk with him at Bombay. Nehru declined the invitation on the ground that he was leaving for Europe tour and a visit to Spain.

In the early part of 1938, there was a long exchange of letters with Jinnah on the interminable communal question, though by now the two were repeating themselves. Nehru's arguments, however, were beginning to have effect at least. Evan a man like S. Wazir Hasan, who had presided over Bombay session of the Muslim League in 1936, had finally reacted against the communalism on February 11, 1938. This propaganda of misrepresentation lies, religious and communal hatred not only between Musalmans and Hindus but also between Musalmans and Musalmans was initiated in the presidential address of the Muslim League session at Lucknow in October 1937. It is being carried on from day-to-day with ever increasing false statements of facts under the guess of the rights of momentous and religious hatred.

Wazir Hasan wanted Nehru and Azad to launch an immediate counter-offensive but Nehru was too tired. The Haripur Congress Session was over, and he decided it was time to indulge in a little wanderlust "to get out of the old rat and cross mountains and seas and make acquaintance with new countries, new people". He wrote a piece on April 7, 1936, published in the *Modern Review of Navy*, about this desire to go somewhere which had possessed him, "It was not physical tiredness but a weariness of mind which hungered for change and refreshment. Political life was an exhausting business and I had enough for a while my mind was elsewhere......". It panted for escape from the troubles and problems that encompassed us, for peace and quiet and the gentle sign of the wind. Nehru was the second most important Indian and Congressman.

He went to the Indian hills, Almora, where "sometimes I would under the pine trees listen to the voice of the wandering wind, whispering many strange things into my ears, and lulling my senses and cooling the fever in my brain." After the Indian hills, his thought turned to Europe. Hitler was marching into Austria and I heard the tramps of barbarian feet over the pleasant gardens of Vienna. This was the prelude to that world catastrophe which had hung over us for long. Was this war?[32]

So the long exchange of letters[33] between the two important leaders wearing a black sherwani and the black Congress cap, leaders produced nothing. But it was made clear how Nehru and Jinnah differed on the problem confronting the country, though both leaders had Western education. Both had different outlook, what Nehru thought, he thought and did for united India and Indian unity. Jinnah only thought for the Muslims of the country. Jinnah was parochial in outlook, but from the correspondence, it appeared that, Jinnah was an Indian nationalist, it was not a fact. Jinnah ceased to be an Indian nationalist in 1928 and he was the President of the Muslim League, a communal organization from 1934. So how Jinnah could be an Indian nationalist in 1938 when he wanted the division of the country in 1940. "It is the duty of every true nationalist", he wrote on March 17, 1938, "to whichever Party or community he may belong to help achieve a united front." In 1940, Jinnah discovered a separate nation of Muslims in India. Now he enunciated the two nation theory devised by Syed Ahmad Khan in 1888. With the coming of two-nation theory, relations between the Congress and the League received such a jerk which was never repaired and India was divided into two separate dominions—India and Pakistan.

This correspondence was finally closed and now another point of dispute appeared. The Congress ministries were functioning from 1937 in eight provinces. In three provinces the Congress had formed the coalition government and in five provinces the Congress government was functioning. The Muslim League brought a charge against the Congress of persecution without waiting for a proper diagnosis; the League established a committee of inquiry headed by the Nawab of Pirpur. It was known as the Pirpur Committee.[34] The committee was doing its work. The year 1939 started, now charges were brought. It was said that the Congress government had permitted the singing of *Bande Matram*, which had been banned by the British Government. The Muslim League did not like the use of Congress flag on public buildings and it protested against its use. Muslims also said that the Congress discriminated against the Muslims in services. The Congress Government showed partiality to the Hindus in communal riots the League did not like that Hindi should be encouraged on flimsy grounds but the Muslim League was pursuing all these points.

But there was no relief from controversy in matters major or minor. Foreign travel always existed as undercurrent of resentment in India, as it was vaguely anti-Indian things to do. Gandhi had putrefied himself in 1890 after returning from abroad. In 1929, a famous Congress socialist as Jayprakash Narayan preferred to appease conservative Hindu sentiment by doing prayers after his return from overseas. Motilal had sneered at the thought and shocked respectable Indians doing so.

Now Nehru started European tour, he visited other places also. He stopped on his way to Europe in Egypt in July then sped off via Italy to Spain as a guest of the Republican Government. The romance of the republican cause was heading stuff. He visited the war front site, met officers and soldiers at General Lester's headquarters and experienced air raids during his five days in Barcelona. Predictably he felt an urge to join the international brigade. He was now convinced that the British Government was tacitly supporting France. He went and addressed on anti-fascist rally at Trafalgar Square in July 17, 1938. He also addressed a public meeting at Barcelona in favour of the Republican government. The meeting condemned General Franco for civil war. So Jawaharlal was fighting for the protection of Democracy in the world.

He came to Britain from Spain. A whole range of people called on Nehru, including Jewish leader, Lord Linlithgow, who was then on home leave, invited him for a chat. Zetland discussed Spain with Nehru naturally the two disagreed.

From London, Nehru went to Paris, Prague (where he supported the resistance to Hitler), Germany and Geneva before coming back to London charged with war fever. He visited the House of Commons to hear Chamberlain announce that he was flying the next day to Munich for talks with Hitler and Mussolini. Nehru was sarcastic about Chamberlain's peace offensive plan and tried out a gas mask, after some time he returned to India.

Now there was a change in the Congress. Subhas Chandra Bose had resigned from the President of the Indian National Congress in the session of the Tripura Congress and Dr. Rajendra Prasad was elected as the President of the Congress on April 30, 1939. The new President was closely watching the Pirpur Committee and the Congress offered to submit all the charges for an important inquiry by the Chief Justice of Federal Court of India, Dr. Rajendra Prasad told to the Muslim League president M.A. Jinnah that this was a proper course and the League would be satisfied. Jinnah rejected this suggestion. The Chief Justice of Federal Court was an Englishman. Jinnah did not agree and he said that the enquiry should be made by the Royal Commission of Judges under the chairmanship of a Law Lord of the Privy Council. The Congress was agreeable but at the instance of the Viceroy the matter was dropped—Viceroy Lord Linlithgow felt that while specific instances might admit of being proved in particular provinces, it would be most difficult for Jinnah to prove any general anti-Muslim action on the part of the Congress governments—furthermore, the provincial Governors—were satisfied that there was no basis for allegation.[35]

The world situation was gloomy from 1931. The world was living in a fool's paradise from 1929. Patches of clouds were seen in the firmament of Europe. The depression of 1929 created a much difficult problem not only for the U.S.A. but for the whole Europe. Hitler had become the Chancellor of Germany from 1933 and he became the President of Germany in 1934. Hitler, Mussolini and Tojo formed the Axis power in 1936. The Axis group did not believe in peace. Hitler annoyed Austria in 1936 and Czechoslovakia in 1938. Japan had conquered Mercharie in 1933. It looked that war might start. Hitler started the Second World War with the attack of Poland on September 1, 1939, the world now got ready for a catastrophe. On Sunday, September 3, at 9 A.M., Sir Nevale Henderson, His Majesty's Ambassador in Berlin, informed the German Government that unless its forces began to withdraw promptly from Poland by 11 A.M., there would be war. Hitler ignored the deadline. At 11.45 A.M. Prime Minister Chamberlain declared that England is at war with Germany. That night his Majesty King Emperor George VI told his empire about the declaration of war against Germany.

In Delhi, Lord Linlithgow, the Viceroy of India did not have the courtesy to wait for the King's broadcast, for having the wisdom to consult Indian leaders, before he declared war on behalf of India. Why did Excellency feel so strongly that India must fight Germany?

Gandhi had been invited to meet the Viceroy through a telegram which reached him at Wardha on Saturday, September 2, 1939. He left for Shimla that night. Other Indian leaders, Jinnah, Bose and others were simultaneously surrendered and informed rather than consulted. Gandhi told the Viceroy that he could not reach any understanding with the Viceroy because the Congress Working Committee had given him no such authority. As far as he was concerned, he viewed the war "within English heart" but the Viceroy wanted to know the national mood and he would have to check with the Congress, which might not necessarily be as generous as him.

Nehru's views on the war were well known. To his relief the Congress government had opposed the Government of India Act amending Bill which aimed at mobilizing Indian resources for war purpose, and he made his views known through speeches, articles and editorials. As he wrote to Krishna Menon on April 26, 1939: "I have been writing in the *National Herald* on the subject also though I have preferred doing so lately in the form of assigned editorials." When Bose was absent from the AICC session in Calcutta on May 1, 1939, Nehru moved the resolution on the war danger which once again committed the Congress in proposing any attempt to drag India into the war without the consent of the Indian people.[36]

France also declared war against Germany, so India was now belligerent country. Without consulting either a single Indian leader or any leader of the eleven provinces enjoying provincial autonomy in India, the British plunged India into a world war against totalitarian oppression at a moment when her own freedom—more cruelly remote then ever before. No Indian was consulted, yet the legislatures of Canada, Australia, New Zealand and South Africa were ready to go to war. The reminder of the contrast with their own position was offensive to Indian politicians, particularly to the Congress. In addition to which an amendments to the Government of India Act, 1935 was rushed through the British parliament. That took only eleven minutes to pass empowering the Viceroy to override the provisions of the Act even with respect to provincial autonomy.

On September 14, 1939, the Congress Working Committee met

to consider the current situation. The Working Committee invited the British Government to declare in clear terms what their war aims were in regard to democracy and imperialism and the new order that was envisaged, in particular how these aims were going to apply and to be given effect to in the present.

On October 17, 1939, the Viceroy, Lord Linlithgow announced that the Government of India Act, 1935 would be modified to the extent deemed desirable by the British. Only Dominion status but not complete independence, would be granted to India after the war. With respect to the Congress desire for Self-Government, Lord Linlithgow declared that the situation must be faced in terms of "world politics".

The Congress Working Committee met at Wardha to consider the Viceroy's statement on October 22, 1939. The Working Committee was of the opinion that the Viceroy's statement was wholly unsatisfactory and calculated to rouse resentment among all those who were anxious to gain India's independence.

The Committee regarded the Viceroy's statement as in every way unfortunate. The resolution went on; in the circumstances the committee cannot possibly give any support to Great Britain, for it would amount an enforcement of the imperialist policy which the Congress has always sought to an end. As the first step in this direction, the Committee called upon the Congress ministries to tender their resignation.

Before the drastic step of resignation of the Congress government in the provinces, the Congress attempted to approach Jinnah and the Muslim League. The Congress leaders met Jinnah but much progress was not made. On the one hand the Congress ministry was gone out of office; on the other hand Jinnah was thinking to celebrate the resignation of Congress ministry as "Day of Deliverance". Pandit Nehru wrote a letter to Jinnah on October 18, 1939 and requested him not to celebrate 22nd December as "day of deliverance".[37] But Jinnah did not agree to this suggestion. Nehru met Jinnah several times but to no avail.

By November 15, 1939, Congress ministries in eight provinces resigned one after the other, in protest against the Viceroy's statement of October 1939. Prof. C.H. Phelps regarded the resignation of the Congress ministries in 1939 as an unwise act. By 1942, the Congress leaders felt that their relinquishment of office in provinces was a mistake. K.M. Munshi differed on the decision of the Congress to resign their office in 1939. Relations between the Congress and Muslims League were on a breaking point. The League now had been leaning towards the British. When the Congress demanded British declaration of war aims, Jinnah disrupted any potential unity by insisting that Congress must first stop its mass contact recruitment campaign among Muslims. Now Jinnah announced the 'Day of Deliverance' to be celebrated on December 22, 1939. Jinnah was glad at the turn of events. Jinnah had been humiliated at the result of 1937 election.

Now he wanted to teach a lesson to the Congress. According to Prof. Coupland, "Hindu-Muslim discord became so bitter that at the time the ministries resigned, it seemed in the United Provinces and Bihar at any rate that with a drastic change of policy, on communal relations, constitutional government might soon become impossible."

For the celebration of the Day of Deliverance, Jinnah made his appeal on December 2, 1939 in this way: "I hope that the provincial districts and primary Muslim League all over India will hold public meetings and pass the resolution with such modifications as they may be advised and after Juma prayers offer prayers by way of thanks giving for being delivered from the unjust Congress regime."[38]

Ambedkar joined Jinnah's Muslim League in celebrating the Day of Deliverance. Nehru was hurt; he believed that Jinnah had become impossible. He dislikes his politics as much as he detached his tactics.

The resignation of Congress ministries ended the uneasy true between the British and the nationalists, represented by the Congress. It handed over India's future to Jinnah who was waiting for such an opportunity. Imaginatively and cleverly, he used this archaeological movement for a call to Muslims to observe Deliverance Day. This was the beginning of the emergence of a new force to be reckoned with in the settlement of the Indian problem. From now Lord Linlithgow began to lean towards the support of the Muslim League. The political environment favoured the building up and strengthening of the Muslim League, where the Congress drifted to finally embark upon the Quit India Movement on August 8, 1942.

Provincial Autonomy at Work

On the whole the Congress ministries had been established in eight provinces. But three deserve special discussion. Talented Congressmen were in the U.P. Ministry. Govind Ballabh Pant was the Prime Minister. Madras had as its Prime Minister C. Rajagopalachari, the only member of the Congress High Command to take up his assignment. The Ministry in Bombay under B.G. Kher was the symbol of collective leadership. The Central Parliamentary Board under Sardar Vallabhbhai Patel's leadership was to keep a watch on the functioning of the Ministries. This direction and control of an extra constitutional character detracted from the democratic freedom of the province, but it was meant to assure adherence to Congress ideology and implementation of its programme.

How the Congress Ministry was formed in U.P.? There was a problem. According to Durga Das, who was the chairman of a Press consultative committee at Lucknow, Purushottam Das Tandon was senior to Pant and he wanted to be the Prime Minister. Tandon was dedicated to the causes of Indian culture, which appeared to Nehru and Rafi reactionary outlook. Tandon was senior to Nehru too. Rafi Kidwai manoeuvred to get Tandon to accept the speakership of the U.P. Assembly and thus cleared the way for Pant, who had been the leader of the Swaraj Party in the defunct provincial legislature.

After assuming the office there was a clash between the Prime Minister, Pant and Governor of U.P., Hanry Haig. The occasion was a directive. Pant had received a Directive from the High Command to secure the release of the remaining political prisoners, and failing that to tender the resignation of his cabinet. This directive had been issued before the Annual Congress session at Haripura in 1938. This was being done by the Congress High Command to satisfy the leftists, who had opposed acceptance of the office. Pant was helpless. The same case was in Bihar and Prime Minister Dr. Shri Krishna Sinha had to face the same problem. Pant kept his letter of resignation ready and he went to attend the Haripura Congress. The crisis was continuing, Gandhi tried to solve the crisis. He suggested that the crisis could be ended if the premiers gave an assurance, after talking with the government that the misunderstanding about interference with their sphere had been removed. Haig was equally anxious for the settlement.

The concept of collective responsibility could not develop in the Pant ministry. Each minister ran his ministry as his or her special preserve. Pant loved to wrestle with rifles, his appetite for notes and memoranda was insatiable. He prided himself on the fact that his own notes were longer than those of the civilians.

The government front bench was very competent. The opposition was not so strong. Pant was an outstanding Parliamentarian. Dr. Kailash Nath Katju, who later on became the Defence Minister and later Home Minister in the Nehru government at the centre, was inefficient administrator and skilful debator. Hafiz Mohammed Ibrahim was a secular leader. He had resigned from the Muslim League to join the Pant Cabinet. He was elected in bye-election on the Congress ticket. Mrs. Vijayalakshmi Pandit was a competent Minister. She applied her own mind. She was articulate and had a gift for the rough and tumble of parliamentary life. Lal Bahadur Shastri was the then Parliamentary Secretary to Pant and Ajit Prasad Jain to Rafi Kidwai. Lal Bahadur Shastri was pre-occupied with petitioners and Party men and those persons wanted Pant's intervention. This process was liked by Nehru.

The Governor of U.P. Hanry Haig and British Civil servants observed the obligations imposed by the constitution. Haig was much impressed with zeal and fair play but the governor felt that Pant "in tackling the problems of law and order had displayed a lack of perspective". Haig also told that Pant meddled in the appointment, transfer and promotion of civil servants. The Indian officers of the service laboured sincerely to help the Congress ministers implement these programmes despite the British civilians, Scepticism about their practicability. There thus grew slowly and invariably a wall between the Indian and British civil servants, the latter in private accusing the former of going over to the rends.

The district administration in the U.P. was highly centralized. The landlords kept peace in the countryside. The British encouraged Muslims of talent and 60 per cent of the junior executive posts under the *Raj* were held by Muslims although they constituted only 14 per cent of the population. The Muslims were being appeased by the British Government to weaken the freedom struggle. Young Hindus, who were denied opportunities for employment in government service, were drawn towards the Congress movement. So also were the millions of tenants to whom the Congress held out promise of hereditary tenancy and abolition of feudal landlordism. Indeed, it was this platform which contributed largely to the Congress success at the polls.

In between 1937-39, the U.P. ministry was genuinely secular.

The Congress wanted to fulfil its pledge, which it had given to the tenantry. This attempt on the part of the Congress created a wedge between the Congress and the Muslims. Rafi Kidwai's Tenancy Reforms Bill encountered stiff resistance from the League landlords, the only propertied class among the Muslims. Nawabzada Liaquat Ali Khan, who became the first Prime Minister of Pakistan, was the leader who opposed this Bill. Liaquat Ali Khan was playing politics on this issue. Now, the Congress regime made it clear to the urban Muslims that they had lost the pre-eminence. They had enjoyed under the Nawab and their British successors.

By this time, Durga Das's article entitled "U.P. in Travail" was published in *The Statesman* on 5th May, 1939. Durga Das summed up the situation at the end of two years of Congress thus; the Congress Party, on assuming office, preceded its pledges into legislative and administrative acts. At once arouse the cry 'this is revolution". The intellectual classes found themselves put in the shelf. The stakeholders asked themselves whether they had supported and financed the Congress for the purpose of promoting their own ruin. The masses inquired if the Congress really intended to play a revolutionary role. The public servants wondered whether the administration would be run on idealistic lines and at the same time avert chaos. Legislatures rubbed their eyes at the disregard shown to the "non-official" opinion voiced by them. The spokesman of the minorities complained that they had asked for liberty and not communal *Raj*. Ministers were overworked, unemployed Congress legislatures were going on the nerves of the ministers and a desperate opposition sacrifices for Party exigencies, the larger issues of a constitutional and financial nature which should be above politics.

On his retirement towards the end of 1939, the Governor Haig wrote to Durga Das, "I have always enjoyed and profited from our talks, for I knew now one who can analyze a political situation so acutely. I have been particularly glad that you have been in Lucknow during these difficult times. Before you came, the exaggerated stories current in Delhi were an embarrassment. You have been able to present U.P. conditions fairly, yet with a benevolent attitude towards the Congress, which was of real value, and you have helped a great deal to a clearer understanding of our conditions."

Durga Das had visited Bombay and Madras to make a study of the Congress regime in these provinces. The Bombay ministry was efficient and the tone of the administration had improved. The Home

Minister, K.M. Munshi, handled a Hindu-Muslim riot within three months of assumption of office. Chakravarti Rajagopalachari, who was the Premier of Madras, was a very dominant figure and his ministry appeared as a one man show. Among all the provinces Madras had a cadre of experienced civilians, both British and Indians, who served the ministries with great loyalty.

The U.P., the Bombay and the Madras set a separate pattern of administration. The collective ministry did not develop in the U.P. A minister ruled a province like an empire and premier looked after all the empires. Bombay was the only province, where collective responsibility was strictly implemented and the ministry functioned like a team. Every minister spoke freely in the meeting, but when any decision was taken, all followed this decision faithfully. Madras was fortunate to have a very experienced Premier. There had been formed a compact ministry under C. Rajagopalachari, whose words were law.[39]

Name of the Premiers under the Provincial Autonomy

	Name	Office
1.	Chakravarti Rajagopalachari (c)	Premier of Madras, 1937-1939.
2.	Bishwanath Das (c)	Premier of Orissa, 1937-1939.
3.	Govind Ballabh Pant (c)	Premier of U.P., 1937-1939.
4.	Dr. Khan Saheb (c)	Premier of N.W.F.P., 1937-1940.
5.	Khan Bahadur Allah Baksh (c)	Premier of Sind, 1937-1939.
6.	A.F. Fazlul Haque	Premier of Bengal.
7.	Sir Sikender Hayat Khan	Premier of Punjab, 1937-1942.
8.	N.B. Khan (c)	Premier of C.P. and Barar, 1937-1938
9.	Dr. S.K. Sinha (c)	Premier of Bihar, 1937-1939.
10.	B.G. Kher (c)	Premier of Bombay, 1937-1939.
11.	Gopi Nath Bardoli (c)	Premier of Assam, 1938-1939.
12.	Ravi Shanker Shukla (c)[40]	Premier of C.P. and Barar, 1938-1939.

Note: 'c' stands for Indian National Congress.

Under the Act of 1935, the Head of the Government in each province was designated as Prime Minister or Premier.

Jinnah accused Congress of destroying Islamic culture and of interfering with Muslim's political rights. But Jinnah cause was not very strong. So he wanted to play his game very carefully. Linlithgow's successor Lord Wavell wrote in his diary in January 1914; "Jinnah is not going to shell out on a rising market, and would be unlikely to temper his demands' until he feels that his influence has reached its peak."

As the Congress ministries had resigned, Jinnah's political power increased. Now he was putting his demands more cleverly. He wrote in a magazine in January 1940 that the British needed to put together a new constitution which should recognized that there are in India two nations who both most share the governance of their common motherland. But his aim was not clear as to what he wanted. His aim became clear after two months, March 1940, when he made a specific claim for the first time for Pakistan. Now he wanted division of the country. The Congress was bent upon independence but the British Government did not like to give independence to India. The All India Congress Committee passed a resolution on February 28, 1940, which ran in this way; "the Congress hereby declares again that nothing short of complete independence can be accepted by the people of India. Indian freedom cannot exist within the orbit of imperialism and Domain status, which is wholly inapplicable to India."

NOTES

1. Aziz, K.K., Rahmat Ali: *A Biogragraphy*, p. 9.
2. *Ibid.*, p. 92.
3. The poet as Patriot by Zoe Ansari, the *Times of India*, April 21, 1985.
4. *Ibid.*
5. *The Times-Archives*, New Delhi, August 11, 1930.
6. *The Gazetteers of India*, Vol. II, p. 577.
7. *Ibid.*
8. Mishra S.G., *Constitutional Devlopment and National Movement,* p. 121.
9. Bruser, Michael, *Nehru: A Political Biography*, p. 229.
10. *Ibid.*
11. *Ibid.*
12. Gopal, S., *Selected Works of Jawaharlal Nehru*, vol. 8, p. 32.
13. Dutta, V.N., *Events belongs to Partition,* published in the *Times of India*, New Delhi, part I, December 21, 1988.
14. Nanda, B.R., *The Partition of India*, New Delhi, Part I, November 21, 1988.
15. Gopal, S., *Selected Works of Jawaharlal Nehru*, Vol. 8, p. 39.
16. A letter written by Jawaharlal Nehru to R. Prasad, July 21, 1937, p. 46, *Selected Ways of Jawaharlal Nehru.*
17. Who had resigned from the National Agriculturist Party in U.P. in 1936 to participate actively in the election campaign of the Muslim League?
18. *Selected Works of Jawaharlal Nehru*, p. 166.

19. *Ibid.*
20. *Ibid.*
21. Dutta, V.N., *Times of India*, New Delhi, December 21, 1988.
22. Nanda, B.R., *Times of India*, New Delhi, November 21, 1988.
23. Gopal, S., *Selected Works of Jawaharlal Nehru*, Vol. IV, p. 199
24. Nanda, B.R., the *Times of India*, New Delhi, November 21, 1988.
25. Those 30 concealed pages were published in 1988.
26. Tandon, P.D., *Times of India*, New Delhi, February 24, 1988.
27. Azad, M.A.K., *India Wins Freedom*, 1988, p. 163.
28. Bruser, Michael, *Nehru*, p. 231.
29. The *Times of India*, New Delhi, May 6, 1991.
30. *Ibid.*
31. *Ibid.*
32. *The Making of Jawaharlal Nehru*, the *Times of India*, New Delhi, November 6, 1988.
33. The Text of Nehru-Jinnah correspondence is to be found in *Indian Annual Register*, Vol. I, 1938, pp. 363-376.
34. Report of the enquiry committee appointed by the All-India Muslim League to enquire into, the Committee was headed by Nawab of Pirpur.
35. Menon, V.P., *The Transfer of Power of India*, p. 71.
36. *The Times of India*, New Delhi, November 6, 1986.
37. Mishra, S.G., *C.D. and National Movement*, p. 127.
38. *The Indian Annual Register*, Vol. II, 1939.
39. Durga Das, pp. 183-188.
40. Mishra, S.G., *Democracy in India*, p. 150.

7

Road to Pakistan

The Muslim League Resolution of March 11, 1940, demanding partition of the country, gave a completely new turn to Indian politics. Jinnah, who once aspired to be a national leader, now took on a sectarian role campaigning for the division of the country on religious grounds. Jinnah's misfortune was that, on the one hand he was considered a Muslim leader by Gandhi, and on other, was heckled by the Muslims at a League conference.[1] In his book *Jinnah of Pakistan* Mr. Stanly Wolpert has discussed the causes that led to birth of Pakistan. Wolpert quotes K. Dwarka Das, who maintained that if Congress leaders could have been friendly worth Jinnah and his ego had not been hurt, Jinnah might have not partitioned the country.[2] That Jinnah's ego was hurt and Gandhi and Nehru underestimated he may be accepted but Gandhi and Jinnah could not have pulled together, parting of ways was unavoidable. Jinnah by his nature could not have taken a second place to Gandhi. He was opposed to mass politics which Gandhi ushered in.

Congress leaders had different views about Jinnah regarding the political set-up in the country. Before the demand of Pakistan, Jinnah was asking for a loose federation with the centre having limited powers and residue powers resting with the states.[3] On the other hand, the whole trust of the nationalist policies of the Muslim League adopted a resolution at Lahore session in March 1940 and that resolution gave a complete new turn to Indian politics. This resolution was later on called 'the Pakistan Resolution'. Indirectly this resolution demanded partition of the country. The implication of the resolution was understood after some time. Congress was in the direction of strong centre. Jinnah could not have gone along with Congress leaders. In his early life, Jinnah had come under the spell of liberal leaders.[4] Jinnah was a great patriot and nationalist, who stood for a free and united India. The nationalist Muslim, the late Mr. Chagla's autobiography, 'Rises in December' throws light on this intriguing problem of why Jinnah changed so much. According to Chagla, Jinnah's besetting fault was his obsessive egoism. To begin with Pakistan was a kind of bargaining counter for Jinnah and if the Congress leader bargained properly, Jinnah might have given up the idea of Pakistan. But it is a controversial statement and others have the right to differ.

According to Chagla, Gandhi's support to the Khilafat movement considerably accentuated the communal and religious aspect of Indian public life. It was again Gandhi who gave Jinnah the title '*Quaid-i-Azam*'.

On March 13, 1940, Lord Linlithgow invited Jinnah for a talk. He assured the Viceroy that the Muslim would not retard the war effort if an understanding was given to them that no political settlement would be reached with the Congress without the *prior* consent of the Muslims. The Viceroy reacted favourly.

Under this political background, the annual session of Muslim League was held at Lahore on March 22, 1940.[5] The session took place in Minto Park in Lahore, the capital of Punjab. Now-a-days it has been renamed as 'Iqbal Park'. M.A. Jinnah, the President of Muslim League, presided over the meeting, around sixty thousands people were present. The people were sitting on the floor in a giant tent. Jinnah sat on a throne, clad in churidar and a traditional Muslim achkan coat. A little below him sat his sister Fatima, wearing a sari of ivory silk. It was the biggest meeting that the Muslim League yet held. It was clear that Jinnah's stature was growing with the adulation he received. Jinnah lit a caravan—a cigarette and addressed the rapt crowd for two hours in English.

The 'Lahore Resolution' was passed on March 23, 1940. this resolution was drafted by Sikender Hayat Khan, moved by Fazlul Haque and seconded by Khaliq-uz-Zaman demanded that geographically contiguous limits are demarcated into regions[6] which should be so constituted, with such territorial readjustments and may be necessary, that the areas in which the Muslims are numerically in a majority as in the north-western and eastern zones of India should be grouped to constitute independent states in which the constituent units shall be autonomous and sovereign. So the resolution envisaged a confederation of two Muslim majority areas of India each with autonomous and sovereign states. By 1940, the Muslim League enunciated the theory that the Muslims 'are not a minority' but a 'nation' and they must have their homeland, their territory and their states. Indeed, the influence of the Muslim League over the Muslims in India had increased much by that time. In Bengal, Fazlul Haque was the leader of the Krishak Praja Party. He had joined the Muslim League under the advice from the Viceroy.

At the Ramgarh session of the Congress, held in March 1940, Maulana Abul Kalam Azad, the President emphasized the heritage of a common nationality between the Hindus and the Muslims in India and significantly remarked: "whether we like it or not, we have now become an Indian Nation, united and indivisible".

The Lahore resolution implied through the deliberate ambiguity of the phrase 'independent states' that more than one independent Muslim state might be created. In other words, there could possibly be an East Pakistan and a West Pakistan without a single Central Government. Fazlul Haque of Bengal thought that the resolution meant an independent Bengal.

The resolution was vague that it was intentionally kept vague, so that the bargaining power for Jinnah should stand intact. The issue was clarified by the Delhi Resolution of April 1941, which proposed that "Pakistan zones[7] where the Muslims are in a dominant majority be constituted into a sovereign independent state". This meant that the administration of East Pakistan would be controlled from West Pakistan. It was disastrous proposition which ultimately brought the Indo-Pak war and the creation of Bangladesh in 1971.

The resolution did not employ the word 'Pakistan' although in his presidential speech Jinnah specifically asserted that the Hindus and Muslims represented different and distinct social orders and could not, therefore, evolve a common nationality. A Hindu correspondent asked him whether the resolution "meant a demand for Pakistan". Jinnah still avoided using the word Pakistan and replied that it was open to him to think so as that he was prepared to accept his interpretations. Durga Das met Jinnah after the session and pointed out that the Sikander Hayat Khan had categorically told him that the resolution was essentially a bargaining counter. Jinnah replied, "a bargain, my friend, is struck between two parties, let the Congress accept the League as the other Party".

Now the Congress and the League had both enunciated their policies. The Congress was prepared not to help the British government in the way effort and the League was ready to cooperate. According to Viceroy invited Jinnah to another talk on June 27. In a statement on August 8, 1940, Linlithgow placed in the hands of Jinnah a veto on constitutional progress by declaring that British Government could not contemplate the transfer of power, to any system of government whose authority is directly denied by large and powerful elements in India's national life. Nor could they be parties to the coercion of such elements into submission to such a government. Jinnah was on top, and when I saw him he disclosed in confidence that the League owed this concession to Leopold Amery, the Secretary of States. Jinnah was remarkably relaxed and leaving back in his chair added, "All I have to do now to wait for the next Congress move and to counter it. I have no doubt that Nehru will play into my hands."

So the meaning of the Lahore resolution was not clear between 1940 and 1946. This resolution was not a detailed or coherent statement of Muslim demands, and Jinnah was careful to maintain the uncertainty. Question of boundaries, population shifts, methods of administration, rights of minorities, and most crucially of all, whether the Pakistan zones and the rest of India would share some kind of control federal authority, were simply not resolved. There is a reasonable ground that it was the failure of Jinnah because he could not prepare any Blue Print of Pakistan. Though Jinnah was vague still he got support from the Government of Punjab and Bengal, because these governments were in complete darkness about the administrative machinery of Pakistan. It is argued that Jinnah never really believed in a totally independent Pakistan and that he used the Lahore resolution merely as a bargaining centre.

Jinnah in his early part of his political career was a nationalist and secular. Sarojini Naidu had called Jinnah as the 'Ambassador of Hindu-Muslim unity'. Motilal Nehru, who was a formidable opposition leader in the central assembly in 1926 had once said before 1920 that Jinnah was showing the way to Hindu-Muslim unity. But now that very Jinnah was determined for the division of the country and became the prophet and founder of the Indian Muslim homeland. Jinnah was a tactful politician, who had very cleverly mixed up the two-nation theory in the Lahore resolution of 1940. By this resolution Jinnah was determined to declare himself as the leader of the entire Muslim population of the country. As Ayesha Jalal has argued in her book "The Sole Spokesman Jinnah".

The Muslim League and the demand for Pakistan, she has written that his use of the communal factor was the political tactics, not an ideological commitment. Asserting that Muslims were a nation avoided the logic of numbers". The Muslim League was never a truly religious Party. The erratic elements within the Millet in several instances denounced the League as ungodly and Jinnah as an unbeliever, few of its prime activities were obvious religious communalist—a figure such as Jinnah or Liaquat Ali Khan could hardly be represented as a mad Mullah.[8]

The obvious problem with the Lahore resolution was that it effectively ignored the fate of Muslim living outside the north-east and north-west of India. There were huge *swadeshi* of the country—in Rajputana, the Central Provinces and the whole of southern India—where Muslims amounted to less than 10 per cent of the population. Were do they migrate to the Pakistan zone or stay out and hope for the best? Jinnah's answer, when passed, was the 'hostage theory', namely that the presence of a Hindu minority in Muslim areas, and *vice versa*, would secure the mutual good treatment of each minority community.

Maulana Azad has written about the Lahore resolution in this way: Mr. Jinnah's Pakistan scheme is based on his two-nation theory.[9] His thesis is that India contains many nationalist based on religious differences, of them the two major nations, the Hindus and Muslims differences, and must as separate nations based on separate states. When Dr. Edward once pointed out to Jinnah that Hindus and Muslims live side by side in thousands of Indian towns, villages and hamlets, Mr. Jinnah replied that this is no way affected their separate nationality. Two nations according to Mr. Jinnah confront one another in every hamlets, village and town and he, therefore, desires that they should be separated into two states.

I am prepared to overlook all other aspects of the problem and judge it from the point of view of Muslim interests alone.[10] I shall still go further and say that if it can be shown that the scheme of Pakistan can in no way benefit Muslims I would be prepared to accept it myself and also to work for its acceptance by others. But the truth is that even if I examine the scheme from the point of view of communal interests of the Muslims themselves. I am forced to the conclusion that it can in no way benefit them to allay their legitimate fears.

Let us consider dispassionately the consequences which will

follow if we give effect to the Pakistan scheme.[11] India will be divided into two states, one with a majority of Muslims and other of Hindus. In the Hindustan state there will remain three and half crores of Muslims scattered in small minorities all over the land with 17 per cent in U.P., 12 per cent in Bihar and 9 per cent in Madras, they will be weaker than they are today in the Hindu majority provinces. They have had their homeland in these regions for almost a thousand years and built up well known centres of Muslim culture and civilisation.

They will awaken overnight and discover that they have become alien and foreigner. Backward industrially, educationally and economically, they will be left to the mercies to what would become an unadulterated Hindu Raj.

To other hand, their position within the Pakistan state would be vulnerable and weak. Nowhere in Pakistan will their majority be comparable to the Hindu majority in the Hindustan states.

Azad says, I must confess that the very term goes against my growth.[12] It suggests that some portions of the world are pure while others are impure. Such a division of territorial into pure and impure is unIslamic and is more in keeping with orthodox Brahmanism, which divides men and countries into holy and un-holy division which is a repudiation of the very spirit of Islam. Islam recognizes no such division and the prophet says: "God has made the whole world a mosque for me".

Further it seems that the scheme of Pakistan[13] is a symbol of defeatism and has been built up on the analogy of the Jewish demand for a national home. It is a confession that Indian Muslims cannot hold their own in India as a whole and would be content to withdraw to a corner specially reserved for them.

When attains her destiny, she will forget the chapter of communal suspicion and conflict and face the problems of modern life from a modern point of view.[14] Differences will no doubt persist, but they will be economic, not communal opposition among political parties will continue, but it will be based, not on religion but on economic and political issues. Class and not community will be basis of future alignments and policies will be shaped accordingly. If it is argued that this is only a faith which events may not justify I would say that in any case the nine crores of Muslims constitute a factor which nobody can ignore and whatever the circumstances, they are strong enough to safeguard their own destiny.

Few prominent Muslims, such as Sir Sikender Hayat Khan came to this conclusion that their vision of Hindu-Muslim-Sikh unity would not succeed, if the Lahore resolution would take a concrete shape. As the Muslims in general were uneducated and poor guided by their religion, so the Lahore resolution get tremendous support. People were under this impression that Pakistan would not be a haven for them. Subsequently the Lahore resolution was popularly described as the Pakistan resolution. The resolution did not make it clear as to what exactly the demand was. The wording was vague and capable of more than one interpretation. The Muslim League demanded that the Muslim majority province should have full autonomy. Sikander Hayat Khan in his support of the resolution had given the same interpretation but now the League leaders gave their demand a much wider connotation. They talked loudly of the partition of the country and the establishment of an independent state for the Muslim majority areas. The Cabinet Mission was not prepared to concede the demand; on the contrary, the mission was in favour of a solution on different lines.

Congress did not like the Lahore resolution. They took it very lightly; Nehru dismissed it as 'fantastic'. Gandhi called it 'baffling'[15] and C. Rajagopalachari condemned it as was the product of a 'diseased mentality'. As Nehru's niece said, the Nehru family regarded the very idea of Pakistan[16] as a joke it seemed absurd to imagine that such a thing could ever happen to India.

So much about the significance of the Lahore resolution but how the resolution was framed and discussed, humiliated by the 1937 election results, the League was now trying to whip up communal frenzy. It was in this state of frenzy that the League announced its Pakistan plan. But who devised in 1940 resolution is an intriguing question? National Democratic Party leader of Pakistan, Khan Abdul Wali Khan, created a sensation in December 1981 by disclosing with documentary evidence, that the Lahore resolution was the handwork of a British agent Sir Zafrullah Khan, an Ahmediya, who died on September 1, 1985 at Lahore. Earlier, on April 2, 1981 Syed Sharifuddin Pirzada[17] had reproduced a letter in the *Dawn* of Karachi, disclosing Jinnah's secret links with Sir Winston Churchill. Who was opposed to giving freedom to India? Dharaminder Gaur in his book *Behind the Enemy Live* published in New Delhi in 1976, clearly established Jinnah's links with the British Intelligence, which was trying to prevent independence.

The communists had supported the demand for partition of the Indian subcontinent raised by the Muslim League. The Communist Party had joined hands with the Muslim League in the assembly election to the Madras Presidency. They had also hobnobbed with Abdul Nazir Madani, who was indicated by the Alavindakshan Commission went into the communal riots in Poonthara, Trivendrum, and by the Bhâskarah Nair Commission which enquired into the Sivigiri incidents. The controversial leader had also campaigned for Chief Minister Nayanar in the 1997-98 election.

Many Muslim leaders, who were closely associated with Jinnah during the Pakistan movement, were not convinced of Jinnah's philosophy. His own sister Fatima Jinnah[18] told Sri Prakasa, India's first High Commissioner to Pakistan in 1949, "I do not know how it was that Quaid-e-Azam thought that Hindus and Muslims could not live together, but he did so". Also the first Chief Minister of Sind, Mohammed Ayode Kuro, who was in the innermost counsels of the Muslim League, made it clear that nobody had really wanted partition of India and creation of Pakistan. The demand for Pakistan was only a policy of bargain to secure "Muslim's future in united India". Jinnah's own right hand man and the Prime Minister of Pakistan Liaquat Ali Khan did not appear concocted of the partition demand. According to Pakistan's ex-Attorney-General, Syed Sharifuddin Pirzada, Liaquat Ali Khan was in secret contact with the leaders of the Congress Parliamentary Party, Bhula Bhai Desai after the failure of Gandhi-Jinnah talk of 1944. Pirzada had served Jinnah as his secretary. On January 11, 1945, Liaquat Ali Khan[19] signed an agreement with the Congress without the knowledge of Jinnah. Pirzada wrote that had this agreement been implemented, the partition plan would have either fizzled out or delayed. When Jinnah came to know about it he was furious, Liaquat Ali had made that bold agreement because he believed Jinnah was going to live long.

Jinnah treated this resolution as the solid basis for Pakistan. Dr. Ambedkar, in his book *Pakistan or the Partition of India* published in 1940 after the Lahore resolution was adopted indicated that the Muslim states would be a part of the Indian Federation. Jinnah agreed with Ambedkar's views. Fazlul Haque himself repudiated the Pakistan concept in 1943 in his book *Indian Politics* published in 1943. Prof. Coupland gave the first serious treatment in English of the idea of Pakistan. Prof. Coupland, Historian of the

British Empire and commonwealth in his book, *The Constitutional Problem of India*[20] published in 1945 made it clear that the resolution was not clear and it could not be said that the resolution called for the division of the country. Mr. Zulfiquar Ali Bhutto,[21] the Executive President, of Pakistan was also of the opinion that the 1940 resolution could not be intercepted for the vivisection of the country.

Nehru's ideas ran contrary to Jinnah's two-nation theory and to the thinking of some of his own Congress colleagues who decried pre-Muslim proclivities. They were a mixed bag 'Hindu Nationalists' traditionalists and Nehru's own view's 'Hindu Communalists' masquery as Congressmen.

The Bangladesh Historian Prof. A.F. Salimuddin has evaluated this phase of Muslim League politics, in the context of the demand for Pakistan which it made in 1940, in a paper presented at an UGC seminar on Bangladesh held in Calcutta in April 1972, Prof. Salimuddin stated, "the movement[22] which led to the creation of Pakistan was not a religious movement. Fear of Hindu political domination which would adversely affect the (Muslim) community's political economic and cultural interests seemed to have been important factor which influenced the movement."

While participating in the symposium on "Religion and politics in India" on December 20, 1984, at Gargi College, New Delhi, Dr. M.K. Hassan, Prof. of History, Jamia Millia University said, the demand for a separate Muslim homeland evolved from fears about the position Muslim would occupy in a "Hindu India". The British no doubt encouraged them in these fears. So Dr. Hassan has echoed the ideas of Prof. Salimuddin, which could not be accepted as correct. Jinnah espoused the cause of Pakistan because of the policy of divide and rule and the 'two-nation theory'. Jinnah was very ambitious and he was interested to establish Pakistan and if not Pakistan, even a truncated and moth-eaten Pakistan, Jinnah felt that after his death, even this kind of truncated and moth-eaten Pakistan would not be established. In the era of freedom struggle, the British Government granted separate electorates to the Muslims and other minorities on the ground of religion. The Muslim League was religious Party and so religion and politics started mingling. In the Khilafat movement of 1920, Mahatma Gandhi completely mixed politics and religion, which proved fatal for the country in the long run. Separate electorates completely antagonized Hindus and Muslims. It was due to the active encouragement of the Muslim leaders from the time of

Sir Syed Ahmad Khan and the British policy that the "two-nation theory" based on religion made progress and the two-nation theory played a dominant role in the Lahore resolution of 1940. So the two nation theory was one of the important causes for the partition of the country.

Chaudhary Rahmat Ali had outlined the idea of Pakistan in 1923. Mr. K.K. Aziz, a senior historian of Pakistan wrote in 1968 on partition. He espoused that the "Indian Nationalism in essence".[23] But Aziz's argument is fallacious. The Indian National Congress was a secular body from 1885. Had it been in the hands of Hindus, only Hindus would have acted as a President of Congress from its inception and resolutions suiting the Hindus would have been adopted. But these allegations have no basis in facts. The first President of the Indian National Congress in 1885 was W.C. Banerjee, not a Hindu but a Christian. The second session of the Indian National Congress was presided over by Dada Bhai Naoroji. He was a Parsi. The third President of Congress was Badruddin Tayabji in 1887. He was a Muslim. The fourth President in 1888 was George Ayub, a British born citizen. The fifth session was held in Bombay in 1889 with William Wedder Burn, as its President, who was a British. So the Aziz's argument is untenable. The Indian National Congress symbolized the "Indian Nationalism" and not a "Hindu Nationalism". Later on Aziz argued that it was responsible for the Muslims to try to establish closer ties with the British, with whom they have greater social intellectual and spiritual affinity then with the "idol worshipping Hindus". What an absurd argument? How the Muslims have greater social contact with the British? These arguments are fallacious. Given this kind of thinking, it is not surprising to find that people like Aziz regard the Partition as *Azadi* from the "fasadat" caused by the Hindus for them the creation of Pakistan becomes a vindication of their presuppositions, history becomes a tautology instead of an explanation.

If the Muslim leaders are historians of the Pakistan movement manipulated facts to justify the existence of a separate Muslim consciousness which 'naturally' constitutes a nation, the historians of Hindu Rashtra conjure up a protest in order to accuse the Muslims of discretion and betrayal, as well as to assert the presence of a Hindu brotherhood which has a primal right to the inheritance of India. But their construction of a fundamental entity called a 'Hindu' who could become the basis of a new collectively of true believers, turns out as confusing and mystical as that of Islamic nationhood.

Thus Bharatendu Harischandra,[24] who was not perhaps a communal thinker but was passionately concerned with the shape of the Hindu civilization, in a lecture of 1884, defines the 'Hindu' as people who lived in Hindustan and includes the Jains, Buddhists, Sikhs, Brahmans and Muslims in his sweep.

In order to give substance to such a meta-religious category, Bharatendu translated parts of the Koran into Hindi in 1884 and wrote brief biographies of the Prophet, Hassan and Hussan in 1875 and a long poem praising Kabir, Tansen and Pirzadi Bibi. It is worth noting here that Sir Syed Ahmad Khan also described the "Hindus" in a lecture in 1884 precisely in the same terms as Bharatendu and included the Muslims in his definition. By 1924, however, Lala Lajpat Rai[25] and Swami Shradhanand began to speak forcefully about the old antagonism between the Hindus and the Muslims and even urged the formation of two distinct religious nations for the sake of peace. As the years went by the term 'Hindu' became sharper and harder, and Mahatma, was eliminated for having tarnishing the glory of Hinduism. On January 30, 1948, Mahatma Gandhi walked out of Birla House, New Delhi, to his evening prayer meeting. As he reached the venue, he was detained by Nathuram Godse,[26] who shot 4 times, point blank at 5.13 p.m. and Gandhi was dead within minutes. After Gandhi's assassination the term 'Hindu' came to be defined, by the more communally committed historians, one who was first an unrelenting enemy of Islam and only after that as someone who had a particular set of ideals and practices. The partition was offered as yet another example in a long sequence of Muslim faithfulness, instead of becoming an exceptional moment of disorder in a continuing history of a life lived together in all its complex variety.

Contrary to the communal histories, the stories about the partition have more to do with the actualities of human experience in barbaric times than with ideologies, and seemed to be bound together by one common thread they find the nation that there was always hatred between the Hindus, Sikhs and Muslims in ordinary life completely incomprehensible.[27]

The Mohammedan Anglo-Oriental College had been established at Aligarh on May 24, 1875, and regular instruction was started from June first. The founder principal was Teodere Beck. In 1920 Jamia Millia Islamia was founded at Aligarh, as it was felt that the M.A.O. College did not fulfil the aspirations of the Muslim intelligentsia and scholars. It was established due to the efforts of nationalist Muslims like Maulana Mohammad Ali, Dr. Mukhtar Ahmad Ansari, Hakim Ajmal Khan and Zakir Hussain. The new institution came up on the other side of the campus of the M.A.O. College separated only by a street. Later on M.A.O. College developed into an university and the Raja of Mohamedabad was the Vice-Chancellor of the Aligarh Muslim University, in pre-partition days, two students of Aligarh Muslim University Azhar and Owais participated in political rallies and enthusiastically shouted the slogan in the university campus "India will be divided, Pakistan will be created". The two-nation theory was very powerful in the campus. Their voices, who wanted Pakistan, had resounded with an unusual note of determination. After the partition, they had begun to talk senselessly and extravagantly and Azhar and Owais migrated to Pakistan.[28]

When the Lahore resolution was passed, Jinnah addressed the crowd for hours in English, a language which very few of the thousands of listeners would have understood, "Brother Gandhi' he told them, has three votes and I have only one vote". He compared the unhappy union of Britain and Ireland to the yoking together of Hindus and Muslims. The needs of the hour had to be protested for; the Musalmans are not a minority. The Musalmans are a nation by any definition. This two-nation theory would have many advantages; not least that arithmetic could be thrown out of the window. As a *quaum* or 'nation' the status of Muslims would be guaranteed throughout India,—regardless of those areas where they were in a minority". In course of the historic speech the word 'Pakistan' was never mentioned but the goal of a separate nation was made explicit. "The problem in India is not of an inter-communal character but manifestly of an international one", he declined Musalmans are a nation according to any definition of a nation, and they must have their homelands, their territory and their state.[29]

Reaction of the British Government

The Lahore resolution of 1940 affected British Government. Telegrams were exchanged between London and New Delhi in April 1940. The Secretary of State for India Lord Zetland told Viceroy Linlithgow that in a forth coming parliamentary speed, he intended pouring cold water on the Muslim idea[30] of partition formally advocated in the Lahore resolution though not necessarily at this state conclusively regretting it. I showed emphasis that this would be a counsel of despair and wholly at variance with the policy of a United India, which British rule has achieved and which it is our aim to perpetuate after British rule ceases.

But the reaction of the Viceroy was quite different. Lord Linlithgow was under this impression that the Lahore resolution would bring advantages to the British Government. Linlithgow thought that the Lahore resolution was very largely in the nature of bargaining,[31] so the British Government should not comment on it because "any overemphasis on unacceptability and faults of Muslim scheme would be politically unfortunate—and I think you will probably feel with me that wise tactics would to keep our hands free until critical moment is reached in future constitutional discussion." By using the Muslim League's demands in this way, the Viceroy was playing a complex game of political brinkmanship, which was to have lasting consequences for the future of Asia.[32] Linlithgow's duty was to nip the effects of the Lahore resolution in the bud. But he did not do this for the benefit of the British imperialism. So Linlithgow was also responsible for the partition of India. Linlithgow acknowledged the strength of Jinnah's position. The Viceroy felt that "Congress was essentially a Hindu Party, though it contains Muslim elements—there is no justification on a broad view for regarding the Muslims within Congress as of any very decisive importance—at the present time the only organization which can speak on behalf of the Muslims of India as a whole is the Muslim League under Jinnah. There are from time to time signs of considerable internal tension in the League but Jinnah remains in complete control and is a person to be negotiated with and the only person in a position to deliver the goods."[33]

But still the blue print of Pakistan was not available. In February 1941 a secret memorandum was prepared for Jinnah called 'what is Pakistan'. The map carved up the parts of India where no one religious group was in a clear majority. This map indicated the thinking of the Muslim League. The Muslim began felt at this stage to beset any individual promote to satisfy other parties. Under this proposal, places like Ambala in the Punjab, which was economically very poor and full of Sikhs and Hindus, were lopped off from Pakistan, which prosperous areas such as Assam, where Muslims represented around a third of the population, were retained. The document also made it clear that the princely state of Hyderabad was very big and it could not be fully independent.

The Muslim League was consolidated daily. The annual session of the Muslim League was held in Madras. It was attended by over a hundred thousand of activists. On a raised platform Jinnah was in the chair. Periyar E.V. Ramaswami Naikar, the leader of the Justice Party sat with Jinnah. The Justice Party was against the Congress and was fighting the Congress from 1920. The Muslim League and the Justice Party had come together to denounce the Congress and all good works done by the Congress. Jinnah's bodyguards were standing on the platform with swords in their hands. In his presidential remarks Jinnah made an appeal to the British Government to stop their policy of appeasement, towards those who were frustrating the war effect, namely the National Congress. But the honeymoon which had started between Viceroy Linlithgow and Jinnah from November 1939, the day the Congress ministries had resigned from the province received a jerk. The Viceroy asked the Muslim provincial premiers to accept the membership of the National Defence Council but Jinnah was not invited.[34] As a result he instructed all the premiers not to attend the council. Most of the premiers who had nominal attachment with the Muslim League, obeyed the instruction except Fazlul Haque of Bengal, who had moved the Lahore resolution in 1940 did not obey the instruction and resigned from the Muslim League. Subsequently he denounced Jinnah on the ground that he seeks to rule as an omnipotent authority even over the destiny of thirty-three millions of Muslims in the province of Bengal. The Nawab of Dacca soon joined Fazlul Haque and they both publicly attacked Jinnah. They called Jinnah autocrat and they said that he was guilty of grossest treachery. Thus the Pakistan movement's of political support in Bengal dwindled and Jinnah was not happy at the turn of events. This event last a long shadow on the Pakistan movement.

At this crucial movement the intelligence bureau had this kind of feeling that Jinnah was a prominent leader and he would play a dominant role in future's political developments. So the intelligent bureau proposed a detailed report entitled "Congress and the Muslim League, a study on conflict". It was based on highly secret sources. This report stated that Sir Sikander Hayat Khan, a prominent leader of the Punjab had made it absolutely clear that he would not tolerate Jinnah's interference in the internal affair of his province, i.e. Punjab and so the report concluded that political progress of the Punjab was, therefore, dependent on Sikander Hayat Khan's attitude and not on Jinnah. The main conclusion of the report was that two political adversarial of the Indian politics Mahatma Gandhi and Jinnah would decide all issues confronting the country, vainglorious, determined, dominating men, impatient of opposition, claver in their various ways but completely obsessed with conflicting ideas, which they are pursuing with almost appalling relentlessness.

The intelligence bureau, however, believed that after the end of the Second World War, a consideration of all available material suggests that they will probably not hesitate to abandon their present entrenched position and to enter the field of negotiation and adjustment immediately the contest for power starts. Whether Gandhi or Jinnah will come out on top in the ensuing fight for political ascendancy depends on circumstances which cannot at present be foreseen.[35]

The Lahore Resolution of 1940—Its Implication not Pakistan

Who among the front-ranking Muslim leaders are to be credited as the first and the last two critics to voice publicly that the geographically concept of the Pakistan territory in the Lahore resolution of 1940 was not what was later officially explained by the League leadership or ultimately drawn on the map.

Now a straight answer can be given by Prof. Amalendu De, Jadavpur University and Peter Hazlehurst, correspondent of the *London Times*, who have done research on the Lahore resolution. Prof. De leaves no room to doubt that the first to protest against twisting the Lahore resolution was none else than its mover, Abul Kassom Fazlul Haque and according to Mr. Hazlehurst, the best critic of the 1940 resolution was President Zulfikar Ali Bhutto of Pakistan.

I take the second first for consideration; one has to read his dispatch, the *Statesman* August 27, 1972, wherein Mr. Hazlehurst writes: in what would have been considered hearsay a few months ago, Mr. Bhutto[36] in a speech in the National Assembly suggested that the founding fathers of Pakistan had envisaged the creation of two Muslim states for the subcontinent. The correspondent further adds in the same dispatch; in completing the somersault Mr. Bhutto has in fact accepted that the Bengalis were correct in their claim for autonomy and independence. It was on the basis of the Lahore resolution which Mr. Bhutto used as rational for his argument that the Sheik Muzibur Rahman first roused his autonomy.

Prof. Amalendu De, in his turn, explained by quoting evidence which cannot be disputed to prove how Abul Kassem Fazlul Haque, soon after the adoption of the Lahore resolution, realized its implication, retracted and disowned the same openly when challenged. Prof. De has explained in his book '*Pakistan*' Prastate O Fazlul Haque, Calcutta, 1972. Fazlul Haque repudiation of the Pakistan concept was made public for the first time in 1943.[37] This repudiation was announced at that time when Fazlul Haque had fallen of the grace of Jinnah.

Even more important than the establishment of the point discussed above has been proved by Prof. A. De, who has explained the Lahore resolution, as moved by Fazlul Haque, was twisted by the League leadership to satisfy their political ambition. Prof. De has traced how and since when this conspiracy was hatched and worked out.[38]

Prof. De quotes Dr. Ambedkar, who in his book *Pakistan or the Partition of India* published in 1940, analyzed the Lahore resolution and concluded, "does the resolution contemplate that those Muslim provinces after being incorporated into states, will remain each one independent sovereign state or will they be joined together into one constitution as members of a single state, federal or unitary". On this point the resolution was rather ambiguous and not self contradictory. It speaks of grouping the zone into independent states in which the constituent units shall be autonomous and sovereign. The use of terms 'constituent units' indicates that what is contemplated it a 'Federation'. [39]

It should be recorded here that Dr. Ambedkar's book was welcomed by Jinnah, although it contained the above analysis of the Pakistan resolution.

Prof. Coupland in his book *The Constitutional Problems of India* has interpreted the Lahore resolution in this way: "It was not clear exactly what this paragraph of the resolution meant. It could scarcely mean that the constituent units of the independent states was really to be 'sovereign', but that it did mean that the states were to be really 'independent' was shown by a subsequent paragraph."

In between the two above-quoted views of two well known experts, Dr. Ambedkar and Prof. Coupland, made public in 1940 and 1945, Fazlul Haque's clear-cut statement on the same point was issued in 1943. Prof. De reproduced it acknowledging the source. It shows in what light the Lahore resolution, when it was unalloyed, was looked upon by its mover. "I want to make one comment" wrote Haque regarding recent utterances about this scheme.

Let me quote from the resolution itself, resolved that it is the considered view of this session of the all India Muslim League that geographically contiguous units are demarcated into regions which should be constituted, with such territorial readjustments as may be necessary, that the areas in which the Muslims are numerically in a majority as in the north-western and, eastern zones of India should be grouped to constitute independent states, to which the constituent units shall be autonomous and sovereign. We have to remember that the three provinces geographically adjoined to Bengal and Assam, Bihar and Orissa. In Assam[40] the Muslims are only 35 per cent, in Bihar 10 per cent and in Orissa hardly 4 per cent.

It is, therefore, evident that Bengal as constituted cannot form autonomous state with the geographically adjacent province. If, however, Bengal has got to be divided into two, the result will be that the Eastern zone which will be predominantly Muslim area will be surmounted by provinces in which, Hindus will be in a majority. It is, therefore, no use hoodwinking the Muslims of Bengal that the formula which may hold well in the Punjab will also hold well in Bengal. At the same time, Bengal Muslims relies that they have got to fall into love with the rest of India.

The controversy whether the Lahore resolution envisaged one state or as Haque explained in his statement that independent states burst out in 1946 at the convention of the Muslim League legislatures. The author makes a reference of that convention of the Muslim League legislatures. The author makes a reference of that convention. He does not mention the name of the person who first raised that point at the convention but Choudhary Khaliq-uz-Zaman in his 'Pathway to Pakistan' leaves no doubt about identifying him. He was Abul Hassen, the then Provincial Secretary of the Muslim League in Bengal. Founding fathers of Pakistan were then pretty satisfied that Pakistan was within a hailing distance and that Delhi convention of Muslim legislatures could solace Hassim who raised the issue with the explanation that the letter 's' added last to the word 'states' in Lahore resolution was "a printing mistake."[41]

Thus the whole game of twisting the Lahore Resolution in the way it was done in 1946 was part of a conspiracy hatched to deprive

Bengalis of their rights has been quoted and his last authority. Lt. Commander Moazzam Hussain, a tragic figure of the Agartala conspiracy case,[42] who in 1969 formed a Party called the "Lahore Praskade Bastahyon co ki Okona".

Today when this conspiracy against history and the crime against a people, whose only fault was that they blindly believed in the Muslim League leadership, are exposed and even men like Mr. Bhutto confessed what the Lahore resolution originally stood for, one is reminded to Fazlul Haque's warning sounded as early as in 1943. "Ever since I moved the Pakistan resolution at the open session of the Muslim League at Lahore on March 24, 1940, "the right of self-determination to all the nationalities of our land would lead to a greater and more glorious unity of India. G. Adhikari had made a statement like this in September 1942.[43] The report by G. Adhikari on 'Pakistan and national unity' supported the Muslim League and advocated partition of Bengal similar to the pattern of Punjab lines, said he, "I have most scrupulously avoided making any observations against the Pakistan scheme. I (Fazlul Haque) have realized ever since, that confusion has been made worse confounded by theorists who have from time to time expounded most fantastic ideas about the Pakistan scheme."

"On many occasions I (Haque) felt that the Muslims of Bengal were being missed by false ideas as to the scheme itself, but I have intentionally kept silent, because I thought my comments may be misunderstood." He then interpreted the Lahore resolution and explained as implication so far as it could be applicable in respect of Bengal. The full text has quoted earlier.

Address: "I must frankly admit[44] that I am a socialist and a Republican and am no believer in Kings and princes or in the order which produces the modern kings of industry, who have greater power over the lives and fortunes of even more than the kings of old, and whole methods are so predating as those of old." Having shocked the more conservative elements, he acknowledged that the Congress could not adopt a full socialist programme now. But 'India will have to go that way if she seeks to end her poverty.'

Just after 11 years in 1940 at the Lahore session the Muslim League adopted the Pakistan resolution under the presidentship of M.A. Jinnah. In theory the resolution envisaged a confederation for two Muslim majority areas of India each with autonomous and sovereign states. But in practice now Jinnah stood for the partition of India on religious lines. It was a victory of 'two-nation' theory Jinnah treated this resolution as the solid basis for Pakistan. When the time came, Jinnah agreed to accept the truncated Pakistan and he was happy at his achievement the architect of Pakistan.

So Lahore gave two kinds of messages for India as well as for the world. The Congress gave the message of complete independence for the whole country. The League sent the message of vivisection of the country on religious lines. The concept of self-determination was the result of the Paris Peace Conference of 1919 held in France. On the basis of one race, the culture, one religion one historical association and one language, the number of sovereign states rose in Europe from twenty to twenty-seven; Jinnah raised the issue of partition of the country on the basis of the concept of self-determination.

The undivided C.P.I. leader G. Adhikari rejected the concept of the united Indian nation advanced by the Indian national Congress. He and other leaders opposed of an India consisting of several nationalists and peoples. They suggest guaranteeing to these nationalities the right of self-determination inclusive for the right of secession from the Indian union. They advocated the proposition that Second World War. ...

The Second World War had started from September 1, 1939. There was constitutional deadlock in India. Churchill became the Prime Minister of Britain in May 1940. He wanted to defeat the Axis power. America entered the Second World War on December 8, 1941 after the Pearl Harbour incident. Roosevelt, the President of U.S.A. suggested Churchill to ease the position in India, as Indian co-operation was essential to defeat the Axis power. The war had taken a difficult turn and Hitler had been fighting against Soviet Russia.

Roosevelt and Churchill met at the Atlantic meeting of Newfoundland in August 1941.[45] They discussed problems confronting the world. The colonial issue was discussed. Roosevelt said,[46] "if we arrive at a stable peace it must involve the development of backward countries, backward peoples. It cannot be done by eighteenth century methods—I cannot believe that we can fight a war against fascist slavery and at the same time not work to free people all over the world from a backward colonial policy". Churchill looked 'apoplectic'; Roosevelt concluded that there must be 'equality of peoples'. Roosevelt and Churchill collided on the issue of the economic autarchy of the British Empire. Soon the two statesmen proclaimed that there should be no aggrandizement, territorial or other. They stated that there should be no territorial transfers without the consent of the peoples concerned. The next point—Article III followed logically,[47] "All peoples should have the right to choose their own form of government. These principles to their authors in August 1941 were not controversial self-determination appeared to be innocuous, but so it appeared that potentially it was the most explosive principle of all. Churchill later argued consistently that he had in mind self-determination for the conquered nations of Europe. Roosevelt subsequently stated repeatedly that the Atlantic Charter applied not only to Europe but also to peoples throughout the world.

Article III reads: "They respect the right of all peoples to choose the form of government under which they will live, they are only concerned to defend the rites of freedom of speech and thought without which such choice must be illusory".[48] Roosevelt himself substituted the phrase and they hope that self-government may be restored to those from whom it has been forcibly removed. On the 11th of August Churchill added the words 'sovereign rights' before the phrase 'self-government'. If it could be argued that Roosevelt's purpose was to make explicit the principle of self-determination, then it could be argued that Churchill's addition of the phrase 'sovereign rights' made the change inapplicable to the dependent British Empire. In the final form the Article reads:

> *"They respect the right of all peoples to choose form of government under which they will live, and they will see sovereign rights and self-government restored to those who have been forcibly deprived of them."*[49]

These were the words affirming the principles of self-determination that Americans and Englishmen read in their newspapers on Saturday the August 16, 1941. So the Atlantic charter promulgated by U.S.A. President, Franklin De Roosevelt and British Prime Minister, Winston Churchill was made public on August 16, 1941.

It was a coincidence that Attlee was addressing a group of West African students in London on August 16, 1941. He told them that the Labour Party had always been conscious of the wrongs done by the white men to races with darker skins. He holds that the opposite idealistic principles of the Atlantic Charter would also apply to all the peoples of the world. Attlee used the word 'freedom'; it was a significant public indication that the Atlantic Charter might have consequences reaching far beyond Europe. Leo Ameny, now Secretary of State for India and Burma was an imperialist. He wrote to the Colonial Secretary, Lord Moyne that the declaration had let loose a lot of questions about its application to the Empire. In his view the declaration pertained entirely to European war issue, but he thought the matter could easily be classified. He proposes that the India Office and colonial office submit a joint memorandum on the subject to the war cabinet. Amery and Monye would merely assure everyone concerned that in British Empire, animated by a spirit of liberty, pursued the goal of self-governing institution. But the colonial office could not accept the ideal of self-government. Moyne was not prepared to give dominion status to Aden, Gibraltar, the Gambia or British Honduras.[50]

The Atlantic Charter thus immediately brought into play within higher government circles divergent ideas about the future and purpose of the Empire. It was clear that self-government could not apply to the following territories. "Gibraltar, Aden, Mauritius, Seychelles, Fiji, the western Pacific islands, the Falklands, British Honduras, Bermuda, the Gambia and Hong Kong all these colonies and probably others (Cyprus, Malta, the dependencies in Borneo and even Malaya) are too small or too important strategically ever to become independent self-governing units". The colonial secretary was not prepared to endorse the principle of self-determination. He argued that it was not for people to decide their fate, people still needed political tutelage.

Churchill was not prepared to accept the principle of self-determination. When the war cabinet discussed the issue on the 4th September, Churchill aligned himself with Amery. The decision was as follows: "the view generally expressed in discussion was that it was clear that the Atlantic Charter was directed to the nations of Europe, whom we hope to free from Nazi tyranny, and was not intended to deal with the internal affairs of the British Empire, or with relations between the United States, and for example, the Philippines". Prime Minister Churchill made a speech in the House of Commons on September 9, 1941. He said, "They had not intended to qualify in any way the commitments of pledges Britain had made to India, Burma or other parts of the Empire.

He then said at the Atlantic meeting, we had in mind, primarily, the restoration of the sovereignty, self-government and national life of the states and nations of Europe now under the Nazi yoke and the principles governing any alterations in the territorial boundaries which may have made Churchill thus had stated explicitly before parliament that Britain was committed to self-government in the colonies, and moreover, that these commitments were 'complete in themselves' and free from ambiguity. The Atlantic Charter thus led to recognition within the colonial office that Britain's basic colonial policy would have to be examined and defined. The argument of the colonial was of the general and agonizing reappraisal of the future of the Empire, a reappraisal that became essentially searching and intense after the disaster of Singapore.

The Atlantic Charter, when promulgated by Roosevelt and Churchill had given great hopes to the national leaders. The Congress leaders hoped that India would achieve freedom at the earliest and Jinnah was under this impression that Pakistan would be formed on the basis of the principle of self-determination. So both political parties' leaders were happy at the signing of the Atlantic Charter. But when Churchill was not ready to apply the provisions of the Atlantic Charter to India, a period of uncertainty started and the period of honeymoon ended. The position was made clear after some time.

Immediately after the signing of the charter, the member of the House of Commons asked the question to Mr. Churchill, Mr. Prime Minister, does Atlantic Charter which grants all countries the right to choose their own form of government, apply to India? Churchill rose and said, no Sir. Churchill excluded India and Burma in his address to the House of Commons. According to the President Roosevelt the Atlantic Charter could be applied to the whole world. This narrow definition of the Atlantic Charter could be applied to the whole world was condemned by the Indian Nationalist leaders. Jinnah was also upset as the Atlantic Charter did not speak anything about Pakistan. The Muslim League did not appreciate the spirit of the Atlantic Charter. At this time Ambedkar was made a member of the Viceroy's Executive Council in July 1942.

Prime Minister, Indira Gandhi talked with a small group of intellectuals in New York in 1982 and expressed her feelings on

Churchill in this way, "She was intrigued by the glaring conditions between Churchill's great care for democracy and freedom in Britain and his stubborn unconnected, even hostility, towards the freedom struggle of Indians."[51]

While the country was passing through the rigours of an intensive struggle, Churchill made a very painful statement in London on November 10, 1942; I have not become the King's first Minister in order to preside over the liquidation of the British Empire."[52] This speech antagonized the Indian people including the Indian National Congress and the Muslim League. Churchill at this stage was not prepared either for freedom of the country or the partition of India. Churchill was a die-hard imperialist. Franklin D. Roosevelt, the American President, made it clear that he deplored British imperialism in India and throughout the world. Amery was among the foremost of British statesman who wanted to preserve the British Empire with in the cabinet, the leader of the Labour Party, Attlee protested against the holding of colonies for the financial advantage. In the opinion of Churchill, nationalist agitators throughout the British Empire should be neither listened to nor encouraged; rather "what those people need is a scrapbook".

In February 1947, a secret memorandum was prepared for Jinnah called 'what is Pakistan'. This memorandum carved up the parts of India where no one religious group was in a clear majority, which shows that even at this stage the Muslim League, realized that individual provinces might have to beseech in order to satisfy other political parties. Ambala remained in India and Assam in Pakistan. The memorandum noted that the state of Hyderabad was large enough, so it would remain independent.

The Quit India Movement, 1942 and the Attitude of the Muslim League

The Second World War was a terrible disaster for the humanity. There was constitutional deadlock in India. Roosevelt was insisting that Churchill should take steps for the improvement of the political situation in India. The Congress desired independence for the country and the Muslim League was determined to establish a separate and independent state. So to ease the situation in India and to break the constitutional deadlock, Cripps, a senior member of the coalition cabinet, reached Delhi on March 23, 1942 with the draft declaration, which had been prepared by the Cabinet. Cripps had been sent to give India's politicians a promise of jam tomorrow in exchange for cooperation today. However the quality and quantity of the jam was not specified. As Amery admitted in his Diary, all Cripps really had to offer was "what is essentially a pro-Muslim and reasonably conservative policy."

Cripps had two things to offer to the Indian leaders: a promise that after the war India would frame her own constitution for independence and the constitution would be ratified by the Parliament and an immediate invitation to the major Indian parties to join the Viceroy's Executive Council. The Muslim League headed by Mr. Jinnah rejected this proposal. The Indian National Congress wanted something tangible immediately. The Congress leaders wanted India to be handed over at once to a government composed largely of Indians. Cripps attempted to make the Congress leaders feel that the offer he was bringing met their demands half-way.

According to Gandhi that the Cripps proposals had all the bad points of the Federation plan of the 1935 Reforms Act and had further introduced the evil principle of partition of India to be divided by people chosen in a very limited franchise. He had told Cripps that his proposals at best offered "an undated cheque on a crashing Bank" and was leaving all power in the hands of the Viceroy and the India Office to govern India, while the war lasted. The American President's personal envoy Col. Louis Johnson reached Delhi in April 1942 and he was functioning behind the scenes.

The deadlock in India persisted. The India Office and the Viceroy were now agreed on building up Jinnah as their crescent card to neutralize the Congress challenge. This was manifest from Sikendar Hayat Khan's disclosure to Durga Das that the Viceroy on instructions from the Secretary of State, had enjoined upon him and Fazlul Haque not to undermine Jinnah's position as "leader of the Muslim community. The League executive almost simultaneously passed a resolution expressing gratification that the possibility of Pakistan is recognized by implication by providing for the establishment of two or more unions in India" and rejecting the Cripps proposals for the reason that they were not open to modifications. Ultimately the Congress leaders also rejected the proposal. The Mission failed and Cripps left for England on April 12.

Churchill was anti-Congress and he was supporting Jinnah right and left. He did not like that Roosevelt take an interest in the affairs of India. Churchill said that he did not like that the Muslims should be governed by the Congress caucus and the Hindu priesthood. In March 1942, Churchill sent Roosevelt an extract of Jinnah's letter attaching Sir Tej Bahadur Sapru and his 'Non-Party conference as a front for Congress and saying a "Hindu Raj" was being planned. Churchill was not in favour of sending any political mission to India. But many circumstances forced Churchill at home and the fall of Singapur compelled Churchill to Agra to send a political mission to India. The "Quit India" movement amounted to the biggest threat to British control in India since the uprising of 1857.

What was the attitude of Muslim League towards the Cripps Mission? Though Jinnah's position had improved considerably, from November 1939 but still Jinnah had no full support in those provinces where Muslims were in a majority. At a Press conference in New Delhi on March 29, 1942, in answer to a question as to whether there was anything to stop two provinces from different parts of India's 'trying to club together and to form a separate union.' Cripps replied: "That would be impracticable as two contiguous provinces may form a separate union." At the same time he stated that it would not be impossible to have 'a rearrangement of boundaries and between the two unions, and exchange of population to get the larger majority in each.' The Cripps Mission increased the chances of the creator of Pakistan.

Jinnah's game had succeeded. The Lahore resolution of 1940 was taking a practical shape. Hardly two years had passed when an important British Cabinet Minister was discussing publicity on the prospect of autonomous provinces staying outside India.[53] It is clear that Cripps had this kind of feeling that many prominent Muslim landlords and politicians were interested more in the future of Punjab and Bengal than in any Indian Muslim unity. He believed that Jinnah might be challenged if the League's feeble grip on the alleged followers was tested. As A. Jalal says, "had the Congress leaders had taken up seriously the Cripps offer, Jinnah would have been in danger of being dumped unceremoniously into a wilderness from which this time there would be no return."

The Congress had suggested that the response of the Indian National Congress to the Cripps offer, should be, "considered to the unanimous demand of the Indian people" and was rejected by

Jinnah, who declared that Congress did not represent Muslims or even all of India's Hindus. The period that followed after the departure of Cripps made it clear that there was a split between the Viceroy and Congress and between Congress and the Muslim League. After the failure of the Mission, Linlithgow wrote a letter to Amery on May 7, "In thinking that the less interested we now appear to be in Indian politics the better".

Linlithgow noted laconically at the end of one document. "Goodbye, Mr. Cripps and also added something significant at the margin." I am myself now quite sure that self-government is income margin: "I am myself now quite sure that self-government is incompatible with unity."[54] This turned out to be true in 1947. Linlithgow personal view of Cripps was summed up by one of gamekeepers of the Viceroy, when he was back in Scotland. He wrote: "The check of the man, to think that he could do in a fortnight what his Lordship has not been able to do in the six years." Linlithgow advised Amery not to let Cripps broadcast about India on the wireless. Linlithgow was in indignation. When Cripps told he had been to blame for undermining the negotiations—the claim was "wholly without foundation and most damaging and embarrassing." At the time of Cripps Mission, the Congress was determined to take liberty or death.

There was profound disappointment in India at the failure of the Cripps Mission. It was felt that the British Government would not grant independence to India even after the end of the war. The future appeared total dark to the Congress. The Congress working committee was called to Wardha on 6 July, to discuss the 'Quit India Resolution'. This resolution was released on July 14; the resolution made it clear that a widespread struggle would be launched under the leadership of Mahatma Gandhi and the AICC would meet in Bombay on August 7, 1942 for ratification. The AICC met in Bombay on the scheduled date and the resolution was adopted after a hot debate on 9th August. The Government of India reacted within a few hours of the adoption of the resolution. All the leaders, who were at Bombay, were arrested in the early hours of the morning of 9th August.

The arrest all went smoothly in the country except for that of Premier Govind Ballabh Pant, who was angry at being woke up so early by the police and gave some trouble with the result that he did not get to the station in time to catch the special train, which left the Queen Victoria terminus station at 7.15 a.m., the D.I.G. was in-charge of the train.

Jawaharlal Nehru was arrested at the family flat in Bombay. He was staying with his sister Krishna Huthee Singh. According to M.J. Akbar, "the household staffs were hardly unfamiliar with the arrests. They quickly laid out the breakfast which Jawaharlal loved, a bowl of cornflakes, eggs, bakery toasts and coffee. The inspector saw the spread and said there was no time for breakfast. 'Shut up', I intend having breakfast before I go." India's future Prime Minister was kept in prison nearly for nine years.[55] With the arrest of the leaders, the quit India movement started, Gandhi was detained at the Aga Khan's Palace in Poona and the committee members were taken to Ahmadnagar Fort. Brian Lapping in his book *End of Empire* has written that 'Quit India' was a retreat by Gandhi that complex problems into the impractical. It was not a proposal of Gandhi, the tough, wily, political negotiator but of Gandhi, the leader of a popular mass movement.

With the arrest of the Indian leaders on August 9, 1942, the political stalemate started in India. The India office in London started to work on a new formula for the future governance of the country. Sir Reginald Coupland, a Prof. of Oxford University, who had spent the winter of 1941-42 in India and was attached to the Cripps Mission as an unofficial advisor, had come out with a report contained a memorandum prepared by an expert showing that Pakistan was financially viable.

The Coupland plan sought to resolve the problem by dividing the country into four broad geographical regions; the Indus Basin, the Gangetic basin, the Delta of Brahmaputra and the Deccan. Two of these regions would have a Muslim majority and the Hindus would predominate in the other two and this would result in a balance of power at the centre for the Princely states he suggested either a single separate Dominion or several Dominions, where viable units were feasible. It is interesting to note that Coupland wanted a statutory guarantcc for the continuance of work of the Christian missionaries in the hill tract of Assam. This lends weight to the suspicion that the present day movement for independence among a section of the Nagas and Mizos in the Assam borders is inspired by missionaries.

The pressure of Second World War and of political happening in the country, however, thrust the Coupland Plan into the background.

But Jinnah seemed to go from strength to strength. Jinnah was happy at the turn of events that now his claim that the League was the sole representative of the Muslims in India had been vindicated for three Muslim majority provinces were being governed by League ministries.

What was the attitude of the Muslim League to the August Movement of 1942? The Muslim League did not participate in this movement. But the Quit India Movement was a blessing to the Muslim League indirectly. The period from 1942-45 was the period of consolidation of the League. The Muslim League utilized the Quit India Movement in its own interest. It was a strange development in the history of the freedom movement.

The Quit India Movement amounted to the biggest threat to the British control of India, since the uprising of 1857. The railway line between Delhi and Calcutta—the main artery of movement—was blown up on in Bihar, where for more than two weeks, the British completely lost control and so could not organize repair teams, supplies could not be sent to the Burmese front, where a Japanese invasion was feared. In many parts of the country, police stations were burnt, policeman killed and British people on the roads stripped by gangs and beaten up. Telegraph wires were cut. In all about a thousand people and almost all Indians were killed.

During the period of the movement, Jinnah stood aloof. This resulted in the communal divide. Hindus claimed that Muslims were not nationalist as they did not join this movement. The Muslim League utilized the Quit India Movement in its own interest. It was a strange development in the history of the freedom movement.

What was the attitude of M.N. Roy and the Communist Party in India? During the war M.N. Roy's support was sought by the Government. He wanted to support the Government, Sir Peraval Griffith described M.N. Roy as "very able unlovable and above all egoistical". But Roy was willing to lend support to the war effort. So his effort to publish 'vanguard' was supported through a subsidy. The money was put to Roy through G.W. Tyson, editor of the *Capital*. Griffith feels that "the money was well spent". Similarly the Communist Party of India was given financial help—the funds coming from the National war front. Griffith told the Home Secretary at the end of the war the fact that the communists had been subsidized could be leaked out and that would do them no good. So the British got the C.P.I. to work for them and then stabbed them in the back.[56]

By 1943, the League ministries were formed in Assam, Sind, Bengal and N.W.F.P.[57] Jinnah was trying to make himself the supreme leader of the Indian Muslims. The British helped the League much in forming the ministries in different provinces. The ministries of Sadullah in Assam and Aurangzeb Khan in the N.W.F.P. were made possible only because most Congress M.L.As. were in jail. Aurangzeb Khan had a nominal attachment to the Muslim League. But the Governor of the province backed Aurangzeb Khan.

The Gandhi-Jinnah Talks or Negotiations (1944)

Finding no response from the Viceroy to solve the political and constitutional problem of the country, Gandhi turned towards Jinnah, since 1942, a prominent member of the Congress had been thinking over the issue of Pakistan. He had come to this conclusion that the present deadlock could be solved only, when any agreement was made with the Muslim League. He had prepared a scheme which was called Rajagopalachari formula. Gandhi saw this formula after his release. He had communicated the formula to Jinnah also. It was published on 10 July. The terms of the formula were that the Muslim League should endorse the demand for independence and co-operate with the Congress in the formation of a provincial interim government for the transitional period, after the termination of the war a commission should be appointed to demarcate those contiguous districts in North West and North East India whereon the Muslims were in absolute majority, and in those areas there should be plebiscite of all the inhabitants to decide the issue of separation from Hindustan, if the majority decided in favour of forming a separate sovereign state, such decision should be given effect to. It would be open to all the parties to advocate their points of views before the plebiscite was held. In the event of separation, a mutual agreement should be entered into for defence, commerce, communication and other essential purposes. Any transfer of population would be on an absolutely voluntary basis. Jinnah denounced the Rajagopalachari's formula in an interview while Gandhi's offer only marred, mutilated, motheaten Pakistan. It was the Pakistan which in the end he had to accept.

After Rajagopalachari's formula, the situation was further complicated with the proceeding of the session of the All India Muslim League at Delhi from 24th April to 26th April, 1943. By this time Jinnah had become more aggressive, more challenging and more authoritative. In application of this point, Jinnah stroke to the working committee where he was able to expose his mind more freely. About the future he told that these were two sets of suggestions:

1. To take direct action here and to force Britain to accept the Muslims demand; and
2. To wait and watch.

Jinnah's assessment about post-War new world order that the end of this war would leave the British more powerful than any of his allies proved wrong, further he extended an invitation to Gandhi to write to him by suggesting an interview.

In response to Jinnah's invitation Gandhi sent a letter to him on May 4, 1943. The letter was sent to Home Department for despatching to Jinnah. It was a great mistake on the part of Gandhi to address Jinnah as Quaid-i-Azam. This new title gave an additional prestige to Jinnah. The letter ran in this way "Dear Quaid-i-Azam, I welcome your invitation. I suggested over the meeting face to face rather than talking through correspondence. I am in your hands."

This letter created a crisis whether it would be delivered to Jinnah or not. Viceroy Linlithgow took a mild view and thought to pass this letter to Jinnah. He sent telegram to Anery on May 13, 1943 justifying his stand that the letter should be sent to Jinnah. He said that there is no analogy between the forwarding to Jinnah of a reply from Gandhi to a public challenge or invitation to Jinnah and a request by irresponsible individuals such as Rajagopalachari, the member of Bombay conference to be allowed to see Gandhi or again an approach by Phillips. He also admitted in the telegram that Jinnah was after all the leader of the second most important Party in India. He concluded by saying that our settled policy had been not to stand in the way of anything that should reasonably facilitate advance towards a settlement. He expressed his desire to let Jinnah have Gandhi's letter.

The Secretary of State for India circulated the text of a letter which Gandhi had asked the Government of India to forward to Jinnah and the Viceroy's proposal of May 14, 1943. War cabinet in its meeting held on May 18, 1943 considered the memorandum of Secretary of the State for India. The Viceroy had recommended that the Government of India should forward this letter to Jinnah. The Secretary of State for India took the view that the letter should not be forwarded and that no meeting between Gandhi and Jinnah should be allowed so long as the Gandhi and the Congress Party maintain their present policy.

The war cabinet agreed that in present circumstance it would be inexpedient to allow Gandhi's letter to go forward a meeting to take place between Gandhi and Jinnah. So Anery sent a telegram on 19th May, informing him of the decision of war cabinet that Gandhi's letter should not go forward. He was instructed that the ground given should be the simple one that the Government, while more anxious to promote agreement between Hindus and Muslims and other political elements were not prepared to give facilities for political correspondence or contact to a person in the detention for promoting an illegally mass movement which he had not disavowed, thus gravely embarrassing Indian war effort at a critical time.

Thus telegram of the Secretary of the State was discussed in the Viceroy's Executive Council on May 23, 1943 and after very considerable agreement in which sharp differences of opinion was disclosed. The Governor General managed to get council to agree that the letter should not be forwarded and Gandhi and Jinnah should be so informed. Gandhi and Jinnah were informed accordingly.

Gandhi was released from Agakhan's palace on May 6, 1944. He now made a fifth attempt to meet Jinnah, Wavell wanted to talk to Gandhi about India's political future but received orders from London not to do so. Gandhi suggested to Wavell that he and Jinnah should meet, which they did in September 1944 at Jinnah's house in Bombay. It was a big mistake on the part of Gandhi to meet Jinnah at his Bombay house.

Roosevelt was taking active interest in the Indian affairs. A confidential report on India submitted by William Philips to Roosevelt created a big storm in New Delhi, London and Washington. Parts of reports were published in the American press by Drew Pearson, though authentic version of it was not available in India. Philips pointed out that the Indian people were at war only in a legal sense as they had to say in their own government and cynically reported the fighting as a clash between fascism and imperialism between which there was nothing to choose. It also said that the Chinese, who regarded the Anglo-American love with distrust, might feel differently, if India was liberated.

Roosevelt had brought about two meetings between Churchill and his special envoy before the report was published, but they had proved unfruitful. Phillips left India a disappointed man and was appointed political advisor to General Eisenhower, supreme head of the Allied forces in Europe.[58]

The Gandhi-Jinnah negotiations which were carried on since September 3, 1944 broke down on 27th September, when Gandhi entered Jinnah's room; he saw a map of Pakistan hanging on the wall back side, both sides were wary. The important reasons for its failure were that the two leaders could not agree on two-nation theory, plebiscite and other issues.[59] Gandhi placed Rajajee's formula for discussion but after some time Gandhi attacked the principle of Pakistan. He wrote to Jinnah, 'I find no parallel in history for a body of converts and their descendents claiming to be a nation apart from the parent stock.[60] If India was one nation before the advent of Islam it must remain one in spite of the change of faith of a very large body of her children." The point of issue appears to be the question of plebiscite. While the Raja's formula insisted on a plebiscite before Pakistan was brought into being. Jinnah was determined on Muslims having the rights to Pakistan without a plebiscite. The talks failed on the issue of Pakistan, Gandhi's impression and Jinnah's intransigence. At the end of negotiation Gandhi told the press that Jinnah was suffering from hallucination,[61] when he imagines that an unnatural division of India could bring either happiness or prosperity to the people concerned. One British official wrote that the negotiations had reached a 'pitiful conclusion' and that the agreement between "these two obstinate old men show that the spirit of accommodation was entirely lacking and each was determined to give nothing away".

Lord Wavel entered this note in his diary on September 30, 1944. The Gandhi-Jinnah talks ended on a note of complete futility. I expected something better, I did not expect statesmanship or practical solution, but I think the two must have got down to something. The two great mountains have met and not even a ridiculous mouse has emerged.[62] This must blast Gandhi's reputation as a leader. Gandhi offered the marred, mutilated Pakistan of the Rajagopalachari's formula, but without real sincerity or conviction.

Jinnah rejected the offer and bluntly told Gandhi that a division of India was on his lips and did not come from his heart. Moreover, Gandhi insisted that any division of India could only take place after the British had left, which was on the line with the Congress aim of wrestling control from the British first and settling with the Muslims, princes etc. afterwards Jinnah believed that once the British had gone the Hindus would never agree to the division of India and that the Muslims would have to fight a civil war to get even a mutilated Pakistan.

Maulana Abul Kalam Azad comments on the Gandhi-Jinnah negotiation in this way: "Gandhi's approach to Jinnah on this occasion was a great political blunder. It gave a new and added importance to Jinnah which he later exploited to the full .... Mr. Jinnah had lost much of his political importance after he left the Congress in the twenties. It was largely due to Gandhi's acts of commission and omission that Jinnah regarded his importance in Indian public life." According to Nehru's political biographer, Prof. Brecher, "The talks strengthened the League; they enhanced Jinnah's prestige and gave him a status of virtual equality with Gandhi, Sikhs and the Hindu Mahasabha was jubilant in the failure of the talks. These two sections did not like Gandhi-Jinnah's negotiations. V.D. Savarkar had asserted that "the Indian province were not the private properties of Gandhiji and Rajaji so that they could make a gift of them to any one they liked".

Wavell wrote a letter to the Prime Minister on October 24, 1944 on political problems. When we started 20 or 30 years ago, on the political reform of India, we laid down a course from which we cannot withdraw. It may have been mistaken cause, and it would probably have been to face prescribed economic development, first it is no late to revise the policy now. Politically Jinnah was rising. It was due to the conditional backing to Jinnah extended by provincial Muslim government and politicians. They had complete control over the administration. The organizations of Muslim League had been weakened in Bengal and Punjab.[63] One factor also helped Jinnah to ascendency. There were no leader to contest for the President of Muslim League, so Jinnah was safe. He was dominant all India leader of the Muslim League.

On October 20, 1944, Wavell completed the first year of his tenure and he wrote a letter to Prime Minister Churchill. He mentioned, 'I feel strongly that the future of India is the problem on which the British Commonwealth and British reputation will stand or fall in the post-war period.' If instead of a friendly partner India became 'lost and hostile', the British were likely to be reduced in the east to the position of commercial bagmen ...... I feel that the vital problems of India are being treated by HMG with neglect, even sometimes with hostility and contempt.

Churchill took a month to reply to this letter. He suggested in the letter the time to consider such matters was at leisure and best of all in victorious piece. The Prime Minister was determined to ignore any such proposals telling Anery that Wevell was merely clinging to Hindus. Hindu, in this context seems to have been an all purpose word for the inhabitants of Britain's Indian Empire.

Wavell recorded in his diary that the government's attitude to India was negligent, hostile and contemptuous to a degree. I had not anticipated and repeated an earlier request he had made to 'flee back to London at once' and state case personally.[64] At last the India Committee gave in and Wevell flew to London on March 24, 1945. Meanwhile an attempt had been made by Vallabhbhai and Liyakat Ali Khan for the Congress League alliance. It was known as 'Vallabhbhai Desai's Plan'. Later it was called Desai-Liyakat Ali Pact, but Jinnah turned down this Pact.

Wavell started his talk with the British cabinet. The cabinet accepted of the Viceroy's plan of conference. Finally on May 31, 1945 Churchill requested and agreed to a conference of Indian nationalist leaders. It was agreed that all political parties of the country would be represented in the conference. It was further agreed that all leaders should be released unconditionally. After the talk was over, he came to New Delhi on 4th June. The British had this kind of feeling in India that the real power lay with the likes of Nehru, Gandhi and Jinnah. Jinnah was the complication, the grit in the nationalist oyster. Jinnah was an opportunist and he had backed the British during the war but only so far as it suited the interest of the Muslim League and at the same time stood in opposition against the British rule. Whenever he supported the Government in the executive council, it was as a tactics and not a policy.

Wavell made a broadcast on June 14, 1945 and said that he proposed to invite Indian political leaders to take counsel with them. With a view to the formation of a new executive council more representative of organized political opinion and including an equal number of caste Hindus and Muslims except for the Viceroy and the Commander-in-Chief, it would be entirely Indian council and for the first time the home, finance and foreign affairs portfolios would be in Indian hands. The council would work within the framework of the existing Constitution. Wavell also announced that orders had been issued for the immediate release of the members of the Working Committee of the Congress, who were still in detention. The members were released on 15th June. The Congress President, Maulana Azad was released from the Ramnibas detention camp on June 15, 1945 at 6 a.m., Jawaharlal Nehru was released on the same day from the Almora District Jail at 8 a.m., Sardar Patel, J.B. Kriplani and Dr. Rajendra Prasad were also released from Yarvada Jail, Karachi Jail, Bankipur Jail respectively.[65] The working committee accepted the invitation to attend the conference.

The Simla Conference, June 1945

It was due to initiative of Wavell that the Simla conference met on 25th June, 1945, twenty-one persons were invited to the conference, the eleven provincial premiers, most of whom were appointees of the Viceroy, because of the resignation of the Congress ministries in 1939, the Congress and League leaders in the central assembly and the council of states, the leaders of the insufficient Nationalist Party and the European group in Sikhs and Gandhi and Jinnah as the recognized leaders of the two main political parties.

The delegates included the Indian National Congress, the Muslim League and regional political parties. Maulana Azad had not been invited earlier, Gandhi debarred to attend the conference on the ground that this was an official conference and he was not even a member of the Congress. However, he agreed to go to Simla as an observer, in response to the Viceroy's persistent request. He gently reminded Wavell that Azad was the official Congress spokesman and error was duly rectified. The delegates came to attend the conference and they returned in hand-pulled rikshaws, and the leader faced their rivals face to face for the first time. They were in different dresses. Khizar Hyat Khan in a elaborate white turban, Azad in achkan and slippers, Jinnah in pale double-basted suit, Gandhi in a dhoti and shawl. The delegates made a strange combination.

LIST OF DELEGATES IN THE SIMLA CONFERENCE[66]

1. Maulana Abul Kalam Azad—President of the Indian National Congress.
2. Dr. P.N. Banerjee—Leader of Nationalist Party in the Central Assembly.
3. Bhula Bhai Desai—Leader of the Congress Party in the Central Assembly.
4. M.K. Gandhi—(He did not attend the Conference on the ground that he was not a member of the Congress Party, but he remained in Simla so as to be available for constitution.)
5. Sir Ghulam Hussain Hidayattullah—Premier of Sind.
6. Hussain Imam — Leader of the Muslim League in the Council of State.
7. M.A. Jinnah — President of the Muslim League.
8. Dr. Khan Sahib — Premier of N.W.F.P.
9. B.J. Kher — Ex-Premier of Bombay.
10. Malik Khaizar Hyat Khan Tiwana — Premier of Punjab.
11. Nawab Zada Liaquat Ali Khan — Deputy Leader of the Muslim League in the Central Assembly.
12. G.S. Motilal — Leader of the Congress Party in the Council of a State.
13. Khawaja Sir Nazimuddin — Ex Premier of Bengal.
14. Pandit Govind Ballabh Pant — Ex Premier of the United Provinces.
15. Maharaja of Parlaki Medi — Ex Premier of Orissa.
16. C. Rajagopalachari — Ex Premier of Madras.
17. Sir Henry Richardson — Leader of the European Group, Central Assembly.
18. Sir Muhammad Saadullah — Premier of Assam.
19. Deo Bahadur Siva Raj — Representative of the Scheduled Castes.
20. Pandit R.S. Shukla — Ex Premier of the Central Provinces.
21. Sri Krishna Sinha — Ex Premier of Bihar.
22. Master Tara Singh — Representative of Sikhs.

Secretaries

1. Sir Evan Jenkins — P.I.V.

2. Rao Bahadur V.P. Menon — Reforms Commissioner.

Wavell came up to Simla on June 22, 1945. On June 24 Wavell had a series of interviews with Azad, Gandhi and Jinnah. It was a long trying day for Wavell. Azad came first in the morning accompanied by Pant as interpreter. (Azad understands English well but is shy of speaking it.) Wavell had a talk with Azad for one and a quarter hours. After lunch, he had 1 and 1/4 hours talk with Gandhi. He asked Mr. Gandhi at the end, whether he proposed to attend the conference in person. He said that he represented nobody except himself and that though he would be prepared to attend the Conference "if I wished" and sit in a corner, he strongly advised Wavell that his presence at the Conference was undesirable. Then Wavell had one and half hour talks with Jinnah. Jinnah who used very harsh words about Gandhi's tactics of claiming to take no part in negotiations saying he pretended not to belong to the Congress when it suited him, but was in reality 'The Dictator of Congress'.

Working of Conference

The working of the Conference met at 11 A.M. on June 25, 1945. The Viceroy made a short address. He said, 'The Statesmanship is having on trial, not merely in the eyes of India but before the whole world.' He has asked them to believe on him as a senior friend of India as one who would labour hard to guide the discussions of the conference in what he believed hard to be the best interest of the country. Soon the conference met with difficulty. The League insisted on the right to appoint all Muslims to the Executive Council. Jinnah was adamant not to allow any Muslims who were not members of the League on a new Viceroy's Executive Council. The Congress refused to abdicate its status as a national organization. Conversation took place between Jinnah and Pandit G.B. Pant, but the deadlock continued. Wavell also did not accept this, he sent a telegram to Amery,[67] "Muslim League does not repeat nor represent all Muslims in India and considerable section of Muslims not only in Punjab but also elsewhere would be outraged by amnesia that it does." According to note of Amery: "the immediate wrecker was Jinnah" he suggests, "but the real wrecker perhaps the long delay before Archie was allowed to try, and so Winston."[68]

On 27 June, Jinnah had a talk with Wavell. On being asked, Jinnah said he wanted a council of 14, with five Hindus, five Muslims, one Sikh and one Scheduled Caste. Wavell finally asked him what was his position regarding the nomination of the Muslim members to the Council. He said that his position was that they now all be nominated by the League and must all the Leaguers. Wavell said that "as I had told him at our first meeting, this was entirely unacceptable to me and asked him bluntly whether he proposed to wreck the whole Conference on this issue" Jinnah did not change his view.

So the Conference was adjourned on 29th June till 14th July. Wavell writes in his Journal 29th June. I am not very hopeful of success unless there is a change of spirit. One of the troubles are that none of the Principal leaders—Gandhi, Jinnah, Nehru, Liaquat, Patel have any administrative experience and they do not understand how the machinery of Government works in practice and think entirely on the lines of all questions being decided by Party votes.[69]

Wavell had one and a half hour talk with Jinnah on July 9, 1945. Again Jinnah told that he could nominate the Muslims on the New Council. Wavell refused to give me his list of names to the Viceroy but in the end he said that the Viceroy might write to him. Wavell wrote on 10th July. Jinnah was deviously in a high state of nervous tension and said to him more than once. I am at the end of my tither. He also said, "I fear I have to record the definite failure of the Conference and so of this time effort to make progress in Indian self-government. On 12th July, he entered in his journal "Rajendra Prasad seems quite ordinary and friendly and not very formidable or outwardly bitter". On July 11, the Viceroy had met Gandhi and said that the Conference had failed on 12th July. The Viceroy explained the position to Hyat Khan, Maulana Azad and Gobind Ballabh Pant. These leaders did not appreciate the policy of the Muslim League.

The final session of the conference met on 14th July, passed of more easily and seriously than Wavell had expected. Azad made quite a temperate statement; Rajagopalachari exhorted me to form a government without a League and then Jinnah made a long exposition of the League point of view. Wavell had a long talk with Nehru after lunch and he put to him that the only hope for India to make best use of an opportunity before her and to him self-government without disruption or civil war was for the Hindus and Muslims to make friends. Nehru was quite friendly and reasonable. The theme of his discourse was that Congress represented a modern nationalistic point of view and the League a narrow medieval conception. After this talk Wavell wrote in his diary that "Nehru is honest and sincere but a theorist and doctrinaire rather than a practical politician."[70]

In his report on the conference Wavell concluded, "Jinnah is narrow and arrogant and is activated by fear and distrust of the Congress. Like Gandhi he is constitutionally incapable of friendly cooperation with the other Party, Azad is an old fashioned scholar with pleasant manners" ...... Has main object is to get even with Jinnah and the League Muslims, who despise him as a paid servant of the Congress. Nehru is an idealist and I should say straight and honest. He adds that although Simla had failed over Jinnah's intransigence about the Muslim representation. The deeper cause was genuine Muslim distrust of Hindus.[71] Their fear that the Congress by passing its national character and using Muslim dummies cannot be dismissed as an obsession of Jinnah and his immediate entourage.

According to Wavell, an underlying reason for the breakdown of the talks was the previous British policy of excluding nationalists from Central Government. One trouble is that none of the principal leaders — Gandhi, Jinnah, Nehru, Liaquat, Patel have any administrative experience and they do not understand how the machinery of government work in practice and think entirely on the lines of all questions being decided by Party votes.

Pakistan on a Platter

After the failure of the conference, Jinnah who was the main instrument of the failure of Wavell confabulations, entered the lift to go upstairs to his suit, I joined him. Durga Das was the joint editor of the *Hindustan Times*. Durga Das was also in the same lift and he asked him why he had spurned the Wavell plan, when he won his point of Party for the League with the Congress. He replied, "I am a fool to accept this when I am offered Pakistan on a platter". I, after on enquiry Durga Das learnt from high officials and political sources that a number of Viceroy's Executive Council had sent a secret message to Jinnah. The rough of League contacts he had framed after the Durga Das went to London.

At London he had quite informal talks with Atlee. The Labour Party had assumed office on 26th July, 1945 with Atlee as a Prime Minister. Attlee told that he, for his part, was clear in his mind that

Britain must quit. He believed that the transfer of power must not be made conditional on India's remaining a position of the British commonwealth. But Attlee should have deep agitation over the Muslim demand for Pakistan and agreed with Durga Das plea that a minority should not be allowed to hold up the progress of majority to self-rule. William Whitley, chief whip of Labour Party, the House of Commons considered the Congress the freedom party and the League disruptions. He wanted to preserve the unity of India.

Failure of the Conference

The Simla Conference failed to expose the real nature of M.A. Jinnah's position. As the Governors of Bengal and Punjab had predicted, Jinnah's conduct during the talks at Simla inflated his credibility, while failing to reveal the fact that he had little serious backing in the two main Muslim majority provinces. The Governors of Bengal and Punjab desired Wavell to 'expose' the possible consequences of the creation of Pakistan, rather than trying to break the Indo-British deadlock by forming an interim government. But Wavell took no immediate step but he felt that validity of their logical argument and subsequently raised the matter with the Whitehall.

In his final address to the conference announcing its failure Wavell said, "I wish to make it clear that the responsibility for the failure is mine.[72] The main idea underlying the conference was mine. If it had succeeded, its success would have been attributed to me, and I can not place the blame for its failure on any of the parties. I ask the Party leaders to accept this view, and to do all they can to ensure that there are no recrimination"......The route cause of the failure was,[73] of course, Jinnah's interagency and obstinacy but Wavell recognized that this interagency represents a real fear on the part of Muslims, including those who do not support Jinnah, of Congress dominion, which they regard as equivalent to a Hindu Raj.

The Simla conference, though it ended in failure, may be regarded in same ways as the greatest achievement of Wavell's Viceroyalty. The idea of holding it, undoubtedly, a right one, was entirely his and it was his dogged persistence that there came the resistance of H.M.G. Once he had detained His Majesty's approval, he encounter little difficulty in assembling the conference, and skilfully got it off to an excellent start in a general atmosphere of goodwill for his initiative had been warmly welcomed in India, and he himself had made a favourable impression on some of the Congress leaders,[74] that he was much struck by Wavell's frankness and sincerity and his obviously genuine desire to open a new chapter in the relations between Congress and the Government.

Nevertheless the conference failed, although Wavell took responsibility for its failure, clearly the fault was not really his. Some critics have, however, contended that by capitulating without a struggle to Jinnah's intransigence and briefly bringing the conference to an end, he needlessly abandoned a great chance of setting India on the road to united self-government. This conclusion implies that if he had ignored Jinnah and continued negotiations with the other parties, Jinnah would have had to give away. Since he could not afford to see a new council formed without the League or alternatively that if he had still refused to come in, he would have lost his hold over the Muslims and more moderate leaders would have come to the fore.

If he would have done like this, his object of forming a united government would have failed. The communal problem would have been more intractable. The Congress dominated council would have not been useful in the persecution of war against Japan. Churchill might have rejected this sort of government so Wavell announced the failure of the conference on 14th July. He said in the end on this way, "I thank you for the help you have given me and for the restraint, patience and understanding by this setback. We shall overcome our difficulties in the end. The future greatness of India is not in doubt."

Jinnah speaking on the failure of the conference observed on a final examination and the analysis of the Wavell plan, we found that it was a snare. There was a combination consisting of Gandhi and Hindu Congress, which stand for India's national independence as one India and the latest exponent of geographical unity. Lord Wavell and Glency and Khizar, who are bent upon creating disruption among the Muslims in the Punjab, and we were sought to be pushed into this arrangement, which, if agreed to, as proposed by Lord Wavell, we should have signed over death warrant.

Jinnah was very discourtcous because he refused to shake hands with Azad at the Viceregal lodge in Simla at the time of the conference. Azad said that he appreciated Lord Wavell's efforts for a solution of the political deadlock. He further said that a firm attitude on the part of the Viceroy alone would have brought a settlement of the communal problem. The Viceroy's present worrying attitude was not helpful. "We are near our goal" he said, and the next stage in the goal itself. It does not matter at all what the intentions of the British Government are."

After Jinnah's statement, Dr. Jayakar wrote to Gandhi in this way: "As I read this speech, where he called the Wavell arrangement a snare, it was clear to me that his apprehension was that . . . . . . if he accepted the interim arrangement . . . . . . in the day-to-day harmony of working the acerbities and animosities, out of which Pakistan is born and fiddled, would be gradually smoothened and Muslim would lose the zest for separate existence on discovering that its basis rests not in realistic but only in long suspicion."

The next result of conference was to introduce the formula of "caste-Hindu-Muslim parity" into practical politics and to strengthen the principle of religious division on the eve of independence.

It is said that Lord Wavell was true and sincere friend of India and he had tried his best to ease the Indian political situation. Leonard Mosley also holds the same view. He has mentioned in his book "The Last Days of the British Raj" that Lord Wavell had made sincere attempts to bring improvements in the political condition of the country. How far this is true? This becomes clear if we study the question and answer of Francis Sayer with Mahatma Gandhi. You will admit remarked Mr. Francis of the United Nations Relief and Rehabilitation Administration in the course of an interview with Gandhi, that Wavell did make an honest attempt to break the deadlock.

> *"An honest attempt should have ended honestly" Gandhi replied. The situation became clearer then a fortnight, when Pandit Nehru received a letter from London. It has been mentioned in the letter, "it is now known that the Wavell offer was maintained in being as part of election necessities."*

"An interim government" Lord Wavell had confided to the Governor of Punjab "might help to dissuade the Muslims from the Pakistan objective". Evidently this possibility was not welcome to Mr. Jinnah. By 1945, Pakistan had ceased to be a bargaining counter for Mr. Jinnah, if indeed it ever was. He was afraid that the League entry into an Interim Central Government could prejudice his case for a separate state.

Thus the Simla Conference failed but Lord Wavell's sincerity, integrity and sense of fairness had remarkable freedom from impressionist blinkers must be admired. But at the same time he had a pathological suspicion and dislike of politicians — especially Indian politicians. Mr. Jinnah stuck him as "too narrow and intransient", Mahatma Gandhi, Malevolent old politician, a very tough politician and not a saint, Sri Krishna Sinha, the least pleasant, rather an aggressive agitator type, Mr. Nehru 'theoretical', Maulana Azad 'ineffective' and Sir Sapru 'intolerant'. The fact is that Lord Wavell himself lacked the agility, flexibility and bionomic needed in those critical years for the difficult task of healing the communal cleavage and creating a bridge to a united and self-governing India.

The Simla conference was a milestone on the road to transfer the power. If it had succeeded, it would have given a new direction to the history of this subcontinent.

The fact is that Lord Wavell himself sacked the agility,[75] flexibility and bonhomie needed in those critical years for the difficult task of healing the communal cleavage and creating a bridge to a united and self-governing India. This was a last opportunity to the forces of nationalism to fight a rearguard action to preserve the integrity of the country. When the battle was lost, the fires of communalism quickly engulfed it.

The General Election

After the breakdown of the Simla Conference there became a sweeping change in the political outlook. Two events transformed the entire scene after the conference. The first was the sweeping victory of Labour Party in Britain; and the second was the dropping of Atom Bomb at the end of the war. The general election in Britain resulted in a victory of the Labour Party. The Conservative Party was defeated and the Labour Party came into power on July 26, 1945. Lord Pethick Lawrence, an old friend of Gandhi, became the new Secretary of State for India.

Congratulating him on the appointment, Gandhi wrote, "If the India Office to receive a decent burial and a nobler monument is to rise from its ashes, who can be the fittest person than you for the work." Lord Pethick Lawrence replied,[76] "I greatly hope that our personal friendship, which has existed for so many years, may bear fruit in harmonious cooperation in achieving the lasting good of India and for people." In a cable to Attlee the new British Prime

Minister, Azad, the Congress President said, "Heartily congratulations to the people of Great Britain on the results of the election which demonstrate their abandonment of the idea and acceptance of a new world. The surrender of Japan was the result of atom bomb. The first atomic bomb to be utilized for war purpose was dropped by a U.S.B.-29 plane on Hiroshima (Japan) on August 6, 1945. On August 8, 1945, Russia declared war on Japan. The second atom bomb was dropped on Nagasaki (Japan) on August 9. Now Japan surrendered unconditionally on August 15, 1945.

The new Labour government headed by Attlee invited Lord Wavell to London in the last week of August in order to review the whole Indian problem. Clement Attlee and his Labour Party had come to the office publicly committed to begin the dismemberment of the Empire. At the same time the announcement was made on August 21, that the general election to the central and the provincial legislatures would be held at the earliest possible. Lord Wavell returned to India soon and an announcement was made on September 19, to the following effect; Provincial autonomy would be restored immediately after the elections, a constitution-making body for India would be established as soon as possible. [77]

The Congress agreed to participate in the elections. In October the Congress High Command issued a 12-point election manifesto. The Muslim League fought the elections on the issue of Hindu domination in a united India and the consequent need of a separate Muslim homeland, i.e. Pakistan. The results were astonishing;[78] the League won all 30 Muslim seats in the central assembly with 86 per cent of the Muslim votes and 427 of the 507 Muslim seats in the provincial legislature with 47 per cent of the Muslim votes. The Muslim League was defeated in the North West Frontier Province. The Congress captured 56 seats in the central assembly with 91 per cent of the "General votes" and 930 in the provinces. The trend in polarization was now evident. The Congress paid a very high price for the August Movement of 1942, which Mahatma Gandhi had called as the "open rebellion". All other groups faded into insignificance.

Elections were held at the end of 1945 for legislative assembly at the centre and in the provincial. The Congress won the overwhelming majority of the unrepresented seats in the Muslim seats. The League majority was almost of the same proportion. The anti-League Muslims, notably the Unionist Party which had formed the government of the Punjab since 1920, were decimated. At last

Jinnah's claim to speak for the Muslims was lacked by the evidence of the ballot box. It was not to diminish his imperiousness. After the general election was over, the question of forming the new government arose in each province. So the Congress President, Mr. Azad began to move the provincial capitals to supervise the formation of the ministers. Azad came to Bihar for the formation of the government. He found the situation complicated by the rivalries of different groups. To this was added the personal problems of important Congressmen. Dr. Syed Mahmud's name was there.

Azad had decided that the Congress should adopt a general attitude towards the Muslim League in the matter of formation of the Ministries. Azad wanted cooperation from the Muslim League elected members. In the many provinces, particularly in Bihar, Assam and Punjab, members of the Muslim League were glad to be in the ministry but Mr. Jinnah did not allow members of the Muslim League to join the Ministry.

The position was very difficult in the Punjab. It was a Muslim majority province but no Party had a clear majority. The Muslim members were divided between the Unionist Party and the Muslim League. Azad held the discussion with both the groups. The League members declined Azad's invitation under the instructions from Jinnah. But Azad carried out negotiations in a way which gave the Unionist Party the opportunity of forming the ministry with the support of the Congress. The Governor Sir Bertrand Glancy was personally inclined in favour of the Muslim League but he had no option and he invited Khizir Hayat Khan, the leader of the Unionist Party to form the government. This was for the first time that Congress ministry was formed in the Punjab. It was the result of Azad's skill in negotiations.

The Congress formed ministries[79] in 8 out of 11 provinces and in the ninth namely, the Punjab it entered into a coalition which cut across communal alignments. The Muslim League was able to form ministries in Bengal and Sind. Wavell was thinking about Pakistan. He had suggested to the Whitehall that the demand for Pakistan should be faced by the government. Wavell had this kind of impression that the Labour Government would handover India to the Congress as soon as possible. In November 1945, Pandit Nehru told Wavell "he could make no terms whatsoever with the Muslim League under its present leadership and policy." Since it was a reactionary body with entirely unacceptable ideas, Wavell was in a fix. Wavell was coming to this conclusion that if there was any movement in the country sponsored by the Congress would be almost impossible to surpass, because the police and the army were demoralized. The Congress wanted a government of their own choice in free India. But Jinnah was adamant and Jinnah announced that 'Pakistan is a question of life and death for us'. Wavell was very clear in his mind that a firm policy should be adopted in the country, let the situation may go out of control.

Wavell sent a secret memorandum[80] to London in early November 1945 and stated we are now faced in India such a situation of great difficulty and danger—Congress leaders elsewhere, but particularly Vallabhbhai Patel in Bombay and Nehru and Pant in the United Provinces, have been making statements and speeches which can be intended to provoke or pave a way for mass disorder.[81] ...... I must accordingly, with the utmost gravity, warn HMG to be prepared for a serious attempt by the Congress, probably next spring, but quite possibly earlier, to subsist by force the present administration in India. Half measures will be of no use in dealing with a movement of this kind, and the choice will be between capitulating to Congress and accepting their demands whatsoever they may be—and using all our resources to suppress the movement.

Around this time, Pandit Nehru declared in a public speech: "India must not wait for the next move of the Labour Government but should prepare herself for a mass battle for freedom". Wavell thought that there were the echoes of 1942 in this statement.[82] He said that Linlithgow had called the August movement of 1942 as 'most serious rebellion' since that of 1857, though the Congress had made little preparation for the August movement.

The Commander-in-Chief in India,[83] Auchinleck reported on December 1, 1945 that conflict was looming. As 1945, was coming to an end, Wavell recorded in his diary that despite the limitations in the approach adopted by Attlee and Cripps, a Labour Government has on the whole made things easier, since rather more attention is paid to India and the outlook is rather more sympathetic. However, I shall consider myself very fortunate if I am writing with any cause for satisfaction at the end of 1946.

Jinnah was a communal leader. This is proved by his statement he issued at the time of the Red Fort Trial, Delhi. In November 1945, the Commander-in-Chief took the fateful decision of committing to trial three officers of Subhas Bose's Indian National Army—a Hindu, a Muslim and a Sikh—before a military court at Red Fort, Delhi. Nehru also appeared before the court wearing the barrister's gown. Jinnah too attempted to figure in the affair. He sent word to Shah Nawaz Khan, the Muslim on trial, that he would defend him, if he dissociated himself from the other accuseds. Shah Nawaz Khan flatly declined, remarking: "we have stood shoulder to shoulder in the struggle for freedom. Many comrades have died on the field of battle inspired by our leadership. We stand or fall together."[84]

NOTES

1. Talwakar Govind, '*The lonely road to Pakistan*', this article has been published in the *Times of India*, New Delhi, November 17, 1984.
2. Wolpert, Stenly, '*Jinnah of Pakistan*', the *Times of India*, New Delhi, November17, 1984.
3. *Ibid.*
4. *Ibid.*
5. French Patrick, *Liberty or Death*, p. 123
6. Mishra, S.G., *Freedom Struggle*, p. 138.
7. French Patrick, p. 124, quotations from both the resolutions was translated from an engraving on a pillar at the '*Minar-e-Pakistan*' in Minto Park, now renamed as *Iqbal Park*, Lahore.
8. French Patrick, *Liberty or Death*, p. 125.
9. Azad, M.A.K., *India wins Freedom*, p. 150.
10. *Ibid.*
11. *Ibid.*
12. *Ibid.*
13. *Ibid.*
14. *Ibid.*
15. French, Patrick, *Liberty or Death*, p. 125.
16. *Ibid.*
17. Proceedings, *Ferrule's Group of Archives*, New Delhi, 1985.
18. *Ibid.*
19. *Ibid.*
20. Mishra, S.G., *Freedom Struggle*, p. 140.
21. *Ibid.*
22. *Ibid.*
23. Bhalla, Alok (edited), *Stories about the Partition of India*, p. xii.
24. *Ibid.*
25. *Ibid.*
26. *The Asian Age*, August 12, 1997.
27. Bhalla, Alok, *Stories about the Partition of India*, p. xiv.

28. *Ibid.*, vol. III, p. 60.
29. *Indian Express*, 26th March 1997.
30. Oioc, Mss, Eur, F125/19, No. 94, April 4, 1940 (quoted by French, Patrick) p. 126.
31. *Ibid.*
32. French Patrick, *Liberty or Death*, p. 126.
33. Oioc, Mss, Eur F125/19, 271, June 30, 1940 (quoted by French, Patrick), pp. 151-152.
34. Quoted Wolpert, p. 193.
35. Enclosure to Oioc, pol(s) s12295/1941 (quoted French, Patrick), p. 135.
36. 'The quarterly review of '*Historical Studies*', Calcutta, Vol. 13, 1973-74, No. 2, p. 117 by Prof. Amalendu De.
37. *Ibid.*
38. *Ibid.*
39. *Ibid*
40. *Ibid.*
41. *Ibid.*
42. *Ibid.*
43. *Mainstream,* October 30, 1993.
44. Norman Dorothy, *Nehru I,* p. 204.
45. Louis W.M. Roger, *Imperialism at Way*, p. 121.
46. *Ibid.*
47. *Ibid.*
48. *Ibid.*
49. *Ibid.*
50. *Moyne to Amary*, August 26, 1941. p. 124
51. *India Today*, December 1984, p. 100.
52. Louis, W.M., Roger Louis, *Imperialism at Bay*, p. 130.
53. *Transfer of Powers*, Vol. III, p. 928.
54. *Transfer of Powers*, Vol. I, pp. 633-634.
55. Akbar, *The Making of India*, 1988.
56. The *Times of India*, New Delhi, September 13, 1997.
57. Sarkar, Sumit, *Modern India*, p. 408.
58. Durga Das, *India from Curzon to Nehru and After*, pp. 211-212.
59. The *Indian Annual Register*, 1944, I, p. 54.
60. Quoted Wolpart, pp. 232-33.
61. *Ibid.*
62. Wavell, *The Viceroy's Journal*, p. 91.
63. French Patrick, *Liberty or Death*, p. 188.
64. *Transfer of Power*, Vol. V, pp. 235 to 260.
65. Exhibited documents, National Archives, New Delhi, December 1985.
66. *The Viceroy's Journal*, pp. 144 to 146.
67. *Transfer of Power*, Vol. V, p. 1125.
68. Barnes, p. 1045.

69. Moon (2), p. 151.
70. Transfer of Power, Vol. V, pp. 1262 to 1263.
71. *Ibid.*
72. Menon, V.P., *Transfer of Power in India*, p. 209.
73. Transfer of Power, Vol. V, pp. 1262 to 1263.
74. Maulana Azad, India wins Freedom, pp. 106 to 110.
75. Mishra, S.G., *C.D. and National Movement*, p. 233.
76. Pyarelal Mastana, I, p. 151.
77. Mishra, S.G., *C.D. and National Movement*, p. 215.
78. Bruser Michael, *Nehru : A Political Biography*, p. 304.
79. *Ibid.*
80. *Transfer of Power*, Vol. VI, p. 699.
81. *Transfer of Power*, Vol. VI, p. 451 to 453.
82. French Patrick, *Liberty or Death*, p. 219.
83. *Ibid.*
84. Durga Das, *India from Curzon to Nehru and After*, p. 224.

8

1946 : Year of Decision

Lord Pethick Lawrence—"1946 will be a crucial year in India's history"

1946 was to be a year of fateful events. During the period immediately following the war it became overwhelmingly evident that the power of the British Empire was rapidly waning. In India, as the areas of South and South-East Asia, it was equally clear that the desire for independence had been growing at such an accelerated rate that the freedom from foreign rule would have to be granted without delay; that the principles enunciated in the Atlantic Charter must be as fully applicable to the awakening East to the West.

With regard to India, in particular, Britain was finding it difficult to maintain her dominant position, if for no other reason than a financial one.

Pandit Nehru issued a statement in February 10, 1946 in the way, "of course I expect a peaceful and friendly settlement with Britain. If such a settlement is needed, India's relations with Great Britain will naturally be closure as there are so many ties already developed between our two peoples, some good, some bad . . . . . . From no point of view can India fit into a current dominion status pattern".

As 1945 was drawing to a close, Wavell wrote in his diary that despite the limitations in the approach adopted by Attlee and Cripps, a Labour Government has on the whole made things easier, since rather more attention is paid to Indians the outlook is rather more sympathetic. However, I shall consider myself very fortunate if I am writing with any cause for satisfaction at the end of 1946.

Parliamentary Delegation

The new proposal put up by the British Government was that a cross-Party delegation consisting of a dozen political persons should visit India to understand the real political situation of the country and submit a report to the government. Pethick Lawrence told Attlee; "there are a good many members of the Party who take a keen interest in India but lack real knowledge about it". "The group arrived on January 3, 1946, many hours late and rather weary," reported Wavell but "I like what I have sure of them".[1]

Mahatma Gandhi's treatment of the parliamentary delegation was not smooth. For some time he did not meet them and when he met, he did not take part in the discussion seriously. When the delegation tried to devise any policy, Gandhi would repeat *mantras* such as "get off our backs" and the "slave clings to his chains", as if that would solve matters. He remained busy "testing the MP's in his own way. As one member of the delegation wrote Gandhi was always testing other people's sincerity but keenly resented any one trying to testify".[2]

Gandhi was in his advance age and he was about 77 years old so he was not in a position to bring changes in his outlook. Now it was clear that India would gain freedom soon. So the new changes required flexibility but Gandhi was still appeared to be in a rebellious mood. The members of the delegation could not understand why Gandhi was behaving in an unfriendly way. The Governor of Bengal told Wavell in December 1945 that during a private interview with him, Gandhi had insisted that all recent violent Congress speeches were outcome of failure at Simla .... The Governor believed that Gandhi lacked realism and balance.[3]

The delegation returned to Britain and after a month went to report to the government. But they had not prepared any report or they had any useful information with themselves. Two members Muriel Nichol and Reg. Sorensen were of this opinion that the British Government should concede the principle of Pakistan. One delegate seriously emphasized and said that if the Muslim League did not participate in the constitution-making, there would be widespread violence in India.[4] Therefore, Pakistan would be carved out for Jinnah on the basis of the Muslim majority areas. It is for the first time that few British MPs were prepared for the division of the country. Instead of protecting the territorial integrity of the country few British leaders instead of fighting separatism which Jinnah wanted, they surrendered to Muslim League; it was very bad for the secular nationalism. Muslim communalism was now supported by these political leaders. They even supported the two-nation theory. The Indian national Congress had categorically rejected the argument that religion was a decisive factor in determining the state affairs, just as it had rejected the two-nation theory that is, that Hindus and Muslims are separate nations. Syed Ahmad Khan, Dr. Iqbal and Jinnah had advocated two-nation theory. Jinnah wanted Pakistan on the ground of two-nation theory. Now two members of the delegation supported the demand of Pakistan. What a tragic approach?

Major Woodrow Wyatt, a young labour M.P. was the originator of this statement. Wyatt's star was rising. He was greatly interested in the future of India. He was thinking seriously about the political development of India. So he went to India personally and studied minutely the political conditions of India. From his study he came to this conclusion that Pakistan was then a fantasy in Jinnah's mind. It was a serious proposition with support from many Indian Muslims. So many British MPs were thinking in terms of the vivisection of India. They were in favour of Pakistan. The cause of a united India was in jeopardy.

Wavell despatched to India Office his own study of the political situation of the country. In his study he had developed his claim that the Congress was serious in wresting power for itself and the Congress was ready for any kind of compromise. If they get opportunity, they could start a revolt against British imperialism exactly in the lines of the August movement of 1942. So Wavell prepared a top secret emergency plan to be used in those circumstances if the Congress and the Muslim League were unable to come to any agreement on the Pakistan issue . . . . . . So it was essential that knowledge of the 'Breakdown plan' should be restricted to the smallest number of people and that there should be no discloser.[5]

The 'Pakistan resolution' of the Muslim League was receiving a momentum. The Aligarh Muslim University students were parading through rural villages, invoking the martyrdom of Imam Hussain, the grandson of the Prophet and telling the people that under the new Congress administration cows would be tethered in their mosque. Urdu poems written and recited, with verses such as 'Do you remember the Delli (Delhi) Wallahas (i.e. the Mugal Emperors). They lived in the Red Fort once. You were kings then, you carrot-eating wretches. But only those who wield a stick can protect their sisters.[6]

Breakdown Award or Plan

There were various observations in this document. The one important observation was that the British Government might be forced by the circumstances into the position of having to impose a unilateral settlement if the Congress and the League would not cooperate with each other. He made it clear that if the Congress and the League failed to agree or of either or both rejected the cabinet mission's proposals. He himself drew up a breakdown plan to meet these possible contingencies and got the mission to accept it and sent it home but HMG declined to comment themselves to it. Later when the mission seemed to be on the point of success, he reminded them that even if the Congress and League were shepherded into an interim government and a constituent assembly, there were many pitfalls ahead, and that circumstances might arise that would compel them to fall back on his breakdown plan, unless something better could be suggested. This break down plan which several writers have quote misrepresented—was to be a recurrent theme during the rest of his time as victory. Wavell had made it clear in this plan that they should concede 'Pakistan' only in those areas where Muslims were in a defined majority. It would not be fair to Sikhs or Hindus to hand over to the Muslim League the whole province such as the Punjab and Bengal: each side of Bengal or the Punjab had a different communal composition. Wavell pointed out to the unnoticed fact that Jinnah would want an exact statement of the boundaries of the proposed Muslim areas. If such a request is made we should keep in hand a detailed demarcation and I will send proposal shortly.[7]

Wavell dispatched these proposals to the India Office on February 7, 1946 in the form of telegram. It suggested possible boundaries to Pakistan covering these areas where Muslims can advance a reasonable claim, modifications in boundaries might be negotiated and no doubt the interest of Sikhs in particular would be carefully considered preventing immediate violence by Sikhs.[8] It was likely that the Viceroy was following the guidance of his Private Secretary George Abele.

Wavell's telegram is considered one of the most important documents in the history of the transfer of power in India, because it was the first serious official attempt to show a rough sketch of the boundaries of Pakistan. Wavell pointed out the areas of the north-east of India which might constitute Pakistan. He recommended the Chittagong and Dacca division, the Rajshahi division excluding Jalpaiguri and Darjeeling, the Syelhat district of Assam and the three eastern districts of Bengal presidency. Wavell was opposed to include 'Calcutta' in Pakistan because this city had a Hindu majority. However, he suggested in the breakdown plan that Calcutta could become a free port in exchange for some concessions over the Central Government by the League. The boundaries that Wavell's telegram gave to the eastern wing of Pakistan corresponded closely to the borders of East Pakistan that was drawn in August 1947.

In the case of north-west of India, Wavell faced difficulties. The reason was that five million Sikhs minority were scattered through the Punjab. Most of the Sikhs were in the east of the province. There were half a million Sikhs in the west, Punjab districts of Rawalpindi, Lyallpur and Montgomery. So he recommended the following areas for the west Pakistan: Sind, North-West Frontier Province, British Baluchistan (the rest of Baluchistan consisted of princely states), and the main administrative divisions of western Punjab—namely Rawalpindi, Multan and Lahore, but less Amritsar and Gurdaspur districts. As Kashmir was a princely state, it was not mentioned.

It is evident from the breakdown plan that the western wing of Pakistan lost the natural border imposed by the Beas and Satlaj rivers. Wavell stated, Gurdaspur must go with Amritsar for geographical reasons and Amritsar being sacred city of Sikhs must stay out of Pakistan.[9] This was a simple point, and had it been agreed at once by the India Office as a matter of policy, much bloodshed might have been averted from August 13 to 15, 1947. Wavell was stressing on this fact that Amritsar and its surrounding districts constituted the heart of the Sikhdom, so it could not be placed within a Muslim homeland that is Pakistan.

Under this situation, Amritsar could not become the part of Pakistan. If Amritsar could stay out of Pakistan, it was natural that Gurdaspur also should not go to Pakistan. Gurdaspur had 50 per cent Muslims. If Amritsar and Gurdaspur would have stayed in the Indian union, Gurdaspur would have given geographical protection to Amritsar.

If Gurdaspur could go to Pakistan, as happened under the Redcliff Award, then Amritsar would look like a lone Sikh island with a threat from the Muslims. On paper the question of Amritsar and Gurdaspur appeared to be a minor but the communal holocaust broke out on this question from August 13, 1947. As Gurdaspur went to Pakistan as a result of Redcliff Award, communal massacres started in free India.

What happened to the breakdown plan in London? Wavell's telegram was received by a junior clerk at the India Office on February 14, 1945. The clerk drew three primitive sketch maps on the basis of information that was furnished by Wavell. By mistake, the clerk marked Gurdaspur district in the potential Pakistan. Except this, everything written by Wavell was incorporated in the map by the clerk. It could not be said that the clerk had done this under political motivation. The main map was simply titled Northern India showing Pakistan conferred to Muslim majority districts, and Gurdaspur did on paper have a Muslim majority.[10] This was simply a clerical error but it had the far-reaching consequences.

Patrick French had written that Wavell's document was read by each civil servant and they made their observations in the margin. They were surprised to see Wavell's document but they had to take the document seriously. Paul Patrick, an influential assistant under Secretary of the State at the India Office wrote in the margin in this way: "It is difficult to believe in the viability of this form the Financial, Economic or Defence stand points".[11] It is clear from the notes of the civil servants that not a single civil servant liked the dismemberment of Indian Empire at the time of Indian independence. They thought that the formation of Pakistan would be beneficial? The claim that the British had secret plans to partition India, Patrick says, cannot be supported from the internal memorandum and documentation of White Hall officialdom.

Wavell had a meeting with the Intelligence Bureau in mid January 1946, the Director reported to Wavell "the Congress is in militant mood and outgunning for the Muslims, confident that they can down them. The DIB thinks they are prepared to take office in the provinces . . . . . . and will then secure control of government servants and make action against Congress impossible". It was the most serious threat assessment I.B. had made.

It has to be noted that in the election of 1945-46, the Muslim League's campaign carried religious edge. Students of Aligarh Muslim University paraded through rural villages. They invoked the martyrdom of Imam Hussain, the grandson of Prophet. They told the villagers that if the Congress government would be formed in the provinces, cows would be tethered in their mosque. Urdu poems were written and recited such as, "Do you remember the Dilli walls (i.e. the Mugal Emperors)". They lived in the Red Fort once. You were kings then, you carrot-eating wretches/but only those who wield a stick can protect their sisters. In the pre-emption days, students of the Aligarh Muslim University enthusiastically shouted this slogan; "India will be divided, Pakistan will be created". Azhar and Owais, two students of A.M.U. always participated in political rallies and they were adamant for Pakistan. After the partition of India, they began to talk senselessly and extravagantly.

Congress won a landslide victory in the provinces that were to be included in Pakistan, conditions were chaotic. It was only in Muslim minority areas such as the United Provinces that Pakistan seemed unreservedly popular. It was seen as a homeland and a safe haven for Muslims. They also thought that if a sovereign nation like Pakistan was established, then the position of Muslims who remained in India, would improve. Many Muslims recapitulated Jinnah's words and they said that Quaid-i-Azam had said that in Pakistan there would be no place for poor Muslims. In Karachi there was no goonda and nobody would be able to throw us out.

By 1946, the Congress and the Muslim League were loosing grip over their followers. The goondas of Bengal and Punjab were under this impression that neither the Congress nor the League was in a position to contain us. At the end of March 1947 the DIB reported to Wavell that the British authorities were living on the edge of a volcano. By March 8, 1947, the Congress Working Committee had adopted a resolution for the divison of Punjab. Any hopeful dream of a united India were killed off for good by a Congress resolution agreed in New Delhi on 8th March, Punjab was burning, communal riots had taken an alarming shape. Throughout the whole country law and order had weakened. The Congress was in a confrontational mood due to the negative policy followed by war time Government. In spite of all difficult situations Wavell was happy by an intelligence report that the Congress Working Committee was in a good mood to reach an agreement with the Government. The reason was that the members of the CWC had this feeling that if nothing was done to reach a settlement, then power might slip into the hands of a younger, revolutionary generation.

From the breakdown plan and Wavell's approach it was clear that Wavell liked that power should be transferred to a united India. He never favoured Pakistan and was anxious as Congress and the British Government to avoid the partition. But like Churchill. Attlee too was not helpful to Wavell. When Wavell went to England in 1946, partition was one of the four possible causes that he purported to the British Government but he did not record it. Only when he came home after relinquishing the change in March 1947, did he say that if a final effort to bring the parties together failed, arrangements should be put in hand for partition.

The Cabinet Mission and Pakistan

On February 1946, it was announced in both houses of British parliament that in view of the paramount importance not only in India and to the British Commonwealth but to the peace of the world of a successful outcome of the discussions with the leaders of Indian opinion, the Government had decided to send out to India a special mission of cabinet ministers to seek in association with the Viceroy an agreement with these leaders on the principles and procedure relating to the constitutional issues. The members of the mission were to be Lord Pethick Lawrence, the Secretary of State for India, Sir Stafford Cripps, the President of the Board of Trade and Mr. Alexander, the first lord of the Admiralty.[12]

Further statements by the British threw additional light upon the nature of the mission's task which was essentially to help the Viceroy give effect to the programme outlined in his statement of September 19, 1945; that is to say, the bringing into being of, first a constitutional making body and secondly, an interim executive council supported by the main Indian parties. There was no intention that the mission should take part in framing a Constitution for India that was the responsibility of India's and themselves. Nor would they like Sir Stafford Cripps, who in 1942, had taken with them definite proposals on which to base their negotiations.

Besides the three members of the Cabinet Mission, eleven civil servants and hangers-on accompanied Sir Stafford Cripps had been sent to the solution of the 'Indian question'. The Labour government was under this impression that Cripps was only person who understood the Indian question. As Nehru had written to a friend in 1942, Cripps had surprising woodenness and insensitiveness. In spite of his public smiles, always he seemed to impress upon us that he knew the Indian problems in and out and he had found the only situation for it. Cripps was confident he could find a settlement in India.

As Secretary of State for India, Pethick Lawrence was the official leader of the delegation, but he had no experience in the art of diplomatic negotiation. Cripps was the only one of the three delegates, who had the capacity to solve constitutional problems. He had great mental ability but poor judgment, as Sardar Patel told Wavell that Cripps told different things to different people. The third member of the delegation was Alexander, who had no previous experience of India. He found politicians who dressed in *dhotis* 'baffling and tricky'.[13] He was a Labour Party imperialist.

The delegation was joined by Wavell in his capacity as Governor General and has its meeting with the Indian nationalist politicians on April 1, 1946. Soon they had meeting with Mohammad Ali Jinnah. Wavell recorded at the end of the meeting that 'we had made no progress whatsoever'. Jinnah's demand was becoming more firm. Alexander observed that Jinnah was the only man I know who walks around with a built-in air cooler. If the delegation talked with Jinnah on the economic validity of Pakistan or on Defence, the talk did not make any progress. He was not ready to give up his demand for Pakistan. Muslims were prepared to start a *Jihad* for the achievement of Pakistan but Jinnah felt that the *Jihad* would be disastrous.

Jinnah's grip on Muslims of the country was tremendous. One prominent member of the Muslim League spoke in a convention in Delhi in April 1946 that a bullet first would pierce a larger member of Muslims than would touch Jinnah. Sardar Shaukat Hayat Khan, son of Sikander Hyat Khan, said: 'I represent the martial claim of Pakistan, who does not believe in words but in actions . . . . . I speak for the Punjab soldier and I say that three-quarter million demoralized soldiers in the Punjab are pledged to achieve Pakistan.' We beg to you to give the words of command.[14] Wavell told Nehru, Congress was asking the delegation to hand over India to a single Party, which was not liked by Muslims. Nehru called the interim government a 'provisional national government' with full sovereignty powers. The Viceroy recorded in journal that Congress so far from giving away anything, have increased their demands, and Jinnah has not conceded an acre of Pakistan.

Since the proclaimed objectives of Congress and the League were diametrically opposite, the mission's task of bringing them to an agreement was difficult, indeed a seemingly impossible one. The Congress wanted a united India. The League wanted India to be divided and the Muslim majority provinces of the north-east and the north-east formed into a completely independent and sovereign state of Pakistan. But the mission believed, not incorrectly and it proved, that the League might accept something less than complete independence for Pakistan, and it was in this belief that they went to work.

After two weeks of discussion, the mission told Jinnah that if he insisted on a fully sovereign Pakistan it would have to be of the truncated variety, excluding most of Assam and half of Bengal and the Punjab. It was said that it would be impossible to include in an independent Muslim state, large areas in which Hindus were in a majority. A truncated Pakistan did not appeal to Jinnah. Then the mission put to him as an alternative proposal for a three-tiered constitution—provinces, groups or sub-federations of provinces and a union under which the groups of provinces—that he claimed for Pakistan would have a large measure of autonomy and would be joined with the rest of India in a union conferred to the control of Defence, foreign affairs and communication. To sweeten this proposal it was indicated that in the all-India union, the Hindu majority and the Muslim majority groups of provinces might have equal representation and that there might be provision for a province to have the right to secede from the union after a period of years. With considerable reluctance the Congress and Jinnah were induced to accept this proposal as a possible basis for negotiation and to agree to send representative to Simla to discuss it.

It appeared from the attitude of the Labour Government headed by Attlee that he wanted to maintain India as a loose and united federation.[15] He did not like Jinnah and his demand for Pakistan. The problem before the Prime Minister was whether Jinnah would accept this compromise formula. On April 11, 1946, Attlee held a meeting of the cabinet and the cabinet gave a formal authorization of Pakistan for the first time. The British Government changed its policy from unity to division, but it could be done as a last resort. It was made clear in the minutes of the cabinet that the cabinet mission should strive to maintain unity, but could accept homeland if they were satisfied that there was no other basis on which an agreement settlement could be reached[16] so the mission was now ready for the Simla Conference.

The Simla Conference, 1946

The mission proved out of the heat of Delhi to the cold climate of Simla at the beginning of May and the second stage of their work began.[17] Those who assembled at Simla, they had to discuss on the basis of the positions that had been outlined in New Delhi; besides the victory and all the three members of the cabinet mission, representatives of the Congress and the Muslim League attended the conference. The Congress had been represented by Pandit Nehru, Maulana Azad, Sardar Patel and Khan Abdul Gaffar Khan and the League by M.A. Jinnah, Liyakat Ali Khan, Sardar Rab Nistar and Muhammad Ismail. Gandhi attended the conference at the mission's request. The mission gave both parties a document containing suggested point for agreement, which elaborated the idea already put forward that there should be a constitutional structure in three tiers, consisting of a union, group and provinces. Wavell, Cripps, Alexander and Pethick Lawrence sat on one side and opposite them four representatives of each Party. There was manifest mutual hostility. Jinnah refusing to shake hands with Azad at the opening session, and calling him as a "stooge" of the Hindus, Muslims called Azad not only as a 'stooge' and 'slow-boy' but also as "the dog of the Hindus". Two Muslims were in the Congress side Azad and Khan Abdul Gaffar Khan. Azad appeared uninfluential to Wavell. Khan Abdul Gaffar Khan, who sat with his head wrapped in a Khadi shawl saying little and Wavell, took him to be 'stupid but obstinate'.[18] The serious negotiation was done for Congress by Nehru who was able and clear in statement and Sardar Vallabhbhai Patel, whom Wavell described as having a Roman face, powerful, claver and uncompromising. Gandhi also intervened, whenever he thought necessary to intervene.[19]

The Simla Conference started from 5th May, as the conference faced difficulties, the cabinet mission suggested further points for possible agreement; that as a concession to the Congress viewpoint, the original list of the union subjects, viz. foreign affairs, defence and communications could be enlarged by the addition of fundamental rights[20] and—that the Union Government should have the necessary powers to obtain for itself. The finances it required for three subjects—to make the union acceptable to the League, it was suggested that the constituent assembly should divide up into three sections, one representing the Hindu majority province, the second representing the Muslim majority provinces and the third representing the states. The first-two sections would then meet separately and decide provisional constitutions for their groups and if they wished group constitution.

To counter balance the Congress objection to the compulsory grouping of provinces in a section, the cabinet mission proposed that a province should have the freedom to opt out of the original group and go to another group or remain out of any group by a majority of the votes of its representatives, if the provincial or group constitution was not acceptable to it. The three sections would then meet to frame the union constitution, under the union constitution, there would thus be three sub-federation; one of the Muslim majority provinces, another of the Hindu majority provinces and the third of the states. The Muslim majority provinces would have the parity of representation in the union legislature as well as in the union government with the Hindu majority provinces irrespective of whether the province in question formed themselves into groups or not. Further, to compensate the Muslims League for the possible loss through opting out of the N.W.F.P. from the Muslim majority group and for exclusion of Assam from the same which the League demanded for the Muslim majority group; it was proposed that there should be the additional safeguard that no measures affecting a communal issue in the union constitution would be passed unless the majority of both the major communities voted in its favour.

The Congress was prepared to accept the formation of groups provided it was entirely optional. It, however, held that this would be for the representatives of the provinces. The Congress was prepared to do anything within the boundaries of reason to remove fear and suspicion from the mind of any province or community but it felt itself unable to endorse any suggestion that went against the basic method of democracy on which it hoped to build up a constitution. Thus on fundamental issue the deadlock was complete. The Congress insisted that the union constitution be framed first, the League, after the group constitutions were drafted. The Congress insisted on the optional character of the groups; the League demanded that they should be compulsory. The Congress insisted on the right of the union to raise revenue by taxation, the League refused.

Failure of the conference seemed inevitable, the Congress, thereupon suggested that an umpire should be appointed by the Congress and the Muslim League to settle matter of differences between them. The suggestion was turndown by the League.

On May 12, 1946, the Second Simla Conference was closed down by Lord Pethick Lawrence, as there was no prospect of agreement. The cabinet delegation issued a statement on 16th May. It was made clear in the statement that the aim of the mission was to create a constituent assembly of elected representative from the eleven provinces who would frame a new constitution. The Cabinet Mission outlined 'scheme A' promoting a unitary state with a weak centre controlling foreign affairs, communications and defence, the provinces being free to form autonomous regional groups. The document opposed the creation of Pakistan. On June 6, 1946 the Muslim League accepted the May statement; while stating it represented 'first step on the road to Pakistan'. It showed that Jinnah was willing to compromise in his search for a better deal.

The Cabinet Mission with the "full approval of his Majesty's Government in the United Kingdom" published their own recommendations. Their plan consisted of two parts. The long term plan for the setting up a constitution making body and the short to decide after the Constituent Assembly had framed the constitution for the all India federal union. The Muslim League, on the other hand, demanded that there should be a separate constitution making body for the six 'Muslim provinces', namely the Punjab, the N.W.F.P., Baluchistan, Sind, Bengal and Assam, although Assam was a Hindu majority province from the very beginning.

After the constitution of the Pakistan federal government and the provinces framed the constitution making bodies of the two groups the Pakistan group and the Hindustan group setting together would deal with the three subjects, namely foreign affairs, defence and communications necessary for defence.

There were other points of differences; the Congress wanted the Union Government to have the power to raise the finances required for the discharge of its functions by taxation. The Muslim League insisted that the federal union should in no event have the power to raise revenues in its own rights but only by contribution.

The League further wished that no decision legislative, executive or administrative—should be taken by the union in regard to any matter of a controversial nature except by a majority of three-fourth.[21]

The Congress agreed to optional grouping of provinces and a Muslim veto on the communal issues in order to allay the anxiety of the Muslims, so that Hindus and Muslims might be able to live together as one nation in their common motherland. The Muslim League regarded the proposals that had been made 'as a strategic gain in its battle for Pakistan'. Congress, on the other hand, was of the opinion that it was not up to the Simla Conference to arrange for the division of India.

As had been feared from the very beginning, the difficulty about parity in regard to the executive or the legislature as between seven Hindu majority provinces, and the five Muslim majority provinces, proved insurmountable.[22] This is worse than Pakistan, wrote Gandhi to Sir Stafford Cripps on the 8th May. As the way out he suggested that an "imperial non-British Tribunal" should make an Award on this issue as on any other matters of difference otherwise incapable of adjustment between the League and the Congress term proposal for the formation of an "interim government".

The issue was whether India was to be partitioned or whether it was to remain undivided. Attlee announced the mission's opposition to Jinnah's claim regarding partition. The Viceroy also favoured a united India. the British Cabinet Mission plan of 16th May, 1946 clearly stated, "A separate sovereign state of Pakistan on the lines claimed by the Muslim League would not solve the communal minority problem—we are, therefore, unable to advise the British Government that the power which at present resides in British hands should be handed over to two entirely separate sovereign states."[23]

In place of Muslim League's demand of Pakistan, the cabinet mission, recommended their . . . . . . "Three-tier scheme" of 16th May 1946 foreshadowed in their, suggested points for agreement at the Simla conference.

According to Dorothy Norman, Muslims in the majority provinces would exercise almost complete autonomy only certain agreed subjects would be dealt with at the section level. Here also the Muslim were assured of a majority in sections B and C and it was hoped that Muslim would be able to satisfy all their legitimate hopes. So far as the centre was concerned, there were only three subjects which from the nature of the case could not be provincially administered.[24]

The long range plan followed the 'fundamental principle' of Pethick Lawrence. It had been mentioned that the sections would meet to form groups and to draft the provincial and group constitution. Each province would have the right to opt out of a group by a simple majority of its legislature after the first elections under the new provincial constitution.

The May 16, cabinet mission plan was an ambiguous one. As Pyarelal has commented; their 16 May plan was fashioned somewhat after the heroine on one of Goethe's classics in whose lineament everybody saw an image of his own beloved.[25] There was in it something for everybody. To the Congress it offered a common centre, though in an alternated form, and freedom of choice to provinces to form groups or not. To the Muslim League it held out the prospect of Muslim Zones to be formed in the north-east and the north-east of India by making it obligatory on the representative of the provinces to sit in sections to settle the provisional constitutions. To the Indian states it offered release from paramount which was not to be transferred to the successor government. To the Sikhs it held out the prospect of preserving intact the integrity of their homeland.

The Muslim League was serious to take advantage of the language of pure Urdu Jinnah declared that he found in the cabinet delegation's plan the basis of Pakistan and accordingly, the Muslim League council, on the June 6, resolved that "inasmuch as the basis and the foundation of Pakistan are inherent the missions plan by virtue of compulsory grouping of the six Muslim provinces in sections B and C, they were willing to cooperate with the constitution—making machinery proposed by the mission". No secret was made of the hope that "it would ultimately result in the establishment of complete sovereign Pakistan" which had been ruled out by the cabinet delegation in their statement. Thus the all India Muslim League council accepted the cabinet mission's proposals by an overwhelming majority.[26]

In the face of deadlock the Cabinet Mission put forward its own recommendation. On June 16, 1946 it proposed the formation of an interim government consisting of six Hindu members of the Congress, one being an untouchable, five Muslims of the League and three representatives of the minorities, one Sikh, one Christian and one Parsi. Jinnah had scored another victory, because all Muslim seats were to be filled up by Jinnah's nominees including the seat of a nationalist Muslim. Further more, all five League nominees were approved but three Congress nominees were replaced without consulting the Party.

This hope had been expressed by the Cabinet Mission and the victory that all parties especially the two major parties would accept this proposal, so as to overcome the present obstacles and would cooperate for the successful carrying on the interim government.[27]

The Congress Working Committee subsequently considered the Cabinet Mission's statements of 16th May and 16th June in its session from 20th June to 25th June.[28] After reviewing both sets of proposal, the committee rejected the mission's plan for an interim government at the centre, while agreeing to the long term plan, but with its own interpretation of disputed clauses. Essentially, Congress continued to desire creation of a free united democratic Indian federation, with a central authority.

The council of all India Muslim League passed a resolution on 6th June, accepting the cabinet the Cabinet Mission's proposals, subject, however, to a host of reservation. The council protested against the references made and the conditions recorded in the statement with regard to the Muslim demand for the establishment of a full sovereign Pakistan, and declared that a separate sovereign Pakistan was still the unalterable objective of the Muslims in India.[29]

Jinnah made a public statement on 17th June, that the leaders of Congress spoke only for the higher castes.[30] They certainly do not represent the Muslims and mere fact that they have a handful of Muslim henchmen for the purpose of window dressing cannot give the national character which they claim, not to represent India. This was followed soon afterwards by an ominous assertion that the Muslim League thought constitutional methods had failed.

Assessment of Cabinet Mission

The Cabinet Mission returned to London on 30th June, 1946. They did not meet Wavell at the time of departure. The Cabinet Mission failed and created more problems than they solved and the last chance to retain a united India disappeared.

This statement is true that Woodrow Wyatt's assertion that the cabinet delegation tried to give away an empire but found that their every suggestion for doing it frosted by the intended recipients. The British intransigence was partially responsible for decolonization. The different Indian leaders had not made up their minds for the term on which they would take independence from the British Government. So the British policy and the attitudes of the Indian leaders were responsible for the failure of the Cabinet Mission. Patrick French commented that in the end "the cabinet delegation created more problems than they solved, and the last chance to retain a united India disappeared". After the departure of the mission Wavell went to Simla for a rest. He was busy for four months in the negotiations. He had also to carry on the administration. Had the cabinet delegation succeeded to some extent, federation might have been established. If a federal government would have been in the office, bloodshed would have been avoided from 16th August, 1946. Punjab and Bengal might have not succeeded. The DIB was furnishing a gloomy picture of the law and order of the country. The DIB had reported to Viceroy Wavell in this way "he considered the country ripe for serious trouble". The chief of DIB Norman Smith ordered the disposal of certain dangerous CID records; the more important documents being returned to London.

On the question of political advisor Wavell added that "if the Prime Minister would rather have a politician than a soldier at the head of India at present, he would be perfect happy. I have no personal ambition."[31] Wavell had his own assessment on the working of the Simla Conference, Wavell had concluded that the failure of the mission had stemmed from the 'duplicity' of Cripps, the 'objective attitude of the delegation as a whole, the 'unyielding' approach of Jinnah and the fact that Congress had known that if it sat tight it could not be dislodged. The mission gave away the weakness of our position and our bluff has been called. The Viceroy wrote in desperation in his journal: 'our time in India is limited and our power to control events almost gone'. Wavell had recorded in his diary in May. "The Muslim League is deeply suspicious of Congress under its present leadership and more particularly of Mr. Gandhi. I think the Muslim League would be prepared to work with the moderate Congress elements, if I could get rid of its extreme left and Mr. Gandhi's influence. The former is only likely to be removed by a violent conflict, the latter only by the normal process of a non-violent old age. So long as the left wing of congress continues to excuse influence, and Mr. Gandhi throws his authority, it is going to be almost impossible to obtain Hindu-Muslim cooperation. Wavell had recorded in his diary in May, "The Muslim League is deeply suspicious of Congress under its present leadership and more particularly of Mr. Gandhi. I think the Muslim League would be prepared to work with the moderate Congress elements, if I could get rid of its extreme left and Mr. Gandhi's influence. The former is only likely to be removed by a violent conflict, the latter only by the normal process of a non-violent old age. So long as the left wing of Congress continues to excuse influence, and Mr. Gandhi throws his authority, it is going to be almost impossible to obtain Hindu-Muslim cooperation."

Wavell had his own assessment on the working of the Simla Conference, Wavell had concluded that the failure of the mission had stemmed from the 'duplicity' of Cripps, the 'objective attitude' of the delegation as a whole, the 'unyielding' approach of Jinnah and the fact that Congress had known that if it sat tight it could not be dislodged. The mission gave away the weakness of our position and our bluff has been called. The Viceroy wrote in desperation in his journal: 'our time in India is limited and our power to control events almost gone'.

Wavell was ruffled in July 1946. He had no clear instruction from the Government. He thought it difficult to control the country which was falling apart. Wavell wrote a letter to King George VI on 5th July, 1946, we must try to leave India united and we must secure the cooperation of the Congress, which represents the great majority of Indian political opinion, what their other views on the past record of that Party.

The important thing of Simla conference was Wavell's own assessment about the Indian leaders. About Gandhi he writes : "he never makes a pronouncement that is not so qualified and so vaguely worded that it cannot be interpreted on whatever sense best suits him at a later stage". Jinnah was lonely, unhappy, arbitrary, self-centred man, fighting with so much resolution what I fear is a losing battle 'Azad was a gentleman and stood for good sense and moderation ...... But up against Gandhi he was a rabbit faced with a stoat', Khan Abdul Gaffar Khan 'whose intelligence and grasp of English are both limited, was regarded by Jinnah as a gratuitous and deliberate provocation', Nehru he found 'sincere intelligent and personally courageous. But he is unbalanced—witness his ploy in Kashmir'. This referred to an episode during the negotiations when Nehru had decamped to the princely state of Kashmir to defend Seikh

Abdullah, the leader of the pro-Congress National Conference, who had been agitating against the Maharaja.

The rest of the Congress Working Committee was dismissed as 'poor staff', with the exception of Sardar Patel, who was 'by the most forcible character among them'. Patel was the only politician, British or Indian, for whom Wavell seems to have had, undimmed respect, despite believing that his nature is fascist and he is always likely to be on the side of direct action and if necessary violence . . . . . . He is communal and has no sense of compromise or generosity towards Muslims, but he is more of a man most of the Hindu politicians.' Later he wrote that although Patel believed "the Muslim League should be fought and suppressed—we respect one another."

By the views of Cripps, Attlee was dissatisfied. Cripps had reported to Prime Minister Attlee that due to Wavell, Party leaders did not come to meet him. Attlee remarked that "if the Prime Minister would rather have a politician than a soldier at the end of India at present, he would be perfectly happy. I have no personal ambition."

NOTES

1. *Transfer of Power*, Vol. VI, p. 739.
2. Wyatt Woodrow, *Confession of an Optimist*, London, 1985.
3. *Transfer of Power*, Vol. VI, p. 789.
4. *Ibid.*, p. 950.
5. *Ibid.*, p. 699.
6. Hassan, Mushirul (edited), *India Partitioned (1)*, vol. I, p. 44.
7. *Ibid.*, p. 701.
8. *Ibid.*, p. 913.
9. *Ibid.*, p. 912.
10. *Ibid.*
11. *Ibid.*, p. 965.
12. Hasan (ii), Vol. I, p. 14.
13. Moon (2), p. 215.
14. Norman Dorothy, *Nehru II*, p. 305.
15. French, Patrick, *Liberty or Death*, p. 228.
16. Pirzada, Syed Shrofuddin, (edited), *Founders of Pakistan*, Karachi, 1969- 1990. p. 230
17. PROCAB 128/5, April 11, 1946.
18. French, Patrick, *Liberty or Death*, p. 238.
19. Wyatt, p. 149.

20. Moon (2), p. 259.
21. Norman, Dorothy, *Nehru II*, pp. 225-226.
22. Pyarelal, *Mahatma Gandhi*, *I*, p. 206.
23. Norman, Dorothy, *Nehru*, *II*, p. 230
24. *Ibid.*
25. Pyarelal, *Mahatma Gandhi*, p. 212.
26. The Annual Indian Delegation 1946, Vol. I, p. 60.
27. Norman, Dorothy, *Nehru II*, p. 233.
28. *Ibid.*
29. Mishra, S.G., *C.D. and National Movement*, p. 259.
30. *Transfer of Power*, Vol. II, p. 1072.
31. *Transfer of Power*, Vol. VIII, p. 167.

9

Nehru's Press Conference in Bombay on July 10 and the London Conference

Pandit Jawaharlal Nehru was elected the President of the Congress for the fourth time in the first week of July 1946.[1] The real story behind the 1946 election was very different. In accordance with the time honoured practice of rotating of presidency, Patel was in line for the post. Many years later Durga Das sought Kriplani's explanation for Gandhi's preference for Nehru as against Patel. Kriplani said that like this saint and holy people, Gandhi wanted significant mind for the President. A legend had grown round and the scarifies made by the Nehru's for national freedom and Gandhi, therefore, preferred him. In so far as Jawaharlal Nehru's election was concerned, Kriplani added, all the PCC's sent in the name of Patel by a majority and one or two proposed the names of Raja Babu in addition, but none that of Jawaharlal. Kriplani knew that Gandhi wanted Jawaharlal to be President for a year and he made a proposal himself saying, some Delhi fellows want Jawaharlal's name. Kriplani circulated it to the members of the Working Committee to get their endorsement. Kriplani played this mischief. Patel never forgave Kriplani for this mischief. Patel was a great executive, organizer and leader. So the Mahatma preferred Nehru, because of his greater international prestige. Gandhi himself had made a remark to a prayer meeting on the eve of partition; Jawaharlal cannot be replaced today, what the charge is being taken from Englishman. He is a harrow boy, a Cambridge graduate and a barrister, is wanted to carry on the negotiations with Englishman.

On being asked, Gandhi said that Patel would have proved a better negotiator and organizer as Congress president but he felt Nehru should head the government. Further Gandhi said that

Jawaharlal is the only Englishman in my camp. In the last Gandhi had said, Jawaharlal will not take second place. He is better known abroad than Sardar and will make India play a role in international affairs, Sardar will look after the country's affairs.[2] Nehru presided over AICC on 6th July and 7th July, 1946 at Bombay, when the AICC met. The AICC was to consider and ratify its ruse decisions. The debate was spirited but outcome was never in doubt. The policy enunciated by the working committee was approved by 204 to 57. Yet the Congress was unhappy about the plans, as evident in Nehru's speech on July 7, 1946. The speech ran as follows: "the Congress idea of independence is certainly different from what the Muslim League or the Viceroy thinks. Our idea of independence is that there must be absolutely no foreign domination in India and that India may even break her connection with British. There is a good deal of talk of the Cabinet Mission's long term plan and short term plan. So far as I can see, it is not a question of agreeing to go into the constituent assembly. We will remain in that assembly as long as we think it is good for India and we will come out when we think it is injuring our cause and then offer battle."[3]

The council of all India Muslim League passed a resolution on 6th June accepting the cabinet mission's proposals subject, however, to a host of reservations. The council protested against the reference made and the conclusions recorded in the statement with regard to the Muslim demand for the establishment of a full sovereign state of Pakistan and declared that a separate sovereign Pakistan was still the unalterable objective of the Muslims in India.

The Congress had accepted the cabinet mission's statements of May 16, with certain reservations. On 10th July, Pandit Nehru held a press conference in Bombay and made a statement, which resulted in a most unfortunate series of consequences.

In reply to a request for implication of the statement made in the all India Congress Committee to the effect that Congress had made no commitment with regard to either the long or the short term plan of the cabinet mission except to enter the constituent assembly.

Pandit Nehru

If you read the correspondence that has passed between the Congress President and the Cabinet Mission and Viceroy, you will be (under) what condition and circumstances we agreed to go into (a) and we have agreed to nothing else. It is true that in going (into) the constituent assembly, the inevitably, we have agreed to a certain process of going into it, that is, election of the candidates of the constituent assembly, what we do there we are entirely and absolutely free to determine, we have committed ourselves (on) no single matter to anybody.[4] The Cabinet Mission reply was more or less 'yes', subject to two considerations (first), proper arrangement for minorities and (second) a treaty between India and England. I wish the cabinet mission had stated that both these matters are not controversial.

In regard to minorities, it is our problem and we shall no doubt succeed in solving it. We shall accept the outside interference, certainly not the British Government's interference.

How to make the role in the constituent assembly a success or not is the only binding factor. It does not make the slightest difference what the cabinet mission thinks or does in the matter.

Of the Power of the Proposed Union Centre

According to the Cabinet Mission's proposal there were three or four basic subjects in it, i.e. Defence, Foreign Affairs, Communications have a large number of industries behind them. So these industries inevitably should come under the union government and they are likely to grow. Defence is such a wide subject that it tends to expand the scope and activities more and more, all that comes under the union government.

Suppose there is trouble between the provinces or states, or an enormous breakdown due to famine conditions. The centre comes in again, neutrally, however, limited the centre might be you cannot help its having wide powers, because the past few years have shown that if there were no central authority conditions would have been far worse in India . . . . . . the scope of centre even though limited, inevitably grows because it cannot exist anywhere.

About the grouping scheme, Nehru was clear. It would probably never come to fruition, he declared, because section A, the Hindu majority provinces, would be opposed, the frontier province would oppose it in section B as would Assam in section C, and provincial realities would thwart it.[5]

Comments

The press conference of Pandit Nehru is considered to be much controversial. Various scholars have interpreted it in various ways. Prof. Michael Brecher, Nehru's first biographer, has commented in this way. There was much politician insight in Nehru's speech. Few would deny that the Frontier and Assam, both Congress provinces at the time, would opt out\of their groups, if given an opportunity to do so in 1946. Has reference to provincial jealousness found ample support in the post-partition history of West Pakistan and India? So to do his observations on a strong centre; both India and Pakistan have had frequent recoveries to 'emergency powers' since independence. Even on October 12, 1999, the Army Chief General Parvez Mussarraf, who proclaimed himself the chief executive of the country after overthrowing Nawaz Sharif's government. This coup of 1979 in Pakistan is a hot empowerment over the earlier coups. There General Parvez Chairman of the Joint Chiefs of Staff Committee and Chief of Army Staff has not proclaimed the martial law on seizing power but simply has declared only a state of emergency as India has done in 1975.[6] Whether it was wise to utter such views in the political atmosphere of 1946 is another question.[7] Nehru's remark certainly cleared the air of confusion and hypocrisy. At the same time they destroyed the façade of arrangements which the Cabinet Mission tried to maintain. In fact the speech sparked the collapse of mission. There was nothing fundamentally new in his speech, but it was a serious tactical error.[8]

Mr. Leonard Mosley has commented in this way: "it was a moment in history when circumspection should have been the order of the day. There was much to be gained by silence. The fortunes of India were in the balance, and one false move could upset them. In the circumstances, Nehru's remarks were a direct act of sabotage.

The Press Conference has also been called 'explosives' and 'historic changing'. According to Maulana Azad 'the Press Conference was one of those unfortunate events which changed the course of history'.[9] In his introduction to the book, Louise Fischer, an American journalist, recounts after the above conference question and answer period, he himself, had addressed Nehru, "you have changed the entire basis of the agreement with England". To which, according to Fischer, Nehru smilingly replied, "I am fully aware of that". Fischer refers to the fact that, in view of what had appeared to be an affirmative vote of the all

India Congress committee with regard to the mission plan, what Nehru said 'changed' everything. It should be noted in this connection that although Fischer, as well as Azad, were perturbed by Nehru's remark of 10th July. Azad himself stated on the same date as also recorded in the Indian Annual Register, 'if unfortunately any inseparable difficulties crop up in direct conflict with our fundamental principles. We shall not hesitate to kill the constituent assembly. Wavell called Nehru's statement as hasty and intemperate.

In reply to a question by Dorothy Norman about Azad's criticism of July 10, 1946 press conference, Nehru said, "I am sorry to confess that I have no very clear idea of the day-to-day occurrence in those days, it was a great burden of occurrences, events, happenings, all over, and tremendous strain under which we are functioning in that interim government as it was called, inside the government, I mean apart from the occurrence outside, because of Muslim League Party were out, as they openly said, to prevent us from functioning satisfactorily, ... So how can I judge how far, I am responsible?"

Mine was certainly part of responsibility, and Maulana Sahib may be completely right in thinking that I acted wrongly, only I would say this, that Maulana Sahib thinks too much in individual terms, sometimes, not in terms of historic forms at work. Individual make a difference and have made a difference but sometimes individuals are only symbol of forces at work.

Though there has been too much comments of this press conference, but Pandit Nehru spoke nothing new here. He had already explained his reservations about the Cabinet Mission plan. The Muslim League had expressed reservations about the mission's statement of 16th June concerning negotiation for an interim government. The League also raised objections, at the same time, both to the mission's long range plans, as well as to Congress reacting to the mission's proposals. It is a different thing whenever Nehru should have opened his mouth on this delicate question or not. But Jinnah made it a plea or refused of the mission's statement.

The Cabinet Mission's Plan and Statement : A Commentary

It was a complicated plan; the three tier scheme was impracticable. This scheme had brought endless friction between the Congress and the League. The administrative machinery should have broken down under this unworkable scheme. Cripps was an intellectual being and he wanted to solve the Indian problem intellectually. He wanted to satisfy both parties. Prof. Michael Brecher's comments runs thus: he was riding two horses at the same time, trying to find a solution on paper which both parties would accept.[10] His proposal, in fact, would have brought Pakistan in through the back door, by the group scheme and would have maintained the façade of the united India. As long as the two Indian parties disagreed on the fundamentals, any plan was doomed. The communal riots caused failure of the Cabinet Mission plan.

The great advantage of British had during this crucial time was their secret intelligence. They had spies and police informers all over the Indian Empire, as well as interrupts of letters, telegrams and telephone calls, which often enabled them to stay one step ahead. Congress had been aware of these underhand activities for many years, and generally used carriers to carry important communications of any kind. The historian Z.A. Zaidi has written that a study of intelligence bureau material soon reinforced my conviction that one of the factors which has sustained British rule in India was the competence of the intelligence service which had been able to penetrate the most difficult and sensitive areas.[11]

Leave Her to Her Fate

The Viceroy's Private Secretary George Abell and Abell's deputy Ian Scott had told him that they have come to this conclusion that our only course is to get out of India as soon as possible, and leave her to her fate, which will be civil war.[12] On August 19, 1946, the Chief of Staff met in Downing Street and was joined by Auchinbek, the Commander-in-Chief in India. They considered a report from the joint intelligence-staff, which suggested that in the event of civil war...... the Indian force as a whole cannot be relied on.[13] Auchinbek's reaction to this was that the situation was a little better than it had been a few weeks before and provided the Indian army remained loyal, he had ample force to deal with any situation that might arise.[14] But this optimistic statement turned false, when the great Calcutta killings began on August 16, 1946.

Direct Action

After July 10, 1946, Jinnah pressed more for Pakistan. Jinnah advanced this argument that Congress would not safeguard the Muslim interest on ground of its tyranny. So the Council of all India Muslim League concluded its three-day session after passing two resolutions, one rejecting the British Cabinet delegation's proposals and the other deciding to resort to 'direct action' for the achievement of Pakistan.[15]

According to M.A. Jinnah and the Muslim League, it appeared that the British and the Congress were slipping back into the belief that they together settle the future of India without concessions to the Muslims. August 16, 1946 was, therefore, fixed by the League as "Direct Action" day.[16] In most of India it passed off without violence but in Calcutta there started that day as uncontainable mass slaughter that spread across most of northern India and lasted for the 16 months, some historians neither Congress nor the League had ever truly accepted the Cabinet Mission's long range plan despite having at one time or another normally approved it—'the British Labour Government and the Cabinet Mission members whom it had sent to India, were in truth in wanting to Transfer Power.'[17]

In 29th July call for 'direct action' to attain Pakistan, the League set up a council of action to remind Muslims that it was in the month of Ram-uh-Zan that the first open conflict between Islam and Hinduism was fought and won by three hundred and thirteen Muslims in Arabia. A leaflet containing a special prayer for the crusade announced that ten crores of Muslims and the British would be starting a *jihad*[18] in this month of Ram-uh-Zan.[19] A leaflet bearing a picture of Jinnah with sword in hand stated, "we Muslims have had the crown and have ruled. Be ready and take your swords . . . . . O Kafir! Your doom is not far and the general massacre will come". Jinnah further told, "what we have done today is the most historic act in our history. Never have we in the whole history of the League done anything except by constitutional methods and by constitutionalism. This day we bid good bye to constitutional methods—today we have also forgot a pistol and are in a position to use it."[20]

Just a week before 29th July resolution calling for 'Direct Action' the Viceroy resumed his efforts to convince both Nehru and Jinnah that a coalition interim government at the centre should be formed, giving assurances that would give the interim government the same consideration as a domain government. On August 6, 1946 the Viceroy acting under instruction from London, invited Nehru to submit proposals for formation of an interim government, because the Muslim League had refused to come in, so at the request of Viceroy, Pandit Nehru went to meet Jinnah at his house in Bombay on the morning of August 16, 1946 to plead with him to forget 'Direct Action' and bring the League into the government.

The meeting lasted for eighty minutes, Pandit Nehru failed in persuading Mr. Jinnah to change his mind. As Morley had said, "Pandit Nehru departed more convinced than ever this man really stood in the way of India's freedom, more determined than ever to destroy him and the myth of Pakistan, which he had created, and yet still unaware of how strong Jinnah really was, how powerful was his hold on Muslim India." Mr. Morley's statement is motivated, prejudiced and far from truth. There is no documentary evidence to support Mr. Morley's charge. In the monumental volume of "transfer of power" and Patrick French's well researched book *Liberty Or Death* there is no reference like this. It is a fact that Pandit Nehru did not like the concept of Pakistan and he was opposed till its formation. To dislike the concept of Pakistan and to destroy Jinnah politically are both separate issues. Therefore, Mr. Morley's statement is open to challenge.

The first inter-religious clash, which has been authenticated by records, took place in 1730 in Ahmedabad. However, the occurrence of communal conflicts as a regular social phenomenon started from 1922 onwards. Thus during 1922-1927 in a period of five years, 150 peoples died and 5,000 were injured in intermittent communal isoline in India. However, the power in which politics in India was perused after 1920 on communal lines creating adverse between these too communities provided process culminated in 1947 with the division of India.[21]

August 16, 1946 had been proclaimed 'Direct Action Day', there were three Muslim dominated province, where the communal handy might flare-up. Karachi and Punjab were Muslim areas but no disturbances could take place due to efficient machinery. The administration was quite efficient in these two provinces. The Chief Secretary of Sind government did not proclaim 16th August as a public holiday. Karachi and Punjab had an efficient British Government; Sir Evan Jenkins did not allow the situation to deteriorate.

But the Bengal Governor was under the control of the Muslim League and Mr. Saheed Suhrawardy was the Premier, Chief Minister from 1950, of Bengal. The Muslims in Bengal were cut, murdered the Hindus and other people. The Premier announced the 16th August as a central holiday in Calcutta. A mammoth rally was held in Calcutta and violence started in Calcutta. Violence was the result of the propaganda of the Muslim League in general and the Bengal League ministry in particular.

Mr. Saheed Suhrawardy managed the mob from the slain. They had come with lathis, knives, bottles and automobile cranks. Violence begin from early morning, the primary cause of outbreak of violence was Jinnah's call for a "universal Muslim hartal" as past of his plan for 'direct action' for the attainment of Pakistan. It was to take place after Friday prayer on August 16. It was to be considered a show of strength by the Muslim *quam* against the so called tyranny of the Congress rule, 1937-1939. Premier Suhrawardy encouraged the Muslims to kill the Hindus. The Muslims dominated the scene till afternoon and then Hindus and Sikhs came out on the afternoon of August 1946. Mr. Suhrawardy addressed the mass meeting in the maidan, Calcutta's main square. The unruly mob returned from the maidan began to interfere with those who did not run the hartal, direct action programme reached its culmination in the great Calcutta killing on 16th, 17th and 18th August.

It was estimated that more than five thousand injured during the great Calcutta killing.[22] Jinnah threw the entire responsibility of the communal frenzy on the cabinet delegation, the Congress and on Gandhi.

The British owned *statesman* of Calcutta placed the blame on the League; "the origin of the appalling carnage and loss in the capital of a great province, we believe the worst communal riots in India's history were a political demonstration by the Muslim League. It wrote on 30th August when the killing had subsided. The bloody shamble to which this country's largest city has been reduced is an abounding disgrace which has inevitably tarnished seriously the all India reputation of the League itself. The *statesman* further writes. This is not a riot. It need a word found in medieval history, 'a funny'. The senior British military officer commented; February's killing had shocked us all but this was different. It was unbridled salvaging with homicidal manias let loose to kill and to maim and bush. The underworld of Calcutta was taking charge of the city.[23] To Jinnah and the League it appeared that the British and the Congress were slipping back into the belief that they could together settle the future of India without concessions to the Muslims. August 16, 1946 was, therefore, fixed by the League as 'direct action day'.

Soon communal violence spread throughout the poorest district of Calcutta, and to the docks, with the minority community in each place coming on the worst. The proper section were killed in larger numbers on the night of 16th August, small gang started with knives and short swords and in the morning of 17th August, several hundreds of corpses were found lying in the gutters, violence were unabated. The Governor of Bengal, Sir Fredrick Burrows, noted in a secret report;[24] I can honestly say that parts of the city on Saturday morning were as bad as anything, I saw then I was with the guards in the some—I actually saw—a crowd clubbing three unfortunate individuals to death—Many corpses were stripped and mutilated. If not until Monday 19th August, that the situation was properly under control with members of Jat, Gurkhas and Green Howard regiments patrolling the streets.

The Governor committed a serious mistake in approving the premier's demand that 16th August, should be public holiday. Burrows was said to be 'steady, sensible, straight,[25] with a slow west country speech', but he was new to the job. He had been working as Governor of Bengal for few months. So the army was in the barracks and there was minimum preparation for the possibility of rioting. The Congress Party subsequently blamed burrows for the killings and considered him as incompetent. Viceroy Wavell came to Calcutta by 23rd August. Wavell doubted whether Burrows could have predicted about the riots. Burrows had a long opinion about Suhrawardy.

By 19th August, the official report stated that four thousand people had been murdered and ten thousand wounded. According to Wavell, five thousand were killed and sixteen thousand injured. According to Patrick French six thousand people were slaughtered in the Calcutta killings. Over a hundred thousands people were left homeless. India's mass migration started for the first time in the country. Terrified groups of people left their hearths and settled in those areas of the country, where their co-religionists were in the majority, the trend still continues.

The Governor blamed the Muslim League for the initial rioting. He thought that it would be fruitless if Bengal was placed under section 93. He thought that it looked uncanny why no British or even Anglo Indian shops were looted and burnt. In February 1946, over the INA trials, European shops were also damaged. The Governor's assessment was that the riots were 'jungs' warfare and the end was politics. Two rival armies of the underworld were most active in the great Calcutta killing. It was wonder that two thousand persons of the 'goonda' type, who had been detained under the Defence of India Rules, 1939 were released between July and December 1946. Most of the killing was done by the goondas, not by mobs. Sikhs were also busy against the Muslims.

The great Calcutta killings were a disaster for the Muslim League. Muhammad Ali Jinnah had requested his people to act peacefully. Jinnah hoped the *hartal* would strengthen the negotiating position of the League through a mass power on the streets. But the consequences were just the opposite and damaged has reputation among Hindus of the country. The Congress leaders had come to this conclusion that Jinnah was guilty. Jinnah knew this fact that his followers were restless, British power was weakening and possibility of the formation of the government by the Indian National Congress was increasing, so he acted in a deliberately communal way. Jinnah was playing the communal game but he had no control in the operation of the events.

The Muslim League was responsible for the killings. There is no evidence that he personally guided the massacres. He had no idea how the criminal underworld of Calcutta might behave. Suhrawardy controlled the Bengal Muslim League and the Muslim League had given charge of direct action to Calcutta's pirs, and mullahs, who had been instructed to mobilize the Muslim community at Friday prayers.

The language of the publicity for 16th August, was clearly religious. Jinnah had forgotten all his secularism and said, let Muslims brave the rains and all difficulties and make the direct action day meeting a historic mass mobilization of the mallet. It was further said, Muslims must remember that it was in Ram-uh-Zan that the 'Quran' was revealed, it was in Ram-uh-Zan that the permission for *jihad* was granted by Allah.[26]

Wavell visited Calcutta and he was certain that rioting would spread across India. There were outbreaks in Bombay and Karachi. The Viceroy was worried that the Calcutta killings had hindered Congress leaders against Jinnah and the Muslim League. Wavell had a meeting on 27th August, he found Mahatma Gandhi 'malevolent' and Nehru 'full of hate' against the League; Gandhi and Nehru's attitudes compelled Wavell to bring the Muslim League into the interim government. Wavell thought that otherwise communal relations would break down. He was hoping that if the League joined the government, the League might be encouraged to co-operate with the Congress to remain in power.

After this meeting, Gandhi sent an angry letter to Wavell accusing him of bias towards the League and threatened that Congress would withdraw from the interim government unless you can wholly trust the Congress the Congress government which you have announced .... The Congress cannot afford to impose its billion worrying elements in India through the use of British arms.[27] Wavell knew that if there was further deterioration in political relations, there would be mass slaughter; circumstances were such that the Congress was dictating terms to Wavell and the British Government had little choice but to accept.

After this event Wavell had written a strong letter to Attlee campaigning about the conduct of the British Government. He included an intercept of the telephone conversation between Sudhir Ghosh in London and Sardar Patel in New Delhi. Sardar Patel was staying at Birla House. Patel had said, Cripps had promised while he was in India that if there was any disturbance in Calcutta he will order for section 93. What is he doing? Ghosh replied that Cripps was out of the country but he would take up the matter with another minister. Patel then told him to remain in London for further instructions. He added ominously; we are taking charge on the second of September.

Wavell was dissatisfied with this secret diplomacy. He felt that secret diplomacy would undermine his authority. He did not know that Attlee was encouraging Ghosh. He wrote a letter to Attlee, "I think it is essential that I should know your mind more fully as regards India and also that I should have a definite policy from HMG .... I cannot continue to be responsible for affairs in India if some members of your government are keeping in touch with the Congress through an independent agent behind my back."[28]

Attlee drafted three different handwritten answers to Wavell but none of them was sent. He simply sent this assurance that we are very conscious of your anxieties and the potential dangers of the situation.[29]

On this occasion in a message to Nehru, he said, "destiny has conspired to test us in new ways and we have assumed this call of destiny with courage and faith in India's future. The death of her freedom that has inspired us for so long, beckons to us again and seems nearer realization. May we prove working servants of India and her people?"

The intelligence bureau played its role in communal riots of the country before the formation of the interim government. On the eve of partition Sir P.A. Smith, Director of the British India government wrote to the Viceroy, Lord Wavell; from the British angle, the game so far has been well played...... the Indian problem has been...... placed into its appropriate plan of communalism. An opportunity for orderly evacuation (by Britain) now presents itself.

Grave communal disorder must not disturb us into action which would reintroduce anti-British agitation. The former is natural, if ghastly process tending in its own way to the solution of the Indian problem.[30]

Interim Government

The formation of interim government proved a difficult task, on August 6, 1946, the Viceroy, acting under instructions from London invited Nehru to submit proposals for formation of an interim government. On 13th August, the Viceroy put out the necessary announcement. Now Nehru made another attempt to woo Jinnah but he failed. The Muslim League refused to join the interim government. After prolonged controversy the interim government was formed on September 2, 1946 with Pandit Nehru as its Vice President. Patel was number two in the government; there were twelve members of the government.

Before the formation the interim government in September 1946, Wavell expressed a 'gloomy view' of the country's future after British withdrawal. In a report to King George VI on the aftermath of Cabinet Mission, he said, "no one can feel much confidence in ability of the Indians who will take over from us to make a strong or prosperous new India.

He added, still we will play our hand well, they are likely to continue to lean on British help, and many maintain some connection with commonwealth, but these three months' close contact with Indian politicians have certainly not enhanced any one's opinion of their political wisdom or foresight. The letter to the King sought to make an assessment of the principle Indian personalities concerned with the negotiations.

Wavell described Gandhi as 'double-tongued', Nehru as 'unbalanced', Jinnah as a 'curious character' and Khan Abdul Ghaffar Khan with 'limited intelligence'.

Wavell had kind words for Sardar Patel and Maulana Azad but dismissed the rest of the Congress Working Committee as 'poor stuff'.

The Muslim League did not join the government at the beginning. With the effort of Lord Wavell, the Muslim League nominee joined the interim government on October 26, 1946. Five Muslim League nominees joined the government, three Congress members resigned and two more were added, now members of the government were as follows :

1. Pandit Jawaharlal Nehru,
2. Sardar Ballabhbhai Patel,
3. Dr. Rajendra Prasad,
4. Mr. Asaf Ali,
5. Mr. C. Rajagopalachari,
6. Liaquat Ali Khan,
7. Dr. John Mathai,
8. Sardar Baldeo Singh,
9. L.I. Chundrigar,
10. Jagjivan Ram,
11. Abdur Rab Nistar,
12. C.H. Bhave,
13. Ghazanfar Ali Khan, and
14. Jogendra Nath Mandal.

Mandal belonged to the Scheduled Castes. The names are not in the order of seniority. The League nominees converted the interim government into an arena of communal conflict.

Jinnah Set Off a Wave of Violence

The interim government had to face the Noakhali riots on the 10th October, 1946. So the scene shifted to the Noakhali district of eastern Bengal. This was the work of the Muslim gangs, who went on rampage, killing, looting, converting Hindus by force and destroying Hindu temples and property. Besides being communal, there were other reasons for the Noakhali disturbances. This disturbances could be traced out from social conflict—debtors against creditors, the landless against the landlords, the bosses against the workers most of all, India's goondas, to badmasses and ruffians took part in the unhappy episode. In a report from a relief centre in Noakhali, in the first week of November, Mess Mural Lister, the English Pacifist and well known social worker of Kingsley hall, wrote; the worst of all was the plight of women. Several of them had to watch their husbands being murdered and then she was forcibly married to someone those responsible for their husband's death. These women had a deadlock; it was not despair, nothing as active as that. It was utter blankness . . . . . . the eating of beef and declaration of allegiance to Islam has been forced upon many thousands as the price of their lives. In Noakhali local things and visiting Hindu 'volunteers' were creating havoc, Gandhi had tried to control the situation. Gandhi went on a prolonged walking tour of Noakhâli, addressing small groups at every village, bringing message to communal harmony and appealing to their sanity. His soothing words were directed to the hearts of each individual. There was no recrimination. Tippera was also affected. There was forced conversion to Islam with Hindus being made to parade wearing a cap inscribed 'Pakistan' and Muslim style lungis. They had there caste marks removed. The conch bracelets of married women were smashed and they were forced to marry Muslim man. At Meerut a police officer's wife and eight children were murdered and the provincial home minister responded by recruiting sixty former INA soldiers as 'special constables' to protect local Congress officials. The communal riots now spread to Bombay, the United Provinces and Bihar. The riots took place in the Chapra district of Bihar from 27th October to 28th October. As a result of the riot, nearly 115 persons were killed and 160 injured. It spread in Patna and Bhagalpur districts also. The violence of Noakhali, for instance was controlled by a local leader, Golam Sarwar, who had been defeated by a Muslim League candidate in the recent elections.[31]

There were two reasons for the Bihar riots. The Government of Bihar had allowed 'Noakhali Day' to be celebrated on 25th October and 26th October, 1946. The servants poisoned the atmosphere of Bihar. The second reason was that Hindu refugees poured into Bihar with tales of programme and looting in Noakhali. So Hindus took revenge on local Muslims, it was a medieval outlook. According to Lord Wavell, the communal riots started due to the criminal folly of the government.[32] According to Sir Dow, Governor of Bihar, who wrote a letter to Viceroy Wavell, the communal riot at Saran at the end of October 1946?[33] But soon spread to Muzaffarpur, Patna, Monghyr, Bhagalpur and northern part of Gaya from September 27, 1946. In Monghyr district, especially in Kharagpur and Tarapur, there had been a worst communal frenzy. Pandit Jawaharlal Nehru, Sardar Patel, Rajendra Prasad, M.A. Jinnah, Liaquat Ali Khan and Abdul Rab Nistar all came to Bihar.[34] Jawaharlal went to the interior part of Monghyr especially Tarapur, thousands came to hear Nehru. He scolded Hindus mercilessly for their brutal behaviour towards those with whom they had lived in peace for centuries. He appealed for a return to sanity but also threatened harsh punishment unless the killing ceased.

Nehru's reaction to the riot was typical of man; deep sympathy for the victims of both communities; stern rebukes to the perpetrators of the ghastly crimes, regardless of the sources; courageous tours of the worst affected areas disregarding his personal safety; appeals for the communal peace supplemented by threats of military retaliation. Nehru was appealed by the crazes resort to mass murder among normally placed peasants. With a long sought prize of independence so near, the riot struck him as a dastardly blow to his hopes for a free India. This appears to be a competition in murder and brutality; he said in the course of a moving report on the riots to the central assembly. On November 4, 1946, Wavell saw Ballabhbhai Patel and Liaquat Ali Khan at 3.15 p.m., when they returned from Patna. Wavell came to Bihar on 7th November, 1946 and reached Patna after lunch. He says that he had a series of interviews with that gangster, the Premier Sinha. Nehru and Prasad were still at Patna. Wavell left Patna on the morning of 9th June.[35] Before he left Patna, Premier Sinha saw him. Wavell told him that his Government had discredited and disgraced Bihar. It was criminally folly to allow Noakhali Day to be celebrated and that the course of action of his government, in insisting on the release of criminals, in prosecuting the government servants and lowering the morale of the police and in failing to control, had been directly to the present tragedy.

In Bihar village after village was purged. The survivors steaming towards areas where they hoped to find their co religionists in a majority. The killing centered on Patna and seems to be committed by gangs organized by local Hindu landlords, while Marwari businessmen in Calcutta provided the funds for the purchase of weapons. The carnage spread through Patna, Monghyr, Saran and down towards Bodh Gaya.

The Muslim League claimed at the time that officials of the Congress administration in Bihar had allowed preparations for slaughter to be made, and Wavell believed that much of the trouble flowed from decision of Premier Sinha. In U.P., Premier Govind Ballabh Pant ordered for the release of a large number of supposedly political prisoners, who were in fact goondas. By the middle of 1947, an estimated twenty thousand Bihari Muslims were dead and tens of thousands were living in makeshift relief camps.

The Muslim League reacted most of this brutal murder of Muslims and with bordered epitaphs in the newspaper *Dawn* exhorted the survivors to remain united enviable against this of murder. They were told that they were martyrs for Islam 'clustering around the throne of God'. Those who were activists and 'helpers' of the Muslim League moved through the refugee camps with political manifestoes. Jinnah raised the possibility of population shifts. He thought that communal problems would be solved through the population transfer. Jinnah like Sir Syed Ahmad and Dr. Iqbal believed that India consisted of 'two nations', Hindu and Muslim and this conception seemed to Jinnah succeed.

Nehru and Nistar had come to Tarapur also. Sir H. Dow, Governor of Bihar had come to Kharagpur on November 1, 1946. From Kharagpur, he came to Tarapur on the same day.

There is a lot of difference on the number of people killed in the communal holocaust in Bihar till December 1946. Prof. Sumat Sarkar in his book *Modern India* says, that in a massacre for more terrible really than Noakhali, 7,000 deaths took place. But it is a statement of facts. According to Jinnah, 30,000 persons were killed. According to Nazimuddin, 10,000 to 20,000 persons were killed. Wavell personally guess had been for 5,000 to 10,000, but the officials estimate is 4,000 to 5,000 only.[36] It was tragic ending of British rule in India.

Bihar was followed by Garhmukteshwar in U.P. where Hindu pilgrims killed 46 Muslims on November 6, 1946. News of such massacre, weakened Congress position in the N.W.F.P., Jawaharlal Nehru, the Vice President of the interim government toured N.W.F.P. in late October 1946 and faced tribal demonstration.

Now the turn of the Punjab came, the Muslim League started a civil disobedience campaign against the Khizar Hayat Khan's ministry from January 1947. The ministry fell on March 4, 1947. On 4th March there was a Sikh demonstration headed by Master Tara Singh. Now large scale riots started in Lahore, Amritsar, Multan, Attock and Rawalpindi. Sikh and Hindu traders and many political leaders were attacked. Large number of persons nearly 5,000 were killed.

Communal riots had been one of the main reasons that influenced Nehru and Patel in favour of partition. By March 10, 1947, Nehru had been telling Lord Wavell in private that though the Cabinet Mission plan was the best solution if it could be carried through the real alternative was the partition of the Punjab and Bengal.[37] After some time, J.B. Kriplani, the Congress President, informed the new Viceroy, Lord Mountbatten, later then have a battle we shall let them have their Pakistan, provided you will allow the Punjab and Bengal to be partitioned in fair manner.[38]

Wavell responded to the spread of violence in September 1946 with a 'withdrawal plan' which he spent to London. He hinted that if things got worst and the British could not govern, they should simply go; this plan appeared to Attlee a military withdrawal and a scuttle. It was not considered at all.

By November 20, 1946, Wavell wrote to Pethick Lawrence; we are very near what will amount to open civil war between the communities. Bitterness between the leaders and the communities generally could hardly be worse than at present. A week later he wrote again in desperation to press London for some sort of guidance. The absence of a definite policy on the part of his Majesty's government is a very serious matter indeed at a critical time like this.[39] Unless there was a political break through of some kind in New Delhi; the Indian Empire would continue to slide into anarchy. The dispute over the structure of the regional groups in a united India had to be clarified or the League would not co-operate in a constitutional making body. Several senior British ministers thought Wavell's insistence on this point was itself a cause of conflict, and it was more important to keep Congress sweet so as to facilitate an orderly British retreat !

London Conference

To remove differences between the Congress and the League representatives, Attlee called the London conference. Attlee assured an invitation to "two representatives of the Congress, two from the League and one Sikh to confer in London in an effect to reconcile the warring parties". Nehru, Jinnah, Liaquat Ali Khan, Wavell and Baldev Singh attended the conference. They flew from Karachi on December 1946. Nehru agreed to attend the conference in order to leave the door open for the League to enter the Constituent Assembly. The London conference continued for four days but the deadlock could not be removed. On 6th December a declaration was made, which went in favour of the League. British constitutional experts backed this interpretation of the May statement over grouping. According to this provinces would be compelled to meet in groups; they could still opt out of the groups but only after the first election under the new group constitution.

The Congress was urged to accept this interpretation. The Congress was declined to accept this. The declaration of December formally destroyed the Cabinet Mission plan. This announcement acted as a green light to the League to persist in the demand for the Pakistan. This declaration, "as Prof. Michael Brecher has called, killed the plan, invited Jinnah to stand fast and spelled the doom of a united India. Arthur Moyle wrote some years later, Jinnah was the only Indian fascist I ever met."

Attlee was not satisfied with Jinnah's style of functioning in the conference. He remained to his confident Arthur Moyle some year later, Jinnah was the only Indian leader I ever met.

Nehru was perturbed by this test of events. The London declaration was a blow to him. He said, "Obstructions were placed in our way, new limitations were mentioned, there was no imagination in the understanding of the Indian problem." After his return from London, the League leaders were no longer interested in a united India. The challenge of Pakistan had become real, and even Nehru with all his anti-Party to the two-nation theory began to have second thoughts. Patel had already reconciled himself to partition. Wavell continued to wave.

The Cabinet Mission—Last Chance for a United India

On December 7, 1946 Nehru and Baldeo Singh flew back to India to attend the first session of the Constituent Assembly of India scheduled to be held on December 9, 1946. The 79 seats that the Muslim League had won remained empty. Sardar Patel was angry with the new interpretation over grouping. It was told that the Constituent Assembly would not be able to meet. But the Constituent Assembly was formally convinced on December 9, 1946 at 11 a.m. the sitting took place at the Constituent Assembly chamber in the Circuit House, New Delhi. The Constituent Assembly started its deliberation with Dr. Sachidananda Sinha, the oldest member of the house, as the provisional chairman. The Governor of Bombay, Sir John Colvelle, who was acting as Viceroy reported to London that the occasion had passed of peacefully without 'Black Flag' demonstrations.

After the London conference, Jinnah stayed in England for some time. He was in indifferent health. He was haggard and ill. He passed his time with caravan a cigarette by his side. Accidentally he met his wife's old friend Kanji Dwarkadas, who was hovering between Congress and the League. At a first glance Dwarkadas found him 'sick and depressed' but he felt that Jinnah had not lost his shrewdness due to failing health.[40] His self-esteem, his pride and his feeling of being personally hurt had embittered him and he had created ghosts of suspicion and distrust all-around him. Dwarkadas felt that much of Jinnah's intransigence and bitterness stunned from the way he had been treated on a personal level by members of the Congress. He saw that the leaders of the Congress and the League did not talk to each other outside formal negotiations.

Dwarkadas was one of such people who believed that Jinnah utilized the Pakistan demand as a bargaining tactics, rather than a fixed policy and a goal of life. He wrote in his book *Ten Years to Freedom* I do not think Jinnah wanted Pakistan. Right till, 1946 he was prepared to work for one united India. So all the time he was talking in terms of Pakistan, this was, I was always believed, a bargaining point for him,[41] under this interpretation, Jinnah only accepted the creation of an independent Muslim state because he had rightly come to the opinion that the Congress leaders did not want any settlement with him.

This question that the Pakistan demand was a bargaining point for Jinnah did not like the partition of the country in fact has been discussed by historian proving this side or that. The Muslim League accepted the cabinet delegation plan before the Congress. It means that Jinnah was not serious for his Pakistan demand; because the aim of the cabinet delegation plan was not Pakistan but a united India. Jinnah was determined to take best from this plan. This is clear from this event; Jinnah was staying at the Cecil Hotel. A waiter at the hotel asked Jinnah; Mr. Jinnah, Sir, do you really want the country partitioned. The Quaid-e-Azam gave a scribbled reply at the bottom of his bill leading question. Barristers do not have opinions—they have briefs.[42]

The British had no Plan to Free India

After the departure of Jawaharlal Nehru and Baldeo Singh from London, the Viceroy stayed in London and talked with the members of the cabinet and Pethick Lawrence. But it was a fruitless discussion. He also attended several meetings of the cabinet and the India and Burma Committee. He felt that he was not getting respect and he was treated like a poor relation. He impressed upon the Secretary of State and members of the cabinet that the Government must take fast decisions. In his opinion, withdrawal from India should be considered like a 'Military plan' made in time of war. But the politicians were not ready for a fast decision. Wavell knew this fact that his friend A.V. Alexander and the Foreign Secretary Ernest Bėvin were strong imperialist. They would not liquidate the British Empire; Wavell was surprised to know that the members of the cabinet were ignorant about India and the political situation of India. Wavell noted in his diary that 'one member of the cabinet had no idea at all that Sikhs were living in Punjab.

Some members of the cabinet were living in the Victorian age. Mentally they were not prepared for the liquidation of the British Empire. Earnest Bevin, a member of the cabinet was an imperialist. Bevin belonged to Labour Party but his attitude towards India resembled with Churchill. Bevin did not like Wavell's tone. He was not prepared to slacken the British hold on India. It was something tragic that the Labour Minister was not ready to accept Wavell's view. He wrote a strong letter to Prime Minister, Attlee about Wavell's 'defeatist attitude'; Wavell's view about political independence to India, he called it defeatist attitude. What a wonder; a soldier victory was doing much for India, whereas a politician Viceroy had done nothing. His predecessor Linlithgow never liked India's freedom. Bevin wanted to turn the clock back. Bevin wanted such category of the Viceroy, who even if he was the last man left, there would come out with dignity and upholds the British Empire. Britannia should not knuckle under at the first blow. The Empire was going to the dogs. In fact you cannot read the telegrams from Egypt and the Middle East now-a-days without realizing that not only in India going but Malaya, Ceylon and the Middle East was going with it, with a tremendous repercussion on the African territories. I do not beg of you to take a stronger line and not give way to this awful pessimism.[43]

Then another problem cropped up—the future Indian Civil Service and the Indian Political Service, which included those British officials who served in the Princely States and certain members of the military and police forces. Wavell discussed this question with his superiors. The Viceroy thought seriously that their loyalty and morale during the present crises would be secured only if they were assured of adequate conversation when British rule ended. But it could be secured only if both categories of services were assured of adequate compensation in free India. The issue was complicated by this fact that under existing legislation, they would have to be paid from Indian revenues but it was felt that the government of free India might not spend compensation on them because they had been oppressed by these government servants in the period of the national movement. It was finally agreed that services would be compensated out of the sterling balances, which was deposited in London.

Wavell had returned to New Delhi. He was anxious what would happen to India. the country was disintegrating and Wavell was not in a position to check the process of disintegration. The authority in London was not in a position to chalk out any policy for India. They were not in a position to take any decision nor do the authorities allow Wavell to take any decision. He recorded in the diary in this way: "1946 had been the most gruelling year. I have ever had...... The cabinet mission was really our last chance to bring about a settlement in India, a temporary one which would have ended us to leave India with peace and dignity."

Wavell felt that "while the British are still legally and morally responsible for what happens in India...... we are simply running on the momentum of our previous prestige...... I have now committed myself, and very nearly committed HMG to a plan of announcing a definite date of termination of our control of India and of withdrawing on a definite plan. It has been my fate for the last 5 to 6 years to have to conduct withdrawal and to motivate defeats, and I have had no real opportunity and to initiate defeats and I have had no real opportunity of success. This is inevitably depressing . . . . . . no rest, no success."[44]

Wavell tried to find out a solution, so he had despatched a 'Breakdown plan'. About Wavell, Mountbatten said, "Wavell writes brilliantly, who had a first class mind, very intelligent and very well disposed, really progressive."

The intellectual and social ferment in Britain of which labour Party's trump in 1945 was an expression, helped in reassuring the merits of traditional British policies towards India. Ideologically the Labour Party had been moving towards a new orientation for quite some time; as far as June 1938. Attlee and Cripps had discussed with Jawaharlal Nehru possibilities of such independence for India and of participation of the Indian National Congress in the Government of India. But the fact of the Indian situation after the Second World War also drove the Labour Party in the same direction.

Speaking on March 6, 1947 in the House of Commons on the condition of India in November 1945, A.V. Alexander, who had been a member of the Cabinet Mission to India, recalled; it might be said that the Indian authorities were literally sitting on the top of a volcano, and as a result of the situation which had arisen after the war, the outbreak of revolution might be expected at any time.

Malcolm Muygeridge, who spent a year in Calcutta in the mid-thirties as Assistant Editor of the Calcutta *Statesman*, writes in his memories that he could not recall meeting a single British businessman of official soldiers or even missionary, who considered it possible that the British Empire in India was to end before the twentieth century had half run its course. The *Raj*, in one form of another would go on for centuries yet. Ten years later, Labour Government decided to transfer power to Indian hands, many British politicians, officials and non-officials regarded it nothing short of a scuttle. According to the novelist, John Masters, who came of a family that had served in India for five generations; glamorous Dickey (Mountbatten) and Attlee with their three month's knowledge between them, breaking up in half a year what it took its centuries to build.

The despair and rage of the 'colonial' unable to reconcile themselves to decolonization in 1947 comes out in the words of John Master's hero Rodney Savage, 'it is time to go' this is the whole sad story. Time to go, that I am not going. Never see? I am not your country, it is more, and I made it for a hundred centuries, I and my grandfather.

NOTES

1. Brecher, Michael, *Nehru: A Political Biography*, p. 315.
2. Durga Das, pp. 430- 431.
3. Brucher, Michael, *Nehru: A Political Biography*, p. 316.
4. *Ibid.*
5. *Ibid.*
6. The *Sunday Observer*, October 17th to 23rd, 1999.
7. Brecher, Michael, *Nehru: A Political Biography*, p. 316.
8. *Ibid.*
9. Maulana Abul Kalam Azad, *India Wins Freedom*, pp. 164-165.
10. Brucher, Michael, *Nehru: A Political Biography*, p. 317.
11. Zaidi, Z.H., (edited), Vol. 3, p. XIII.
12. Moon (2), p. 336.
13. *Transfer of Power*, Vol. VIII, p. 225.
14. *Ibid.*
15. The Indian Annual Register, 1946, II, July 29th, p. 9.
16. *The Times of India*, New Delhi, July 1985.
17. Norman Dorothy, *Nehru II*, p. 243.
18. Holy war fought by Muslims against unbelievers.
19. The ninth month of Muslim year, during which Muslim fast from sunrise to sunset.
20. Leonard Mosley's, *the British Raj*, p. 29.
21. *Mainstream*, January 5, 1999.
22. Pyarelal, *Mahatma Gandhi I*, p. 236.
23. Brecher, Michael, *Nehru*, p. 319.
24. *Transfer of Power*, enclosure to document, p. 197.
25. Moon (2), p. 220.
26. *Transfer of Power*, Vol. VIII, enclosure to documents, p. 197.
27. Gandhi, M.K., Vol. (2), p. LXXXV.
28. *Transfer of Power*, Vol. VIII, pp. 328-329.
29. *Transfer of Power*, Vol. IX, p. 919.
30. Quoted in J.N. Dixit, *Anatomy of a Flawed Inheritance*, *Times of India*, New Delhi, December 7, 1997.
31. French, Patrick, *Liberty or Death*, p. 268.
32. Moon, P., *Wavell, the Viceroy's Journals*, p. 372.
33. *Transfer of Power*, Vol. IX, p. 451.
34. *Ibid.*
35. *Ibid.*
36. *Transfer of Power*, Vol. IX, p. 140.
37. *Wavell, the Viceroy's Journal,* edited by Moon P., pp. 426-427.
38. Hodson, H.V., *The Great Divide,* London, 1969, p. 236.
39. *Ransfer of Power*, Vol. IX, pp. 119 and 197.
40. French Patrick, *Liberty or Death*, p. 271.

41. Dwarkadas, *Ten Years to Freedom*, pp. 199-191 and 224.
42. Kesavan, Mukul, *Looking Through Glass*, London, 1995, p. 576.
43. *Transfer of Power*, Vol. IX, pp. 431-432.
44. Moon P., (2), pp. 412-413.

10

Lord Mountbatten presided over the Partition of India : An Introduction

Lord Wavell was anxious to terminate the British Raj in India. But Prime Minister could not agree with Wavell's views. The interim government could not tackle law and order problems of the country. Several parts of northern India were under the impact of communal riots. Bihar was worst affected province. At this critical time, the leader of the Congress Socialist Party, Jai Prakash Narayan spoke in a press conference that the interim government would disintegrate within six months. He added that the Muslim League was a "British front" and the country needed a 'revolutionary struggle'.

Lord Wavell was in a great mental tension. On February 4, 1947, while Wavell was making preparation for his daughter's wedding in New Delhi, a King's messenger came from London carrying a fatal letter. A conservative M.P. Harold Macmillan was staying in the Viceroy's house. The letter mentioned 'I think you may agree that the time has come to make a change in the Viceroyalty'. Attlee asked Wavell that he would agree if his name is submitted for the dignity of an Earldom, Wavell response was blunt. He said that this was an undignified way to shock him. He had in the past made several offers to retire but the Prime Minister told him that he would remain on this post. In the end Wavell pointed out the divergence, as I see it, wrote the Field Marshall, and is between my wanting a definite policy for the interim period and HMG refusing to give me one.[1]

When Wavell learnt that his successor was Lord Mountbatten, Wavell wrote in his diary: 'an unexpected appointment' but a clever one from their point of view, and Dickie's personality may perhaps accomplish what I have failed to do. Though Wavell had said at his dismissal, he was glad at Mountbatten's appointment. He knew him as supreme allied commander in South East India during the Second World War. Japan had surrendered before Mountbatten on August 15, 1945. The Viceroy had also received help from Mountbatten in tackling the Bengal famine of 1943. Both agreed on one point and that point was decongestion. It was only several months after India's independence that Wavell concluded his successor had very much given a way to the Congress side.

Attlee did not follow a straight policy towards Wavell in matters of the change of Viceroy. While Wavell was in London in December 1946, Attlee had offered the post of Viceroy to Mountbatten but the Prime Minister did not tell this fact to Wavell. He ought to have informed him the Government was in search of his successor. Mountbatten laid down his terms of appointment. Attlee assured him of support but at the same time he was trying for his dismissal. In mid January 1947. Attlee told Wavell it would not be advisable to fix a day for India's independence.[2] Attlee was concealing the true fact. The fact was that few days earlier than mid-January, Mountbatten had written a letter to Attlee; it makes all differences to me, to know that you propose to make a statement in the House, terminating the British Raj, on a definite and specified date. His only concern, he continued was that I am not really sure, however, that HMG wish me to try and achieve in India.[3]

In a letter of instruction to Mountbatten, Prime Minister Attlee had said, it is a definite objective of His Majesty's Government to obtain a unitary government for British India and the Indian states, if possible within the British commonwealth, through the medium of a Constituent Assembly set up and run in accordance with the Cabinet Mission's plan, and you should do the utmost in your power to persuade the parts to work together to this end ...... "If by October 1, you consider that there is no prospect of reaching a settlement on the basis of a unitary government for British India either with or without the cooperation of Indian states, you should report on His Majesty's Government on the staffs which you consider should be taken for the handing over power on the due date."

Thus the date of handing over of power and the dead line for the negotiations were laid down. Mountbatten was expected to persuade the Indian leaders to agree to implement the Cabinet Mission plan, failing which he was to report to the British Government on how best to transfer power by the said date.[4]

Mountbatten's letter was the centre of the problem. The solution of India's problem depended on the content of the reply from the Prime Minister. Like Mountbatten, Wavell had the same type of the problem. Mountbatten refused to go to India under unless a clear instruction on Indian independence was assured to him. Till Wavell's period, Attlee had no fixed policy regarding India. It was this reason why Wavell was not happy with the white hall's policy. Attlee's policy always changed, the policy was always in a state of perpetual flex. Attlee disliked Wavell, mistrusted his judgment and ignored his advice. It was a tragedy that Wavell and Attlee always differed. But it was an irony of the situation that when Mountbatten placed the same kind of demands, Attlee accepted them.

By this time events were moving so fast that Pathick Lawrence found it difficult to keep peace with Mountbatten. Mountbatten appeared to be a man of hurry. So Pathick Lawrence resigned the job of the Secretary of State and Lord Listowal was subsequently appointed as the Secretary of State for India at the time of Indian independence. As Attlee's biographer states, the Prime Minister was in fact his own Secretary of State for India.[5] After receiving the offer, Mountbatten made it a condition to Attlee for accepting the post that he should be given plenary powers and that there should be a deadline for the handing over of power. Before Mountbatten's arrival, the Viceroy himself was never allowed to negotiate with any sort of authority. It all had to be referred back and it was always open-minded. So he demanded plenary powers. The Government accepted both the conditions. So he accepted the offer on January 3, 1947. In a letter of instructions to Mountbatten on 18th March, Attlee had said, "it is the definite objective of his Majesty's Government to obtain a unitary government for British India and the Indian States, if possible, within the British Commonwealth, through the medium of a constituent assembly, set up and run in accordance with the Cabinet Mission's plan and you should do the utmost in your power to persuade all parties to work together to this end. If by October 1, 1947 you consider that there is no prospect of reaching a settlement on the basis of a unitary government for British India, either with or without the cooperation of Indian states, you should report on his Majesty's Government on the steps which you should be taking for the handing over of power on the due date. Mountbatten believed in a unified India.

Thus the date of handing over of power and the deadline for the negotiation were laid down. Mountbatten was expected to persuade the Indian leaders to implement the Cabinet Mission's plan, failing which he was to report to the British Government how best to transfer power by the said dates. It had been decided to demit British authority by the end of 1948. Wavell had suggested March 1948 avoiding the chaotic condition in India; the British must depart from India by March 1948. In June 1946 Wavell had even suggested January 1, 1947 as a suitable date for British departure.

The problems before the Indian leaders were, would India remain united? But the dream of united India was dashed for ever, when the Congress Working Committee resolved on March 8, 1947 to partition the Punjab.[6] Nehru and Patel agreed to divide the Punjab. Gandhi was in a peace mission in Bihar. The Working Committee resolved that "there should be a division of Punjab into two provinces, so that the predominantly Muslim part may be separated from the predominantly non-Muslim part". Jinnah could get Pakistan, but it could be a 'moth eaten', truncated Pakistan. So the Congress proposed partition of the Punjab into two provinces and invited the League to a joint conference for this purpose. Ostensibly this was suggested to lesser communal friction. But in perspective the Congress had taken a very long step towards partition of the entire country. The decision to partition was taken even before the acceptance of the Mountbatten plan by the Indian leaders. Mountbatten had not even reached Delhi.

Mountbatten was given greater discretion than Wavell. Mountbatten could reach any decision without referring to the India Office. Not a single Viceroy had got this kind of discretionary power as Mountbatten. He could meet and talk to anybody in India without prior permission from London. A conversation with Attlee supposedly went as follows, "You were asking for plenipotentiary powers over His Majesty's Government". No one has been given such powers in this century. Attlee was silent for some time. Cripps gave a nod, then Attlee continued further, "all right, you have got the powers and the job".[7] The need for the plenipotentiary powers in India had disappeared seventy years earlier, when the first telegrams were sent from London to Calcutta. By 1947, communication was almost instantaneous. The result was that Mountbatten left London with far clearer instructions[8] than his predecessors had ever been given even if the policy that Wavell had initiated remained essentially unchanged. This helped to mitigate his ignorance of Indian politics. As one of the inner circles wrote at the time; Mountbatten, in briefing himself for the political talk that lies ahead of him, is starting from scratch.

Mountbatten's Early Career

Mountbatten has been regarded as a man of destiny. There can be few greater success of our time than that of Mountbatten, whose father was a German Prince, who was known to his friends as Dickey, and who ended his career as Admiral of the Fleet, Earl Mountbatten of Burma.

A great grandson of Queen Victoria related to most of the royal houses of Europe, the inheritor by marriage, of much wealth and the famous county estate of Broad lands. He was a man whom the gods continually smolder. He was the son of the Lord Milford Haven and a second cousin of the British King Emperor, George VI. He was born on June 25, 1900 at Windsor. The queen attended the baby's christening. Six months later, her long reign ended. In the childhood he was known as Dickey Battenberg. His father and his elder brother George, was in the Navy. Mountbatten joined as a cadet in 1913. His brilliant father was First Sea Lord. The First World War broke out on June 28, 1914 and his father prince Louise of Battenberg felt compelled to resign. Mountbatten was at Osborne Naval College and this news gave a terrible shock to him. Later in the war Prince Louis[9] changed his name to Mountbatten and the King created him Marques of Milford Haven. Dickey now became Lord Louis Mountbatten.[10]

After the war and a spell at Cambridge, young Lieutenant Mountbatten became a close friend of the then Prince of Wales and was his ADC. He went to India in 1920 with the Prince on two goodwill missions to the Empire. It was in Delhi on the second Voyage that Mountbatten became engaged to the girl, he was to marry after some time in 1922. The girl was the beautiful heiress Edwina Ashley. From her grandfather the rich German Jewish financier, Sir Ernest Cassette, she was left a fortune of several million pounds. She was the daughter of Wilfred Ashley, a conservative member of parliament. In 1924, Mountbatten became a special side officer. After promotion to commander and a tour of duty commanding destroyers, Mountbatten came home in 1936 and joined the Admiralty.

When Lord Mountbatten visited the Delhi University for its silver jubilee celebration held on March 7, 1948, he is said to have disclosed, it is curious, but to my wife and myself it is very pleasant incidence that Delhi University should be celebrating the silver jubilee of its foundation in 1923 for we win marriage in that year and have just celebrated our silver jubilee wedding. The connection between these two events may not be immediately apparent until I tell you that the room in which I asked my wife to marry me was Room No 13, which is now the Registrar's office.

In 1956, when Lady Mountbatten visited Delhi, the then Vice Chancellor, Dr. Mahajan invited her to visit the place and got inscribed the above quotation on a marble slab still adorns corner of the Registrar's room, coupled with the stones of the institution which celebrated its platinum jubilee in 1997.[11]

The New King, Edward VIII had been on the throne, but he could not approve of what his old friend and shipmate had decided.

Mountbatten loved him very much. He was his friend. He had the greatest possible love for Simpson, a twice divorced American woman and charm. But Mountbatten thought that his laying down on his job and abdicating from the throne was wrong. He told him so. The fascinating part was that he made a very good Prince of Wales but not a good King.

Now the Second World War broke out on September 1, 1939. Mountbatten was now to command of the brand new destroyers. For the fleet of coverage and seamanship, he was awarded the DSG in December 1940; Mountbatten again went to the sea and rejoined at Plymouth. In the autumn of 1940, he became Naval officer. On the recommendation of the new Prime Minister Churchill, Mountbatten was propelled sharply upwards, first as Advisor then as chief of combined operations with the acting rank of Vice Admiral and equal status to the chiefs of staff, he was only 41.[12]

After the invasion of Sicily and Italy in 1943, Mountbatten's work at combined operations was more or less completed and when a supreme commander was needed for the stagnant South-East Asia command, he seemed the ideal man for the post. He would have a million men under his command, of mixed nationality, most of whom had never heard of him. How would he impress himself on them? At the age of 43, he was sent to South-East Asia as Supreme Allied Commander in late 1943. Winston Churchill searched 'a young and vigorous mind' and appointed him supreme allied commander. The authority and responsibility that command placed on his youthful shoulders had only one counterpart, the supreme allied command of twilight Eisenhower. While going to join his new assignment, Mountbatten came to Delhi. Wavell had supported Mountbatten's appointment from the outset. Delhi was his temporary headquarters but in mid 1944, Mountbatten transferred his headquarters from New Delhi to Kendy in Cylone. Mountbatten came to see Wavell in September 1944. He told that Churchill had been as intractable as ever about India.

After the end of the War, Mountbatten played an important part in the decolonization of Burma and Indo-China.[13] Although he was not a political theorist and did not share, Edwin's socialism' he took a firmly pragmatic approach towards colonial rule. He saw that nationalist forces were in the ascendant in Asia in 1945, so he was not in favour that Asia should revert to *status quo anti.* Mountbatten experiment his thought in Burma. He treated Aung Sen, the father of the nation in a dignified way. The result was his treatment of Aung Sen provided temporary stability to Burma and the country remained free from revolution. At this time Jawaharlal Nehru paid a visit to Singapore on behalf of the Congress in 1946. Lord Wavell informed Mountbatten that Jawaharlal Nehru would be Prime Minister of India, so he should be treated well. When Nehru reached there for a week's visit to Malaya, Mountbatten received him on the March 18, 1946 in a dignified way.[14] By treating him courteously, he reduced the scope for tension and unrest locally, and wooded Nehru for the future. Nehru was impressed with Mountbatten's behaviour. Now both knew each other in a fine way. After some time Mountbatten assumed the charge of the office of the Viceroy of India on March 24, 1947. As Mountbatten was known to Nehru, Mountbatten held Jawaharlal Nehru in high esteem. Jawaharlal Nehru became the Prime Minister of India, when India got freedom on August 14/15, 1947. By this time Jawaharlal Nehru was the Vice President of the interim government. Mountbatten was mentally razor sharp and tremendously resourceful.[15]

Mountbatten's Appointment as Viceroy and Wavell's Departure

I have already mentioned that the British Government headed by Attlee had offered the job of Viceroy of India in December 1946 and Mountbatten accepted the offer after some time. Attlee had accepted both of Mountbatten's conditions. A new initiative on Indian independence was necessary. The incumbent Viceroy, Lord Wavell was not the man to make it. Attlee looked around for a successor and sent Mountbatten to India. Mountbatten knew that the challenge was difficult. He knew this fact that he was handed a poisoned chalice but the offer was irresistible. His all friends and well wishers including Lady Mountbatten were opposed that Mountbatten should accept this offer but Mountbatten had taken a decision already.

Mountbatten had the capacity for making and implementation tough decisions. He was not a deep thinker.[16] He was extremely good at analyzing a problem and formulating an immediately strategy to tackle it. The duty of Mountbatten was simply to arrange imperial withdrawal. His work was to give Britain, which had been reduced to second rate power in the world, freedom from the Indian Empire. As David Can Nadine has written, most members of the royal family are employed to open things. But Mountbatten was quite brilliant as the much more difficult and important job of doing things down . . . . . . As such he was pioneering an important job of doing things down. As such he was pioneering and pre-eminent, de imperialist, which was followed, in the next quarter century, by many other mortieious of empire.

Before Mountbatten's assuming the charge of Viceroy, an historic declaration has been made in the House of Commons on February 20, 1947. British Prime Minister Attlee made a famous statement 'announcing His Majesty's Government's definite intention to make the necessary steps peacefully to transfer power into responsible Indian hands by a date not later than June 1948'[17] It wished to hand over its responsibility to authorities established by a constitution approved by all parties in accordance with the cabinet plan, but unfortunately there was no clear prospect that such a constitution and such authorities would emerge. If then, it should appear that an agreed constitution would not have been worked out by June 1948, it would have to consider to whom the transfer of power of central government for British India or in some areas to the existing provincial governments or in such other way as may seem most reasonably and in the best interest of the Indian people.

The inference that Attlee's statement of February 20 proved the way for partition and even represented an indirect concession to the League demand for Pakistan is shared by various English officials prominently connected with the last stage of British rule. The prevalent feeling in London by February 1947 seemed to be that Pakistan was the only way out of impasse. Attlee was instantly conservative over India.

Tory spokesman led by Churchill and Sir John Anderson were of this opinion that the Cripps offer of 1942 should be implemented in place of Attlee's statement. Churchill himself had no illusion about the meaning of Attlee's statement. India is to be subjected not merely to partition but to fragmentation and to haphazard fragmentation, he declared, referring to the freedom of action granted the princely states.

Churchill's attitude to Indian politicians was reaffirmed in words which Nehru and other leaders have probably never forgotten, in handing over the government to these so called political classes we are handing over to men of straw, of whom, in a few years, no trace will remain. And in a passionate outburst he appealed to the house ...... 'Let us not add ...... by shameful flight, by a premature hurried scuttle ...... at least, let us not add, to the pangs of sorrow now so many of us feel, the taint and smear of shame. The labour benches were unmoved'. One aspect of Attlee's statement which puzzled his audience was the summary dismissal of Wavell.[18]

The transfer of power to the subcontinent was the toughest assignment Mountbatten ever handled. It was a heart breaking task, so dramatically had Hindu-Muslim relations deteriorated that the country was teetering on the brink of a virtual civil war. Mountbatten had quickly to take a number of critical decisions, the most important being weather he should stick to the date fixed by the British Government for the transfer of power or to advance. He decided to advance it. His critics held this and other decisions by him responsible for the communal holocaust that followed. This was an unjust view. Delay in the transfer of power would have only heightened the communal tension already beyond control. I shall answer all these problems which I have raised in this chapter.

Attlee had wanted Mountbatten as a new man to bring renewed energy to a basically uncharged policy. But Mountbatten, by the demand over timing, in fact charged his policy, although this was not generally realized at the time. By announcing a date by which they would go, come what may, the British government was effectively processing something else, the British government was effectively announcing something else, that if no agreement was reached between Congress and the League. The British would hand over to the existing provincial governments. Jinnah, having lost the powerful role in a united India, that the cabinet mission had almost secured for him was likely to accept those provinces that opted to join Pakistan. Mountbatten's purpose in asking for definite, final date had been to concentrate the minds of the Indians and make them get on with it. The granting of his request made the creation of Pakistan inevitable if the negotiations breakdown.[19]

It is doubtful, if without Gandhi's gimmicks—to borrow Sir Algernon Rumbold's phrase —the British would have wound up the Indian Empire in 1947.[20] The British historian Arnold Toynbee has, therefore, a point when he says that Gandhi was as much a benefactor of Britain as of his own country; he made it impossible for the British to go on ruling India, but at the same time he made it possible for us to abdicate without rancour and without dishonour ...... In helping British to extricate themselves from this imperial entanglement Gandhi did them a single service for it is easier to acquire an empire than to disengage from one.[21]

As Gandhi had hoped and predicted, the liberation of India in 1947 turned out to be a prelude to the liquation in imperialism in Asia and Africa. In this process of voluntary decolonization and transmutation of their all-white Empire into a multiracial commonwealth and British were guided by a sound political instinct. As Queen Elizabeth in her speech at Philadelphia on July 6, 1976 on the occasion of the United States bicentennial said, "the British lost the American colonies[22] in 18th, century because we lacked that statesmanship to know the right time, and manner of yielding, what is, impossible to keep."

The British Empire has been a unique phenomenon in history.[23] The saying that it was acquired in a fit of absent mindedness was an obvious exaggeration. But it was not acquired in pursuit of a grand design either. A nation of shopkeepers proud of its pragmatism could not possibly have produced and pursued a grand design. And the manner of its disposal was as remarkable as its acquisition, though in a different sense. It was wound up deliberately and we can say, relatively painlessly. Shopkeepers would not stick to an enterprise which had ceased to be profitable such a phenomenon can never cease to fascinate, certainly not those who have been involved in it whether as rulers or as subjects.[24]

Mountbatten now expected to reach Delhi. He was coming with clear instructions from London, this helped him to find out a solution to the problem. Patel reacted to Mountbatten's appointment. When he learnt that Mountbatten was a politically radical aristocrat, he murmured, Ah! He will be a toy for Jawaharlal to play with—when we arrange the revolution.[25] Before Mountbatten could reach Delhi, Patel dismissed Norman Smith and replaced him his own nominee as director of the Intelligence Bureau. So he now had an Indian director of the Intelligence Bureau.

Between the announcement of his appointment and his departure, he met Churchill. Churchill said to Mountbatten, whatever arrangement you may make, you must see that you do not harm a hair on the head of single Muslim. He said, I have no wish to harm the hair on anybody's head.[26]

Mountbatten arrived at Delhi in the afternoon of March 22, 1947. They were driven by open landrace with cavalry escort to Viceroy's house. Lutyen's palace was to be their home and headquarters. On 22nd March, Lord Wavell went out on his usual early morning horse back ride from Hauz Khas, accompanied by members of his staff and that afternoon his successor arrived, like Gandhi, Mountbatten travelled with an entourage. Mountbatten's case it consisted of smooth thrusters and high profile fixers rather than goat milkers and *bhajan* chanters. They were named as the 'Dickey Birds' by the Staff of Viceroy's house, who did not like the interpolers from London. The very presence of in New Delhi of these two minds Wavell and Mountbatten represented a break with tradition. Normally, an outgoing Viceroy sailed with due pomp from the Gateway of India, while the next steamer bore his successor towards its spans, thus sparing India the embarrassment of having two gods upon its soil at the same time. Mountbatten himself had insisted on this breach of custom so he could talk with the man he formally bowed his head as he reached the top of the stairs.

Wavell reviewed his efforts to reach a solution. He stood up and opened his safe, looked inside were the only two items he could bequeath his successor. The first was the—diamond crusted badge of the Grand Master of the Order of the Star of India, the emblem of Mountbatten's new office and the second was the operation Madhouse. The Viceroy and the Viceroy-designate had a short and intense discussion, at which Wavell said, I am sorry for you. I have only one solution, which I call 'Operation Madhouse'[27]—withdrawal of the British province by province, beginning with women and children, then civilians, then the Army. I can see no other way out, afterwards Lord and Lady Mountbatten escorted Lord and Lady Wavell to Palam airport. The Batten has mounted remarked the Field Marshal cryptically to his ADC David Walker as he said farewell. Walker was given exclusive permission to record the departure for posterity on his cine-camera. Wavell was seriously worried about the situation in the Punjab as he flew back to Britain. The province had deserted into communal slaughter in the struggle for the political ascendancy, with Sikhs as the principle target. Before his departure, Wavell told to Mountbatten about Jinnah in this way. Oh, he said absolutely helpless, don't forget this about Jinnah; he is pure Englishman by education, by outlook and by affection. He speaks English and as far as I know, talks to other dialect of any sort.

The usual feature of the ceremony was that Mountbatten followed the example of Lytten, 1876-80, and made a short speech. He began by referring to the government's resolve to transfer by June 1948 and adding that since many administrative questions had to be settled before power could be transferred. This in effect meant a solution had to be reached within the next few months.

The most glorious event which marked Mountbatten's destiny had probably been the great Durbar's ceremony held in the Durbar hall of Viceroy's House on March 24, 1947 when he and Edwina were officially installed as Viceroy and Viceraine of India. After the ceremony thirty one guns were fired. Before coming to India, Churchill had told one thing to Mountbatten. Whatever arrangements, you may make; you must see that you do not harm a hair on the head of a single Muslim. Mountbatten said, I have no wish to harm on anybody's head.[28]

Mountbatten's Style of Functioning

Mountbatten's instruction did not go very far. Attlee and his colleague in London were still committed to the cabinet mission plan for the constituent assembly that would create a unitary government acceptable to all.[29]

Indian parties and Mountbatten was instructed to persue this directive to the utmost of his power only if by October 1947 he found it to be impossible and he was to consider alternatively. He thus arrived to find his instruction overtaken. The cabinet still required him to stand seven months fighting for a unitary state,[30] when the Congress supposedly a prime beneficiary of this policy, had given up the struggle. Mountbatten introduced a radical change until now the Viceroy was isolated from all contact with the masters. The new Viceroy announced he and his wife or daughter would take their morning rides unescorted. His words sent a wave of horror through the house, and it took him some time to get his way. But he did, and suddenly the Indian villagers along the route of their rides began to witnessing a spectacle so unbelievable as to seem a mirage; the Viceroy and the Viceraine of India fretting past them, waving graciously, alone and unprotected.

Then he and his wife made an even from revolutionary gesture. He did something no Viceroy had disagreed to do in two hundred years; visit the home of an Indian who was not one of a handful of privileged princes. To the astonishment of all India, the Viceregal couple walked into a Garden Party at the single New Delhi residence of Jawaharlal Nehru. While Nehru's aides looked on dumb with disbelief. Mountbatten took Nehru by the elbow and strolled off among the quests, casually chatting and shaking hands.

The gesture had a stunning impact. 'Thank God' Nehru told his sister that ever as, 'we have finally got a human being for a Viceroy and not a stuffed short.'

Anxious to demonstrate that a new esteem for the Indian people now reigned in Viceroy's house, Mountbatten accorded the Indian military, two millions of whom had served under him in South East Asia, a long overdue however. He had three Indian officers attached to his staff as ADC. He offered the doors of Viceroy's house to be opened to Indians, only a handful of who had been invited into his presents before his arrival. He instructed his staff that there were to be no dinner parties in the Viceroy's house without Indian guests. Not just a few token guests, henceforth, he ordered, at least half the faces around his table were to be Indians.

His wife brought an error more dramatic revolution to the Viceroy's dining table. Out of respect for the ordinary traditions of her Indian guests, she ordered the house's kitchen to start preparing dishes, which in a century of imperial hospitality, had never been offered in Viceroy's house, Indian vegetarian food. Not only that she ordered the food to be served flat Indian trays and servants with the traditional wash basins, jugs and towels to stand behind her guests so they could, if they choose, eat with their fingers at Viceroy's table, they wash their throats with a usual gargle.

Not long after their arrival the *New York Times* noted, "No

Viceroy in history has so completely won the confidence, respect and liking of the Indian people". Within a few weeks, the success of 'operation seduction' would be remarkable that Nehru himself would tell the new Viceroy only half jokingly that he was becoming a difficult man to negotiate with because he was 'drawing longer crowds than anybody in India'.[31]

Mountbatten introduced a new procedure. He decided to resolve the Indian problem by establishing relationship of understanding and trust with the big five key Indian leaders Gandhi, Nehru, Jinnah, Liaquat and Patel. He began with grand entertainments, more Indians were invited to Viceroy's house than ever before. There were garden parties, dinners and luncheons, to which all manner of people came, by invitations, rather then by command. Mountbatten put his all into making them feel welcome. He was a sparkling socialized and this part of his task came easily to him. He put on the uniforms and his medals and quickly won personal credit not only with the princes; who had been accustomed to come to the Viceroy's palace but with political, social, administrative and industrial leaders.[32] Many years later countess Mountbatten's lady in waiting Jaya Thadani remembered the last Viceroyalty. Everything moved so well because they themselves were both very proficient. He had the German quality of extreme discipline and everything had to be perfect. It was a social household. There were dinner parties and drink parties. Everybody in that house knew that it was the end of era; that when Mountbatten left there was going to be prohibition. So everybody was determined to drink the Viceroy's Cellar dry.[33] That did not make for a clear hand early in the morning, except that Lord Louis, as Mountbatten was called and Lady Louis always were clearheaded and knew exactly what hey were going to do with the rest of the day. We would follow rather bleary-eyed and often muddled along as best we could.

He had the German quality of extreme discipline and had to be perfect. He was extremely good-looking. He was 46 years old only. He had only to walk into a room and every female heart flattered. He knew that and he would stand there with a very 'look of me' sort of attitude and charm everybody in the room. He enjoyed the way he looked and the ADC who walked behind him would generally carry a comb so that when Lord Louis stopped out of a plane or a car he could see that his hair was in place. In sharp contrast, Lady Mountbatten never really cared how she looked. She did not care whether her hair looked right or her make up often way, you have only got two dresses, do not you ought to have a few more. She never cared about that way of living thing and that too was very endearing.

George Abele, who was a triple blue and first at oxford, said Mountbatten that India, was heading for a civil war and she could be saved by bounding the rapidest of resolutions to her problems. He explained that the most administrative machine governing India was collapsing. There was the shortage of British officers caused by the decision to stop recruiting during the period of the Second World War and the rising antagonism between the Hindu and Muslim members meant that the vaunted institution, the Indian civil service, could not survive the year. The time for discussion and the debate was past speed, not deliberation, was needed to avoid a catastrophe. The Chief of Staff, General Lord I.S. May pointed out "India was a strip on fire in mid-ocean with ammunition in her hold. The question, he told Mountbatten, was could they fire out before it reached the ammunition."

The first report Mountbatten received from the British Governor of Punjab warned him there is a civil war atmosphere throughout the province. Five days after the new Viceroy's arrival incidents between Hindus and Muslims took 99 lives in Calcutta. Two days later, a similar conflict broke out in Bombay leaving 41 mutilated bodies on its pavements.

Confronting by these outbursts of violence, Mountbatten called India's senior police officer to his study and asked if the police were capable of maintaining law and order in India. "No, your Excellency" was the reply, "we cannot" shaken, Mountbatten put the same question to Field-Marshal Sir Claude Auchinbek, commander-in-Chief of the Indian Army. He got the same answer.

Mountbatten quickly discovered that the Government with which he was supported to govern India, a coalition of the Congress Party and the Muslim League put together with enormous effort by his predecessor, which was in fact an assembly of enemies so bitterly divided that its members hardly spoke to one another. It was clearly going to fall apart, and when it did, Mountbatten would have to assume the appalling responsibility of exerting direct rule himself with the administrative machine required for the task collapsing underneath him.

Mountbatten saw each of the Indian leaders alone and devoted his first meeting to relaxed discussion[34] about the past, their shared interest and cultural and personal matters. They always sat in armchair in an informal and friendly arrangement as he could devise. The only major Indian leader he met before and the first to join in Delhi was Jawaharlal Nehru, whom he had got to know in 1946 in Singapore, where Mountbatten was Supreme Commander and Nehru a visiting Indian politician fresh out of prison officials had their advised against his seeing Nehru, but Mountbatten was sympathetic to nationalists and arranged a meeting.[35] The two men at once got on, as did Nehru, a widower with Lady Mountbatten, as Brian lapping says in his book "End of Empire"!

For the new Viceroy, Nehru was the key. He was a superb orator and writer, a man who treasured words as a courtesan. Not only was he the leader of the interim government and Gandhi's chosen successor to lead Congress, he became a closed personal friend of Lady Mountbatten in a relationship that transcended their families political business. Richard Hough, author of books on naval history and on Mountbatten, writes in 'Edwina' his biography of Countess Mountbatten, that Nehru was "Edwina's first and only great love".[36] Between the two men the close understanding and trust that developed were not unparallel among British rulers and their nationalist successors but nowhere else did a British Proconsul need so quickly to establish a firm rapport with a nationalist leader. Mountbatten had liked Nehru and respected each other and frankly surveyed the problems and personalities of pre-partition India.[37]

Now Mountbatten started interviewing all Indian leaders and their politicians' timely turn. His interview with Jawaharlal Nehru took place on March 24, 1947.[38] The interview took place at Viceroy's House, the present Rastrapati Bhawan, in whirl of publicity. The press advisor had been directed to arrange for photographers, whose duties were to photograph the meeting. This procedure was mentioned in the minutes of the new Viceroy's staff meeting. Notes were dictated after each interview and circulated among Mountbatten's team. Mountbatten was determined that he should establish a personal rapport with the politicians with whom he would be negotiating, and hoped to make it clear through the media that he would not be operating in the side of an old fashioned imperialist. As I have mentioned earlier that Mountbatten had arranged garden parties, dinners and luncheons. Mountbatten called these 'goodwill campaign'. This new style of functioning of Mountbatten had a very important effect on Delhi's new editor "Nehru's niece Nayantara Sahgal remembers a letter from her mother which told her that the new Viceroy and his wife had dropped informally to my uncle's house in New York Road, and sat in the garden eating strawberry ice-cream. P. French could not believe it and thought she must be joking." These events may not be important today but it was full of meaning in March 1947, when India was marching to independence. This event indicated that Mountbatten was genuine to do for India.

In this background his first interview began with Nehru. Nehru struck him as most sincere. He asked him as most sincere. He asked him about Jinnah. Nehru gave him a remarkable word power of Jinnah's character and described him as one of the most extraordinary men in history. Further he told that Jinnah was a financially successful through mediocre lawyer and found success late in life after the age of sixty. Further Nehru explained Jinnah's creed, which he admitted had scored enormous success, as always to avoid taking any positive action which might split his success. In the end, he said Jinnah had negative qualities. How far Nehru was right in the assessment of Jinnah? Jinnah was Nehru's political rival but to call him as a mediocre lawyer was not right. Jinnah was a successful lawyer. He had a very good practice at Bombay and London. Jinnah practiced at the Privy Council, London. Out of his practice he built a fine building at Malabar Hill in 1939 and purchased a fine house at London. He was an outstanding lawyer. He was not an unsuccessful politician. He was in politics when Nehru was a student at Harrow in London. Jinnah was a member of the Indian National Congress from 1906 and of the Muslim League from 1913. He was responsible for the Lucknow Pact of 1916. It was due to his initiative that the Indian National Congress and the Muslim League held the session at Lucknow. Whatever may be the help from the British Government, Jinnah succeeded in partitioning India into two dominions—the Indian Union and Pakistan. So Jinnah should be considered as a successful politician but he was an enemy to united India. it is a fact that success came late to Jinnah. Jinnah's success started from 1940, when the Lahore session of the Muslim League adopted a resolution which was called later on—the Pakistan resolution. Jinnah got success from this time and it continued till 1947, though he could not get Pakistan according to his own scheme, he got a 'moth eaten and truncated Pakistan'.

Mountbatten spared no effort to win Nehru's support; on none of India's leaders would 'operation seduction' have more impact than Jawaharlal Nehru. A friendship that proved decisive to the months to come was beginning that afternoon.

Taking Nehru to the door Mountbatten told him Mr. Nehru, I want you to regard me as the last British Viceroy winding up the *Raj*, but as the first to lead the way to a new India. Nehru turned and looked at the man he had wanted to see on the Viceregal throne. Ah! He said, a faint smile creating his face, now, I know what they mean when they speak of your charm as being so dangerous.[39]

According to Brian Lapping, Mountbatten next saw Liaquat Ali Khan, Jinnah's number two and than benefiting from Nehru's advice, he saw Gandhi. According to No. 7 of the transfer of power Vol. X, Mountbatten's interview with Patel began after Nehru's interview on 25th March. The interview began; Patel had a well earned reputation for toughness. Emotion formed no part of his character, as is recorded in *Freedom at Midnight*, p. 94. The remark was not wholly exact Patel was an emotional man but he never let the emotions break through the composed faced he turned to the world. Mountbatten deemed Patel as 'most charming'. Patel had high opinion for Sir Stafford Cripps. He said to Viceroy that he opposed Jinnah's view on the Muslim problem on this condition that 80 per cent of India's Muslims were simply 'forcible converts' from Hinduism. When asked about the purpose of forced religious conversion, Patel was very frank and said he could not discuss the matter, because he had no idea of the Muslim mentality. The press attack Alan Campbell, Johnson thought the Home Minister was at least straight forward in his opinions. His approach to the whole problem was clear and decisive. India must get rid of the Muslim League.

Mountbatten considered this meeting with Gandhi very important and so wrote to the Mahatma inviting him to Delhi even before the ceremony enthroning him as Viceroy. Gandhi accepted the invitation. The Viceroy had offered to send his personal aircraft to Bihar to fly Gandhi to Delhi. Gandhi, however, had declined the offer. He had insisted on travelling, as he always did in a third class railway carriage.

Gandhi was invited to see Mountbatten on March 31 at 5 p.m., Gandhi came to see him accompanied by Miss Patel.[40] Miss Patel can be identified as 'Manu Ben Patel'. The talk started with Lord and Lady Mountbatten. The interview ended at 7.15 p.m. They talked purely on social and friendly matters. Again Gandhi came to see Mountbatten on April 1, 1947 at 4 p.m., trailed ever by a retinue of three dozen loyal disciples. Gandhi was the VVIP. Person in the Indian subcontinent and Gandhi could be recognized only because of the loin cloth that he wore according to Valet Charles Smith' he stayed on for afternoon tea, which was arranged on the lawn—Gandhi did not touch either the cakes or sandwiches, but chose to eat a bowl of goat's curd which he had brought with him. He even persuaded the Viceroy to sample a mouthful![41]

The conversation started, Gandhi first told about his past life in details, and then he spoke on political matters. While discussing political matters, Gandhi stressed on those parts of activities, where Gandhi was involved and played a part in political matters. Mountbatten was delighted to hear all these events from the mouth of Gandhi. During the course of the discussion Mr. Gandhi gave it as his considered opinion as a student of history and of world politics that never before, in any case of history he had read about in recent or past-times, had so difficult or responsible a task been imposed on anyone man as that which now faced me. I thanked him sincerely for realizing the position to which I was placed.[42] Gandhi discussed the Tripuri Congress of 1939 and Subhas Chandra's declaration that he could contest for the second time for the office of the President of the Congress. He made strange proposal to remove the political deadlock prevailing in the Central Government. He told Mountbatten on April 1, 1947 that should dismiss the present central government and invite Jinnah to form the government.[43] Congress would co-operate, Gandhi promised so long as all the measures that Mr. Jinnah's cabinet bring forward are in the interest of the Indian people as a whole. If Mr. Jinnah rejects this offer, the same offer to be made *mutasis mutandis* to Congress.

Mountbatten was surprised to hear this strange proposal but after some time he understood its implications. George Abele pointed out to him that this proposal would provoke open civil war. George Abele argued that the Congress had a majority in the central legislature and cabinet would not be able to function. There would be a deadlock and it would lead to civil war. V.P. Menon was a constitutional advisor to the Viceroy. Menon had a soft corner for the Congress but still he wrote that this move would certainly place Jinnah in a position of having to adjust his views to those of the Congress. This is perhaps not unintended by Gandhi . . . . . . It is no solution to suggest that power should be transferred to the Congress to the exclusion of the Muslim League. If the proposition were as simple as that, it would have been solved long ago.[44]

Mountbatten gave his first interview to Jinnah on 5th May but this meeting was not a success. Mountbatten complained that his guest alternated between a most rigid haughty and disdainful frame of mind and 'a gracious tea Party hostess manner'. Liberal ideas of Mountbatten and his charming personality had some effect on Jinnah but still his attitude was rigid and he had his own conception what the Muslim would accept or would not accept. The meeting ended, Mountbatten said to his advisors that still he was unsure what type of recommendations he would make to the British government, although at present I was utterly imperial.[45] Jinnah was the evil genius in this whole thing. Everyone of these interviews lasted one hour. They were reduced in Mountbatten's notes to three or four pages. They represented each page 15 minutes of talking. Therefore, one- eighth of what was said was compressed into this.

Mountbatten gave second interview to Nehru on April 1st from 3 p.m. to 4.20 p.m., it was interview number 20. Mountbatten gave second interview to Patel on 1st April from 7 p.m. it was interview No. 21. Mountbatten gave third interview to Gandhi on 2nd April from 3.30 p.m. to 4.30 p.m., on 3rd April there was another interview between Mountbatten and Gandhi from 2.30 to 4.30 p.m., and it was interview No. 28.[46] Mountbatten gave fifth interview to Gandhi on April 4, from 2.30 to 4.30 p.m. On 11th April Mountbatten gave an interview to Liaquat Ali Khan from 5.30 p.m. to 6.40 p.m., it was interview No. 52. Mountbatten granted three interviews to Jinnah on 5th, 6th and 7th April. On 5th April Jinnah remained till dinner and even after that past midnight. Again Mountbatten interviewed Jinnah on 7th April from 4 to 6.30 p.m. On 8th April Mountbatten talked with Jinnah from 6 to 8 p.m. Mountbatten argued endlessly the case for a 'unified India' Jinnah offered no counter arguments. He gave the impression that he was not listening. His attitude was an affront to Mountbatten's conviction that everyone was susceptible to reason until he had not thought it possible that a man with such a complete lack of sense of responsibilities could hold the power which he did. The Viceroy had nine meeting with Jinnah till the Mountbatten plan. Jinnah gave the impression to Mountbatten that he wanted full Pakistan. Mountbatten told him that I regarded it was a great tragedy that he should be trying to force me to give up the idea of united India. He told Jinnah that he wanted Pakistan. Mountbatten records his impression nevertheless he gives me the impression of a man who has not thought out on single piece of the mechanics of his own scheme and he will have the stack of his life when he really has to come down to earth and try and make his vague ideas.[47] Mountbatten felt that Jinnah had the faculty of closing his mind to the thing—he could see points, he was an able debater, he had a well trained mind, he was a lawyer. But he gave him the impression of having closed his mind, closed his ears, he did not want to be persuaded, he did not want to hear.

What happen to Gandhi's scheme that Jinnah should run the central government on 9th April? Mountbatten made a tentative suggestion to Jinnah. This suggestion had greatly tackled his vanity and that he had kept turning over a proposition in his mind. Gandhi's scheme had the support of Maulana Azad and Abdul Ghaffar Khan. But it was unacceptable to Nehru, Patel and other Congress leaders. The Congress working committee turned down Gandhi's proposal. So Gandhi wrote a letter to Mountbatten asking him to withdraw the scheme. The extract of letter is as follows: Gandhi's letter to Mountbatten, Bhangi Colony, New Delhi, April 11, 1947—

Dear friend,

I had several short talks with Pandit Nehru and an hour's talk with him alone and then with several members of the CWC last night, about the formula I had sketched before you. I am sorry to say that I failed to carry of them with me except Badshah Khan. I do not know that, having failed to carry both the head and heart of Pandit Nehru with me. I would have wanted to carry the matter further. But Panditjee was so good that he would not be satisfied until the whole plan was discussed with the few members of the CWC who were present. I felt sorry that I could not convince them of the correctness of my plan from every point of view. Nor could they dislodge me from my position, although I had not closed my mind against every argument. Thus I have to ask you to omit me from your consideration. Congress men, who are in the interim government, are stalwarts, seasoned servants of the nation and therefore, so far as the Congress point of view is concerned, they will be complete advisors. On Gandhi's scheme Mountbatten says in his report; I must say that "I was speechless at this immoral suggestion and shook my finger at him (Gandhi). But he only blinked and smiled".[48]

Mountbatten had six meetings with Mr. Jinnah, averaging between two to three hours each and the conversations continued. Jinnah made it abundantly clear that the Muslim League would not in any circumstances reconsider the cabinet mission plan and he was intent on having Pakistan. Mountbatten got Jinnah to see May and he gave him his ideas on Pakistan. Is May produced his notes he had made, Mr. Jinnah said 'that is your scheme not mine'. Mountbatten told him that if he accepted his arguments on the need for partition of India, then he could not resist the arguments that Congress were putting forward for the partition of the Punjab and Bengal. Jinnah was quite hurried at this argument and argued at great length on the need to preserve the unity of the Punjab and Bengal, pointing out that the Punjab and Bengal regarded their provinces as unified territories which they would hate to see split up.

Then Mountbatten told him that he had been so impressed by his arguments that he was prepared to accept them. Jinnah was delighted but only until Mountbatten pointed out that his arguments had also convinced him that the partition of India would be criminal. Then Mountbatten and Jinnah started going round the mulberry bush again. Mountbatten hastened to assure him that he should not allow his personal feelings on that was good for India to interfere with working out a solution which would be acceptable to the people of India in their present frame of mind. But he warned Jinnah categorically that if he finally decided to recommend to His Majesty's Government that there should be partition, then that principle would be applied right through the provinces and that partition follow the boundaries of the communal majorities since I was convinced that the non-Muslim communities in the Punjab and Bengal would be just as likely to fight if put under Muslim domination as Muslim League would be likely to fight under Congress domination.

Although Jinnah did not lose his friendly attitude, his argument became more and more futile, and he ended by saying "if you persist in chasing me with your ruthless logic, we shall get no where".

The Viceroy summed up by pointing out the choice before him was likely to be—

- The cabinet mission plan which gave him all five provinces of Pakistan with complete autonomy and with only a very weak centre to which they would have allegiance for three subjects which might be covered by the general term defence.

Or

- A very moth-eaten Pakistan, the eastern and North West frontier parties of which were unlikely to be economic proposition and which would still have to some centre for general defence subject for a long while after we had left.

Jinnah ended up in a rather more reasonable frame of mind regretting his inability to reconsider the cabinet mission plan. He said it could only have been worked in a spirit of the utmost co operation and mutual trust which might have been portable a year ago but that the atmosphere how so far from improving was continuously worsening and it was clear that into the circumstances did Congress intend to work the plan since in accordance with the spirit or the better,[49] with Gandhi having distanced himself from May 10, 1947, the Party was supported by two equally dominant pillars, Pandit Nehru and Sardar Patel. But the Mahatma's detachment did not prevent him from casting a vote of preference. He unambiguously chose his spiritual son, the Urbana Kashmiri Pandit over the dour landlord from Ahmedabad.[50] Sardar Patel had the sharpest of minds elegant, erudite and socially committed; Jawaharlal Nehru was just the man of destiny a nation needed as it hurtled into the rendezvous with self-destiny participated in the political discussion came practically to an end.

Jinnah was insisting on Pakistan in all interviews. He wanted two Muslim states—one in the east and the other in the north-west. Bengal and part of Assam was to compromise the eastern wing and in the north-west, the whole of the Punjab, Sind, N.W.F.P. and Baluchistan. Mountbatten was tired at Jinnah's demands and told Jinnah at interview No. 46 that in case of partition, the Punjab and Bengal would be partitioned. It was told that Bengal and the Punjab had communally mixed population. Jinnah was most upset at this 'moth-eaten' and truncated Pakistan.[51] He said that this demand for partitioning the Punjab and Bengal was a bluff on the part of the Congress to try and frighten him off Pakistan. Jinnah had fixed determination and he was of this opinion that Bengalis and Punjabis could not be divided. They had so much of common elements that the two provinces could not split in two. The Viceroy was losing patience with Jinnah. He perceived him not as the chosen spokes- man of a substantial minority of the Indian people, but as a trouble maker.

The Viceroy's staff meeting was held on April 11, 1947 at 10 a.m.[52] the proceedings are as follows, the Viceroy said that it had always been and would remain his main desire to hand over power to an unified India with a strong centre. The next best to this would be to hand over to a unified India with a week centre. He had now six meetings with Mr. Jinnah. He had brought all possible arguments to bear on Mr. Jinnah but it seemed that appeals to his reason did not prevail. He had presented view to Jinnah the enormous advantage of retaining a unified India—as one; India could be immensely powerful and in the front rank of world powers. He had asked Jinnah why he could possibly wish to throw away such advantages. Jinnah had not been able in his presence to adduce one single plausible argument in favour of partition.[53] In fact he had offered no counter arguments. He gave the impression that he was not listening. It was impossible to agree with.

Mountbatten granted another interview to Jinnah on 9th April. Hindu-Muslim riots were continuing. The Viceroy liked that to restore communal harmony, a joint communiqué should be issued. Mountbatten liked that Gandhi and Jinnah should sign the communiqué. Both leaders were not ready to put their signatures. Mountbatten wrote a letter to Lord Pathick Lawrence on April 15, 1947. He pointed out that Gandhi and Jinnah were not to issue a joint communiqué. At last Mountbatten efforts succeeded. Mountbatten wrote a letter to Lord Pathick Lawrence on April 15, 1947 in this connection, "after a fairly stormy passage I obtained the signature of Jinnah and Gandhi to a public statement deploring recent acts of violence and lawless ness among all communities and denouncing for all time use of force to achieve political ends." Jinnah signed in English and Gandhi in Hindi, Urdu and English. This appeal vindicated Gandhi ideals.[54]

Soon Mountbatten sent a report to London, "I regard Jinnah as a psychopathic case (Viceroy's papers). In fact until I had met him I would not have thought it possible that a man with such a complete lack of administrative knowledge or sense of responsibility could achieve or hold down for a powerful position". Mountbatten felt Jinnah had not throughout one single piece of the mechanics of his own great scheme, and he would have the shock of his life when he really has to come down to earth and try and make his vague idealistic work on a concrete basis. I will then make one final determined effort to secure some compromise on the basis of the cabinet mission plan. If I fail, I shall to fire my last shot in the shape of our announcement of partition.[55]

The social aspect cannot be overlooked, Mountbatten and Lady Mountbatten liked and identified with Nehru but they found Jinnah difficult to handle. Jinnah was rich and he was an elitist. But he was not in the British mould despite his honour square suits. As Patrick remarks, for all the propaganda of Congress, he was never an insider in British governing circles and was considered a spy by many ICS officers. He was no more anglicized than somebody like Patel. For instance, he breached protocol by walking out of a function in front of their Excellencies something that Jawaharlal Nehru would never have done. Even after independence, Nehru was happy to stand and toast King George VI at dinner, despite having once (in the Lahore Congress of 1929) made a famous speech declaring himself no believer in kings and princes.[56]

Lord Wavell also did not like Jinnah. Like Wavell, Mountbatten preferred Liaquat Ali Khan to Jinnah. Mountbatten thought that it was easier with Liaquat than Jinnah. According to the Viceroy papers, his Excellency, the Viceroy pointed out to Jinnah that all these arguments in favour of non-partition of provinces applied equally to the non-partition of India. According to Mountbatten's papers dated April 24, 1947, Miss Jinnah spent an hour and a quarter with me. She talks always politics she made violent attacks on Congress and the Urdu controversy as a whole. Like Mr. Jinnah, she has of course a persecution mania. She seemed almost fanatical at times in her attitude. According to Mountbatten's papers Viceroy's interview with Patel took place on April 24, 1947 from 11 a.m. to 12.55 p.m. Finally Patel said, "since you have come out here the things have got much worse. There is a civil war and you are doing nothing to stop it. You won't govern yourself and you won't let the central government govern. You cannot escape responsibility for this bloodshed."[57]

Mountbatten did not resist Patel's comments and asked him to tear up the minute. Then Mountbatten asked that he would resign. Then the document was torn up. This event ticked out Patel.[58] A study of Mountbatten papers from April 23 to April 28, 1947 convinces that the situation was really critical. The situation was going out of control. There is V.P. Menon's note attached in Mountbatten papers and the note points out that the alternatives before us are a united India on the basis of the cabinet delegation's plan and if that is not so viable a divided India.[59]

As the Cabinet Mission's plan had to be cast away, Mountbatten informed British cabinet that with the communal situation getting worse day by day it was imperative that a new plan of partition had to be worked out but he emphasized that effective power would have to be transferred even before the due date of June 1948. He had already set his administrative machinery in motion. In this phase, two Menon's proved to be of great help to Mountbatten one was V.P. Menon and the other Krishna Menon.

Mountbatten's interview with Suhrawardy took place on April 28, 1947. It was interview No. 98. Mountbatten told him that I was ardently against all forms of partition.[60] I wanted above everything a united India. If I could not have a united India, then I would like the Cabinet Mission plan. If I could not have the Cabinet Mission plan, I would then put it to the provinces to decide. I had been called up to partition the Punjab, Bengal and Assam. Mountbatten talked with Jinnah on April 26, 1947 from 5 to 6.20 p.m. it was interview No. 100. Mountbatten told Jinnah that "Suhrawardy wanted a unified Bengal on condition that it joined neither Pakistan nor Hindustan.[61] Jinnah agreed with this proposal and said that 'they would be on friendly terms with us'. Jinnah told to Mountbatten, "in fact the leaders of the Congress are so dishonest, so crooked and so obsessed with the idea of smashing the Muslim League that there are no lengths to which, they will not go to do so and the only way of giving Pakistan a chance, is to make it an independent nation of the British Commonwealth". [62] According to Mountbatten papers, Mountbatten said that although he considered Mr. Jinnah about the most difficult and unreasonable man with whom he had ever had to deal, did face that Mr. Jinnah's fears had some foundation.[63]

On May 1, 1947, the President of the Constituent Assembly, Dr. Rajendra Prasad made a statement at the outset in which he said that the assembly must be prepared not for a division of India but also a division of some provinces. Due to the problem of Bengal, Dr. Rajendra Prasad had issued this statement. In order to undermine the plan of partitioning Bengal and the Punjab, S.P. Mookerjee wrote a letter to Mountbatten on May 2, 1947, "we are opposed to Pakistan and we like that Bengal should not be partitioned". Jinnah suggested that there should be an eight hundred mile corridor between the two wings of Pakistan and that Calcutta should become a 'free port'. The Congress leader's reaction was hostile and so the idea was soon foundered. It had another effect. The concept of Bengali politicians to keep Bengal united also evaporated. Nehru and Jinnah did not like to weaken their position in New Delhi. On 23rd May, Patel wrote a letter to a political associate in Calcutta, "talk of the idea of sovereign public of independent Bengal was a trap to induce the unwary to enter into the parlor of the Muslim League". Bengal had to be partitioned, if the non-Muslim population is to survive. When Suhrawardy later proposed that Calcutta might remain a free port for six months after the British had left, Sardar said he would not permit such a thing for even six hours.[64] Various political leaders and claimants met the Viceroy in the office. An embassy on behalf of the princely states, a delegation from the North West Frontier Provinces led by Abdul Gaffar Khan and a contingent of Sikh lumens led by Master Tara Singh put their claims before the Viceroy. Dr. B.R. Ambedkar was speaking on the Scheduled Castes.

Viceroy had come to this solution on the basis of the cabinet mission plan was not possible. By this time he had seen the principal Indian leaders. So he called a conference of the eleven provincial governments in mid-April.

The Governor's Conference—3rd April, 1947

The eleven governors assembled around the oval table in the conference chamber presided over by Mountbatten. These governors were capable and dedicated men. They offered India the responsible exercise of authority acquired by a life time of service. India, in its turn, offered them an opportunity to live in a splendour utmost regal in its dimension. The official residences in which they dwelled were places staffed by scores of retainers. Their rights ran our territories as vast and as popular as the largest nations of Europe. They crossed their territories in the comfort of their railway cars, their cities in Rolls Royas with turbaned escorts and their jungles on elephant's back.

The governors had ranged around the table in order of procedure. The first were the heads of the three great presidencies of Bombay, Madras and Bengal. The other provinces then followed: the Punjab, then Sind with its port at Karachi, United Provinces, Bihar and Orissa, Assam, site of the famous tea plantations on the Burmese frontier, the Central Province (currently M.P.) and finally the North West Frontier Province guarding the Khybar Pass and the Afghan Frontier.

Lord Mountbatten, at 46, was the youngest man at the table. He had a brilliant parliamentary career and he had a background of administrative achievement. Most of the eleven governors had devoted an entire career in India. They were proved man, certain to be sceptical of any plan put before them by the neophyte in their midst. Yet Mountbatten was personally convinced his lack of expertise was the disadvantage it seemed, he began by asking each governor to describe the situation in his province. Eight of them pointed a picture of dangerous troubled areas but in these provinces the situation was still under control. It was the portrait offered by the governor of the three critical provinces, i.e. the Punjab, Bengal and North West Frontier that sobered the gathering.

The Governor of the North West Frontier, Sir Ulof Caroe spoke first. Almost Ulof Caroe's career had been spent on that edge of the Empire. No westerner alive could reveal his knowledge, of its unruly pathetic man, their tribes' man, their culture and language. He warned that the provinces were close to disintegration and if this happened there might be invasions from the North West. Sir Evan Jenkins, the Governor of Punjab was even grimmer. It is absurd to predict that Punjab will go up in flames, if it is partitioned he said, 'it is already in flames'.

The Governor Sir Frederick Burrows of Bengal was ill in Calcutta. But the briefing in the province's situation was offered by his Deputy was very disquieting as the reports from the N.W.F.P. and the Punjab.

When these reports were finally finished, Mountbatten's staff passed out a set of papers to each governor. They carried the details. Mountbatten announced one of the possible plans under examination. It was called for easy references, Plan Balkan and it was the first draft of the partition plan. Mountbatten had ordered his chief of staff Lord Ismay to prepare a week earlier.

All the assembled governors were shocked to go through the papers. These Governors were the architects of Indian unity. Most of them had spent their lives in strengthening the ties and they learnt painfully that Indian unity would be dismantled by the departing Britain.

The plan was called after the Balkanization of the states of central Europe after the First World War. This plan would allow each of India's eleven provinces to choose whether it wished to join Pakistan which was to be created as a separate dominion or remain in India or if a majority of both its Hindus and Muslims agreed became independent. Mountbatten told his assembled Governors that he was not going lightly to abandon hope for a united India. Mountbatten said that he wanted the world to know the British had made every effort possible from March 1947 to keep India united and if Britain failed it was of the utmost that the world know it was 'Indian opinion rather than British decision that made partition the choice'. He made it clear that a future Pakistan was so inherently enviable that it should be given a chance to fall on its own demerits, so that later the Muslim League would revert to a united India with horror.

These Governors did not display any enthusiasm for the partition of India nor did they oppose it. The fact was that they had no other solution to propose. (*Freedom at Mid Night*, pp. 111 to 114)

Partition and the High Command of the Congress Party

The High Command of the Congress Party was deliberating the issue of the partition of the country. Mahatma Gandhi was not satisfied with the trend of the discussion. These leaders felt that the partition was the only alternative. Gandhi felt that the parting of the ways between him and these men had come. Gandhi was pained and told a friend; they call me a *mahatma* but I tell you I am not even treated by them as a sweeper.

Like Mountbatten, Nehru, Patel and the others all felt a catastrophic, overtook India and partition was the only to save the country. Gandhi believed that they were wrong. Even if they were right, he would have preferred—choose to partition. Gandhi was a voice crying in the wilderness, it was an irony of history that Nehru and Patel, who always stood together since 1920 were not ready to hear him for the last time. Patel had been prepared to concede partition, even before Mountbatten's arrival. He was ageing. He suffered two heart attacks. He likes to cure these endless debates and got down to the talk of building an independent India. Give Jinnah his state, he argued it would not survive any way. In five years, the Muslim League would be knocking at their door for India's reunification.

At this critical moment of history, Nehru was a torn and

anguished man. He was caught between his deep love for Gandhi and his admiration and friendship for the Mountbatten. Gandhi spoke to his heart; Mountbatten's to his mind respectively. Nehru detested partition, yet his national spirit told him, it was the only answer. One argument was vital. If Pakistan is created, Hindu India could have the strong central government. It would then be possible as Nehru thought to build the socialist state of his dreams. The result was that ultimately, Nehru too stood out against the man (Gandhi) he had followed so long from 1920.

With Nehru and Patel in favour of the partition of the country, the rest members of the High Command quietly fell into line. Nehru was authorized to inform the Viceroy that while Congress remained passionately attached to the idea of a united India. It would accept partition, provided the two great provinces of Punjab and Bengal were divided. Collins and Lapierre has remarked in *Freedom at Midnight*, p. 20; the man had led to victory to their triumph was left alone with his tarnished victory and his broken dream.

On May 2, 1947 at 6 p.m. the Viceroy's Chief of Staff Lord Ismay started for London with the 'Balkan Plan' for the division of India. This plan was to be submitted to His Majesty's Government for consideration.

Mountbatten was not happy with this plan. Now it was certain that he would go down in history as the man who divided India. Had Mountbatten knew of Jinnah's fatal illness, which had been referred by Lord Wavell in his Diary, things would have been different?

Partition, Mountbatten wrote 'is sheer madness' and no one would ever induce me to agree to it were not for this fantastic communal madness that has seized everybody and leaves 'no other course open'.

The responsibility for this mad decision he wrote, must be placed squarely on Indian shoulders in the eyes of the world, for one they well bitterly regret the decision they are about to take. (*Freedom at Midnight*, pp. 119-120)

After the provincial autonomy of 1937, a central intelligence officer in each province had been appointed, who reported directly to the director, Intelligence Bureau, who passed any intelligence to Sardar Vallabhbhai Patel, the Home Minister, Government of India from 1946.

The Viceroy had to find out a solution of the present crises but the choice was that the Viceroy must do what the oldest Party of the country liked. The Viceroy could not displease the Indian National Congress. The Second World War had reduced Britain to a second rate power. Hence Britain was not in a position to impose any kind of political settlement on India. Britain was powerful in 1942 to impose a settlement on the country. But it was not possible for Britain to impose a solution in the post-1945 period.

Indian National Congress did not accept the recommendation of the Cripps Mission and the Congress started an 'open rebellion' in August 1942. But that was not possible in April 1947. As Mountbatten admitted to a 'top secret' meeting of the staff on May 1, 1947, in the past when the situation was not fluid, at the instance of Mountbatten, the words were deleted from the minutes. But 'now if he fell foul of Congress it would be impossible to continue to run the country—it was evident—that anything but a clean partition would produce enmity on the part of Congress'.[65] Lord Pathick Lawrence was still continuing as the Secretary of state. Prime Minister Attlee replaced Pathick Lawrence by the Earl of Listowal, Listowal continued in the office for four months only.

Mountbatten had daily meetings with all the political leaders not only of the two major political parties, but with those of all the minorities and with many of the Rulers and Dewans of Indian States. He conferred with all the Governors and residents as well as the army commanders and most of the senior Indian officers of the Armed Forces.

Mountbatten's first course, in all his discussion had been to urge the political leaders to accept the Cabinet Mission plan unreservedly. For in his opinion that plan provided the best of arrangement that could be devised to meet the interests of all the communities of India. But it had been impossible to obtain agreement between the leaders of the two main parties either on the Cabinet Mission Plan or on any other plan that would preserve the unity of India.

Mountbatten was tired with these interviews. Each session with an Indian leader lasted about an hour. He then spent 15 minutes dictating a note, which was usually circulated to his staff.[66]

NOTES

1. *Transfer of Power*, Vol. IX, p. 583.
2. French, Patrick, *Liberty or Death*, p. 276.

3. *Transfer of Power*, Vol. IX, pp. 510 and 451, Mountbatten was responsible for propagating the term 'the British Raj' or 'The Raj' as a way to referring to Britain's Indian Empire. It rarely appears before 1947, and is not generally used in India today, since '*Raj*' simply means rule and could apply equally with to '*Ram Raj*', Congress Raj. 'Angrej Sarkar' was the term used at the time for Indians, for whom the British usually reformed to the 'Indian Empire'.
4. *The Times of India*, New Delhi, December 1981, XX Govind Talwalkar *'it was an immoral suggestion'*.
5. Harries Kenneth Attlee, London, 1995, p. 362.
6. *Congress Bulletin*, No. 3, March 26, 1947.
7. Gregg, John, (edited), *Nehru Memorial Lectures*, 1966-96, New Delhi, 1992, p. 22.
8. Campbell, Johnson Alan, *Mission with Mountbatten*, London, 1972, p. 29.
9. Mountbatten's original name.
10. A tribute by Ludo Vir Kennedy titles *Mountbatten: A Man of Our Time*, published in the *Times of India*, New Delhi, September 7, 1977—courtesy, *The Listener*, London.
11. *The Times of India*, New Delhi, August 15, 1947, *India, the First 50*.
12. A tribute by Ludo Vir Kennedy titles' *Mountbatten: a man of our time*, published in the *Times of India*, New Delhi, September 7, 1977—courtesy, *The Listener*, London.
13. French, Patrick, *Liberty and Death*, p. 285.
14. *Ibid.*
15. Doon Campbell Diary, the *Asian Age*, August 7, 1947.
16. French, Patrick, *Liberty and Death*, p. 285.
17. Collins and Lapierre, *Mountbatten and the Partition of India*, p. 22.
18. Brecher, Micheal, *Nehru : A Political Biography*, pp. 336-337.
19. Lapping's Brian, *End of the Empire*, a review published in the *Times of India*, July 1, 1988.
20. Nanda, B.R., *the British had No Plan to Free India*, published in the *Times of India*, New Delhi, May 26, 1985.
21. Nanda, B.R., *A Time to Go*, published in the *Times of India*, New Delhi, June 9, 1985.
22. *Ibid.*
23. Brian, Lapping, *India No More Jewel in Crown*, published in the *Times of India*, June 16, 1985.
24. Mosley, Leonard, *The Last Days of the British Raj*, p. 81.
25. *Ibid.*
26. Mountbatten and the Partition of India, p. 27.
27. Hudson, H.V., *The Great Divide Britain-India-Pakistan*, p. 204.
28. Collins and Lapierre, p. 27.
29. Brian, Lappings, '*End of Empire*' a review, 'Jinnah sets off a violence',

the *Times of India*, July 7, 1985.
30. *Ibid.*
31. *Freedom at midnight*, pp. 79-80.
32. Brian, Lappings, '*End of Empire*' a review, 'Jinnah sets off a violence', the *Times of India*, July 7, 1985.
33. *Ibid.*
34. *Ibid.*
35. *Ibid.*
36. *Ibid.*
37. *Ibid.*
38. Transfer of Power, Vol. X, Interview No. 3, p. 11.
39. *Freedom at Midnight*, p. 88.
40. *Ibid.*
41. Durga Das, *Sardar Patel's Correspondence IV*, p. 43.
42. *Transfer of Power*, Vol. X, p. 197.
43. *Ibid., Interview No. 19*, pp. 69 and 141.
44. *Transfer of Power*, Vol. X, pp. 124-125.
45. *Ibid.*, p. 138.
46. *Ibid.*
47. *Ibid.*, Interview No. 28, p. 102.
48. *Transfer of Power*, Vol. X, p. 197, Editor in Chief, Nicholas Manseargh, Revised this volume by G. Talwalkar.
49. *Mountbatten and the Partition of India*, Report No. 3, April 17, 1947.
50. *The Times of India*, August 15, 1997.
51. *Transfer of Power*, vol. X, p. 284.
52. *Ibid.*, p. 199.
53. *Ibid.*
54. Durga Das, *Curzon to Nehru and After*, p. 243.
55. *Transfer of Power*, Vol. X, p 300.
56. Sahgal, Nayantara, *Prison and Chocolate Cake*, London 1981.
57. *Transfer of Power*, Vol. X p. 388.
58. *Ibid.*, p. 398.
59. *Ibid.*, p. 438.
60. *Ibid.*, p. 448.
61. *Ibid.*, p. 451.
62. *Ibid.*, p. 453.
63. *Ibid.*, p. 507.
64. French Patrick, *Liberty or Death*, p. 555.
65. *Ibid.*, p. 511.
66. Excerpts from Brian Lapping, *End of Empire*, the *Times of India*, July 7, 1985.

11

Plan Balkan—The Balkanization of India

Mountbatten had been emphasizing that the cabinet mission plan would keep India united and with a loose centre the Muslims would get Pakistan in substance though not in name.

Nehru and Patel claimed that the Congress had accepted the Cabinet Mission Plan. Though they had reservation initially, they agreed to the British interpretation. So they demanded that the Muslim League should join the constituent assembly. But despite this we find from the reports of the talks which Nehru had with the Viceroy as well as his letter to him that he was not reconciled to the idea that the provinces should first decide on the group constitution and then freely exercise their right to opt out. He wanted them to exercise their right before joining the group. The Viceroy could not agree to this procedure and Jinnah did not wait the Cabinet Mission Plan which he all in while maintained was dead as mutton.

Jinnah's demand was Pakistan. He wanted two Muslim states one in the east and the other in the north west. Bengal and part of Assam were to comprise the eastern wing and in the north west, the whole of the Punjab, Sind, North West Frontier provinces and Baluchistan.

In fact, Jinnah had been told by the Cabinet Mission in clear terms that if he insisted he would have to agree to the partition of the Punjab and Bengal and also, to sacrifice Calcutta. When Mountbatten pointed out that Bengal and the Punjab would be partitioned. Jinnah remarked on 8th April that it would be a 'moth-eaten Pakistan' but Mountbatten suggested that it would be a 'truncated Pakistan'.

As the Cabinet Mission's plan had to be cast aside, Mountbatten informed the British cabinet that with the communal question getting worse day by day. It was imperative that a new plan of partition had to be worked. He came to this conclusion that Jinnah would stick to the demand of Pakistan till the last moment and the Congress leaders were amenable to compromise. He also came to this conclusion that the Indian situation was rapidly deteriorating into chaos and that the cabinet plan for a united India would have to be scrapped. But the further instruction to go on pressing it until October 1947 made an impact on him.

By early April 1947, it was clear that partition was inevitable. By mid-April Mountbatten had begin to evolve the plan that he hoped would resolve existing difficulties in India. Now he was of this opinion that a united India would be maintained only as a result of a bitter and costly civil war. It was known as the Balkan Plan. 'Balkanization' as by word of the earlier half of the twentieth century was a much greater threat in India in 1947. The broad bases of the plan was the demission of the authority to the provinces or to such confederations of provinces as might decide to group themselves in the intervening period before the actual transfer of power. The plan had adopted a special method in Bengal and the Punjab.

Mountbatten formed a special committee consisting of Ismay, Mieville and Abele to produce a plan under his general supervision. This would include the draft of an announcement by HMG on how they intend to transfer power on the due date. This committee headed by Mountbatten met one of the principal leaders each day from 7th April to 14th—Liaquat on Monday, Nehru on Tuesday, Jinnah on Wednesday and Patel on Friday. Mountbatten found that a single leader who came to tender evidence before a small committee, "They are reasonable and go out of their own way to be helpful" not only in pointing out difficulties which would encounter from their own Party, but also frequently drawing attention to the difficulties which would be raised by the other Party.[1]

The plan had also made an arrangement for the holding of an election in the North West Frontier provinces to ascertain the wishes of the people of the province.

Krishna Menon and V.P. Menon had helped the Viceroy to prepare the 'Balkan Plan'. Krishna Menon was the friend of Mountbatten and V.P. Menon was the Reform Commissioner, George Abele, Principal Private Secretary in a note to the Viceroy had said that Mr. Krishna Menon has an encyclopaedic knowledge of every thing to do with the Indian Constitution on the basis of Dominion status.

This plan had been prepared by Mountbatten with the help of Lord Ismay, Chief of the Viceroy's Staff, who had been Churchill's Chief of Staff throughout the war. Sir George Abele, Private Secretary to the Viceroy, a distinguished scholar and triple blue whose knowledge of India and Indians was great. The broad outline of the plan had been discussed with the prominent Indian leaders. The view of Pandit Nehru, Sardar Patel, M.A. Jinnah and Liaquat Ali Khan had been obtained at the series of meetings with the Viceroy. The Viceroy had formulated a plan for rapid departure from India. This plan would have enabled his Majesty's Government to cut loose from India under the guise of delivering liberty.

The plan was supposedly based on the Cripps offer (1942). It was construed out of a variety of conflicting ambitions and intention. Plan Balkan intended to satisfy all units of the country but it did not succeed in its intention. Various drafts had been prepared at several stages, various people in New Delhi got chance to go through it. On May 2, 1947, Mountbatten's Chief of Staff, Lord Ismay accompanied by George Abele departed for London with the plan 'Balkan' for the consideration by the British Government. It was presented to the cabinet on 3rd May for immediate approval. On 3rd May the draft of the plan had been shown to Nehru and Jinnah. But they had not been allowed to retain the document. Apart from them, the outline of the plan had been discussed with Sardar Patel, Liaquat Ali Khan and Sardar Baldev Singh. On 4th May Mountbatten had an interview with Gandhi from 4 to 5.30 p.m. and discussed with him the outline of the plan. He wanted to know his views on the plan. Gandhi said that he opposed to the partition of the country. By 6th May, Mountbatten had 133 interviews with the Indian leaders.

The essence of the plan was to make it apparent to the people of India, and to the world in general that we are allowing, so far as possible, Indians themselves to choose how they wish us to transfer power, provinces will have the right to decide whether they will all work with the present Constituent Assembly; whether only some will adhere to it (Hindustan); and whether others will wish to sit up a new constituent assembly (Pakistan). In the case of the three provinces, Punjab, Bengal and Assam on which partition has been asked for if Pakistan takes place, I am opposing machinery to allow the provinces themselves to decide if they want partition. There is a reluctance to accept any formula, which I believe to be due to the desire of the Indians to the force the British to make a decision on how they will transfer power, so that we may get the blame of things ultimately go wrong.[2]

The chief characteristics of the plan were to break India into constituent parts and then to put them back together again. There was this provision that each of the eleven provinces of British India would decide its own fate. Bengal and the Punjab could divide down the middle if they chose to. The Indian states would have the choice of standing alone or forming alliances with any state or any province if they thought so. If once this process had been completed, all the parties could reunite, according to taste. If the 'Plan Balkan' would have been approved and implemented, its natural result would have been that the constituent assembly would have died a natural death and in the process a collection of miniature autonomous warring states across India would have been created.

Attlee personally and many members of his cabinet had no idea about India and its politics and they tried to re-work the whole plan. Few things were added to the plan. An option was introduced which would enable the North West Frontier provinces to become independent if it chose so. It was decided that the future of Baluchistan was to be settled by a handful of nominated landlords. Few amendments and clarifications were added by the parliamentary draftsman. When cabinet approved 'The Plan Balkan' with amendments, it was sent to India. Mountbatten announced that he would call a meeting of the Indian leaders in the middle of May, with a view to securing their rapid agreement to the proposals.

On 9th May, Sardar Vallabhbhai Patel announced that "the current British policy of remaining neutral, but holding power is a way of propagating a civil war and that control should be transferred immediately to the Central Government as it now stands with the Viceroy act . . . . . . If there were conflicts in the cabinet on any question, the majority would rule".[3] On the same day an officer of the Indian army, Brigadier Carriappa, suggested at a private meeting that once the British had left there should be a military dictatorship in the country. The forces, with either Nehru or Jinnah as Commander-in Chief should take over power. Mountbatten replied that such a course of action would be not only wholly impracticable but highly dangerous.[4]

The Viceroy pointed out that the only other possible reason for the last minute rejection by Mr. Jinnah would be a sudden realization that Pakistan was not practicable. When faced with the full horrors of a truncated Pakistan, he might conceivably try to get out of it, but this was most unlikely.[5]

Simla

It was the summer season and the Viceroy came to Simla on the evening of Tuesday, 6th May, accompanied by V.P. Menon, the Reforms Commissioner and Sir Fric Mieville. Gandhi wrote a letter to the Viceroy on May 8, 1947; it would be a blunder of first magnitude for the British to be Party in any way whatsoever to the division of India. The Viceroy had moved to Simla for a week. Mountbatten had asked Nehru to come as my guest as he thought that he was nearing a breakdown from overwork and he spent four days at Simla with the Viceroy. Nehru arrived on Thursday, 8th May to stay as state guest for four days. Jawaharlal Nehru was accompanied by his daughter Indira, his confidant Krishna Menon, and his south Indian secretary M.O. "Mac" Mathai. They stayed at Viceregal lodge and spent much of their time at 'The Retreat', resting place at Mashobra. The Viceroy's establishment at Simla held Jawaharlal Nehru in high esteem. Dickey and Edwina were close to Nehru. Nehru was highly elated. He remembered events of 1942 to 1945, when he had been languishing in prison, and now the circumstances had turned and he was the personal house arrest of the Viceroy, the King's cousin. As Mathai recorded; one thing that I could not fail to notice was that whenever Nehru stood by the Lady Mountbatten, he had the sense of triumph.[6]

The visit was the definite social success. 'Jawa' as the Mountbatten called him, consolidated his instinctive bond with Edwina. Mountbatten came close to Nehru and like Nehru; Mountbatten exhibited inability to walk fast backwards uphill. We have made real friendly with him and whatever else happens I feel this friendship is sincere and will last. So Mountbatten and Nehru were enjoying holiday at Simla. In London events were moving fast. The India and Burma Committee met in the Prime Minister's room, House of Commons on 8th May at 5.30 p.m. with Attlee in the chair and considered the draft paragraph by paragraph. Further amendments were suggested and approved. Attlee despatched a letter to the Dominion Prime Minister on 8th May, the partition of India is eminent. Lord Ismay sent a telegram to Mountbatten on May 9th; the cabinet committee suggested the meeting with the big five might start on May 17th. So Mountbatten invited Nehru, Patel, Liaquat Ali Khan and Sardar Baldev Singh to meet him round the table in Delhi at 10.30 a.m. On 17th May the Viceroy's Press Advisor, Campbell Johnson announced that the Viceroy would present to the big five leaders the plan which His Majesty's Government had approved for the transfer of power to Indian hands.

Mountbatten and Nehru were on good terms. Mountbatten invited Nehru on the night of 10th May into the Viceroy's study for a drink. On 10th May, the final amended text of 'Plan Balkan' had been telegraphed to Simla. Mountbatten was determined on this point that the Indian leaders should accept this plan. Mountbatten had taken precaution that an announcement of the acceptance of the plan must be made on 20th May at 7.30 p.m. it should be announced simultaneously on the floor of the House of Commons. The Viceroy had a distinct lunch and he wanted that Nehru should look at the London draft. Mountbatten was not sure whether the Indian leaders would approve the plan? He broke with both protocol and even handedness by allowing Nehru to see a copy of the document 'as an act of friendship' and even to 'take the draft to bed'.

Nehru read the draft in the night and sent the reply in the morning of 11th May in the form of a 'personal and secret note to Mountbatten'. When Mountbatten was in the middle of a meeting with the Governor of Punjab, Nehru sent him a letter. This is a copy of the letter from Pandit Jawaharlal Nehru to His Excellency The Viceroy; you were good enough to speak to me frankly and in a very friendly manner last night and to give me an opportunity to see the tentative proposals. I need hardly to tell you how much I appreciate your confidence to me or that I am convinced of your earnest desire to help India to achieve her freedom as early as possible. It has been a privilege to get to know you better and I hope that our understanding of each other will be helpful to both and to the wider courses we have at heart.

I read the draft proposal you gave me with the care. They deserve and with every desire to absorb them and accept them in so far as I could. But with all the goodwill in the world I reacted to them very strongly. Instead they produced a devastating effect upon me. The relatively simple proposals that we had previously discussed now appeared, in the garb that HMG had provided for them, in an entirely new context which gave them an ominous meaning. The whole approach was completely different from what ours had been and the picture of India that emerged frightened me. In fact much that we had done so far was undermined and the cabinet mission's scheme and subsequent developments were set aside, and an entirely new picture presented a picture of fragmentation and conflict and disorder, and unhappily also, of a worsening of relations between India and Britain. That, I am wholly convinced, was and is not your intention, nor can I believe that is HMG's intention. But HMG seems to function in an ivory tower of own isolated from realities in India. They precede apparently on certain assumption which his little relevance and ignore the basic factor of the situation in India.

If my reactions were so powerful, you can well imagine what my colleague and others will think and feel. I think it will be a disaster if something is done now which will dam up the river of progressively friendly relations between Britain and India and reverse the current.

I have written rather hastily note on the tentative proposals. This is necessarily rather crude as I am in a hurry to let you know now I feel about it all. I tried to make the note brief but it strengthened itself. As soon as it is ready I shall send it to you. Meanwhile, I am sending this letter to you for some indication of how upset I have been by these proposals, which I am convinced, will be resented and better all over the country.[7]

In his diary Mountbatten called Nehru's role as 'Bombshell'. Campbell Johnson noted, Nehru having read it has vehemently turned it down and is convinced that it involves a major departure in principle from the original draft prepared by Mountbatten and his staff. The Viceroy told his press attaché that he had only given the plan to Nehru on a lunch...... without that lunch, Dickey Mountbatten, he said would have been finished and could have packed his bag,...... He said, that most of his staff, with natural caution, had been against his running over his plan with Nehru, but he following his advice rather than their advice he had probably saved the day.

It is the credit of Nehru that he saved India from Balkanization into so many smaller units.[8] But for Mountbatten it was a personal and most humiliating relief. But Mountbatten was not daunted. He called a crisis meeting of officials of Viceregal Lodge in the afternoon of 11th May. Mountbatten told the meeting that the 'Plan Balkan' was based on the Cabinet Mission Plan, under which provinces could opt out of groups within the union of India. But in reality the "Plan

Balkan" offered numerous successors states and later on these states could rein groups if they so desired. As Nehru told one official, it would create 'Ulster's' all over the subcontinent. The Viceroy had assured Attlee that the Plan would be approved by all political parties of India but it failed to win support only in the first round.

Nehru Foiled Plan to Balkanize India

> *"Records prove beyond doubt that it was Pandit Jawaharlal Nehru, who had foiled a British plan to Balkanize India", Mr. M.J. Akbar says in his latest book "Nehru—The Making of India".*

According to M.J. Akbar, this secret plan was limited to a handful of Indians. Maulana Azad had little idea of all this and his understanding of partition was, therefore, limited. Nehru and Patel worked in harmony on this issue and kept this secret to themselves.

According to the little known British Plan, the provinces would initially become successor states and inevitably this would influence the negotiating powers of the particularly the larger princely states, which in any case would have the right to strike deals with the centre integrating into the union.

"At least a dozen confused nations would have emerged, at the very minimum" if the plan was executed, says Akbar in his book.

In a separate chapter on "Plan Balkan" Mr. Akbar says, Sardar Vallabhbhai Patel, the strong man of India, had accepted the idea of partition even before Pandit Nehru.

V.P. Menon had convinced Patel that a United India was impossible, "Jinnah would never agree to anything except Pakistan and it was better to save what could be saved of India rather than gravitate towards civil war."

With Sardar Patel's broad concurrence, V.P. Menon forwarded the 'Partition plan' to the British Government. The British Viceroy, Lord Mountbatten saw this plan before it was sent.

Mountbatten took a short trip to the hills of Simla. Pandit Nehru along with Indira and Mr. Krishna Menon joined them as their personal guests on 8th May and were put up at the Viceregal lodge.

> *"On the evening of 10th May, Lord Mountbatten and Pandit Nehru retired to the Viceroy's study after dinner. They were*

alone. It was at that meeting Lord Mountbatten decided to show Pandit Nehru a copy of the secret 'Plan Balkan'. Lord Mountbatten's staff was strongly opposed to showing the Plan to Pandit Nehru. The staff argued that it would be 'breach of faith' to reveal it to Pandit Nehru in advance without showing it to Mr. Jinnah too."

Pandit Nehru did not have the remotest suspicion about what he was going to see when he took the file Lord Mountbatten preferred. They continued their conversation and Pandit Nehru began reading it when he had returned to his bedroom. He was horrified shaking with rage. He stormed into Mr. V.K. Krishna Menon's room, until composed himself. He felt cheated, betrayed. So for the only plan the British had discussed with him, had been of Mr. V.P. Menon which had the approval of Sardar Patel too.

On 8th May and 9th May they had formally discussed these proposals at meeting with Mr. V.P. Menon also being present but even this Indian did not breathe a word about the alternative scheme which was certain to 'Balkanize' India, as he was under instructions not to.

At the Viceroy's 11th miscellaneous meeting on 10th May, Pandit Nehru accepted transfer of power on the basis of Dominion states, and though he claimed that the only real difficulty would be in regard to Pakistan, he said it was most clear Pakistan would have to be conceded.

When Mr. V.P. Menon saw Pandit Nehru in the morning of 11th May, recalls in his memoirs, "I found that his usual charm and smile had deserted him and that he was obviously upset". It was a civil servant's understatement. But Nehru was in no mood to talk to a civil servant. He rushed a "personal and secret" letter to Lord Mountbatten. The proposals, he said had procured a devastating effect upon me. "The whole approach was completely from what ours had been and the picture of India that emerged frightened me, a picture of fragmentation, and conflict and disorder and unhappily also, of a worsening of relations between India and Britain."

According to the book, Pandit Nehru's violent opposition shook Lord Mountbatten and there was the collapse of the Balkan Plan. Lord Mountbatten then met Pandit Nehru alone and agreed that Mr. Jinnah would get Pakistan, with Punjab and Bengal truncated. But power in the rest of the country would be handed to only one central successor government.

It sounds one of those very dramatic things to say which immediately arouse suspicion, but the record proves beyond doubt that Pandit Nehru with the help of Mr. Krishna Menon performed a unique and immeasurable service to his country, a service which has not been sufficiently recognized. Pandit Nehru had gone to Simla for a pleasant break, not a crisis. It came upon him suddenly. In fact, he was lucky to be there. In Delhi, the environment may not have existed for such an exchange of confidence. Only one other man knew what was happening that day and he too did not disclose the details to a soul. Sardar Vallabhbhai Patel, who was being secretly informed through the telephone, Mr. V.P. Menon, Pandit Nehru and Sardar Patel gave their commitment that they would bring the Congress round; the only trouble was now to force Jinnah to accept a divided Punjab and Bengal.

At the Congress Working Committee on May 31, 1947, the Muslim Congress man felt the tragedy (of Pakistan) to perhaps a greater degree. It was they, who felt themselves bewildered and felt Jinnah had destroyed their dream.

On June 14, 1947, the All India Congress Committee met to ratify the June 3, plan. Sardar Patel delivered a key-note address. Sardar Patel and Nehru were one on this point. If they had not accepted partition, he said, India would have been shattered. Pandit Nehru pointed out the prevailing madness of violence.

Menon Plan

At this critical moment, Mountbatten turned to Menon. Rai Bahadur V.P. Menon was the Reforms Commissioner from 1942. He was a clerk in the Government of India's Reforms Office. He had been promoted to the post of Reforms Commissioner. Menon was close to Patel from the time of the interim government. On 11th May, Mountbatten entered his office in a state of high emotion and Menon was summoned and asked to revive a proposal he had been floating for some time. This plan proposed that power shall be transferred to two central governments, one in India and one in Pakistan. Both governments would get the status of Dominions in the British Commonwealth. Provincial assemblies of Bengal and Punjab would decide if they were in favour of division. Pending a constitution to be framed by the constituent assembly, authority would be handed over without any delay to the two new governments and two governments would function under the terms of the Government of India Act, 1935.

Nehru was to leave Simla that very night. So Menon was given three hours time to prepare the plan. From the Viceroy's residence Menon came to the hotel, where he was staying. Then he started his work and Nehru's time of departure reached. Menon dashed off a few pages on his typewriter. Nehru examined them and returned to New Delhi satisfied with the draft. It was known as the 'Menon Plan'.[9] Within three hours Menon prepared a Draft, which many eminent politicians had failed to prepare. Menon wrote letter; I was keeping Vallabhbhai informed of the development in Simla and he was delighted by the turn of events.

At this turn of events Mountbatten sent a telegram to Attlee on 11th May, for postponing invitations to Monday, 2nd June. He sent another telegram to Ismay informing him that the plan was rejected by Nehru. Mountbatten was happy at Menon's draft and referred to him as 'my brilliant Indian staff officer'. With Attlee and the cabinet in a state of dismay over these developments, the Viceroy was ordered back to Britain to offer an explanation. So he flew out from Delhi on 18th May and Edwina and Menon were with him. Mountbatten was meeting ministers and took a 'trembling Rai Bahadur Menon to meet the King Emperor. The Viceroy was present at the India and Burma Committee on May 18, 1947 at Downing Street London. Jinnah made a remark on Pakistan in an interview with Reuters on May 21, 1947. He said that the Muslim League would demand a corridor through Hindustan to connect the two wings of Pakistan. Secondly, the League would 'fight every inch' against the partition of Bengal and Punjab. On May 21, 1947 the Viceroy's draft statement was approved by the British Government. Attlee had told Mountbatten when asking him to see Churchill, holds the key in England. Neither I nor any of my government would possibly persuade him, but he is fond of you. He trusts you. You have a chance.

The Viceroy had an interview with Churchill on May 22, 1947. Churchill agreed that the Conservative Party would facilitate legislation on the basis of this discussion. Finally, Churchill declared that if Mountbatten really would deliver the formal public acceptance of all the Indian parties to this plan, then the whole country would be behind him. He and his Conservative Party would join Labour in cramming through parliament the historic legislation. Mountbatten needed before its summer recess, India could become independent not in years or months, but in weeks, even days.[10]

Before his departure to London, Jinnah defined Pakistan to Mountbatten in an interview on May 17, 1947.[11] He said, P for Punjab, A for Afghan (Pathan in NWFP), K for Kashmir, I for nothing because the letter was redundant in the word in Urdu, S for Sind and Tan for Baluchistan. Liaquat Ali Khan, who was also in the interview said that the literal meaning for Pakistan was 'pure land'. It was interview No. 140.

Though Wavell had spoken of the partition scheme as "Operation Madhouse" and Mountbatten considered it 'sheer madness', but the partition of the country was now a settled fact. The draft statement laid down that the provincial legislative assemblies of Bengal and Punjab should meet in two parts, one representing the Muslim majority districts and the other the rest of the provinces. The members of two parties of the legislative assembly sitting separately would be empowered to vote whether or not the province should be partitioned. It was decided that a small conference consisting of leaders of the Congress, the Muslim League and Sikh would be conversed by the Viceroy on 2nd June for presenting the plan. On 30th May, after a last meeting with members of the India and Burma Committee, Mountbatten returned to India. Till June 22, 1947 Mountbatten had nine interviews with Gandhi, five interviews and four meetings with Nehru, nine interviews with Jinnah and five interviews with Patel.

On May 23, 1947, the British cabinet approved in principle the terms of draft plan, in the event of a failure to secure compromise on the basis of the cabinet mission plan. While the date of June for the Viceroy's meeting with the Indian leaders was already settled, some final arrangements had still be made on his return from London.[12] First, the importance was the question of attendance. Nehru had suggested that Acharya Kriplani as President of Congress should be invited in addition to Nehru himself, Patel, Jinnah, Liaquat Ali Khan and Baldev Singh. But the Viceroy pointed out his difficulty in according to the request. Jinnah when sounded was most averse to the idea. Nehru on behalf of Congress Working Committee insisted upon its adoption. The matter was finally resolved. An invitation was issued to Acharya Kriplani on Congress side and Abdul Rab Nishtar on behalf of the Muslim League.

Mahatma Gandhi was still opposed to the partition of the country. He, in his address, after evening prayer in New Delhi on May 26, 1947 urged 'every patriot' and certainly the British power, to out face the worst violence and leave India, as it be left, under the Cabinet Mission document of May 16, Congress President, Acharya Kriplani made a statement on 28th May, 1947, New Delhi, "We do not want this division to be carried out by the British Government. It will be the duty of free government to decide whether India shall be partitioned or not. If partitioned, on what principle partition is to be effected."

Mountbatten's Plan

On May 23, 1947 the Cabinet approved in principle the terms of a draft plan. In the event of failure to secure a compromise on the basis of the cabinet mission plan, the Viceroy was authorized to lay before the conference of Indian leaders convened for 2nd June. On 30th May after a long meeting with members of the India and Burma Committee on outstanding problems, the Viceroy had returned to India.

On 2nd June, conference of seven leaders had been invited to attend Nehru, Patel and Kriplani on behalf of the Congress, Jinnah, Liaquat Ali Khan and Abdul Rab Nishtar on behalf of the League and Sardar Baldev Singh representing Sikhs. All the eight signatories set round a small table, while Ismay, Mievelle and the Viceroy's secretary set immediately behind the Viceroy. The atmosphere was tense and got the feeling that the less the leaders talked the less the chance of friction and perhaps the ultimate breakdown of the meeting. The meeting of the Viceroy with the Indian leaders opened at 10 a.m. on 2nd June and lasted for two hours. At the outset the Viceroy remarked that he should remember no meeting at which decisions had been taken which would have such a profound influence on the world history.[13] He told that he would remember no meeting, however, at which decisions had been taken whose impact upon history had been profound as would be the impact of the decision before them.[14]

For record and history, Mountbatten formally asked Jinnah last time if he was prepared to accept Indian unity as envisaged by the Cabinet Mission Plan. He would not, he said, ask them to go against their conscience and give their full approval to a plan, parts of which went against their principles. He asked only that they accept it in a peaceful siprit and vow to make without bloodshed.

Copies of the plan were then handed round to the leaders. The Viceroy asked that they should take them acting for discussion with their respective working committee and let him know of their reactions by mid-night. He did not ask for specific agreement to the terms of the plan but for assurance that leaders and parties do their best to have it out peacefully.

Gandhi made no direct comment on the Menon plan, but suggested that; they might reconsider the cabinet delegation's proposals, he had so hastily opposed the previous year. He also asked Mountbatten to sack the Governor of North West Frontier Province on the grounds of his supported pro-Muslim League was. Mountbatten was mentally upset lest Gandhi might torpedo his plan. But he was completely relaxed, when Gandhi did not protest at all about the Menon plan. Mountbatten sent a letter to Lord Listowel on 2nd June at 5 p.m., the letter ran in this way 'God might be on our side' since Gandhi, who came to see me after the conference, presumably to implement his declared policy of stopping the present agreement, was afflicted by a day of silence. But he wrote me a friendly note of personal regards.[15]

The Earl of Listowel replied to Mountbatten "it seems that Gandhi is at loggerheads with the CWC. At the moment it may be that everything you achieve will be the result of CWC rejecting Gandhi's opinion."[16]

After some time, Jinnah entered the Viceroy's study inhaling one of the Caravan cigarettes. Jinnah kept insisting, he could not give an indication of the Muslim League's reaction to Mountbatten's plan, until he had put it before the Leaguer's council. He needed at least a week to bring its members to Delhi.

Mountbatten said that it was incredible. He had got his demand Pakistan. Even the Sikhs had swallowed it. Finally, he got everything, but at the eleventh hour, he was preparing it all, to bring the whole thing crashing down to articulate rust one word 'yes'. Mountbatten simply wanted his agreement. Attlee was standing by in London waiting to make his historic announcement in the House of Commons in less than 24 hours. He had pledged Attlee and his government that this plan would work. He had coaxed a reluctant Congress with enormous difficulty to accept partition. Even Gandhi had temporarily allowed himself to be bypassed; Mr. Jinnah,

Mountbatten said, if you think I can hold this position for a week while you summon your followers to Delhi, you must be crazy. You know this has been drawn out till we are at boiling point. You have got your Pakistan, which at one time no one in the world thought you would get. I know you call it 'moth-eaten' but it is Pakistan. Now all depends on your agreeing tomorrow along with everyone else the Congress has make their acceptance on your agreement. If they suspect your holding out of them, they will immediately withdraw their agreement and we will be in the most troubled mess.

'No, No', Jinnah protested that everything had to be done in the legally constitutional way; I am not the Muslim League' he said. 'Now, Mr. Jinnah come on' said Mountbatten, icily calm despite his growing frustration do not try to tell me that, you can try and tell the world, but please don't try to kid yourself that I don't know who's who and what is what in the Muslim League. Mr. Jinnah said Mountbatten, I am going to tell you something. I do not intend to let you work your plan. I cannot allow you to throw away the solution you have worked so hard to get; I propose to accept on your behalf.[17]

Now at that point, Mr. Jinnah, Mountbatten continued, I shall turn to you. I don't want you to speak; I don't want congress to force you into the open. I want you to do only one thing. I want you to nod your head to show that you are in agreement with me. 'If you don't nod your head, Mr. Jinnah, Mountbatten concluded then you are through and there will be nothing more I can do for you. Everything will collapse. This is not a threat, it is a prophecy. If you don't nod your head at that moment, my usefulness here will be ended, you will have lost your Pakistan, and as far as I am concerned, you can go to hell'.

Reaction by Different Political Parties

The Congress Working Committee had felt that the temporary Dominion status with the British Empire under the Menon would bring advantages to the country, the interim government would be strengthened and the diseased liner of East Bengal and West Punjab would be cut off. Attlee had directed the Viceroy that India should keep a link with the British Empire. So Mountbatten stressed this fact and Indian leaders agreed to be the part of the British Empire. The reactions of the Congress was conveyed to the Viceroy on the morning of 3rd June in the form of letter from the Congress President J.B. Kriplani, socialist leader Jaya Prakash Narayan, Ram Manohar Lohia and Achut Patwardhan were special invitees to the committee. The Congress working committee accepted the plan. Baldev Singh also accepted the plan.[18] Jinnah simply had given verbal assurance. So Mountbatten was feeling shaky. Ismay wrote in his diary that he and Mountbatten had to leave dinner early in the evening of 2nd June to go and wrestle with Jinnah. Mountbatten was in trouble. After a good deal of 'horse trading' the most of the Viceroy could squeeze out of him was the admission that Prime Minister Attlee might safely be advised that he could go ahead with his announcement about plan to the House of Commons on the following day.[19]

Jinnah was in desperate condition. He knew this fact that he was not in a position to break the Congress hold at the centre and he had to reconcile himself to a 'moth-eaten' Pakistan. Now there was no other alternative simply to accept this kind of Pakistan. Jinnah was feeling that now the British Government was departing from India and the British power would not remain in the country to implement any agreement. Jinnah's dream of greater Pakistan had been destroyed by the 2nd June meeting at the Viceroy's lodge chaired by Mountbatten. The Congress had accepted the decision of the meeting. Mountbatten was interested to implement this decision. Jinnah felt that the Indian leaders and the British Government had killed the idea of a greater Pakistan. Cripps had recommended for a 'unified India' with strong regional autonomy but the decision of 2nd June had destroyed the Cripps offer. Hence Jinnah accepted the decision of 2nd June with heavy heart.

At the provincial level the Muslim League was not strong. Local leaders in the Punjab were not interested to maintain the unity of the province. These leaders wanted to maintain their hold on the administrative level. Chaos had started in the province. In the village League supporters were being killed by Hindus and Sikhs. In Bengal the local League wanted an independent and united Bengal and did not accept Jinnah's policy at the centre. The Viceroy's original wish to frighten Jinnah into cooperation on the basis of the short length of the time available had been realized and he gave a provisional acceptance at a meeting the following morning.

If Jinnah had been the man who destroyed hopes of India united, Gandhi was the man who could destroy his hopes of dividing it. On the day Mountbatten had left London, Gandhi had told in his evening prayer meeting "let the whole nation be in flames, we will not concede one inch of Pakistan". Gandhi believed that the portion was wrong.

A few days later, Gandhi had awakened by mistake at half past three, half an hour before his morning prayer. His great niece Manu was with Gandhi lying beside his straw pallet on the floor of their New Delhi sweeper's hut. Manu listened as Gandhi had agonized alone in darkness; today I find myself alone he said, his voice so low it was a whisper to the night. Even Patel and Nehru think I am wrong and peace is sure to return if partition is agreed upon.

They wonder, he said, if I have not deteriorated with age, there was a long pause. Then Gandhi sighed and whispered. Maybe all of them are right and I am alone floundering in the darkness. Again there was a long pause, then Manu heard a last phrase slip from his lips; 'I shall not be able to witness it' but should evil overtake India and our independence is imperilled, as I apprehend, then let the posterity know the agony of this old soul thinking about the matter.[20]

June 3rd, Meeting

The second session of the meeting started on 3rd June at 10 a.m. He said, all three parties had its acceptance, so too, had Sikhs, he said in a long and friendly conversation the previous evening with Mr. Jinnah, who had assured him the plan was acceptable.

At these words, Mountbatten turned to Jinnah, seated at his right. At this instant Mountbatten had absolutely no idea what the Muslim leader was going to do. For an endless second, he stared into Jinnah's impassive and expressionless face. Then slowly Jinnah indicated his agreement with the faintest nod he could make. His chin moved half an inch downward, the shortest distance it could have travelled consonant with accepting Mountbatten plan.

This was the plan received its final sanction. An imposing document entitled 'the administrative consequence as of partition' has been prepared by a note by the Viceroy that it was his initiative that the act transferring power to the new dominions should be brought into operation not later than 15th August. This document consisted of 34 pages and it was single spaced. It was before each man, the leaders were stunned and now they understood the significance of partition. The Viceroy informed Attlee on 3rd June at 3.30 p.m. about the acceptance of the plan.[21]

The question is why Jinnah accepted the husk, mutilated, moth-eaten and truncated Pakistan. I have already discussed its causes few pages back. The other reason was that Jinnah was suffering from tuberculosis. Jinnah was a chain smoker. One Doctor named Commander Jai Patel had treated him some years earlier. He had been X-rayed and he was living under a sentence of death. But no leader including Mountbatten knew this fact that Jinnah was on a point of death. The Government had no intelligence report on this point. If the Congress leaders knew about the fatal health of Jinnah, they would not have agreed for June 3rd Plan. By 1948 he was suffering from bronchitis and he died on autumn 1948. Jinnah knew that even truncated Pakistan would not be formed after his death. So he accepted truncated Pakistan.

When Indian leaders accepted the Menon's plan and when Prime Minister Attlee announced this plan in the House of Commons, the newspaper called it 'Mountbatten Plan' and not Menon's plan. Gandhi met Mountbatten after his prayer meeting on 3rd June at 7 p.m. Mountbatten told him that the newspapers have called it 'the Mountbatten Plan' but it should be described as 'Gandhi Plan'. I did on advice of Gandhi and Gandhi gave me the idea. Then Gandhi spoke to Mountbatten 'you and your magic tricks' in getting Congress and the Muslim League to agree on everything. As the result of 3rd June Plan, the political and geographical unit of India disappeared. When the plan was to be implemented, Congress would represent that it was not a question of one India with area sending from the centre. These areas would be known as Pakistan.[22]

Gandhi and Mountbatten

Gandhi walked into Mountbatten's study at 6 p.m. his prayer meeting was at 7 p.m. Mountbatten felt at his first glance that Gandhi was deeply upset. Gandhi was in the chair. Gandhi kept raising and dropping one hand, 'lamenting in an almost inaudible voice', it is so 'awful' ! Mountbatten was apprehensive that a public denunciation of his plan would be disastrous. So he started his argument by telling Gandhi now he understood and shared his feelings at scaring the united India, he had worked for all his life destroyed by his plan. As he spoke an inspiration struck him. The newspaper had called his plan 'Mountbatten Plan', he said, but they should have called it the 'Gandhi Plan'. It was Gandhi, Mountbatten told, who had suggested to him all the major ingredients of the plan. Mountbatten continued and said that Gandhi told him to leave the choice to the people of India and the plan continued this provision. It was the elected provincial assemblies that would decide India's future. Each assembly would vote on whether it wished to join India or Pakistan. Gandhi had urged British to quit India at the earliest and dominion states would accomplish this.

> *"If by some miracle the assemblies vote for unity, Mountbatten told Gandhi, you have what you want. If they do not agree, I am sure you do not want us to oppose their decision by force of arms."*[23]

Mountbatten put his case before Gandhi with realizing, pleading and employing all his charm. Gandhi was still vehemently opposed to the partition but he was shaken by the Viceroy's strong argument. Gandhi was uncertain of his grip of India's masses and on the Congress leaders. He was searching for an answer from his conscience but at this stage his inner voice was silent. Gandhi was in doubt, should he remain faithful to his instincts, denounce partition, and even at the price of plunging idea into violence and chaos? Or should we listen to the Viceroy's desperate plan?

Mountbatten had not finished his argument when Gandhi became ready to go to the prayer meeting. He told Mountbatten, he never allowed himself to be late for a prayer meeting.

Gandhi reached prayer meeting ground and he delivered his verdict on the issue of partition. Many in the crowd wanted to hear from the lips of Gandhi. Gandhi said, it was no use blaming the Viceroy for the partition. Love to yourself and in your own heart for an explanation of what had happened.[24]

All the political parties had accepted the June 3rd Plan and they had all accepted that India would be free on August 15, 1947. But after some time the parties called this steps blunder when the communal riot started from August 13, 1947 in an acute form, the parties started saying that it was blunder to achieve freedom on 15th August. Why 15th August was selected? The reason was that Mountbatten felt that as the agreement had been reached among the different political parties, there was no need that the British should stay in India to rule. If the British decide to go early, the administration would settle down and all uncertainties would disappear.

It was clear that before the transfer of power, the interim

government controlled and managed by the Congress would rule without any hindrance. Pakistan was still in the process of being created. This process might have given certain advantage to the interim government over Muslim League. It was clear that a re-constitutional of the central administration on the basis of communal Party would never be accepted by either Nehru, Vice President of the interim government and Sardar Patel, the Home Minister. Jinnah knew that he should take control of the Pakistan territory as early as possible. Hardly there were ten weeks left, when liberty would come to India. But before liberty could come, death through communal riots began to spread in town and villages of the Indian subcontinent.

Partition was undoubtedly a tragedy but a worst tragedy would have been to try to impose a unity unacceptable to the great majority of 100 million Muslims that was a widely held detachment view of the implication of portion at that time. Mountbatten succeeded, at the prayer meeting that June night, Gandhi said, the British government is not responsible for partition. The Viceroy had no hand in it. In fact he is as opposed to division as Congress itself, but if both of us 'Hindus Muslims' cannot agree in anything else, then the Viceroy is left with no choice.[25] Jinnah's dream of greater Pakistan had been destroyed by the decision of both Congress and the British Government and the unified India with strong regional autonomy that Cripps had proposed the previous summer, May-June 1946, was no longer an offer.[26]

The open diplomacy of Mountbatten had brought the partition. The Viceroy had urged the political leaders to accept the Cabinet Mission plan unreservedly, for in his opinion that plan provided the best arrangement but he could not obtain agreement between the leaders of the two main parties on the Cabinet Mission or any other that would have preserved the unity of India. So the partition was the only alternative.

Muslim League

The Council of All India Muslim League met in the ball room of Imperial Hotel in Delhi to make their decision. But a gang of Khaksars, a militant Punjabi Muslim group entered the meeting hall and their purpose was to disrupt the meeting. They wanted Delhi to be included in Pakistan. They rushed into the room wielding knives and overturning tables and they wanted to stab Jinnah. 'The Muslim League guard took position' reported one witness 'as soon as the Khaksars rushed in, some were badly dabbled and thrown out. It was indeed pathetic to see some of them bleeding or dealt with severely by the police. Although Bengali merchants and the Pakistan national movement back in Cambridge had denounced the plan as 'the greatest betrayal in the history of the millet.' It was accepted by the delegates. After the meeting Nehru and Patel complained to Mountbatten about the wording of the resolution adopted in the meeting and they raised objections to the content of some of the League's speeches. What was the source to Nehru and Patel? The Intelligence Bureau agent had been sent by Patel to the meeting and so the source was highly authenticated.[27]

Comments on the 3rd Plan

The elder politicians of the country Mr. Chakravarti Rajagopalachari told to Mountbatten, "if you had not transferred power when you did, there would have been no power to transfer. George Abele, who did not like or trust Mountbatten, wrote privately that it had been a triumph for the Viceroy."

On June 20, 1947, the members of the Bengal legislative assembly met and decided on the partition of Bengal. At the preliminary joint meeting it was decided by 126 votes to go that the province if it remained united, should join new constituent assembly, i.e. Pakistan. At the separate meeting of the members of the West Bengal Legislative Assembly on the same day, it was decided by 58 votes to 21 that the province should be partitioned and by the same majority that West Bengal should join the existing constituent assembly should partition eventuate. It was also decided by 105 votes to 34, that in the event of partition, East Bengal would agree to amalgamate with Sylhet.

NOTES

1. *Viceroy's Personal Reports*, No. 4, April 24, 1947.
2. *Mountbatten and Partition of India*, p. 140.
3. Man Singh and Moon, *Transfer of Power*, Vol. X, p. 738.
4. *Ibid.*, p. 755.
5. Viceroy's Staff Meetings, May 7, 1947, p. 142.

6. Mathai, M.O., *Reminiscences of the Nehru Age*, New Delhi, 1978, p. 209.
7. *Mountbatten and Partition of India*, pp. 146 to 148.
8. *Transfer of Power*, Vol. X, p. 756.
9. Menon, V.P., *Transfer of Power in India*, p. 365.
10. *Freedom at Midnight*, p. 150.
11. *Transfer of Power*, vol. X, p. 873.
12. *Ibid.*, p. 949.
13. Man Singh and Moon, *Transfer of Power*, Vol. II, Introduction.
14. *Freedom at Midnight*, p. 155.
15. *Transfer of Power*, Vol. XII, p. 53.
16. *Transfer of Power*, Vol. XII, p. 60.
17. *Freedom at Midnight*, pp. 155 to 159.
18. *Transfer of Power*, Vol. II, p. 69.
19. Ismay, Hastings, *The Memoirs of Lord Ismay*, London, 1960, p. 424.
20. *Freedom at Midnight*, p. 157.
21. Transfer of Power, Vol. II, p. 86.
22. Campbell's Diary, *The Asian Age*, August 1947.
23. *Freedom at Midnight*, p. 163.
24. *Freedom at Midnight*, p. 164.
25. Reuter, *the Asian Age*, August 6, 1947.
26. French, Patrick, *Liberty or Death*, p. 303.
27. *Transfer of Power*, Vol. II, pp. 129, 130 and 153.

12

Orderly Partition of India and Transfer of Power

Now India was to get freedom on August 15, 1947. There was too much to bad one within such a limited time, the verdicts of the provinces had to be ascertained. Complex machinery was set up to affect the partition. In June 1947, a Partition Council was set up consisting of Dr. Rajendra Prasad and Sardar Patel for the Congress, Liaquat Ali Khan and Abdul Rab Nishtar for the League with Mountbatten as the Chairman. The Partition Council had been formed with the impossible task of implementing the division of assets of the Government of India which consisted of everything from railway lines, food stocks, ships and bulldozers to printing presses, chairs and type-writers. A Steering Committee had also been set up under two senior civil servants, H.M. Patel and Chaudhary Mohammad Ali. A separate committee to deal with assets was also set up under the chairmanship of *Sir Patrick*. Sir Cyril Radcliff had been sent from London to divide the country.

The Secretary of State, Lord Listowel had admitted it would be 'unfair to Pakistan' to accept Hindustan as the successor of the former India, exactly such move was agreed by Attlee's India and Burma Committee on the assumption that there will be a financial adjustment of the assets involved.[1] This was a doubtful constitutional decision, however, since legally no 'Indian union' existed at this point and so it was not clear from what Pakistan was seeding. This matter was never entirely resolved and was overtaken by the rush of events. The Congress had divided to call their new nation "India" rather than 'Hindustan' the impression of continuity was complete. As Alan Campbell Johnson remembered, Pakistan was cutting itself from India. I cannot pretend we thought of it any differently.[2]

The interim government was not in a position to govern. So the interim government was reconstituted on July 10, 1947, one for the new India and one for Pakistan. This came into effect immediately. Now there was split in the administration. Every employee of the Government of India and from provincial Governors to peons had to choose between India and Pakistan. The 'optees' as those who choose Pakistan came to be known. Liaquat Ali Khan told the Viceroy I now wish to God you could get partition through by August 1.[3]

The process of division started in the provinces. The Legislative Assemblies of the Muslim majority provinces had to cast their votes in both Bengal and Punjab, members generally divided along communal lines; Muslims voting against the division of their province but in favour. If joining Pakistan and Hindus and Sikhs favouring partition as a means of remaining in India. The Mountbatten Plan was based on the principle that the Muslim provinces should be separated and formed into a separate state.

It was considered in the Punjab Legislative Assembly. There were 168 members of the Punjab Assembly. 91 members voted to join a new separate Constituent Assembly. The members consisted of 88 Muslims, 2 Indian Christians and one Anglo-Indian, 72 members from east Punjab meeting in separate session rejected by 50 votes to 22, a motion by the Muslim League leader, Khro of Mamdot that a province should remain united. East Punjab members decided to join the existing C.A. Hindu, Sikh and representatives of one Scheduled Caste numbering in all 77, voted for the present Constituent Assembly. As anticipated, the Sind Legislative Assembly at its special sitting on June 26 decided by 33 votes to 20 that Sind should join the new Pakistan Constituent Assembly so the creation of Pakistan was now as legally decided upon. Baluchistan did the same and joined Pakistan. The Sikhs did not like the partition of Punjab. India's Sikhs bore black arm bands on July 8 and prayed in their Gurdwaras to protest against the threat to split their community under the British plan for India. The Viceroy sent a report to the Secretary of State, Listowel on 13th July about Sialkot referendum results. By a majority of votes, Sialkot gave its verdict in favour of Pakistan. The Boundary Commission for Bengal was to demarcate the Muslim majority areas of Sialkot district and contiguous Muslim majority areas of adjoining districts.

North-West Frontier Province

The case of NWFP was peculiar. Though a Muslim province, it had a Congress ministry under Dr. Khan Sahib Khan. The tribal chairman Abdul Ghaffar Khan was the tallest leader of the province. He was a member of the Indian National Congress and at this time he was a member of the Congress Working Committee. He was an associate of Gandhi and Nehru in the Indian independence struggle. Ghaffar Khan also known as the Frontier Gandhi started campaigning against the British in 1920. But what will be fate of N.W.F.P. under the Mountbatten Plan. Muslims were in the overwhelming majority in the Frontier Province. Lord Mountbatten had said that the province would be given a chance to opt. He suggested that a referendum might be held to decide whether the frontier would join Pakistan or India. Lord Mountbatten told Dr. Sahib Khan, a premier of N.W.F.P. to hold a plebiscite and asked Dr. Sahib if he had any objection. He could not object to the proposal for a plebiscite. However, he raised a new issue. He said that if there was to be plebiscite, the Pathans of the frontier should have the right to opt for Pakhtoonistan, as a state of their own.[4]

The fact was that the Khan Brothers were not as strong in the frontier as the Congress thought. There influence had waned after the agitation for the partition began.[5] Now that Pakistan was in slight and Muslim majority provinces had been promised the opportunity of forming an independent state, an emotional upheaval swept through the frontier. The movement for Pakistan was further strengthened by the activity of the British officers who openly supported Pakistan and persuaded the majority of tribal chiefs in the frontier to side with the Muslim League. Dr. Khan Sahib saw that his only chance for retaining the leadership of the frontier was to raise the demand for Pakhtoonistan. Many Pathans would prefer a small state of their own as they feared the domination of the Punjab. Mountbatten did not like any fresh demand.

The Congress Working Committee had endorsed the decision of the Frontier Congress authorizing Khan Abdul Ghaffar Khan to take whatever action he thought necessary to deal with the situation in the province. The Frontier Congress now demanded the creation of a free Pathan state with a constitution framed on the basis of the Islamic conception of democracy, equality and social justice.[6] So Dr. Khan Sahib and Khan Abdul Ghaffar Khan stood for an independent

Pakhtoonistan. Neither Mr. Jinnah nor Lord Mountbatten was, however, prepared to accept this demand. Lord Mountbatten made it clear that the frontier could not form a separate and independent state but must be included either in India or Pakistan.[7] The Khan brothers then declared that their Party could take no part in the plebiscite and called on the Pathans to boycott it. Their opposition was, however, of no avail. The plebiscite was held and a large proportion of the people voted in favour of Pakistan. The result of North West Frontier Province referendum is as follows:

1.	Valid votes for Pakistan	2,89,244
2.	Valid votes for India	2,874
3.	Total electorates	5,72,798
4.	Majority	2,86,370
5.	Votes for Pakistan (P.C.)	50.49 %

In this way N.W.F.P. became a part of Pakistan. If the Khan Brothers had not boycotted the plebiscite and the supporters had worked earnestly, nobody can say for certain what the result would have been. However, the result went in favour of the Muslim League and the British Government immediately accepted it. It would have been better if the Pathans would have taken part in the referendum. Abdul Ghaffar Khan had ordered a boycott. More than half of the electorates voted to join and the power of the Khan Brothers was temporarily broken. Thus officially Pakistan was created but not inaugurated as yet.

The Boundary Commission was instructed to demarcate the boundaries of the two parts of the Punjab on the basis of ascertaining the contiguous majority areas of Muslims and non-Muslims. In doing so, it was to take into account other factors. The Boundary Commission was further instructed to demarcate the boundaries of the two parts of Bengal on the basis of ascertaining the contiguous majority areas of Muslims and non-Muslims. It was to take into account other factors also.

The Radcliff's Award—The Boundary Lines of Pakistan

The dangerously unsettled state of whole country was continuing from April 17, 1947. The British Government appointed Sir Cyril Radcliff K.C. (later Lord) who had been called to bar Inner Temple in 1924 and was the Vice Chairman, general council of the Bar, to divide India from Pakistan. He was the men who drew the border line between India and Pakistan. He belonged to the ruling Labour Party. He arrived in Delhi on July 8, 1947. He was to do his difficult, job in five weeks. Nehru, Jinnah and the Boundary Commission had all agreed that the work should be completed by August 15th and Sir Cyril Radcliff concurred. Radcliff was initially chosen as the chairman of an arbitral tribunal, which was to adjudicate over the division of assets between India and Pakistan, but he soon moved into chairing the Boundary Commission instead, since they were communally split, it was agreed in the Indian Independence Act that the Award of the commission would mean the decision of the chairman. A pair of Boundary Commissions, one for Punjab and another for Bengal were set up. The Punjab Boundary Commission consisted of two Muslim High Court Judges and Bengal Partition Commission consisted of two Hindu High Court judges under Sir Cyri's guidance. Justice C.C. Biswas and B.K. Mukherjee (for Congress) and Saheb Mohammad Akram and S.A. Rahem (for the Muslim League) would partition Bengal and Justice Mehr Chand Mahajan and Tejah Singh (for Congress) and Din Mohammad and Mohammad Munir (for Muslim League) would partition the Punjab.

On the evening of his arrival, Sir Cyril was summoned by the Viceroy to meet the Indian leaders. He pointed out that the division of the country would take considerable time. So he wanted 'how long had he got', the Viceroy replied that the partition would be completed in five weeks. Before Sir Cyril Radcliff could reply, Nehru said, if a decision could be reached in advance of five weeks, it would be better for the situation.[8] It was very difficult task to divide the country in such a short time. He was given 36 days in which to dissect the subcontinent, Radcliff asked some more time.

Radcliff and Mountbatten both maintained that they were impartial in the partition of the country and they did not have any discussion about the boundaries. However, according to Mountbatten's Deputy Private Secretary Jan Scott, the Viceroy attended a meeting of the Boundary Commission in Lahore on July 22. So Mountbatten did not keep himself aloof from the activity of the Commission. I do not intend to say that Radcliff was corrupt or independent. Radcliff was a barrister following a brief. He was an upright proud, naughty British Judge. But despite his encyclopaedic knowledge of vast areas of subjects, however, Radcliff knew virtually nothing about India. But he was a man with a deep sense of duty. The need for a precise border line between India and Pakistan had been felt at a very late date either by the Indian leaders or by the Viceroy. Wavell was the first Viceroy who felt the necessity for a demarcation of Pakistan, which was still in the air. Wavell had sent a telegram on February 7, 1946 to the British Government embodying the detailed demarcation of projected Pakistani territory. Attlee's Government did not either confirm or reject the telegram. So when Radcliff started his work in July 1947. Nobody had an idea about the map of Pakistan. So there was lack of precision in determining Pakistan. So in the election of 1946 Muslims cast their votes in greater numbers than 1937 elections for the formation of a truncated Pakistan. The election of 1946 brought Pakistan. The Muslim League captured overwhelming seats in the Muslim majority provinces.

Mountbatten asked Radcliff to draw his boundary lines ascertaining the contiguous majority areas of Muslims and Non-Muslims. In doing so he would take into account other factors. No one had any intention of spoiling out for him what those other factors should be or what weight he gave him. To do so would have led Nehru and Jinnah into another of their unending agreements. Mountbatten further explained that it was imperative that his decision be ready by 15th August a date only weeks away. Mountbatten's words meant that he would never be able even to glimpse the lands he was to divide. Radcliff told that if this awful haste was really forced on him, he warned Mountbatten, errors and mistakes, some of them perhaps grave, were bound to creep in.

Radcliff was a stubborn and independent man and was not prepared to take the Viceroy's words as final. He called personally on both Nehru and Jinnah. To each he put the same question: was it absolute necessary to have definite partition lines, however, defective, drawn by 15th August. Both insisted it was. Given their insistence Radcliff had no choice but to comply. It was not, he realized, a surgeon's scalpel he was going to require to perform his vivisection of Punjab and Bengal. What he would need was a butcher's axe.

The significance of the Radcliff line was felt by July 1947, when partitioned Punjab and Bengal, N.W.F.P., Sind, Baluchistan and Sylhet became part of Pakistan. In May 1947, Nehru had told Mountbatten that when Congress referred to the partition of the Punjab, they had not gone into the question in any great detail. Even in June 1947, it had been assumed in all sides that relations between India and

Pakistan would remain cordial and the boundary between the two countries would be settled by a negotiation. Nehru said in June 1947 that at some points in the future, India and Pakistan would "mutually consider modification and verification of their frontiers so that a satisfactory arrangement might be arrived at. That is likely to be fairly lengthy process involving the ascertainment of the wishes of the people in any particular area affected."[9] Most Muslims saw Pakistan as a homeland front. They would at come and go from Dominion to another freely. They thought that they would at leisune come from Lahore to Delhi, Delhi to Lahore, Aligarh to Karachi and Karachi to Aligarh, Bombay to Lahore and Lahore to Bombay. It was this thinking that prevented, Jinnah from selling his Malabar Hill in Bombay.[10] Jinnah was under this impression that he would flirt between India and Pakistan. But with the growth in communal violence, which took an acute form from August 13, 1947. It became too much clear that give and take between the two nations was not possible and by the end of August 1947 with the beginning of Kashmir aggression by Pakistan and of the communal slaughter in both Dominions, the prospect of friendly co-existence disappeared and this friendly co-existence has not been restored as yet.

The terms of appointments were as follows. As he was making Rs. 60,000 a year at the Bar, Radcliff was anxious that his plan for exemption from income tax and surtax should not be affected by the appointment. Apart from his salary, he wanted 'living allowance' suitable accommodation and free travel for his wife and step children, to enable them to live in comfortable style without expense to him.[11]

It had been agreed by the Congress and the Muslim leaders that Radcliff should draw his boundaries on the basis of contiguous majority areas of Muslims and Hindus, while taking into account other factors which methods did Radcliff follow.[12] He destroyed all his papers which had helped him to demarcate the boundary by the end of 1947. It is apparent that he followed the detailed demarcation produced by Wavell in February 1946. But the question is who had prepared this Wavell's demarcation plan. Wavell's document had been prepared by the Reforms Commissioner, V.P. Menon, who had been helped by Sir Benegal Race.[13] There was no other map of demarcation available to Radcliff. The national boundary that was laid down in the second schedule of the Indian Independence Act corresponded exactly to Wavell's line, except that it placed the district of Gurdaspur in Pakistan.

After some days he prepared his map. This map was based on original plan with certain changes. In Bengal he gave the tribal Chittagong hill tracks in the Far East to Pakistan (presumably in order to safeguard the security of the crucial port of Chittagong), while he allocated a small amount of Muslim territory to the north of Calcutta in India. He followed Wavell's document in the Punjab and even included Gurdaspur and a small portion of the holy city of Amritsar.[14]

Meanwhile the Viceroy informed the Secretary of State that the Awards even before publication were causing problems on the question of Gurdaspur in Punjab and Chittagong hill tracts in Bengal and he had decided to keep them under wraps till the two dominions had been inaugurated to us not to vitiate the atmosphere on the occasion of such historic event.[15]

Radcliff had done his work. It has been decided that the Radcliff Awards would be announced few days earlier before 15th August. Mountbatten did not like to publish the Awards earlier, let the Congress may boycott the independence celebrations. He said that he had not received the Awards yet. It was presented to the nine leaders on 16th August. So when the Dominions were formed on 14th August and 15th August, neither Pakistan nor India knew what their boundaries were. It was said that the border was altered at Mountbatten's thinking. There is powerful and detailed evidence that Mountbatten was responsible from source such as the diary of his Secretary John Christie, the 1992 testimony of Radcliff's assistant Christopher Beaumont, a footnote in Penderel Moon's book *Divide and Quit* and the dubious retrospective assertions of various Pakistan officials.

The fixation of boundary between the two Dominions was a very difficult work. Had Wavell's document been followed literally in better spirit, there would have been no communal massacres. Some hidden facts are like this. At a lunch at the United Services Club in Simla with his commissioners in early August, Radcliff said that he would award a portion of Ferozepur district with a nominal Muslim majority to Pakistan, in return for giving Gurdaspur and part of Lahore district to India.

This boundary line of Radcliff brought the communal massacres on 8th August George Abele sent a rough map indicating the Ferozepur salient to the private office of Sir Evan Jenkins to enable him to make security arrangements along the new border. There was a letter attached with the map and it was signed by Abele. Abele had remarked there will not be any great changes in the final award. Mountbatten later claimed this was done without his knowledge, but this has been contradicted. It is pointed out that at two separate staff conferences he had told Abele that Jenkins should have the earliest possible notice of the line, so that he could make police and Military dispositions.

For two or three days the alterations in the border continued due to the representations from V.P. Menon, Jawaharlal Nehru, the chairman of Punjab waterways, ministers from the princely state of Bikaner, and various other suspects. In practice experienced officials such as Abele liked the changes on either 10th or 11th August, Jenkins received a scrap home message from Viceroy's house telling him to eliminate salient, meaning that the whole of Ferozepur district would now remain in India. So Radcliff adjusted his Awards on 11th and 12th August.

India was Born Amidst Slaughter

There was one variation. The Wavell line of February 1946 and the second schedule of the Indian Act placed parts of Ferozepur district in Pakistan. The Maharaja of Bikaner had told Mountbatten the salient should not be put under Pakistan. Radcliff was aware of this fact that his work was of a butcher's, not a surgeon's one. Since his Hindu and Muslim colleagues had disagreed on almost every controversial issue, he had been forced to take most of the decisions and he had done his best to reconcile the demand of race, tradition and economic necessity. It was realized by everyone that his Award would cause anguish to many millions of people on the side or another of the new frontier and appear deeply unsatisfactory to the Governments of India and Pakistan.

Radcliff's Boundary Award was sent to the leaders of the two new Dominions at 2 p.m. on 16th August. Three hours later Liaquat Ali Khan, Pandit Nehru and Sardar Patel, the Congress Party boss and Sardar Baldeo Singh for the Sikhs gathered in the council chamber of Government House. It quickly became clear that Radcliff had proved his impartiality. Everyone was displeased.

Liaquat Ali Khan was outraged over the allocation of Gurdaspur to India. Patel equally put out at the loss of the Chittagong hill tracts to Pakistan. It was quite clear to me, reported Mountbatten, that if we had not brought the leaders together to hear each other's indignation we might have had as serious a blow up as V.P. Menon feared.

As it was, Mountbatten was able to argue conveniently that India could not have done so badly if Pakistan were so dissatisfied and Pakistan could have nothing to complain about in a solution that caused India such dismay...The leaders were sufficiently impressed to accept the Awards under protest and to agree that they should immediately be published.[16]

It was at this point that the Punjab fell apart, only an insane optimist would have supported that the announcement of the new frontier would bring to a halt the violence which had been mounting over the previous weeks. Even a pessimist like Evan Jenkins, the Governor of Punjab, had presumed, on the other hand, if that the lines of partition were accepted by both parties things would gradually settle down and their might be some movement of population over the next few years, but for the part Hindus and Muslims, even Sikhs would continued to co-exist in reasonable harmony. The pessimistic proved over optimistic.

Philip Ziegler in his book *Mountbatten* has mentioned that incidents multiplied in the last few days before the transfer of power. In the East Punjab, Sikhs were alleged to have raped Muslim women and paraded them in the streets before murdering. In West Punjab, a Muslim male surrounded a Sikh temple and burnt it to the ground with all its occupants, such atrocities may have been grossly exaggerated and never have taken place at all, but the rumours were enough. Philip Ziegler continues to mention that on both sides of the frontier, thousands, hundreds of thousands, eventually millions of peasants concluded that they could find safety only by abandon their homes and fleeing to the homelands which had been so arbitrarily called into existence on both sides of the frontier, the new citizens of India and Pakistan looked with hatred at the river of refugees flowing across their land and determined to avenge the wrongs being done to their compatriots. Trains packed with refugees were set upon and their passengers massacred those who fled on foot ran the gauntlet of hands of murders. Each incident provoked a new wave of refugees; each wave of refugees generated its own crop of bloody incidents.

Too late, the Indian and Pakistani leaders realized what horrors had been unleashed. At a meeting of two new countries joint defence committee, Mountbatten persuaded the two Prime Ministers to discuss what could be done to check the violence. Liaquat and Nehru went to Amritsar, in the heart land of the Sikhs and jointly appealed for peace, they sat but failed to catch the wind . . . . . . their visit may have done some good, but harshly enough to be noticed in the tornado of evils. The police split upon communal lines. All that was left was the army, and army too was gravely weakened by the revenges of partition and infected by the plague of communalism.

On the other side of problem, Radcliff had returned to London on 17th August. The decisions of the Boundary Commission were published, when Radcliff was in London, Radcliff did not disclose the reasons why he gave Gurdaspur to India and the Chittagong hill track to Pakistan. He never spoke even in London about the reasons. A newspaper interviewed him a few months earlier before his death. He asked him "whether he would ever like to return to India" he answered, "God forbid, not even if they asked me. I suspect they would shoot me out of hand both sides. He died in 1977; without Gurdaspur, India would have no practicable land access to Kashmir and the Maharaja of Kashmir, Hari Singh, would have no choice except to link Kashmir's desting to Pakistan.

Pakistan raised a question in 1948 in the United Nations about the last minute changes in the boundary lines. A question was raised in the House of Commons about the propriety of the alteration? Radcliff personally drafted the reply on behalf of the government and the concerned minister replied, I understand from Sir Cyril that he found the treatment of this area a question of considerable difficulty and on this point he reached a final conclusion differing from that which he was disposed to adopt at the time when Sir George Abele asked him for advance information. In an accompanying private note, Radcliff pointed out quite reasonably that the concept of 'provisional' *versus* 'final' boundary was meaningless. Since his decision was an 'award' which had no status until it was formally presented to the Viceroy 'earlier drafts' he wrote and there were quite a few wise drafts and no more.

There is no need of commenting on Radcliff. He was an English man and he was given an impossible task of dividing country within six weeks. He had no idea about Geography of India. There was not a single map of Pakistan available. If he had seen any map of Pakistan in 1945 or 1946, his task would have been much easier. He would have been given more time with a team of experienced advisors. Then he would have prepared the awards, which might have satisfied both parties.

On August 29, 1947, a Joint Committee at Lahore agreed that the boundary force should be disbanded. With its disappearance Mountbatten's last operational responsibilities had ended. He was now free to perform his function as Governor General in the manner he felt most appropriate. He made his intention manifest in his decision to take a long delayed holiday in Simla. With Edwina he went there directly from Lahore.

"Lazed in bed all morning" was his triumphant diary entry for the start of his holiday. It was the first time he had been able to say as much since he had left England and it was to be last for several weeks. The crisis had been left behind him but its clamour reverberated in his ears. So India was born amidst slaughter.

Comments on the Radcliff Award

The Congress had claimed for West Bengal about 59 per cent of the area and 46 per cent of the population of the province. Under the Radcliff Award, only 36 per cent of the area and the 45 per cent of the population were assigned to West Bengal of the total Muslim population of Bengal only 16 per cent came under the West Bengal, while as many as 42 per cent of non-Muslims remained in East Bengal.[17]

The Hindus of the Punjab, specially the Sikhs, resented the loss of Lahore and the canal colonies of Sheikhpura, Lyallpur and Montgomery, while the Muslims protested against the retention of the Mandi Hydro-electric project by East Punjab.

So the Radcliff Award satisfied none of the parties. The *Hindustan Standard* of Delhi censured it as 'self-contradictory, anomalous and arbitrary' and as unjust to the Hindus of Bengal and Punjab. The *Dawn* the Muslim League organ declared that Pakistan had been cheated, that the Award was biased decision, an act of shameful partiality.[18] The Sikhs criticized the Award as unjust to the Sikhs. The Award was, however, accepted by all the parties concerned because everyone began to feel the futility of these protests.

In seven weeks it was done, the frontier decided a continent for better or worse divided. The next day he sailed for England where he quickly forgot. The case as good lawyer must retain and he is not afraid, as he told his club, that he might get shot.[19]

Auden composed another poem about Radcliff who "shut up in a lonely mansion, he got down to work, to the risk of settling the fate of millions. The map at his disposal was out of date and the census returns almost incorrect but there was no time to check them, no time to inspect contested areas. The weather was frightfully hot. And a bout of dysentery kept him constantly on the trot.

It will be difficult for the people of India to forget the incalculable damage caused by the Radcliff Award.[20]

The Punjab—A Lawless Province

The internal situation of the Punjab was alarming. Trouble again fixed up in Lahore, Amritsar and the Gurgaon district. Jinnah begged Mountbatten to be utterly ruthless in suppression trouble in Lahore and Amritsar. He said, "I don't care whether you shoot Muslims or not. It has got to be stopped. On 24th June, Nehru came to see him and talked in the same strain. He suggested turning over the cities to the military, withdrawing the police and declaring martial law. The meeting of the cabinet on 25th June was a very difficult one. Mountbatten was attacked by leaders of both parties for the complete failure of the "British" to maintain law and order under Section 93. Nehru as usual, completely lost control of himself and demanded the sacking of every official, from the Governor downwards, that same day Mountbatten had to reprimand him publicly for this irresponsible suggestion; Mountbatten admitted Nehru took the rebuke very well.

The Mountbatten plan of June 3, 1947 and the press conference of June 4 made it clear that India would be partitioned and at the same time India would achieve freedom on 15th August. Bengal and Punjab were going to be partitioned. The Sikhs and the Hindus did not like the partition of Punjab. So it looked a civil war had started in the Punjab.

Master Tara Singh, a seventy-two old former Hindu was the leader of the official Akalis. Lord Wavell regarded Master Tara Singh as 'stupid and emotional'. Sir Evan Jenkins, the Governor of Punjab considered Master Tara Singh as 'eccentric old man'. The Sikhs could not reconcile themselves to the idea of a Muslim homeland. In August 1944, Giani Kartar Singh proclaimed in August that 'if Pakistan was foisted upon the Sikhs with the help of British bayonets, we will tear it into shreds as Guru Govind Singh tore up the Mughal Empire'.[21] Master Tara Singh has forwarded a demand to the cabinet delegation of 1946 that there should be a 'province' in which Sikhs would be in a 'domination or almost dominant position' and able to federate with either India or Pakistan but the delegation did not take this demand into consideration.

Just after the Cabinet Mission's departure, an attempt was made to find out a solution between the Muslim League and the Sikh leadership. A meeting was held in Delhi between Jinnah, Tara Singh, Kartar Singh and the Sikhs of Patiala and his senior ministers. Jinnah pleaded for support for the cause of Pakistan and expressed his desire that the Sikhs would enjoy full autonomy within Pakistan but the Sikhs rejects it and said they would not accept Pakistan under any circumstances. The Sikhs further said that they did not like either a Congress dominated India but they also felt that they would not be able to form an independent Sikh state. Jinnah also could not do anything for the Sikhs. So there were riots all over Punjab in February 1947. Tara Singh threatened a Sikh uprising and he ordered for a celebration of 'Anti-Pakistan Day' on 11th March.[22] Premier Sir Khizer Hyat Khan Tiwana could not control the situation. The Governor of the province, Jenkins took administration of the province in his hand under Section 93 of the Government of India Act, 1935. The Unionist Party, which was an anti-communal organization, had disintegrated after the fall of Premier Sir Sikander Hayat Khan and now the province had become communal. Violence broke out in March 1947 and several thousand Sikhs were murdered by armed Muslim gangs, in the rural areas in the district of Rawalpindi. This violence was the result of the provocation speech of Master Tara Singh. He said our motherland is calling for blood and we shall satiate the thirst of our motherland with blood . . . . . . I have sounded the bugle, finish the Muslim League.[23]

Whatever may be the cause of this massacre, the Sikhs around Rawalpindi suffered and there was an exodus of around 80,000 refugees into East Punjab. By this time paramilitary Muslim League guards were parading in Lahore. The ailing Jinnah was not in a position to control the situation. The situation was taking an alarming shape. By April 1947, Tara Singh declared publicly that the Sikhs were bitter and angry and would fight for their survival. Muslims had become very aggressive and they set fire in the beards of the Sikhs. They taunted the Sikhs that they have degreased and grown rich. Punjab's Hindus were feeling shaky about their future and they were preparing to save themselves from the attacks of the Muslim League guards. There were RSS in the Hindu group and they felt that "We Hindus have to change, if we are to survive and rule

India . . . . . . the only language a Muslim understands is that of a knife and a grenade."[24]

After August 1945, the Governor of the Punjab Sir Bertrand Glancy was replaced by Evan Jenkins. On 5th August, Jenkins sent a police officer to Delhi. His name was Gerald Savage and he belonged to CID. He told the Viceroy that he had reports of Sikhs plans to derail trains and detonate bombs. There was a plot even to assassinate M.A. Jinnah on 13th August at the time of the independence celebration in Karachi. Ex-INA soldiers and the RSS were involved in this conspiracy with Master Tara Singh as leader. The matter was reported to Mountbatten. He informed Jenkins that Tara Singh and other activists involved in this conspiracy be arrested at the suitable time. That you fix up, the Governor made full preparation for their arrest but later on decided not to arrest them because they had taken shelter in the Golden Temple where police action caused much excitement.[25]

The creation of the 'Ferozepur salient' further vitiated the atmosphere. As the result of the Ferozepur salient, the Sikhs were losing their properties in Sialkot, Gujrawala, Shekhpura, Lahore, Lyallpur and Montgomery districts. This Ferozepur salient also snatched the two sacred Sikh battlefields of Soleroan and Ferozshah into Pakistan. This advance news of Radcliff's draft plan produced an upsurge of violence.

The Punjab province looked like a lawless state. The administration was completely paralyzed. On 12th August, Jenkins telegraphed to the Viceroy about the Lahore city and pointed out that the condition was unbelievably bad and 'Inspector General tells me that now the DIB was not sending any report to the English Officers'. Sardar Patel was personally being informed by his new appointee DIB. Patel received all information from the Central Intelligence officers.

On 13th August, Jenkins reported that almost 400 people had been murdered in the province and Amritsar was burning. His telegram concluded: 'general situation deteriorating'. The communal holocaust was now underway.[26]

Intelligence Failure for the Viceroy

Mountbatten did not even know the name of the Intelligence Bureau. His predecessor not only knew and controlled the Bureau but received all kinds of informations. But Mountbatten had no access to the report of the intelligence officers and he did not know the *vital* information. Of course, he received some scraps of local intelligence via provincial Governors but he had no access to the DIB. Now the DIB was under the control of Sardar Patel. As H.U. Hudson has written, "Lack of intelligence, such as had always reached district officers, magistrates, police men and criminal investigation departments cost many Indian lives . . . . . . in the disorders of the 1946 and 1947".[27] Hudson did not know at the time of writing was just how profound the breakdown of communication had been.

In New Delhi the intelligence Bureau continued to function under the control of the Home Minister, Vallabhbhai Patel.[28] The British were able to crush without difficulty the disturbances of 1942; they failed to deal in the same way the communal riots of 1947. The disturbances of 1947 were initiated by the communities against one another in the presence of a government which was to transfer power to an unknown successor or successors not later than June 1948. It is essential to understand the Punjab background from 1921 to the end of 1942. The Punjab was dominated by homegrown Muslim leaders powerful enough to control or at least to influence very greatly, the policy of the Muslim League as a whole. These leaders saw clearly that the Punjab could not be governed by a communal Party, Muslim or non-Muslim. They, therefore, developed the unionist idea—a united Punjab, with a Unionist Party open to members of all communities, under Muslim leadership. As the Muslim League gained strength, the Muslim unionists were driven to equivocation. They could not deny Pakistan and endeavoured to treat it as a matter external to the Punjab. But it was clear from the first that Pakistan was a vital internal issue and that sooner or later the Punjabi Muslims would have to accept it fully and run the League, or reject it and maintain it the unionist idea under the period of Sir Sikander Hyat Khan, the Unionist Party was very strong. The Unionist Party of the Punjab—consisting of Hindu, Muslim and Sikh landed interests—had a majority headed by Sir Sikander Hyat Khan, only assisted by Sir Chhotu Ram. At the instance of the Viceroy, Sir Sikander joined the Muslim League, but he was no communalist. Sir Sikander Hyat Khan was the Premier of the Punjab from 1937-42. At the end of 1942, the Unionist Party began to disintegrate. The last Unionist ministry under Malik Sir Khizar Hyat Khan Tiwana continued until the general election of

1945-46, which was fought on the bitterest communal lines only eight or nine Muslim unionists survived with one or two exceptions Hindu unionists were defeated or absorbed by the Congress Party, and Sikh unionist joined the Panthetic Party. The Punjab had reached the worst possible position, so long avoided, in which practically all Muslims were on one side of the fence and practically all non-Muslims on the other.

The situation might have been saved by a genuine coalition between the Muslim League on the one hand and the Congress or the Panthic Party on the other. But communal feeling was too strong, and both the Muslim League and the Congress were under orders from outside the Punjab. It was most unfortunate that a country with thirty millions inhabitants was sucked into the vertex of all India politics. Punjabis ceased to be Punjabis and become Muslim, Hindus and Sikhs—the Sikhs alone retaining their political independence. The new ministry took office on March 1946 under the leadership of Malik Sir Khizar Hyat Khan Tiwana.

There was highly explosive condition in Punjab. The news of communal disorder of unprecedented scale in Bombay, Calcutta, Noakhali, Bihar, the Western United Provinces and the N.W.F.P. caused great alarm. The coalition ministry took strong action. The ministry saw that private armies would play a large part in communal strife. Two of these the Muslim National Guards and the Rastriya Swyam Sewak Sangh were prominent and were growing rapidly. The Sikhs had disbanded their Akali Sena in about 1940, and it was thought undesirable that they should have an excuse for reviving it. In January 1947, the ministry accordingly banned the Muslim League National Guards and the Rastriya Swyam Sewak Sangh under the Criminal Law Amendment Act, 1908.

Meanwhile, HMG announced their intention of leaving India not later than June 30, 1948. The Muslim League had started the civil disobedience movement. The ministry was losing its grip on the administration. So the premier resigned on March 2, 1947. Now Iftikar Husain Khan, leader of the Muslim League was asked to form the ministry. The non-Muslims believed that the Muslim League Ministry would destroy them. The Congress and the Panthic Sikhs held a large meeting in Lahore in the evening of 3rd March and the rioting started on the morning of 4th March in Lahore, Amritsar, Multan, Rawalpindi, Jullundur and Sialkot cities. Rural areas were also affected. On the evening of 4th March, the outgoing ministers refused to carry on in accordance with the usual convention. The new ministry could not be formed. So a proclamation under Section 93 of the Government of India Act, 1935 was announced on the evening of 5th March.[29] Non-Muslims were massacred and there was serious rioting and burning in Amritsar from 11th April to 13th April.

Lahore.

Before the attainment of independence by India, the streets of Lahore were burning. They were full of smoke. Groups of panic-stricken frightened the people, passed through them under the protection of the army. But there was also a soldier who joined large gatherings of hooligans and laughed with them; dead men lay piled everywhere like garbage. Bodies of naked women lay scattered in the deserted streets. The silence of the city was broken by slogans—slogans which screamed loudly.[30]

By the end of 1947, the few Muslims who used to live there have been killed, and now since the Muslim customers no longer came there. The Muslim shopkeepers in Ganju-ki-Gali had abandoned their business. After the second week of August there was a dramatic change in Sayyidmalthe Bazaar. It had been attacked by hordes of Muslims. Many of the shops and houses owned by Hindus had been burnt. By the August 13, all the Hindu families living in Ganju-ki-Gali had run away. The intoxication of Independence Day did not last long. Even as the of Independence Day were being sung, Amritsar, Lahore and Sialkot, one after another were the cities, towns and settlements burning.

The British Government carried on the administration of the country on the report of intelligence; with Patel taking charge of the Home Ministry, everything had changed, until now the DIB[31] was an English man and the Viceroy had the free access to the DIB. There was another institution which carried out the intelligence work. Till the interim government was formed on September 2, 1946, the Indian political intelligence and the Director, Intelligence Bureau was carrying on intelligence work. Before Mountbatten's arrival, things had started to change. Norman Smith was the DIB. Patel dismissed him from the post and appointed Rai Bahadur T.G. Pillai as DIB. Pillai was district Superintendent of Police from Madras. He was loyal to Patel. Patel blocked the "personal access" of the DIB to the Viceroy; DIB's intelligence was now available to the Congress ministers only. The

Viceroy began to depend on the reports of the eleven provincial Governors, the quality of which varied according to circumstances. The DIB had reported to Wavell at the end of March 1947 that the British authorities were living on the edge of a volcano. The Viceroy was further reported that the Congress Working Committee was anxious for settlement, since its members felt that power might be slipping into the hands of a younger, more revolutionary generation. By the time Mountbatten assumed the charge of the office of Viceroy on March 24, 1947, things had changed drastically. The Indian political intelligence had virtually stopped functioning and there was the Indian DIB. On Patel's orders, Mountbatten was not permitted to see him. So Mountbatten did not personally know how communalism had been taking the heavy toll. Jenkins reports were the only source; he knew what was happening in the Punjab. It is a matter to be pondered whether Patel received all reports from the DIB and if he received all reports, why he did not take any action. Patel was an efficient administrator but why he slept over these reports?

Patel's private conversation is reported to be missing. Jenkins had told Mountbatten in June 1947, "a minister in the coalition government told me he had heard him say that Hindustan could quickly make an end of its Muslim inhabitants if Pakistan did not behave."[32] Jinnah believed that Patel would welcome trouble from the Sikhs in the central Punjab.[33] Sardar was certainly adamantly opposed to the planned arrest of the unstable Master Tara Singh, despite the fact that Congress was to imprison the Sikh leader five times during the years following independence.

The Implementation of the Plan and Indian Independence Act

The provincial governments of India and Pakistan were formed on 20th July. Amidst these developments the constitutional formalities were hastily completed in London. Pakistan was created officially on June 4, 1947. The Indian Independence Bill was introduced in the House of Commons by the Prime Minister on July 4.

On the same day the Secretary of State Lord Listowel addressed a press conference at the India Office and said; this is a Bill unique in the history of legislation in this country. Never before has such a large portion of the world population achieved complete independence through legislation alone. He went on to say that on 15th August India would achieve complete independence.

Indian Independence Bill was passed by the House of Commons on 15th July and by the House of Lords on the following day. The Bill received the royal assent on July 18, 1947. The Government of India Act, 1935, as modified and adapted, was brought into operation by the India (Provisional Constitution) Order, 1947, made by the Governor-General on August 14, 1947. The Bill in its final form consisted of only twenty sections and three schedules. The Indian Independence Bill was a model of consensus and simplicity. To give India her freedom, Members of Parliament required only twenty changes and sixteen type written pages. Never had so momentous a measure been drafted and erected with comparable speed. Clement Attlee had told the house at the time of the historic bill. In such a state at the point of a sword has been forced to surrender power to another people but it was very rare for a people who had long enjoined power over another nation to surrender it voluntarily. Winston Churchill paid a rare tribute to his rival Attlee for the wisdom he had displayed in searching Louis Mountbatten as his Viceroy. It may be said of the 'British Raj' he noted, as Shakespeare said of the Thane of Cawdor; 'nothing in his life become him like the leaving it'.

When Mountbatten had been appointed as Viceroy, Winston Churchill as a leader of opposition had told the House of Commons that the whole thing wears the aspect of an attempt by the government to make use of brilliant war figures in order to cover up a melancholy and disastrous transaction .... In handing over the Government of India to so called political classes we are handing over to men of straw of whom in a few years no trace will remain ...... a richly ironic statement, given that Congress was to retain power in India for forty-six of the fifty years following independence.[34]

The Indian Independence Act provided for the setting up of two new Dominions on August 15, 1947 powers hitherto exercised by the British Parliament, and the government in British India, would be transferred to the two new Dominions, also on August 15th. The new Act substituted certain new provisions for previous ones contained in the Government of India Act of 1935.

As the Bill was enacted into law on July 18, 1947, Prime Minister Attlee despatched a tangled metaphor to 'my dear Dickey', I am very conscious that I put you into bat on a sticky wicket to pull the game out of fire. Few people would have taken it on; and few, if any, could have pulled the game round as you have.[35]

In spite of the changed political situation, it was a mirade that

India was to attain freedom on August 14/15, 1947. Lord Curzon, who had taken a hand in drafting the declaration of 1917, thought it would take India 500 years to qualify for self-government. A few years later S.P. Sinha, a brilliant lawyer and the first Indian member of the Viceroy's Executive Council, suggested that India would become a Dominion in 300 years. In 1943, the outgoing Viceroy Lord Linlithgow told his successor Field Marshall Wavell that British rule in India would last for another 30 years.

But History falsified their prophecies and India attained Dominion Status at the midnight of August 14/15, 1947.[36]

In the 1947 Independence Act the territories of the Dominions were defined with appropriate qualification for the areas to determine their choice by referendum or by vote of their legislature. Each Dominion was to be headed by a Governor General, but it was expressly stipulated that one person might serve in a dual capacity, in the hope that Mountbatten would be acceptable to both. The absence of a legally constituted parliament in either of proposed Dominions was overcome by giving both constituent assemblies the duel status and function of legislature and constitution-making body. The Government of India Act, 1935 and its accompanying orders-in-council would remain in force (pending alteration of the drafting of new constitution by the successor authorities), subject to the removal of the reserved and special powers vested in the Governor General and the Provincial Governors. All laws in force in British India on August 15, 1947 would remain in force until amended by the new Dominion legislatures. There was also a provision for continuity in the terms of employment of members of the services . . . . .[37]

Two provisions of the Act gave rise to vigorous controversy, even before the formal transfer of power, the Governor Generalship and the constitutional future of the princely states.

Congress proposed Mountbatten as Governor General of the Dominion of India, undoubtedly on the assumption that the League would do likewise. To the consternation, Jinnah decided to occupy that post in Pakistan. In reality, it made little difference to the power pyramid in Pakistan during the first year, for Jinnah remained the dominant personality until his death in September 1948.[38]

The all India committee approved Nehru's strong line by "stating that it could not admit the right of any state in India to declare its independence and to live in isolation from the rest of India". By default the Indian Independence Act seemed to give the princes freedom to accede to India or to Pakistan, or to become dependent. The vagueness involved with respect to the present difficulties that might well have led to in stability and fragmentation.[39]

All laws in force in British India on August 15, 1947 would remain in force until amended by the new Dominion legislature. These were also a provision for continuity in the terms of employment of members of the service. Prof. Michael Bracher has commented that indeed, the Indian Independence Act was remarkable for the degree in which it assured continuity in political institutions, the legal and judicial system and the constitutional fabric of British India.

Two Weeks to Partition and Freedom

Two weeks to freedom were very crucial period in the history of the Indian freedom movement. Meeting of the cabinet constituted for Pakistan presided over by the Viceroy and attended by Liaquat Ali Khan, I.I. Chundrigar, Abdul Rab Nistar, Ghanzafar Ali Khan, Jogendra Nath Mandal, Mohammad Ali and Osman Ali took place in New Delhi on August 1, 1947 and the question of the formation of a new ministry in North West Frontier Province was discussed. The question arise which Dominion either India or Pakistan will be the successor government. The Secretary of State said that His Majesty's Government had all along accepted that the new Dominion of India would be a successor Government of India with rights and obligation of the all India including membership of the United Nations. On 23rd June the Punjab assembly had voted in favour of partition. On 4th August Pandit Nehru submitted to the Viceroy names of 13 ministers for the first cabinet of Independent India which together with the total of 14.

On 6th August the leaders of both the Dominions took note of the statement and agreed in principle to initiate discussions and agreed that the delegation should visit India as soon as the present pressure of the business had slackened. In view of the deadlock in the Partition Council on the division of assets and liabilities, it was decided to refer the matter to the Arbitral Tribunal.

On behalf of HMG, the Viceroy welcomed India's offer to take over the international obligations and liabilities of the country as they existed on 15th August. Pakistan agreed to the Indian Dominion inhabiting India's membership of international organizations like the United Nations Organization, while Pakistan would apply for membership of such organization as she desired to run. Both Nehru and Jinnah agreed with the Viceroy that the princes and their nominees would continue to receive decorations and honours from the King after August 15, 1947.

On 7th August Jinnah, the Governor General designate of Pakistan arrived in Karachi. The Muslim League flag was unfurled over the Government House. Before he left Delhi for Karachi in a farewell message he said, I wish Hindustan's prosperity and peace.[40] I bid farewell to the citizens of Delhi among whom I had many friends of all communities and I earnestly appeal to everyone to live in this historical city in peace. The past must be buried. Let us start a fresh as two Independent sovereign states of Hindustan and Pakistan.

On 8th August few important changes were on the anvil. It was just one week before the deliverance day and while the whole people of the Punjab and Bengal looked to the future with trepidation, the rest of the country was busy making big plans for the celebrations of the historic day.

By August 9, 1947, the rumours that the creation of the Ferozepur was circulated at Delhi and central Punjab, the Sikhs were demoralized and this was devastating news for them. The Sikhs were losing their countless forms and properties in Sialkot, Gujrawala, Sheikhpura, and Lahore, Lyallpur and Montgomary districts and also a long part of land before Amritsar. The advance news of Radcliff's draft plan provided an upsurge of violence.

During the night of August 9, an awful scene appeared. The 'Pakistan special No. 1' train carrying senior civil servants of the new Muslim homeland from Delhi to Lahore was derailed by a Sikh Jatha, with several people being killed.[41]

Now 10th August started, it was the last Sunday before independence. The Pakistan Constituent Assembly met in Karachi for its inaugural session with Jogendra Nath Mandal being elected unanimously as its chairman pending the election of the President. He said the minorities would not be treated justly and fairly but generously in Pakistan.

Eleventh August started, the British Raj entered its last week. Kashmir too did not remain quiet when Prime Minister Kak was replaced by Janak Singh. The Pakistan Constituent Assembly affirmed the National flag of Pakistan and also unanimously elected M.A. Jinnah as its President. Jinnah reiterated the equality of rights for minorities, a promise of equal citizenship for all in Pakistan irrespective of caste, creed or colour. The Governor-General issued a notification 'Joint Defence Council Order, 1947' constituting the council, defining the scope of its functions, rules of procedure etc. it will cease to operate from April 1, 1948.

Even after he went to Karachi as Governor General of the Dominion of Pakistan, Jinnah never gave up the hope that he might return to the mansion he built for himself on Malabar hills. Jinnah had an affinity for the house which he built and occupied in 1939.

Sri Prakash was India's First High Commissioner in Pakistan. Sri Prakash met Jinnah in his house at the direction of Prime Minister Jawaharlal Nehru. Sri Prakash talked on the question of Bombay house. Jinnah said, "you don't know I love Bombay. I still look forward to going back there".

The following are the excerpts from the address of Quaid-i-Azam M.A. Jinnah in the Constituent Assembly of Pakistan in Karachi on August 11, 1947:

> *"You are free, you are to go to your temples, and you are free to go to your mosques or any other place of worship in the state of Pakistan. You may belong to any religion or caste or creed ...... that has nothing to do with the business of the state ...... We are starting in the days when there is no discrimination between one community and another, no discrimination between one caste or creed and another. We are starting with this fundamental principle that we are all citizens and equal citizens of state. The people of England in course of time had to face the realities of the situation and had to discharge the responsibilities and burdens placed upon them by the government. Today, you might say with justice that Roman Catholics and Protestants do not exist, what exists now is that every man is a citizen and equal citizen of Great Britain, all members of the nation."*

Equal Citizens

If you change your past and work together in a spirit that everyone of you, no matter to what community he belonged, no matter what relations he had with you in the past, no matter what his colour, caste or creed, is first, second, and last a citizen of this state with equal right's, privileges and obligations, there will be no end to the progress. You will make . . . . . . we are starting with this fundamental principle that . . . . . . we are all citizens and equal citizens of one state. Now I think we should keep that in front of us as ideal and you will find that in course of time Hindus would cease to be Hindus and Muslims would cease to be Muslims, not in the religious sense, because that is the personal faith of each individual, but in the political sense as citizen of the state. I shall always be guided by the principles of justice and fair play without any, as is put in the political language prejudice or ill will, in other words, partiality or favouritism. My guiding principle will be justice and complete impartiality, and I am sure that with your support and co-operation I can look forward to Pakistan becoming one of the greatest nations of the world.

All the same in this division it was to avoid the question of minorities being in one dominion or the other. Now that was unavoidable. There is other solution now what we shall do? If we want to make this great state of Pakistan happy and prosperous, we should wholly and solely concentrate on the well-being of the people and specially the masses and the poor. If you will work in cooperation, forgetting the past, burying the hatchet you are bound to succeed.

I cannot emphasize it too much. We shall begin to work in that spirit and in course of time all these angularities of the majority and minority communities, the Hindu community and the Muslim community . . . . . . because even as regards Muslims you have Pathans, Punjabis, Sias, Sunnis and so on and among the Hindus you have Brahmins, Vaishanavas, Khatris, also Bengalis, Madrasis and so on . . . . . . will vanish. Indeed if you ask me this has the biggest hindrance in the way of India to attain the freedom and independence but for this would have been free peoples long ago.

The first and foremost thing that I would like to emphasize is this . . . . . . remember that you are now a sovereign legislative body and you have got all the gravest responsibility as to how should take your decisions. The first observations that I would like is this: you will no doubt agree with me that the first duty of a government is to maintain law and order so that the life, property and religious beliefs of its projects are fully protected by the state.

Curse of Corruption

The second thing that occurs to me is this, one of the biggest curses from India is suffering is bribery and corruption, this really is a poison.

We must put that down with an iron hand and I hope that you will take adequate measures as soon as it is possible. Black marketing is another curse. I know that black marketers are frequently caught and punished. Judicial sentences are passed or sometimes fines only are imposed. Now you have to tackle this monster, which today is a colossal crime against society, in our distressed conditions, when we constantly face shortage of food. A citizen who does black marketing comments, I think a greater crime than the biggest and most grievous of crimes. These black marketers are really knowing, intelligent and ordinarily responsible people. I think they ought to be very severely punished because they undermine the entire system of control . . . . . . and cause wholesale starvation and want and even death.

History's Verdict

The next thing that strikes me is this. Here against is a legacy which has been passed on to us . . . . . . the evil of nepotism and gibber. This evil must be crushed restlessly. I want to make it quite clear that I shall never tolerate any kind of gibber, nepotism or any influence directly or indirectly brought to bear upon me . . . . I know there are people who do not quite agree with the division of India and the partition of Punjab and Bengal. Much had been said against it but now that it has been accepted. It is the duty of everyone of us to loyally abide by it and honourably act according to the agreement, which is now final and binding on all, but you must remember, as I have said mighty revolution that has taken place is unprotected.

But this question is, whether it was possible practicable to act otherwise than what has been done . . . . A division has to take place on both sides in Hindustan and Pakistan, there are sections of people who may not agree with it, who may not like it, but in my judgment there was no other solution and I am sure future history will record its verdict in favour of it. And what is more it will be proved by actual experience as we go on that was the only solution. Any idea of a united India could never have worked and in my judgment it would have led us to terrific disaster. May be that view is correct; may be it is not; that remains to be seen.[42]

Jinnah made an extraordinary speech to the first Constituent Assembly of Pakistan in Karachi on August 11, 1947. Jinnah seemed to guestion the basis on which his new kingdom had been established. In that speech, he suddenly called upon all those gathered there to struggle for the equal rights. This was declared by a man who had fought so hard for the creation of a separate Muslim state and in the midst of religious massacres. The extract of his speech is as follows: I know there are people who do not quite agree with the division of India . . . . . . but in my judgment there was no other solution and I am sure future history will record its in favour of it . . . . . . may be that view is correct; may be it is not; that remains to be seen. He went on to say that his ambition was that Pakistan should become a nation in which there were no discrimination of colour, caste or creed.

> *"You are free, you are free to go to temple, you are free to go your mosques or to any other places of worship in this state of Pakistan. You may belong to any religion or caste or creed that has nothing to do with the business of the state . . . . . . we are starting in the days when there is no discrimination, no distinction between the community and another, no discrimination between one caste or creed or another. We are starting with this fundamental principle that we are all citizens and equal citizens of the state . . . . . . now, I think we should keep that in front of us as our ideal and you will find that in course of time Hindus would cease to be Hindus and Muslims would cease to be Muslims, not in the religious sense, because that is the personal faith of each individual but in the political sense as citizen of state."*

The 'secular' Pakistan of Governor General Mohammad Ali Jinnah's celebrated speech of August 14, 1947 inaugurating the new state lasted for all of 24 hours only. The idiom of religion based politics could not be crossed. And the ruthless logic of basing nationalhood on religion took on dynamics, and momentum of its own. The central dilemma of Pakistan has since its conception been one, how to have a Muslim nation but not on Islamic state. Two, if the state has to be Islamic, which word of God, would prevail.

It was a magnificent vision for the new nation. Jinnah did his best to cope with the effects of the massacres and migrations. He lived in Karachi and his sister Fatima stayed with him. He had little or no appetite, and had even lost his ability to will himself to sleep. He began his day discussing these mass killings with Fatima. Jinnah was a frustrated and disappointed man, Jinnah concluded in this way. But the question is, whether it was possible or practicable to act otherwise than what has been done. A division had to take place on both sides, in Hindustan and Pakistan. There are sections of people who may not agree with it, who may not like it, but in my judgment there was no other solution and I am sure future history will record its verdict in favour of it. And what is more it will be proved by actual experience as we go on that was the only solution. Any idea of a united India could never have worked and in my judgment it would have led us to terrific disaster. May be that view is correct. May be it is not, that remains to be seen.[43]

This view was clearly contrary to Two-Nation Theory, which was the basis of the new state of Pakistan. And it had come from the father of Pakistan. His close friends and advisers were against it. Douglas, a Deputy Principle Information Officer of the Government of India who had gone to Karachi as the publicity chief, and others decided that this portion of speech to the Constituent Assembly be blacked out; censorship at the very beginning of Pakistan.[44] The editor of *Dawn* protested and threatened to go to the Quaid-e-Azam. It is well known that this portion of Jinnah's speech was not published in most of the newspapers in Pakistan. It was mentioned later by Mr. Justice Munir in one of his judgments.

It would not be irrelevant to mention that once when Jinnah went to Sind where he was welcomed by a big procession of peasants and they cried 'Maulana Mohammad Ali Zindabad' Jinnah halted the procession, pointed his finger at the crowd and said, stop calling me Maulana. I am not your religious leader. I am your political leader. Call me, Mr. Jinnah or Mohammad Ali Jinnah, no more of that Maulana. Do you understand me?[45]

Pakistan Constituent Assembly affirmed the national flag of Pakistan and also unanimously elected Jinnah as its President. Jinnah reiterated the equality of rights for minorities, a promise of equal citizenship for all in Pakistan irrespective of caste, creed or colour.

Dr. Khan Sahib, Premier of North Western Frontier Province described the rumours that he intended to decline Pathanistan on 15th August, as 'nonsense'. He clarified that while Congress would not participate on the celebration of Pakistan, the minister would attend official business.

On August 12, 1947 the Boundary Commission reports were ready for submission but it had leaked out that in the Bengal Award, Chittagong hill tracts were allocated to East Bengal, which had caused a major problem for the Congress and the Viceroy was anxious to avoid any problem at this stage with the Congress and sent his officers to Radcliff, requesting him to postpone the submission of the report but he was in no mood to help, when it was well known that the reports were ready. Finally, the Viceroy asked Radcliff[46] to date his reports 13th August, which would mean that by this time the reports were submitted, Mountbatten would have left for Karachi to participate in the Pakistan celebrations and return only in the evening of 14th August, considering the time required for printing of reports and the two intervening holidays on account of independence celebrations, the reports would not be ready for being public until 16th August. The Viceroy instructed his staff to inform the Government of the Punjab and Bengal that reports would be delayed and would not be available until 16th August and, therefore, the two governments of Bengal would take charge according to the national boundary on 15th August and adjust later where necessary.[47]

Punjabis were the Crown Jewel of India

The Punjabi Governor in a telegram to the Viceroy and Secretary of State reported on the fast deteriorating situation in Punjab, particularly Lahore, and felt that the strength of the Punjab boundary force was inadequate for the task ahead. The Punjab boundary force had been established on August 1, 1947 and the boundary force consisted of twenty-three thousand persons.[48] It consisted of Rajputs, Baluchs, Gorkhas and Dogras. The accounts of the Boundary Forces attempt to maintain law and order made depressed reading on 14th August. They found the bodies of thirty five Sikhs who had been knifed at Lahore railway station. By the time the Punjab Boundary Force reached Amritsar, many Muslim women had been dragged from their homes and hacked to death.

The Governor General issued a Gazette notification 'Arbitration Tribunal Order 1947' defining its composition, organizations and functions.

The Pakistan Constituent Assembly adopted a hotly detailed resolution conferring the title of Zakir-e-Azam on Jinnah from August 15.[49] Most Congress members from East Bengal opposed the resolution. On the afternoon of 13th August, Mountbatten flew to Karachi to bid Godspeed and farewell to Pakistan. His main work was to inaugurate the dominion of Pakistan. The Pakistan cabinet requested to Viceroy and Governor General to dismiss provincial governments and assume the power himself through the Governor which the Viceroy thought would be a fraud on the Indian Independence Act and after consulting the Secretary of State, Lord Listowal informed Pakistan that this could as well be done by the Pakistan Constituent Assembly itself.[50]

In the evening of August 13, 1947 there was a banquet at Government House, Karachi at the end of which Jinnah read a long speech. This state banquet was attended by 80 persons. Karachi had been identified as the capital of Pakistan, only later was it to shift to Rawalpindi and then Islamabad. Truck loads of personnel and tonnes of files had been transferred to Karachi from New Delhi.[51] It was followed by an alcohol-free reception attended by some 1,500 of the leading citizens of Pakistan, which included some very queer looking Jungle man, accompanied by sweet music played by a band of bearded warrior in Kilts.[52]

14th August was the last day of colonial rule in India. The state of Pakistan came into being today. On August 14, 1947, Mountbatten addressed the new Pakistan[53] Constituent Assembly, and then came the procession. After completion of the procession Mountbatten flew across the emptying Punjab to New Delhi, to launch the other part of the subcontinent into independence. In the midst of all-round excitement, there was an air of poignancy as millions of refugees were moving across the borders of the new dominions, still not sure where the dividing line was. Meanwhile the Viceroy informed the Secretary of State that the Awards even before problems on the Gurdaspur in Punjab and Chittagong hill tract in Bengal and he had decided to keep them under wraps till the two dominions had been inaugurated so as to vitiate the atmosphere on the occasion of such a historic event.

The Governor General issued the Indian independence (internal arrangement) order,[54] 1947 giving effect to the agreement as to the devolution of international rights and obligations upon the dominions of India and Pakistan, whereby membership of the international organizations together with the rights and obligations attached to such membership devolved solely upon India. Another notification called the 'Indian Independence (Rights, Property and Liabilities) Order 1947 was issued by the Governor General to provide for initial distribution of rights, property and liabilities.[55] Lord Mountbatten as Crown representative advised the British High Commissioner in New Delhi to clarify to the Government of India that since paramount was not being inherited by the successor dominions, the records containing information on the private lives of the rulers and internal affairs of the states would also not be inherited by them. Even list of such files would not be provided since the list would contain significant reference to matters which breach confidence if disclosed.[56]

The Viceroy speaking in the Pakistan Constituent Assembly inaugurated the new dominion of Pakistan and said Pakistan was 'parting between friends who have learned to honour and respect one another even in disagreement'.

The Indian Constituent Assembly met at 11 p.m. with the singing of *Vande Matram* and unanimously adopted a resolution appointing Mountbatten as the new Governor General of India. This should be known regarding the appointment of India's first Governor General in free India. Gandhi an affectionate man himself had scaled Mountbatten's warmth and responded to it. 1st July afternoon, the man who had spent so many years in British Rules walked into the Viceroy's study. There Gandhi asked Mountbatten to accept Congress invitation to become the first Governor General of the nation it had taken him 35 years to wrest from his countrymen.

Gandhi's words were an immense personnel tribute to Mountbatten and an equally immense tribute to British. Looking at him, lost in his armchair, Mountbatten was overwhelmed, we have jewelled him, we have humiliated him, we have scorned for him, we have ignored him, he thought, and he still has the greatness of spirit to do this. Touched almost to tears, Mountbatten thanked Gandhi for his encouragement. Gandhi acknowledged his words with bard a nod and concluded his speech. Prisoners were released to mark the occasion. Dr. Rajendra Prasad took the chair. The Constituent Assembly functions also as parliament of free India, 256 members of the Constituent Assembly rose to take pledge just after midnight. The pledge of dedication was repeated in three languages English, Hindi and Urdu. It was here that Nehru delivered his famous "Tryst with Destiny" speech. Rising to the height of the occasion, Pandit Nehru in the capacity of India's first Prime Minister made a speech which was at once notable and a masterpiece of literature.[57] The new cabinet of India consisting of 14 persons was formed. Thus there was the birth of India's freedom. He said, "Long years ago we made a tryst with destiny and now the time comes when we shall redeem our pledge, nor wholly or in a full measure but very substantially. At the stroke of midnight, when the world sleeps India will awake to life and freedom. A moment comes which comes but rarely in history, when we step out from the old to the new, when an age ends and when the soul of a nation long suppressed finds utterances. It is feeling that at this moment we take the pledge of dedication to the service of India and her people and to the still larger causes of humanity."[58]

Within 10 years unbridled communalism had created a religion based state on the subcontinent. It was not the Muslim masses who brought Pakistan into being. It was the elitist electoral politics of British India based on separate electorates and restricted to the enfranchisement of the propertied few that resulted in the formation of Pakistan.[59] If it is true that the Muslim elite voted with their hands for Pakistan, it is equally true that unless driven out by physical violence, the masses Muslim or Hindu voted with their feet to stay where they were. Thus Pakistan came into existence on August 14, 1947.

Was the birth of Pakistan a Muslim majority state? The Pakistan movement that brought it into being was deeply divided on why a Muslim state was at all necessary. A function of the Pakistan movement—the Mullah element wanted Pakistan because it would constitute a Dar-ul-Uloom in what was otherwise a subcontinent given over to the Dar-ul-Harb. The other and much larger factor of the Muslim League led by Zoroastrian-minded Quaid-e-Azam) wanted Pakistan for much more mundane reasons. The Muslim community could secure advancement freed of competition from other communities. The Muslim elite, especially of the Muslim minority provinces, were also quick to grasp the point that in Muslim majority Pakistan they would not only constitute the creamy layer but be happily positioned to take off all the creams themselves. But of course, it would not do to say so. And so the materialist Muslim element of the Pakistan movement found itself obliged to pay up services to the idiom and etiquette of religion based politics. The Quaid-e-Azam himself, who had in any case forsaken his Zorastrian family, gave up wine, and discarded to showiness fur cap, perhaps he even read the Namaz and observed the Raga certainly, if he did not do so the new Pakistan government were not going to advertise the fact.

The consequence was that the secular Pakistan of Governor General Mohammad Ali Jinnah's celebrated speech of August 14, 1947 inaugurating the new state lasted for all of 24 hours. The idioms of religion based politics could not be crossed. And the ruthless logic of basing nationhood on religion took on dynamics and momentum of its own. The central dilemma as of Pakistan has since its inception been one, how, to have in Muslim nation but not an Islamic state?

The chapter has been closed. The unification and the division of India was the result of the British policy. Other important factors were also responsible for the partition of India. The partition of India was great sorrow to Lord Mountbatten, the Viceroy, who presided over the partition of the country in 1947.

Road to Freedom and Partition

India was now a new nation on August 14/15, 1947. Lord Curzon, who had taken a hand in drafting the declaration of 1917, thought it would take India 500 years to qualify for self-government. S.P. Sinha, a brilliant lawyer and the first Indian member of the Viceroy's Executive Council, estimated that India would become a dominion in 300 years. Lord Linlithgow in 1943 told his successor Field Marshall Wavell that British rule in India would last for another 30 years. But history falsified them all and history moved very fast with the result that India achieved dominion status on August 14/15, 1947.

In this way India got freedom on August 14/15, 1947 and Pakistan was born as a new nation. Freedom did not come overnight. It was a long restlessness battle against odds; with the plight of the struggling Indian fighters a poor match against the might of the colonial forces. Along with the freedom fighters were those who took out newspapers peppered with inspiring stories, risking the wrath of the rulers. While the war for freedom took of a physical tussle on the streets, newspapers kept the desire for independence burning bright.

The physical partition of India is an accomplished political reality. The Muslim League made religion based demand in the election manifesto of 1937 and the religion based state of Pakistan was established on August 14, 1947.

Partition of British India was brought about by foreign powers, the British and the Muslim League. The mistake of Congress Party was also one important factor. Indian union rejected the argument that religion was a decisive factor in determining the issue of statehood, just as it had rejected the two-nation theory, which is that

Hindus and Muslims are separate nation. India opted for secularism in 1947. In spite of the fratricidal carriage which preceded and followed the partition. The birth of Pakistan represented the triunes and the colonization of Muslim communal politics in the Indian subcontinent. The result was that West Pakistan was left with virtually no Hindu population, whereas India continued to have very sizable Muslim population.

British rule came to an end with the creation of Pakistan on August 14, 1947 and India obtained its freedom on August 14/15, 1947 with Jawaharlal Nehru's speech 'Tryst with Destiny'. It was the end of protected struggle against British colonial rule. There was widespread communal violence and it resulted in a worst migration in human history. No doubt independence brought joy to millions but it plunged Bengal and Punjab into an agony unknown in India's history. As months passed both Hindu and Muslim on either side of the Radcliff line, realized that partition might have solved the constitutional tangle, but at a price immeasurable in terms of human misery. The uprooted did not know where to go. To many of them it was a journey to doom. Protection was guaranteed to the minorities by the infant's dominions; but no dominion was able to implement it. In the wake of the holocaust came the Radcliff Award, demarcating the boundaries between the two states, but instead of settling the dispute it only fanned the flames of communal frenzy, especially in the border areas.[60]

According to Zakaria, more than half a million people died in search of rehabilitation, those who survived came to a new soil free, but not their own. Amrit Lal in his article has written: Lakhs of men had died, lakhs of children had been orphaned, lakhs of women had lost their homes and honour. Now all that remained were their stories, which were told and heard by people as they smacked their lips with an epicurean's delight.[61]

As trainloads of refugees from West Pakistan poured into India, the atmosphere of Delhi and East Punjab became charged with hatred. There was indiscriminate looting and even murder and rape. Gandhi was a disillusioned soul. His faith in the intrinsic goodness of humanity was completely shaken. As he saw those orgies he was appalled by the cruelty of man to man. Everyday, at his prayer meeting, he spoke on peace and communal harmony. People heard him but he did not find in them the proper response.

Prime Minister Nehru, as he confessed in a broadcast, was able 'full of horror with the things I saw and that I heard'. To the Prime Minister, it was a challenge, to his leadership and to the secular character of India. He was distressed to find even some of his own colleagues in the Congress and the cabinet warning in this faith in secularism. But in no circumstances could he be untrue to himself; in that flood of hostility he stood firm as a rock. Alone he gave battle to the communalists, without ruth or fear. He braved the wrath of fanatics with danger in hand, sought to stab at the back of his secular state. He declared, unmindful of his popularity, that whatever Pakistan might have done, he would not let India shape as a Hindu state. He said, "India is not a communal state, but a democratic state in which every citizen has equal right". To this pledge, he received the unequivocal support of Mahatma Gandhi. In retrospect, it emerges as a miracle how the master and disciple, Gandhi and Nehru, stopped back the dark forces of communalism that had gripped the people from one end of the country to another. Was freedom worth the price of partition?[62]

The partition of subcontinent in 1947 was the single most traumatic experience in recent Indian history. The violence it unleashed was unprecedented and barbaric. The memory of those days still marks the social behaviour, the political judgment and the sense of moral righteousness of everyone in the region.

The result of the migration was that West Pakistan was left with virtually no Hindu population, whereas India continued to have a very sizable Muslim population, and this was by all accounts the most conclusive testimony of India's secular approach even at the tense and critical juncture of the partition of the country. Having proclaimed its adherence to secularism at time of partition and inspire of the partition, the dominant political Party in India chose to regard the creation of Pakistan as an allusion. Even though it was prepared to be reconciled to Pakistan as an accomplished fact, it was not prepared to act on the communal and theoretic principle on which the two-nation theory was based.[63]

Karachi, August 13/14, 1947

Jinnah, the Governor General designate of Pakistan arrived in Karachi on August 7, 1947. The Muslim League flag was unfurled over the Government House. Before he left Delhi for Karachi, in a farewell message he said, I wish Hindustan prosperity and peace. I bid farewell to the citizens of Delhi among whom I had many friends of all communities, and I earnestly appeal to everyone to live in this great and historic city in peace. The past must be buried. Let us start a fresh as two independent sovereign states of Hindustan and Pakistan.[64]

The Pakistan Constituent Assembly met in Karachi on August 10, 1947; for its inaugural session with Yogendra Nath Mandal being elected unanimously as its chairman pending the election of the President. Jinnah was elected as its President on 11th August the Pakistan Constituent Assembly adopted a hotly decided resolution conferring the title of Quaid-i-Azam on Jinnah from August 15. Most Congress members from East Bengal opposed. This resolution was adopted on 12th August.

Mountbatten and Lady Mountbatten arrived in Karachi in the afternoon of August 13, 1947 to bid goodby to Pakistan. There was a large crowd at the airport to receive the Viceroy. Colonel Burney, Military Secretary to M.A. Jinnah told them that the crowds were noticeably thicker than those which had greeted Jinnah, when he made a similar entry a few days before. [65]

Less agreeable, he also reported that a plot had been discovered to throw a bomb into Jinnah's open car during the state procession on 14th August. The police saw little hope of arresting the conspirators before the procession took place. Jinnah was ready to go through with it, if the Viceroy concurred. He at once agreed that the arrangement should be unaltered.[66]

Jinnah made an impromptus speech. He proposed the health of Pakistan. He made a very fine speech. No one present could have detected that he had been taken by surprise. "For ten minutes the appropriate phrases and thoughts blow from him in smooth sequence" wrote Alan Campbell-Johnson, Mountbatten's Press Attaché "he is a born raconteur and his informal but quick firing eloquence" is ideally adopted to after dinner speech making.[67]

After the banquet; Mountbatten returned and between Jinnah's sister, Fatima and the wife of Liaquat Ali Khan, Jinnah's right hand man. These ladies enjoyed themselves mocking the credulous Hindus, who had allowed astrologers to dictate to them, when India would begin life as an independent nation. The joke rebounded on them. According to Mountbatten, when it was realized that Jinnah had forgotten the rules of Ramzan and a luncheon Party he had planned for the following day, i.e. 14th August had hurriedly to be cancelled.[68]

Fatima Jinnah was much impressed with the behaviour of Lady Mountbatten and when Mountbatten and Lady Mountbatten left them, Fatima embraced Lady Mountbatten. Fatima Jinnah's embrace was a natured gesture of warm affection.[69]

The independence celebration was to start on 14th August, it was a great trial. Mountbatten, Jinnah and Liaquat Ali Khan had all been informed about the plot to assassinate Jinnah. Now the open car procession was to start. Jinnah was determined not to cancel the open car procession. Mountbatten could not help thinking that he was going to have to risk his life in a few moments because of the obdurate man to whom they were addressed. The victory had no more success in persuading Jinnah to cancel their threatened procession then he had a trying to get him to abandon his dream of Pakistan. To cancel the ride or to rush through the streets of Karachi in a closed car would have been, Jinnah felt, an act of cowardice come what may, and he was ready for the procession. Mountbatten was going to expose himself to an assassin's bomb in an open car, at the side of a man he disliked, to celebrate the birth of a nation to whose creation he had been so vehemently opposed.

Now Mountbatten and Jinnah proceeded to the waiting car. They had to go Rolls Royce the Government House. Waiting before them was the black open that was to carry them through their ordeal. For a brief moment, Mountbatten fixed his eyes on his wife. He had given her driver orders to stay well behind his car. He was certain she would find a way to thwart them.

The Punjab CID officer G.D. Savage had informed Louis Mountbatten about the plot to kill Jinnah on August 14 at Karachi at the time of the open car procession. He had informed that a group of Sikh extremists had linked with the Rastriya Swyamsevak Sangh (RSS), as their head stood Master Tara Singh, a third grade school teacher. Tara Singh had called on his followers to drench Indian blood at the Sikh's secret convocation in Lahore. It had been decided that the RSS would infiltrate an unidentified number of their supporters into the city of Karachi. Each had been given a British Army Mill's hand-grenade. None of them was aware of the other's existence so that the arrest of one man would not compromise the plan.

On 14th August, those men were to station themselves along the route which would carry M.A. Jinnah in triumphant procession through the street of Karachi from Pakistan's Constituent Assembly to the official residence of the new Governor General. The plan was that one of the RSS followers was to assassinate the founder of Pakistan by hurling a grenade into the open carriage. The RSS had this idea in mind that the assassination of Jinnah would launch the entire subcontinent into savage civil war from which the numerically superior Hindus were bound to emerge as undisputed rulers.

Liaquat Ali Khan excitedly demanded that Mountbatten arrest the entire Sikh leadership stunned the Viceroy could not decide what to do. If Master Tara Singh was arrested, Mountbatten feared, might well start the civil war, which the RSS wanted.

Turning to the CID officer, Mountbatten said, suppose I ask the Governor to arrest the Sikh leaders? The officer replied that the Sikh leaders were isolated in Amritsar Golden Temple. No Sikh police would obey the order to go in after them and to send a Muslim police was unthinkable.

'Sir' the officer replied, "I am sorry to have to say there are not enough reliable police left in the Punjab to accomplish an order of that sort. I have to say it, but I can see no way to carry out such an order.

Mountbatten pondered a moment. He announced he would ask for a joint recommendation on that to do from the Punjab's Governor, Sir Evan Jenkins, Pandit Nehru and Liaquat Ali Khan. Liaquat Ali Khan rose from his chair at Mountbatten's words, you want to murder the Quaid-i-Azam he protested, 'If that is really the way you feel about it, I will go along in the same car and get murdered with him.' Mountbatten replied, but I am not going to throw the leader of five million Sikhs into jail without the agreement of the Governor.

The CID officer carried the Viceroy's letter to Lahore and gave to Governor Jenkins. He read the letter whatever can we do? Replied Sir Evan Jenkins, how we can stop them?

Five days later during the night of 11th/12th August, the Sikhs of Tara Singh successfully executed the first phase of the programme, they had agreed with the RSS.[70] During the Independence Day celebration Ex-INA soldier were operating in connection with the RSS and Master Tara Singh to assassinate Jinnah in Karachi.[71]

In the morning of 14th August Mountbatten addressed the Constituent Assembly. It was a colourful assembly. Beside Jinnah sat the Viceroy Mountbatten glowed in his white naval uniform and to the decorations are so loved to wear. Mountbatten rose to deliver the king's good wishes to his newest dominion. Then he declared, the birth of Pakistan is an event in the history. History seems something to move with the infinite slowness of a glacier, and sometimes to rush forward in a torrent. Just now in this part of the world, our united efforts have melted the ice and moved some impediments from the stream and we are carried in the full flood. There is no time to look back. There is only time to look forward.

With these words, the Viceroy looked sideways towards Jinnah and Mountbatten declared: if I would like to express my tribute to Mr. Jinnah. Our close personal contact and the mutual trust and understanding that has grown out of it are, I feel the lost errand for future good relations. He concluded in this way the time has come to bid you farewell, may Pakistan prosper always . . . . . . and may she continue in friendship with her neighbours and with all the nations of the world.[72]

Viceroy by speaking in the Pakistan Constituent Assembly inaugurated the new dominion of Pakistan and said Pakistan was parting between friends, who have learned to honour and respect one another even in disagreement.[73]

Then it was Jinnah's turn, it was the last day of colonial rule in India and Pakistan came into being. Jinnah with his white sherwani buttoned up to the base of his emaciated throat and said Britain and the peoples she had colonized were parting as friends and I sincerely hope that we shall remain friends. Pakistan, he declared would not be found wanting in friendly spirit by our neighbours and all the nations of the world.[74]

Then the state procession took place in the open cars. It was the black open Rolls Royce that was to carry them through their ordeal. Jinnah and Mountbatten sat side by side and Edwina and Fatima Jinnah in the car immediately behind them. For a brief second, Mountbatten fixed his eyes on his wife. He had given her driver strict orders to stay well behind his car. He was certain. She would find away to thwart the assassins. His eyes met Jinnah as the car started. They did not speak. Jinnah was in a tense.

A 31 gun Viceregal salute followed them down the drive out into Karachi's streets. To drive for three miles through dense crowds, knowing that every window, every group of figures might conceal an assassin, would have tested the nerves of anyone. The car came on the Victoria Road. There Mountbatten saw a young man, who tightened his grip on the Colt 45 swelling his coat-pocket. He also saw the faces waving from the windows of the building opposite. At this Mountbatten flicked off the safety catch of his weapon

Mountbatten's car neared the balcony of the building. The CID officer G.D. Savage saw this scene and put up a prayer for the safe ride.

Mountbatten and Jinnah were both so preoccupied with the risks they had taken that they had not sent a word to each other since getting into the car. The strain was mounting and Mountbatten was telling himself, "After all, I have given them their independence". He could not believe there were men in that crowd willing to kill him. His presence he sincerely thought, might save Jinnah 'they just won't kill him' he insisted to himself, 'when they realize it became killing me at the same time'.

On his balcony, G.D. Savage held his breath as the car rolled under his feet. He kept his hand fixed on his weapon until the Rolls Royce had passed beyond the range where he could offer its occupants any protection. So he went into his room for rest.

Ahead of the car now, the 'huzzah's and zindabad' gave way to a menacing silence. It was a Hindu area. Mountbatten told himself this is where it will happen. The Hindu area covered the Elephinston Street, Karachi's principal commercial thoroughfare. The car took five minutes to cross it. Almost all its stops and markets belonged to Hindus and they were embittered by the event their Muslim neighbours were celebrating.

Nothing happened and the gates of Government House rose in front of the Rolls Royce. The most harrowing drive of Louis Mountbatten's life was over. Mountbatten and Jinnah passed the test by the slightest gesture that the occasion was anything but one of the euphoria. "Bomb attack reported never materialized" noted Mountbatten briefly in his diary.[75]

As the car ceased to stop, for the first and only time in their intense, difficult relationship; Jinnah relaxed, his glacial façade disappeared and a warm smile illuminated his features.[76]

With an unusual display of emotion, Jinnah placed his hand on the Viceroy's knee, when they reached their destination and murmured, "Thank God! I have brought you back alive?" Mountbatten retorted and pointed out, how much more serious it would have been if he had been bumped off.[77]

An intensive efforts, by Collins and Lapierre to discover in 1975, why the plot in Karachi was not executed?, revealed only one indirect testimony offered by Pritam Singh, a bicycle repair man in Jallandhar was arrested by CID in connection with the Sikh's part of plot, the derailment of the Pakistan trains. The RSS had indeed, claimed, infiltrated its men into Karachi, but the leader whom I relied for explosion was to pass the signal to the others to hurl bomb these lost their courage when the car passed them.[78]

The independent celebration was over at Karachi and Mountbatten and Edwina were back to Delhi in the afternoon of August 14, 1947 to launch the other part of the subcontinent into independence.[79]

In the midst of all round excitement, there was an air of poignancy as millions of refugees were moving across the borders of the new dominions, still not sure where the dividing line was. Meanwhile the Viceroy informed the Secretary of State that the Awards before publication were causing problems on the question of Gurdaspur in Punjab and Chittagong hill tracts in Bengal and he had decided to keep them under corps till the two dominions had been inaugurated so as not to vitiate the atmosphere on the occasion of such a historic event.

New Delhi, Astrologers and Indian Independence

As a staff meeting after his press conference held on June 4, 1947, New Delhi, the Viceroy had noted with a smile that there was 'a complete lack of high level adviser's on astrology in his staff; insisting this he remedied forthwith, he assigned his able young pass attaché, Alan Campbell Johnson, the additional responsibilities of viceregal astrologer.

Most vexing problem was that posed by Mountbatten's impetuous selection of August 15, 1947 as the date for India's Independence. A congeries of astrologer, finally advised India's politician that though 15th August was a wholly inauspicious day on which to begin their nation's modern history, August 14 represented a considerably more favourable conjecture of the stars. A relieved Viceroy accepted the compromise the Indian politician proposed to propitiate the celestial bodies. India and Pakistan would become independent dominant on the stroke of Midnight, August 14, 1947.[80]

The Viceroy, Louis Mountbatten chose August 15, 1947 out of the blue for one-fifth of humanity to awake to freedom. Pandit Jawaharlal Nehru, seen to be India's first Prime Minister, did not believe in astrology and Nehru told the Viceroy, he had chosen an unpropitious day for one of the most momentous transfer of power ever to take place in modern history. Never mind Nehru, if you agree to take place a midnight meeting and just before midnight strikes, we will transfer power. As midnight approached, Mountbatten signed the last telegram as Viceroy, and the old Legislative Assembly was passing the resolution proclaiming independence.[81]

Mountbatten had made a broadcast on the evening of June 3, 1947. He said that India would achieve freedom and India would be partitioned. At a press conference, Mountbatten announced that India would achieve freedom on August 15, 1947. As soon as the date was announced, astrologers all over India began to consult their charts. Astrologers of Banaras and the Southern India immediately proclaimed August 15th a date so in auspicious that India would be better advised to tolerate the British one day longer than risk eternal domination.

In Calcutta, Swami Madanand rushed to his celestial charts as soon as he heard the date announced. He took at his 'Navmash' on enormous circular charts composed of a succession of concentric circles on which were plotted the days and months of the year, the cycle of the sun and the moon, the planets, the signs of Zodiac and the position of the 27 stars influencing the destiny of the earth. At the centre was the map of the world. He twisted the circles on his chart until they were all set for 15th August then, from a map of India in the charts Cora, he began to draw a series of lines out towards the edge of the wheel. As he did so, he set up aghast. His calculations were foretold disaster. India on 15th August would be under the zodiac sign of Makara, Capricorn a sign one of whose particularities was its unrelenting hostility to all centrifugal forces, hence to partition. For worst that day would be passed under the influence of Saturn, a notably inauspicious planet, dominated by Rahu, scornfully labelled by astrologers the star with no neck, a celestial body whose manifestations were almost wholly malign. From midnight, 14th August throughout August 15th, Saturn, Jupiter and Venus would all lie in the most accursed site of the Heaven. The young astrologers looked up from his chart overcome by the magnitude of the disaster they had revealed.

Despite the discipline acquired in the years of *yoga*, meditation and tantric studies in a temple in the hills of Assam, the astrologers lost control to him. Seizing a piece of paper he sat down and wrote an urgent appeal to the man inadvertently responsible for his celestial catastrophe. 'For the love of god', he wrote to Louis Mountbatten, 'do not give India her Independence on 15th August. If floods, droughts, famines, and massacres follow it will be because India was born on a day cursed by the star'. [82]

New Delhi, August 14, 1947

The Union Jack was never formally lowered during the historic night of August 14th/15th in Delhi. It was lowered on the evening of 14th August folded up respectfully, and handover to a British agent. Thousands of flag staff at sunset was quiet and they did not protest. At sunrise of 15th August its place was taken by the banners of an Independent India. The flag on the palace of the new Governor General of India was allowed to have the royal British crest.

In the evening of August 1947, two *sanyasis* with their brachiates and foreheads streaked with ashes and uncut hair, tumbling to their shoulders came to York Road, New Delhi to sprinkle Pandit Jawaharlal Nehru with holy water, smeared his forehead with sired ash, led their scepter on his arms and dropped him in the cloth of God. The man who had no faith in traditional religion submitted himself to the *sanyasis* with almost cheerful humility.[83]

Mountbatten had made clear that it was his firm policy that the British flag should not be ceremoniously hauled down, Nehru had agreed. If the lowering of the Union Jack in any way offended British susceptibilities, it should not take place.

The tower of residency, Lucknow was the only spot in the British Empire, where the Union Jack was never lowered from 1857. The tower had become the shrine of imperial India. At 10 p.m. on the evening of 14th August, the tower's care-taker, Warrant Officer, J.R. Ireland, had hauled the Union Jack down for the last time.

At 17 York Road, Jawaharlal Nehru had finished washing the *sanyasi's* ashes from his face and sat down to dinner, when his telephone rang. His daughter Indira and his guest Padmja Naidu could hear him in his study showing to make him heard over a hot line.

Indira and Padmaja Naidu gasped. When to return, he was unable to speak and he was in tears. The caller had been telephoning from Lahore. All the water in the old city's Hindu and Sikh quarters had been cut. People were going mad from thirst in the troubled summer. Stunned, he said, "How am I going to talk tonight; how am I going to pretend there is ray in my heart for India's Independence, when I know Lahore our beautiful Lahore is burning."[84]

New Delhi, Midnight, August 14, 1947

At the midnight of August 14, 1947, the fire was burning in the New Delhi garden of Dr. Rajendra Prasad, the President of the Indian Constituent Assembly. It was sacred fire consecrated and purified by the Vedic rites by the Brahmin priest who sat aside and rhythmically chanting the *mantras* "Oh, Fire, intend the Brahman beside it; you are the countenance of all the gods and of all learned men. Yours is the power to penetrate the innermost recesses of the human heart and discover the truth."

As the Brahmin priests repeated his atonal chant, the learned men and women who would shortly become the first minister of an independent India, filed past the fire. A second Brahmin sprinkled each with a few drops of water. Then they stopped over to a woman waiting with a copper vassal, its exterior white washed, its top covered with palm leaves. As the minister paused before her, she dipped her right fore finger into the vassal, then with the liquid on her finger drops, pressed a bright vermillion dot on to their foreheads. It was the ancient Hindu symbol of the 'third eye' which was really behind appearances, a device to shelter its bearer from the influence of the evil eye on the malevolent designs of those who wished them ill. This prepared for the cruel burdens awaiting them, those men and women Flag wrapped filled into Constituent Assembly hall.[85]

Dream of New India, 'Tryst with Destiny' Reaffirmed

Celebrations for the freedom weak started with the unfurling of the national flag at Gandhi ground in New Delhi on August 9, 1947 by Dr. Rajendra Prasad, Vande Matram was sung on the occasion.

The Constituent Assembly started its session at 11 p.m. Dr. Rajendra Prasad took the chair. The session was being held in the central hall of the council house (central house of Parliament), which witnessed 'Transfer of Power' from the British Crown to people's representatives, all of whom were members of the then

Constituent Assembly. In all 296 members of the Constituent Assembly after the Muslim League representatives had departed for Pakistan attended the ceremony.[86]

Really a great burden had fallen on the minister for the governance of the country. The men upon whom those burdens would now begin most heavily rose to speak. Nehru had dictated this speech before delivering it and showed it to Mahatma Gandhi, C. Rajagopalachari, Rajendra Prasad, Maulana Azad and other leaders. Even though Mathai, in his book, claimed that the "Tryst with Destiny" was his creation, which was totally untrue.[87]

Patrick French in his book *Liberty or Death* has mentioned at page 318 that Nehru's speech had gone through a number of drafts. He had started with the phrase a date with destiny but his secretary M.O. Mathai suggested this might be construed to have romantic connotations. They had tried a rendezvous with destiny instead, but Nehru finally settled for; long years ago we made a tryst with destiny, and now the time comes ...... [88] Tryst with Destiny before the Constituent Assembly transferred power for the governance of the country. The speech was notable and a masterpiece of literature. The joy of the members was mingled with sorrow. They were conscious of the partition, of the enormous burden of responsibility they were to shoulder in ushering the nascent democracy into an era in which people would be free from poverty, ignorance, disease and inequality.

Before making his celebrated speech, which was part of the resolution he moved on the occasion. Nehru made a reference to the communal fighting which broke out in several cities. He said, "We know there is rejoining in the whole of the country. Not far from Delhi, big cities are ablaze and its heat is reaching us here. Our happinesscan not be complete. We have to face all these things with a brave heart. We are not to raise a hue and cry and get perturbed."

When we are on the threshold of freedom, we should remember that India does not belong to any one Party or group of people or caste. It does not belong to the followers of any particular religion. It is the country of all, every religion and creed. All Indians shall have equal rights. If any one is oppressed, we shall stand by his side.[89]

In an impressive ceremony, Nehru delivered the address. This is the text of his speech; long years ago we made tryst with destiny and now the times comes when we shall redeem our pledge, wholly or in full measure, but very substantially. At the stroke of the midnight hour, when the world sleeps, India will awake to life and freedom. A moment comes, which comes but rarely in history, when we stop out from the old to the new, when an age ends, and when the soul of a nation, long suppressed, finds utterances. It is fitting that at this solemn moment we take the pledge of dedication to the service of India and his people and to the still larger cause of humanity.

Unending Quest

At the dawn of history, India started on her unending quest, and trackless centuries are filled with her striving and her success and her failures. Though good and ill fortune alike she has never lost sight of that quest or forgotten the ideals which gave her strength. We end today a period of ill fortune and India discourse herself again. The achievement we celebrate today is but a stop, an opening of opportunity, to the great triumphs and achievements that await us. Are we enough and wise enough to grasp this opportunity and accept the challenge of the future?

Freedom and power bring responsibility. The responsibility rests upon this assembly, a sovereign body representing the sovereign people of India. Before the birth of freedom we have endured all the pains of labour and our hearts are heavy with the memory of the sorrow. Some of these pains continue even now. Nevertheless, the past is over and it is the future that backones to us now.

That future is not one of ease or resting but of incessant striving so that we may, fulfil the pledges we have so often taken and one we shall take today. The service of India means the service of the millions who suffer. It means the ending of poverty and ignorance and disease and inequality of opportunity. The ambition of the greatest man of our generation has been to wipe every tear from every age. That may be beyond us, but as long as there are tears and suffering so long our work will not be over.

And so we have to labour and to work hard, to give reality to our dreams. Those dreams are for India, but they are also for the world, for all the nations and peoples are too closely knot together today for anyone of them to imagine that it can live apart, peace has been said to be indivisible to its freedom, so its prosperity now and so also is disaster in that one world that can no longer be split into isolated fragments.

To the people of India, whose representatives we are, we make an appeal to join us with faith and confidence in this great adventure. This is no time for petty and destructive criticism, no time for ill will or blaming others. We have to build the noble mansion of free India, where all her children may dwell.

I beg to move, sir

That it may be resolved that

After the last stroke of mid night, all members of the Constituent Assembly present on this occasion do take the following pledge:

"At this solemn moment, when the people of India, through suffering and sacrifice, have secured freedom,

I . . . . . . a member of the Constituent Assembly of India, do dedicate myself in all humanity to the service of India and her people to the end that this ancient land attain her rightful place in the world and make her full and willing contribution to the promotion of world peace and the welfare of mankind.

The appointed day had come . . . . . .

The day appointed by Destiny—and India stands forth again after long slumber and struggle, awake vital, free and independent. The past clings to us still in some measures and we have to do much before we redeem the pledges we have so often taken. Yet the turning point is past and history begins a new foe us, the history which we live and act and others will write about."

Fateful Moment

It is a fateful moment for us in India, for all Asia and for the world. A new star arises, the star of freedom in our east, a new hope comes into being, and a vision long cherished materializes. May the star never sat and that hope never is betrayed.

We rejoice in this freedom, even though clouds surrounds, and many of our people are sorrow stricken and different problems encompass us. But freedom brings responsibilities and burdens and we have to face them in the siprit of a free and disciplined people.

On the day our first thought go to the architect of this freedom, the Father of Our Nation, who embodying the old sprit of India, hold a loft the torch of freedom and lighted up the darkness that surrounds us. We have often been unworthy followers of him and stayed from his message and bear the imprint in their hearts of this great son of India, magnificent in his faith and strength and courage and humility. We shall never allow that torch of freedom to be blown out, however, high the wind or stormy the tempest.

Our next thought must be of the unknown volunteers and soldiers of freedom who, without praise or reward have served India even unto death. We think also of our brothers and sisters, who have been cut off from us by political boundaries and who unhappily cannot share at present in the freedom that has come. They are with us and will remain of us. Whatever may happen and we shall be sharing in their good and ill fortune alike.

Justice for All

The future belongs to us, whether do we go and shall be our endeavours? To bring freedom and opportunity to the common man, to the peasant and workers of India, to fight, and to end the poverty and ignorance and disease, to build up a prosperous, democratic and progressive nation and to create social, economic and political institutions which will ensure just and fullness of life to every man and woman.

We have hard work ahead. There is no resting for anyone of us till we redeem our pledge in full, till we make all the people of India what destiny intended them to be. We are citizens of a great country, on the verge of bold advance and we have to live up to that high standard. All of us to whatever religion we may belong are equally the children of India with equal rights, privileges and obligations. We cannot encourage communalism or narrow mindedness for no nation can be great whose people are narrow in thoughts or in action.

To the nation and the people of the world we send greetings and pledge ourselves to co-operate with them in furthering peace, freedom and democracy. And to India, our much loved motherland, the ancient, the eternal and the ever now, we pay our reverent homage and we blend ourselves afresh to service. Jai Hind! [90]

As the function was going in the Constituent Assembly, outside a rippling wave of thunder clattered across the midnight sky and drenching monsoon rain spattered the thousands of ordinary Indians ramming the area around the hall. A large number of persons had assembled outside the hall. As the clock struck 12, head bowed and the representatives sat in meditative silence.

In the hall, the hands of clock, over the spike's stand crept up to the Roman XII hands bowed, the representatives sat in meditative silence, waiting for the crams of midnight. Not a figure stirred as those twelve heavy tolls marked the end of a day and an era. To the Indian politicians, the conch shell's bleat heralded the birth of the nation. To the world, it played retreat for the passing of an age.

Outside of the hall, the rain had stopped and a jubilant mood swept over the crowd. As Nehru emerged, thousands of happy people rushed forward, threatening to engulf him and the ministers behind him in their embrace. Watching the thin screen of policeman trying to hold people back, an enormous smile animated Nehru's face. Nehru said, you know to an aide standing behind him exactly ten years ago in London, I had a fight with Lord Linlithgow, the Viceroy, I got so mad. I shouted, I will be damned if we do not have our independence in ten years. He answered, "Oh! No, you won't". The Prime Minister recalled with a laugh India will not be free in my time, Mr. Nehru, he said nor in your either.[91] New Delhi became the capital of the Republic of India. New Delhi was the imperial capital from 1931 to 1947.

All the leaders stood united and single-minded in a row to march towards 'Tryst with Destiny'. When indeed India reached the Promised Land, politics as the people knew, would vanish. The leaders hoped that it would be a nation with no scam, crime or political deception. It would be dream world and everyone was singing out of joy about the type of Destiny that we wanted to have for ourselves? We should have decided what was the nature of the civilisation that we wanted to build and what cultural values, what motivation and what frame of mind would be needed to create and sustain that civilization. Our primary task should have been regeneration of the power of the Indian mind, recreation of the ancient nobility of temper and reconstruction of those ideals and concepts, which has inspired men like Swami Vivekananda and Mahatma Gandhi, and which had led Arnold Toynbee that India would conquer the conquerors in the twenty-first century.[92]

The stage was set out for Nehru and Rajendra Prasad to enter the room. All members took the pledge of dedication either in English or Hindi or Urdu. At the conclusion of the sitting, Dr. Prasad and Pandit Nehru motored to Government House to convey the Constituent Assembly's twin message to Lord Mountbatten intimating to him the assumption of power by the Constituent Assembly and endorsement by that sovereign body of the recommendation that Lord Mountbatten be Governor General of

India from August 15, 1947. Mountbatten agreed to the Governor General of free India.[93]

Before the winding up of session of the Constituent Assembly, its President, Dr. Rajendra Prasad had said; the country which was made by God and nature to be one, stands divided today separated from near and dear ones, even from strangers after some association is always painful. It would be untrue to me if I did not at this moment confess to a sense of sorrow at this separation.

> *"To those who feel like us but are on the other side of the border, we send a word of cheer. They should not give a way to panic. They have no reason to fear that they will not get protection and just and fair treatment and they should not become victims of doubt and suspicion, they accept the assurances publicly given and win their rightful place in the polity of the state, where they are placed by their loyalty."*

Chaudhary Khaliq-uz-Zaman said, "Now the time has come when we have to shoulder great responsibilities, when there will be no room for clapping and high sounding slogans. After today the task before this house, before the leaders of the country will not be spectacular one but one that requires diligence, industry and service to the people."

Dr. S. Radhakrishnan said, "While India is attaining freedom, she is attaining it in a manner which does not produce joy in the hearts of people or radiant smile in their faces. Some of those who were charged with responsibility for the administration of this country tried a bid to accentuate communal consciousness and bring about the present result (partition), which is the logic outcome of the policies adopted by the lesser minds of Britain. Were we not victims, ready victims, so to say, of the separatist tendencies frosted on us?"

Now that India is divided, it is our duty not to indulge in words of anger. They land us nowhere; we must not lose our passion. The body politic may be divided but the body historic lives on. Political divisions physically partitions are external but the psychological divisions are deeper. The cultural cleavages are the more dangerous. We should not allow them to grow.

"A free India will be judged by the way in which it will serve the interests of the common man." Jawaharlal Nehru spoke about the nations 'Tryst with Destiny' and immediately began working for a democratic, secular and united India which could play its role in the world befitting a great people. In his own way, Mahatma Gandhi had fine tuned the destiny idea and talked about building a nation which could wipe off the tears of the poorest, the loneliest and the destitute of the land.

They had different views of what a free India should be like national aims and the question of ends and means, Gandhi was most concerned with whatever their view points, conception or otherwise. Gandhi and Nehru wanted to work for an India where none died for lack of food, where everybody had shelter and some clothes to put on, where every child would go to school to learn skills and ideas for a bright future.

Gandhi, Nehru, Patel, Dr. Rajendra Prasad and many other leaders who came from different streams of thought and millions of people who suffered with them in the struggle for freedom shared a common dream of building a new India and society based on some values. Idealism was in the air. There was purpose and a sense of direction that helped the leaders and they get over the birth pangs of freedom.

It will be befitting the occasion to mention that a grateful Nation celebrated the Golden Jubilee of India's Independence and the celebration on August 14/15,-1947 at the stroke of midnight with a stirring call by President K.R. Narayanan. The function was held in the central hall of Parliament, which on the same time and day 50 years ago had witnessed the transfer of power. The 45 minutes function included playing of taped speeches of Gandhi, Nehru and Subhas and Nehru's celebrated address 'Tryst with Destiny'. The number of invited were far more than the seats available in the central hall. There was complete confusion with several hundred guests, including a large number of ministers.

The function began at 11.55 p.m. with the President escorted by the Prime Minister and presiding officers of the Rajya Sabha and Lok Sabha. British Speaker of the House of Commons, Betty Boothrayed was present at the function. Besides the President, the Prime Minister L.K. Gujral, Lok Sabha Speaker P.A. Sangma, Rajya Sabha Deputy Chairperson Najma Heptullah and the entire union cabinet, M.P.'s, a galaxy of VIP's including former Presidents, Prime Minister, Supreme Court Judges and senior serving and retired bureaucrats attended the function. In a lofty tone the President made a touching reference to the country's partition, which had ever shadowed the birth of independent India in 1947 and sacrifices made by leaders like Rajendra Prasad, Sardar Vallabhbhai Patel, Maulana A.K. Azad and B.R. Ambedkar. Reminiscent of the pledge taken in 1947 by the founding father of the Constitution, the President said, "At this moment of the midnight, let us bow our heads to Bharat Mata, whose children we are and also to take a vow to serve her and the people of India, regardless of caste, class, religion, language or region."

Mountbatten had agreed to be the Governor General of India from August 15, 1947. It was the second Honour that Mountbatten had received that evening. A few minutes before, he had learnt that his cousin George VI, in recognition of his accomplishments in India had elevated him to a rank in the peerage from Viscount to Earl.[94]

Mountbatten took out a decanter of port and personally filled his visitor's glasses. When he had done so, he raised his own and said, 'To India', after a sip. Nehru in turn raised his to Mountbatten "to King George VI", he said.

Before this event, Mountbatten had accepted Dr. Prasad's invitation, pledging to serve India as if he were himself an Indian. Then Nehru gave Mountbatten an envelop containing the list of the man who, with his approval would constitute the first government of an independent India. When they had left, before going to bed, Mountbatten opened the envelop Nehru had handed over to him. As he did so, he burst into laughter. In the haste of this great evening, Nehru had not had time to write down the names of independent India's first cabinet. It consisted of a blank sheet of paper.[95]

Mahatma Gandhi

It is our duty to know how Gandhi passed the night of August 14/15, 1947. Gandhi was staying at 151 Bittaghat Road at Hydari House, Calcutta. A handful of non-violent Hindu and Muslim Volunteers stood to watch the Indian independence celebration which was going on in New Delhi and other places had not influenced Gandhi at all. Not a single lamp bulb, not even a candle flickered from the broken window at Hydari House. Nothing, not even the event of the independence night, which itself was a momentous, had been allowed to intrude into the daily routine of the men and women inside the

Hydari House. In the spacious room which served as their communal dormitory, they lay stretched out on straw pallets. On one of them, next to his neatly aligned wooden clogs, his *Gita*, his dentures and his steel rimmed spectacles, was the familiar, bald headed figure. When the clock had struck 12 and India had awakened to life and freedom, Mohan Das Karam Chand Gandhi, the architect of the Indian freedom and whom the nation addressed as Bapu, had been found asleep.[96]

New Delhi, August 15

There was great enthusiasm in the country; August 15, 1947 was a very solemn day for the people of the dominion of India. It was the end of a long and protracted struggle against British colonial rule. India attained independence after partition. Queen Victoria's great grandson advanced towards the throne, where he would assume the charge and an honour unique in the coming annals of decolonization. For Louis Mountbatten, the most remarkable and inspiring day in his life was beginning, the day he would be handing over change of the heart land of his great grand father's empire.

His wife walked by his side in a silver lame garden gown, a diadem set on her brown hair. He was fully determined that the 'day' would go off with the utmost pomp. Mountbatten had supervised every detail of India's independence ceremonies with his love of pageantry and his Teutonic zest for detail. A colourful uniformed escort proceeded. The regal pair as they flowed towards those crimson thrones in which five months before they had been installed as Viceroy and Vicerine. Ranged to their right and left on the marble dais under a velvet canopy were the new minister of India, the swearing in ceremony was to start at 8 a.m.

Swearing-in-Ceremony

Mountbatten had written a letter to the Secretary of State, Earl of Listowel from New Delhi on 16th July; in order to arrange the ceremonies of 15th August, I should be grateful for guidance on the following points; do I cease to be Governor General, the moment past midnight on the night of the August 14/15.[97] In this case will it be necessary for me to be sworn in again, before I proceed in state to the Constituent Assembly on the morning of 15th? Will you please also send the form of oath which I shall be required to take? Listowel replied to Mountbatten on July 23, 1947; you will cease to be Governor General immediately, after mid-night of August 14. It will be necessary to be sworn and to take the oath of Allegiance on 15th August before proceeding in state to the Constituent Assembly.

All the new ministers of India were waiting for the swearing-in. The swearing-in-ceremony was to start at 8.30 a.m. in the Durbar Hall in front of the official audience of some 500, including a number of ruling princes. The official guests including Ambassadors, princes and the cabinet then drove in procession from Government House to the council chamber.[98]

Mountbatten took oath first. He swore of true allegiance to His Majesty King George VI, his heirs and successors and to the Constitution of India as by law established. The ministers swear of allegiance to the Constitution of India as by law established. Pandit Jawaharlal Nehru took the oath of the office of the Prime Minister. There were 13 Ministers and their names were as follows:

1. Sardar Vallabhbhai Patel
2. Maulana Abul Kalam Azad
3. Dr. Rajendra Prasad
4. Dr. John Mathai
5. Jagjivan Ram
6. Baldev Singh
7. C.H. Bhabha
8. Rajkumari Amrit Kaur
9. Rafi Ahmad Kidwai
10. Dr. B.R. Ambedkar
11. Dr. S.P. Mukherjee
12. Sir S. Chatty
13. N.V. Gadgil

The politicians who took over in 1947 were talented idealists who had provided their credentials in their struggle for independence. After the swearing in ceremony, Mountbatten delivered his address to the Indian Constituent Assembly. Heavy responsibilities lie ahead of you, but when I consider the statesmanship you have already shown in the great sacrifice you have made. I am confident that you will be worthy of your destiny. In your first Prime Minister, Pandit Jawaharlal Nehru you have a word renowned leader of courage and vision.[99]

His trust and friendship have helped me beyond measure in my task under his able guidance, assisted by the colleagues whom he has selected and with the loyal co-operation of the people. India will now attain a position of strength and influence and take his rightful place in the comity of nations. At this historic moment let us not forget all that India owes to Mahatma Gandhi—the architect of her freedom through non-violence. Nehru was in cotton Jodhpuri dress and a linen vest. Sardar Patel looked like a Roman emperor in his white dhoti and all the others in their white Congress caps. Mountbatten had become the humble and faithful first servant of an independent India.

Outside, the echoes of the 21 gun salute marched the events, waiting for Mountbatten at the foot of the red-carpet steps. Leading out of Durbar hall was the gold state carriage. The great procession jangled downed the drive of Viceroy's house. It was an India such as no English man had seen three centuries.[100]

According to Mountbatten, never have such crowds been seen within the memory, I have spoken to. Not only did they line every roof top and vantage point, but they pressed so much as to become finally quite unmanageable. At the council chamber, it had been arranged that there should be two guards of Honour of 100 men each. These 200 men joint with the police were just able to keep the crowd back sufficiently to let get out of the state coach without being physically lifted out, if it by the crowds.[101]

The ceremony in the council chamber was dignified and Mountbatten's speech was well received. Fortunately two more Guards of Honor of the Indian Army were due for the departure ceremony and Mountbatten gave orders that the four Guards of Honor were to pile arms inside the council chamber and then endeavour to keep the crowds back. As we were about to depart they saw that it was doubtful whether the 400 men of the Guards of Honour could keep the way clear to the coach. So Nehru went on to the roof and waved to the crowd to go back, the door was then opened and surrounded by the staff, Mountbatten made his way through to the coach.

It took them half an hour to go to the short distance back they had to go slowly through the crowds. Once, Mountbatten and his Party were held up for five minutes by the pressure of the crowd. Apart from the usual cries of 'Jai Hind' and 'Mahatma Gandhi ki Jai' and 'Pandit Nehru ki Jai' a surprising member shouted out

'Mountbatten ki Jai' and more than once 'Pandit Mountbatten ki Jai'.[102]

After lunch Mountbatten's Party decided to pay an impromptus visit to the great children's fete being held in the Roshnara Park. This was an unqualified success. Thousands of children gathering all round us cheering and yelling and trying to shake hands. I felt that it would be a good idea to get out of the function and informal surroundings for at least one of the Independence Day celebrations.

Durga Das wrote in the *Hindustan Times*; Pandit Nehru as the first Prime Minister and Lord Mountbatten as the first Governor General was the hero's of the drama. They got receptions which any monarch or President would ever have envied. The outburst of popular joy was like the burst of calm and the mighty torrent breaking through all banners.

India Gate

At 6 p.m. the great event of the day was to take place—the salutation of the new Dominion Flag. It was the official raising of the Indian flag. This function was to be held in open space near the India Gate. It was estimated that 30,000 people would attend. The figure was wrong, not by thousands but by well over about a million. Never before had anyone ever seen anything remotely like it in India's capital city. The function was to be held near the flag pole.

All arrangements had been made—the visitors gallery and guide ropes. But all arrangements were swept away by the surging crowds. Helpless, the police looked on as banners were trampled, chairs smiffed, like tags under a man's foot. The flag hoisting[103] took place at 5 p.m. and function[104] took place at 6 p.m.

Pamela Mountbatten, the 17 years old daughter of the Governor General arrived with two of her father's staff. With enormous difficulty, they worked their way towards a wooden tramline. Hundred yards away they came on an impossible barrier of people, all seated, and squeezed so tightly that there was barely a breath of all between them.

Spotting her from his place on the tramline, Nehru shouted at her to cross over the people to the platform. How can I? She shouted back, I have got high heels on! "Take them off" replied Nehru. Pamela could not dream of doing something as undignified on such an historic occasion. 'Oh!, she gasped', 'I could not do that?' 'Then leave them on', said Nehru, 'just walk over the people'. They won't hind. 'Oh!'

replied Pamela, 'the heels well hurt them'. 'Don't be silly girl', snapped Nehru, 'take them off and across!'

With a sigh, she kicked off her shoes, picked them up and set off across the carpet of human beings separating from the platform. The Indians over whom she was treading help her along, steadying her shaking legs, guiding her elbow pointing with delight to her shiny high heels.[105]

In the meantime Mountbatten's state carriage appeared on the horizon. There was connotation from the women's side. Women's were afraid lest their babies would be crushed by the mob's surge. From the state carriage, Mountbatten realized that it was not possible to hold all planned rituals. He himself could not even get out of the carriage. "Let us just hoist the flag", he shouted to Nehru, the bands swamped. They cannot play. The guard cannot move.

The man on the platform heard his call. The saffron white and green banner of free India climbed up the flag pole. Mountbatten marked its progress with a formal salute. Half a million people were watching the flag hoisting ceremony with happiness. Even the heavens seemed ready to brighten its historic impact. As India's new flag neared the peak of its flag staff, a rainbow suddenly flashed across the sky. The appearance was interpreted as a manifestation of Divine. One man murmured, when God himself gives us a sign such as this. Who can stand against us? It was the proud day for Louis and Edwina Mountbatten. Mountbatten's achievement was wonderful and simply unparallel. No Englishman had received this honour. He received something neither Queen Victoria nor George VI had received the homage, the real homage to the people of India; 'Mountbatten ki Jai'—'long live Mountbatten'.[106]

Now Louis and Edwina Mountbatten were returning to Lutiyan's Palace. The golden carriage was ready. Nehru himself was pushed up into the carriage to ride with them. Nehru fought his way to the coach and climbed in to tell Louis and Edwina that Pamela was safe. George Abele described how Nehru came to their rescue, when they were overwhelmed by the crowd, fighting like a maniac, striking people right and left and eventually taking the tepee of a man who had annoyed him particularly and smashing it over his head.[107]

Prime Minister Clement Attlee had every reason to feel satisfied. India's Independence had been accompanied by an outpouring of goodwill and friendship towards Britain, such as no one had thought possible six months before.

There are two other significant facts which have to be recorded. The first is that the President of the Constituent Assembly, Dr. Rajendra Prasad invited Lord Mountbatten on behalf of the assembly to send back a 'loyal message' of thanks to His Majesty saying that India and Britain would always be the greatest of friends. The other was that at a state banquette consisting of 100 persons, Nehru made a speech in the most friendly terms possible prior to proposing the toast of the King. At this Mountbatten proposed the toast of the dominion of India.

An evening Party had been arranged at Government House attended by 3,000 dignitaries and stayed till after 2 O'clock in the morning. At 9.15 p.m. 3,000 guests were individually presented with Mountbatten.

This is one statement of a person who had participated in the Delhi celebrations on August 14/15, 1947. H.P. Nanda, who carried on business in Lahore and who had to come to India after the division of the country had expressed his feelings in this way; we flew to Delhi from Lahore, where he had 600 buses, to share in the celebration of independent India. We saw the Union Jack go down and the Indian flag go up at the Viceroy's palace, now known as Rashtrapati Bhawan. The Viceroy and the Viceraine, Lord and Lady Mountbatten with Pandit Jawaharlal Nehru arrived in the 16-Horse buggy at Parliament House followed by riders on horses, all the colourful gold and red uniforms. There was a sea of people at India Gate and the air resounded with the chorus of the national anthem of India. There was much jubilation and for a while, people forget the national grief at the bloody carnage happening in all corners of the subcontinent.[108]

Banaras — August 15

Large numbers of persons assembled at the ghats. In the city, as it did every morning, the honour of being the first person to step across the threshold of the temple of God, Benaras, foremost shrine, belonged this morning to Pandit Bhawani Shanker. Few men in Benaras felt more intensely the joy of this dawn than this Pandit. Pandit Shanker had offered Indian nationalists fleeing away from the British CID, the sanctuary of his shrine.

A flask of Ganges water and a vial of sandal wood paste in his hands, Pandit Shanker marched through his temple's gloom towards a stumpy gamete outcropping. That heavy thumb rising in the darkness was the most precious Hindu relic in Benaras. Shanker's forefather had earned for their descendants the right to be its perpetual custodian by hiding it from the Mughal Hordes of the Emperor Aurangzeb. That he bowed before it this August morning humbly thanking the gods for the birth of Modern India, the cult that piece of stone represented is the oldest form of worship. It was the '*Lingam*' where Pandit Bhawani Shanker was bowing his head. At the sun's first rays, thousands of Hindus joined Pandit Shanker, expressing their gratitude at the reincarnation of their ancient nation by lovingly caressing the *Lingam* with sandalwood pastes, Ganges water and cow dung, garlanding the *Lingam* with marigolds, offering them rose petals and the betel leaves of Shiva's favourite tree, the '*bilva*'.[109]

Just after Indian Independence celebrations, Mountbatten was raised in rank from Viscount to Earl, taking the title 'Earl Mountbatten' of Burma. Lord Kalleam, who had been nominated Governor of Assam, wrote to Ismay to say how well deserved he felt the honour was. 'He and Edwina are simply terrific', he wrote and no other living man could have got the things through.[110]

Mountbatten became a legend in his life-time. The transfer of power to the subcontinent was the toughest assignment Mountbatten ever handled. The country was on the brink of a virtual civil war, so he decided to advance the date fixed by the British Government for the transfer of power. Delay in the transfer of power would have only heightened the communal tension already beyond control. India's march towards and as it happened towards partition was a complicated affair. It involved an interaction between British policy, the Indian National Congress and powerful personalities such as Gandhi, Nehru and Jinnah.

London—post-August 15, 1947

15 August was the day scared into the memory of many a British citizens, it was a day for some touched with imperial nostalgia, a mixture of pride and uncertainty and even, for few, by frustration. Several of those who saw themselves and leaders in their generation had cited the Viceroyalty of India as the pinnacle of their public careers. This was a prospect now denied to them. They bewailed the passing of the Raj even more than the fact of the partitions of Punjab and Bengal, which accompanied the lowering of the Union Jack.

There was a curious assortment of frusteted would be British Viceroys of India, whose ambitions were thwarted by Britain's demission of power in 1947. Enoch Powell, classical scholar, Prof. of Greek in Austria, learnt Urdu while serving as a soldier in India during World War Two. Afterwards, he confessed that he walked around St. James's Perkins London and wept on that fateful 15th August, not only because of the passing of the British Raj but because he could never be Viceroy. The post of Viceroy was regarded as a very prestigious post and the Viceroy drew a salary which not a single man more fortunate enough to draw. The Viceroy's residence was a Palace. Sir John Deeth, the Scottish giant and the first director of the BBC was another British citizen. Who mourned the passing of the Raj? It was not only as a theatre in which many a Scotsman had made their fortunes, and reputation, but its passing meant he could never become Viceroy himself. Rab Butler, a left-wing of the conservative Party, was born in India. As a relatively young junior Minister, he had piloted the parts of the Government of India Act, 1935 through the House of Commons and which later on became the Constitution of India in 1950. He was also an aspirant for the post of Viceroy. Butler was nursing in his old age about his faded ambitions which certainly included the wish that he had been Viceroy, though no doubt he regretted twice Prime Ministerial office in Britain even more.[111]

Only the British Government could have aborted the casual chain that led to partition and the massacre. Perhaps they should have defied world opinion and their own principles. Yeasty reinforced their presence in India, resolved to set it out until a truly united and independent India became a possibility. If they had done so, they would have had to have friend another Viceroy, Mountbatten did not go to India to maintain the power of the Raj, and would never have taken on the task. The job he was given to do instead he did supremely well.

Partition it the deepest of national traumas, was brought about by foreign powers, the British and the Pakistanis. Though Pakistan was created but the Congress leaders did not accept the 'two-nation theory', that is, Hindus and Muslims are separate nations. The Indian leaders categorically rejected the argument that religion was the decisive factor in determining the issue. The birth of Pakistan represented the triumph and the culmination of Muslim communal politics in the Indian subcontinent. Undeterred by the division of the nation on the basis of the two nation theory which proceeded on the basis that the Muslims in India and particularly those in Muslim majority provinces were entitled two separate homeland, Indian National Congress under the leadership of Jawaharlal Nehru and Sardar Vallabhbhai Patel and with the inspiration of Mahatma Gandhi struck to its philosophy of secularism and the composite nationhood of India.[112]

Nehru was the better opponent of very conception of Pakistan. He used to say that the two-nation theory was fantastic nonsense. What of one Jinnah, he said, when a thousand Jinnah would not be able to take it from him! But, ultimately, one Jinnah received Pakistan on a plate from Nehru, having tactically forced the Congress into accepting the scheme.[113]

Peaceful Transfer

Let us be thankful for one great blessing. It is one of the biggest triumphs of democracy that freedom has come to the people of this country without a violent and bloody upheaval. We do not forget the struggles of the past, nor the fact that they occasionally led to bloodshed; to Mr. Gandhi again must go the credit for the non-violent from which mass agitations generally took. Yet never before in history has so vast transfer of power been accomplished with so much speed and with so much goodwill on both sides. Mr. Attlee, the British Prime Minister, described his Government's action as the fulfilment of a mission. For many years past, successively British-government has proclaimed their intention of leading India to self Government. The dispute was not so much over the goal as over the speed and method by which that goal would be achieved.

It is doubtful, if without Gandhi's gimmicks—to borrow Humboldt's phrase—the British would have wound up the Indian Empire in 1947. The British historian Arnold Toynbee has, therefore, a point, when he says that Gandhi was as much a benefactor of Britain as of his own country. He made it impossible for the British to go on ruling India, but at the same time he made it possible for us to abdicate without rancour and without dishonor . . . . . . in helping British to extricate themselves from the imperial entanglements. Gandhi did them a signal service for it is to acquire an empire than to disengage from one.

As Gandhi has hoped and predicted, the liberation of India in 1947 turned out to be a prelude to the liquidation of imperialism in Asia and Africa. In the process of, voluntary decolonization and transmutation of, their all white empire into a multiracial Commonwealth. The British were guided by a sound political instinct. As Queen Elizabeth in her speech at Philadelphia on July 6, 1976 on the occasion of the United States bicentennial said, the British lost the American colonies in the eighteenth century because we lacked that statesmanship to know the right time, and manner of yielding what is impossible to keep.[114]

NOTES

1. *Transfer of Power*, Vol. II, pp. 347 and 481.
2. French, Patrick, *Liberty or Death*, p. 314.
3. *Transfer of Power*, Vol. II, pp. 347 and 481.
4. Azad M.A.K., *India wins Freedom*, p. 211.
5. *Ibid.*
6. *Ibid.*
7. *Ibid.*
8. Mosley, Leonard, *British Raj*, p. 195.
9. *Transfer of Power*, Vol. II, p. 292.
10. French, Patrick, *Liberty or Death*, p. 323.
11. *Transfer of Power*, Vol. II, p. 342.
12. *Ibid.*
13. French, Patrick, *Liberty or Death*, p. 325.
14. *Ibid.*
15. The *Asian Age*, August 14, 1947.
16. The *Times of India*, New Delhi, March 10, 1985.
17. Menon, V.P., *Transfer of Power in India*, p. 403.
18. Rai, Satya M., *Partition of Punjab*, pp. 57-58.
19. Quoted by Peter Lyons in his article "*Partitions Reconsidered*" a British Prospective, published in India, the First Fifty Years, 1997, London, pp. 17 and 894.
20. The *Times of India*, New Delhi, May 8, 1998.
21. Quoted, Singh, Khuswant, *A History of Sikhs*, Vol. II, p. 252.
22. French Patrick, *Liberty or Death*, p. 333.
23. *Ibid.*
24. Mehta, Ved., the Ledge Between the streams, London 1984, p 313.
25. *Transfer of Power*, Vol. II, p. 657.
26. Patrick French, *Liberty or Death*, p. 338.
27. Quoted Hudson, Appendix II, p. 350.
28. Campbell Johnson, p. 150.
29. *Mountbatten and the Partition of India*, pp. 197 to 211.
30. Bhalla, Alok, *Partition of India*, Vol. II, p. 137.
31. Director of Intelligence Bureau.

32. Durga Das, (ed.), *Sardar Patel's correspondence*, 1945-50 (ten volumes), vol. IV, p. 141.
33. *Transfer of Power*, Vol. XII, p. 559.
34. Campbell, Johnson, pp. 28-29.
35. *Transfer of Power*, Vol. XII, p. 215.
36. The *Times of India*, New Delhi, June 2, 1985.
37. Mishra, S.G., *Constitutional Development and National Movement*, p. 317.
38. *Ibid.*
39. *Ibid.*
40. The *Asian Age*, August 7, 1947.
41. Patrick French, *Liberty or Death*, p. 337.
42. The speech appeared in the Indian Press 50 years ago on August 15, 1947. These views are today not publicly acknowledged by the Pakistani establishment.
43. Jinnah, M.A., "Quaid-i-Azam's Pakistan", *Times of India*, New Delhi, August 15, 1947.
44. Gopal Madan, "Jinnah's Secularism II", *Times of India*, New Delhi, July 29, 1994.
45. *Ibid.*
46. The *Asian Age*, August 12, 1947.
47. *Ibid.*
48. Jaffrey, Robin, *Modern Asian Studies*, Vol. V, 1974, p. 499.
49. The *Asian Age*, August 12, 1947.
50. *Ibid.*
51. Reuters correspondent, "Doon Campbell's Sixth Article", published in the *Asian Age*, August 10, 1947.
52. Mansingh and Moon, *Transfer of Power*, Vol. XII, London, 1988, p. 770.
53. The *Asian Age*, August 14, 1947.
54. *Ibid.*
55. *Ibid.*
56. *Ibid.*
57. Exhibited documents, *National Archives of India*, New Delhi, 1985.
58. *Ibid.*
59. "Pakistan Paper" by Mani Shanker Aiyer, *Times of India*, New Delhi, June 26, 1994.
60. Rafiq Zakaria, *A Study of Nehru*, pp. 67-68.
61. *Partition of India*, Vol. I, p. 115.
62. Rafiq Zakaria, *A Study of Nehru*, p. 68.
63. *India, the First 50 Years*, p. 66.
64. The *Asian Age*, August 7, 1997.
65. The *Times of India*, New Delhi, March 10, 1985.
66. Philip Ziegler, *Mountbatten*, the *Times of India*, March 10, 1985.

67. The *Times of India*, New Delhi, March 10, 1985.
68. *Transfer of Power,* Vol. XII, p. 770.
69. *Mountbatten and the Partition of India,* p. 108.
70. *Freedom at Midnight*, pp. 209 to 211.
71. French, Patrick, *Liberty or Death*, p. 337.
72. *Freedom at Midnight*, p. 236.
73. The *Asian Age*, August 14, 1997.
74. *Freedom at Midnight*, p. 236.
75. Extract from '*Mountbatten's,* by Philip Ziegler, *Times of India*, New Delhi, March 10, 1985.
76. *Freedom at Midnight*, p. 239.
77. Philip, Ziegler, *Times of India*, New Delhi, March 10, 1985.
78. *Freedom at Midnight*, p. 239.
79. *Transfer of Power*, Vol. XII, p. 771 and the *Times of India*, March 10, 1985.
80. *Freedom at Midnight*, p. 195.
81. Deen, Campbell (3), Diary, the *Asian Age*, August 8, 1947.
82. *Freedom at midnight*, pp. 166 to 169.
83. *Ibid.*, pp. 242-243.
84. *Ibid.*, p. 245.
85. *Ibid.*, pp. 246-247.
86. Exhibited documents, *National Archives of India*, December 1985.
87. The *Times of India*, New Delhi, May 12, 1993.
88. Mathai, M.O., *Reminiscences of the Nehru Age*, New Delhi, 1978.
89. The *Times of India*, New Delhi, August 16, 1949.
90. The *Times of India*, New Delhi, August 11, 1947.
91. *Freedom at Midnight*, pp. 251-253.
92. The *Times of India*, New Delhi, August 15, 1947.
93. Exhibited documents, *National Archives of India*, December 1985.
94. *Ibid.*
95. *Freedom at Midnight*, p. 258.
96. *Ibid.*
97. *Transfer of Power*, p. 771.
98. *Ibid.*
99. *Ibid.*, p. 776.
100. *Freedom at Midnight*, pp. 266-267.
101. *Transfer of Power*, p. 772.
102. *Ibid.*
103. Collin and Lapierre, *Freedom at Midnight*, p. 275.
104. Prof. Manseargh and Moon in, *Transfer of Power*, p. 772.
105. *Freedom at Midnight*, p. 276.
106. *Ibid.*, pp. 277-278.
107. *Transfer of Power*, vol. XII, p.772.
108. The *Times of India*, August 15, 1947, India, first 50, p. 27.

109. *Freedom at Midnight*, p. 261.
110. The *Times of India*, New Delhi, March 10, 1985.
111. *India—The First 50 years*, pp. 19-20.
112. *Ibid.*, p. 66.
113. Rafiq Zakaria, *A Study of Nehru*, p. 233.
114. The *Times of India*, June 9, 1985.

13

Partition through the Pages of History

Peter Lyon an academic secretary of the Institute of Commonwealth Studies and Reader in International Relations, University of London, 1997, have defined partition as a principle of fission not fusion. To take on a valued general significance a definition of partition needs to be comparative and relational and swell as contextual. Partition certainly needs to be seen as but an aspect of the much wider and ever ramifying tussle between centripetal and centrifugal forces and thus of the endless tension between elements of political fission and fusion.[1]

Peter goes on to say: partition involves the tearing of a previously united politic co-territorial unit apart, ostensibly for dynastic, imperial nationalist or religious or ethnic reasons. In one way or another partitioning was a device familiar in the history of European statecraft over many centuries.

Charlemagne (C.742-814) was Emperor of the West (800-14) and King of the France (768-814). After the coronation he was known as Charles I after defeating the Lombard (774), he conquered Saxony (772-804). He ruled a vast empire bounded by the North Sea, the Elle, Bavaria, Caranthia, Lombardy, the Mediterranean, the Pyrenees and the Atlantic. He intervened (789) to save Pope Leo III from deposition and was rewarded with the title Holy Roman Emperor (800). At the end of his reign he had to defend his frontier from attacks by Vikings and Saracens. His reign was notable for administrative, judicial and ecclesiastical reforms.

According to the treaty of Verdun (1843), three sons of Emperor Louis I divided up, Charlemagne's empire among them. According to this partition, Louis II 'the German' received the eastern port. Charles II 'the Bald', the Western part and Lothario II, the centre and the imperial crown. This division prefigured much of the political history and subsequent boundary making of Western Europe. It prefigured much in the political history and subsequent boundary making of Western Europe. And it has often been remarked that many of the present day boundaries of Europe can trace a lineage back not to Charlemagne, but even earlier to Roman Public Administration.[2]

Peter examines partition in the historical perspective. According to him partition treaties were part and parcel of the dynastic politics of Europe, especially between the fifteenth and eighteenth centuries, when territory was frequently transferred because of deaths or marriages affecting particulars dynasties. The partitions practiced by dynasties in seventeenth and eighteenth century Europe (and especially the swallowing in three units of Poland in the late eighteenth century) produced extensive justificatory excuses and exculpations.

The study of Poland is very interesting. In 1138, the first partition of Poland took place. It was split up into a number of Dutch's. The Teutonic knights conquered East Prussia (thirteenth century) cutting off Poland's access to the Baltic. Poland was reunited (fourteenth century), under Calmer III. Lithuania was united to Poland (1386). The kingdom was enlarged to include parts of White Russia and the Ukraine. A constitutional monarchy was established. An elective monarchy was instituted in 1572. Gradually it was weakened and was finally annihilated when Austria, Prussia and Russia agreed to partition Poland. In the first partition (1772) Prussia took north western Poland except Gdansk. Austria took Galicia and Russia took land east of the Dvina. In the second partition (1993) Prussia and Russia took more than half of what remained. A revolt (1794) led by Kosciusko prompted the third partition (1795) in which Austria, Russia and Prussia annexed all the remainder and Poland completely disappeared.

Albert Sorrel, inclusive incisive analytical historian of the French revolution (1789) commented sardonically but appropriately that the practitioners disregarded the difference usually considered to exist between judges and thieves.[3]

Generally partition merely connotes territorial redivision and re-apportionments as with the scramble for Africa by the European imperial powers of the mid-1880. Undoubtedly, however, for many it carries more emotionally laden politically surgery. Here the classic paradigms a Poland in the late eighteenth century, Ireland in the early twentieth century, Punjab and Bengal in 1947. In Punjab and

Bengal it is the fusion of religion and nationalism. Indeed, the prime justification for such partition is that there is no longer mutually acceptable, viable, lasting alternative partition may take many forms but partitioners tend to talk as if a particular partition is the only viable option, necessity mother its expression.[4]

A recently published historical dictionary of the British Empire and Commonwealth asserts that partition was a principle "tacitly accepted in the nineteenth century. India under the system of paramount" which involved the division of the subcontinent into directly ruled provincial and princely states, with the later was retaining some autonomy. While discussing partition, the dictionary has discussed Ireland, Cyprus, and Punjab in 1947 but the partition of Bengal in 1905 which was the product of Curzon's rule has not found a place in this dictionary.[5] Perhaps it was not discussed because it was a short lived partition.

According to the Oxford Roman's lecture of 1907 it was Curzon who was an autocrat left his mark on the map and memoirs of the subcontinent, not least regarding both Punjab and Bengal.

The Punjab was the last of the Governor's provinces of India proper to come under British control together with the North West Frontier Province, which was not separated from it until Curzon's decision of 1901. This was historically the area which had borne the brunt of landward attack upon India.

At the very beginning, the boundaries of the British defined province of the Punjab stretched from the Afghan frontier to Delhi.[6] Five frontier districts were separated in 1901 to form the North West Frontier Province. Delhi district was cut out a decade later in 1911, when the Government of India transferred its administrative capital from Calcutta to New Delhi. Even after these severances the province of the Punjab remained territorially larger than Great Britain and compared slightly less than 10 per cent of British India's total area and population which providing as was well known, the bulk of recruits into the British army in India. Bengal was the political unit of British India which experienced more changes of boundary than any other. At different times the Bengal Presidency included Bihar, Orissa, and Assam.

Curzon (1899-1905) remains one of the most controversial of the British Viceroys. Most Indians regard him as the archetype of western imperialism—self-assured, totally committed to the theory that it was the white man's vision to civilize the Asian. Even today he is remembered, above all for the partition of Bengal (1905) which had subsequently to be annulled in the Delhi Durbar of 1911. But India has much to be grateful to him for our frontiers along Tibet which may have remained undefined. For Curzon partition was an administrative imperative. For Curzon, dividing Bengal was his desire to readjust several provincial boundaries. It was his view that the existing boundaries of Bengal, Assam, the Central Provinces and Madras were antiquated, illogically and productive of inefficiency. He told one of his senior officers, "I should like to fix the provincial boundaries for the next generation", an ironically ambition in respect of Bengal as partition based only seven years. It was defeated by an upsurge both of local nationalism and British criticism.[7]

The partition of India was in a different setting. The Indian Independence Act, 1947 brought to India on August 14/15, 1947 and Pakistan was born on August 14, 1947. Several books and articles are available on the partition of India. Still controversies persist regarding interpretation of work on the Punjab and Bengal Boundary Commission presided over by Sir Cyril Radcliff; though there are several books on partition available, but serious readers are few who have aptitude to read those books written by specialist historians. In Britain also standard books are not read to a great extent. People read Paul Scott's novels on partition but they don't read authentic books. In India the scene is more pathetic. Research books are not utilized and cheap books are read. The time has come to read well documented books; otherwise it will be difficult to understand why partition took place. Prof. Manseargh's edited *Transfer of Power* in 12 volumes is indispensable and these books are monumental works.

How partition takes place? Partition is conceived and implemented not in a vacuum. It is a product of "weary men"—a tired and desperate generation—and they want to find out a solution of the complicated problem. This view is of T.G. Fraser, a British historian. Fraser says that partition provided one drastic way out of contemporary dilemmas in 1947. But the underlying problems—whether in Kashmir, Ireland, Cyprus or elsewhere—remain to reappear in different forms, thus confirming the view that there is no ultimate and permanent solution in human affairs, merely a series of imperfect expedients.

In 1947, there was the tussle between centripetal and centrifugal forces, and there was tension about political fission and fusion. These two features are still prominently in the international politics of the countries of South Asia. Partition involves division of a political territorial unit, and there have been several partitions in South Asia since 1947—involving parts of Kashmir, and massive states reorganization in India in 1956 to mention but two examples.[8]

In the Paris conference of 1919, many new nations were created. Partition further came, Poland which had disappeared from the map of Europe as a result of the three partitions, which I have discussed earlier was created again in 1919. Yugoslavia and Czechoslovakia were also created as separate nations. Australia added to Yugoslavia, Bosnia, Herzegovina and the Dalmatian and to Czechoslovakia, Bohemia, Moravia, and Austrian Silesia and parts of Lower Austria and last to Rumania, Bukovina. So Austria lost several areas as the result of drastic partition of 1919.

After the end of Second World War in 1945, process of partition further appeared in Indo-China. Indo-China was a French colony, in 1939 a small nationalist organization, Viet Minas or the League for the Independence of Vietnam had appeared under the leadership of Chin Minh. In 1945, Ho Chi Minh declared himself as the President of the Republic of Vietnam. In July 1954, a cease-fire agreement was signed with France. As a result of this agreement, the French withdrew from Vietnam north of the 17th parallel of latitude, leaving to the Viet Minh the area of Tonkin and Annam. In the southern areas the non-communist regime of Bao Dai, ex-emperor of Annam, was preserved by French power till October 1955. No truce could be reached between North and South and legally partition was mentioned.

As a result of the Second World War, Germany finally surrendered to the Allies (May 8, 1945). The Allies divided Germany into four occupation zone (America, British, French and Russia). The Soviet blockade of Berlin (April 1948 to May 1949) led to the division of Germany (1949) into East and West Germany. This partition contained for a long period—Germany was unified.

By the Independence Act of 1947, the partition of India took place. Pakistan was created on August 14, and India was declared a free country on August 14/15, 1947. This partition is still continuing.

This partition is in detail a unique event, but each partition also tends to conjure up a spiralling methodology, a meta-history, which may become more complex and fanciful and not entirely impotent with the passing of the year even 50 years or more. The recent reunification of Germany and of Vietnam indicates that partitions never last for ever. Partitions are not a permanent thing. Peter Lyon comments at these reunification in these words: "do either of these examples after instructive analogies for Ulster or Cyprus or Kashmir or Bengal? I suspect not. We can at least say that it is of great importance that the suppression of partition lines should be proved by conciliation and agreement, not by war and bloodshed and the cutting of golden knots."

As a student of History, I feel that the partition of India is a temporary phase and at some distance of time as the result of the people's movement there will be reunification of India and Pakistan. If Poland could emerge a separate nation after three partitions and if Germany and Vietnam could be reunited, then there is a strong possibility that India and Pakistan will establish one Government. It may adopt administrative Machinery known as federation or confederation.

Let the last words be those of the English poet, now dead, Wystan Auden:

> "Unique events that once took place
> Within a unique time and space
> In the new field they occupy
> The unique serves to typify
> Becomes, though still particular
> An algebraic formula
> An abstract module of events
> Derived from dead experiments
> After life must itself decide
> To what and how it is applied."

Explaining the Responsibilities for the Partition of India

August 14/15, 1947 is indeed a memorable day in the history of India as it marked her deliverance from alien domination by the mutual consent of the British nation and the Indian statesman. The devastation of partition and the words it left below on the sub-continental psyche created like a democracy for the Indian unit.

The last British Governor of the North West Frontier Province. Sir Olaf Caroe, still lament over the partition of India. He says; I still sorrow, for each side had much to give to the other. Sir Olaf's remark was occasioned by an article that the birth of Pakistan was inevitable. The Ex-British Governor did not agree with this.

Lord Listowel, Secretary of State for India at the time of Indian Independence described the partition of India as a 'tragedy' and blamed the lack of political vision on the part of a succession of conservative governments for throwing the opportunity they had of completing the transfer of power to a united India.

In the contemporary period the partition of India is such a controversial subject that British Historians and the Historians of the subcontinent find themselves in difficulties in taking a detached view of the problem. The question that comes to the uppermost mind of a researcher is that, was the partition just a product of British imperialism or was it a natural culmination of historical process? It also needs to be studied whether the partition was a product of policy or of accident or both? Again, was the partition a solution or in other words, was it inevitable?

The British historians have often emphasized the incompatibility of Hindus and Muslims and thus presenting an apologetic view of events, which led to the partition. Indian historians blame British imperialism as its connivance with the Muslim League. In India a view that the creation of Pakistan was a defeat, may be a dismemberment of mother India. An analysis of Hindu-Muslim relations can form crux of study of the partition of India. The writers in Pakistan seem to agree that the creation of Pakistan was the logical conclusion of the Hindu-Muslim relations through the centuries. Some of them in this category are M. Hasan, Choudhary Mohammad Ali and K.K. Aziz, a respected historian of Pakistan writing in 1968 begins his version of the events leading up to the partition by reasserting that the 'Indian nationalism' espoused by the Congress was, from its very inception, a "Hindu nationalism in essence" which the Muslims could not possibly have supported. He quoted with approval a statement by Amir Ali, published in 1906 when the Congress was not yet incomplete control of the national movement urging not to rein from its very inception, a Hindu nationalism in essence which the Congress for otherwise tied to the Juggernaut of majority they would in the end be crushed out of the semblance of nationality.

Since this declaration has little historical substance and can only be proved by repetition. Aziz goes on to do so by evoking the authentic of an article by Maulana Shaukat Ali published in the *Empire Review* in 1931. In this article Maulana Shaukat Ali calls upon the Muslims to place their faith in the British because the Hindus were trying to coerce them into accepting a subordinate position in the nation. After this conventional call to the faithful to be vigilant against Hindu subversion, Maulana Shaukat Ali's arguments, which Aziz accepts without a murmur of dissent, becomes a little baroque unlike the Hindus who are used to be subjects, Maulana Shaukat Ali says, the Muslims are remarkably free from servility and know how to maintain their poise and dignity in adversity. The Muslims, being a constitutionally minded people should trust the British because they have made fair laws and treated them justly. Moreover, Hindu agitation politics, as advocated by the votaries of *satyagraha*, is not only unconstitutional, it is also against the Islamic injunction about obeying the rulers. Indeed, it is reasonable for the Muslims to try to establish closer ties with the British, with whom they have greater social, intellectual and spiritual affinity than with the "idol worshipping Hindus". The most bizarre part of this argument is that stance the British had established the 'greatest Muslim empire in the world' and 'intimate relations with all the independent Muslim States'. It was to be expected that the Indian Muslims would wish to remain within the security of the empire for their own well being. Given this kind of thinking, it is not surprising to find that people like Aziz regard the partition as '*azadi*' from the '*fasadat*' (riot) caused by the Hindus for them the creation of Pakistan becomes a vindication of their presuppositions, history becomes a tautology instead of an explanations.[9]

If the historians of Pakistan movement and a historian like the stature of Prof. Aziz manipulate facts to justify the existence of a separate Muslim consciousness which 'naturally' constitute a nation, the historians of the Hindu Rashtra mentally conjure up a past in order to accuse the Muslims of desecrations and betrayal, as well as to assert the presence of Hindu brotherhood which has a primal right to inheritance of India. Recently Prof. Rajendra Singh, chief of the RSS gave a statement on September 15, 1999 that the Muslim invaders has destroyed 3,000 temples and we want only three to be returned from the Muslim—Ayodhya, Mathura and Varanasi. This kind of propaganda is against the Indian democracy. This kind of 'Hindutwa' is as dangerous as the approach of Prof. Aziz and other historians. This kind of thinking is as confusing and mythical as that of Islamic nationhood.

Thus Bharatendu Harish Chandra who was not perhaps a communal thinker but was passionately concerned with the shape of the Hindu civilization, in a lecture in 1884, defines the "Hindus as people who lived in Hindustan and included the Janis, Buddhist, Sikhs and Muslims in his sweep. In order to give substance to such a mete-religious category, Bharatendu translated parts of the Koran into Hindi (1884), wrote brief biography of the Prophet, Hasan and Hussain (1875), and a lag poem praising Kabir, Tansen and Pirzadi Bibi. It is worth noting here that Sir Syed Ahmad Khan also described the "Hindus" in a lecture in 1884 in precisely the same terms as Bharatendu and included the Muslims in his definition. By 1924, Lala Lajpat Rai and Swami Shradhanand began to speak forcefully about the old antagonism between the Hindus and the Muslims and even urged the formation of two distinct religious nations for the sake of peace. As the years went by, the terms "Hindu" became sharper and Mahatma Gandhi, the architect of the Indian freedom and who was one of the finest witnesses to the possibility of a Hindu spiritual and democratic life in modern times, was ruthlessly eliminated for having tarnished the glory of Hinduism on January 30, 1948 just after 5.50 p.m. Mahatma Gandhi was shot by a Hindu at Birla Bhawan, New Delhi. The 'Hindu' came to be defined by the more communally committed historians, as one who was first an unrelenting enemy of Islam and only after that as someone who had a particular set of ideals and practical. Thus partition was offered as yet another example in a long sequence of Muslim faithlessness, instead of being an exceptional moment of disorders in a continuing history of a life lived together in all the complex variety.

Contrary to the communal histories, the stories about the partition have more to do with the actualities of human experience in barbaric terms than with ideologies, and seem to be bound together by one common thread they find the nation that there was always hatred between the Hindus, Sikhs and Muslims in ordinary life completely incomprehensible.

The partition of India subcontinent was the single most traumatic experience in our recent history. The violence it unleashed was unreasoned, unexpected and barbaric provoked by the hooligan action of a few, the vengeance that ordinary Hindus, Muslims and Sikhs wracked on each other coarsened our social sense, distorted our political judgments and deranged our understanding of moral rightness.

The writings of Prof. Aziz and other leaders will not help us to discover the causes that led to the formation of Pakistan. There are writers in India like G.W. Choudhary, Aziz Ahmad, I.I. Qurashi, and K.K. Siddiqui who denied any complicacy of the British Government in the creation of Pakistan. All these writings tend to be more political than historical and the historiography of Pakistan also lacks criticism.

In India on the other hand, one view is that while independence of India was inevitable, partition was not. Another view often expressed in this view of the subcontinent is that the unity of India was exaggerated as an appeal. So was the disunity as a tactic.

Finding scapegoat is an old practice quite known in the realm of historiography. Partition of India is attributed to the Roman Imperialism of the British. Ram Gopal in his book *How India Struggled for Freedom* emphasis the dividing role of the British. Pattabhi Sitaramayya lays emphasis on the character of British policy of supporting one element of society against another.[10] Dr. S.B. Chaudhary (Prof. of History, Burdwan University, Bengal) is of opinion that the British by counter poisoning the Hindu against Muslims, the Princes against the activities, wanted an early demise of the Congress.[11] Dr. Tara Chand finds the British primarily responsible for the communal rift which was accentuated by constitutional reforms from 1909 to 1935. By which time the communal consciousness developed into the consciousness of nationality and concept of political unity into that of federal unity. Muslim nationality blossomed under Britain's warm sympathy into the idea of the Muslim nations whose expression demanded full-fledged Independence and sovereignty.[12]

One may feel that singling out the British for dividing India does not speak high of the political acumen of Indian leadership. Dr. Majumdar is enclosed to say that British did not create the communal problem, they only exploited it.

However, to some, the birth of Pakistan came as a surprise because its demand was actually a bargaining counter. It is also true that the leaders of the Indian freedom movement did not try seriously to eliminate the prevalent contradictions of the Indian society. The national movement with democratic slogan never attempted consistently to take into account the different and often conflicting element of society.[13]

Thus what I have attempted is an explanation of responsibility of the partition of the country. There were three parties to this tangle and which parties or leaders were responsible? The British Government, the Indian National Congress and the Muslim League were the parties to this problem. I have already explained in a previous chapter that the policy of 'Divide and Rule' is to be traced from the Simla deputation of October 1, 1906, the granting of its request that the Muslim community be treated as a separate and historically important element in India's population and acceptance of the principle of separate representation mark the beginning of Muslim separatism in Indian politics. The introduction of the principle of separate electorate accented the difference between the two communities. The Hindus and Muslims stood in two different camps, hopes of unity between the two for political purposes receded in the background. Minto, thus succeeded in dividing and weakening the forces of nationalism and winning over a large majority of the Muslims to the side of the Government assuring them that their interests were safe with the British. In a letter to the King, Minto proudly wrote, "His Majesty's Mohammedan subjects have been the most loyal supporters of the Raj throughout the recent seditious agitation."

The British Government followed this policy till 1947. The conservative opposition and Muslim intransigence whipped up by the British prevented the Round Table Conference of 1931 from arriving at any compromise and the dominion status was doomed to failure. During the Second World War period when the Congress ministers resigned the office by November 1939 owing to Lord Linlithgow's war policy. After this the central government tried to woo Jinnah more and more. The Cripps proposals in 1942 indirectly accepted the Muslim demand for Pakistan. During this period the British nurtured the growth of the plant of Muslim separatism and finally brought it to fruition. The strength of the Muslim League had increased from August 11, 1942 because all the prominent Congress leaders have been interned. The British were happy at the growing strength of the Muslim League as a significant factor in the Indian political scene.

The failure of Gandhi-Jinnah talks in September 1944 seemed to rub out for the time being the possibility of an agreement between the Congress and the League on the main constitutional issue. The chief hurdle Lord Wavell realized was Mr. Jinnah's intransigence on the Pakistan issue. Lord Wavell found Jinnah intractable at the Simla Conference of 1945. At Simla, Jinnah seemed to be unusually tense and unsure.[14] In July 1946, Jinnah almost single handed blocked

Lord Wavell's plan for which the Viceroy had laboured for eight months. If the Viceroy had mastered the courage to override Jinnah's objection and gone ahead with the reconstitution of his Executive Council, it was not impossible that the League leader might have fallen in line. But Wavell did not like to go so far for fear of Churchill. He thought that Churchill would not support him in case he would displease Jinnah.

The policy of 'Divide and Rule' reached a climax in the period of Lord Louis Mountbatten. He was the last Viceroy and Governor General of independent India. He found that Jinnah was not amenable to compromise. The Mountbatten plan was accepted by the Indian leaders on June 3, 1947. The Indian Independence Bill, 1947 was passed by the British Parliament and signed by the King on July 18, 1947. On the basis of this Act, Pakistan was born as a separate nation with dominion status on August 14, 1947. India obtained freedom on August 14/15, 1947 at midnight. The independence was tagged with the partition of India. In the 24th Montagu-Burton lectures on international affairs, Prof. C.H. Philips, Director, London School of Oriental Studies, examined the circumstances which led to the partition of India. He was inclined to hold that the failure to implement the federal provisions of the Government of India Act, 1935 at the central level was the basic cause that led to the partition of India. He is perfectly right in his conclusion. The resignation of the Congress Ministries by November 1939 was an important for the division. The policy of 'Divide and Rule' was another reason for the vivisection. Jawaharlal Nehru also held the British policy responsible for the partition of the country. He told Prof. Michael Brecher in 1956; I think now looking back, that partition would have been avoided if the British Government's policy had been different about a year or eighteen months before Mahatma Gandhi looked upon partition as the result of Britain's long drawn out policy of 'Divide and Rule'.

Was the Partition of India Inevitable?[15]

The Indian Independence and unity were irreconcilable and neither the Indians nor the British could be blamed for the partition of India is the view taken several commentators in the soul searching that has gone during India's 50th anniversary celebrating in 1997. Since in democracies, various sections of the population have to settle their political differences among themselves, the hidden fissures in society—

as here between Hindus and Muslims—come to the surface, as the election processes advance.

Nevertheless one may wonder whether unity could not have been preserved if, only if, in 1934 the British had not decreed the communal Award giving extraordinary weightage to Muslim votes in elections and later Churchill's Government had not so doggedly supported Mr. Jinnah's separate demands (Hindustan, Muslimstan and Princesstan as Churchill used to say). The Communal Awards had been announced in 1932 and not in 1934.

In 1939 the Congress Party Government, held power from 1937, in eight of the eleven British Indian provinces had resigned, thereby reducing the British need to depend on the Congress Party's help to mobilize Indian resources for the war and in return pay heed to its demands.

In 1942, Mahatma Gandhi had not launched the Quit India Movement as yet, which was taken in Britain as a stab in the back at the moment of their direct peril and turned them decisively against Mr. Gandhi and towards Mr. Jinnah, who was quick to promise that he would try to ensure the loyalty of Muslim troop—nearly 40 per cent of the British Indian Army—in the war.

In the post-war, after 1945, negotiations for independence, the Congress Party had on the one hand given a clear indication to a weakened and insecure Britain that their government of a free India would cooperate on issues of Britain's vital interest in the world, i.e. in the Middle East and remain in the Commonwealth provided they abandoned ideas of partition; and to threaten them with a general revolt which Britain had neither the resources nor the will to suppress, if they did not and refused to enter the Viceroy's Executive Council till the matter was clarified.

By 1946, the Congress Party abandoned the creed of passive resistance and prepared the masses to resist partition. Subhas Chandra Bose had shown that on a different platform Hindus and Muslims would work together for Indian freedom and unity.

The problem of Muslim separatism was not the result of economic factors or capable of being solved by socialism or secularism. It had to be tackled politically in the run-up to independence, not least with the help of the third Party Britain. After all, this was the track finally adopted in 1847 with Mountbatten and it was through British cooperation that four-fifths of India was saved as one unit and the Indian princely states brought in.

It is a mistaken view expressed by some commentators that any policy of 'give and take' with Britain during the period 1939 to 1946 would have aborted the people from the Congress Party because the masses trusted Mahatma Gandhi and have followed him. After all the Congress did not fracture when in finally in 1947 a policy of compromise with Britain and even partition and membership of the commonwealth were agreed to.

It is also not correct that the acceptance of the Cabinet Mission Plan because it denied Pakistan would have ensured Indian unity. Under this plan was a built-in option for the whole of Punjab, Sind, the N.W.F.P. and Baluchistan on the one side and the whole of Bengal and Assam on the other, which were then under Muslim League government to secede after British withdrawal.

Mr. Woodrow Wyatt, then a British Member of Parliament and who accompanied the Cabinet Mission, has recently revealed in an article in the '*London Spectator*' when Mr. Jinnah expressed reservation about the plan as it denied Pakistan, I put it to him that though the statement (announcing the plan) ruled out Pakistan, it was the first step on the road to it—when I finished, his face lit up. That is it. You have got it and it was after this talk that the Muslim League accepted the plan.

I am convinced that if these two groups of provinces had broken away under fear or rigged elections the Congress Party at the centre would have sunned to suppress the cessation for fear of a civil war—look at how they fumbled at Kashmir and India would have lost the whole of Bengal and Punjab and also Assam, instead of only half of Punjab, half of Bengal, Calcutta remaining in India and none of Assam gave one district and finally happened.

Partition could possibly have been avoided if a different course was followed by the Congress Party since 1930.[16] But by 1947, tied as we were to a non-violent approach, two alternatives faces us; the Cabinet Mission plan as defined by Lord Ismay which Mountbatten showed to Pandit Nehru in Simla on May 10, 1947 during the dinner time and Nehru rejected and the partition plan with a smaller Pakistan which Mountbatten produced with the help of V.P. Menon adding the verbal assurance to the Indian leaders that he would help in the territories of the Princely States.

In the given circumstances, the Congress leaders forgetting pride and prejudice adopted the less harmful course. Lord Mountbatten had told Mr. Narendra Singh Serila soon after the Bangladesh war that he had prophesied to Pandit Nehru and Sardar Patel that East Pakistan would break away from Pakistan within a quarter of a century.

Actually enormous progress has been made in the past 50 years in the scaling down the ambitions of the two-nation theory.[17] And if India remains firm and patient, in probably another quarter of a century our erstwhile compatriots will start seeing the advantages of cooperating with us.

An Alternative to Pakistan

Fazl-i-Hussain, an architect of the Unionist Party in Punjab, evolved a model inter-communal partnership in politics different from Jinnah's two-nation theory. He did not want the division of the country. This point has been discussed by Prof. V.N. Datta in this article: an alternative to Pakistan, which was published in the *Hindustan Times*, August 11, 1997, p. 7.

Was Pakistan inevitable? Was it a logical consequence of the policy 'Divide and Rule' which the British had adopted in India from 1906? Was it the cash of two personalities, the Mahatma and Quaid-i-Azam that led to the creation of Pakistan? Was the partition of India into two sovereign independent states a failure in statesmanship? Could the partition had been avoided or defined and if so at what point of time and how? These Questions are baffling for historians but I have tried to analyze this question in my own way.

After the Lahore resolution of March 1940, the rift between the Indian National Congress and the Muslim League widened. Jinnah was determined to struggle for an independent sovereign state, while the Congress wanted to maintain the unity of the country. The Cripps proposals of 1942 failed to reconcile the contending parties. The Quit India Movement of 1942 led to the arrest of the Congress leaders and they were in jail from 1942-45. This was a blessing in disguise for the Muslim League and Jinnah came very close to Viceroy Linlithgow. The Muslim League emerged as a very strong force during 1942-1945. The Pakistan had caught the imagination of the Muslims and the British felt that the Muslim could not be ignored.

Jinnah did not matter much in the Indian politics from 1920 to 1931. He had no political base in the country. He has resigned from the Congress in 1920 and he was not popular in the Muslim League till 1933. He knew little of provincial politics and his main interest lay in central politics. He was a 'consultative politician' anxious to offer ready made formulas in constitutional questions. A man of few words, proud and formal, he could seldom inspire confidence. It was to Sir Fazl-i-Hussain that the Muslim looked for leadership in Indian politics. His decisive influence would be traced from the Government of India Act, 1935 which strengthened the Muslim position in politics and determined the political destiny of the country.

Fazl-i-Hussain was the architect of the Unionist Party in Punjab. A shrewd politician and a brilliant tactician, Fazl-i-Hussain evolved a model of inter-communal partnership in politics, which was entirely different from Jinnah's two-nation theory of separatism. Fazl-i-Hussain did not like to divide the country for he firmly believed in the unity of India. The governing principle of the Unionist Party was economic, not religious. Despite the British attempts to stroke the fires of communal passions, the Unionist Party, with ups and downs in its fortune managed to govern Punjab in peace and unity, Prime Minister Clement Attlee regarded the Unionist performance as the biggest democratic experiment in India.

Initially a Congressman, Fazl-i-Hussain disassociated himself from the non-cooperation movement and resigned from the Congress. He believed that non-constitutional methods of wresting power from the British were quite detrimental to the interests of the country. He had great faith in parleys and negotiation to settle constitutional issues. He championed the Khilafat cause and believed that it could be settled round the table. Fazl-i-Hussain was determined to safeguard Muslim interest. He thought that 'separate electorate' which the Congress had accepted in 1916 in the Lucknow session of the Congress, provided adequate protection to 'Muslim interests'. Hence he condemned the 'Nehru report' of 1928, which had limited separate electorate, and recommended Adult Franchise.

In the late twenties and thirties the communal question eluded the grasp of Indian politicians. It was left to the British to introduce the Communal Award (1932), which was prelude to the Government of India Act. Three Round Table conferences (1930-32) failed to resolve the constitutional question. As a member of the Viceroy's Executive Council (1930-35), Fazl-i-Hussain exercised great influence in the formulation of the Government of India Act, 1935. He enjoyed the confidence of Lord Irvin and Lord Wellington. During the Round Table Conference in London he gave timely directions to the Muslim representatives, the Aga Khan, Sir Mohammad Zafrullah and Sir

Shafiat Ahmad Khan as to how Muslim interests could be adequately safeguarded.

Fazl-i-Hussain firmly believed that the coalition made of governance was the panacea of India's ills and was most suitable way of protecting the interests of various communities. He has been criticized for injecting a communal virus in Indian politics by his insistence on raising Muslim representation in the Punjab and Bengal Legislatures and increasing separate provinces of Sind and the North West Frontier Province. The fact is that Indian politics worked within the framework of communal representation. The framework could not be overthrown it was an integral part of the prevailing Indian political system. That is why Nehru Report of 1928 which had rejected 'separate electorate' was not accepted by the Muslims. Fazl-i-Hussain recognized that sharp differences existed among parties on constitutional issues. As a realist he evolved a formula by which representatives of various communities would share and administer power on the basis of economic, not religious interests.

Fazl-i-Hussain thought that Jinnah was out of touch with the reality of Indian politics. He found it different to deal with Jinnah. In his diary dated March 2, 1936 he noted: "Jinnah could not get on with anybody. He is no leader, I am afraid I will not go out of my way to be nice to him." He depreciated Jinnah's participation in the Round Table Conference and wrote to Sir Malcolm Haiby on May 20, 1930 that he disliked Jinnah's doing all the talking in the Round Table Conference. He recorded in his diary on January 11, 1931 that "Jinnah was doing mischief" but he was determined to counteract it. It was at his suggestion that Sir Shafait Ahmad Khan ensured the burial of Jinnah's Parliamentary Board in 1936, much to Jinnah's chagrin.

After serving for four years as a Viceroy's Executive Council he returned to Punjab. He was distressed to see the Unionist Party torn by factional politics. He called up on Sir Sikander Hyat Khan to resign from the Governorship of Reserve Bank and returned to Punjab to prepare the Unionist Party for 1937 elections. He prepared the election manifesto, restructured the Party, and produced a pamphlet 'Punjab politics' which laid down some guiding principles for his Party members. It is a tribute to Fazl-i-Hussain that the Unionist Party won 96 out of 175 seats in the 1937 elections in Punjab and formed a ministry that lasted for about nine years. The Muslim League could only secure one seat then.

With the coming of Second World War on September 1, 1939, the character of Indian politics changed and the intrusion of external factor greatly influenced the course of Punjab politics. Jinnah launched the 'Direct Action Day' movement from August 1946 in Bengal and also the Civil Disobedience Movement in July 1947 to topple the Punjab Coalition Ministry. But unfortunately Hyat Khan died at this time. So the Unionist Party was fragmented and the way was open for Pakistan.

Views of Contemporary Persons

Intizer Hussain was one of them. He was born in the 1920s in U.P. (India). He migrated to Pakistan after the partition. He is one of the most important writers in Urdu.

Intizer Hussain, for instance, does not think that there was anything either 'Historically inevitable' about the creation of Pakistan or 'natural' about its emergence. Instead, he has said repeatedly, that to assert the Muslim identity in the Indian subcontinent has always been utterly distinct from Hindustan and has been formed in antagonistic relationship with it, making the formation of Pakistan a political necessity and a logical outcome of cultural difference is not only bad history, but is also bad metaphysics. Such poor faith towards the past, such thoughtless disregard for the long history of the daily and peaceful intermingling of communities which worshipped different gods, he believes, always buds to disaster.

"I have no idea what a purely Islamic culture is", Intizar Hussain said to Prof. A. Bhalla, when he met him in Lahore in 1992. The best of Muslim minds, like the best minds of any community with the 'God'. They realized that in a place like India before 1947, where there was a plurality of gods and a plurality of 'truths' ethically and religiously were not the expletive preserves of any single community or sect.

Bhisham Sahni has written in his paper, the train has reached Amritsar that the decision to create Pakistan had just been announced and people speculated about the shape of things to come. Some people rejoiced at the creation of Pakistan, others rejoiced at India's independence.[18]

At the Railway Station of Wazirabad, a roar went up from the crowd, "Pakistan Zindabad? Islam Zindabad! Quaid-i-Azam Zindabad".

Divide and Quit

There were two books which deal with the theme "Divide and Quit". The first book is *The Original of the Partition of India (1936-1947)* by Anita Inder Singh (published in 1987) and the other is *Making the New Commonwealth* by R.J. Moore (1987). Mrs. Singh holds opinion that before the 1937 elections, the Congress and the Muslim League had different objectives but after the elections the gap widened between the two parties. The League was dominated by feudal lords opposed to land reforms. Mohammad Ali Jinnah held the Congress programme of land reforms all sham. Jinnah wanted a national Government instead of independence in 1937.

The election result shocked Jinnah.[19] In no province could the League form a cabinet. The League wanted a coalition with the Congress in U.P. but it could not be elated with the electoral success, Nehru started taking of Muslim mass contact movement which infuriated Jinnah who had realized the importance of mass contact by then. Jinnah blasted the Congress and did not miss a single opportunity to shape at the Congress premiers who happened to be Muslim.

Jinnah's accusation that the Congress ministers were anti-Muslim did not convince even the British officers. But the Muslims felt pray to this propaganda and felt alienated. The war came to the rescue of Jinnah. The Congress ministers resigned by November 1939 as protest against Lord Linlithgow's war policy though the Congress wanted a national government, Jinnah refused to co-operate with them. Both the Congress and the League did not join the Viceroy's Executive Council but unlike the Congress, the League did not follow a confrontationist course. Hence the Viceroy became more inclined towards the League. By holding talks with Jinnah, the Congress leaders strengthened his position which led him to demand Pakistan.

The Rajaji's formula and Liaquat-Desai Pact and other moves on the parts of the Congress consolidated Jinnah's position. When the Second World War came to an end in 1945, the Attlee Government ordered election in India. At this time the Communists were close to the Muslim League and how Dr. Adhikari, the communist leader, helped in drafting the election manifesto of the League.

The League consolidated the position considerably.[20] The Party won 78 per cent of the Muslim seats. The great Calcutta killings of August 1946 further wakened the Congress opposition to the partition which it ultimately had to accept finding no other alternative.

It may safely be concluded that by always underestimating the seriousness of the call for a sovereign Pakistan, neither the British nor the Congress formulated a strategy to challenge or resist it. India paid a heavy price and even then could not resolve the communal problem.

U.K. tried to Divide Gandhi and Nehru

The British Government secretly thought of creating a division between Mahatma Gandhi and Jawaharlal Nehru as early as 1938 to perpetuate their rule in India, according to a book on 'Nehru' by noted freedom fighter, Mrs. Aruna Asaf Ali.

The book *Private Faces of a Public Person* written in association with Mr. G.N. Raghavan quotes hitherto unpublished letters from American journalist, Mrs. Francis Gunther, to Nehru telling him that 'nothing encourages the British so much as the thought of a split between you and Gandhi'.

Mrs. Gunther writes in her letter to Nehru that during conversation with the Viceroy "his general feeling was Nehru has the brains but Gandhi the people.[21] If they can be separated we are safe."

Quoting extensively from the letter, Mrs. Asaf Ali says during Mrs. Gunther's conversation with the Viceroy "so many questions about Nehru so keenly."

The Viceroy had told Mrs. Gunther, "Confidentially that he had tried to meet him (Nehru) while in Calcutta during Christmas but it had not gone through."[22]

The letter says, "The V (Viceroy) said you were very brilliant etc. but Gandhi was a great man. He wanted to know how far you would go and how far the people would follow you".

On the need for a strange image of unity between the two leaders, Ms. Gunther writes: "This must be specially underlined for public consumption. You must stand together in public like Siamese twins. Nothing encourages the British so much as thought of a split."

"You on other the hand are considered as dangerous that if the British Empire ever fails it will all be laid to you—wherever we went, interest—and fear—central on you—your thought, your plans, your projects, your influence" Ms. Gunther wrote.

"That is why, since so many of them think that, it seems imperative for you and Gandhi to do the Siamese twins act, no mater what", Ms. Gunther advises Nehru. She says it was also imperative for Nehru to succeed to Gandhi's place in the affections of the people after his death.[23]

Among the fascinations in the book is the correspondence between the two in January 1928 marking the "trauma that preceded Jawaharlal unconditional acceptance of the Mahatma's leadership?"

Mrs. Asaf Ali writes that the conflict between the two leaders was over Gandhiji's sympathy for moderate elements in the Congress who were content for dominion status, his disapproval of modern industrialization and his apparently weakened reformist attitude towards Indian princes and capitalists."

In a letter on January 11, 1928 Jawaharlal Nehru wrote a letter to Mahatma Gandhi to which he gave free expression both to his immense admiration for and basic difference with Gandhiji.

Nehru writes, "You know how intentionally I have admired you and believed to you as a leader who can lead this country to victory and freedom. I have done so in spite of the fact that I have hardly agreed with anything that some of your previous publications like India Home Rule contained."

Nehru continues; "It passes my comprehension how a national organization can have as its ideal and goal domination status.[24] The very idea suffocates and strangles me."

On Khadi he says; "Khadi will grow slowly and if war comes it will grow very fast but I do not see how freedom is coming in its train—I neither think that the so-called *Ram Raj* was very good in the past—nor do want it back."

"You have criticized strongly the many obvious defects on industrialization and heavily paid any attention to its merits.[25] It is the opinion of most thinkers in the West that these defects are not due to industrialism as such but to the capitalist system which is based on exploitation of others. You do not say a word against the semi-feudal zamindari system which prevails in a great part of India or against the capitalist exploitation of both workers and the consumers.

Mrs. Asaf Ali says that Gandhiji responded to this letter which he described as a frank and honest document—by suggesting that they had perhaps reached the parties of the ways.

In a letter of January 17, 1928 Gandhiji says, "Though I was beginning to detect some differences in view point between you and me. I had no whatsoever of the terrible extent of those differences."

> *"I see quite clearly that you must carry on open warfare against me and my views—but this dissolution of comradeship—if*

dissolution must come—In no way effects our personal intimacy. We have long become of the same family, and we remain such inspire of grave political differences. I suggest a dignified way of unfurling your banner. Write to me a letter for publication showing your differences. I will print in Young India and write a brief reply".

Mrs. Asaf Ali says Jawaharlal shrank back from the very thought and wrote to Gandhiji "there can be no question of our personal relations suffering. But even in the wider sphere, am I not your child in politics, though perhaps a truant and errant child."

Mrs. Asaf Ali says Gandhiji's assassination orphaned Nehru.[26] "He was thrown entirely on his own spiritual resources and thought deeply on the phenomenon of saintliness and the need to combine the values of socialism and science with humane and critical values."

She says some of the most eloquent and deeply felt of his utterances was about Gandhi, whom he saw as the latest in a line of moral geniuses that India had thrown up beginning with Siddhartha Goutam, the Buddha.

The Partition of India—Two-Nation Theory and its Origin

My first chapter deals with the Two-Nation theory and Sir Syed. As two-nation theory was one of the important causes for the vivisection of India, so I started with two-nation theory. As Sir Syed Ahmad developed his two-nation theory, so it has been argued that Syed Ahmad sowed the seed of partition.

The fact is that the roots of Muslim separatism of which the partition of the country was the culmination could be traced back to the "Simla Deputation" of 1906, the demand for separate electorates and the foundation of the Muslim League in 1906. Syed Ahmad threw his powerful influence in favour of the coalition of his community from national movement. Since the national movement started, Sir Syed Ahmad raised a great question mark, which was to shadow Indian political till 1947.

Anti British Feeling

The Balkan wars (1912-13), defeat of Turkey in the First World War (1917-18), the Jallianwala Bagh Tragedy (1917), the Government of

India Act (1918) and the Khilafat issue (1914-20) around anti-British feeling among Indians. The Muslims were highly enraged at this time. After the failure of the Khilafat movement, circumstances changed. In 1919-20 Hindu-Muslim unity reached its high water-mark. After the end of the Khilafat movement, the one successful experiment in bringing the Muslim community into the heart of the nationalist movement failed to break its psychological isolation, and indeed confirmed its tendency to view political problems from a religious angle.

The failure of Hindu-Muslim unity for which Gandhi had laboured hard evaporated after the failure of the non-cooperation movement in 1922 and the abolition of the caliphate in 1924. Now communalism started in the country and Gandhi's voice was drowned.

Petty Politics

The All-Parties Conference of 1928 failed and communalism became more strong force. Jinnah called this event as "Parting of ways".[27] The unity could not be resorted between the two communities.

The second Round Table Conference of 1931 could nothing to improve the relations between the two communities. In 1932 the British Government imposed a solution in the form of the communal Award, which was published by the British Government on August 17, 1932. The Communal Award treated the untouchables as politically separate from the Hindu. Gandhi protested and went in a personal fast.[28] Untimely Communal Award was modified and the Poona Pact was signed on September 24, 1932. The Poona Pact coincided for more parliamentary representation to the untouchable.[29] The British Government set its seal of approval on the Poona Pact on 26th September Muslim separatism dominated and distorted the course of Indian politics; the central figure in this drama during the next decade was Mr. Jinnah.

But the Muslim League did not do well in the 1937 elections. Jinnah had met with an electoral disaster of the first magnitude in 1937. Not only did the Muslim electorate fail to vote the Party to office in the Muslim majority provinces but even in the Muslim minority provinces his Party was routed. As B.R. Nanda remarks "Jinnah was not the man to let History pass over his head". Nanda's remarks continue and he wrote that Jinnah set out to achieve through a propaganda blast what the ballot box had denied him. He decided to use the dynamite of religious emotion to acquire political influence and power.

As a result of the 1937 elections, Congress ministries had been functioning in eight provinces. Hardly ministries had functioned for some weeks; the Muslim League brought the charge of tyranny over Muslims. Jinnah's allegations were as the Moulana Azad says absolutely unfounded. But they brought untold mischief. The cry of Islam in danger, the reiteration of Congress tyranny and the specter of 'Hindu Raj' created the climate in which Jinnah propounded his two-nation theory and the proposal and the proposal for the partition of India at the Lahore session in 1940.

The vision of a sovereign Muslim state in Indian subcontinent was reminiscent of the past glories of Muslim rule. It was too fascinating a proposal, the Muslim middle class, which for historical reasons, had been left behind in the race for the plums of government service. Trade and industry in certain areas was attracted by the idea of a Muslim state, Muslim landlord in Bengal and Punjab saw the prospect of deliverance from progressive politicians like Pandit Jawaharlal Nehru, who indulged in dangerous talk of abolishing zamindari. Muslim officials were glad of the new vistas which were expected to open to them in a few states without the Hindu seniors having over their heads. Muslim traders and industrialists began to cherish visions of free fields for prosperous ventures without the intrusion of Hindu competitors.

Separatist Ideology

The outbreak of the Second World War on September 3, 1939 helped the propagation of the separatist ideology. The Viceroy Lord Linlithgow and his advisors anticipating a show-down with the Congress were in search of friends. It was during the war period that Jinnah strengthened his position because the Congress leaders were interned as the result of the Quit India Movement of August 1942. He was careful not to embody himself with the British and outwitted and outmanoeuvers such seasoned provincial politicians as Sikander Hyat Khan and Fazal-ul-Haq. When the Congress went into the political wilderness, Jinnah with the help of the British Governors, succeeded in installing Muslim League ministries in Assam, North West Frontier Province, Sind and Bengal. From every attempt at a solution of the constitutional deadlock between 1939 and 1946, he extracted political gains and his Party. The Cripps Mission in 1942 mattered to him only in so far as the provision for the non-accession of provinces signified an indirect endorsement of the principle of partition. The ill-fated Bhulabhai-Liaquat Pact was repudiated by him, but it introduced the idea of parity between the Congress and the League in an interim Government. The Gandhi-Jinnah talks in 1944 were useful to the League leader only in so far as they raised his prestige with his own following. It was his veto which made the Simla Conference in 1945 a futile exercise.

It is not surprising that in their long-drawn-out struggle with the Indian National Congress, the British had a soft corner for the Muslim League. They were glad to use Muslim separatism—just as they used the princely order—to the nationalist gains. As a British historian, Peter Hardy points out in his scholarly study of "Muslim politics in India" to expect them the (British) to encourage the ideals and the growth of non-communalism and thus to hasten their own demise as the rulers of India with all that would mean for the British political and economic condition in the world, was to expect a degree not merely of altruism, but also of prophetic insight out of the world of the history of governments.

Misinterpretation of Events in 1946

In Maulana Azad's 'India Wins Freedom' some of the severest strictures have been reserved for Jawaharlal Nehru for certain comments he made at a press conference in Bombay on July 10, 1946. According to Azad, this was one of those unfortunate events which change the course of History and to Jinnah it came as a burnished because the remarks 'provoked' Jinnah and led to the withdrawal of the Muslim League from the Cabinet Mission Plan and thus ultimately to the partition of India.[30] The Maulana further tells that all this would not have happened if he had not made the greatest blunder of his life in proposing Nehru's name for the presidentship of the Congress in 1946.

The Maulana had been elected to preside over the Ramgarh Session of the Congress in 1940. The normal term of the Congress presidency was only one year and in ordinary course a fresh election would have been held in 1941. But it could not be, as Gandhi launched the individual Civil Disobedience Movement in 1941. The Government had arrested many Congress leaders so election was not held. Again the election was due in 1942. But the Quit India Movement started from August 9, 1942. In the morning of August 9, all the leaders who had assembled and participated in the AICC session of the Congress in Bombay were arrested. Pandit Nehru, Sardar Patel, Abul Kalam Azad and other leaders were arrested. The August movement started in the country. All the leaders who were arrested they were released in June 1945.[31] So the election was now to be held. The election of a new President for the 1946 session of the Congress was due.

It is surprising that the Maulana should have forgotten the procedure for the election of the Congress President. It may be that due to advanced age, he had become senile. Never in the history of the Congress had an outgoing President proposed the name of the successor through a press statement. A definite procedure existed for election to the highest office of the Congress. Recommendations were submitted to the provincial Congress Committee to the AICC office by a certain date. The choice was usually made from among the recommended names before the meeting of the AICC by informal Congress leaders and after taking Gandhi's advice.

Two Versions

As for the sequence of events in 1946, we have a first hand version from Acharya J.B. Kriplani (who was the General Secretary of the Congress at that time), which is totally at variance with that of the Maulana. According to Kriplani, three names were received from the provincial Congress Committees, those of Sardar Patel, Pattabhi Sitaramayya and Kriplani himself. Nehru's name had not been recommended but according to Kriplani, "Gandhiji had expressed a wish that at that juncture Jawaharlal should be President". The last date for receiving recommendations from the provincial Congress Committee was already over. However, fifteen members of the AICC could propose a name. Kriplani obtained the signatures of the members of the Working Committee, and of a few local members of the AICC and duly proposed Nehru's name.

Patel was in line for the post. Fifteen years had elapsed since he presided over the Karachi session in 1931, whereas Nehru had presided at Lahore, Lucknow and Faizpur in 1929, 1936 and 1937 respectively. Patel was the overwhelming choice of the provincial Congress Committees. Nehru's election was due to Gandhi's intervention. Patel was persuaded to step down. The Mahatma's decisive influence was confirmed by his own remarks to the AICC on July 6, 1946; I told Jawaharlal that he must wear the crown of thrones for the sake of the nation and he has agreed. The following day, i.e. 7th July while taking over the chair from Azad, Nehru declared: I was for long time unable to make up my mind—but the day before yesterday I persuaded myself to shoulder the responsibility on the advice of Mahatmaji and also my colleagues in the Working Committee.

The general consensus is that the Mahatma preferred Nehru because of his greater international prestige. Gandhi himself strengthened this belief by his remarks to a prayer meeting on the eve of partition. Jawaharlal cannot be replaced today, whilst the charge is being taken from Englishmen. He is a Harrow boy, a Cambridge graduate and a Barrister, is wanted to carry on the negotiation with Englishmen. A close colleague of Patel minimized this factor and stressed the point that Nehru could speak with greater authority for a united Congress than Patel, who allegedly disliked Azad and was inclined to distrust nationalist Muslim in general.

A long discussion would convince any one that Azad had nothing to do with the election of Nehru as the President of the Congress in 1946 and Azad's remarks are factually incorrect. Nehru was elected by the AICC.

Careful Study

Now I came to the press conference of Jawaharlal Nehru dated June 10, 1946. Three days before the press conference, Nehru had addressed the AICC, a careful study of his speech shows that he was replying to criticism levelled by his socialist critics in the Congress Party. The Congress socialists were critical of the Cabinet Mission plan. The socialists had questioned the status and power of the proposed Constituent Assembly on the ground that it was being convened by the British Government. When the resolution on the Cabinet Mission plan was being discussed in the AICC the Congress socialists opposed it vehemently.[32] They brought Yusuf Meharacelly in a stature, which was ill. He also spoke against the Cabinet Mission plan. He said that the Constituent Assembly could exist on its surface.

Some press representatives asked Jawaharlal Nehru: whether with the passing of the resolution by the AICC the Congress had accepted the plan *in toto*, including the compositions of the interim Government. In reply he stated that Congress would enter the Constituent Assembly unfettered by agreement and free to meet all situations as they arise. Press representatives further asked if this meant that the Cabinet Mission plan could be modified. Jawaharlal replied emphatically that the Congress had agreed only to participate in the Constituent Assembly and regarded itself free to charge or modify the Cabinet Mission plan as it through best. Jawaharlal made it clear that the Constituent Assembly would be a sovereign body. About the grouping scheme, he said that it would probably never come to function; because Section A, the Hindu majority provinces would be opposed, the frontier provinces would oppose it in Section B as would Assam in Section C and provincial jealousies would thwart it.

Azad considered the press statement of Jawaharlal as a bombshell. How far Azad's comments are justified? I have already stated that Nehru had made these statements only to silence the Congress socialists who were against the Cabinet Mission plan. Nehru was of this opinion that these statements would clear the doubts from their minds and they would accept the Cabinet Mission plan. The oft-quoted sentence from his speech would make it clear that Nehru's speech was meant for the success of the Cabinet Mission plan; we are not bound by a single thing except that we have decided to silence the critics within the Congress Party and not to provoke the Muslim League. The whole tenor of Nehru's 6,000 words speech was to justify the acceptance of the Cabinet Mission plan.

The Muslim did not like Nehru's interpretation on Cabinet Mission plan and passed a resolution on July 27, 1946 withdrawing its acceptance of the mission's long term plan and called for 'Direct Action' to achieve the goal of Pakistan. It is interesting to note that the meeting of the council, which passed this resolution, had called by the General Secretary, Nawab Liaquat Ali Khan, before Nehru held the press conference in Bombay. Thus it is evident that the Muslim League had made up its mind earlier to withdraw its acceptance of the plan. Nehru's statement was made as an excuse by the League. The League was never sincere in accepting the plan. In his speech to the Muslim League council on June 2, 1946, Jinnah said: "Let me tell you that Muslim India will not rest content until we have established full, complete and sovereign Pakistan".[33] Accepting of the Mission's proposal was not the end of their struggle till Pakistan was achieved, if this was the true intention of Jinnah and if Jinnah was determined to torpedo the Cabinet Mission plan, then there is no justification in Azad's remark that "It was one of those unfortunate events which changed the course of history". Azad has blamed Nehru without any reason. Prof. V.N. Datta says that the effect of Nehru's statement on the minds of Jinnah was devastating. Michael Brecher, Nehru's first biographer has agreed that Nehru should have avoided a public discussion of political probabilities which could but provoke the League. Brecher has called Nehru's speech of July 10 as "one the most fiery and preventive statements in his forty years of public life".[34]

Many Checks

A three tier constitution such as the Cabinet Mission had outlined a delicate mechanism with humorous checks and balances. Under the two major parties, the Congress and the League entered the Constituent Assembly with tremendous goodwill and determination to cooperate. It was impossible to draft a workable constitution much less to enforce it. This would have created the ideal conditions in which units could break off. The Congress leaders had of course no intention of letting the League get away with the Pakistan of its own conception with six provinces, but disguising them as groups of provinces in the first instance. This was the background of the opposition to Gandhi, Nehru and Patel, and indeed of the entire Congress leadership to compulsory grouping of provinces. This opposition might have softened if Jinnah had tried to assure his critics. By failing to give such an assurance, Jinnah sealed the fate of grouping scheme; and that of the Cabinet Mission plan. It is true he thus made sure of Pakistan, but it was to be a Pakistan minus East Punjab, West Bengal and a major portion of Assam.[35]

Azad and Nehru and the Partition in the Light of "India Wins Freedom"

Nehru had told Leonard Mosley in 1960; the trust is that we were tired men, and we were getting on in years. Few of us could stand the prospect of going to prison again and if we had stood out for a united India as we wished it, persons obviously awaited us. We saw the fires burning in the Punjab and heard everyday of the killings. The plan for partition offered a way out and we took it.[36]

The Indian National Congress was a national and secular organization and it stood for a unified India. The Congress had adopted a resolution of complete independence at the Lahore session in 1929 under the Presidentship of a progressive and young leader Pandit Jawaharlal Nehru. The Muslim League was a communal Party established in Dacca in 1906. Jinnah, who had taken the membership of the Indian National Congress in 1906, had resigned from the Indian National Congress in 1920. Jinnah had become a member of the Muslim League in 1913. So after 1920, Jinnah moved to the Muslim League and became the President in 1934. M.A. Jinnah in his Presidential address on March 23, 1940 at Lahore session of the Muslim League demanded a divided India. It was made clear in the resolution that there would be two autonomous states in the country. It was said that "Hindus and Muslims can never become one nation". All the leaders of the Congress were opposed to the partition of the country. The Congress President, Maulana Abul Kalam Azad spoke on the Pakistan scheme on April 25, 1945 in this way: "the very term Pakistan goes against my grain.[37] It is harmful not only for India as a whole but for Muslims in particular. And in fact it creates more problems than it serves." Mahatma Gandhi, Pandit Jawaharlal Nehru, Sardar Patel and Dr. Rajendra Prasad were all opposed to the partition of the country. But under the compulsion of circumstances, the Congress leaders agreed to divide the country. Sometimes an individual moulds the currents of history and sometimes the current of history overtakes an individual. So the leaders of the Indian National Congress succumbed before the currents of history and they accepted partition.

India wins Freedom

The title of Maulana Azad's book *India wins Freedom* is a misnomer. Autobiography is a hardly suitable medium for writing history, especially of such a turbulent period as the last phase of British rule in India. My bone of contention is that "India wins Freedom" cannot be regarded as Azad's autobiography on the following grounds:

1. Azad died on February 22, 1958 and *India wins Freedom* was published in 1959. Nowhere does the manuscripts of the book bears Azad's signatures signifying his approval of the text. The book's sub-title is not 'Autobiography' but an 'Autobiographical Narrative'.[38] The focus of the book is

not on freedom of India but the transfer of power. The book's title does not fit with inside contents.

2. The book *India wins Freedom* is not in the Maulana's word. It is apparent from Humayun Kabir's preface that the Maulana was relying entirely upon his memory.[39]

Even in 1958, there was a vast reservoir of source materials available in the country, but these vast materials on the Indian freedom movement were not utilized either by the Maulana or Prof. Kabir. Maulana was depending on his memory, a dangerous expedient in recapitulating those events of hectic political activity. A long prison sentence (1942-45) during which period his wife and his sister died, had shattered his health. His 'memory was also failing' in the words of Prof. Kabir and when, towards the end of his life, he was dictating to Prof. Kabir, the incident recorded by the latter, he was deeply distressed by the political situation in the country. It is also likely that there was a communication gap between them. Prof. Kabir's understanding of the Maulana's elegant Urdu was as inadequate as his literary English was to the Maulana. Actually the Maulana did not write the book himself but related the story to Prof. Kabir. He makes it clear that the English text was approved by the Maulana, but some portions of the text containing incidents and reflections of a personal character were taken out and deposited under sealed cover in the National Library, Calcutta and the National Archives, New Delhi. It was on 22nd February, when Maulana was on the death bed, he had willed that the thirty pages be released for publication after thirty years on February 22, 1988. These thirty pages were released in September 1988 by a Court's directive and the book was released on November 7, 1988.

Indictment of Nehru

The strong indictment of Jawaharlal Nehru by the Maulana has surprised historians to a great extent, though the rest of it as I consider is merely an elaboration of what was already in book *India wins Freedom*. There is one portion in the book entitled as "Prelude to Partition'. Azad has written in this way: "this was one of the greatest tragedies of Indian history and I have to say with deepest of regrets that a large part of this responsibility for this development rests with Jawaharlal."[40] Azad holds Nehru responsible for the countries partition in 1947. This is a personalized view of history which ignores the larger, impersonal and as this case, incisively currents and this makes nonsense of history.

Criticizing Nehru for two mistakes—one in 1937, when he failed to accept the cooperation of the Muslim League and another one in 1946, when Pandit Nehru stated that the Congress would be free to modify the Cabinet Mission plan, which inspired Jinnah to withdraw from the League's earlier acceptance of the plan and demand for a Muslim state (Pakistan). Azad says, "These reopened the whole question of political and communal settlement" and finally, led to 'one of the great tragedies of Indian history of partition'.[41] but with the publications of *Selected works of Jawaharlal Nehru*, Vols. 8 and 9 by Dr. Rajendra Prasad's *Correspondence and Select Documents*, Vols. 1-2, edited by Valmiki Chaudhary, *The Transfer of Power*, Vols. 1-12 edited by Nicholas Manseargh, E.M.R. Lumaly and P. Moon, *Liberty or Death* by Patrick French, it is now possible to set the record straight.

Maulana tells us that "Nehru's opposition to the inclusion of two, instead of one, Muslim League legislatures in the Congress ministry in U.P. was a blunder". If the (U.P.) League's offer of co-operation had been accepted, Maulana writes, "The Muslim League Party would, for all practical purposes would have merged in the Congress. Jawaharlal's action gave the Muslim League in the U.P. a new lease of life".[42] Mr. Jinnah took full advantage of the situation and started an offensive which ultimately led to partition. The reasoning is naïve but it has such a wide currency that it needs to be investigated thoroughly.

1937 Elections

These elections took place under the Government of India Act, 1935. The following numbers of seats were won by the Congress in the Legislative Assemblies of the six provinces. Madras 159 out of 215, U.P. 134 out of 228, Bihar 98 out of 151, Bombay 86 out of 175, Central Provinces 70 out of 112, and Orissa 36 out of 60 seats. Out of 564 candidates for the 228 seats in the U.P., 152 were from the National Agricultural Party as against 168 Congressmen and Muslim League. The National Agricultural Party won 21 seats and the Muslim League 27.[43]

As a result of elections the Congress emerged as the strongest Party to form the Ministry in the U.P. but out of 64 provincial seats reserved for Muslims, 26 were won by the Muslim League, 28 by independents, 9 by the National Agricultural Party and only one by the Congress.[44] The Muslim League led by the Jinnah, however, met with an electoral disaster. It won 39 out of 107 Muslim seats in Punjab, 3 out of 33 in Sind and 10 in Madras. It did not win a single Muslim seat in the legislatures of Bihar, C.P., Orissa and N.W.F.P. In U.P. and Bombay, it did not comparatively better. In Bombay it won 27 out of 60 Muslim seats and 20 out of 29 in the U.P. with this poor showing the League hardly qualified for a coalition in any province.[45]

In case of U.P. should be understood thoroughly because Azad has accused Nehru on the formation of the U.P. Ministry. In this election in the U.P. the Indian National Congress and the Muslim League were facing challenges from the N.A.P. The National Agricultural Party of Awadh and Agra was formed in 1934.[46] On the eve of the General Election Sir Malcolm Haibey, the Governor of the U.P. had inspired the big landlords supported by business interest to form the National Agricultural Party in the U.P. to fight the Congress.

During the general elections, there was not much conflict between the Congress and the Muslim League. It was the desire of both parties to avoid a conflict as much as possible and to accommodate each other. In the early stages of the election campaign a number of Muslim who were more or less Congressmen were doubtful if they would stand on behalf of the Congress or the League. So they drifted gradually to the League side. The League election board in UP was a curious affairs. There were some fairly good and old Congressmen in it. This election was a tussle with the Agricultural Party which was wholly a Government Party. The League was also opposing them and so the Congress opposition to the League weakened.

There was no kind of arrangement between the U.P. Congress and the League, but a kind of convention had developed.[47] In one or two instances the Congress opposed the League candidates and defeated them. During the election the outstanding and most powerful worker on behalf of the League was Maulana Husain Ahmad, who was very close to the Congress.

After the elections there was a tussle inside the League and the reactionary elements seemed to gain the upper hand. Relations between the U.P. Congress and the U.P. League became more strained. During the convention at Delhi this matter was discussed by the Congress with the Jamiat leaders who had so far supported the League fully but who were worried at the reactionary turn it was taking.

After the convention in the U.P. League board became even more reactionary and its President Raja Shaben Ali Khan of Salimpur (who had resigned from the National Agricultural Party in U.P. in 1936 to participate actively in the election campaign of the Muslim League) had joined the interim ministry. This created a crisis in the League which resulted in the resignation of many members from the Parliamentary Board. Among those who resigned was Maulana Hussain Ahmad. Most of those who resigned were not MLAs but one MLA Hafiz Ibrahim, who resigned and formally joined the Congress Party.[48]

Walli a Congressman of Lucknow, in his letter of March 28, 1937 informed the Congress President, Jawaharlal Nehru that Khaliq-uz-Zaman had been drifting from the Congress and should not be brought back through any alliance or coalition with the Muslim League in the Assembly. Further, Walli wrote a letter to Jawaharlal Nehru on March 30, 1937 informing him that "a scheme is being hatched with the help of Pantji and Mohan Lal. I am personally convinced that any kind of pact or coalition between us and the Muslim League will be highly injurious."[49]

In this perspective, Jawaharlal wrote a letter on March 30, 1937 to Govind Vallabh Pant, the leader of the U.P. Congress Party in this way: "I have been informed that a scheme is being hatched with your help and Mohan Lal. I am personally convinced that any kind of pact or coalition between the Congress and the Muslim League will be highly injurious." Nehru issued a statement on April 25, 1937 at Allahabad: "those who talk entering into a pact or alliance with Muslim or others, fell to understand of the new forces that are moving our people."[50]

Towards the end of June 1937, the UP Muslim League leader Khaliq-uz-Zaman and Nawab Mohammad Ismail Khan made an approach towards the Congress. This had obviously some connection with the possibility of ministers. They pointed out that their parliamentary board had offered co-operation to the U.P. Congress Party on the basis of the "Wardha Programme" as laid down by Working Committee and were prepared to work under discipline of the Congress Party.

At this stage Maulana Abul Kalam Azad went to Lucknow from Wardha.[51] Azad was a member of three man Congress parliamentary subcommittee. Khaliqu-uz-Zaman was negotiating on the coalition ministry formation with Azad. Azad had authorized by the Congress

Working Committee to deal with Congress affairs in U.P. and Bihar. The Maulana was in charge of negotiation in U.P. and nothing seems to have been done against his wishes. Pant was also with Azad.[52] Azad saw Khaliq, who told him that he was practically prepared to give him a blank-cheque; provided, two of their members were included in the Ministry himself and Nawab Ismail Khan, the President of the U.P. Boards. Azad looked at all with some suspicion. But he felt attracted by the possibility of the whole Muslim League causing to exist as a separate group and being practically absorbed by the Congress.

After this Maulana Azad and Govind Ballabh Pant came to Allahabad. They discussed the question of the formation of the coalition Ministry with Jawaharlal Nehru. Nehru disliked this bargaining for seats in the Ministry. Azad and Pandit shared the feeling of Nehru. All of them disliked taking the two persons, who from the Congress point of view were weak. They feared reaction among them, Congressmen in general and the Congress Muslims in particular, who would have been irritated at their being excluded in preference for those who had been fighting the Congress. What of those who had stood by the Congress during all these years. What of the Jamiat which was supporting the Congress and opposing the League?[53]

Nehru, Azad and Pant thought over this matter seriously and they decided to a workable proposition. This was the winding up of the Muslim League in U.P. and its absorption in the Congress. This would have the great effect not only in up but all over India. This would mean a freehold for the Congress programme without communal troubles. This would knock over the British Government which relied so much on these troubles. After much discussion in which two other members of the U.P. (Acharya J.B. Kriplani and Narendra Dev) joined. They all came to the conclusion that the Congress should offer stringent conditions to the U.P. Muslim League group and if they accepted them *in toto*. Then we should offer to two ministers in their group. Besides them, one minister, would be Rafi Ahmad Kidwai.

So the conditions were drawn up. The March resolution of the Working Committee and the Congress policy in the legislature were to be accepted. The Muslim League would be wounded up including the U.P. Parliamentary Board. The entire Muslim League M.L.As. were to become full members of the Congress Party. All of them were to be abided by the discipline of the Party, but did not ask them to sever all connections with the present Muslim League.

The Maulana and Pant went to Lucknow. They sent for Nawab Ismail Khan but he was ill in Meerut and could not come. There was talk with Khaliq, who agreed to all the conditions except two, the winding up of the Parliamentary Board and not to set up separate candidates at bye-election. These were vital conditions. Khaliq said that he personally could agree but he had no authority to do so. Then he said that he could not give final answer and Azad and Pant returned to Allahabad.

Meanwhile rumours had spread that Azad and Pant were talking with the Muslim League. There was consternation among all Congress people especially the Muslim Congressmen, the Jamiat people and young Muslims. At this stage Nehru felt that trouble follow and the settlement would be temporary only. Azad was also distracted. Ultimately a word was sent that "We regretted, we could not alter our previous conditions at all, if they were accepted *in toto*, we would agree. But otherwise, we had no authority to go beyond this without consulting the Working Committee. So the matter dropped and Azad went off to Bombay. Khaliq said that he was unable to agree.

Nehru's Role

To blame Jawaharlal Nehru for the failure of the negotiations with the Muslim League of U.P. is unjustifiable. Azad was in charge of negotiation with Khaliq. His memory played back with him, as facts are otherwise. He twisted them to blame Nehru. His role in these negotiations was relatively small. He was keeping an indifferent health. He was being consulted by Azad, who was in touch with G.B. Pant, R.A. Kidwai, K.M. Ashraf, P.D. Tandon and other important members of the U.P. legislature. The most important consideration with provincial Congress leaders as with Nehru was that if the Muslim League with its landlord support came into cabinet, the Congress programme for agrarian reforms particularly the abolition of zamindars would be jeopardized.[54]

There is no doubt on this point that if a coalition ministry had been formed with the Muslim League in U.P. in 1937 and other provinces on Jinnah's terms, the paralysis which struck the interim Government at the centre in 1946-47 would have overtaken the provincial cabinets ten years earlier. But it is difficult to agree with

Prof. V.N. Datta, who has suggested in his article that "a successful working of the Congress League coalition would have prevented the possibilities of Pakistan resolution of 1940." Under no circumstance there should be an alliance of a secular Party with a communal Party. If there is any alliance between them, this alliance is not permanent. But the question is how far Nehru can be blamed, if the coalition ministry could not be formed in U.P.

The Congress wanted the League to accept the principle of joint responsibility which the League refused. The League also wanted itself to be accepted as the sole arbitrator of matters pertaining to Muslims. Fortunately, P.D. Tandon, a journalist and Congressman of Allahabad is still alive and his mind is still alert. He was involved in this negotiation with the U.P. Muslim League. P.D. Tandon covered Congress politics as a journalist, commenting on Prof. Humayun Kabir, Tandon said, "Kabir had some hidden hostility towards Nehru". Commenting about the proposed released pages 30 years after Azad's death, he said, how will it help history to realize a doubtful document. Those who could do no harm to Nehru in his life time now will have some sadistic pleasure defaming after his death."

Gowher Rizwi in his book (published in 1988) *Linlithgow and India* has contested Abul Kalam Azad's claim that "failure to form a Congress-Muslim League coalition in the U.P. turned Jinnah into an implacable foe of Congress, revitalized the League and ultimately led to partition".[55] Rizvi said that a close examination of the evidence it is possible to conclude that there was no breach of faith, when Congress failed to include League nominees in the U.P. cabinet. He says in the end that it is surely difficult to attribute partition to so trifling a cause. An error or a series of error in tactical judgment cannot explain such a momentous event. There were more fundamental forces at work.

Dr. B.B. Misra in his standard book *The Indian Political Parties* has examined some hitherto unpublished papers on the formation of the coalition ministry in the U.P. Dr. Misra supported those who are critical of Pandit Jawaharlal Nehru for his role in the ministry making fiasco in Lucknow in 1937. He also blames Nehru for his generally abrupt and impatient attitude towards Mr. Jinnah, a much older man.[56] But I have tried to show that a committee headed by Azad had been set up to look into the affairs of the ministry formation in U.P. Nehru was consulted, when it was felt necessary. Otherwise the

Committee was fully competent to take a decision. This negotiation went on from March to June 1937. Nehru advised the Committee from March 30, 1937 to June. Nehru was not in haste. Four months were a very long period. Nehru was never impatient. He gave due consideration to the League's point of view. The ministry was going to be formed in July 1937. So the discussion was closed and no nominees of the League was taken in the cabinet. This is the fact behind the formation of the ministry.

But mercifully, Dr. Mishra retains from adding, as some others have done in the past, that had two Muslim nominees been invited to join the cabinet of Pandit Govind Ballabh Pant, the formation of Pakistan would have been avoided. In any case one may agree or disagree with Dr. Mishra's conclusion but no one can say that they have not been supported with strong arguments.

So there is no doubt on this point that the discussion of the 1937 election in *India wins Freedom* is flawed by numerous errors of facts as well as of judgment. There are no evidence to hold this opinion that the negotiation with the Muslim League failed, because of Nehru's interference and obstinacy. Prof. C.H. Philips, Director of Oriental Studies, London University has observed in the introduction to the book *Partition of India* (1970) and has centred Azad's conclusion in this way: "In the light of the success at the polls, there was justification in the refusal of its leaders to accept any policy of forming coalition ministries with other parties, and certainly not with the Muslim votes, had been humiliated in the general election. On the contrary, by offering places to many Congress Muslims in its new ministries, was able to point the morale, and in this context Nehru's declaration that Congress must actively pursue a policy of mass Muslim contact made excellent sense.

In the book titled "*Gandhi, His Life and Thought*" (1970) Acharya J.B. Kriplani, who was the General Secretary of the Congress, described the account of the events in the Maulana's book "*India wins Freedom*" as a curious mixture of facts and fancies and says, it is not a question of correcting a passage here and there. It would require a volume as big as he had written to correct all his misstatements and misconceptions.

Jawaharlal Nehru may have been opposed in 1937 to any opportunistic alliance by the Congress with the Muslim League in the then United Provinces but no personal responsibilities could be fixed on him for the failure of negotiations for League's co-operation with the Congress Government in return for two seats in the state cabinet says Dr. S. Gopal, former university professor of contemporary History, at J.N.U., New Delhi. Dr. Gopal contests the stand taken by the Maulana that Nehru's action gave the League in the U.P. a new lease of life and enabled Jinnah to start "an offensive which ultimately led to Pakistan".

Till his dying days, Jawaharlal Nehru maintained that the 1937 decision was right; a non-communal nationalist Party had no need to share power with the Muslim League that was so patently without popular support. Justifiable through it was in terms of British constitutional practice, however, the 1937 decision had damaging consequences. The Viceroy looked into the many complaints and found that none was substantial but to a great many Muslims it seemed that a Hindu Raj might take complete control

At a press conference before his death, Nehru said, the Maulana's thinking that I was deciding and ordering things was not quite correct. These things are seldom done by an old individual. I was neither in the ministry nor going to be in the Ministry. There were others too, senior people. May be my views counted to some extent. I will tell you quite frankly what I was worried about at that time. I was anxious that since Congress ministries came in, they should take up the question of the land reforms, viz., zamindari abolition and I did not want that question stymied by any agreement with the Muslim League which was largely representative of the big zamindar of the U.P. Therefore, it was not so much a question of principle but politics to be adopted by the Congress ministry.

Press Conference of July 10, 1946

In Azad's *India wins freedom* some of the severest structures have been reserved for Nehru for certain comments, he made at a press in Bombay on July 10, 1946. I have already discussed the implications of the press conference. Dr. S. Gopal, the second biographer of Nehru says in his book *Jawaharlal Nehru* that Jinnah had not been in the first instance happy about a commitment from he had not drawn all the advantages he had expected and used Nehru's statement as the chance to break out of the acceptance. He adds that Nehru's assertion effectively deals with a difficulty created by the Cabinet Mission's unwarranted and clandestine assurance to Jinnah that a majority vote in a section (of the Constituent Assembly) would ensure compulsory grouping of the provinces. Dr. Gopal asserts that Pakistan was not made inevitable Nehru's statements. They at the most provided Jinnah with an opening. The record as researched by Dr. Gopal demonstrates that differing an anti-Congress prejudices of Viceroy Wavell during the crucial years (1945-47) had already strengthened Jinnah's position. So Azad's interpretation is not correct. His statement had nothing to do with the birth of Pakistan.

The Presidentship of the Congress

The Maulana tells us that 'I proposed his (Nehru) name for the Presidentship on April 26, 1946 and this was perhaps the greatest blunder of my political life'. I have examined this allegation and have found it completely devoid of facts. As Azad's memory was failing, so he has written imaginary things.

Further he writes, "I have regretted no action of mine so much as the decision to withdraw from the presidentship of the Congress at this critical juncture. It was a mistake which I can describe in Gandhi's words as one of Himalayan dimension." Here Azad has placed wrong facts. His name had not been recommended by any provincial Congress Committee. So Azad was not a candidate for the 1946 Presidential election. I have also examined this event in the historical perspective. So Azad is incorrect, when he says that he withdrew his candidate from the 1946 election. There is no question of withdrawing. He was out of picture.

> *"The Maulana has mentioned the wrong fact that Congress circles in Bengal, Bombay, Madras, Bihar and the U.P. openly expressed the opinion that I should be charged with the responsibility of free India in its course." The Maulana further writes that there would have been no partition, if I had not proposed the name of Nehru for the presidentship of the Congress. The entire observation is unhistorical. B.R. Nanda has called this discussion of Azad as "misinterpretation of events in 1946".*

NOTES

1. Lyon, Peter, *Partition Reconsidered: A British prospective, India: the first 50 Years*, London,1997, p. 17.
2. *Ibid.*

3. *Ibid.*
4. *Ibid.*
5. *Ibid.*
6. *Ibid.*
7. *Ibid.*
8. *Ibid.*
9. Bhalla, Alok, *Stories about the Partition of India*, Volume I, p. XIII.
10. Mishra, S.G., *Constitutional Development and National Movement*, p. 341.
11. *Ibid.*
12. *Ibid.*
13. *Ibid.*
14. *The Gazetteer of India,* vol. II, p. 583.
15. The author of this article is Narendra Nath Sarila, a former Diplomat, who was also on the staff of Lord Mountbatten in 1948. This article was published in the *Times of India*, New Delhi, September 15, 1947.
16. Quoted by Narendra Nath Sarila in the *Times of India*, New Delhi, September 15, 1947.
17. *Ibid.*
18. A. Bhalla, *the Partition of India*, Vol. I, pp. XXVII to 148.
19. Govind Talwakar, *Divide and Quit India,* published in the *Times of India*, New Delhi, November 23, 1988.
20. *Ibid.*
21. An article entitled 'UK Tried to Divide', *'Gandhi and Nehru'* published in the *Times of India*, New Delhi, November 23, 1988.
22. *Ibid.*
23. *Ibid.*
24. *Ibid.*
25. *Ibid.*
26. *Ibid.*
27. Sarkar Sumit, *Modern India*, p. 263.
28. *The Gazetteers of India,* Vol. II, p. 577.
29. *Ibid.*
30. Nanda B.R., *Misrepresentation of Events in 1946, II,* published in the *Times of India*, November 22, 1988.
31. *Ibid.*
32. *Ibid.*
33. Data, V.N., *Events Leading to the Partition, Part II*, p. 22.
34. Brecher Michael, *Nehru—A Political Biography*, p. 316.
35. Nanda, B.R., *Misrepresentation of Events in 1946 II*, published in the *Times of India*, New Delhi, November 22, 1988.
36. Bhattacharya A., *Countdown to Partition*, pp. XXV-XXVI.
37. Azad, M.A.K., *India wins Freedom*, p. 150.
38. *Ibid*, p. 251.

39. *Ibid.*
40. *Ibid.*
41. *Ibid.*
42. *Ibid.*
43. Gopal, S., *Selected Works of Jawaharlal Nehru,* Vol. 8, p. 32.
44. Dutta, V.N., *Events leading to the Partition,* Part I, published in the *Times of India*, New Delhi, December 21, 1988.
45. Nanda, B.R., *The Partition of India,* Part I, Published in the *Times of India*, New Delhi, November 21, 1988.
46. Gopal, S., *Selected Works of Jawaharlal Nehru,* Vol. 8, p. 19.
47. *Ibid.*
48. *Ibid.*
49. *Ibid.*
50. *Ibid.*
51. Dutta, V.N., *Events leading to the Partition,* Part I, published in the *Times of India*, New Delhi, December 21, 1988.
52. Nanda, B.R., *the Partition of India,* Part I, published in the *Times of India*, New Delhi, November 21, 1988.
53. Gopal S., Selected Works of Jawaharlal Nehru, vol. 8, p. 19.
54. Nanda, B.R., *the Partition of India,* Part I, published in the *Times of India*, New Delhi, November 21, 1988.
55. Maulana Abul Kalam Azad, *India wins Freedom*, p. 43.
56. "Journey to the Beginning", the *Times of India*, New Delhi, March 20, 1977.

14

Jawaharlal Nehru and Edwina's Relationship

Azad's statement runs as follows: "without a month of Lord Mountbatten's arrival in India, Jawaharlal, the firm opponent of partition had become, if not a supporter, at least acquiescent to the idea. I think one factor responsible for the change was the personality of Lady Mountbatten. She is not only extremely intelligent but has a most attractive and friendly temperament." Azad had tried to create an atmosphere of such kind, which might be interpreted that Lady Mountbatten exerted certain influence on Nehru.

Thus Azad has touched Nehru's personal life and he has maligned Nehru. How far Azad's statement is correct? Aruna Asaf Ali, a valiant freedom fighter has written a book in association with Mr. G.N.S. Raghavan titled *Private Face of a Public Person*. This book sketches the development of Nehru's personality as well as his philosophy of life. Mrs. Asaf Ali says, "Jawaharlal has just a faint regret in middle age that his personal life has been a much neglected affair."[1] Asaf Ali quotes it from Nehru's diary dated November 14, 1940 written at Gorakhpur jail on his 51st birth anniversary. Mrs. Asaf Ali says, "though the question of physical intimacy in Jawaharlal's relationship with woman friends had received wide attention, the fact remained that woman friends were to Jawaharlal not play things but persons endowed like himself, with a mind and with social and ethical concerns."

On being asked at a press conference, before his death, about Azad's observation that Lord and Lady Mountbatten had influenced him to accept partition. Nehru said, "I say it is quite conceivable for people to have different recollection as to who influenced whom.[2] The real fact is that how I am influenced I cannot judge it. But I think the real factor was the situation itself and the bitterness and the conflicts that were growing and the feeling that even some arrangements could be arrived as to prevent partition, those conflicts and inner descriptions would continue and might come in the way of any marked progress on the economic or other plan later. So how can I judge, how far I was responsible? Apart from this responsibility, Maulana Sahib thinks too much in individual terms of historical forces at work. Individual makes a difference and have made a difference but sometimes individuals are only symbols of forces at work. To Azad assertion that it was the Mountbatten who had influenced Mr. Nehru to agree to partition, C. Rajagopalachari, former Premier of Madras and former Governor General of India, said to a journalist, Morica Felton in 1962, "that it was in very bad taste to publicize that statement. And the statement is itself untrue. Partition had already been agreed before Mountbatten's arrival and the decision was not influenced by personal consideration. These things came about as the result of the working of historic forces. Neither the Prime Minister nor Patel could have influenced in a way that Azad said they were."[3]

Lady Mountbatten and Mountbatten

Philip Ziegler's book *Mountbatten* is useful for this period. Edwina was the daughter of Wilfred Ashley, a Conservative Member of Parliament and she was the granddaughter of Sir Ernest Castle, who had been born in Cologne, son of a Jewish money lender and small-time banker. In a career as remarkable he batted his way to immerse fortune and through his role as private banker and financial adviser to the future Edward VII, lodged himself in the innermost temples of the establishments. He was one of the richest and most powerful men in Europe. On February 13, 1922 while accompanying the Prince of Wales on the India tour, it was in room No. 13 of the then Viceregal Lodge that Mountbatten, who was the ADC to the Prince of Wales,[4] asked Edwina (who had come as a guest of the Viceroy Lord Reading) to marry him. It is now the office of the Registrar, University of Delhi. She said she would, this was entered in the Mountbatten's diary on February 14, 1922.

Nehru first encountered Edwina, when he visited Singapore (1946), when Mountbatten was still supreme commander in South-East Asia. She was there to meet him when, accompanied by her husband, he arrived at the Indian Y.M.C.A. The excited crowd broke into what had started as polite exchanges (between them). Mountbatten recorded; "A roar as if a dam bursting fell upon. Our ears and crowd burst through every door and window of the Y.M.C.A. In no time they were upon us. Edwina was the first to be knocked down, and disappeared under the mob. Pandit Jawaharlal screaming "Your wife, your wife, we must go to her". He linked arms with me and together we charged into the crowd in an endeavour to find her. Meanwhile she had crawled between the people's legs, and had come out at the far end of the room, get on a table, shouted to us that she was all right.

Eventually the Party escaped to a kitchen and barricaded the door with a table from which Nehru addressed the crowd, "that was an unusual introduction" remarked Nehru afterwards.[5] When they got back to Government House, Mountbatten was enraged at the mismanagement of the visit to the Y.M.C.A. and the scratches all over his brand new car. Edwina quieted him with the aid of a soft drink and assurances that Nehru himself was delighted at the way things were going. She was right, when he returned for dinner, their visitor was conspicuously effable and on the way home he said, "he had not enjoyed an evening with English people as much since he had come down from Cambridge more than 30 years ago."

That he was sincere seems certain that Mountbatten out to please were a formidable combination, when they genuinely liked and admired the person whom they wished to charm, the effect was irresistible. Nehru left Government House and in the convocation he had met an English couple, whom he could trust and who understood and sympathized with the needs of India asked what impression he had formed of the supreme commander, Nehru delivered before replying; "A very noble specimen of British Imperialism".

When Mountbatten became Viceroy on March 24, 1947, Edwina worked hard in the world of health and welfare, and established a strong rapport with the Indian leaders and their wives. Mahatma Gandhi was touchingly by fond of her. But her close relationship with Nehru did not begin until India obtained her independence on August 14/15, 1947. Gandhi was dead on January 30, 1948 by assassination. After Gandhi's murder, Mountbatten urged Prime Minister Nehru to come to live with them at Government House, where adequate security could be more easily maintained. Nehru refused, but with the death of the man who had so strongly influenced him, he began to see more and more of the Mountbatten's and to draw them some of the moral sustenance which he used to draw from the Mahatma. Their effect on him was subtle but persuasive.

I am afraid how Delhi and more specially you and Dickey have civilized me too much and you have humanized me a little also. He wrote to Edwina in June 1948 that the humanizing part is welcome but the civilizing process is not so welcome, however, desirable it might be. The wild animal in me tame through it has grown, resents it and along to break away. I remembered when I was not so tame, and had greater freedom of action, though within a limited sphere. I was rather like a flame burning myself and scorching others and oblivious of both. The flame grows dim and smokes and the bright point which gave me faith is no longer there.

In the Mountbatten's Nehru found companions who were not only congenial but secure. They had no axis to grind in India, no relations to advance, no home towns to favour, no covetous eyes on the occasion, no covetous eyes on the accession. But their view was as nearly objective as Nehru was likely to hear. The Prime Minister respected their judgment, had absolute confidence in their goodwill, and drew comforts from their support.[6] "I want someone to talk to me sanely and confidently, as you can do so well" he wrote in April; "For I am in danger of losing faith in myself and the work I do...... What has happened is happening, to the values, we cherished, where are our brave ideals?"

This letter was addressed to Edwina but applied to both of them. A month later it would have been different. On May 15, 1948, Nehru drove with the Mountbatten to spend a few days with them in the country near Simla. "Suddenly I realized and perhaps you did also" he wrote nearly 10 years later to Edwina that there was a deeper attachment between us, that some uncontrollable force of which I was only dimly aware, drew us to one another. I was overwhelmed and at the same time exhilarated by this new discovery. We talked more intimately, as if some will had been removed, and we could look into each other's area without fear or embarrassment.[7]

So began a relationship that was to endure until Edwina Mountbatten's death; intensely loving, romantic, trusting, generous, idealistic even spiritual. If there was any physical element, it can only have been of minor importance to either party.

Mountbatten's reaction was one of pleasure; "please keep this to yourselves but she and Jawaharlal are so sweet together" he writes to his daughter, Patricia. They really dote on each other in the nicest way and mummy and I are doing everything we can do to be tactful and help. Mummy has been incredibly sweet lately and we have been such a happy family. He liked and admired Nehru; it was useful to him that the Prime Minister should find such attractions in the Governor General's home. It was agreeable to find Edwina almost permanently in a good tamper; the advantages of the alliance were obvious.[8]

How did Nehru feel that his love for Edwina in any way diminish his respect and affection for her husband. On the contrary it heightened in the Prime Minister; Edwina seemed sometimes to be almost conspirators in ensuring that Mountbatten got all that he wanted out of life and was not made to feel excluded from their relationship.

Nehru wrote to thank her for a suitably silver cigarette box.[9] "For your private care I might tell you provided do not tell Dickey, that the spelling of my name was all wrong I make no grievance of it. Indeed in a way I like this mistake which makes the inscription characteristic of Dickey, who has thus far failed to grasp completely how my name should be written or pronounced."

Though Mountbatten knew how close this relationship was between Nehru and his wife. Edwina knew that Mountbatten knew, they were for several years reticent about discussing the matter except by wiles references. Thus in 1952 Edwina wrote to ask Mountbatten to keep Nehru's letters for her.

> *"You will realize that they are a mixture of typical Jawaharlal's letters full of interest and facts and really historic documents. Some of them have no personal remarks at all. Others are love letters in a sense, though you yourself will realise the strange relationship most of it spiritual—that exists between us. Jawaharlal has obviously meant a very great in my life, in these last years and I think I in his too. Our meetings have been rare and always fleeting, but I think I understand him, and perhaps him, as well as any human being can ever understand each other."*

It is rather wonderful that my affection and respect and gratitude and love for you are really so great that I feel I would rather you had these letters than any one else, and I feel you would understand and not in any way be hurt rather the contrary. We understand each other so well although so often we seem to differ and to be miles apart you have been very sweet and good to me, and we have had a great partnership. My admiration and my devotion to you are very great.

Mountbatten did understand and was not hurt indeed, this letter repaired the only injury that the relationship had done him, which sometimes he had felt himself not merely excluded but kept.

I am glad you realize that I know and have always understood the very special relationship between Jawaharlal and you made the easier by my fondness and admiration for him and by the remarkably lucky fact that among my many defects. God did not add jealously in any shape or form. I honestly do not believe, I have ever known that jealously means universal as it seems to be—and if it concerns the happiness of any one I am as kind of as you, then only my desire for your happiness exists. That is why I have always made your visits to each other easy and been faintly hurt when at times—you did not take me in your confidence right away.

There is an element of self-deception in this letter. There had been times when Edwina's behaviour with other man had caused Mountbatten sharp pain that was certainly akin to jealousy. Nor did his wife's relationship with Nehru leave him entirely unmoved. After Edwina's death he asked his daughter Pamela to look first at Nehru's letters, so fearful was he that he might find them some proof that the love between the two had not been as platonic as he had imagined.

Yet for the most part he felt not even a tremor of regret. He had never hankered after an exclusive relationship with his wife. He was happy, proud almost, to open it to a man he esteemed so highly, to call it a triangle or Mountbatten complaisant husband would be to be little relationship to all concerned.

Suddenly I realized and perhaps you also, Nehru wrote nearly 10 years later to Edwina, "that there was a deeper attachment between us, that some uncontrollable force, of which I was only dimly aware, drew us to one another. I was overwhelmed and at the same time exhilarated by this new discovery. We talked more intimately, as if some veil had been removed, and we could look into each other's eyes without fear or embarrassment."

Pamela Mountbatten had her own perceptions about her mother Edwina's relationship with Jawaharlal Nehru. An extract concerning the Nehru-Mountbatten episode from the book *Story of Freedom* (BBC TV Series) reads, "with Jawaharlal, however it was true love, and the love of equals—their relationship was passionate but also intellectual. It was deep but also light-hearted, their conversation full of giggles and sideling glances—much of their relationship was conducted in front of others, members of their family and servants and there was no secret about their physical closeness; they would hug and he would take her arm and press her hands as they spoke."

Mrs. Morgan and Azad's Allegation

Mrs. Jennet Morgan's recently published book *Edwina: A Life of Her Own* (1991) was clearly falsified Azad's allegation brought against Jawaharlal Nehru. Mrs. Morgan taught political history at Oxford University and then moved into the cabinet office in Whitehall; she is now a non-executive Director of various public companies. She had access in England to Nehru's letters to Edwina. The assassinated Prime Minister Rajeev Gandhi had placed all Edwina's letters addressed to Nehru to Mrs. Morgan. Mrs. Vijayalakshmi Pandit had persuaded Rajeev Gandhi to let Mrs. Morgan have Edwina's letters. These letters reflected the relationship between Edwina Mountbatten, wilful heiress and Nehru, Indian intellectual.

When Mountbatten was appointed Viceroy, Edwina's diary entry reads; 'Possible new horror job', she did not want to go to India. But after 15 months stay in India she did not want to leave. On their last night, the cabinet gave a banquet for the Mountbatten, when Nehru and Dickey spoke, Edwina would not restrain her tears. Nehru was too upset to take any word of her farewell speech, "India has given me many things" she told him, and "the most precious was bestowed on her at the very end. Nehru had shown her how to speak about her feelings to him she unlocked her and her emotions." Her parting gift to him included two of her prized possessions; a small eighteenth century; French Box of enamel and gold, an emerald ring and the silver St. Christopher medallion her mother had once given her father. Nehru gives her an ancient coin, which she attached to her bracelet, a box of mangoes and a copy of his autobiography.

Mrs. Morgan had raised one important question—was their love consummated? In so far as a third person can never know, I think it went as far as hugging—Nehru was a great hugger, patter and striker. There is a sort of view of the relationship in this country that first of all Nehru and Lady Mountbatten had an affair and the affair began while Dickey was Viceroy and that influenced the whole shape of the independence to come. Maulana Azad also holds this kind of view that Lady Mountbatten changed Nehru's view towards partition and Nehru accepted partition because of Lady Mountbatten. But this is absolute nonsense. When they met Nehru was nearly 58 and she was her late 40s. He may have considered it disloyal, ill mannered and wrong to have an affair with the wife of his friend. If Lady Mountbatten longed for the consummation, but soon it downed on both of them, when she left, there was no time. The relationship then developed through the passionate letters, whichever available at London and Delhi. It is almost as if the passion from her side is sublimated in these letters. She would not have wanted to degrade it. Then as the years passed, it grew deeper.

Mrs. Vijayalaxmi Pandit told Mrs. Morgan that "Nehru liked to be a teacher to women—wanting to share knowledge, to communicate ideas, wanting to nourish." Edwina was like a school girl, whose hero had wanted to educate her. Nehru's had a complex personality. One minute you would be dealing with a Kashmiri Pandit, but the next minute you seemed with the sort of person who had been to English Publish School and University. Mrs. Morgan told in an interview to the editor of the English paper "The Independent that I do believe that she had a non-sexual relationship with Nehru inas much as a third person can ever know." Thus it is clear that the relation between Nehru and Edwina were platonic. Letters gave pleasure to both. Both knew this fact that their 'destiny' will keep them separate. It was the special feature of Nehru's relationship that established his relations with those women who were of a strong temperament. Padmja Naidu, Kamla Devi Chattopadhayay, Rajkumari Amrit Kaur and Madam Chiang-Kai-Shek were such type of women. Lady Mountbatten also belonged to this category.

So Maulana Azad's assessment on Nehru's relations with Lady Mountbatten is based on conjecture and not on facts. It is the result of Azad's figments of imagination. As Nanda says, "His ability to empathies with women from culture is possibly accounted for by the fact that there was in his psyche 'a gentleness an aesthetic dimension, a love of all things beautiful however trivial they appear to the ordinary eye', which according to his associates made women gravitated towards him."

There are no evidences on record to show that Jawaharlal Nehru had ever an extra marital affair with Edwina. A personal affair should not be turned into a political issue. The private life of a political leader should not be a political subject. The private life had nothing to do with the political issues facing the nation. In Britain personal life of a leader is completely separated from his political career and as the events indicated in February 1992 with reference to Mr. Paddy Ashdown, the liberal democratic leader, who had a brief affair with his secretary. In the latest public opinion poll held in Britain on February 9, 1992, it was proved that the British voters fancy 'loving leaders'.

Edwina possessed a fine intellect, most penetrating some thought than her husband, Edwina Mountbatten sued to have been sought out for the blessing of a cupriferous providence.

A 13-year Tryst with Edwina, who was 45

The tale of profound relationship belongs to the India of the age of innocence. Nehru's interaction with Lady Mountbatten for 13 years was an important part of his life and the literary legacy. Extracts from his letters to Lady Mountbatten's revival is a moving love story.

To read about it presented with great sensitivity by Lady Edwina Mountbatten's biographer, Ms Janet Morgan was an ennobling experience. Lady Mountbatten seemed to share Nehru's vision of a new India. She had an understanding of India's problems and seemed to have craved for an Indian identity.

'*Edwina Mountbatten—A Life of Her Own*' published by Herbert Collins portrays the last Viceraine of India as capable, hard working progressive, compassionate, tough, arrogant, serious frivolous and passionate.[10] Lady Mountbatten emerges as a woman with political judgment and a keen sense of humour. She knew the British system and the high society too well. The biographer M.S. Morgan does not hide Lady Edwina's flaws. The heroine is unfaithful, spoiled, temperamental and a difficult wife.

The book documents in detail the interaction between Nehru and Lady Edwina. Its first glimpse is provided by the biographer saying that it was not unusual for Lady Edwina to drop in at the Prime Minister's house. Since partition, they had worked together on relief and welfare policy and by now they were good friends.

A fortnight after the Independence Day, Lady Mountbatten suddenly realized how fond she had become of Nehru. She had called on Mrs. Amrit Kaur to discuss the riots in New Delhi and later at night. They heard that the Prime Minister had gone out to investigate and had disappeared. They searched the dark street and found him standing by the road side calming a crowd of angry men armed with knives. We brought him back. Edwina wrote triumphantly in her diary; she had liked Nehru's recklessness and he liked being rescued.

In the wake of Mahatma Gandhi's assassination, Nehru was invited by Lady Edwina to join the family in their retreat at Mashobra. In a reply note to Lady Edwina, he spoke of needing some one to talk, 'to me sanely and confidently as you can do so well. I am in some danger of losing faith in myself and in the work I do, what has happened is happening to the values we cherished? Where are our brave ideas? Lady Edwina was to write to him later. You have left me with a strange sense of peace and happiness. Perhaps I have brought you the same.

The biographer says Nehru found it difficult to face the prospects of Lady Edwina's departure. She reminded him that he had told her to be practical. And so it will be and it has to be—otherwise and right you are. But wisdom brings little satisfaction. A feeling of acute malice is creeping over mc and horror me, when I look at a picture in my mind of your shaking thousands of hands on the night of 20th and saying your final good-bye. Dickey you cannot bypass your fate. Just I as I cannot bypass mine. So you will shake hands pleasant memories of the stay in India. Her parents chose interaction with Indian leaders. So necessary for the success of their mission was construed as class disloyalty, when they returned home to Britain.

An important aspect of Edwina's attraction for Nehru was the supportive role. She played in the transfer of power and the post-partition riots.[11] Her untiring efforts to over succour to the refugees revealed a dimension to the personality of the heiress, which Ziegler seems to have totally ignored. When he describes her as restless, egocentric, intolerant rarely a comfortable person to be with yet, equally, never boring. Even Tyabji speaks with administration of how well-informed, she was in world affairs, enlightening him on the political scenario in Indonesia just before he left for that country on a diplomatic assignment.

As B.R. Nanda puts it, while she may have "sown her wild Oats" as a young woman, in later years, she had matured into an intelligent, compassionate human being with whom a sensitive person like Nehru could relate without reserve.[12] In the same way that he could interact with other women of substance like Padmja Naidu, Kamla Devi

Chattopadhayay, Rajkumari Amrit Kaur and Madam Chiang-Kai-Shek. His ability to sympathise with women from diverse culture is probable accounted for by the fact that there was his psyche gentleness, anesthetic dimension, alive of all things beautiful, however, trivial they may appear to the ordinary eye. Which according to one of his associates made women gravitate towards him? Like the American journalist Frances Gunter, whose profile of him in life made him the toast of New York's gitterati for weeks on end?

And yet he was not merely a figure to be venerated but an intimate friend. Gunter writes to him in September 1943[13] thus I had to turn on the bed light, and took out your letters that lie in my bed table drawer—the real letters in your own hand. I have made typed copies of your letters that I keep for every day reading—I took them and read them—you would think I would know them by heart by this time—they warm me and made me strong. I tackled them with my hand, and feel the touch of your hand, warm and string and comradely, like the sun.

If he warmed women like sun, they too made his heart sing. Veteran communist and parliamentarian Renu Chakravarti recalls an unforgettable vignette she witnessed in 1928, during the Congress session in Calcutta. Both Padmaja Naidu and Nehru were staying over in our home. Suddenly, Mrs. Naidu had one of her fainting fits and the girls were in a hurry. Do you know what Nehru did? Just picked her up in her arms and laid her on the sofa. It was a relationship full of twists and turns, she recalls but we were all hoping some how that they would get married. They were both so lonely but some how it did not work out.

Why indeed, did not it work out? Could it be because Nehru himself sat an unreachable for most human beings. Dr. Kakar has an explanation. "The reason why he forged relationship with women who were unavailable and independent is possibly because he did not want to give too much of himself away to enter into commitments which would involve a surrender of self." The conventional reason offered is that it was his sense of political mission which stood in the way of any of the relationships turning permanent. As Tyabji says, "why did he even need a permanent companion?" He was quite happy as he was. He could enjoy the company of intelligent, attractive women who gave him the solace he needed in moments of emotional turmoil. This lack of personal commitment enabled him to devote all time to his political mission.

Indeed Nehru's unusually intense relationship with some of the most intelligent and creative women of his time would seem to have more than made up for the misgivings had expressed in an entry in his prison diary on November 14, 1940. Perhaps there is just a faint regret at what I have missed through life—my personal life has been a much neglected affair.

Nehru and Edwina (Exchange of Letters)

After Lady Mountbatten's departure to London, Nehru wrote, "I am convinced that[14] we have to function in our respective orbits or else or both of us will lose our roots and feel terribly unhappy. The biographer, Mrs. Morgan concludes that for Nehru, India came first but Edwina has tightened the load. You came and unlocked the doors and windows. Nehru said in one of his daily letters, which he wrote past midnight after finishing his official papers. The biographer says, "Nehru write freely to Lady Edwina. His letters were poems, his own and those of other people. Yeats, Swinburne, Euripides, Auden, Joyce Blake, the song of Solomon. Nehru loved words Lady Edwina was his inspiration. Writing to her about his solace from Kashmir to sent her gift, not shawls or silver, but a piece of India birch bark." In olden times it was used in place of paper for writing manuscripts on paper, Nehru had been carried away. His relationship with Lady Edwina had been shaped by their letters. Words, words—and, as he said there were still a thousand ideas to discuss. After a meeting in London, Nehru was relieved to find that their reunion was marvellous as their correspondence had led them to expect—a heavenly weekend.[15] Lady Edwina records ecstatically—but chaste alluding only in general terms to the physical passion they denied themselves. Nehru could not work unceasingly. It was pleasant to have an intelligent woman friend in whom he could confine. It delighted him to be of service to bring Lady Edwina sugar from America (in Britain it was rationed). To Nehru it was a great relationship. No great adjustments need be made. This was not a marriage, with us infringements and compromises. He had been a widower for many years and liked his privacy.[16]

Lady Edwina wrote to Nehru in May 1949, you have brought me all I was yearning for happiness, balance, misery even but we know the reason and we would not change it and there is infinitely more power and purpose in life. At one stage Nehru commented on the decline in the frequency of letters during the previous 10 years and wondered whether poetry has turned into prose. It was not so. Lady Edwina said; ten years—monuments in their history and so powerful in their effects on our personal lives. All the incidents you mentioned the strange courts of events—I seem steeped in them, wrote Lady Edwina in March 1957.

At one stage when Lady Edwina thought she might be dying, she wrote to her husband I have been thinking all those letters I have from Jawaharlal and what should be done with them. I would like you to have them for your life time. You will realize that they are a mixture of typical Jawaharlal letters; full of interest and facts and really historic documents. Some of them have no 'personal' remarks. Others are love letters in a sense though you yourself will realize the strange relationship—most of it is spiritual—which exists between us. Jawaharlal has obviously meant a very great deal in my life in these last years and I think I in his—our meetings have been rare and always fleeting, but I think I understand him and perhaps he me, as well as any human being can ever understand another, particularly, when two like us are generally thousands of miles apart and in such different lives and circumstances.[17]

The biography should satisfy to a large extant those who were curious about the extent of the Nehru-Edwina relationship. J. Morgan, historian, who had unlimited access to Lady Mountbatten's papers, was also permitted by Rajeev Gandhi to see Lady Edwina's letters to his grandfather. Quotations from those letters reflect arrested desperation of a highly-strung and extremely intelligent woman, who loved India as much as she loved Nehru. The biographer had produced overwhelming evidence to justify her conclusion; India and Nehru and India; in her they were intertwined.[18]

The extracts of her correspondence between Nehru and Edwina, frequency of letters, their meetings and holidays spent together after the Mountbatten left India and the contact maintained for 13 years all testify to the intensity of their feelings for each other. In the context of the discreet gossip and scandalous speculation after her death in 1960, the biography—an academic, a woman and someone had unlimited access to the personal papers of Lady Edwina, has something to say.[19]

During the five years that she worked on the book, she did find herself in people's drawing rooms talking about Lady Edwina's sex life. Mrs. Morgan says, "I dare say she would have liked him to become her lover; to reassure her that she was still desirable. But Nehru was a tremendously honourable man with very good manners. Some people may laugh at this, but good manners can see you through almost anything. They contain you. Nehru liked having these emotionally and intellectually close friendships. Why miss it up any thing more?[20] And I wonder if it would have lasted so long for otherwise? But he did love her that odd, awkward difficult words means—and when she died, he was grief stricken.

For the Indian readers, there is more in the book than the personal emotion—intellectual ties between the first Prime Minister and the last Vicereine. It is the way Lady Mountbatten perceived India and its problems and in the extent she devoted herself to those with considerable thought and feeling and with ruthless efficiency, discarding some of the old traditions of the Viceroy's house. This she did while associating her Viceroy husband engaged in the most difficult assignment of his career during a very critical phase in India's history. It is an account that may still inspire India's civil and foreign services and its voluntary relief organizers.[21]

Lady Edwina did not pull her punches. For example, she declared that much of the trouble between Hindus, Muslims and Sikhs was artificially emerged and a result of previous policies, missed opportunities and mistake made on all sides. When trouble broke out in any part of country; Lady Edwina headed for it to see things and to do something about it. Lady Edwina recorded these developments in her diary with astute—. She was always very well informed.

At her own request, Edwina was buried at sea. Her body was taken aboard the frigate 'wakeful' at Portsmouth and then out to the open sea. The Archbishop of Canterbury read the burial service and she was committed to the waves. From 'Tresul' an Indian frigate sent by Nehru, a wreath of marigold was cast upon the sea.

A Survey of Philip Ziegler's Book *Mountbatten* and Janet Morgan's Book *Edwina Mountbatten*.

Mr. Azad's allegations have found a place in *India wins Freedom* regarding Jawaharlal Nehru and Edwina Mountbatten and those allegations have been examined by Philip Ziegler and Janet Morgan's in their respective well-researched books. Ms. Morgan has taken five years to complete her work. Both authors have written dispassionately and deceptively. Morgan's biography of Edwina Mountbatten has reopened the debate on Lady Mountbatten's relationship with Jawaharlal Nehru. Thee controversy created by Azad's writing has been closed by Mrs. Morgan work. I have discussed Lady Mountbatten and Nehru in my previous three sub-chapters. Still I felt the need to have a fresh look on this controversy. In India people discuss this question not in an objective way and I hope that this short treatment will clear away the mist forever, unless a new well-researched book is not published. Janet Morgan's book throws new light on the celebrated relationship between Jawaharlal and Edwina Mountbatten.

Did the 13-year relationship between Jawaharlal Nehru and Lady Mountbatten cross the sexual Rubicon? Philip Ziegler's *Mountbatten* published in 1985 left the question unanswered, merely stating that it was an intensely, loving romantic, trusting, generous, idealistic even spiritual interaction, and that if there was any physical element it can only have been of minor importance. This sparked off considerable speculation about where the truth actually lay. Now at least in a recent biography of Lady Mountbatten. *A Life of Her Own* (1988) the author, Janet Morgan, who was given an access to the letter written by Edwina to his grandfather has suggested that the relationship was 'non-sexual' to the best of her understanding.

It was possibly because of this non-controversial interpretation that the book (the type script of which had been sent to Rajeev Gandhi) met with his approval. But for two or three modifications, Nehru's grandson apparently found the book quite objective and suitable for public consumption.

There are some, however, who do not buy this theory. To former diplomat, Badruddin Tyabji, who claims to have known Nehru closely, this imposition of a sexual halo around our leaders is unhealthy.[22] "As long as they confirm to horns of decency, I do not see why they should not be allowed to live their private lives as they will." He asserts, in fact I would be extremely wary of a leader without a sex life, because he would be nothing short of abnormal. And Nehru, he maintains was certainly not an ascetic, but a man who lived life to the full, who enjoyed the company of women especially if they embodied a continuation of beauty, wit, independence and strength.

But definitions of normality themselves are open to debate, according to psycho-analyst Sudhir Kakar,[23] while no relationship can sustain itself without the 'erotic change', this does not imply only consummated desire. All too often, an unfulfilled erotic change (manifesting itself through intimate conversations, correspondence, even the physical embrace of the loved one) can keep a relationship going longer than a consummated one.

For historians,[24] the question is redundant. B.R. Nanda, for instant explains that a serious historian would deign to discuss such sensitive areas of public figure's private life, only if he has access to hardcore evidence, and even then, it has to be explored with great subtlety, he cautions. For instance, in my biography of Gandhi I have commented on Gandhi's intensely, close relationship with Mirabehn. But I have revealed that when one was confronted with the prospect of her marrying a fellow inmate at the Ashram, his response was positive, he ran into similar predicament in his biography of Jamnalal Bajaj. In Gandhi's food steps, when decline with the difference between the Gandhi an industrialist and his wife. One must take care never to allow one's judgment to be clouded; to respect the sanity of fact, even while one is being critical.

Going by this criterion, Janet Morgan would seem to have come off with flying colours. The letters she has referred to in the broad lands Archives within the Mountbatten estate in Britain, are intense passionate poignant but offer no indication that the relationship between the great Indian leaders and the former Vicereine was 'anything' but 'platonic'. After all, as Dr. Kakar points out, if it had been otherwise, it would have been impossible to keep out any reference to that dimension of their love from the correspondence—their only link after the Mountbatten's left India.

From the published extracts of the letters, it appears that the Nehru-Edwina episode was also lined with anguish and soft denial. Even while their bond was a source of ecstasy for both, they had to come to terms with the fact that their destinies could never merge, the political compulsions would come in the way of their spending lives together interestingly. Mountbatten, a peripheral figure in this love saga, also paid a price. Prof. Ravinder Kumar, Director of the Nehru Memorial Museum. Recalls the Mountbatten's daughter Patricia disclosing during a visit to India a few years ago that while the family had pleasant memories of the stay in India,[25] her parents close interaction with Indian leaders, so necessary for the success of their mission was construed as class disloyalty, when they returned home to Britain.

B.R. Nanda has written about on this aspect of Nehru's life. Nehru was a figure to be venerated. Inspite of this he was an intimate friend. The Nehru-Edwina correspondence is invaluable in another context—literature. From what little I have read, it reveals the poetic sensibility of the leader, his multidimensional psyche. His approach in love was not the 'P' and gets out attitude that John F. Kennedy, for instance displayed says Kakar; Nehru, he argues, understood and experienced the emotion of love in all its contradictions and richness. He thus elevated it to a lace which a mind devoid of imagination could never hope to attain.

Years later, British author Leonard Mosley, recounted a conversation that he had with Nehru in 1960, when Nehru was Prime Minister. Nehru had said that truth is that we were tired men and we were getting on in years. Few of us could stand the prospect of going to prison again and if we stood out for a united India as we wished it, prison obviously awaited us. We saw the fires burning in the Punjab and elsewhere heard everyday of the killings. The plan for the partition offered a way out and took it.

So Azad's statement is untrue on the basis of published documents and contemporary publications. Nehru was not alone responsible for the partition of the country. To me it appears that partition was not the result of minor accidents as Azad has narrated in *India wins Freedom* but of broad and big forces of history.

Conclusion

Maulana Azad had grievances against the leaders of the Indian National Congress. He felt grievously hurt that he was not allowed by Gandhi to complete his term as Congress President. It should be remembered that Nehru and Azad were staunch supporters of Gandhian nationalism, love, human brotherhood and unity. But in pre-independent India Nehru was one of the prominent Congress leaders and certainly important. But there were many other stalwarts like Sardar Patel, C. Rajagopalachari, Dr. Rajendra Prasad and Acharya Kriplani, who also mattered in the affairs of the Congress. So Nehru alone would not have been isolated for the partition of the country.

Maulana Azad's indictment of Nehru put a question mark on his own role in the freedom movement; the basic question is why

Azad did not assert himself in 1937 and 1946. Azad had a very effective say in the Congress organization. Mahatma Gandhi was against partition of the country and the Maulana could have taken the support and procured definite decisions by the Congress Working Committee. On June 14, 1947 the All India Congress Committee met to ratify the 3rd June plan. Govind Ballabh Pant moved the official resolution on the partition of the country and Maulana Azad seconded it.

If Azad has such strong feelings about the role of Nehru in the partition of the country, he should not have merely deposited the thirty pages of the *India wins Freedom* in the National Library, New Delhi for thirty years but would have openly opposed partition in the crucial AICC meeting, and he should have joined the Government of free India led by Jawaharlal Nehru as a cabinet minister.

It is no use blaming others for commission of certain wrongs, when one is guilty of one's duty, it is easy enough to blame others fortyone years after the event.

Why Nehru and Patel agreed to Partition?[26]

Maulana Azad has raised the question of responsibility for the tragedy of partition; he describes Sardar Patel as its author. This is an extraordinary statement, because no one was more consistently opposed to the 'two-nation theory' and the partition of the country than Patel. It was after his experience of working as a Home Minister with the representatives of the Muslim League in the interim government of 1946, and the series of communal holocaust in Bengal, Bihar and the Punjab, that Patel came to the conclusion that while the British would not leave India without a settlement with the Muslim League there was no chance of the Congress being able to effect a *modus vivendi* with the League.

The partition of India, as demanded by the League, was bad enough but even worse possibilities had begun to loom ahead. As Patel saw it, the question was whether India was to have one or more division. In the twilight of the British Empire some of the princes in central and western India were nursing new ambitions. It was the intrigue by the ruler of the small state Bastar, in Central India with the Nizam of Hyderabad and the attitude of the political department to it, which convinced Patel that it was imperative to secure immediate British withdrawal even if it meant the acceptance of partition.

Mental Alliance

A similar conclusion was reached by Nehru after his frustrating experience in the interim government, where he found a 'mental alliance' between British officials and the League members. The riots in the Punjab in March 1947 proved the last straw. By the time Mountbatten assumed the charge of the office of the Viceroy of India on March 24, 1947 the Congress leadership sobered by its experience in the interim government and the growing lawlessness in the country was becoming reconciled to the idea of salvaging three-fourths of India from the chaos which threatened the whole.

It has been suggested that Nehru and Patel agreed to the partition of the country because they were avid for power. The decision in favour of 3rd June plan was, however, not that of Patel and Nehru alone. It was endorsed by the Congress Working Committee. According to Acharya J.B. Kriplani, who was then President of the Congress, the only member of the Working Committee, who opposed the resolution, was Abdul Ghaffar Khan; even the Maulana did not oppose it. At the meeting of the All India Congress Committee, 157 votes were for it and only 13 against. It was a painful decision taken with a heavy heart, but in an overwhelming majority of the members there seemed no alternative to it. The immediate problem, as Nehru saw it, "to arrest the swift drift to anarchy and chaos". At the meeting of the AICC Gandhi advised the members to accept the decision of the Working Committee, though he was himself opposed to it? "I cannot challenge the present Congress leadership", he said "and demolish the people's faith in it, unless I am in a position to tell them. Here is an alternative leadership. I must, therefore, swallow the bitter pill." An ageing Nehru and an important Patel swallowed the bait.

Congress Acceptance

In retrospect it appears that Congress acceptance of the partition in June 1947 was not a sudden development. It was the culmination of a process which had begun immediately after the passage of the Pakistan resolution at the Lahore session of the All India Muslim League in March 1940. Gandhi had opposed the partition theory and the vivisection of India, but he wrote as early as April 1940.

> *"I know no non-violent method of compelling the obedience of eight crores of Muslims to the will of India, however, powerful a majority the rest may represent. The Muslims must have the same rights of self-determination that the rest of India has. We are at present a joint family; any member may claim a division."*

This was perhaps the only possible position for a man of non-violence but it could not but encourage Jinnah to believe that if he persisted in his demand and was able to mobilize Muslim opinion. Pakistan would become reality.

But another leader might have taken the line of Abraham Lincoln, President of U.S.A. (1861-65) and insisted that there could be no compromise on the unity of the country. Two years later, the Congress Working Committee in its resolution on the Cripps Proposals (1942) affirmed that "it cannot think in terms of compelling the people of any territorial unit to remain in the Indian union against their declared and established will."

Under the impact of the League propaganda and the political deadlock with the Government, the Congress position on the question of partition went on softening. In 1944 (Gandhi-Jinnah talks) Gandhi in his talks with Jinnah not only accepted the principle of partition, but even discussed the mechanism for the demarcation of boundaries. In 1946, the Congress accepted the Cabinet Mission plan with its loose three-tier structure, and a Central Government which was unlikely to have the powers of the resources to maintain the unity of the subcontinent.

The Cabinet Mission plan proved still born. The interim government, which was functioning from September 2, 1946, revealed the incompatibility of the two major parties. Henceforth, there were only two options, partition or the country as demanded by the League, or a moratorium on all political controversy for a couple of years to allow tempers to cool and to produce the climate in which a compromise solution could be acquitted, unfortunately, the unrepresented communal rioting on the land from August 16, 1946 after the Muslim League's "Direct Action" day made a respite impossible. One man still hoped to build bridges of understanding between the communities. Gandhi toured the villages and towns of Bengal and Bihar, condemning violence, irrespective of the perpetrated it, rehabilitant refugees and restoring confidence. He was convinced that the tension, however serious it might seem, was a temporary phase; and that the British had no right to impose partition on India, temporarily gone mad.

Gandhi met Mountbatten on April 1, 1947 and suggested that Jinnah be invited to form the central interim Government. By this supreme gesture the Mahatma hoped to win over Jinnah. Mountbatten considered Gandhi scheme as "Immoral".[27] This scheme had the support of Maulana Azad and Abdul Ghaffar Khan. But the technical question was how a person, who was not the leader of the majority Party, could be appointed Prime Minister ignoring the majority. So it was unacceptable to Nehru, Patel and other Congress leaders. The Congress Working Committee turned down Gandhi's proposals. So Gandhi wrote a letter to Mountbatten from Bhangi Colony, New Delhi on 11th April asking him to withdraw his scheme.[28] With this Gandhi's participation in the political discussion came to an end. Nehru and Patel who had worked with the League in his interim government could not dream of holding overall powers to Jinnah.

Now or Never

The crux of the problem in the summer of 1947 was whether the delay, such as Gandhi suggested could have staved of the partition. The political temperature had risen; it did not suit the Muslim League to have it lowered, for the League, it was a case of now or never. Gandhi's plea that there should be 'Peace before Pakistan' did not impress the League. In fact, the League's argument was that there could be no peace until Pakistan was established, that it was either to be a 'divided or destroyed India', having declared their resolve with an historic declaration in the House of Commons on February 20, 1947 to leave India by a date not later than June 1948.[29] It wished to hand over its responsibility to authorities established by a constitution approved by all parties in India in accordance with the Cabinet Mission plan but unfortunately there was no clear prospect that such a constitution and such authorities would emerge. "If then, it should appear that[30] an agreed constitution would not have been worked out (by fully representative Constituent Assembly) by June 1948, it would have to consider to whom (the) transfer (of) the power of the Central Government (should be made) whether as a whole to some form of Central Government for British India, or in some areas to the existing provincial government, or in such other way as may seem most reasonable and in the best interests of the Indian people." At this stage, when the announcement was made, the British Government did not want to and perhaps could not antagonize the Muslim League, or compel it to a particular cause of action. During the period of Lord Linlithgow before the Lahore resolution of 1940, the British Government could have exercised a moderating influence on the Muslim League; but now the scope for such influence was limited. Especially after the 1945-46 elections, in which all the 30 Muslim seats in the Central Legislative Assembly and 439 seats out of 494 Muslim seats in the provincial assemblies had won by the Muslim League.

There is remarkable document in *India wins Freedom*, it was a manifesto addressed to Indian Muslims in 1946 by Maulana Azad giving his critique of the Pakistan scheme. In its lucidity, irrefutable logic, and impassionate eloquence, it would not have been improved upon, but it was all in vain. His wordings remained unheeded, he wrote.

The Muslim League had carried on propaganda to arouse religious fanaticism and communal passions. This clouded the political issue so much so that Muslim who stood on Congress or other ticket had difficulty even in securing a hearing from the people.

As the Maulana brooded in the evening of his life on the events of those years, it must have been a galling thought to him that his word has not carried weight with his own community. This could not but have added to the sadness and bitterness which are reflected in *India wins Freedom*.

Nehru's acceptance of the partition was the result of compulsion of events and the pressure of circumstances which made him to succumb to it than any change in his outlook or conviction. In fact, in less than year after India was divided, he wrote to the Nawab of Bhopal in a letter dated July 9, 1948; partition came and we accepted it,[31] because we thought that perhaps that way, however, painful it was, we might have some peace to work along our own lines. Perhaps we acted wrongly. It is difficult to judge now. And yet, the consequences of the partition have been so terrible that one is enclosed to think that anything else would have been preferable. That partition has come, and it brought in its train other vast changes. There can be no going back now to India as it was before the partition. Organic changes have taken place in India which prevents that going back.

Nevertheless, all my sense of history reveals against the unnatural state of affairs that has been created in India and Pakistan. I cannot see it continuing for long as it is. Something that was inherently wrong and unnatural was done and it brought disastrous consequences in its train. There is no setting down to it and conflicts are due to folly or litheness of those in authority in India or Pakistan. I feel, however, that it is something deeper than that and not all the wisdom of statesman could end these conflicts in the present context because they are inherent in the situation. Ultimately I have no doubt that India and Pakistan will come close together and it may be that there is some kind of federal link between them or at any rate certain common subjects. There is no other way to peace. The alternative is an ever deteriorating situation and incessant conflict.[32]

A prophet of secularism, Nehru never wavered, despite the partition, in his opposition to the two-nation theory. He stood firmly against the forces of communal reaction in India, and though the creation of Pakistan made his task more difficult. He remained as steadfast as ever in his determination to preserve India as a secular state and to see that the Muslims, who remained in India, did not suffer.

By January 1947, the Congress tried to woo Jinnah by comprising on the grouping issue, but the League was no longer interested in a united India. The challenge of Pakistan had become real and even Nehru with all his anti Party to the two-nation theory began to have second thought.[33] Patel had already reconciled himself to partition. Wavell continued to waver and was eventually replaced by Lord Mountbatten to bring a fresh mind to the problem. In a moment reflection, almost a year after the partition, Nehru stated, "We consented because we thought that thereby we were purchasing peace and good, though at a high price."

To Prof. Michael Brecher, Pandit Nehru confessed in 1956 "well, I suppose it was the compulsion of events and the feeling that we could not get out of that deadlock or morass by pursuing the way we had done, it became worse and worse, further, a feeling that even if we get freedom for India, with what background, it would be a very weak India, that is, a federal India with far too much power in the federating units. And also the fact that we saw no other way of getting our freedom in the near future, I mean.[34] And if others do not want to be in it, well, how can we and why should we force them to be in it.

But perhaps Pandit Nehru came nearer the truth in a conversation with Mosley Leonard in 1960 when he said; the truth is that we were tired man and we were getting on in years too.[35] Few of us could not stand the prospect of going to prisons again and we had stood out for a united India as we wished it, prison obviously awaited us. We saw the fires burning in the Punjab and heard everyday of the killings. The plan for partition offered a way out and we took it.

He adds, "but if Gandhi had told as not to, we would have gone fighting, and waiting, but we accepted that partition would be temporary, that Pakistan was bound to come back to us. None of us guessed how much the killings and crises in Kashmir would embitter partition."

Pandit Nehru had reflected further on this issue in this way: "I think, now looking back, that partition could have been avoided if the British Government's policy had been different, about a year or eighteen months before."

Thus it is clear that Nehru and Patel played a dominant role and they carried the Party in favour of partition. Gandhi was opposed to partition and it was an irony that having followed him faithfully for almost 30 years with very few expectations, Nehru and Patel should have broken with the master on the most significant issue afflicting India in modern History.[36] Nehru was also perturbed at the prevailing madness and he came to this conclusion that partition was better than the murder of innocent citizens. Patel had also thought in the same line that partition would make the way for peace. Nehru also brought that "if they (the League) are forced to stay in the union no progress and planning will be possible.[37]

It was felt by the Congress leaders that partition would be short lived. As Prof. Brecher has told that the Congress leaders believed that Pakistan would not be the viable state politically, economically, geographically or militarily and that sooner or later, Pakistan would be merged into the Indian union. Acharya J.B. Kriplani thought in the same way. Calling on the Party to make India a strong, happy, democratic and socialist state, he declared, "Such an India can win back the seceding children to the lap. For the freedom we have achieved cannot be complete without the unity of India."[38] The Congress Working Committee had also passed a resolution to the same effect. The resolution ran in this way: "the committee believed that the destiny of India will yet be realized and that when passions have cooled, a new and stronger unity based on goodwill and co-operation will emerge." But these were ideas and this could never happen. Though sixty-two years have passed, but the trends towards unity or confederation are not encouraging.

The Congress leaders believed that they would reject the Mountbatten's plan the British Government might impose another plan, which might bring more calamity for the country.

Most of the prominent Congress leaders had spent their lives in jail going and imprisonment. These leaders after a long struggle got an opportunity to serve the country, when the interim government was constituted on September 2, 1946. These leaders, especially Pandit Jawaharlal Nehru found an opportunity to translate their ideas into action. So if they would have rejected the Mountbatten plan, then they would have been out of office. But as these leaders wanted to serve the country, so they did like to part with power. The Mountbatten plan provided an opportunity to these leaders to develop the country in their own ways and according to their political thoughts.

These leaders did not like to follow Mahatma Gandhi's advice of civil disobedience in 1947. So they had no any other alternative except the Mountbatten Plan. As Prof. Brecher has remarked that it was ironic that in this situation, Gandhi, the great compromiser, acted as the pure revolutionary, while Nehru, the acknowledged revolutionary in the Congress, accepted a compromise situation in 1947.

Had these leaders followed Mahatma Gandhi, perhaps the vivisection of the country might have been avoided, Mahatma Gandhi's counsel might have maintained the unity of the country. Nehru, Patel, Prasad and some prominent leaders wanted a composite India. These leaders had been advocating their view points for three decades, why could not wait for a couple of years more. Jinnah was dead within a year of Pakistan's foundation. Perhaps after the death of Jinnah, the issue of Pakistan would not have been raised. Perhaps Mosley's opinion seems to be right; a little patience and all the troubles might have been avoided.[39]

Though Gandhi protested against the partition throughout his life, but it is wonder that Gandhi supported the Mountbatten plan in the All India Congress Committee session on the issue of partition. But if Gandhi had told us not to, we would have gone on fighting and waiting.[40]

Hence these factors led to the establishment of Pakistan. Jinnah, whose grandfather was a Hindu and who himself was as second generation Muslim, had been called as the architect of Pakistan. But to call Jinnah as the builder of Pakistan is far from truth. Pakistan was the creation of British policy of 'Divide and Rule' and the mistakes committed by the Indian leaders in the period of the freedom struggle. I do not feel either Clement Attlee or Lord Mountbatten was individually responsible for the partition of India. A long line of their predecessors had laid the lines of a policy that could have no other consequences; the special British contribution had consisted in exploiting the discordances in Indian social life.

Events Leading to Partition

Prof. V.N. Dutta, former university professor and Head of the Department of History, Kurukshetra University, and Haryana has replied to B.R. Nanda, who has written four articles on the partition of India. Prof. Dutta has advanced his own argument that the coalition ministry in 1937 in U.P. would have prevented the adoption of the Lahore resolution in 1940. I have examined the problem of the coalition ministry in detail and concluded that the Congress did a wise thing in not forming a Ministry in U.P. with the help of the Muslim League. I have tried to show that Jinnah took shelter in the Muslim League from 1928. Jinnah could not be regarded a secular in 1937. He was the President of the Muslim League from 1934. A man, who was the President of the communal Party, can not be regarded as a secular leader. If he was not secular, then he was a die-hard communalist. So Prof. Dutta's arguments that Jinnah was not a die-hard communalist in 1937 could not be accepted. However, my duty is to put Prof. Dutta's writings in the historical perspective. His first point is Coalition Ministry.

Mr. Nanda rules out the possibility of a Congress-Muslim League coalition ministry in U.P. in 1937 on the following grounds; the Congress had a radical agrarian programme which the Muslim League could not accept. Jinnah would have wriggled out of the commitment even if Chaudhari Knaliquzzaman efforts for a negotiated settlement with the Congress had matured; the coalition Ministry, if formed, would have been paralyzed by internal squabbles which later characterize the Interim Government in 1946-47.

Prof. Dutta has replied to Nanda on some points. He said that the 1937 electoral manifestoes of the Congress and the League did not differ on social and economical matters such as industrial development, the uplift of the rural population, the rural ineptness and civil liberty. The Congress had the programme of Zamindari Abolition. The League would not have co-operated on this point. The Muslim League was a feudal organization. It was not a mass Party like the Congress. Zamindars were dominating the Muslim League. Many landlords in turn looked to the leadership of the League for security. Jawaharlal Nehru said that the Muslim League represented a group of Muslims, no doubt highly estimable persons, functioning in the higher regions of the middle class and having no contact with the Muslim masses. He further said, may I suggest to Mr. Jinnah that I came into greater touch with the Muslim masses than most of the members of the Muslim League. Nehru's disposal of land distribution and socialist thinking as a way of dealing poverty was anathema to Jinnah. For the rich and influential Muslim landlords of the United Provinces, the typical Congress worker was not an alluring prospect, with their homespun clothes, Gandhi caps, aggressive vegetarianism and Hindi speech they remained the Muslim with any pretension to gentility. The Congress was being influenced by the all India Kissan Sabha and the Kissan Sabha was demanding the abolition of the zamindari, so how the Congress could allow the League to join the ministry. Prof. Dutta should approach this problem in a radical way. It was good that the League nominees could not join the ministry in the U.P. Even Acharya Narendra Dev had been consulted on this issue. The Muslim League did not agree to the terms laid down by the Congress. It was essential that the Muslim League should disappear as a political Party in the U.P. but Khaliq-uz-Zaman did not agree to this. The Muslim League nominees paralyzed the Interim Government in 1946. If the coalition ministry functioned in Bengal and Punjab, did secularism succeed? Fazlul Haque of Bengal encouraged the Lahore resolution in 1940 and in the Punjab, communalism because a strong force after the death of Sikander Hayat Khan. Jinnah persuaded Sikander Hayat Khan, Premier of the Punjab and Fazlul Haque of Bengal to ally their forces to the League. This was done for expediency and amounted to a sacrifice of the League's internal coherence in exchange for possible future influence. But this experiment failed. So the Congress did a wise thing by declaring to give two seats to the Muslim League in the U.P. ministry. All these facts should be taken into consideration by Prof. Dutta. It is not proper to say that after the failure of the negotiations, Gandhi, Nehru, Subhas Bose and Rajendra Prasad tried to open unity talks with Jinnah. To quote Prof. Dutta, now Gandhi, Nehru, Subhas Bose and Rajendra Prasad was desperately keen to open unity talks with Jinnah but he was unwilling to oblige them. These leaders wanted to remove differences with the League. They did not like unity with the League. What Prof. Dutta means unity? Does he think amalgamation of the two? The Congress leaders did not like merger. Gandhi met Jinnah and the negotiations between Gandhi and Jinnah started from September 3, 1944 and continued till 27th September. The negotiations broke down on two-nation theory, plebiscite and others. Jinnah wanted Pakistan without any plebiscite but Gandhi wanted plebiscite first and Pakistan next. So they could not agree and this negotiation failed. The question of unity did not crop up at all. During the Second World War, 1939 to lesion the growing rift between the Congress and the League, Nehru met Jinnah in October-November 1939 several times, but to no avail. The League leader liked Nehru, spoke of his personal regard for him and even admired "his character and integrity" but he disapproved of his politics and compared him to "Peter Pun" who never grows up. Meanwhile as a cleavage between the Congress and the government widened, Congress ministerial resigned by November 1939. Jinnah, as a shrewd politician, exploited the situation and proclaimed December 22, 1939 "Day of Deliverance" for the Muslims. Nehru was hurt; he believed that Jinnah had become impossible.[41] He disliked his politics as much as he detested his tactics.

When the Muslim League adopted the 'Direct Action' resolution and Jinnah announced 16th August as 'direct action day', Nehru approached Jinnah directly in an effort to cut the Gordian knot of suspicion. The two leaders met in Jinnah's home in Bombay on August 15, 1946 but their goal could not be reconciled. Little did either realize that exactly one year later the impasse would be broken in the cataclysm of partition and communal war. The parties resumed their propaganda with renewed vigour. Wavell was distracted by the turn of events and prelisted in his attempt to square a circle. So the Congress leaders liked to remove differences with the League. They did not like 'unity' with the League.

Prof. Dutta has discussed the press conference of July 10, 1946, that as a result of his statement at the press conference; another opportunity was lost by the Congress for setting the constitutional crisis through its tactless handling. It could be urged that if the Cabinet

Mission recommendations had worked, there would have been no partition! I have examined the press conference in my previous chapter but how far Prof. Dutta's conclusion is correct? The question is, what Nehru said at the conference?

Nehru said that the Congress was committed to participate in the Constituent Assembly and nothing else. And the assembly would be a sovereign body, regardless of policy statements from London. Of course, the Constituent Assembly would take steps for the protection of the minorities. As regards for a treaty with Britain he said that this depends on the British attitude. If the British Government was not prepared for the immediate transfer of power, there would be a direct clash. If they treated Indians as equal, there would be a treaty. About the grouping scheme, Nehru was clear. He said it would probably never come to fruition, he declared, because Section A, the Hindu majority provinces, would oppose, the frontier provinces would oppose in Section B, as would Assam in Section C and provincial jealousness would thwart it. He also stressed the likelihood of a very powerful Government than that envisaged by the Cabinet Mission. The scope of the centre, even though limited, inevitably grows, because it cannot exist otherwise.[42]

There was much political insight in Nehru's observation. It is very difficult to deny that the frontier and Assam, both Congress provinces in 1946, would opt of their groups if an opportunity was given. Nehru's reference to provincial jealousy found adequate support in the post-partition history of India and Pakistan. India opted for emergency provision more than 110 times. In Pakistan military dictatorship was established for more than 25 years. So Nehru was right that the centre should be very strong. The Simon Commission had recommended in 1930 that India should have a nerve centre. So Nehru was perfectly correct in his assessment.

The question is whether Nehru should ventilate his ideas in the political atmosphere of 1946 or not; Nehru's remarks certainly cleared the air of confusion and hypocrisy. At the same time they destroyed the façade of agreement which the Cabinet Mission tried to maintain. In fact, his speech sparked the collapse of the mission.[43] There was nothing fundamentally new in his speech, but it was a serious tactical error. This statement did not prepare the ground for Pakistan. The Lahore resolution had been adopted on 1940 and since then he wanted Pakistan. But Nehru's statement provoked Jinnah to start the Direct

Action Day from 16th August. Had the Central Government been strong in 1946, the Direct Action Day would have been nipped in the bud. But the Central Government was a weak one. The Premier of Bengal was a communalist and direct action day was observed in Bengal only. The League withdraws its acceptance of the Cabinet Mission's long plan and the League had not accepted the short-term plan. So Pakistan was not the result of Nehru's statement but there were fundamental causes for the partition of the country. I do not agree with Prof. Dutta's conclusion that the birth of Pakistan had nothing to do with separatist tendency. Even during the period of Lord Mountbatten, Jinnah did not agree to the Cabinet Mission's recommendations. Mountbatten tried his best that the Congress and the League should accept the Cabinet Mission plan. The Congress had no objection but the League rejected the Cabinet Mission plan. So if the Cabinet Mission's formula did not work properly, Jinnah was responsible for this. When Mountbatten came to this conclusion that Jinnah wanted Pakistan and he was not interested to maintain the unity of the country, he said to Jinnah that in case of Pakistan, Bengal and Punjab would be partitioned. So Jinnah did not get Pakistan, but a 'moth-eaten and truncated Pakistan'.

Last Week of British Rule

The last week of British Rule in India was the most hectic of any. The government officers had been working longer hours and under more trying conditions. On Tuesday, the 12th August, Viceroy Mountbatten was finally informed by Radcliff that his Awards would be ready by noon the following day; it was too late for him to see before leaving for Karachi. This matter was discussed in a meeting of the Viceroy's staff on the evening of the 12th. The question was what should be done with the report? The Reforms Commissioner V.P. Menon was able to warn the Viceroy of the Disastrous effect that the award was likely to have on the Congress leaders, he went so far as to say that Nehru and Patel were certain to blow up; since they had assured a delegation from the Chittagong hill tract that there was no question of their being allotted to Pakistan. V.P. Menon went on to say that if the details of Awards were given to the Indian leaders before the 15th, he thought they might refuse to attend the meeting of the Constitution Assembly which the Viceroy was to address. If given to them later in the day—V.P. Menon thought they would refuse to come to the state banquet and the evening Party. In any case, he said that unless the situation was handled with the utmost care, Congress would blow up.

So on 13th August, the Viceroy wrote to Jinnah and Nehru telling them that he had not received all the Awards by the time and he left for Karachi. He suggested that there should be a meeting at Government House on 16th August to decide upon the timing and method of publication, and also the method of implementations the undertaking of the Partition Council to accept the Award and enforce the decisions contained in it.

Khan Abdul Wali Khan, the leader of the National Award Party and son of the late Frontier Gandhi, Khan Abdul Ghaffar Khan has written a very well-researched book on the partition of India known as *facts are facts*, inside story of the partition of India. The book was first written in Pushtu and translated by his wife Naseem into Urdu and later into English and was published first in Peshawar. The book was released on the eve of Wali Khan's departure for Bombay to see his ailing father, Frontier Gandhi. The author has systematically outlined the role the British played in fanning communal tension in separating the Muslims from the Hindus. 'Britain pursued the policy of communal politics to its logical end' concluded Wali Khan. "When there was no way for it to continue to rule it could at least divide and leave, leaving behind a trail of horrendous communal bloodshed and an intensity of hostility so pervasive and deep running that it will leave its mark on generation to come."

Zafrullah prepared Partition Plan

The plan for India's partition into two Dominions was sponsored by the British and drawn up by Sir Chaudhary Zafrullah Khan, who later became Pakistan's first Foreign Minister.

According to Mr. Wali Khan's book, a top opposition leader, Sir Zafrullah prepared the plan on the condition that its authorship would remain secret. The argument was that since Sir Zafrullah knowing that it was his handwork, will make it suspect in their areas from its very start. A copy of the plan had gone to Mohammad Ali Jinnah and also to Sir Akbar Hydari, the Prime Minister of Nizam of Hyderabad (for financing it) obviously; it was much the same scheme that was adopted as the Pakistan resolution on March 23, 1940 contends Wali Khan.

The research conceded out by Mr. Wali Khan at the India Office Library in London is apparently based on documents declassified by the British Government under the 30-year rule. When the Muslim League adopted Sir Zafrullah's plan, the then Viceroy appointed by British became assured that they could depend on the League in promoting their policies and in its facing up to the Congress, Mr. Wali Khan surmises discussing the British tilt towards the Muslim League, he pointed out the British decided that it might not be a sound strategy to keep lending strength to Hindus who were the country's preponderant majority.

There was also another consideration. There were no Hindus in other countries of the world, whereas the Muslims were spread in four countries of the world. Thus Muslims were a strong and organized world force, the book says. The Englishmen's worry was that the Muslims were scattered among various organizations. They were willing to accept the supremacy of the British but none was ready to find accommodation with each other.

In those days the Muslim League was divided into two groups. One was led by Sir Mohammad Shafi and the other by M.A. Jinnah. Once convinced that Jinnah could be on the government side. It became very easy for the British to start coaxing unity within the Muslim League fighting the Congress required organization. It had to be one of the Muslims. The Englishman cast himself in the role of Godfather who issued instructions from behind, Mr. Wali Khan writes, the Englishman's game was to get the Muslims come together in a sort of confrontation with the Congress and make it appear to the world that the Indians were among themselves, so what the Government could do, the book says, this analysis is quite correct.

During the First Round Table Conference (1930) the British made full use of the communal differences. When the Second Round Table Conference was called (1931), the strategy was pursued to further points. The author points out that Harijans were also similarly sought to be involved in castes issues and alienated from the Congress to further weaken the Congress and the Hindus. It would give the British great joy if like the princes, the Harijan leader, Dr. Ambedkar also fell into their hands. An excited Secretary of State for India writes on December 28, 1932; Ambedkar has behaved well at the Round Table Conference and I am most anxious to strengthen his hands in every reasonable way.

But Mahatma Gandhi foiled the British gambit by launching a fast unto death. It was a terrible for the country. Ambedkar agreed with the leaders of the Congress and the Communal Award was replaced by the Poona Pact. The Harijan continued to be the part of the Hindu fold. The strategy having failed, the British Government now depended mere on the Muslims. As the Congress did not support the Government policy in the Second World War, so the government turned towards the Muslim League. The Congress ministry resigned in all the provinces by November 15, 1939 and the League came very close to the Government and the Muslim League became very powerful from 1942-45. The League did not support the Quit India Movement of 1942. At this time Viceroy Linlithgow lifted the ban on the Communist Party of India. The bargain struck was that the Party's leader, Mr. M.N. Roy would be released and M.N. Roy would not support the Congress policy, as the Congress had been weakened during the Second World War. So the Muslim League captured sufficient seats in the 1945-46 election.

The British Government supported the Muslim League openly till 1946. When Jinnah did not agree to maintain a united India, then Mountbatten agreed for a 'Truncated Pakistan'. Mr. Wali feels that the American global strategy threatens the very existence of Pakistan and undergone regional stability by encouraging an arms race with India. According to him it was the 'global imperialist conspiracy' which led to the partition of India whose real author was Lord Linlithgow and Zafrullah Khan and not Quaid-i-Azam Jinnah. It is an issue which has been sharply contested in a dispatch in *Pakistan Times*.

Based on the study of the India Office papers in London over a total period of some 75 months its hide affairs to be as controversial as the author's own towering personality. Khan Abdul Wali Khan, leader of the National Award Party of Pakistan and son of the Frontier Gandhi, the Late Khan Abdul Ghaffar Khan feels that the very existence of the Pakistan state is threatened by a global imperial conspiracy, which was also responsible for the partition of India.

Answering a question, Mr. Wali Khan squarely blamed the British for creating the communal virus in the subcontinent. He also said, "That we have been duelled as agents of India in our country but history is history which none can change. In Pakistan history is not recorded but fabricated and manufactured. According to him, the book is compiled mainly on the basis of documents available at the

Commonwealth Foundation Library at London; well exposed the people responsible for the partition of India."

He said the British had not spared anyone while preserving the documents and he had spared time in writing the book "which would reveal when and who were responsible for the unfortunate partition not of the country but in fact of the Muslims of India". The Second Round Table conference broke up in utter failure on December 1, 1931, and Gandhi told Prof. Laski he would return to India helpless, homeless and empty handed. For Laski, the debacle was inevitable result, he wrote. Justice Holms of Sir Samuel's Hoare's belief that the "White man ought not to be asked to give way to the Black and Gandhi's hunting fear that the white man in India will always take a yard for each inch of compromise" Laski predicted an India in flames for the next few years and out of that tragedies too vast even to think of. Gandhi left London, travelled through Europe, arrived in India and immediately renewed his campaign of passive resistance.

The evening before he left London, Gandhi met with a group of Labour Party sympathizers that included Kinslay Martin, Leonard Woolf, and H.F. Nevinson, H.N. Brailsford and Prof. Laski. Gandhi asked the group what course he should follow on his return to India? he asked each person in the room to tell him now as they read the break-up of negotiations, what he should do; Leonard Woolf's account in his autobiography of what then happened provides a fascinating contemporary portrait of Gandhi's friend Harold Laski.

When we had all said there followed one of the most brilliant intellectual and pyrotechnic displays which I ever listened to. Gandhi thanked us and said that it would greatly help him if his friend Harold Laski, who was one of us, would try to sum up the various lines of judgment and advice which had emerged. Harold then stood up in front of the fireplace and gave the most lucid, faultless summary of the complicated, diverse exposition of ten or fifteen people to which he had been listening in the previous hour and a half. He spoke for about twenty minutes. He gave a perfect sketch of the pattern into which the various statements and opinions logically composed themselves; he never missed a point. There was a kind of beauty in his exposition, a bowless certainty and simplicity which one feels in some works of art.

After the collapse of the Round Table Conference on India Laski continued to advocate Indian Independence, while Churchill regarded the Indian Raj and the 'Crown Jewel' in the glorious British Empire, it was for Laski 'the slum of empire'. He protested the cycle of arrests and repression in India. Laski ridiculed, not by the quality of our rule, not by a reciprocal interest born of mutual goodwill. We hold India by the sword, no country is held by goodwill, when fifty thousand people have to be sent to jail. The British were unwilling to recognize, he wrote, that Indian nationalism is part of a basic revolt of the east against western tutelage, to which there is no answer save that of freedom.[44]

NOTES

1. The *Times of India*, New Delhi, September 29, 1991.
2. *Ibid.*
3. *Ibid.*
4. The *Times of India*, New Delhi, October 30, 1999.
5. *Ibid.*
6. *Ibid.*
7. *Ibid.*
8. *Ibid.*
9. "13-year Tryst with Edwina", the *Times of India*, New Delhi, January 31, 1948.
10. Sharma, L.K., *'A 13-Year Tryst with Edwina'*, published in the *Times of India*, June 13, 1991.
11. P. Viswanathan's article, 'Knight in Story A Man', published in the *Times of India*, June 21, 1991.
12. *Ibid.*
13. Quoted in Aruna Asaf Ali's *Biography of Nehru*, Private face of a public person.
14. P.Viswanathan's article, *Knight in story a man*, published in the *Times of India*, June 21, 1991.
15. *Ibid.*
16 *Ibid.*
17. *Ibid.*
18. *Ibid.*
19. *Ibid.*
20. *Ibid.*
21. *Ibid.*
22. *Ibid.*
23. *Ibid.*
24. *Ibid.*
25. *Ibid.*
26. Based on B.R. Nanda's article published in the *Times of India*, New Delhi, November 21 to 24, 1988.

27. Nicholas Manseargh, editor-in-chief, the *Transfer of Power*, Vol. X, p. 69.
28. *Ibid.*
29. Collins and Lapierre, *Mountbatten and Partition of India*, p. 22.
30. Norman, Dorothy, *Nehru* Vol. II, p. 303.
31. Zakaria, Rafiq, *A story of Nehru*, New Delhi, 1997, p. 7.
32. *Ibid.*
33. *Ibid.*
34. Brecher, Michel, *Nehru,* p. 377.
35. Mosley, Leonard, *British Raj*, p. 274.
36. *Ibid.*
37. *Ibid.*
38. *Ibid.*
39. Mosley Leonard, *British Raj*, p. 274.
40. *Ibid.*, p. 248.
41. Zakir, Rafique, *A Story of Nehru*, 1997, pp. 54-55.
42. *Indian Annual Register*, Vol. II, 1946, pp. 145-147.
43. A comprehensive account of the Cabinet Mission is to be found in V.P. Menon's book, *Transfer of Power in India*, pp. 280-284.
44. *Mainstream*, July 31, 1993, pp. 10-11.

15

Jinnah as a Man, as a Politician and his Achievement

Millions of people living on both sides of the Radcliff line of 1947 were uprooted from their homes in history's most massive migration. They underwent killings, arson and unparallel in the annals of man's inhumanity to man. The wounds of some of them have healed. There are some others who are still grappling with them or are seeing their scars. However, there is no denying the fact that by and large, some of the heat generated at that time has ebb and the dust raised has settled down. The younger generation, who are born either in India and Pakistan after 1947 does not know about the cause that led to the horrible nightmare and why the Indian National Congress and the Muslim League behaved as they indeed did and also who were the real villains of the peace, while most of those on the Indian side of the Radcliff line think that it was all because of the villainy of M.A. Jinnah; those on the other side think that it was the perfidy of Nehru and Jinnah.

It is much difficult to unravel the enigma of M.A. Jinnah, who shaped India's destiny more than half-a-century ago, he remaining the most elusive of chain-smoker, gaunt, thin lipped and slightly sinister in appearance. He managed to create a new nation by perseverance and political cunning. In Pakistan Jinnah the Quaid-i-Azam is revived almost a secular saint. He is sacrosanct, beyond reproach; speaking ill of the father of the nation is no more acceptable than insulting Gandhi has pride to be on this side of the border.

On the other side of the partition line, Jinnah is often demonized but for him, it is suggested all would have been well. India would have remained undivided and whatever tensions there have been between Hindus and Muslims never have happened.

But what type of man Quaid-i-Azam was? A brilliant Barrister, a gifted politician, fastidious, stubborn and a little austere what should not be overlooked is the remarkable triumph which crowned his political career. He won nationhood for Indian Muslims just seven years after he had first publicly espoused that aim. It was one of the most astonishing achievement in modern Indian history. Jinnah had complained about being given a 'moth-eaten' Pakistan, but it was at the time of its creation the biggest independent Islamic nation in the world.

Earlier Political Career and Mode of Living

Son of a dealer in manufactured goods of Karachi, Mohammad Ali Jinnah, who was born in around 1876 in a modest house and who was seven years younger than Mahatma Gandhi, had been actively interested in politics ever since he heard from the visitor's gallery of the House of Commons the speech by the first Indian member of British Parliament, Dadabhai Naoroji in 1892. Gladstone and Disraeli also made an impression on him. Jinnah was 16 and a student of Law in London. Dadabhai Naoroji was his hero and he tried to emulate. Fourteen years later, when Jinnah had made a name at the Bombay High Court, Naoroji presided over the 1906 session of the Indian National Congress. Jinnah worked as secretary of India's grand old man. Jinnah's grandfather was a Hindu, who became a convert to Islam.[1]

Patriot

Jinnah was a member of the Indian National Congress from 1906. He took the membership of Muslim League in 1913. When Mahatma Gandhi, who was in South Africa from 1893-1914, returned landed in Bombay on January 9, 1915, Jinnah was among them who received him. Jinnah was the President of Gujrati Sabha. The Gujrati Sabha felicitated M.K. Gandhi. While expressing his gratitude, Gandhi said that he was glad that a Muslim was the President of the Sabha. Wolpart says that this hurt Jinnah as he thought himself as a national leader. Jinnah's misfortune was on the one hand, he was considered a Muslim leader by Gandhi, and on the other, he was heckled by Muslims at a conference and was asked to speak in Urdu if he was a true Muslim. In 1913, Jinnah decided to join another political organization, the Muslim League. By this time he insisted that Hindus and Muslims should battle together for end of colonial rule. He was a staunch Congress man. A politician of great ability, he was a patriot to the core. Like Gopal Krishan Gokhle, another hero he believed in constitutional methods for the achievement of India's independence. Handsome, lean, erect, this clear headed and distinguished looking man, lived like an English gentleman. His life style was European. He drank regularly and avoided the mosque on Friday. The holy Quran had no place in his vision of the world. He knew less of the verses of Quran than Gandhi. He was proud and arrogant. He was always impeccably dressed in western attire. In the words of the American journalist Louis Fischer, he was the best dressed man in the British Empire. He was an armchair politician not a man of masses. He had few disciples or friends, only followers.

His Marriage

Jinnah lost his first child wife, while he was a student in London. After his return from London, he came to Bombay to practice as a barrister; Jinnah attended a meeting of the political campaigning organization of the Indian National Congress at Bombay in 1904. Jinnah was married for the second time in 1917. He fell in love with Ruttie Peti. She was the daughter of Sir Dinshaw Peti, one of Bombay's richest Parsi merchant. The father was opposed to the marriage but they were married at Jinnah's house on Malabar Hill in Bombay. She was 18 only and Jinnah was then 41 years of twenty five years older than her. The marriage of a great socialite beauty and the lawyer politician, who talked only of law and politics, proved unhappy. They were incomplete. Mrs. Ruttie Jinnah shifted to her parent's house in 1928 and stayed away from him. They had one daughter, Dina Wadia born on August 14, 1919. Dina Wadia lives in New York. She has a son. Jinnah's only grandson Nasli Wadia has home in Bombay. Jinnah had affection for his grandson. He was the head of the Bombay Dyeing. He was four years when Jinnah died in 1948. Ruttie Jinnah died in Taj Mahal Hotel. Jinnah was away from Bombay. He reached for the burial of his wife. It is typical man that he packed away everything with her memory, even the photographs.

Jinnah's Outlook and Approach

Jinnah was not a Muslim fundamentalist.[2] He was an ambitious lawyer. Muslim and Hindu fanatics were also distasteful to him. He openly followed Muslim-Hindu marriages and he married a Parsi girl. He drank whisky. He wore a stiff-white collar even in the hottest weather and when making a speech, he would fix his monocle to his eye to add emphasis to a pause. He had been an active lieutenant of the Congress moderate, Gokhle and in the 1920s he was described as the Ambassador of Hindu-Muslim unity, in the words of Sarojini Naidu. But as the 1920s advanced and Gandhi's campaign brought the Congress widespread mass support. Jinnah found himself displaced due to Gandhian technique. His fastidious taste was offended by the organization's changing tone. He was bitter at studying a brief and drafting an opinion then at responding to popular moods.

Furthermore he became convinced that the change in Congress from the middle class group into a mass Party marked also its evolution and an orgy of Hindu fanatical power. Jinnah tried to persuade Gandhi and the Congress to make concessions that might have claimed Muslim fears. When he failed, he at first quit both politics and India, settling down in 1931 to a successful practice as a barrister in London.

Two years later, a Muslim landowner, Liaquat Ali Khan, came to London to persuade him that the Muslim League needed him back in India as their leader. He returned still hoping for cooperation with the Congress. He hoped good result from the 1937 elections but the League had won less than 5 per cent of the Muslim votes. Jinnah having reluctantly agreed to lead a communal organization like the Muslim League. Gandhi and Nehru without any thought had insulted a man whose iron will more than equalled that of Robert Clive, who for forty-nine days heroically defended Arcot till the besieging forces of Chand Sahib withdrew.

His Political Activeness

He returned to his life of bachelor and he remained bachelor throughout his whole life. His sister, Fatima remained with him till the end. Jinnah was very actively involved in politics. He was a member of the Home Rule League set up by Tilak. He was largely instrumental in the signing of the Lucknow Pact of 1916. He genuinely believed that Hindu-Muslim unity was possible and advisable. He resigned from the Congress in 1920. In 1928, he finally parted with the Congress. He became the President of the Muslim League in 1934 and continued on this post till Pakistan was created on August 14, 1947.

Disillusionment

Under the Government of India Act, 1935, provincial autonomy was introduced in all the provinces of the country. The provincial elections were held in 1937 and in this election the Muslim League was defeated. Jinnah was disillusioned in politics and frustrated in his personal life. The British Government felt that the most formidable opposed to them was the Congress. It was thought that to check the Congress Party it was necessary to bring into another Party opposed to the Congress. It was understood that this could be only the Muslim League. The League was now leaning towards the British. The Secretary of State for India Lord Zetland observed that he would steadily growing conviction that the dominant factor in determining the future form of Government would prove to be the all-India Muslim League.

Lord Linlithgow and the Muslim League

Second World War broke out on September 1, 1939 and without consulting the Congress Party or the premiers, Viceroy Lord Linlithgow declared India to be a belligerent country on September 3, 1939. The implementation of the federal part of the Government of India Act was put on cold storage for the period of the war. The policy of the later Government of India under Lord Linlithgow was to put the Congress and the League on par to build a Muslim leader so that he may attain the same status as Mahatma Gandhi had attained.

Linlithgow played a dirty game to achieve his goal. Gandhi sought an interview with Viceroy. His request was granted on this condition that Jinnah also asked for an interview. The Viceregal House communiqué was issued that the two names of Gandhi and Jinnah together as being granted interview. In pursuance of the Congress parliamentary decision, the Congress ministers resigned in all provinces by November 15, 1939. In the provinces, where the

Muslims were in the majority, the Muslim League had not been in a position to form Government in provinces. However, Jinnah took up the role of a spokesman for these provinces at New Delhi. In any case these provinces were already playing an important role in the war effort. The Unionist Party in the Punjab under Sikander Hyat Khan had assured support to the Muslim League at the central level but only on condition that the League did not interfere in the Punjab affairs.

Linlithgow leaned on Jinnah and it is on record that he was grateful to him for help extended by him against the Congress. He continued to tell Whitehall that so long as the Congress was not able to meet the Muslim demands, it would be a mistake to try 'sleeping horses' or doing anything which might lose the Muslim support. He asked Jinnah in February 1940 to put forward constructive proposals. The League conferred for four days and rejected any move to draw up a constitution based on counting on heads. It took into account the fact that the Muslims were in a minority in India, and would remain a minority. The only way to get over this status was by-pass the arithmetical process. And this could be done only by declaring the Muslims 'to be a nation' by which argument the League would claim parity with the Congress at the central level.

Federation provision of the Government of India Act, 1935 was to be scrapped and a call given to reconsider *de novo* by repudiating that Muslims was minority. It also virtually conceded the power of veto to M.A. Jinnah as the sole spokesman of the Muslims in India. The Congress leaders were put behind the bars as a result of the August Movement of 1942. At this critical time, Jinnah had a field day. Jinnah was free to project the Muslims demands day in and day out. Editors of national dailies were put behind bars and the Anglo-Indian press generally gave Jinnah the highest publicity. Recognizing that he did not have the support of the Muslim majority provinces, he kept his statement in regard to future policies vague and imprecise. Dr. Mohammad Iqbal, whose name has been associated with the concept of Pakistan, had observed that only possible solution of the future Muslim majority provinces was to have a bold social and economic programme for the amelioration of the lot of poor Muslim masses based on the law of Islam.

Although the Lahore resolution[3] of 1940 demanding Pakistan and the growing effectiveness of Jinnah's campaign brought new strength to the Muslim League, it still tried some way to go to achieve real political effectiveness. The Muslim League received a major and unexpected Bonus in 1942. Sir Stafford Cripps in his draft declaration which spilled the British cabinet's decision of his mission announced that after the war any province could stay out of the proposed independent Indian Union and form its own Government. This meant that if the Muslim League could persuade the government or voters of the seven provinces, which could set up Pakistan. Nobody thought they could do it but this was a major concession and came as a surprise. Jinnah could claim to wavering Muslims that the principle having been conceded, he was home and dry as far as the British were concerned. The opt-out clauses in the Cripps Declaration pleased British Prime Minister Churchill because he wanted both to upset the Congress and to encourage the loyalty to Britain of Muslim soldiers. Both Viceroy Linlithgow and Sir Archibald Wavell, the Commander-in-Chief in India, had said they were uneasy about the opt-out provisions. They warned of the danger of encouraging communalism and separatism.[4]

Within four years Jinnah had established him. In 1940 he had been the leader of the League that had failed to win a substantial share of the Muslim vote and had just adopted the apparently chimerical and impracticable policy opposed both by the British and the Congress of a separate Muslim state of Pakistan. By 1944 his Pakistan policy was winning him mass support among Muslims and had been conceded in principle by British. His star seemed to be rising. What the leaders of the Congress, formerly determined to make him look insignificant one, now themselves looked out of sight.

Jinnah's assertion of his own primacy paid-off equally with the British. Linlithgow turned to him as the all India leader of the Muslims, even though did not get anything like the authority over its provincial Ministerial that the Congress had exercised. Similarly Cripps turned primarily to Jinnah for a Muslim view of his draft scheme—waiting about—plainly progress towards independence in India was low on the cabinet's agenda. It was not until May 1945 that Wavell initially got permission to bring Congress and League representatives (instead of individuals chosen periodically by the Viceroy, as hitherto) onto his Executive Council.

At the Lahore session of 1940, a resolution was passed demanding partition of the country. This gave completely new turn to Indian politics. A leader, who once aspired to be in charge of his nation's affairs turned into a sectarian leader campaigning for the division of the country on religious grounds, and also it is bad to discriminate people on the grounds of religion. In 1942, when Cripps came to negotiate a settlement with the Indian leaders, Jinnah could sense that his demand for Pakistan was within his reach. With the Pakistan resolution Jinnah brought changes in the Punjab and Bengal ministries.

A golden map of India with a couple of Muslim green splashes and the word 'our demand' set above the fireplace in Mohammad Ali Jinnah's study room in a White House on the Aurangzeb Road. Within days, the words would read 'our realization', the splashes marked East and West Pakistan, chunks of land on either side of independent India which Jinnah had fought hard for. There was a sort of partition obsession in Delhi from May 1947. It covered everything, from the most efficient army to typewriter ribbons. There were special committee's glaring every aspect of the split. Since July thousands of Muslims working in Delhi's imperial red sandstone secretariat had been involved to the West. Sixteen chartered train covered 900 miles to Karachi.[5]

Basically secular in outlook, Jinnah did not wish to get involved in traditional remedies and advices his followers also not to advocate such idea from the public platform because he knew that any appeal for economic programme might deprive him of support from the vested or business interests. In 1944, the Ali hordes offered to support Jinnah provided he gave assurances that the state of Pakistan would be based on Islamic principles. Jinnah turned down their offer. He could give no such assurance. It suited him to keep his position as vague and imprecise. This suited the Viceroy, whose sole interest was the war effort.

Wavell and Step towards Pakistan

Lord Linlithgow was succeeded by Lord Wavell and Wavell assumed the charge of the office of the Viceroy on October 20, 1943. Though a military man, Wavell was determined to change the face of India. He wanted to bring an improvement in the political situation. Wavell felt that it was not possible to keep India in bondage for more time. So he sent a top secret document to the India Office, London on February 7, 1947. It was marked 'breakdown plan'. He made it clear in this plan that Britain would be able to exercise control over India for longer and on administrative grounds. We could not govern the whole of India for more than a year and a half from now. The Cabinet Mission Plan of 1946 had accepted this plan. The Second World War ended in 1945. In the general elections of 1945 in Britain, the Labour Party won the election and a Labour Government was formed in 1945.

To Jinnah and the Muslim League, it appeared that the British and the Congress were stepping back into the belief that they could together settle the future of India without concessions to the Muslims. August 16, 1946 was, therefore, fixed by the League as "Direct Action Day". In most parts of India it passed off without violence but in Calcutta started the uncontrollable mass slaughter, which spread across most of northern India and lasted for the next 16 months. Both the British and the Congress, Jinnah explained, had held pistols at his head—today we have forged a pistol and are in a position to use it. This day we bid goodbye to constitutional methods. In this way Jinnah set off a wave of violence to achieve Pakistan. The Prime Minister of Britain, Mr. Clement Attlee made a famous statement on February 20, 1947 announcing His Majesty is Government's definite intention to take the necessary steps peacefully to transfer power into responsible Indian hands by a date not later than June 1948.[6]

Lord Mountbatten and Creation of Pakistan

Lord Mountbatten was appointed as the Viceroy of India and he assumed the charge of the office of the Viceroy and the Governor General of India on March 24, 1947. Mountbatten had been directed to arrange the transfer of power on the basis of the Cabinet Mission plan of 1946. Mountbatten did his utmost for a united India but Jinnah was determined for the division of the country, so Mountbatten felt that it was difficult to keep India united. After the failure of the plan 'Balkan', another plan known as the Mountbatten plan was prepared. The Working Committee of the Congress, Jinnah and Baldeo Singh accepted the plan by the morning of January 3, 1947. The plan was announced by the All India Radio on June 3 at 7 p.m. the open diplomacy of Mountbatten brought partition and the independence of the country. The Viceroy had 142 interviews by this time with all the political leaders of the country.

According to Indian Independence Act of July 1947, India was to achieve freedom by August 15, 1947. Pakistan was to be established along with the freedom of the country. It was now certain that India would be vivisected and Pakistan would be formed as a separate dominion. Jinnah had succeeded in his aim. The partition of India was now an accomplished fact. But he could not achieve full-fledged Pakistan. He succeeded in getting a 'moth-eaten and truncated' Pakistan. Thanks to British collusion, Jinnah had achieved his so-called goal in less than a decade. The Indian National Congress achieved freedom after decades of three mass movements in 1920, 1930 to 1932 and 1942. The credit of Jinnah was that he was the sole leader to struggle for Pakistan. The Congress leaders had never expected that India would be free in their life-time but freedom came in their periods.

On August 7, 1947, Jinnah, the Governor General designate of Pakistan arrived at Karachi from Delhi, the silver D.C. 3 plane given him by the Viceroy for the historic flight to Karachi. As he reached the top of the steps, he turned back for the last glimpse of the city in which he had waged his relentless struggle for his Islamic state. 'I suppose Jinnah murdered', this is the lást I will be looking at Delhi. The Muslim League flag was unfurled over the 'Government House.' Before he left Delhi for Karachi, in a farewell message he said, "I wish Hindustan prosperity and peace. I bid farewell to the citizens of Delhi among whom I had many friends of all communities, and I earnestly appeal to everyone to live in this great and historical city in peace." The past must be burked, let us start a fresh as two independent, sovereign states of Hindustan and Pakistan. M.A. Jinnah, while flying from Delhi, he said to his ADC Ahsan in this way: "I never expected to see Pakistan in my lifetime. We have to be grateful to God, for what we have achieved." He entered the Government House which was now his official residence.

On 10th August, the Pakistan Constituent Assembly met in Karachi for inaugural session with Jogendra Nath Mandal being elected unanimously as its Chairman pending the election of the permanent President. He said the minorities would not only be treated ruthlessly and fairly but genuinely in Pakistan. Jinnah made a speech to the first Constituent Assembly of Pakistan on August 11, 1947. Following are excerpts from the address of Quaid-i-Azam Mohammad Ali Jinnah,

> You are free; you are free to go to your temples or to any other place of worship in this state of Pakistan. You may belong to any religion or caste or creed—that has nothing to do with the business of the state. We are starting in the days when there is no

discrimination between one community and another, no discrimination between one caste or creed and another. We are starting with this fundamental principle that we are all citizens and equal citizens of one state. The people of England in course of time had to face the realities of the situation and had to discharge the responsibilities and burdens placed upon them by the Government. Today, you might say with justice that Roman Catholics and Protestants do not exist, what exists now that every man is a citizen and equal citizen of Great Britain, as members of the nation. The above speech appeared in the Indian press 52 years ago. These views are today not publicly acknowledged by the Pakistani establishment.[7] But the question is, whether it was possible or practicable to act otherwise than what has been done. A division had to take place on both sides, in Hindustan and Pakistan, there are sections of people who may not agree with it, who may not like it, but in my judgment there was no other solution and I am sure future history will record its verdict in favour of it. And what is more it will be proved by actual experience as we go on that was the only solution. Any idea of a united India could never have worked and in my judgment, it would have led us to terrible disaster. May be that view is correct, may be it is not, that remains to be seen.

After Jinnah's death, Prime Minister Liaquat Ali Khan took over the administration of the country in his hand. The administrative machinery was weaker even in Jinnah's period. Liaquat decided to continue secular democracy, which Jinnah liked to establish. But destiny did not like this and in October 1951 he was assassinated in Rawalpindi. Since then Pakistan has launched from disaster, until in 1958 the Commander-in-Chief, General Ayub Khan led a coup and attempt to establish secular democracy was foiled. The experiment of democracy failed and the Army rule started. Democracy was subverted for the fourth time on October 12, 1999 and Parvez Musharaff was the ruler of the country. Again for the fifth time when Mrs. Benazeer Bhutto tried to take the command of the country in her own hand was brutally killed in a bomb blast and subsequently her husband Mr. Asif Ali Zardari took over the command as the ruler of the country.

This speech indicated that communal Jinnah was died and secular Jinnah was born on August 11, 1947. Pakistan was created as a separate dominion under the British Commonwealth. Had Jinnah remained alive for few years more, Pakistan would have functioned as a secular and democratic country. Jinnah's speech was a challenge to the two-nation theory. Jinnah's close friends and advisers were against this speech. Mr. Douglass, a Deputy Principal Information Officer of the Government of India, who had gone to Karachi as the Publicity Chief and others decided that this portion of the speech to the Constituent Assembly be blacked out. It was a tragedy that censorship was considered on the first day of Pakistan. The editor of *Dawn* protested and threatened to go to the Quaid-i-Azam. It is well known that this portion of Jinnah's speech was not published by most of the newspapers in Pakistan. It was mentioned later by Mr. Justice Munir in one of the judgments.[8]

Jinnah followed the policy under which there was no discrimination between Hindu and Muslim. His Parsi friend Jamshed Nassarwanjee, who had seen Jinnah in tears at the all parties' conference in Calcutta in 1928, reported that Jinnah was again in tears in 1948. Jinnah went in January 1948 to see an encampment of Hindus along with Jamshed when he saw the misery of Hindus. At this Jinnah had tears on his cheeks. Jinnah had been to Sind and there the people called him 'Maulana'. Jinnah stopped and said to the people that they need not address him as Maulana. He was not their religious leader but a political leader. They should call him Mr. Jinnah and not Maulana Jinnah.

A film on Jinnah was released in Islamabad on June 2000. The producer of the film is Akloor Ahmad who is now Pakistan's High Commissioner in Britain. The Pakistani citizen well assess Jinnah, the founder of Pakistan, I believe that Jinnah wanted a liberal Muslim state and not a conservative state in Pakistan. I hold this opinion that Jinnah had a vision of a liberal democratic country.

End of Jinnah

Jinnah did his best to cope with the effects of the massacres and migrations. He was basing himself in Karachi. His sister, Fatima was with him. He was keeping a very indifferent health. He was losing his appetite. Practically he was living in a state of sleeplessness. By 1948, he became very weak.[9] He was suffering from bronchitis but still he consumed endless packet of Craven A cigarettes. Everybody knew that he was in a poor state of health. Even the press reported about his shattered health. In the autumn of 1948, Jinnah was under rest in Baluchistan. His bronchial condition worsened on September 11, Fatima seeing the critical stage of his health decided that the Governor General should be back to Karachi. The Governor General and Fatima were accompanied by several oxygen cylinders and a terrified entourage. They had a long flight followed by a journey in an Army ambulance. They reached the city in the same night. The seventy-one year Jinnah died a few hour later.[10] Along with his death, secular democracy also died. It was greatest misfortune for the two nations. After Jinnah's death secular democracy weakened and in course of time Dictatorship was established. The army took over the administration of the country in their hands and for the fourth time in October 12, 1999, General Musharaff toppled the civilian Government of Sharif and proclaimed him the chief executive of the country. The Constitution has been suspended in Pakistan; the first coup took place by General Ayub Khan in 1958.

Jinnah's Political Achievement

Patrick French write in his book *Liberty or Death* about Jinnah, his political achievement had been colossal and more remarkable in several respects than that of his opponents in Congress. Jinnah's achievement was the creation of Pakistan. The Pakistan movement started from 1940 and a separate nation like Pakistan was established in 1947. But full credit for the formation of Pakistan should not go to Jinnah only. The British Government contributed a lot to the creation of Pakistan, as I have narrated in several chapters. The policy of 'Divide and Rule' started from the Simla deputation of October 1, 1906. I have discussed in detail how the British Government helped Jinnah to divide the country. The policy of 'Divide and Rule' should be analyzed clearly. French rejects the policy of divide and rule and suggests that Britain had no hand in deliberately keeping communities divided. Anthony Read and David Fisher in his book *The Proudest Day* also dismiss the divide and rule policy as 'pure myth'. But I do not agree with the views of French and Read in this context, the policy of 'Divide and Rule' helped the British Government to weaken the nationalist movement and also in the consolidation of the Muslim League. There are enough references in my writings to convince the readers that the British Government helped Jinnah to succeed in his aim.

Judged in this background Jinnah's achievement was not colossal but it was certainly an achievement for Jinnah that he succeeded in creating a 'moth-eaten and truncated' Pakistan in his life time. As regards Congress leaders had to fight on two fronts first the British Government; and the second, the Muslim League. The Congress leaders had struggled for emancipation of the country from 1920 to 1947. Even a leader like Pandit Jawaharlal Nehru had been assaulted by the police. The Congress leaders spent the best period of their lives in jail. Nehru's mother Swarup Rani and the wife Kamala Nehru were also assaulted. Nehru remained in jail for nearly nine years. Gandhi's wife Kasturba Gandhi died in jail (the Aga Khan Palace) in Poona on February 22, 1944 at 7 p.m. while Maulana Abul Kalam Azad was in jail at the Ahmadnagar Fort from 1942; he lost his wife and sister. So the Congress leaders had suffered much for the cause of the country, but Jinnah was an arm chair politician and he did not go to the jail even for a day for the attainment of even the truncated Pakistan. Then how Jinnah's achievement was colossal? The Congress resisted till the end against the division of India. But circumstances were beyond their control. The communal riots which started from August 16, 1946 as a result of the Direct Action Day enunciated by Jinnah, took a very serious shape and the Interim Government was not in a position to control it. Viceroy Wavell could not control the situation. The administration had broken down. Finding no other alternative they decided to accept Pakistan in order to save the remaining parts of India. So it cannot be accepted that the achievement of the Congress leaders was insignificant. Hence, Patrick French's argument could not be accepted valid in both parts.

When Pakistan came into being in 1947, the country was foisted with a leadership that had no roots in its soil. Jinnah was originally a Gujarati and Prime Minister Liaquat Ali Khan hailed from Karnal and his wife was a Christian from U.P. The Muslim League had no firm base or a grassroots organizational structure in any of the four provinces in West Pakistan—Sind, Punjab, Baluchistan and the N.W.F.P. Further, rather than abiding by the 1940 resolution, which promised two 'autonomous and sovereign' states.

In the end a 'mutilated and truncated' Pakistan was created on August 14, 1947. Stanley Wolpert in his book *Jinnah of Pakistan*[11] has quoted from Kanji Dwarkadas who held this opinion that if Congress leaders could have been friendly with Jinnah and his ego had not been hurt; Jinnah might not have partitioned the country. That Jinnah's ego was hurt and Gandhi and Nehru underestimated as Wolpert has remarked. But it is a fact that Gandhi and Jinnah would not have pulled together.[12] Basically Gandhi had no faith in the law of the country. Gandhi was determined to destroy the law for the freedom of the country. He started three movements in the country from 1920 to 1942. The non-cooperation movement of 1920, the civil disobedience movement of 1930, which continued till 1932 and the August movement of 1942 were carried on outside the framework of the law, which was prevalent in the country. Jinnah was basically a constitutionalist. He resigned from the Congress because Gandhi decided to start a movement in 1920 by breaking the law. Jinnah argued and said that Gandhi should not break the law, but Gandhi did not agree. So Jinnah ceased to be a member of Congress. Only once in his political career, he broke the law on August 16, 1946 and stated the 'Direct Action Day'. Jinnah was ambitious. Jinnah had a desire to capture the Congress organization after 1915. It was a peculiar time, nearby all founder leaders of the Congress had died by 1915. Some of them had become blind and some of them had become physically invalid. So Bal Gangadhar Tilak, Annie Besant, Madan Mohan Malviya and M.A. Jinnah were in the race to be the supreme leader of the Indian Congress. Mohandas Karamchand Gandhi who had returned from South Africa in January 1915 had not made a mark in the Congress. But Gandhi proved a better tactician and organizer than these leaders. Even Jinnah could not stand before Gandhi and Gandhi pushed them to wall. Gandhi became the sole leader of the Congress in 1920 and he continued as the unchallenged leader till 1947. Subhas Chandra Bose had challenged Gandhi in 1938 and ultimately Gandhi emerged victorious. Jinnah was not happy at these developments. So Gandhi and Jinnah could not have pulled together. Parting of ways was unavoidable. Jinnah by his nature could not have taken a second place in the Congress organization. Jinnah considered himself senior to Gandhi in the Congress. Jinnah had taken the membership of the Congress in 1906. Gandhi was in South Africa from 1893 to 1914. While he was in South Africa, he attended few session of the Congress. Jinnah was opposed to mass politics which Gandhi ushered in 1920.

Congress leader had different views when Jinnah regarding the political setup of the country. Before the demand of Pakistan at the Lahore session in March 1940, Jinnah was asking for a loose confederation with the centre having limited powers and the residue powers resting with the states. On the other hand, the whole thrust of the nationalist politics of the Congress was in the direction of a strong centre. Jinnah could not have gone along with the Congress leaders on the issue of functioning and the concept of a strong centre.

But was Jinnah happy with the achievement of Pakistan? Jinnah was to boast that he won Pakistan with the help of his typewriter. But it was only for dramatic effect. One aspect of Jinnah's political life has to be understood before this chapter is closed. The Calcutta killings proved how tenuous, Governmental power was once any community resorted to organized violence as a matter of policy. Gandhi went to Noakhali and camped in Calcutta, when the whole nation was celebrating the Indian independence on August 15th, Gandhi was fasting in Calcutta. Nehru threatened to bombard Patna, if the riots did not stop. But Jinnah did practically nothing to protest against the mindless violence, when he signed the peace appeal with Gandhi he did so with reluctance. Wolpert is silent on this aspect of Jinnah's political carrier. But the question is, was Jinnah happy with the achievement of truncated Pakistan? Subsequent events proved it was not so. At the height of glory, he was lonely, a disillusioned and physically ruined man. He was on the point of death. Wolpert has written that when the Nizam's embassy Liaquat Ali met Jinnah, the Pakistani leader was in tears and he was painfully aware of the plight of the refugees. Jinnah knew this fact that he was painfully aware of the plight of refugees. Jinnah knew this fact that he was under the shadow of the death and might have felt worried at the poor calibre of the Pakistani leadership. Jinnah himself thought his Prime Minister Liaquat Ali was a mediocre. He also had no faith in him. Hence, when Liaquat Ali went to see him, he was on his deathbed. Jinnah thought that Liaquat Ali had done so only to know the seriousness of the illness and whether he would die or not.

In the early life, Jinnah had come under the spell of liberal leaders but he threw aside liberal ideals when Pakistan was formed and combined the powers of the Governor General and the Prime Minister. When Pakistan was born, he was an autocrat and cast his state in the same mould. Parliamentary democracy could take root in Pakistan as Jinnah himself sowed the seeds of autocracy.

Jinnah's misfortune was that, on the one hand, he was considered a Muslim leader by Mahatma Gandhi and on the other was heckled by the Muslians at a League conference. When Gandhi was assassinated, Jinnah's reaction was that a great Hindu leader had died. But after a while, when he met an American banker, he was much more generous and said that Gandhi's death was a great loss to Muslims. Jinnah chalked out his strategy reliantly and pursued it relentlessly. The circumstances also favoured him but at the end of the day he was to be consented with what he had not called a motheaten Pakistan and by strange coincidence, he himself was devoured by a terminal disease in September 1948 at Karachi.

While reviewing *Genesis of Pakistan* by V. Nagarkar, Inder Malhotra remarked on February 15, 1976 in the *Times of India*, New Delhi that the partition of the subcontinent into India and Pakistan could have averted if only someone had the good sense to do some little thing or to avoid doing it. India's march towards freedom and as it happened towards partition was a complicated affair.

The Pakistani authors hold different opinion about Jinnah's contribution. About Jinnah, Pirzada says that he was not the creator of the forces but the obvious leader who guided rather than endangered the movement for Pakistan. Aziz Ahmad also projects Jinnah as a clear headed lawyer who could formulate and articulate in precise terms what he really wanted. Salim M.M. Quereshi assassins Jinnah's role in the situation aspect of the meteoric rise in popularity since 1937, while after 1940 he developed a distinct identity of his own. K.B. Sayeed says that Jinnah had two personalities, one in the twenties and early thirties which looked for compromise and safeguards and who had undergone emotions trauma of life; and two, in the late thirties and forties when he changed his personality and negotiated from the position considered considerable strength which was based on the political power that he had accumulated since 1937.

In the second phase stage of study, Shariful Mujahid extols the role of Jinnah who appears at the critical junction of history to give vent to the long passion force separate and distinct religio-political existence of the Muslims. He says that as late as in June 1946, the alternative path of united India seemed to be probable but it was Jinnah who averted this. K.B. Sayeed avers that Jinnah showed extraordinary courage to coordinate the rural and the urban forces and made the Unionist Party of Punjab to accept the League's libel to enhance his prestige. His objective was to win a crushing victory for the League in the heart land of Pakistan to concretize the claim of Pakistan. Hamza Alavi reveals that Jinnah's political genius laid perusals in his ability to orchestrate a loose, volatile and unpredictable coalition of forces. He is generally pictured as a man with a firm grip over the group that he was landing. But that was a myth made possible by his powerful personality. His hold over the various groups was quite tenuous and he had to take them on their own terms. Ayesha Jalal maintains that Jinnah's career in the 1920 shows that at every step he had to band policies as he possessed no solid political base. Jinnah's effectiveness depended upon his ability to act as a power-broker between the Muslim interest in the provinces and safeguards against his rival Congress politicians at the centre. After 1937, Jinnah had a different stature and since 1940 he became his sole spokesman of the Muslim community. His political strategy was to win safeguards at the centre for the Muslims in the minority provinces assuring other communities the same status in the Muslim majority provinces. But Jalal says that Jinnah's two-nation theory was a sword which cut his Pakistan down to size. The two men casualties were Jinnah's hopes of bringing all the Muslim within the Indian Union and the portion of Punjab and Bengal. She defends Jinnah by suggesting that he tried to remain above communal considerations all through his political career. It was only in the end that he had to play the communal card of 'Direct Action' which he was quite reluctant to use.

As far as the Pakistan movement is concerned, authors like I.H. Qureshi, Hafez Malik, S.M. Aziz, Aziz Ahmad, Pirzada, etc., all unanimously that the Pakistan movement was a result of religious nationalism, the folly of Congress Party and the leadership of Jinnah which resulted in the Muslim claim for a separate nation.

Finally, when the heat and dust of the partition trauma have settled down the heroes have receded from the centre stage of politics to the pages of history. Blood and tears shed at length have dried up; a cool dispassionate analysis would conclude not the partition was the product of the propertied claves, studiously cultivated, to begin with, by the feudal processional and colonial interest. It was left to the Muslim Saltnat to lead it to its successful conclusion under the leadership of Jinnah and his politics since 1937-47. Jinnah was an astute Barrister, who dressed like a British aristocrat—three piece suit, tie and manacle. Jinnah was far from a deviate Muslim. In fact he used Islamic a bait to attract the Muslim Ulemah. Liaquat Ali, who became Prime Minister of Pakistan, was assassinated for being a U.P. Mujahid.

Pakistan was no achievement for Muslims. It marked their retreat into a narrow shell of their own. Chaudhary Khaliq-uz-Zaman admitted in his memoirs that the two-nation theory 'never paid any dividend to us' and that it proved positively injurious to the Muslims of India, and on a long term based for Muslims everywhere adding "that but erstwhile comrades-in-arms in Muslim majority areas in the fight for Pakistan" were to busy thinking of their own future in the new state. Evidently, they had never serious thought to the fate of Muslims who were going to be left in India.

The trauma strengthened Nehru's opponents in the Congress. He fought back valiantly and with considerable success, but without compromise, though "All of us" held that it seems to be getting infested with the RSS mentality. This is a curious finale to our careers. If the present Hindu outlook does not change radically, I am quite sure that India is doomed. The Muslim outlook may be and I think is often worse. But it does not make very much difference to the future of India.

Jinnah was exhausted by the trip. He seemed barely able to lift himself from the seat, when the DL3 rolled to stop. One of his aides offered him his arm to guide him out of the aircraft. Jinnah spurned it. The Quaid-i-Azam was not coming home to Karachi on the arms of the other man. With another effort of his indomitable will, Jinnah stiffly erect walked slowly down the steps and through the sticking almost hysterical mob to his waiting car. A large number of people had come to receive the 'father' of Pakistan. He walked slowly on the steps of Government House, which was now the official residence of Pakistan's first Governor General. Pausing at the top of the stairs to catch the breath, he turned and looked at his new aide. His eyes seemed to glow and for just an instant something vaguely, like a smile passed across his face. "Do you know, he whispered hoarsely to Syed Ahsan," I never expected to see Pakistan in my lifetime."[13]

Conclusion

A book has been published on Fatima Jinnah by Surayya. The name of the book is *Fatima, Jinnah Ke Shab-o-Roz*, 1978. Surayya Khurshid had interviewed Miss Fatima Jinnah. Fatima told many things about Pakistan and her statement shows she was not happy with the political situation of Pakistan. She says, "A dog is more faithful than man. At least it does not forget its benefactor. Pakistanis have forgotten their benefactor, who gave them this country. They are doing things for which this country was not meant."

"In Bombay, we always had pai (trotters) in the morning. This was the Quaid's favourite breakfast."

"Quaid was seriously ill in those days. There was the burden of (communal) riots and the problems facing the new country on him."

"Right or wrong, this (Pakistan) was our choice but the spirit with which we created could not be carried forward in the direction we had wanted. I am glad the Quaid-i-Azam did not live to see all this." Jinnah's daughter, Mrs. Dina Wadia lives in the U.S.A. told a channel for documentary film that Jinnah never really wanted Pakistan.[14] The reference is available in the National Archives of Pakistan.

NOTES

1. *Freedom at Midnight*, p. 101.
2. An extract from *End of Empire* by Brian Lapping.
3. An extract from *End of Empire* by Brian Lapping, published in the *Times of India*, June 30, 1985.
4. *Ibid.*
5. Campbell's article, The *Asian Age*, August 9, 1947.
6. Mansergah and Moon, *Transfer of Power*, Vol. X, p. 670.
7. The *Times of India*, August 1997.
8. Jinnah's Secularism- II, by Madan Gopal, *Times of India*, July 30, 1994.
9. French, Patrick, *Liberty or Death*, p. 364.
10. *Ibid.*
11. Stanley, Wolpert, 'Jinnah of Pakistan', the *Times of India*, September 17, 1984.
12. *Ibid.*
13. *Collins and Lapierre*, p. 227.
14. *The Asian Age*, August 9, 1997.

16

BBC Documentary on Jinnah

A British Broadcasting Corporation documentary on Pakistan's leader Mohammad Ali Jinnah has been accused of distorting facts to justify the two-nation theory. Made by the London based Pakistani scholar Akbar S. Ahmad, the two-hour long documentary Jinnah 'the making of Pakistan' came under attack from scholars on Monday evening at University of Mumbai's convocation hall, where it was shown to a select gathering on May 6, 1998, the show was organized by the Ambedkar Centre for Justice and Peace, Canada.

Dr. Rafiq Zakaria, who was interviewed for the film in 1947, accused the documentary makers of taking his views out of context to appease the advocates of Partition. I am shocked. They interviewed me for nearly two hours. My views on Jinnah's role in the creation of Pakistan have been twisted. Based on the interviews with Jinnah's daughter Dina Wadia, Iqbal's son Javed Iqbal, writers Khuswant Singh and Mulk Raj Anand and many others who were witnesses to the events leading to partition, the film attempts to portray the founder of Pakistan as a great statesman and a saviour of millions of Muslims in the subcontinent. Dr. Zakaria said that Pakistan was created on hostility and Jinnah did an unforgivable disservice to Indian Muslims. Ten million people were killed at the time of partition. It orphaned Muslims and Jinnah was to a great extent responsible for one of the major blunders in history, he said adding, it would have been better had we gone for a civil war than this dismembering of India. The repercussions can be seen even today.

Shot in India and Pakistan, the film encompasses major events of the freedom struggle such as Mahatma Gandhi's arrival from South Africa and the momentum he gave to the Indian National Congress, the role of Sir Syed Ahmad Khan and his Aligarh movement in creation of a separate Muslim nation and the Allahabad Conference of May 1946 which was the last attempt to make Jinnah change his mind on partition. Jinnah has been shown as a liberal, who enjoyed music, smoked cigars and played billiards. As the film progresses, the man whom Sarojini Naidu called an 'Ambassador of Hindu-Muslim unity' becomes Quaid-i-Azam. Social reformer Asghar Ali Engineer, who also participated in the discussion which followed after the screening of the film, said that creation of Pakistan negated the secular ethos which was evident in music, culture and language.[1]

A discussion on Jinnah had been arranged in Bombay on May 8, 1996. The discussion had been initiated by Prof. V.N. Datta (Retd. Professor of Kurukshetra University), he raised the eternal question was Jinnah's demand for Pakistan based on his inner conviction or was it the consequence of political compulsions and lack of personal equation with Gandhi and Nehru? As expected there was no unanimity. A 90-minute documentary on Jinnah which was recently in London suggests that Jinnah was more ambivalent about the creation of the Muslim nation than has previously been recognized.

"Mr. Boy, you are an Indian first and then a Muslim" said M.A. Jinnah in 1925, while admonishing the Raja of Mahmudabad, who had been claimed that he was a "Muslim First". It was the same Jinnah who sought to give pre-eminence to the Muslim identity at the residence of the Raja of Mahmudabad, twelve years later, when he persuaded himself that this could be promoted by shedding his Seville Row suits and by doming a Sherwani dark and Persian lamb cap. Jinnah had then sought to give himself this new identity after the Muslim League could secure only 109 out of the 482 seats reserved for the Muslims in the election to the provincial Assemblies held earlier that year.[2]

What Jinnah found particularly in 1937 was that his claim was the exclusive voice of the Muslims of the subcontinent had been rejected throughout the country. What constituted a particular setback for him was the triumph of Congress Party, which had advocated a similar platform in the Muslim majority North-West Frontier Province—the same Congress Party, at whose hands, Jinnah claimed, the Musalmans could not expect any justice or fair play.

The quest for separate identity for the Muslims of the subcontinent which rejected in 1925 and championed in 1937 inversely led to the demand for a separate state for the Muslims. This found expression in the famous Lahore Resolution of 1940. This was a resolution, passed by leaders largely drawn not from the Muslim-majority provinces, but from the Muslim-minority provinces. Punjab was then ruled by Sir Sikander Hayat Khan and the Unionist Party, who had routed the Muslim League in the 1937. Provincial assembly election and who framed the whole thought of partition not only unthinkable but also ludicrous.

When Pakistan was created on August 14, 1947, the country was foisted with a leadership that had no roots in its soil. Jinnah was a Gujarati and Prime Minister Liaquat Ali Khan hailed from Karnal and his wife was a Christian from U.P. The Muslim League had no firm base or grassroot, organizational structure in any of the four provinces of West Pakistan—Sind, Punjab, Baluchistan and the N.W.F.P.

Interestingly, in his last days Jinnah appeared to be in favour of converting the Muslim League into a secular Party and remaining it as the 'Pakistan National League'. My advice to Muslim brother in India is to give inflicting loyalty to the state in which they happen to be, he said by advocating a secular state for Pakistan and urging the Indian Muslims to their faith in their welfare and progress in a secular India, Jinnah in effect repudiated all that he had earlier said about the need for a separate state for the Muslims, if their separate identity was to be preserved and their rights guaranteed.[3]

Of all those who shaped India's destiny half a century ago, Mohammad Ali Jinnah remains the most elusive. A chain-smoker, gaunt, then lipped and slightly sinister in appearance, he managed to create a new nation by perseverance and political cunning. He made religion the bases for nationhood. He won nationhood for Indian Muslims just seven years after he had first publicly espoused that aim. It was one of the most astonishing achievements in modern history. Jinnah may have complained about being given a 'moth-eaten' Pakistan but it was at the time of its creation in 1947 the biggest independent Islamic nation in the world.

Jinnah was bundle of contradictions. He advocated making Urdu the official language of Pakistan (to the funny of Bengali speakers), even though he was not comfortable speaking in it. Even though he went to Karachi as Pakistan's Governor General, he never gave up the hope—according to Nusli Wadia, Jinnah's only grandson that he might return to the mansion he had built for himself in Bombay Malabar hill.

During the period of Second World War, columnist Kuldip Nayyer had a chance to see Jinnah at close quarters, when the Quaid-i-Azam came to talk to law students in Lahore. There was a Tea Party. And Kuldip Nayyer asked him a question, suppose Pakistan is a reality and India was attacked by some other power, what would the attitude of Pakistan be? Jinnah said young man, "Blood is thicker than water, and we shall stand for you." Had this friendly mental attitude would have continued in Pakistan after Jinnah's sad demise, India and Pakistan would remained as friends and would have prospered much. Pakistan's rulers should take a lesson from Jinnah—the Father of the Nation of Pakistan.[4]

Jinnah's Political Thought from 1947

Even after the formation of Pakistan the Congress leaders including Mahatma Gandhi, subscribed to the ideals of common Indian nationhood and a composite culture as a matter of basic principle, which they were not prepared to forsake even after the partition. It is significant that after the creation of Pakistan, the founding Father of Pakistan, M.A. Jinnah did not envision a theocratic society. Jinnah, the Quaid-i-Azam of Pakistan, echoed the sentiments of Indian secularism in his speech on August 11, 1947 in the Constituent Assembly of Pakistan. To quote a few excerpts from that historic speech, in which the Quaid-i-Azam said. If you change your past and work together in a spirit that everyone of you no matter to what community he belongs, no matter what relations he had with you in the past, no matter what is his colour, caste or creed, is first, second and last a citizen of this state with equal rights, privileges and obligations, there will the no end to the progress you will make. I cannot emphasize it too much, we should begin to work in that spirit and in course of time all these irregularities of the majority and minority communities, the Hindu community and the Muslim community—because even as regards to Muslims you have Pathan, Punjabis, Shias, Sunnis and so on and among the Hindus you have Brahmins, Vaishnavas, Khatris, the Bengalis, Madrasis and so on will vanish. Indeed, if you ask me this has been the biggest hindrance in the way of India to attain freedom and independence and but for this we would have been free peoples long ago. No power can hold another nation, did especially a nation of 100 millions souls in subjection, nobody could have continued hold it on you for any length of time but for this.

Jinnah's dream of a secular civil society, which might seem to be conceptuality self-contradictory, was eclipsed in Pakistan by the thematic concept of Islamic state. It is noteworthy that the emergence of Bangladesh and the end of East Pakistan in 1971 was a remainder of the inadequacy of the religious tie by itself although Bangladesh too became an Islamic state, when it abandoned its original constitution. In the words of L.M. Singh, the former High Commissioner for India in U.K.; the words of Quaid-i-Azam, however, continue to ring in what remains of Pakistan and in the lonely and desolate corridors of History.[5]

I conclude that Jinnah gained a nation without damaging the crease of the trousers, like some Lord of England.[6] Before the birth of Pakistan, Jinnah paid lip-services to the idiom and etiquette of religion-based politics. The Quaid-i-Azam gave up pork, eschewed wine, discarded his Seville Row suits, took to Sherwanis and lent his name to the fore cap. Perhaps he even read the Namaz and observes the Roza.

Jinnah's Blunder

On the basis of report published in the *Frontier Mail*, Peshawar, the *Muslim India*, New Delhi, edited by Syed Shahabuddin, I.F.S. has quoted Col. Elahi Baksh, who had attended on Jinnah during his last illness, as having made the revelation that Jinnah considered the creation of Pakistan to be the biggest blunder and wanted to go to Delhi and tell Nehru to forget the foulness of the past and become friends again.

He revealed, one day we learnt that Prime Minister Liaquat Ali Khan was coming to visit the Quaid-i-Azam (during his last fatal illness Mr. Jinnah had gone to Ziarat near Quetta). The next day the P.M. arrived and he greeted the Quaid to which the Quaid made no reply. Now face to face he (Liaquat Ali Khan) asked how the Quaid was. The Quaid blew up and said, you have started thinking of yourself as a big man. You are nothing. I have made you Prime Minister of Pakistan. I have made it. But I am now convinced that I have committed the biggest blunder of my life. If now I am I get the opportunity I will go to Delhi and tell Jawaharlal to forget the follies of the past and becomes friend again. At that point the Quaid lifted his hand as if in a handshake and was shivering with emotion. Elahi Baksh said to Liaquat Ali Khan that the excitement was not good for the patient. Liaquat Ali came out of the room and remarked, "the old man has now discovered his blunder".

Ratification of Mountbatten Plan

The Congress Working Committee had agreed to the Mountbatten Plan and it had been conveyed to the Viceroy early morning on June 3, 1947, in the form of a letter from the Congress President, J.B. Kriplani, socialist leader Jay Prakash Narayan, Ram Manohar Lohia and Achyut Patwardhan were special invitees to the meeting of the CWC. The Congress Working Committee had accepted this plan. Now this resolution was too ratified by the All India Congress Committee. The AICC met on June 14, 1947 with Acharya Kriplani in the chair. The Indian National Congress, which had always fought for the unity and independence of India, was now considering an official resolution for the division of the country. Pandit Govind Ballabh Pant moved the resolution. He said that the acceptance of the June 3 plan was the only way to achieve freedom and liberty for the country. The resolution was seconded by Maulana Azad and Sardar Patel.

Maulana Azad said that the decision which the Working Committee had taken was the result of a most unfortunate development. Partition was a tragedy for India and the only thing that could be said in its favour that we had done our best to avoid division but we had failed. Now there was no alternative and if we wanted freedom here and now, we must submit to the demand for dividing India. We must not, however, forget that the nation is one, and its cultural life is and will remain one, politically we had failed and were, therefore, dividing the country. We should accept our defeat but we should at the same time try to ensure that our culture was not divided. Sardar Patel argued that the resolution for division did not arise out of weakness or compulsion but it was only true solution in the existing circumstances of India. Patel delivered the keynote address. He used the analogy of a discussed body and argued that if one limb was poisoned it must be removed quickly lest the entire organism suffer inoperably. The speech was typical of the man—pointed, brutally frank, and unemotional.

Purushottam Das Tandon opposed the resolution vehemently and the ground he gave was that cultural and national life of India could not be divided. Further he said that the decision of the Working Committee was an admission of weakness and that it arouse out of a sense of despair. He concluded that accepting the one-third plans would benefit neither the Hindus nor the Muslims.

Pandit Jawaharlal Nehru intervened in the debate and said that there was no question of any surrender to the Muslim League. It was wrong to say that the Congress Working Committee had taken fright and so surrendered.

Khan Abdul Ghaffar Khan spoke a few words. He expressed his sorrow over the fact that his colleagues had the plan of partition. As a small mercy, he wanted them to find out if the proposed plebiscite on the North West Frontier would include the alternative of independence along side of the two other choices of accession to India or Pakistan.

Jay Prakash Narayan made remarks against partition in a few words only. Ram Manohar Lohia opposed the resolution persistently and seriously. He was vocal in his opposition. The socialist group certainly opposed it but the house was not with them.

After the first day's debate, there was a very strong feeling against the Working Committee's resolution. Hence, Gandhi had to intervene in deliberations. Gandhi was the unhappiest person present; he could not approve of the plan but was too unharmed to say anything. Apparently, he did not have either the heart or the courage to oppose his own portages and plunge the country into another struggle. Gandhi said that he had always opposed partition; no one could deny this fact. He felt, however, that a situation had now been created, when there was no alternative. Political realism demanded the acceptance of the Mountbatten plan and he would appeal to the members to accept the resolution moved by Pandit Pant. Further, he told that consequences of rejection would be the finding of a new set of leaders, who would not only be capable of constituting the Congress Working Committee but also assuming the charge of the Government.

Gandhi had made a moving speech. Hinting at the socialist group, he said that although he opposed the plan, he did not have the strength to take over the Party from the existing leadership and carry the burden forward on his weakened shoulders. He told the opposition to throw out the resolution if it had the strength to do it. He pleaded, if you had the strength, I would also be with you, and if I felt strong enough myself, I would alone take up the flag of revolt.[7]

After two days of debate the Mountbatten plan was put to vote and it was approved by 153 to 29 with 36 abstentions. In the second count it was 157 to 29. The socialists remained neutral in voting. Narendra Deo contended that our neutrality was not the result in decision but came from mature thinking. The most crestfallen was the small but dedicated bands of national Muslims who felt betrayed. A rare photograph portrays Nehru's anguish as he pondered the meaning of partition.

Acharya Kriplani was President of the Indian National Congress at that time. He made a most force-fed and memorable speech, in the case of which he answered the charge that the Working Committee had taken the decision out of fear. He said, I must admit the truth of this charge, but not in the sense it is made. "The fear is not for the lives lost or of the widow's wall". or the orphans cry or of the many houses burnt. The fear is that if we go on like this, retaliating and heaping indignities on each other we shall progressively reduce ourselves to a stage of capitalism and worse. In every fresh communal fight, the most brutal and degraded acts of the previous fight became a norm.

Thus wrote V.P. Menon was the plan accepted. But acceptance was one thing; its implication was a different matter altogether. Here was the task, which normally should have taken yours to accomplish, but which had to be compressed into the short space of a few weeks. It was a task before which anybody would have qualified for it was one which seems to tempt the Gods.

Nehru was an idealist and an optimist, who believed that there would be reunion later. He wrote a letter to K.P.S. Menon on April 29, 1947; I have no doubt sooner or later India will function as a united country. Perhaps, the best way to reach that stage is to go through some kind of partition. He reported this to General Carriappa as well,[8] that the Congress acceptance of Pakistan, however, unfortunate, did not amount to an acceptance of the two-nation theory on which the demand for Pakistan was based. The Congress had accepted partition as unavoidable, while keeping the hope alive. "We often have to go through the valley of shadow before we reach the sunlight mountain tops" wrote Nehru to Carriappa. It had neither accepted defeat in the battle against communalism nor scarificed its secular principles. The Communist kisan leader Keryanand Sharma warned in a speech in Narkatiaganj, Champaran, Bihar in early November 1947 that 'by raising the slogan of Hindu Raj,' the people will support the two-nation theory of Mr. Jinnah, which was still unaccepted by Gandhi and Nehru.

Nehru knew that communalism not only posed a threat to law and order but to the very secular nature of the Indian state. Muslim communalist had earlier tried to get the Congress to compromise on its secularism but only secured from the Congress an acceptance of partition, not of the two-nation theory. Hindu communalists had taken up the battle, where their Muslim counterparts left off and tried to subvert the building of a secular free India. If the Congress had succumbed to the pressure to establish a Hindu state, that would have been the complete victory for communal forces.[9]

India's march towards freedom and it happened towards partition was complicated affair. It involved an interaction between British policy, the Indian National Congress, the Muslim League and powerful personalities such as Gandhi, Nehru and Jinnah. Indeed, neither the British Government nor its chief opponent, the Congress was a monolith. Neither was free from an internal debate, occasionally better and prolonged. It is necessary to bring all these strands, at once complementary into a discussion of the subject to make it reasonably truthful. Brian Lapping has done this difficult job in his book *End of the Empire*. This well documented book is a systemic study of the partition and independence of India. Till his dying day Jawaharlal Nehru maintained that the 1937 decision was right; a non-communal nationalist Party had no need to share power with a Muslim League that was so patently without popular support.[10]

Lord Mountbatten became a legend in his own life time quite justifiably. The transfer of power in the subcontinent was the toughest assignment, Mountbatten ever handled. It was a heart breaking task so dramatically had Hindu-Muslim relations deteriorated that the country was teetering on the brink of a virtual civil war. Mountbatten had quickly to take a number of critical decisions; the most important being whether he should stick to the date fixed by the British Government for the transfer of power by June 1948 or to advance. He decided to advance it. His critical hold this and other decisions by him responsible for the communal holocaust that followed. This was an unjust view. Delay in the transfer of power would have only heightened the communal tensions already beyond control.

In Jinnah, Mountbatten found no flexibility to compare with Nehru, who had presented Jinnah as a monster of negativism, a man who could agree to nothing because it might split his followers if he did. In this he underestimated his adversary; Jinnah used negativism to achieve positive ends. Nehru tried to break this by a talk with Jinnah. Jinnah did not agree. The result was that Pakistan was born amidst slaughter.[11]

This is an unfortunate tendency to see 1947 primarily as a power of sorrow or even as a blemish on the nation's face. If partition was the most traumatic event of the twentieth century, their independence was surely the most significant turning point. The Council of All India Muslim League met in the ballroom of an Imperial Hotel in Delhi on June 10, 1947 to take decision on the Mountbatten Plan. Hardly the meeting had started; it was disputed by a Ganj of Khaksars, a militant Punjabi Muslim group, who wanted Delhi to be included in Pakistan. The member of this group rushed into the room wielding knives and overturning tables. They wanted to stab Jinnah. The Muslim League guards took the position; some were bodily doubled and thrown out. It was indeed pathetic to see some of them bleeding or dealt with severity by the police.[12]

Although Bengali merchants and the Pakistan National Movement back in Cambridge had denounced the Plan as 'the greatest betrayal' in the history of the millat, the plan was accepted by the delegates. After the meeting Nehru and Patel complained to Mountbatten about the wording of the Muslim League's resolution and objected to the consent of some of the leaders speeches. Their source, it should be noted, was an Intelligence Bureau agent who had been sent by Home Minister Patel to infiltrate the meeting. [13]

Who Conceded Pakistan?
Who Divided United India?

Though fifty-three years have passed and the partition is now a settled fact but this question torments the citizens of the Indian Republic, why India was partitioned and who were the leaders who agreed to divide the country, some name one person, some the other. But in point of fact, there is no simple and straight answer. The new generation will be interested to know and understand this knotty problem. It became evident if one goes through the pages of the freedom struggle that partition provided one drastic way out of contemporary diligences.

The Indian National Congress stood for a united India. Mountbatten did his best for maintaining the unity of India. The Congress leaders tried their best to take help from the Muslims on this point. Though the Congress was opposed to the principle of separate electorate, but still to woo the Muslims accepted the principle of separate electorate in the Lucknow Pact of 1916. The Muslim were not reconciled to the idea of one nation and resolution in the Lahore conference of the Muslim League in March 1940, which was called 'the Pakistan resolution' later on Mountbatten interviewed Jinnah seven times and asked him not to press for Pakistan. He asked Jinnah to accept the recommendation of the Cabinet Mission. Mountbatten did not like to divide the country but Jinnah was adamant and the division took place. The British Government planted the seed of partition by conceding separate electorate under the Morley-Minto's Reform Act, 1909. The communal representation which was introduced in 1909 destroyed the concept of unity of the country.

Mahatma Gandhi, who has been called the architect of the Indian freedom, was the first Congress leader to concede to the Muslims at the Ramgarh Congress session from 17 to 20 in 1940 the right of separation as in a Hindu joint family. He suggested the setting up of a Constituent Assembly based on adult franchise and proposed that the Muslim members be allowed to decide whether they wanted to live separately or as members of a joint family. Gandhi's offer was essentially a move in the political game of outbidding and outwitting the British.

Gandhi made it clear that the Congress would have no objection for the division of the country, if the Muslim League expressed its desire for the vivisection of the country. But the British Government were astute than Gandhi. The British outbid Gandhi in August 1940, when Leopold Armory through Linlithgow, placed in Jinnah's hands a Vito in advance to self-government. This was done both to tide over the period of war and checkmate the Congress. But it had the effect of fixing a pointer to the need to partition.

The year 1942 brought difference of outlook among Gandhi, Rajagopalachari and Nehru. Japan had been fighting against the British and Japanese warships appeared in the Bay of Bengal. Nehru favoured guerilla warfare. Rajagopalachari was convinced that progress in the country was impossible without agreement between the Congress and the League. He managed to get two resolutions passed by the Congress members in the Madras legislature on April 23, 1942. The first recommended to the All India Congress Committee (which was to meet in Allahabad) that Congress men should acknowledge the Muslim League's demand for Pakistan and that negotiations should immediately be started with the Muslim League for the purpose of arriving at an agreement and securing the installation of the national government to meet the present emergency. The resolution urged that to sacrifice the chances of the formation of a national government for the doubtful advantage of maintaining a controversy over the unity of India in the most unwise policy and that it had become necessary to choose the lesser evil.[14] Azad did not like the Madras resolution. Dr. Rajendra Prasad described Madras resolution No. 1 as premature, if not perverse on April 26, 1942. The AICC met in Allahabad on 29th April, 1942. It was a stormy session. The Congress was not in favour of partition of the country and it rejected this treasonable suggestion by 120 to 15 and adopted resolution on May 2, 1942 that the proposal to disintegrate India by giving liberty to any component states or territorial unit to side from the Indian Union or federation would be detrimental to the best interests of the people of the different states and provinces and the country as a whole and the Congress, therefore, cannot agree to any such proposal. This resolution emphasized the unity of India.

As a protest against this resolution Rajagopalachari resigned from the Congress on July 15, 1942. The resolution reaffirmed its faith in the united India. Nehru came next under the pressure of American President; Churchill the British Prime Minister; and dispatched Cripps to India who reached Delhi on March 23, 1942. He came with a proposal that envisaged partition as a possibility and gave political content to the veto placed in Jinnah's hand. The draft declaration stated that the right of secession from the Indian Union was a concession to the Muslim demand for Pakistan. A concession like before the actual establishment of an Indian Union was calculated to vitiate the very scheme of an Indian Union and damp the ardour of large section for the Indian Union. The Congress Working Committee rejected the proposals made by the British war cabinet with regard to India and the alteration of them by Sir Stafford Cripps. The novel principle of non-accession for a province was also a severe blow to the conception of Indian unity and an apple of discord likely to generate growing trouble in the provinces.

A resolution was drafted by Nehru in this connection. The resolution formally conceded for the first time the principle that it did not believe in keeping within the Union any race against its expressed wish. The draft towards partition, therefore, received a push when Bhulabhai Desai and Liaquat Ali Khan in March 1945 and entered into an agreement providing for equal representation to the Congress and the League in the reconstituted cabinet. But Jinnah turned down the pact. Gandhi blessed the proposal but Wavell transformed it into equality between Muslims and caste Hindus—as against equality between two political entities. Gandhi then disowned the pact, but the damage was done.

Rajagopalachari, who had resigned from the membership of the Indian National Congress on 1942, now intervened with Gandhi's blessings to resolve the deadlock by offering the matter of partition to be settled by a referendum. In essence, this gave concrete shape to Gandhi's plan vaguely enunciated at the Ramgarh session as a tactical move.

Viceroy Wavell almost succeeded in preserving the unity of India in co-operation with the Congress with his plan for a war time coalition. But his effort was frustrated at the eleventh hour when Jinnah relieved the secret offer of 'Pakistan on a platter' from his friends in Whitehall and in Delhi. I have discussed the theme of "Pakistan on a Platter" in my last chapter. Slowly the country was moving towards the division.

Jawaharlal Nehru, Sardar Patel and Rajendra Prasad next acknowledged Jinnah's two-nation theory in March 1947, by advocating in a resolution adopted by the Congress Working Committee the division of the Punjab into Muslim majority and Hindu majority areas. From March 4, 1947 communal riots had started in the Punjab and on the 5th, the Governor of the Province Jenkins took over the administration of the province. The Punjab was burning and serious rioting broke out in Lahore, Amritsar, Multan, Rawalpindi, Sialkot and Jullundur. It was against this background that the Congress Working Committee met early in March 1947. Attlee's statement of February 20, 1947 compelled the Congress Party to take a decision regarding the Punjab. There was a growing feeling within the Congress leadership that the alternative to partition was chaos. There will to preserve the unity of India was being undermined, so on March 8th the Working Committee finally acknowledged the essence of the British Government's policy dedications. It has been made clear that the constitution framed by the Constituent Assembly will apply only to those areas which accept it. However, in an effort to salvage the non-Muslim majority areas of the Punjab and Bengal, it must also be understood that any province or part of a province which accepts the constitution and desires to join the Union cannot be prevented from doing so.[15]

To remove any doubt of its intention, the Congress proposed partition of the Punjab into two provinces and invited the League to a joint conference for this purpose. Nehru, Patel and Prasad were responsible for the division of Punjab. These three leaders did not consult Gandhi, who reacted sharply and considered this to be an hour of great humiliation.[16] It can be said in perspective that the Congress had taken a very long step towards partition of the entire country. And these three months before the Mountbatten plan was formally approved by the Indian leaders. Indeed, it happened even before the new Viceroy, Mountbatten arrived in New Delhi to take over the charge of the office of the Viceroy.

Mountbatten took over the charge on March 24, 1947 and interviewed the Indian leaders. The plan for a 'united India' did not succeed. Nehru declared in a public speech on April 20, 1947 that the Muslim League could have Pakistan "on condition that they do not take away other parts of India which do not wish to join Pakistan". At this announcement Durga Das asked Nehru whether he had taken into account the effect his statement would have on Gandhi. He said Gandhi had fully supported the objection raised by Gopinath Bardoli, Congress Premier, Assam to that State's inclusion in the eastern zone envisage in the plan for the Cabinet Mission. That was the major difference. Nehru explained in the Congress and League interpretations of the plan.

The issue was clenched when Prasad, as the President of the Constituent Assembly, read out on April 28, 1947 an authoritative statement of the Congress stand, that no constitution would be forced in any part of the country that was unwilling to accept it. "This may mean the statement ended not only a division of India but a division of some provinces. For this, we must be prepared and the assembly may have to draw up a constitution based on such division." He came to this conclusion that Jinnah was determined for the partition of the country. So 'the Plan Balkan' was prepared and he informally consulted Nehru, who rejected it. Nehru accepted the Menon's Plan. As Mountbatten himself stated in the Nehru Memorial Lecture; Nehru realized that this would mean a much earlier transfer of power even though there were to two Governments and left a good chance for the essential unity of India to be maintained.

Why Nehru consented to Partition?

When Nehru had gone to attend the London Conference in 1946, Dr. Zakaria led a delegation to him and requested him to address the Majlis. Nehru was extremely busy. But he agreed to speak and spoke for more than an hour. Zakaria spoke to him of the pain and anguish that the Indian students felt at the talk of partition and their fear of its consequences. Nehru analyzed first the whole political situation to the members of the Majlis and then assured us that the Congress would never agree to any kind of partition. He stated that we would rather go on fighting for our freedom with the British for many years than submit to such a situation. The students were then satisfied. But his subsequent change to the division came as a shock to the Indian students in London. Dr. Zakaria has analyzed this question in this way : I still believe it was more the compulsion of events and the pressure of circumstances which made him succumb to it than any change in his outlook or conviction. In fact, like Gandhi, I do not think he forgave himself for having given into a scheme which instead of solving the communal problem, only aggravated it.[17]

In fact, in less than a year after India was divided, Nehru wrote to the Nawab of Bhopal in a letter dated July 9, 1948; partition came and we accepted it because we thought that way, however, painful it was, we might have some peace to work along our own lives. Perhaps we acted wrongly. It is difficult to judge now. And yet, the consequence of that partition have been so tenable that one is inclined to think that anything else would have been preferable. That partition has come and it brought in its train other vast changes. There can be no going back now to India as it was before the partition. Organic changes have taken place in India, which prevented going back.

Nevertheless, all my sense of history rebels against this unnatural state of affairs that has created in India and Pakistan. I cannot see it continuing for long as it is something that was inherently wrong and unnatural was done and it brought disastrous consequences in its train. There is no settling down to it and conflicts continue. Perhaps these conflicts are due to the folly or littleness of those in authority in India or Pakistan. I feel, however, that it is something deeper than that and not all the wisdom of statesman could end these conflicts in the present context because they are inherent in the situation ultimately. I have no doubt that India and Pakistan will come closer and it may be that there is some kind of liberal link between them or at any common subjects. There is no other way to peace. The alternative is an ever deteriorating situation and incessant conflict.[18]

Nehru ruefully admitted, we consented to partition because we thought that, thereby, we were purchasing peace and decency.[19] Nehru was a bitter opponent of the very conception of Pakistan. He used to say that the two-nation theory was fantastic nonsense. What of one Jinnah, he said when a thousand Jinnahs would not be able to take it from him. But ultimately one Jinnah received Pakistan on a plate from Nehru, having tactically forced the Congress in accepting his scheme.[20]

Even after Mountbatten's assuming the charge of the office of the Viceroy and the Governor General of India on March 24, 1947, communal riots were still continuing in the Punjab. Mountbatten's negotiations were continuing with the Indian leaders. Nehru was convinced that the partition was the only alternative to the chaotic condition of the country. The speech to the all India States people's conference in April 18, 1947, he declared, the Congress have recently on practical considerations passed a resolution accepting the division of the country, presumably referring to the Working Committee of March 8th. Later in the month he asserted; the Muslim League can have Pakistan if they want it but on the condition that they do not take away other parts of India which do not wish to join Pakistan. [21]

Another disturbing note was contributed by Gandhi who informed his prayer-meeting on 31st May; even if the whole of India burns, we shall not concede Pakistan, even if Muslims demanded it at the point of sword. But these were mere words, for power in the Congress now lay with Nehru and Patel.

Why? Nehru

After some time Nehru spoke on partition. Seven districts but closely related factors emerged from his speeches at the time. Perhaps the most compelling fear was that a tragic civil war would ravage the subcontinent unless the deadlock was broken swiftly. Along with this concern was the belief that acceptance of the League demand would ensure security for the minorities. The use of violence to maintain unity, Nehru declared, would have meant civil war and would have checked the progress of India for a long time to come. On another occasion he stated that the Congress had not surrendered to the riots but they are very much disturbed at the prevailing madness—partition is better than the murder of innocent citizens.[22] In the same spirit Patel said, 'we were promised peace if we accepted partition'.

A third reason was Nehru's conviction that, the problems before India were of such a serious nature that no delay could be tolerated. The situation in the country had deteriorated very fast and the Interim Government of 1946 had been paralyzed with the unparliamentarily tactics of the League representative. Partition seemed to him the only way to the daily conflicts within the cabinet. The League policy of obstruction reaped rich rewards.

This concern about the consequences of the existing impasse was strengthened by another source of anxiety, namely grave doubts about the implications of an artificial unity. If any (the League) are forced to stay in the Union he said, no progress and planning will be possible. To his colleagues and followers, Nehru added that it was necessary to face reality. A section of the population wanted to secede, and unity could not be achieved by compulsion nor was it in accordance with democratic procedure or desirable in terms of India's long range interests. Further he was besieged by urgent pleas from Hindus and Sikhs in the Punjab and Bengal to accept partition of these provinces in order to safeguard them against permanent discrimination and possible annihilation in a Muslim majority Pakistan. Finally, they thought that Indian freedom itself might be jeopardized or at least delayed weight heavenly in his decision. The Mountbatten Plan seemed to provide a way out of the tangled web of chaos and frustration. It seemed honourable and ineffective partition, he reiterated time and again, was the lesser of two evils.

There is striking consistency in Nehru's stated views on the motivation of his decision. Nine years after the decision the act occurred, he remarked, well, I suppose it was the compulsion of events and the feeling that we could not get out of that deadlock and worse, further, a feeling that even if we got freedom for India, with that background, it would be a very weak India, that is, a federal India with far too much power in the federating units. A larger India would have constant troubles, constant disintegrating pulls, and also the fact that we saw no other way of getting our freedom in the near future, I mean. And so we accepted and said, let us build up a strong India. And if others do not want to be in it, how can we and why should we force them to be in it.

To this array of factors which shaped Nehru's outlook on partition may be added four others, in the atmosphere of confusion, of fears and of hopes which pervaded India throughout 1947. There was a web spread belief that partition would be short lived. Most of the Congress leaders and Nehru among them, subscribed to the view that Pakistan was not a viable state—politically, economically, geographically or militarily—and that sooner or later, the areas which had seceded would be compelled by force of circumstances to return to the fold. Nor was this appraisal confined to the Congress. Most impartial deservers, sympathizers with the Pakistani cause and perhaps, some League leaders themselves were pessimistic about its future.

The hope of reuniting India was also expressed by the Congress President, Acharya J.B. Kriplani just after the Congress accepted the Mountbatten plan on June 3, 1947. He called the Party to make the Indian Republic a strong, happy, democratic and socialist state, he declared, such an India can win back the seceding children in the lap—for the freedom we have achieved cannot be complete without the unity of India! Nehru himself did not speak directly on this issue, but a Working Committee resolution, in the drafting of which he was undoubtedly involved, continued the following passage. The committee believes that the destiny of India will yet be realized and that, when passions have cooled, a new and stronger unity based on goodwill and co-operation will emerge. It is possible that this was merely a relationship for their acceptance of partition. Prof. Michael Brecher asserts that he had conversation with many Indian politicians and he came to this conclusion as the result of the conversation that this was a sincere conviction but this conviction was misguided and revealed a misreading of the forces at work within India and abroad.[23]

There was one unstated consideration in Nehru's dilemma at this time was the belief that if the Congress rejected the Mountbatten plan, the British Government would impose an award, which would have been more disadvantageous. Having rejected Gandhi's alternative of mass civil disobedience, their bargaining position was weakened. Fear of the British response to Congress intransigence helped to condition their acceptance of partition.

A positive inducement was the imminent acquisition of power after a long struggle. The alternatives were to accept advised but independent India or to follow Gandhi into the political wilderness—but the Congress leadership, declared Kriplani the Congress President, a few months after partition! Found the prospect of an immediate and peaceful transfer of power too tempting and chose the first alternative.[24]

According to history for those who have been in opposition most of their political life, the prize of power is tempting. The Congress leaders had already tested its fruits and were naturally reluctant to part with it at the moment of triumph. This applies to Nehru as well as to his colleagues, for he is not averse to the benefits it confers. But his attitude to the assumption of power in the Provincial Government in 1937 and his record in the freedom movement strongly suggests that he sought power primarily to translate his ideals into reality. Many events, the habit of power had not yet been formed, for during the period of the Interim Government (1946), his influence was severely limited by the Viceroy's presence and that of the League members.

The attitude of Nehru and his worthy colleagues to Gandhi's alternative policy was embarrassment coupled with the belief that it was unworkable in the conditions of 1947. Today also I feel that he (Gandhi) with his supreme fearlessness is correct and my stand is defective. Why then am I not with him? It is because I feel that he has as found no way of tackling the problem on a mass basis.[25] The words were of Kriplani's but the thought was shared by Nehru, Patel and most, if not all of the Congress High Command in the early summer of 1947. They had followed Mahatma in civil Disobedience movement four times since 1920. But in the greatest crisis of the nationalist movement they refused to take the plunge lest Gandhi should have miscalculated and the country be overrun by uncontrollable civil war. They chose the way of compromise in the hope that large-scale disorder could be avoided. By the end of the year of decision they had ample cause it question the wisdom of their choice, though none did to in public. It is ironic that in this situation Gandhi, the great compromiser, acted as the pure revolutionary while, Nehru, the acknowledged revolutionary in the Congress, accepted a compromise solution.

It is easy to speculate on what might have been but in terms of their often stated goal of a united India would it not have been wiser for Nehru and his colleagues to reject the Mountbatten plan which, in any case, was on the verse of collapse. By so doing they would probably have won independence—and unity. Having waiting for thirty years, should they have not waited a little longer, as Gandhi suggested. Perhaps they did not because they had been totally demoralized by the events of 1942 and post-1942 events.

Partition Days (June to August 1947)

Some people say that the carnage of partition could have been avoided if the date of transfer of power had not been advanced from June 1948 to August 15, 1947. Those who have lived through those crucial months vividly recollect that riots had started in Punjab three months before, and not after June 3, 1947, the date on which the plan for the partition (superseding the Cabinet Mission Plan for the United India) and the advancement of the date of transfer of power had been announced. The disturbances started on March 4, and spread within days to other parts of the province.

Once the partition had been agreed to, there was none left with any authority for the governance of the entire country for any length of time. At the centre, the interim government which had been functioning from September 2, 1946 was tottering one of the many examples is Liaquat Ali's budget, which was presented in February 1947, without consulting his colleagues in the Government. It was becoming increasingly impractical for the Congress and the Muslim League to govern jointly. By then the British had neither the moral authority nor the required machinery to undertake administrative tasks. Both the bureaucracy and army which any government needed for governance were divided into as many as three segments; pro-Congress Indians, pro-League Indians (who later on became Pakistanis) and the British. The first two elements as Sardar Patel stated in his well-known statement stood bitterly opposed to one another from the secretary down to the peon; the third, viz. the British were badly demoralized. In such a volatile situation, how a country of 450 million could be kept under control for as many as 12 months until June 1948. The number of killings, spread over a longer period, would surely have risen. A shorter period actually provided a better opportunity for an orderly transfer. If the Muslim League, instead of adopting a triumphant air over the achievement of Pakistan had inspired in their followers mood humility and worked in close co-ordination with the Congress, things would have turned out differently. Mahatma Gandhi had shown the day in Noakhali. The adoption of a similar approach on the western front could have saved more lives and laid the foundations for a better relationship between the two emerging nations.

I remember vividly those periods of 1947, when India achieved independence. I was a post-graduate student of Patna College in the Department of History. How riot had spread from Calcutta and Noakhali to Bihar and U.P., Punjab was already burning. India appeared to be a lawless state. If Mountbatten would not have advanced the date of independence, India would have been fragmented into many parts and so Mountbatten did a very nice thing by dividing India into two Dominions and by arranging orderly transfer of power to India. India remained a continuing entity.

The division of Indian subcontinent was the biggest blunder in the history of mankind, said Altaf Husain, Muttahida Qaumi Movement leader in London in September 2000 but the New India had evolved as a modern nation-state and had emerged stronger than what it was at the midnight of August 14/15, 1947.[26]

Conclusion

In the final analysis, the Congress leaders and Party were too tired to carry on the struggle any further and were, in their heart of hearts, anxious to grasp power and enjoy its fruits without further delay. As Badshah Khan told Durga Das in Kabul in 1967 in so many words, "some of my colleagues in the High Command did toy with the idea of going ahead with the fight. But the majority accepted the view that they might then miss the bus. In the next elections in Britain, it was feared, the Labour might be thrown out of office and the diehard Tories voted back to power...... [27]

Unknown at the time, Churchill played a key role in the creation of Pakistan. As soon as the Second World War started in 1939, Churchill felt that India could not be ruled indefinitely. This point has been made clear by King George VI in his book, *His Life and Reign*. The King decided, "To give up India to the Indians after the war". Churchill and his colleagues decided, at the same time to save what they could out of the wreckage and it was this conviction that lay behind the offer to Jinnah of 'Pakistan on a platter'. It was thought that Pakistan would give them a foothold in the subcontinent.[28] As the historian Charley has written, 'Churchill stood for the British Empire, for British independence and for an 'anti-socialist' vision of Britain.

Prime Minister Attlee and his colleagues in the government did not agree with the policy of the Conservative Government that functioned in the country. So the Labour Government attempted to maintain a unified India, however fragile its federal structure. Mountbatten also tried his best to maintain the unity of India till the first week of may 1947. But the compulsion of events went beyond control of the main British and Congress actors in the final scene of the freedom. The Punjab was burning from March 1947. Communal riots had been taking huge lives. The law and order had completely broken down. Circumstances compelled the Congress leaders to accept the demand of the Muslim League and so destiny helped Jinnah to get a truncated Pakistan.

NOTES

1. *The Asian Age*, May 6, 1998.
2. *Mainstream,* January 21, 1990.
3. *Mainstream*, June 2, 1990.
4. *The Indian Express*, March 3, 1997.
5. *India: The First 50 Years*, pp. 61-66.
6. Patrick, French, *Liberty or Death*, p. 351.
7. *Frontline,* January 9, 1998.
8. *Ibid.*, p. 75.
9. The *Times of India*, September 3, 1997.
10. The *Times of India*, June 20, 1985.
11. The *Times of India*, New Delhi, March 10, 1985.
12. Pirzada, Vol. III, p. 129.
13. (1) *Transfer of Power*, Vol. II, pp. 129,130, 153., (2) Patrick, French, *Liberty or Death*, p. 307.
14. Nicholas Manseargh, the *Transfer of Power*, London, 1970, p. 632.
15. Brecher, *Nehru,* p. 340.
16. Durga Das, *India from Curzon to Nehru and After*, p. 254.
17. Zakaria, Rafiq, *A Study of Nehru*, p. 7.
18. *Ibid.*, p. 8.
19. *Ibid.*, p.69.
20. *Ibid.*, p. 234.
21. Brecher, Michael, *Nehru*, p. 345.
22. Bose, D.R., *New India Speaks*, p. 184.
23. *Congress Bulletin* No. 5, November 7, 1947.
24. *Congress Bulletin* No. 6, December 31, 1947.
25. *Congress Bulletin* No. 4, July 10, 1947.
26. *The Pioneer*, Lucknow, October 6, 2000.
27. Durga Das, *India from Curzon to Nehru and After*, p. 255.
28. *Ibid.*

Hence, Mountbatten took a right decision to create Pakistan on 14th August and independence to India at the midnight on August 14/15, 1947.[1]

NOTE

1. The *Times of India*, New Delhi, August 1947.

APPENDIX II

Liaquat Ali Khan wanted to Avert India's Partition

Nawabzada Liaquat Ali Khan, who later becames the Prime Minister of the Dominion of Pakistan, wanted to avert the partition of India as he thought that Jinnah would die soon.

A controversy has been raging in Pakistan about the role of Liaquat Ali Khan before and after the partition. Pakistan's former Attorney General and Law Minister Sharifuddin Pirzada, who had served Jinnah as his Secretary, has sensationalized this controversy by issuing a long press statement claiming that the founder of Pakistan died as a heart broken man due to the attitude of Liaquat Ali Khan. The text of his statement was partially published by the Government owned morning newspaper *Jung*; other papers used only a few paragraphs.

According to Pirzada, Liaquat Ali Khan had gained the confidence of Jinnah to such an extent that in 1943 he called on (Liaquat Ali Khan) his right hand man. However, in 1944, when the Congress Working Committee members were in jail for launching the Quit India Movement in August 1942 and the Gandhi-Jinnah talks of 1944 had failed, Khan had expressed his keenness to come to terms with the Congress without the knowledge of Jinnah. The desire was conveyed to the leader of the Congress Parliamentary Party, Bhulabhai Desai, in a letter written by Dr. Syed Mahmud. According to the letter, Liaquat Ali Khan was keen to come to terms with the Congress after the installation of the Interim Government and joining of the representatives of the Muslim League in the government.

The result was the Liaquat-Desai pact in January 1945, while Desai had obtained the approval of Mahatma Gandhi, Liaquat Ali did not inform Jinnah about the talks leading to the pact. Sir Mohammad Yemen Khan in whose house the Muslim League had met to finalize the pact wrote in *Name-i-Amal* that the question of seeking Jinnah's approval was not discussed in the meeting because Liaquat Ali had been told by Doctors that Jinnah had only a few days to live. Jinnah came to know of the pact through the leakage in the press. He was very angry. Liaquat told him that the pact was only a draft.[1]

NOTE

1. The *Times of India*, New Delhi, November 6, 1945.

APPENDIX III

Jinnah's Blunder

On the basis of the report published in *The Frontier Post*, Peshawar, the Muslim India, New Delhi, edited by Syed Shahbuddin, has quoted Col. Elahi Baksh, who had attended to Mr. Jinnah during his last wrath at Ziarat'neer Quetta, Baluchistan, as having made the statutory reservation that Jinnah considered the creation of Pakistan to see his biggest blunder and wanted to go New Delhi and tell Nehru to forget the follies of the past and become friends again.

He revealed: one day we learnt that Prime Minister Liaquat Ali Khan was coming to visit the *Qaid at Ziarat*. The next day the Prime Minister arrived and he greeted the Qaid to which the Qaid made no reply. Now face to face, Liaquat Ali Khan asked how the Qaid was. The Qaid blew up and said, you have started thinking of yourself as a big man. You are nothing; I have made you the Prime Minister of Pakistan. You think you have made Pakistan but I have made it. But now I am convinced that I have committed the biggest blunder of my life. If now I get the opportunity, I will go to Delhi and tell Jawaharlal to forget the follies of the past and become friends again. At that point the Qaid lifted his hand as if in a handshake and was shivering with emotions!

Elahi Baksh said to Liaquat Ali Khan that the excitement was not good for the patient. Liaquat came out of the room and remarked, 'the old man has now discovered his blunder'.[1]

NOTE

1. The *Times of India*, New Delhi, September 1950.

APPENDIX IV

If Churchill had won in 1945–Would he agree to part with Pakistan?

Several persons have given the assessment but the most convincing has been provided by a former British Prime Minister, James Callaghan (1976-79). Mr. Callaghan was a junior minister then and with his closeness to Mr. Attlee other senior Labour leaders was in a position to know the full facts. He has recorded his views frankly in his book *Time and Chance*.

Supposing Churchill had won the 1945 General Elections instead of the Labour Party, what would Jawaharlal Nehru have made of Churchill's defiant statement issued on November 10, 1942? I did not welcome the King's first minister to preside over the legislature of the British Empire. Would Churchill have refused self-government to India? Lord Mountbatten recorded in his diary that some years later in conversation, Churchill complained that Britain had India away, and said that it would have given him pleasure to fight for it. If he had been Prime Minister and followed his instructions, post-war Britain might have been involved in a long and debilitating conflict in a vain attempt to hold down the whole subcontinent by force. Such a conflict would have weakened Britain's exhausted economy and further.

We would not have prevented India from gaining her independence but it would have been won by her people after a wordy conflict, leaving behind better feeling between them and us. Fortunately the election of the Labour Government spared both India and Britain from the possibility of any such folly. It fell to Clement Attlee to take the momentous decision to offer India her freedom.

With his knowledge of India, he had no hesitation and his leap into the unknown proved to be the wisest as well as the most courageous decision in the whole lifetime of the Labour Government.

I write this despite the timeless slaughter that followed the partition of the country and the creator of Pakistan since those days, Pakistan has left the commonwealth although from time to time there have been hints that she would not be averse to the regressing. At present this would not be possible, though I hope it would not be ruled out in different circumstances.

India on the other hand, under Pandit Nehru, took the decision to remain a member of commonwealth with the result that the friendship of India and British perhaps has grown as the years pass and I, like thousands of others, have been the recipient of the many tokens of genuine and sincere Indian affection. Indeed, I am proud to say that in Andhra Pradesh a housing state is named after him.

When the Bill to grant independence to India came before parliament, Churchill framed his opposition in a speech which contends a memorable phrase. He spoke of the grief with which he watched clattering down of the British Empire. But his followers were divided; some agreed with him, most did not. How were they to vote on the Bill? The Conservative Party did what every opposition does in such a situation. It put down a so called 'reserved amendment' which blurred the differences between its members and under which they could all huddle in safety. The amendment did not oppose the grant of independence in principle but it attempted to assuage those conservators who were opposed by bearing out any date for its implantation. A toothless beast indeed and it was rejected by an overwhelming vote.[1]

If it had been carved it would have aroused intense anger in India. A story went around at the time that may be apocryphal but illustrate perfectly, Churchill's wit and his prejudices. It was said that when the Tory shadow government to consider whether it should oppose the Indian independence Bill, the former Colonial Secretary, Oliver Stanley, who was the Principle Tory spokesman was not present at the beginning of the meeting. Churchill took advantage of his absence to deliver a diatribe and by the time he had frustrated.

NOTE

1. The *Times of India*, New Delhi, July 10, 1988.

APPENDIX V

The Transfer of Power and Partition

Prof. R.J. Moore is a recognized scholar of modern Indian history. His latest book of essays *End Games of Empire* (1988) reflects, like his other books, his painstaking research and objective analysis.

Moore deals with the period between 1920 and 1947, crucial both for India and Britain. It is commonly believed that the Muslim leaders demanded strong provisions and a weak federation in the last stages of the transfer of power. But Moore rightly pointed out that this demand was voiced by the Muslim leaders as early as the late 1920s. Congress, on the other hand, favoured a strong with adequate safeguards for the provinces.

British spokesman was talking about federation and dominion status but this idea of a federation was hazy and they were reflected to concede the logical corollary to Dominion States, namely secession from Empire. It was Lord Willingdon as Viceroy who put a break on reforms that could have led to dominion status. The Conservatives not only played the Muslim card but also that of the princes who were resented to join the federation.

Congress resorted to Civil Disobedience Movement (1930-32) which was used by the British to bring the Muslim cover to them. Separate electorates had given ministerial powers to Muslims in Bengal and Punjab. Though British statement favoured a strong centre, as long as they had power, they did not discourage the Muslim parts from demanding a weak centre. As the Congress boycotted the first Round Table Conference, the Government of India Act, 1935 favoured the Muslims and the provinces. Once the princes discovered the federation being envisaged would be weak they were smart enough to reverse their stances and expressed their willingness to accept the formula.

The *Manchester Guardian* (London) correspondent wrote as far back in 1931, 'Many Muslims do not believe in—a federal India and they foresee a Muslim state in the north stretching from Karachi to northern Bengal. The federation did not come about before independence. Who was to blame? Lord Halifax thought the federation might have saved the situation between 1930 and 1940. He blamed Lord Willingdon for obstructing constitutional progress though he agreed that Churchill too was responsible for blocking the plan.

It can be summoned that the British Government was not serious about the idea of a federation which was put forth as a counter to the Congress demand for dominion status. Lord Listowel, the last Secretary of State for India, was candid enough to remark that the British lost a chance in the 1930s by denying dominion status. It is said by some that the Cabinet Mission Plan should have been accepted by the Congress and that Mountbatten did not want partition. It is pertinent to note in this connection the mental makeup of Mountbatten. Lord Ismay had observed that it was impossible to get Mountbatten to go through the alternative drafts methodically. He was a grand clap in a thousand ways but clear in thought and writing was not his strag suit.

As such Mountbatten created problems for himself and others when he misunderstood Nehru with regard to the ultimate constitutional set-up. His scheme was in similar to that of the Cabinet Mission and was rejected by the Congress. So Nehru did not suffer from amnesia or go back on his promise when he rejected Mountbatten's plan.

Moore with his usual inclusive logic brings out the uncertainness of Mountbatten's gossip of the plan and the Fundamentals of established policy and how he was slow to appreciate the essential demands of the Congress. He maintains that the constructive role of the Congress on the emergence of the 3rd June Plan has never been understood and in particular the nature and significance of Mountbatten negotiations with Nehru have been misconstrued.

Prof. Moore's analysis of the relations between Jinnah and the Pakistan movement clarifies many doubts. Probably for the first time it has been revealed that some of the passages in Jinnah's speech on the Lahore resolution were drawn from the representations of Ahmad Basher and the Aligarh group. Those who claim that Jinnah and the Muslim League accepted the Cabinet Mission plan should ponder over the following findings of Moore, 'Jinnah received written letters of advice from Aurangzeb Khan and Jamil-ul-din Ahmad that emphasized the advantages of accepting the Muslim's schemes. Ahmad, then the convener of the League's committee of writers expressed the prudent strategy vigorously. The League should work the plan up to the group stage and to create a situation that forces the hands of the Hindus and the British to concede the Pakistan of our conception. Congress leaders saw through the game and opted for outright partition.[1]

NOTE

1. Govind Talwalkar, the *Times of India*, New Delhi, October 30, 1988.

APPENDIX VI

History was on Nehru's Side (Inside of the Simla Conference, 1945)

After the end of the Second World War in 1945, the Viceroy like a statesman called a political conference in June 1945. In the middle of the June 1945, the Viceroy sent off telegrams to India's notables, inviting them to sit together later that month and discuss with him the subcontinents future. And since it was scheduled for June, he invited them to Simla. Mukul Kesavan learnt that the Cecil was chosen as the lodging place of the League delegation. The representation of the Congress were not staying at the Cecil, though the management offered to make room for them. They were separately housed in bungalows spruced up for the conference. The Muslim Leagues arrived in the evening of 24th. Jinnah, Liaquat Ali Khan and Hussein Imam reached the Cecil.

Mukul Kesavan supervised the laying of their table. The vase at the centre had to be changed because the gardener had supplied an arrangement of red rose buds, the flower patented by Nehru for his buttonhole. Dinner was scheduled for seven, as the clock chimed the four, Jinnah led his colleagues into the room, where is Gandhi? Burst out Liaquat Ali Khan, midway through the soup. Next to Jinnah's whopper leanness looked more than ever like an overfed peg. He also looked worried.

In Simla, Hussein Imam, dubbing at his mouth with a napkin, Manohar Villa to be peruse, he added finically his spoon in the soup bowl. Then why, is not he attending the conference? Demanded

Liaquat aggressively looking at the others in turn, no one bothered to answer. The question was rhetorical. The Mahatma had been reiterating has reasons to press for days now. He had written to the Viceroy explaining that he could not represent the Congress for the reason that he was not a member of that party. He was not biased at all or if he was, he was simply on the side of freedom.

Old hypocrite, offered Hussein Imam, why not Nehru then? Why, not him? This is not Ludo or marbles, said Liaquat wrathfully, how can they be so . . . . . . so non-serious? Azad is going to lead them into the conference. Azad! For approval but has said nothing. He had coined that sneering token Muslim label for Azad some years ago and it had struck; now he let his lieutenants chorus it.

Liaquat was still shaking his head. He was not the only one puzzled leader-writers, Lord Wavell leaguers like Liaquat, layman like me, even literate ladies, had all been wondering why the father of the not-yet nation and his protégé were not playing helms man for this critical meeting. At stake was the conversation of the Interim Government which the Viceroy hoped would oversee the transition to self-governing India.

There was a lot to play for—why had not Congress sent its champions? What are they up to? Growling Liaquat worrying a chicken breast for its secrets, how can they afford to be so casual? Because Nehru believes he has history on his side, one sinter and Jinnah had their whole attention. You must understood, he continued dialectically that Nehru is a Whig, all socialists and that communist, who was changed in Kanpur conspiracy case. His trial statement ran to five hundred and seventy-two pages. It began with the rise of capitalism and ended with the inevitability of violent class struggle of which, he argued the conspiracy for which he was being tired was but a single instance. If class struggle was predestined, his part in it was inevitable—not culpable. It was most remarkable argument I have ever heard in court. What happened to him? Asked Liaquat interested, he hogged, said Jinnah absently. The point is, he believed he had history on his side, so does Nehru, he can send Azad to Simla without a qualm because it is written that the Congress will inherit an undivided country, like he inherited Motilal's money because the Congress is mother India's only son. He leaned back as I served him the pudding and staled his fingers.

Like that communist, Nehru knows he has history under rein. It was not an accident that he first called for complete independence, what on horseback. You remember Liaquat? How he rode to Lahore Congress session on a white charge? That horse was history. For himself, Jinnah favoured history without capitals, History not as live agent but as dead record which supplied precedents for his great political brief. When he (Mukul Kesavan) returned with the coffee, he (Jinnah) was patently rehearing his conference strategy for the creatures at his tale.

The British owned this country, he said, speaking his words, not the Congress can give us nothing. Ignore it, the British can, but they won't until they are forced to. We are too small to face them to do what we want, but big enough to veto anything that does not suit us. When we sit at that table tomorrow, remember what we are working towards. Deadlock till they learn to listen, till they show their hands. Jinnah paused to ask for cigars, when I (Mukul Kesavan) came back with them five minutes later, Hussein Imam, was picking his teeth and Liaquat had nearly nodded off. The Qaid had a jolt on his hand.[1]

NOTE

1. Mukul Kesavan, The *Times of India*, New Delhi, January 29, 1995.

APPENDIX VII

Diaries of a Troubled Time (1829–1945)
The Empire at Bay

This volume contains the inside story of Second World War and the transfer of power to India as witnessed by leading British politician. During the war as Secretary of State for India, L.S. Amery had to carry out the politics of the Government headed by Winston Churchill, who had a blind spot for India. Amery thus invited a lot of criticism in Britain but the diaries revealed that he was no die-hard imperialist like his leader.

In fact it is learnt that Amery opposed Churchill's stand on India for a long time before the war. The Conservatives were divided; not only on internal issues but on foreign policy matters too. Sir Stanley Baldwin was a parallel Prime Minister with Beaverbrook asking for imperial preference and Churchill for a strong stand against the Indian demand for independence.

In fact it is surprising that the Government was pressured by two press Lords Beaverbrook and Rothermore. As Baldwin was forced to preside over a divided party he remained a weak Prime Minister. At the same time nobody in the Conservative party could replace him. Baldwin's vacillation on the stand he took regarding India alarmed Amery who thought that the forces of nationalism could not be washed away or crushed. Amery often classed with Churchill, who did not see any wisdom in meeting the demand for self-Government in India halfway.

By 1930, Mahatma Gandhi launched his Satyagraha movement which culminated in an agreement with the Viceroy Lord Irwin. The

Round Table Conference followed with talk in granting provincial autonomy to India. Amery found these fatties and thought that the ultimate goal should be a federal Government in India and Indian leaders should be asked to share responsibility at the centre with provincial autonomy, the authority of the central government would have been weakened. However, Baldwin felt that something more than provincial autonomy must be given to India to keep her in the commonwealth. Stanley Hoare also agreed with this stand. The Gandhi-Irwin pact was a godsend to Baldwin who would have been in a weak position, had there not been any agreement.

Here it must be noted that the Labour party did not think of granting Domain Status to India. However, the provincial autonomy experiment could not run its full course as the Second World War broke out and the Congress ministers resigned on the question of more meaningful sharing of power both in the provinces and at the centre.

Churchill assumed power as Prime Minister and Amery became Secretary of State for India though the Prime Minister did not favour radical constitutional changes; he was of the view that the Viceroy Council should be more representative. Arthur More, the then editor of the *Statesman* in a personal letter summed up the situation in India. He writes, I am convinced that the Viceroy could get War coalition Government at the centre. He is determined not to have it, let the Indians be finally convinced of that and we are lost. The British half of the Government of India is completely ignorant of the true state of feelings.

In the initial period of Churchill's coalition Government, the Labour and Liberal parties did not press for more powers being given to the Indians but once the Japanese launched an offensive under which the British defences fell. Attlee was alarmed and suggested somebody should be sent from London to negotiate with the Indian leaders.

By this time the Muslim League had passed a resolution demanding Pakistan which resulted in a stiff attitude in the Congress. Some thought that Amery himself should visit India. It was also suggested that Churchill should go to India and make the political announcement there but he and his Government had no definite policy and Churchill would not consider giving any concessions.

Later, Sir Stafford Cripps came to India on a political mission but the mission failed. Amery admitted the Cripps plan was to pave the way for Pakistan. Gandhi was shrewd enough to grasp this and was successful in scotching it. He launched a movement called the

Quit India Movement of 1942 against British domination which ruled out all possibilities of a settlement.

Meanwhile the War was intensified and with Amery joining the war as the result of the 'Pearl Harbour incident' it was a matter of time before victory was gained. Victory over Germany brought about the end of the national Government in Britain and under the Labour Government, India was partitioned and gained freedom.[1]

NOTE

1. The *Times of India*, New Delhi, August 28, 1988.

APPENDIX VIII

Nizam considered Pakistan Shadow without Reality

The Nizam of Hyderabad, Mr. Usman Ali Khan, considered the concept of Pakistan a shadow without reality. He thought it was impracticable and had opposed it. The Nizam had conveyed these views to the then Viceroy, Lord Wavell in 1946, a year before Pakistan was born. He had told him he did not believe in Pakistan. These facts have been received in the eighth volume of *the Transfer of Power* from July 1946 to November 1946 when Lord Wavell was trying to form an interim Government.

After Mr. Nehru and Mr. Jinnah failed to reach an agreement on the question of the participation of the Muslim League in the Interim Government, the Congress was faced with a grave crisis. At time the Nizam wrote to Lord Wavell: I do not at all believe in Pakistan. In fact, it is impracticable, or, I consider it is a shadow which has no reality. In my opinion, Mr. Jinnah must see things in right perspective or understand their reality and should not waste his health and time in trying to achieve something which is not practicable.

Muslims Share

Instead of this, he should demand proportionate share in the Government for Muslims along with other communities . . . . . . Mr. Jinnah cannot succeed in his struggle until he takes to a correct course. Wisemen have said that one should desire only what is good or is possible, the Nizam told the Viceroy.

The Nizam had advised Lord Wavell to do his best to get the Muslim League into the Interim Government and this would stop

APPENDIX IX

Last of the Imperial Lords

An Interview of Govind Talwalkar with Lord Listowel

Lord Listowel was the last Secretary of State for India and he had piloted the Bill of Indian Independence. Govind Talwalkar met him in the House of Lords and put him few questions. This is an extract of interview :

1. Why it was that Lord Attlee had devoted very few pages in his autobiography to the transfer of power in India, was it, because Attlee as some hold did not care much for India? Lord Listowel could not subscribe to this theory. He said the fact that Attlee had given only very few pages to Indian independence was nothing strange. He was very self-effacing and a man of few words. It was not correct to say that he did not care much for India in fact, accordingly to Lord Listowel it was because of Attlee's powerful support that Lord Mountbatten and the India Office could take the various important far-reaching elections that they did in such a short time. Besides, Attlee was burdened with the stupendous task of post-war reconstruction at home.
2. Whether it was true that his predecessor, Lord Pethick Lawrence had not been agreeable to British handing over power to India in the stipulated period and so had been replaced by him as Secretary of State. Lord Listowel said this was not true; Pethick Lawrence was an old and tired

any future crisis, I must make it very clear that Indian
always remained loyal to the British Government and h
it in all crises and have thus proved their firm loyalty
King and the Throne. Therefore, in my view they deser
some consideration by the British Throne. As against tl
said, the Congress was an 'enemy' of the British. Lo
not commend on this letter, he only sent the acknowle

NOTES

1. The *Times of India*, New Delhi, October 25, 1979.

man. He could not keep pace with Mountbatten. This was known beforehand and it was dicided that he should be replaced by a younger person, when Lord Mountbatten took over Lord Listowel was in his forties and as a member of the parliamentary delegation which precedes the Calumny Mission, had toured India and acquainted himself with the Indian problems.

3. There is a feeling, at least in India that because Lord Mountbatten was a man in a hurry, he decided to divide and quit India within a couple of months of his arrival? Lord Listowel would not agree with this theory. He said that the decision to divide and quit was not that of Mountbatten. It was a deliberate decision on the part of the Calumny. The Indian administrative machinery had run down. Then were riots in large parts of the country and the British could not hold on for long. If the division had been postponed the severity of the holocaust would not have been blessed but, on the contrary, would have increased. However, Lord Listowel agreed that in a different situation the partition could have been planned in advance. As it was, it could not be, when it was found that the partition of India was invited. Attlee did not want to put off the date. In the London the parliamentary as well as the executive machinery was put under great stress to hurry up with the legislation. It was a race against the clock.
4. The final question was whether the partition of India was undividable and whether the British could escape their share in the responsibility? Lord Listowel referred to his article 'Indo-British Review' where he says, the Punjab tragedy was an inevitable consequence of the division of British India and it could only have been avoided if the unity of India had been preserved. By the time Mountbatten went out it was too late. The divisive became increasingly difficult to reverse from the movement when the Muslim League became connected to Pakistan in 1940. There will be continue to be endless and inclusive argument about the degree to which the mistakes of Indian and British political leaders constituted to the consummation of this process. But there can be no doubt that the British alone had the power to transfer their sovereignty to a united India or that they were responsible

> for the welfare of all its inhabitants regardless of creed or castes. Gandhi, it will be remembered a skid for dominion status at the Second Round Table Conference in 1931 and he was the voice of the majority. Before 1940, the transition would undoubtedly have been made without providing separate homelands for the religious communities. But British statesmanship in the province or decade was at the lowest ebb that I can remember in forty-five years of public life. It was not surprising that the vision was lacking and that the last opportunity was thrown away. The 1935 India Act might have been the opportunity, if we had insisted on its implementation instead of allowing the princes to exercise the Veto. Instead of granting self-Government which was promised since 1917 or insisting on federation, we clung to power under the clock of responsibility to part with it by our own reduced circumstances, after four years of war. In the context of history, the transfer of power in 1947 was no more than a mitigation of the failure of British policy to part with it earlier and to a united India.

Now Mr. Govind Talwalkar took his leave. He felt that he was face to face with the last representative of colonialism who was a willing party to the dissolution of the Imperial rule.[1]

NOTE

1. The *Times of India*, New Delhi, August 1988.

APPENDIX X

August 15, 1947—Freedom
One Era Ends and a New Begins

Today the people of India achieve their freedom and that freedom is complete. By passing the Indian Independence Act, the British Parliament transferred to the two new Indian Dominions full powers to look after their own affairs and as dominions they have the right, if they do desire, to leave the British Commonwealth of Nations at any time in the future, thus ends a long political struggle movement by many varying phases. On this day it believes people of the two new states to remember with gratitude those grants of the past who sowed what their descendants are reaping. No brief list of their names can pretend to the conflict, but among them we would recall Dadabhai Naoroji, Pherozshah Mehta, Gokhale, Tilak, Annie Besant, W.C. Banerjee, C.R. Das, Motilal Nehru, and a host of others.

Today we happily have with us many who see the frustration of their life's walk including Mr. Gandhi, Pandit Jawaharlal Nehru and Sardar Vallabhbhai Patel to mention only a few. Mr. Jinnah has not got Pakistan nor must we forget the tremendous service rendered by Lord Mountbatten in the final stages. But it is Mr. Gandhi whom the majority of his fellow country men will regard as the architect of their freedom and the object of their veneration. Before Mr. Gandhi weaned the dominant influence in the Indian National Congress, the man who advised the country's political claims were a group of what might be termed intellectuals. To Mr. Gandhi must go the credit for making the movement for political freedom a mass agitation? It was he who took it out of the hands of the few and gave it to the many.

From the day that Mr. Gandhi brad-based has appeal, its success despite mistakes and reversals was eventually certain.

Partition

The one disappointment to Mr. Gandhi as to millions of his fellow countrymen is the fact that freedom comes to India divided into two separate states but the roots of that unhappy division lie deep in history.

Peaceful Transfer

Let us be thankful for one great blessing. It is one of the biggest triumphs of democracy that freedom has come to the people of this country without a violent and bloody upheaval. We do not forget the struggle of the past, nor the fact that they occasionally led to bloodshed to Mr. Gandhi again must go the credit for the non-violent form which mass agitations generally took yet before in history has so vast transfer of power been accomplished with so much speed and with so much good will on both sides. Mr. Attlee, the British Prime Minister described his Government's action as the fulfilment of a mission. For many years successive British Government has proclaimed their intention of leading India to self-government. The dispute was not so much over the goal as over the speed and method by which that goal could be achieved. The people of the subcontinent freed from outside control will develop in future according to their own genius and in their own best interest. Yet they inherit from British rule three things which are worth adding to in the interests of the common people—freedom from external aggression, a sound administrative system and the rule of law.[1]

NOTE

1. From the *Times Archives*.

APPENDIX XI

New Insight into History of Congress

Prof. S.R. Mehrotra has written a well documented book *A History of the Indian National Congress*, Vol. I. The Late Pattabhi Sitaramayya's History of the Congress used to be regarded as a standard work but so much new material is now available that a new history of the Congress is overdue. Prof. Mehrotra has accomplished this task with great competence. He is convinced that the credit for forming the Indian National Congress must go to A.O. Hume, a civil servant, who had some enemies and critics in the administration. He had the advantage of receiving administrative reports which understood unrest among the people and apprehended the repetition of the uprising of 1857. Hume thought it advisable to have a national platform which would eventually play the role of the opposition in the House of Commons. Though some Viceroys and Governors were sympathetic to the Congress, the official attitude changed quickly.

Newspaper Reports

Prof. Mehrotra quotes newspaper reports to give the reader a feel of the proceedings of the first Congress. The tone of the speeches was moderate. Some demands were made about recruitment to the civil service and representation in the Advisory Congress. With the passage of time, Home Rule became the objective of the Congress wrote one correspondent, it seemed to me that as if every member had inwardly resolved upon having less words and more work. There was an attempt in almost every speech to be brief concise and to the point, an anxious care to assist them to complete the discussions.

Another fact that K.T. Telang was bright and lively and one reporter work about Dadabhai Naoroji, the grey haired patriot in short and thin, but full of spirit, enthusiasm and good sense. The old man is full of sparkle, wit and shies however and sarcasm with rare fluency of speech and curt expressions, he harmonized all conflicting points raised in the discussion. Sessions were held in big crities and sometimes there was competition over the honour and privilege of playing host.

What about expenditure? The first session spent Rs. 3,000 but the expense increased afterwards and between 1888 and 1914, it ranged between Rs. 40,000 and Rs. 60,000. We find that an Englishman was preferred as President and a member of the provincial reaction committee was mildly admonished by Dineshaw Wacha, the Secretary of the Congress for insisting on an Englishman as President.

Generally, the session was exceptional, that is why Rabindranath Tagore remarked that Indians were unwilling to forego the sweetness of human relationship even in there link and that at their political gatherings they were less improved by the business done than the hospitality received. So also with the Congress that much of it which is truly national its hospitality has played an abiding part in the national representation, which its work ends with the three-day session and is heard of no more during the rest of the year. Some others also did not want the Congress to be a three-day affair. It was Gopal Krishan Gokhale, who first devoted Congress to full term work for the organization.

The author has done well to reproduce the full text of the Constitution of the Indian National Congress and can test the working of the organization or whatever is left of it today. Great storm was set by the work of the British Committee in London, towards advocating Englishman. But eventually, Hume himself was alarmed at the prospect in India. He sent a circular expressing fear that there might be widespread revolt. He was prevailed upon to withdraw this by his Indian and European colleagues.

While there was, yet no sign of a revolt in the country, once in the Congress was already evident. The Moderates who dominated the organization were opposed by the extremists, who advocated a countrywide boycott after the partition of Bengal. They classed in Surat in 1907 and the Congress split afterwards. Tilak was sentenced for six years (1908-1914) for 'seditious' writings. But he became stronger after his incarnation. Moderate leaders could not stem the tide and Tilak did not advised the Congress but demarcated it.

Lucknow Pact

Muslims in small number used to attend the sessions of the Congress from 1885 but the First World War (1914-18) on which Turkey was not on the side of the allies made all the differences. In anticipation of administrative reform Hindu and Muslim leaders raised hands. The result was the Lucknow Pact of 1916. The mood of not only Congressmen but the entire country had changed and most moderates could not gauge it properly. The British Government was not helpful either and Mintage who was the Viceroy admitted that the resume fell short of expectations. But when the Rowlett Act also came, followed by the Amritsar Massacre of 1919, the Moderates were swept off their feet.

It should not be forgotten that many of the Moderates were inspired by a great ideal. As Gokhale put it, let us not forget that we are at a stage of the country's progress when our acknowledgements are bound to be small, and our disappointment frequency and trying—it will, no doubt, be given to our countrymen of future generation to serve India by their success or of the present generations to serve India by their success, we of the present generation must be contended to serve her mainly by our failures. However their failures were nobler than the achievements of present day leaders.

APPENDIX XII

Gandhi and Ambedkar
Commercial Awards and the Poona Pact

Till the time of the memorandum of May 1928 to the Simon Commission, Ambedkar was in favour of territorial constitutions in which citizen belonging to all religions and castes would reasonably choose their representatives on the basis of adult franchise. The various systems of separate communal electorates in which the support of members of a religious community or caste would be sought by candidates of community or caste would be sought by candidate's competitively espousing their interest against other communities and castes had been introduced in respect of Muslims under the Indian Councils Act of 1909.

However, by the time of the Second Round Table Conference convened by the British Government in London in September 1931, Ambedkar had become a proponent of separate electorates for the depressed classes. Opposing this, Gandhi said in a speech at the Indian Majlis of Oxford on October 24, 1931: "I am certain that the question of separate electorate for the untouchables is a modern manufacture of a satanic Government. The only thing needed is to put them on the voters list and provide for fundamental rights for them in the constitution. Separate electorates will perpetuate the stigma. Do you want the untouchables to remain untouchables forever?"

Gandhi also said that Ambedkar has a right to spit upon me, as every untouchable has and I would keep on smiling if they did so but I may inform you that Dr. Ambedkar speaks for that particular part of the country where he comes from. He cannot speak for the rest of India.

On the failure of the delegates to the RTC, who had been handpicked by the British Government to find an agreed solution? Prime Minister Ramsey McDonald gave his Communal Award on August 18, 1932. It provided any other things for a total of 780 reserved seats for the depressed class in the provincial legislature of these 71 seats in the areas where these voters chiefly prevail would be filled by the Depressed Class voting as a separate electorates. Gandhi, who had been put under detention on return from London, undertook a fast unto death in protest. The British Prime Minister had said while announcing the Award that if the communities concern came to an agreement between them, the Award would be suitably modified. Gandhi's fast was clearly armed not only at the British Government but at inducing a change of attitude among the caste Hindus and untouchable's leaders. From a conference of these leaders in Bombay emerged a compromise formula that was a hybrid of separate and joint electorates. In the 71 constituencies related to in the Award, there would be a primary election in which the depressed class voters would choose a panel of three or four candidates. This panel would then be put before a joint electorate of the depressed class and caste Hindus voters for that choice.

Gandhi not only agreed to the formula but offered to apply to all the 148 seats reserved for the depressed classes. Ambedkar accepted this. He explained later that he had agreed only in order to save Gandhi from certain death. The Poona Pact was signed on September 24, 1932. Ambedkar signed the Poona Pact, which concedes for more parliamentary representations to the untouchables. Then they had been allotted under the British Award. The British Government set its seats of approval on the Poona Pact on the September 26, 1932. Now Gandhi broke the fast. The Hindu joint electorates continued with reserved seats for untouchables. The compromise formula was incorporated in the Government of India Act of 1935.[1]

NOTE

1. *Mainstream,* July 16, 1994.

APPENDIX XIII

Legacy of the Raj

There is no unanimous British view on the imperial past; the eighteenth century founders of the Empire like Clive never pretended that they were in India for the benefit of Indians. Much later, 'Divide ET Empera' as description of British policy in India came not from the Indian nationalists but from Conservative British politicians like Lord Salisbury. The Viceroy, Lord Curzon claimed that India won by the sword could be held by the means of the same instrument not lay before the transfer of power, Penderel Moon an idealistic young ICS member was informed by the ICS members in the India Office that the British were in India not to teach Indians the art of Self-Government but to protect massive British investments in the territory.

As the Indian nationalist movement gathered momentum, British writings focused on the opportunism of the nationalist and their unrepresentative character as vine the impossibility of nation's land for India, hopelessly divided by language and religion.

In the book *The Proudest Day* published in 1947, Anthony Read and David Fisher has dismissed the Divide and Rule policy as "Pure Myth" but this book is based on secondary sources and hence this view cannot be accepted. Patrick French's book *Liberty or Death* is well documented and so Read's view is untenable.[1]

NOTE

1. *Frontline*, October 1997 and *Mainstream*, March 23, 1996.

APPENDIX XIV

Acharya Narendra Dev

After the martyrdom of Pandit Ganesh Shanker Vidyarthi during the communal riots in Kanpur, the U.P. Congress movement split into two factions, one led by Acharya Narendra Dev and consisting of the young and progressive persons; and the other of conservatives led by Purshottam Das Tandon. The Congress victory in the U.P. Assembly elections under the Government of India Act, 1935 brought in the question as to who will be premier of this most important province. But these leaders threw door the gauntlet.

Acharya Narendra Dev, having the backing of the youth and the blessings of Jawaharlal Nehru, gained an edge over Tandon. As this was not to the liking of the conservative group inside the Congress, it somehow influenced Rafi Ahmad Kidwai, but Kidwai did not agree to the elevation of Tandon to premiership. A compromise formula was found. Tandon was coaxed into accepting the assembly's speakership and Govind Ballabh Pant was chosen for the Prime Ministership of U.P. since the Pant considered Acharya Narendra Dev as his political rival.[1]

NOTE

1. *Frontline*, October 1, 1997.

Appendix XV

Sardar Patel

Balwant Singh Mehta is one of the six surviving members of the Constituent Assembly and who turned 100 on felly, 8,200 has praised it for Sardar Patel. He is the one who has tabled the motion relating to the Constitution of India, full of praise for Sardar Patel. He says that Sardar was more qualified to become the country's Prime Minister, but for the lack of statesmanship and straightforwardness he fads for the role of Pandit Nehru. Sardar Patel who brought in B.R. Ambedkar as a member of the committee that drafted the constitution, Ambedkar, who was not even a member of the Constituent Assembly, then became prominent.[1]

NOTE

1. The *Times of India*, New Delhi, January 6, 2000.

APPENDIX XVI

Jai Prakash Narayan

According to the Viceroy, Lord Louis Mountbatten, Jai Prakash Narayan asked for Finance, Home and States Department portfolio and 25 seats in the Legislative Assembly as a price for his party joining the government.[1]

NOTE

1. The *Asian Age*, August 1, 1947 (republished on July 29, 1997).

APPENDIX XVII

Communist Role in Freedom Struggle

The collapse of the Soviet Union and numerous other socialist regimes in Eastern Europe brought with it a flood of academic and non-academic literature on the past, present and future of the commonwealth parts all over the world.

The Communist Party in India, unlike in the erstwhile Soviet Union, has not had the opportunity of being in power, except the state level. The communists have been unable to identify their own roots, both due to their dilemma-prone relationship with the national movement and initial near-total identification with the Bolsheviks. As K. Damodaran points out, the Comintern did not grasp the specific nature of the Indian social formation, wrongly assessed the strength of bourgeois nationalism of the Congress and underestimated the relative autonomy of the Indian bourgeoisie and its political instrument, the Indian National Congress. The Indian communists inherited this lack of understanding at that juncture and they became completely isolated from the mainstream of the nationalist movement in the late twenties and the early thirties.

As a result, the Communist Party in India failed to use whatever opportunities it got to play its part in proportion with its effective power of intervention as the transformative part of a left tendency in the Congress movement, which led the struggle for hegemony in India during the freedom struggle. But it was alienated from the mainstream to its wrong conception that the members of Congress were bourgeois. So the role of the Communist Party in the national movement was marginalised. Some of the points are as follows:

1. The communists in India viewed 'nationalism' as a bourgeoise ideology and they identified the Indian bourgeoise as the ruling class. But they have not expressed on what basis a Marxists identity, the Indian bourgeoise as the ruling class?
2. That the communists failed to perceive the ground reality and their own role in the ongoing struggle is evident from their understanding of Gandhi's strategy. Gandhi was able to link the constitutional method and non-constitutional method—that is, mass movements—to create a new strategy for the national movement. The colonial policy was to acquire the consent of as many sections of the Indian people and draw them into the constitutional part of activity. In attempting to hagemonise the national movement the state sought to possess moral prestige and retain legal authority by proving channels and institutions for the constitutional tendency to express itself and carefully handling the mass movement. Gandhi's strategy to counter hagemonise the national movement was by a 'war of position', that is period of mass movements and intervals of truce. In this way the Congress acquired a hegemonic influence over a widespread anti-imperialist conciousness. The communists, showing a lack of understanding of the socio-political reality in India then, and lost in their 'sectarian' ideological debates, propogated a 'war of manoeuvre' position, that is, a seizure of power model which was most suitable at that juncture. The communists saw the role of Gandhi, Nehru and the Congress Socialist party as part of a 'bourgeois manoeuvre'.

But the role of the Communist Party in the national movement should not be underplayed. If the Communist Party did at that juncture commit 'mistakes' to an incomplete understanding of the socio-political reality in India, and depend on the Bolshevik view of India, it does not mean that they had no relevance in the struggle. The Communist ideology was not an indigenous product and this led to a lack of understanding of its philosophy and principles amongst the Communists in India, and thus its direct application to the Indian situation without analyzing its relevance. Subjective and objective factors were not taken into consideration at that time. But it is evident that the Communist committed mistake in the freedom struggle and it is hoped that realization of these will result in some amount of rethinking in the communist movement in the twenty-first century.[1]

NOTE

1. *Mainstream,* September 26, 1992.

Appendix XVIII

Dandi Revisited: A Monument and a Memorial

Dandi is a desolate site now. Clumps of thorned bases have taken over the salt pan that was once the site of an empire defying act. The sea has receded some distance. The house in which Gandhi spent the night before the day he broke the salt laws is a museum rarely visited.

On March 12, 1930, after prayers Sabarmati Ashram, Ahmedabad he sat out with his followers men and women. They walk out of the gates of the Ashram, the procession then turned left, crossed the bridge across the Sabarmati River and briskly moved south, along what is now called Ashram Road. On March 26, near Bharuch, the Satyagrahis crossed the Narmada in boats. Jawaharlal Nehru walked with them for some distance. At last the procession reached Dandi on 4th April. All of them assembled under a banyan tree by the sea and prayed.

On 5th April, Gandhi stayed at Safai Villa, a two-storied building that belonged to a Muslim family with business connections in South Africa. That evening, Gandhi held a public meeting under the banyan tree and prayed with the Satyagrahis. Early next morning, along with the other marchers, Gandhi walked towards the sea. After a ritual bath in the sea, he walked back and picked up some salt from the pans in front of Safai Villa. Other volunteers followed, Wevele Millar, the journalist who witnessed the Satyagrah wrote; suddenly at a word of command, scores of native police rushed down upon the marchers and rained blows on the heads with steel shod lathis. Not one of the marchers even raised an arm to fend off the blows, they went down like terrapins.

By voting the monopoly of the British in collecting salt, Gandhi gave a signal to the nation. Like a tidal wave, the Satyagrah spread to other ports of the country. In Ahmedabad, the salt collected by Gandhi was auctioned and Dr. Kanungo brought for Rs. 1,600.

After Gandhi picked some salt at Dandi, he came to Karaadi village about 10 km. from Dandi. A hut was built by the side of a small pond and he stayed there from 14th April to 4th May. From this hut he wrote to the Viceroy of his intention to march to Dharasana and raid the salt godown there. The police came to the Karaadi hut at the dead of night on 4th may. Gandhi was arrested and the police took him to a railway level crossing four kilometres away. There the Frontier Maal going towards Mumbai was stopped and he was taken to Pune. The police burnt down the hut, Mira Behn wrote, at the dead of night, like thieves they came to steal him away, for when they sought to lay their hands on him. They feared the multitudes because they took him for a prophet. Gandhi was kept in the Yervada Jail, Poona.

On April 6, 1961, a monument built near the banyan tree under which Gandhi prayed with the Satyagrahis was inaugurated by Prime Minister Nehru. Safai Villa was converted into a museum. In 1973, the silver jubilee year of India's independence, 24 survivers of the Dandi March gatherd in Delhi and met Prime Minister Indira Gandhi. The group included R. Raghavan and Abbas Vattaji. A monument was built on the spot where Gandhi picked up the salt which was opined in 1976 by K.K. Viswanathan, Governor of Gujarat. A momento commencing how salt was prepared in a big pan was presented to the nation by family members of late C.F. Desai on April 6, 1988.[1]

NOTE

1. By Theodore Baskaran, *Frontline*, December12, 1997.

APPENDIX XIX

Mahatma Gandhi was not chosen for the Nobel Peace Prize

Mahatma Gandhi, the strongest symbol of non-violence in the twentieth century was never chosen for the Nobel Peace Prize. Gandhi was nominated in 1937, 1938, 1939, 1947 and finally a few days before he was murdered in January 1948. In 1937, a member of the Norwegian Storting (Parliament) Ole Colbjornsen (Labour Party) nominated Gandhi for this year's nobel prize and he was one of 13 candidates on the Norwegian Nobel Committtee's short list. The Committee's advisor, Professor Jacob Worm-Muller, who wrote a report on Gandhi, was much more critical. On the one hand, he fully understood the general administration for Gandhi as a person, he is undoubtedly a good noble and ascetic person, a prominent man, who is deservedly honoured and loved by the masses of India. On the other hand, when considering Gandhi as a political leader, the Norwegian Professor's description was too favourable. Therefore, he wrote, sharp turns in his policies, which can hardly be satisfactorily explained as follows.

He is a freedom fighter and a dictator, an idealist and a nationalist. He is frequently a Christ, but then suddenly an ordinary politician! Gandhi had many critics in the international Peace Movement. The Nobel Committee advisor referred to these critics in maintaining that he was not consistently pacifist, that he should have known that some of the non-violent campaign towards the British would degenerate into violence and terror. This was some- thing that had happened during the first non-cooperation campaign in 1920 and 1921 for example, when this was the Chauri-Chaura event and Gandhi withdraws the movement in 1922.

A frequent criticism from non-Indians was also that Gandhi was too much of an Indian nationalist. In his report, Professor Worm-Muller expressed his doubts as to whether Gandhi's ideals were meant to be unusual or primarily Indian. One might say that it is significant that his well known struggle in South Africa was on behalf of the Indians only, and not of the blacks whose living conditions were even worse.

The name of the 1937 Nobel Peace Prize laureate was to be Lord Cecil of Chilwood Ole Colbjornsen renominated him both in 1938 and in 1939 but ten years were to pass before Gandhi made it to the committee's short list again.

In 1947, the nominations of Gandhi came by telegrame fron India via Norwegian Foreign Office. The nominators were B.G. Kher, Prime Minister of Bombay, Govind Ballabh Pant, Premier of the United Province and G.V. Maveankar, Speaker of the Lok Sabha. Their motivations were written in telegraphic style, like the one from Govind Ballabh Pant, recommended for this year Nobel Prize. Mahatma Gandhi, architect of the Indian nation, the greatest living exponent of the moral order and the most effective champion of world peace today. There were to be six names on the Nobel committee's shortlist, Mohandas was one of them.

The Nobel committee's advisor, the historian Jens Arup Seep, wrote a new report which is primarily an accent of Gandhi's role in Indian political history after 1937. The following ten years Seep wrote from 1937 up to 1947, led to the event which for Gandhi and his movement was at the same time the greatest victory and the worst defeat—India's independence and India's partition. The report describes how Gandhi acted in the three different but mutually related conflicts which the Indian National Congress had to handle in the last decade before the independence, the struggle between the Indians and the British the question of India's participation in the Second World War and finally the conflict between the Hindu and Muslim communities. In all these matters, Gandhi had consistently followed his own principles of non-violence.

The Seep report was not critical towards Gandhi in the same way as the report written by Worm-Muller ten years earlier was. It was rather favourable, yet not supportive Seep also wrote briefly on the on going separation of India and the new Muslim state Pakistan and concluded—rather prematurely it would seem today. It is generally considered as expressed for example in the times of August 15, 1947, that if the gigantic surgical operation constituted by the partition of India has not led to bloodshed of much larger dimensions. Gandhi's teachings the efforts of his followers and his own presence should get a substantial part of the credit.

Having read the report, the members of the Norwegian Nobel Committee must have felt rather updated on the last phase of the Indian struggle for independence, however, the Nobel Prize for Peace had never been accorded for that sort of struggle. The committee members also had to consider the following issues; should Gandhi be selected for being a symbol of non-violence and what political effects could be expressed if the Peace prize was awarded to the most prominent Indian leader relation between India and Pakistan were from developing during the action of 1947.

From the diary of Committee Chairman Governor John, we now know that when the members were to make their decision on October 30, 1947 two active committee members, the Christian Conservative Herman Smith spoke in favour of Gandhi. However, in 1947, they were not able to convince the three other members, the Labour politician Martin Tranmael was very reluctant to award the Prize to Gandhi in the midst of the India-Pakistan conflict and former Minister Birger Braedland agreed with Tranmael. Gandhi was, they thought; too strongly connect to one of the belligerents. In addition, both Tranmael and John had learnt that one month earlier, at a prayer-meeting, Gandhi had made a statement which indicated that he had given up his consistent rejection of war, based on a telegram from Reuter, the *Times* on September 27, 1947, under the headline Mr. Gandhi on 'war' with Pakistan. Mr. Gandhi told his prayer meeting to-night that though he had always opposed all warfare. If there was no other way of securing justice fron Pakistan and if Pakistan persistently refused to see its proved error and continued to minimize it, the Indian Union government would have to go war against it. No one wanted war, but he could never advise anyone to put up with injustice. If all Hindus were annihilated for a just cause he would not mind. If these were war, the Hindus in Pakistan could not be fifth columnists, if their loyalty lay not with Pakistan they should leave it. Similarly Muslims whose loyalty was with Pakistan should not stay in the Indian Union.

Gandhi had immediately stated that the report was correct but incomplete. At the meeting he had added that he himself had not changed his mind and that he had no place in a new order where they wanted an army, a navy, an airforce and what not. Both John and Tranmael know that first report had not been complete, but they had become very doubtful. John in his diary quoted himself as saying, whole it is true that Gandhi is the greatest personality among the nominees—plenty of good things could be said about him. We should remember that he is not only an apostle for peace but he is first and feremost a patriot. Moreover, we have to bear in mind that Gandhi is not naïve. He is an excellent jurist and a lawyer. It seems that the committee chairman suspected Gandhi's statement made one month earlier to be a deliberate step to deter Pakistan aggression. Those of five members being against awarding the 1947 prize to Gandhi, the committee unanimously decided to award it to the Quakers.

1948: A Posthumous Award Considered

Mahatma Gandhi was assassinated on January 30, 1948, two days before the closing date for that year's Nobel Peace Prize nominations. The committee received six letters of nominations naming Gandhi. For the third time Gandhi came to the committee's shortlist—this time the list only included three names including Gandhi. The committee advisor Seep wrote report on Gandhi's activities during the last five months of his life. He concluded that Gandhi through the converse of life, had put his profound mark on an ethical and political attitude which would prevail as a large number of people both inside and outside India. In this respect Gandhi can only be compared to the founders of religions.

Nobody had ever been awarded the Nobel Peace Prize posthumously but according to the statutes of the Nobel Foundation in force at that time, the Nobel Prize could, under certain circumstances be awarded posthumously. Thus it was possible to give Gandhi the prize. However, Gandhi did not belong to an organisation, he left no property behind and no will, who should receive the prize money. The director of the Norwegian Nobel Institute August Schov asked another of the Committee's advisors, Lawyer of Torleif Reed to consider the practical consequence of the committee were to award the prize posthumously. Reed suggested a number of possible solutions for general application.

Subsequently, he asked the Swedish Prize Awarding Institute for their opinion. The answers were negative, posthumous Awards they thought, should not take place unless the laureate died after the committee's decision had been made.

On November 18, 1948, the Norwegian Nobel Committee decided to make no award that year on the grounds that there was no suitable living candidate. Chairman Gunnar John wrote in his diary to me it seems beyond doubt that a posthumous award would be contrary to the intentions of the testator. According to the chairman, three of his colleagues agreed in the end, only Oftadal was in favour of a posthumous award to Gandhi.

Owing to this tragic assassination, Gandhi could not receive the Nobel Peace Award. Had he remained alive even for few months more in 1948, he would have been a Laureate. The brutal assassination deprived Gandhi of this prestigious Award.[1]

NOTE

1. An article by Oyvind Tonnesson, *Frontline,* March 3, 2000.

APPENDIX XX

Gopal Krishan Gokhale's Ideas have Continuing Relevance

Mr. Gokhale was the greatest leader that India has ever provided writes in the *Ststesman* on February 21, 1915 'perhaps her greatest man' it has to be admitted that at the time of his death and for at least a decade before it. Gokhale occupied a unique place in the public life of India. You know Mrs. Besant had pleaded with him in 1914 that India cannot spare you and a month or so of rest may these years of work. You must remember Rabindranath Tagore to Gokhale in December 1913, that for a man like you to live in it is a service to your country, for your life is not merely useful, but is a light to others. A month earlier, the poetess Sarojini Naidu, when her own life was hanging precariously in the balance sent a message of love and gratitude to Gokhale. You have been beacon light of hope to the young generation.

It was no mean achievement for a man who had started life without the advantages of birth or fortune to have attained such pre-eminence. Gokhale's political ideals and methods were the ideals and methods of the founding fathers of the Indian National Congress. The formative influence in his life was of course Ranade, who in turn been inspired by the example of Dadabhai Naoroji. Gokhale used to describe himself as an intellectual grandson of Dadabhai Naoroji. In the conflict between two generations of the Congress politicians Gokhale did not join the rabel band of angry youngman instead, he became the spokesman of the old guard.

The conviction and the courage with which Gokhale spoke up for his country raised his stock high with the Indian educated class.

Gokhale had visualized an India of expanding industry of awakened faculties and increasing prosperity and mere widely distributed comfort and wealth. In his 'Indian Economic Thought' Professor B.N. Ganguli draws our attention to the surprising modern character of Gokhale's thinking and analysis and describes him as a bridge between the nineteenth century Economic theory and the Economic thought as it developed in the twentieth century. He desired political or economic reconstruction of the country.

He died on February 22, 1915, after taking his B.A. degree from the Elphinston College. He was drafed on to the staff of the Fergussan College, Bombay, where he lectured on English literature, Mathematics, History and Political Economy. After some time he was appointed as a professor in the Fergussan College. He was returned by the Central Division as its representatives to the Bombay Legislative Council. He remained only two years in this Council. Then he was elected by his non-official colleagues to succeed Sir Pherozshah Mehta as the representative of Bombay in the Viceroy's Legislative Council. From 1902 to the day of his death, Gokhale continued to be a member of the Viceroy's Legislative Council. He became also a member of the Royal Commission or the Public Service of India.[1]

NOTE

1. The *Times of India*, February 4, 1997.

APPENDIX XXI

The Film that could have averted India's Partition

If only Lord Mountbatten had known in 1947, that Mohammad Ali Jinnah was strikem with lung disease and would not have more than one or two years to live, the awesome decision to cut up India into two might have been avoided, according to two foreign political researchers (1975).

In their book *Freedom at Midnight* Larry Collins and Domique Lapiere record the knowledge of Jinnah's illness at that crucial period, when the new and the last Viceroy were having individual talks with the Indian leaders. The secret was frozen on to the gray surface of a piece of film, a film which could have upset the political equation and would almost certainly have changed the course of Asian history. The author says 'yes' so precious was the secret that even the British CID, one of the most effective investigative agencies in the world, was ignorant of its existence.

It was known only to Dr. J.A.L. Patel, a Bombay physician who kept in a sealed envelop the X-ray films that revealed that Jinnah, the 70 years old Muslim leader who had frustrated Louis Mountbatten's efforts to preserve India's unity, was living under a sentence of death from tuberculosis. Jinnah's sister, Fatima Jinnah only knew about the film. No third person knew it.

Finding no other alternative, Mountbatten agreed to the plan of Pakistan 'partition'. Mountbatten wrote is sheer madness and no one would ever induce me to agree to it were it not for this fantastic command madness. Patrick French in his book *Liberty or Death* (1997) has described Jinnah's illness also. According to him Jinnah's poor state of health was a closely guarded secreat is absurd, because Jinnah's photo always appeared in the press. Patrick holds this opinion that Collins and Lapiere's account regarding Jinnah's journey to Bombay in May or June 1946 was incorrect because Jinnah was not busy in negotiating with Cripps nor he says there was any Doctor in Bombay by the name of J.A.L. Patel, though there was one Doctor called Commander Jai Patel. But Patrick accepts this view that Jinnah had tuberculosis in 1946. Had Lord Mountbatten or the Indian leaders learnt about Jinnah's fatal illness, they could have rejected Mountbatten plan and joined Gandhi in rejecting this plan.

But it was not known to them till Jinnah died on September 11, 1948 due to bronchitis at Karachi. So had the Indian leaders knew about the film and the bronchifis condition, perhaps India's partition would have been avoided.[1]

NOTE

1. The *Times of India*, November 17, 1978.

APPENDIX XXII

Jinnah's Negativism and Partition

One factor which played an important part in the history of partition was the personal ambition of Jinnah, shrewd and sharp as he was; he knew that in united India he could not be a second fiddle to Gandhi and Nehru, whereas in independent Pakistan he would be the supreme. Louis Fisher, an American journalist has also called Jinnah a politician of limitless ambition. It was difficult for Jinnah to remain in a position of a toothless tiger with claws carefully manicured would have been worse than death.

Jinnah's major demo, Liaquat Ali Khan is on record as having said that he would sooner have a few acres of sand desert provided it was his very own, rather than have a united India with a majority rule. Philips Zieglar is perhaps nearer the truth when he says in his book *Mountbatten* Jinnah used negativism to achieve positive ends by saying 'no' he inexorably closed all avenues except the one leading to the only affirmative he would accept—all independent Pakistan.

Maulana Azad's assessment that Nehru and Patel were responsible for India's partition is not corroborated by the well documented research books.[1]

NOTE

1. The *Times of India*, 1997.

APPENDIX XXIII

Jawaharlal Nehru's Call for Socialism in India

In his Presidential address to the Congress on Sunday night Pandit Jawaharlal Nehru said, for many years now I have been a distant looker on this Indian scene where once I was an actor and many a thing has happened that has failed me with distress and anguish. Temporary failure has little significance where the arm is high and the struggle bound to long one. It is but the inactive to further effort often it teaches us more than a victory easily won and becomes a prelude to a great success. Real failure comes only when we forget our ideas and objectives and principles and begin to wander away from the real which leads to their realization.

Sixteen years ago, under the inspiration of our leader, we took a new and long step converting this Congress from an ineffective body, feebly functioning amongst the upper classes into a powerful democratic organization with its roots in the Indian and the vast masses who live on it. Yet our struggle was that part of a far wider struggle for freedom and the forces that moved us were moving millions of people all over the world and driving them into action.

Of one thing I must say a few words for to me it is one of the most vital things that I value. That is the tremendous deprivation of civil liberties in India. I can never adjust myself to it, I find it intolerable. And yet I find many of my own countrymen complacent about them. Some who have made the practice of sitting on a fence into a fine art, being natural when such questions are discussed? We in the Congress welcome all cooperation in the struggle for the Indian freedom; our doors are ever open to all who stand for that freedom and are against imperialism. But they are not open to the allies of imperialism and the supporters of repression and those who stand by the British Government in its suppression of civil liberty. We belong to opposite camps.

In course of his speech he stressed socialism in India and Congress as organization of masses. Concluding he said: we have forgotten for the moment the larger ideals we stood far and we quarrel over petty issues. We have largely lost touch with the masses and deprived of the life giving energy that flows from them. We dry up and weaker and our organization shrinks and loses the power it has.[1]

NOTE

1. The *Times Archives*, April 1936.

APPENDIX XXIV

CPI and Partition

It is a fact that Indian communalists had supported the creation of Pakistan or the Muslim League's demand for Pakistan. The Indian communists became the staunch supporters of the demand for Pakistan put forward by the Muslim League in 1940. They supported the demand till the country was actually partitioned in the name of the principle of self-determination.

In the elections to the central assembly and provincial assemblies held in November 1945 and February 1946, the Indian communists supported the Muslim League candidates. Similarly they had opposed the Quit India Movement in August 1942 and dubbed the Congress a fifth columnist of the fascist powers.

APPENDIX XXV

The Man Behind Socialist Movement

The idea of founding the Congress Socialist Party was conceived in Nasik Central Prison during 1932-33 but the first conference was held only in 1934 in Bombay which was attended by Acharya Narendra Dev, Jaiprakash Narayan, Dr. Ram Manohar Lohia, Kamla Devi Chattopadhyaya, Achyut Patwardhan, S.M. Joshi, N.G. Gorang and Minoo Masani. For many a socialist, Yusuf Meherally was the conscience of the movement to the late first President, Rajendra Prasad who was a devoted servant of the country and to Nehru a 'loved friend'.

Yusuf Meherally front ranking socialist of pre-independence era, founder member of the Congress Socialist Party and tolerant of religions and man of the masses, he incurred the wrath of his own community. Though his spirit of reform and revolution so much so that they deserted and disowned him during his last journey to the burial ground and some of them even closed their windows angrily as the funeral procession passed. He died of tuberculosis in Bombay in 1950 at the age of 47. The Congress Socialist Party challenged the Indian communist's monopoly of socialist ideology, laid down in dictum that every socialist must fight for India's freedom and that the Congress was the broadest based organization for the anti-imperialist struggle.

Meherally and his friends defused and enlarged the role of Socialists written the Congress. The CSP was formed after the birth of the Communist Party of India in 1924, which branded the Congress as an organization demarcated by the Indian interests. Meh[illegible] along with leaders like Lala Lajpat Rai, prepared the groun[illegible]

Salt Satyagraha with a nationwide demonstration against the Simon Commission in 1928.

In 1931 when the Second World War broke out and Meherally strongly flavoured a massive struggle against the imperialist war into which India was dragged without consent. However, he finally did go along with the restricted individual Satyagraha proposed by Mahatma Gandhi. Acharya Narendra Dev, Ram Manohar Lohia, Achyut Patwardhan and others were also touching socialist leaders, who helped the movement to develop.

APPENDIX XXVI

Patel's Letter to Golwalkar

Expressing his views about the RSS and its leaders, the then Union Home Minister, Sardar Patel in his letter of September 11, 1948 wrote, all their speeches were full of communal poison. It was not necessary to spread poison in order to stir up the Hindus and organize their protection. As a final result of the poison, the country had to suffer the significance of the individual life of Gandhi.

The Sardar said that there was not even an 'iota of sympathy' in the Government of the people for the RSS and the opposition in turn more severe when the RSS men expressed joy and distributed sweets after Gandhi's death. The virulence of the RSS opposition to the Congress, disregarding all considerations of personality, decency or decorum, had created a kind of sense of unrest among the people. In the concluding part of his one page letter in which he points out that there is no place for party conflicts. The Sardar says: "I am thoroughly convinced that the RSS men carry on their patriotic endeavour only by joining the Congress and not by keeping separate or opposing."

Sardar Patel had written another letter to Dr. Shyama Prasad Mukherjee in reply to his entirety on behalf of the RSS and the Hindu Mahasabha. The relevant excerpts is as follows, as regards the RSS and the Hindu Mahasabha, the case relating to Gandhi's murder is *subjudice* and I should like to say anything about the participation of two organizations but our report do confirm that as a result of the activities of those two bodies particularly the former, an atmosphere was created in the country in which such a ghastly tragedy becomes possible.

There is no doubt in my mind that the extreme section of the Hindu Mahasabha was involved in the conspiracy. The activists of the RSS constituted a clear thrust to the existence of the Government and the state. Our report show that these activists despite the ban have not died down. Indeed, as time has marched on, the RSS circles are becoming more defiant and are indulging in subversive activities in the increasing measure. In 1947, Golwalkar, Godse and others viewed Gandhiji as the main obstruction in achicving the goal of a Hindu Rashtra and so Gandhiji was removed from the scene.

APPENDIX XXVII

The Hindu Mahasabha and the RSS

The Hindu Mahasabha was started in 1915 as a forum for a variety of Hindu interests. Its early membership included Lala Lajpat Rai, Pandit Madan Mohan Malviya and Bhai Parmanand. But the group got a well defined political orientation only after Veer Savarkar, a Hindutwa, became president in 1937. Even after the Gandhi's assassination, the Mahasabha was still important to win five Lok Sabha seats in 1952 and emerged as the main opposition party in the old Madhya Bharat State.

The RSS was formed in 1925. The RSS as an organization never participated in the freedom struggle. Not one of the leaders went to jail and fought against the British. The RSS did not even participate in the August movement of 1942. The RSS cadre was taught that it is the Muslims who have enslaved India and Hindus. All the stories and folklore narrated to the youngsters at the RSS Shakhas were directed towards Muslims and Islam. They said nothing against the British and justified their non-participation in the freedom struggle on the ground that RSS was a cultural organization and not a political one.

The doctrine of the RSS was to keep Hindus away from the freedom struggle and this attitude benefited the British Government. The Indian National Congress was established in 1885. If the RSS had participated in the National Movement, the British imperialism would have suffered a lot. Sir Syed, like the RSS men, advised Muslims not to participate in politics and concentrate only on education.

APPENDIX XXVIII

Rise of Urdu and Partition

The synthesis of the Hindu and Muslim cultures that had been spontaneous taking shape for over 500 years at the grassroots, however, came to nothing. Right from the beginning the Muslim ruling class, with the exception of small enlightened sections of them in every period, knew like the British later, that they could hold political power over their subjects, who vastly outnumbered them, only if they remained aloof from them underpinned their status as rulers by a distinct cultural identity. This gave an opportunity to the intellectuals and the Ulema, who came in great number from Central Asia, to continually reinforce the already existing conservative and racist—indeed facist-tendencies of the Muslim rulers and elates.

In a book *Bane Saghir Maen Muslman Maashray Ka Almaye*, Dr. Mubarak Ali has given an insight into the Muslim society and cultural history during the Sultanate and the Mughal periods. Few references are in this way, as a result of the Mongol invasion of Central Asia, large numbers of the ulema migrated to India. They were followers of the Sunni faith and in the matters of 'Figh' held extremist views on arriving here, they compelled the sultans of Delhi not to treat Hindus as 'Zimmis' because that treatment is permissive only towards the people of the book, since Hindus were not the people of the book, they ought either to be slaughtered or else convicted to Ashram. And if this was not possible then at least they ought to be kept in a state of humiliation and degradation.

Ruling Class

The centre of the Muslim ruling classes' political and religious loyalties remained outside India. After Sind was conquered in 712 A.D. by Mohammad Bin Kasim and King Dahir was killed, the Governor and other administrators of Sind were still officers of the Omayyed and Abbasid Caliphates. Even when independent Arab governments were established in Sind, they regarded the Abbasid Caliph as the source of their politics and spiritual authority and his name used to be mentioned in the Khutba.

When the Truks established their rule in Northern India they too retained political allegiances to authorities outside India, to the Ghazni and Ghori Dynasty. Even after this connection was ended, the Sultans of Delhi kept sending for certificates from Baghdad and Cairo to legitimate their rule in India.

While the Ulema has successfully managed to insulate Muslim politics and outlook from the developments that were taking among the Indian masses at large and turned them into channels that were essentially destructive of those developments, a similar and similarly unequal, conflict was going on the fields of language and literature.

From the time that Humayun returned from his exile in Persia with an Army of Persian scholars and poets and artists in 1554 A.D., any hope that any of the burgeoning vernaculars could one day become the official language were doomed, so far as the Persian intellectuals and poets were concerned by and large neither India nor Indian language existed. Persian and Persian way of life reigned supreme at the court and indeed Persian was made state language in 1582.

Nevertheless, the supremacy of the Persian-orientated conservative forces did not go unchallenged; the conflict between the need to overcome religious divisions and create an integrated Hindu-Muslim culture of India on the one hand and the efforts of the orthodox ulema and intellectuals to prevent this from happening on the other erupted in the context of Persian literature itself, and for a time it looked as if the orthodox forces had lost the fight.

As is well known Akbar inspired by the Sufi teachings, invented the Din-e-Ilahi, with the specific purpose of bringing Hindus and Muslims together, he took great interest in the translation of Sanskrit works into Persian. The intellectual's atmosphere at court underwent a radical transformation. An open mindedness towards other religions begins to make its appearance among scholars and literates. Abul Fazal translated many religious works, including the *Bhagvat Gita* and the *Bible*. It even seemed that the age of the enlightenment was approaching.

In the form of another, this thrust towards idealization and towards a composite Hindu and Muslim culture was continued during the reign of Akbar's successors and, in the literary sphere culminated in Dara Shikoh's translation of the *Upanishads* into Persian under the title of *Sirr-i-Akbar*. In Annemarie Schimmel's words, it was 'a most remarkable work which became one of the sacred scriptures of European idealists and philosophers after Anquatil Duperron translated it into Latin in 1801.

The orthodox sections of the Muslim elite could not stomach these developments for too long. Their revenge first took the form of an attack on the Shias (the poets and scholars who had been coming in large numbers from Iran, and had assisted Akbar in his literary and religious experiments were Shias). Abul Fazal was murdered and the orthodox elements find triumphs came with the ascension of Aurangzeb to the throne in 1658 after he had blinded and thrown into prison his brother Dara Shikoh, the translator of the *Upanishad* a and the rightful heir to the throne.

Islam-fundamentalism and reaction now reigned supreme. It was in this atmosphere that Urdu—the Indian vernacular—that had been growing and maturing among the Indian people for the previous five or six centuries arrived in Delhi in the Person of the poet Wal Dakhni, and hits fate was a foregone conclusion.

Urdu was literally usurped by the ruling classes and reshaped to serve their own narrow, reactionary aims. All that was genuinely popular in its make-up, all that was popular in origin, all that had made it a living expression of an ongoing Hindu-Muslim rapprochement, was suppressed or purged from it. And it was thus that it now emerged as 'the language of the Muslims' an instrument that divided a people and a continent where once it had promised their unification.

New Language

The character of this new language is precisely portrayed by Aziz Ahmad; this rejection of the Indian and Hindu elements was an unconscious operation of group psychology, an instinctive effort to preserve in a culturally alien and hostile milieu its own cultural roots, signs, symbols and insular patterns of expressions. In this process imaginary was drawn exclusively from Persian precedents, i.e. from the unseen and unexpected sights, sounds and smells of Persia and Central Asia, rejecting totally the Indian sights, sounds and season's experiences as materials regarded not sublime enough for poetic expression.

The state of poetic mind which works entirely in terms of this exclusively non-Indian magic symbolism can perhaps be illustrated by an occasional poem of Gandhi (1796-1869), the greatest of Urdu poets, on an object so purely Indian as a roasted betelnut. He used eight metaphors to describe it, seven of which are of non-Indian cultural origin.

Urdu created for itself, by a process of mathematical multiplication an inexhaustible wealth of symbols, images and designs which compared to generalized necessities of emotion and intellect. It was a desperate unconscious clinging to the origins of the symbols of Muslim India's cultural experience which had begun abroad and an instructive escape from the fear of submergence into the Hindu culture milieu, with, its strange gods, its almost pigeon love of the actual Indian nature, its startling realism, and its tempting fragrance and rhythm.

To conclude it may be said that the origin of Urdu began about 1000 A.D. and Khadi Boli, which was dominant, around Delhi when the Muslims came formed the bases of Urdu. In the time of Mirza Asadullah Khan Ghalel (1796-1869 A.D.), Urdu progressed. In the reign of Shah Alam II, Oudh became a centre of the Urdu knowledge, many Urdu poets in the nineteenth and twentieth centuries discussed contemporary problems, cultural conflicts and social turmoils in the ghazal. Mohammad Iqbal (1873-1938) was one such poet. Iqbal was a politician also and he was in favour of Pakistan. The period of 1936-1947 was one of revolt and experimentation. A new direction was given to old poetic forms and many new forms were attempted in order to develop socio-consciousness through literature. But the growth of the Urdu literature killed the spirit of the composite culture which had started from the time of the Mughal Emperor, Akbar. Aurangzeb was an opponent to the composite culture. The orthodox section of the Muslim elite did not like the composite culture and this elite group favoured Urdu to develop. The Hindu-Muslim rapprochement was now coming to an end and Islamic fundamentalism was reigning supreme. It was in this hostile atmosphere that the idea of partition took a concrete shape. M.A.

Jinnah also backed Urdu and when Pakistan was formed, Urdu became the official language of Pakistan. The people of the East Pakistan did not like Urdu and they revolted and the Bangladesh was formed. Had the Urdu literature supported the spirit of the composite culture, the result would have been different in 1947. So the rise of Urdu was one factor for the partition of India.

In this process only that was vanquished was not merely the 'Indian and Hindu element', but the Indian people both Hindus and Muslims. And they will keep being defeated, until they snatch the skate out of the clutches of religion.

The distinguished scholar Abdul Hague, speaking in Karachi on February 15, 1961, had said that Pakistan was not created by Jinnah nor was it created by Iqbal, it was Urdu that created it. For, the fundamental reason for the discord between Hindus and Muslims was the Urdu language. The entire two-nation theory and all other difficulties of this nature issued solely from Urdu. Therefore, Pakistan owes a debt of gratitude to Urdu. It would be relevant to note here that while the creator of Pakistan, Mohammad Ali Jinnah, always spoke and broadcast in English, it was Pandit Jawaharlal Nehru who addressed the Nation in Urdu, called by some as Hindi and by others as Hindustani.

Index

Abdul Ghaffar Khan, 225, 231, 263, 385, 387
Abdul Rab Nishtar, 249–250, 260
Acharya Kriplani, 249–250, 428, 430
Administrative machinery, 114, 184, 230, 330, 413, 465
Administrative reform, 471
Aga Khan, 36, 67–68, 340
Agartala conspiracy case, 128
Agra Muslim, 35
Agricultural Party, 88, 357
Ahmad Khan, 15, 21, 34, 120–121, 333, 341, 423
Alavindakshan Commission, 118
Ali, Liaquat, 78, 118, 418, 420, 427, 442, 445, 448–449
Ali, Maulana Shaukat, 39, 331–332
Ali, Mohammad, 281
Ali, Rahmat, 78
Aligarh Institute Gazette, 22
Aligarh movement, 30, 423
Aligarh Muslim University, 122, 162, 165–166
Aligarh Party, 38
Allan Octavian Hume, 71–72, 75
All-Party Conference, 65, 97
Al-ttilal press, 37–38
Ambedkar Centre for Justice and Peace, 423
Ambedkar Commercial Awards, 472
Ameny, Leo, 131
Ancient Monuments Preservation Act, 42
Anglo-Indians, 59, 261
Antagonism, 219
Anti-British agitation, 35, 192
Anti-communal organizations, 273
Anti-Pakistan Day, 273
Arbitration Tribunal Order, 288
Archaeological movement, 104
Army rule, 413
Ashley, Wilfred, 209, 368
Ashram, 43, 86, 382, 481, 501
Asian Nationalism, 81
Assessment of Cabinet Mission, 175
Atlantic Charter to India, 130–132, 160
Atom bomb, 153–154
Attlee campaigning, 191
Attlee, Clement, 154, 279, 392, 411, 451
Attlee's policy, 207
August Movement, 138, 154, 156, 162, 350, 408, 417, 500
Aurangzeb Khan, 139, 455
Ayub, George, 120

Backward colonial policy, 129
Badruddin Tyabji, 72, 74, 381
Badshah Khan, 225, 443
Balkan Plan, 234, 239, 246
Balkanization of India, 238

Bangladesh War, 338
Bargaining centre, 114
Bargaining powers, 113
Basher, Ahmad, 454
Bengal Muslim League, 190
Besant, Annie, 39, 41, 45, 73, 417, 467
Bhagat Singh, 61–62
Bhaskarah Nair Commission, 118
Bhumihars, 94
Bihar Muslim Independent Party, 95
Bihari Muslims, 196
Black marketers, 285
Blake, Joyce, 378
Bombay Legislative Council, 489
Boothrayed, Betty, 310
Boundary Commission, 263–264, 270
  for Bengal, 261
  Lahore, 264
Bracher, Michael, 281
Bradlaugh, Charles, 72
Brahmanism, 1, 116
Brecher, Michael, 183, 185, 198, 336, 353, 389, 440
British Broadcasting Corporation, 423
British Commonwealth, 150, 167, 206–207, 230, 247, 413
British education, 10
British element in India, 49
British Government's policy, 336, 390
British imperialism, 35, 95, 97, 123, 162, 331, 369, 500
British India, 42, 86, 192, 206–207, 212, 241, 279, 281, 291–292, 327, 465
British Indian Empire, 73
British Labour Government, 186
British period, 14–15, 35
British policy, 43, 65, 120, 149, 176, 241, 292, 318, 334, 336, 392, 431, 466, 474
British power, 190, 250, 253
British Raj, 44, 48, 152, 205–206, 279, 282, 319
British rule, 14–15, 48, 97, 123, 144, 201, 212, 293, 312, 468
British war cabinet, 434
Brother Gandhi, 122
Buckingham Palace, 59–60
Burdwan University, 334
Bureaucracy, 48, 442, 446
Burma, 41, 132, 209, 211, 318

Cabinet delegation, 172, 174–176, 188, 272
Cabinet Mission, 5, 117, 167, 169–176, 181–183, 186, 192, 198, 201, 214, 238, 257, 273, 338, 395–396
  and Pakistan, 167
  and Viceroy, 181
  to India, 202
  scheme, 244
Calcutta killings, 185, 188–190, 343, 418
Callaghan, James, 451
Calumny Mission, 465
Capitalism, 430, 457
Capitalist system, 345
Caste
  fabric, 9
  fragmentation, 2
  system, 9
  issues, 398
Cease-fire agreement, 329
Cecil Hotel, 200
Central National Mohammedan Association, 17
Central Parliamentary Board, 105
Central Telegraph Office, 58
Champaran movement, 41
Charter of slavery, 86
Chittagong hill track to Pakistan, 270
Chittagong hill tract in Bengal, 289

Churchill, Winston, 36, 117, 130–131, 143, 210, 279, 409, 459
Civil disobedience movement, 57, 196, 276, 342, 349, 417, 441, 453
Civil disorders, 10
Civil services examinations, 71
Civil society, 426
Civil war, 49, 100, 143, 148, 185, 219, 223, 229, 241, 245, 272, 297, 338, 423, 438
Clive, Robert, 406
Coalition governments, 10, 99, 278
Collective interests, 5
Collins, Herbert, 375
Colonial policy, 479
Colonialism, 466
Commercial Awards, 472
Commercial organizations, 70
Commonwealth of India, 51
Communal Award, 84–85, 97, 337, 340, 347, 399
Communal cleavage, 153
Communal conflicts, 187, 193, 445
Communal disorder, 35, 192, 276
Communal electorate, 49, 84
Communal factor, 115
Communal organization, 37, 53, 99, 406
Communal Party, 31, 66–67, 91, 257, 275, 354, 361, 392
Communal riots, 100, 118, 166, 185, 192, 194–195, 197, 205, 256–257, 275, 416, 435, 438, 444, 475
Communal state, 97, 294
Communal war, 394
Communalism, 8, 21, 27, 30–32, 36, 41, 46, 82, 85, 98, 153, 192, 270, 347, 430
Communist Party in India, 118, 138, 399, 478–479, 496
Composite culture, 3, 67, 426, 504–505
Compromise formula, 48, 169, 473, 475
Conciliatory policy, 54
Congress Democratic Party, 55
Congress domination, 226
Congress League coalition, 91, 361
Congress-Muslim League coalition, 92, 361
Congress Nationalism, 36
Congress organization, 46, 384, 417
Congress Party, 20, 25, 55, 66, 88–90, 94, 107, 141, 189, 233, 337–338, 351–352, 358–359, 407, 424
Congress policy, 90, 359, 399
Congress rule, 188
Congress Socialist Party, 205, 479, 496
Conservative groups, 475
Conservative Party, 153, 248, 319, 452, 459
Constitution of India, 85, 313, 319, 476
Constitutional deadlock, 129, 133, 348
Constitutional methods, 175, 186, 405, 411, 479
Constitutional Problems of India, 126
Constitutional progress, 114, 454
Constitutionalism, 186
Cotton, Henry, 39
Council Act, 32, 37, 76, 472
Coupland Plan, 137
Criminal Law Amendment Act, 276
Cripps Declaration, 409
Cripps Mission, 135–137, 235, 348
Cross-Party delegation, 161
Cultural conflicts, 504
Cultural development, 8, 14
Cultural organizations, 500
Curzon's rule, 327
Czechoslovakia, 84, 101, 329

Day of Deliverance, 103–104, 394
Declaration of independence, 55
Defence of India Rules, 190
Delhi convention of Muslim legislatures, 127
Delhi University, 210, 368
Deliverance day, 104, 282
Democratic organizations, 493
Depressed caste, 59
Desai-Liyakat Ali Pact, 144
Discovery of India, 80–81
Divide and rule, policy of, 35–36, 76, 119, 335–336, 339, 392, 415
Dominion Parliament of India, 50
Dominion Status, 48
Double votes, 84
Durbar Hall, 313–314

Economic factors, 337
Economic theory, 489
Education, western, 34, 70, 99
Election campaign, 88, 357–358
Election Commission, 10
Election manifesto, 87, 292, 341, 343
Electoral organization, 26
Electoral system, 32, 85
Element of society, 334
Elite groups, 70, 504
Emergency powers, 183
English educated classes, 70–71
English education, 16, 24, 34, 70
  growth of, 24, 70
English language, 9, 70
English literature, 489
English Pacifist, 194
Englishman's game, 398
European war issue, 131

Favouritism, 284
Fertile soil, 7
Feudal
  landlordism, 106
  lords, 343
  organizations, 393

Fiji Indians, 14
First World War, 38–39, 209, 233, 346, 471
Foreign domination, 6, 16, 181
Free India, 49, 52, 96, 156, 165, 195, 200–201, 290, 306, 309–310, 316, 337, 384, 431
Freedom movement, 3, 38, 59, 80, 138, 383, 441
Freedom struggle, 3, 8, 14–15, 43, 45–46, 106, 119, 133, 392, 423, 432, 478–479, 500
French power, 329
French Revolution, 9
French, Patrick, 31, 35, 53, 56, 165, 176, 187, 189, 304, 356, 415, 490
Friday prayers, 188, 190
Frontier Congress, 262
Functional leadership, 8
Fundamental principles, 5, 174, 184, 283–284, 286, 413
Fundamental rights, 4, 49, 171, 472

Gandhi
  and Hindu Congress, 151
  and Jinnah, 15, 111, 141, 144, 147, 228, 394, 407, 416–417
  and Nehru, 111, 262, 294, 310, 344, 406, 416, 424, 430, 492
  Chauri-Chaura event and, 484
  deprived, 487
  Indira, 132, 482
  negotiation, 142
  and Nehru, Divide, 344
  Rajeev, 379, 381
  and Swami Vivekananda, 308
Gandhian nationalism, 383
Gandhian technique, 406
  activities of, 486
  assassination of, 121, 346, 376, 500
  blessings of, 435
  campaign of, 406
  emergence of, 44

failure of, 59, 61
friend Harold Laski, 400
hunting fear of, 400
ideals of, 484
impression of, 142
influence of, 176–177
intervention of, 350
-Irwin Pact, 54, 56–57, 59–60, 62, 460
-Jinnah negotiations, 142–143
Kasturba Gandhi (wife), 416
letter of, 15, 140–141, 225
mastery of, 45
monologues of, 58
precious life of, 85
preference of, 180
scheme of, 225
strategy of, 479
tactics of, 147
teachings of, 485
Ganges water, 8, 317–318
Garden Party, 73, 217
General Ayub Khan, 413, 415
General Smith, 43
Germany, 7, 39, 100–102, 329–330, 461
Ghaffar Khan, 262
Gibraltar, 131
Gokhale, Gopal Krishna, 39
Golden Temple, 274, 297
Goodwill campaign, 220
Government of India Act, 39, 54, 65, 67, 86, 102–103, 248, 273, 277, 279–280, 319, 336, 340, 356, 407–408
Governmental power, 418
Great Britain, 5–6, 103, 154, 160, 327
Group constitution, 171, 174, 238
Gunther, Francis, 344
Guru Govind Singh, 272

Hakim Ajmal Khan, 45, 51
Haque, Fazlul, 112–113, 118, 124, 126, 128, 134
Harbour, Pearl, 129
Hardy, Peter, 349
Hari Singh, 270
Haripur Congress Session, 98
Hasan, Wazir, 82, 98
Haven, Milford, 209
Hayat Khan, 117, 124, 168, 425
Hazlehurst, Peter, 125
Hill tracts, 137
Hindu and Muslim-communal models, 3
Hindu brotherhood, 120, 332
Hindu community, 76, 85, 284, 426
Hindu domination, 87, 154
Hindu fanatical power, 406
Hindu Mahasabha, 3, 20–21, 47, 53–54, 81, 96, 143, 498, 500
Hindu majority provinces, 116, 171–173, 182, 352, 395
Hindu-Muslim
cooperation, 177
riots, 108, 228
unity, 53, 114, 347, 406–407
-Sikh unity, 117
Hindu Nationalism, 16, 120, 331
Hindu-Nation State, 2
Hindu Nationalists traditionalists, 119
Hindu Party, 123
Hindu Raj, 20, 135, 150, 348, 363, 430
Hindu Rashtra, 120, 332, 499
Hinduism, 1–2, 9, 18, 186, 222
Hoare, Stanley, 460
Home Rule, 469
Hough, Richard, 220
House of Lords, 279, 464
Hume, Joseph, 72
Hunter Commission, 44
Husain, Fazli, 66–67
Hussain, Zakir, 122
Hyat Khan, 148, 275, 341–342

Idealism, 310
Iftikar Husain Khan, 276

Ilbert Bill, 72
Imperial Lords, 464
Imperial rule, 466
Imperialism, 103, 109, 141, 214, 320, 493
Imperialist war, 497
Income tax, 266
Independence Act, 280, 329
Independence Day, 277, 375
Independent Bengal, 113, 231
Independent nation-state, 6
India Muslim League, 25, 29, 37, 83, 127, 139, 174–175, 181, 186, 257, 432
Indian association of Lahore, 18
Indian Freedom Movement, 14, 58, 281, 334, 355
Indian Independence Act, 264, 266, 278–279, 281, 289, 328, 467
Indian National Army, 157
Indian National Congress, 6, 16, 36–41, 44–46, 59, 75–76, 93–95, 120, 133–135, 221, 235, 353–354, 403–405, 430–432, 469–470
Indian National Federation, 5
Indian National Union, 72
Indian nationalism, 6, 24, 41, 46, 120, 331, 401
Indian nationalist movement, 474
Indian Patriotic Association, 19
Indian Political Service, 201
Indian politics, 28, 31, 85, 111, 136, 209, 339–342, 347, 409
Indian secularism, 426
Indo-Pak war, 113
Industrial development, 393
Industrialism, 345
Industrialization, 67, 345
Institute of Commonwealth Studies, 325
Intelligence Bureau Report, 35
Interagency, 150
International Peace Movement, 483
Iqbal Park, 112
Iqbal, Rahmat Ali, 78
Islamic
  fundamentalism, 503–504
  nationhood, 120, 332
  pantheism, 83
Ismay, Lord, 240, 242, 338, 454

Jadavpur University, 125
Jamia Millia University, 119
Japan, 7, 13, 101, 151, 154, 206, 433
Jenkins, Evan, 269, 274
Jihad, 168, 186, 190
Jinnah
  blunder of, 427, 450
  campaign of, 408
  career of, 53, 420
  character of, 221
  conduct of, 150
  contribution of, 419
  death of, 413
  demand of, 97, 168, 227, 238, 424
  dream of, 253, 257, 426
  ego of, 111, 416
  fears of, 230
  game of, 135
  grip of, 168
  illness of, 234, 490–491
  interagency of, 150
  interference of, 124
  invitation to Gandhi, 140
  League of, 68
  letter of, 135
  misfortune of, 111, 404, 418
  Muslim League and, 339
  negativism of, 492
  objection of, 336
  outlook of, 406
  philosophy of, 118
  plan of, 67
  policy of, 253
  presidential speech of, 113
  rejoinder of, 15
  resignation of, 45

secret links of, 117
statement of, 152
stature of, 112
terms of, 91, 360
Johnson, Alan Campbell, 260, 295, 300
Joint families, 13, 386, 433
Judicial system, 281
Justice Party, 124

Kalhiawor Agency of British India, 42
Kanpur conspiracy case, 457
Karaadi village, 482
Kayasthas, 94
Kennedy, John F., 383
Khaliq-uz-Zaman, 89–91, 112, 358, 393
Khan Brothers, 87, 262–263
Khan Sahib Khan, 262
Khan, 99, 162, 448
Khilafat movement, 46, 112, 119, 347
Khizar Hayat Khan, 145, 155, 196
Krishak Praja Party, 113
Krishna Menon, 230, 239, 245–247
Kurukshetra University, 20, 392, 424

Labour Government, 155–156, 160, 167, 169, 202, 411, 444, 451–452, 461
Labour Party, 55, 130, 133, 149–150, 153–154, 168, 200, 202, 400, 411, 451, 460, 483
Lady Mountbatten, 210, 218, 220, 242, 296, 367, 374–375, 378, 380–381
Lahore Conspiracy Case, 61
Lahore resolution, 93, 112–115, 117–118, 120, 122–128, 135, 388, 392–393, 395, 408, 424, 454
Lahore session, 32, 55, 78, 128, 221, 348, 354, 385, 409
Land reforms, 87, 93, 343, 363
Lapping, Brian, 137, 220, 222, 431
Large-scale disorders, 441
Lawrence, Pathick, 207
League board, 88, 358
League policy of obstruction, 439
Liaquat Ali Khan, 107, 115, 118, 144, 170, 195, 240, 249–250, 260–261, 268, 295–297, 427, 448, 450, 456
Liaquat-Desai Pact, 343, 448
Liberalism, 19–20
Lincoln, Abraham, 386
Linlithgow, 92, 114, 123, 136, 156, 361, 407–409, 433
London Conference, 180, 197–199, 437
London declaration, 198
Lord Attlee, 464
Lord Cecil, 484
Lord Chamberlain, 60
Lord Curzon, 24, 42, 280, 292, 474
Lord Daffrin, 21
Lord Dufferin, 73–74
Lord Halifax, 454
Lord Irvin, 57, 340
Lord Irwin, 459
Lord Kalleam, 318
Lord Lander, 32
Lord Linlithgow, 36, 100–104, 112, 123, 292, 308, 335, 343, 348, 388, 407, 410
Lord Listowel, 251, 260, 289, 331, 454, 464–465
Lord Louis Mountbatten, 209, 336, 477
Lord Lytton, 16, 24
Lord Mayo, 71
Lord Milford Haven, 209
Lord Minto, 24–25, 28, 31–32
Lord Mountbatten, 197, 205, 210, 232, 245–246, 262–263, 289, 292, 308, 315, 317, 338, 367, 464–465, 490–491
Lord Moyne, 131

Lord Pethick Lawrence, 153, 160, 167, 172, 228, 235, 464
Lord Randalph Churchil, 73
Lord Reading, 45, 368
Lord Salisbury, 71, 474
Lord Wavell, 142, 151–154, 192–194, 197, 205, 211–212, 215, 229, 234, 272, 335, 457, 462–463
Lord Willingdon, 340, 453
Loyal organization, 76
Lucknow Congress, 40, 86
Lucknow Pact, 34, 38–41, 221, 407, 433, 471
Lyon, Peter, 325, 330

Macaulay's education policy, 10
Macmillan, Harold, 205
Maharaja Lakshmeshwar Singh Bahadur, 75
Majesty's Government, 172, 197, 206–208, 212, 226, 234, 240, 243, 281
Majority provinces, 173, 320, 425
Malabar hills, 221, 266, 283, 405
Malthusian Indians, 14
Mandal, Jogendra Nath, 281–282, 412
Mangal Singh, 47
Manseargh, Nicholas, 356
Mass-based campaign, 43
Mass contact recruitment campaign, 104
Mass disorders, 156
Master Tara Singh, 197, 231, 272–274, 296–297
Materialist Muslim elements, 291
McDonald's Communal Award, 53, 84
Menon Plan, 247–248, 251
Militant Punjabi Muslim group, 257, 432
Minto Park in Lahore, 112
Moderate elements, 345
Mohammedan Anglo-Oriental College, 16, 121
Mohsin-ul-Mulk, 25
Money power, 58
Montagu-Chelmsford Act, 43
Moore's analysis, 454
Morgan, Janet, 380–382
Morley-Minto era, 32
Morley-Minto's Reform Act, 433
Mosley, Leonard, 152, 183, 353
Moth-eaten Pakistan, 238, 253, 404, 425
Mountbatten, Edwina, 316, 370, 373, 375, 380–381
Moyle, Arthur, 198
Mullah element, 291
Multi-nation-state, 6
Mumbai University, 423
Munir, Mohammad, 264
Musalman of India, 37
Muslim
  communalism, 35, 162
  domination, 226
  education, 21
  elements, 123
  faithfulness, 121
  fanatic, 47
  fundamentalist, 406
  gangs, 193
  Hamdard, 78
  henchmen, 175
  homeland, separate, 87, 119, 154
  landlords, 96, 135, 348, 393
  majority provinces, 117, 138, 155, 169, 171, 261–262, 265, 347, 408, 420
  majority zone, 66
  mass contact movement, 343
  merchants, 35
  nation, 15, 286, 292, 334, 424
  power, 39
  provinces, 80, 86, 126, 172, 174, 261–262

rights, 26
rule, 348
seats, 87, 154, 175, 343, 357, 388
separatism, 76, 335, 337, 346
society, 501
states, 20, 80, 118, 125, 227, 238, 291, 348, 356, 454
style lungis, 194
unionists, 275–276
veto, 173
votes, 87, 92, 154, 337, 362, 406, 409
women, 288
zones, 174
Muslim Raj, 20
Muslim India, 20, 187, 352, 427, 450, 504
Muslims League, 127, 171, 184, 356
Mussolini, 100–101
Muttahida Qaumi Movement, 443
Mutual agreement, 85, 139
Muygeridge, Malcolm, 202

Nagpur Congress, 44, 46
National Agricultural Party, 87–88, 96, 356–358
National Award Party of Pakistan, 397, 399
National Defence Council, 124
National Democratic Party, 117
National liberation movement, 83
Nationalism, 1, 4–6, 11, 14, 17, 20, 25, 30, 41, 44, 83, 153, 327, 335, 459
active, 83
arrival of, 6, 10
bourgeois, 478
religious, 420
Nationalists, 18, 35, 53, 67–68, 81, 99, 104, 112, 114–115, 129, 138, 149, 220, 474, 483
movement, 66, 347, 415, 441, 478
Muslims, 37–38, 51, 96–97, 112, 122, 175
policy, 111
Nationhood, 7–9, 13, 292, 404, 425
Nawab Ismail Khan, 89–90, 359–360
Nawab of Dacca, 32, 34, 124
Negativism, 431
Nehru, Jawahar Lal
action, 93, 363
aides, 217
arguments, 98
assertion, 363
attitudes, 96, 191
conviction, 439
diary, 367
dilemma, 440
disposal, 393
election, 350
ideas, 119
interaction, 375
interference, 92, 362
interpretation, 352
interview, 222
and Jinnah, 99, 186, 231, 240, 265, 282, 318, 403, 431
letters, 82, 371–373
-Mountbatten episode, 372
Nayantara Sahgal (niece), 221
observation, 395
opposition, 356
outlook, 440
personality, 367
Press Conference, 180
reference, 395
relations, 374
relationship, 374
Sardar Patel and, 247
speech, 181, 183, 304, 352–353
statement, 184, 352–353, 395–396
Subhas Bose and, 48
Swarup Rani (mother), 416
vision, 375
Nehru Memorial Lecture, 436

Nehru Memorial Museum, 382
Nehru Motilal, 44, 63, 114, 467
Nepotism, 285
Nicholson of Cambridge University, 83
Noakhali Day, 194–195
Nobel Peace Award, 487
Non-Brahmin movement, 76
Non-communalism, 349
Non-cooperation movement, 43–46, 340, 347, 417
Non-Indian nationalism, 6
Non-Party conference, 135
Non-violent campaign, 483
Norman, Dorothy, 173, 184
North West Frontier, 232, 238–239, 241, 429

Operation Madhouse, 215, 249
Operation seduction, 218, 222
Opportunism, 474
Orderly evacuation, 192
Orthodox elements, 503
Oxford University, 137, 373

Pakistan National Movement, 78, 432
Pakistan policy, 409
Pakistan resolution, 91, 111, 117, 126, 128, 162, 221, 361, 385, 433
Pakistan
- birth of, 79, 111, 291, 293, 297, 319, 331, 334, 364, 396, 427
- defined, 249
- seeds of, 66

Pant, Govind Ballabh, 19, 89, 105, 384, 475, 484
Panthic Party, 276
Parliamentary institutions, 54
Partition Council, 260, 281, 397
Partition of India, 54, 80–81, 92, 118, 133–134, 205, 226, 292, 328–331, 336, 348–349, 392, 397, 399–400, 465
Partition scheme, 249
Partition theory, 385
Partition treaties, 326
Patel, Vallabhbhai, 156, 170, 234, 241, 245, 247, 311, 313, 320
Patrick, Paul, 165
Patriotic association, 19
Peasant movement, 43
Philips, William, 141
Pilgrimage centre, 45
Pirpur Committee, 99, 101
Plan Balkan, 232, 238, 240–241, 243–246
Pluralism
- cultural-religious, 2
- religious, 3

Poet-Patriot of India, 80
Political
- baptism, 6, 11
- congregation, 81
- consciousness, 12
- elements, 141
- independence, 200, 276
- mission, 135, 377, 460
- power, 2, 108, 419, 501
- realism, 429
- separatism, 16

Poona Pact, 65, 84–85, 347, 399, 472–473
Poona Sarvajanik Sabha, 71
Porbander, 42
Post-war Britain, 451
Post-war period, 143
Powell, Enoch, 319
Power-broker, 420
Power pyramid, 280
Power triangle, 66
Praja Krashak Party, 67
Pre-independence era, 496
Princely States, 42, 201, 338
Privy Council, 50, 78, 101, 221
The Proudest Day, 415, 474
Provincial
- autonomy, 48, 93, 102, 104, 108, 154, 234, 407, 460

cabinets, 51, 53, 360
governments, 52, 91, 212, 214, 231, 278, 387, 441
governors, 101, 261, 275, 278, 280
legislatures, 50, 85, 87, 105, 154, 473
reaction committees, 470
Public holidays, 187, 189
Pun, Peter, 394
Punjab Nationalist Unionist Party, 48
Punjab waterways, 268

Quit India Movement, 104, 133, 135, 137–138, 337, 339, 348–349, 399, 448, 461, 495

Radcliff Award, 165, 263, 267–268, 271–272, 293
Radical groups, 52
Rai, Lala Lajpat, 20–21, 39, 41, 121, 496, 500
Rajagopalachari, 105, 108, 117, 139–140, 142, 148, 304, 368, 383, 433, 435
Rajendra Prasad, 36, 41, 53, 94, 101, 145, 148, 195, 230, 290, 303–304, 309–311, 313, 317, 354
Rajguru, 61–62
Rajputs, 94, 288
Ramnibas detention camp, 145
Ram-uh-Zan, 186, 190
Rastriya Swyamsevak Sangh (RSS), 1, 273–274, 296–297, 300, 332, 498–500
Reactionary elements, 60, 88, 357
Read, Anthony, 415, 474
Referendum, 262–263, 280, 435
Refugee camps, 196
Refugees, 269, 273, 289, 293, 300, 376, 418
Relief centre, 194
Religious
fanaticism, 388
fundamentalism, 22
groups, 32, 123, 133
institutions, 52
movement, 119
practices, 2
Rennin, Ernest, 7
Republican Government, 82, 100
Reservation of seats, 49, 67, 85
Revolutionary movement, 24
Rig Veda, 8
Right of self-determination, 15, 80, 128–129
Rioting, 189–190, 276
Riots, 188–190, 194–195, 273, 332, 375, 385, 418, 422, 438, 442–443, 445, 465
Road, Victoria, 298
Roman Imperialism, 334
Roosevelt, Franklin D., 129–130, 132–133, 135, 141–142
Roshnara Park, 315
Rothney Castle, 72
Rowlett Act, 41, 44, 471
Royal Commission, 489
Ruling classes, 5, 479, 501, 503

Sabarmati, 43
Saheed Suhrawardy, 187–188
Sahib Khan, 262
Salimuddin, 119
Samuel, Raphael, 15
Satyagraha movement, 459
Sayer, Francis, 152
Scepticism, 106
Second World War, 101, 125, 129, 133, 137, 202, 206, 210, 219, 235, 329, 343, 394, 399, 459–460
Sectarian leader campaigning, 409
Secular states, 49, 294, 389, 425
Secular-democratic country, 3
Secularism, 3–4, 41, 46, 82, 190, 293–294, 320, 337, 393, 431

Self-government, 48, 103, 130–132, 136, 148, 280, 292, 433, 459, 466, 468, 474
Self-rule, 36, 45, 48, 70, 150
Separate electorates, 20, 26, 29–31, 35–37, 40–41, 51–52, 59, 65, 67, 76, 85, 119, 340–341, 432–433, 472–473
Separate nation, 6, 99, 115, 122, 162, 293, 319, 329–330, 336, 415, 420
Separate sovereign Pakistan, 175, 181
Separate union, 135
Separatism, 3, 162, 340, 409
Separatist movement, 9, 81
Serila, Narendra Singh, 338
Settled policy, 140
Shafi, Mohammed, 51
Shah Nawaz Khan, 157
Shastri, Lal Bahadur, 106
Sikh unionist, 276
Simla Conference, 145–146, 150, 152–153, 170, 173, 176–177, 335, 349
Simon Commission, 47–48, 54, 57, 68, 395, 472, 497
Simon report, 54
Singh, Baldeo, 198, 411, 445
Singh, Baldev, 250
Singh, Giani Kartar, 272
Singh, Janak, 282
Singh, Kartar, 273
Singh, Khuswant, 423
Singh, Krishna Huthee, 137
Singh, Pritam, 299
Singh, Rajendra, 332
Singh, Tara, 273–274, 296–297
Sir Abdur Rahim, 62
Sir Cyril Radcliff, 260, 264, 328
Sir Samuel Hoare, 59–60
Sir Stafford Cripps, 167, 222, 409, 434, 460
Social conflicts, 194
Social reforms, 70
Socialism, 82, 337, 346, 493
Socialist groups, 429
Socialist Movement, 496
Socialist revolution, 83
South Africa, 40, 43, 404, 417, 423, 481, 484
Sovereign Pakistan, 169, 344, 352
Sovereign states, 5, 80, 113, 128–129, 169, 412
independent, 126, 295, 339
separate, 139, 173
Sovereignty, 12, 49, 132, 334, 465
Soviet Union, 478
Spanish Civil War, 82
Spiritual founders of Pakistan, 79, 84
Stanley, Oliver, 452
Statehood, 12, 292
independent, 12
Subhas Chandra's declaration, 223
Sufi teachings, 502
Swadeshi movement, 24
Swami Shradhanand, 46, 121
Swaraj Party, 63, 105
Swearing-in-ceremony, 312–313
Swedish Prize Awarding Institute, 487
Syed Sharifuddin Pirzada, 117–118

Tagore, Satyendra Nath, 71
Tea Party, 426
Tea plantations, 232
Territorial boundaries, 132
Thaper, Romila, 2
Theoretic principle, 294
Thompson, Edward, 79–80
Tilak, Bal Gangadhar, 39, 45, 417
Tinkathia system, 43
Toynbee, Arnold, 308
Transfer of Power and Partition, 453
Transfer of power, 114, 150, 164, 187, 212–213, 239, 243, 256, 260, 269, 303, 310, 318, 355–356, 431

Tribal groups, 8
Tripura Congress, 101
Tuberculosis, 86, 255, 490–491, 496
Two-nation theory, 12, 15, 17, 20–22, 99, 114–115, 119–120, 122, 162, 319–320, 339–340, 346, 389, 420–421, 430–431
  advocated, 162
  defining, 12
  discussed, 80
  divisive, 22
  and its origin, 20
  and Jinnah, 129
  propounded, 21
  Sir Syed and, 346
Union Jack, 302, 317–318
Unionist Party, 67–68, 154–155, 273, 275, 340–342, 408, 425
United Indian Patriotic Association, 19
United Nations Organization, 281
University of London, 325, 362
Untimely Communal Award, 347
Untouchables, 48, 76, 84–85, 347, 472–473
Usman Ali Khan, 462

Valid votes
  for India, 263
  for Pakistan, 263
Vedic people, 8
Viceroy Council, 460
Viceroy Minto, 26
Viceroy Wavell, 176, 189, 195, 364, 416, 435
Vietnam, 329–330

Wadia, Dina, 405, 422
Wali Khan, 397–399
War cabinet, 131, 140–141
War coalition government, 460
War time coalition, 435
Wardha Programme, 358
Warsaw Programme, 89
Web, Alfred, 41
Wedderbeum, William, 39, 72
Whitley, William, 150
Wolpert, Stanley, 416
Woolf, Leonard, 400
Worm-Muller, Jacob, 483
Wyatt, Woodrow, 338

Yemen Khan, 449
Yoga, 301
York Road, 302
Young India, 61, 346
Yugoslavia, 329
Yule, George, 41, 75
Yunus, Mohammed, 95

Zafrullah Khan, 67, 397, 399
Zamindari abolition, 91, 93, 363, 393
Ziegler, Philip, 269, 380